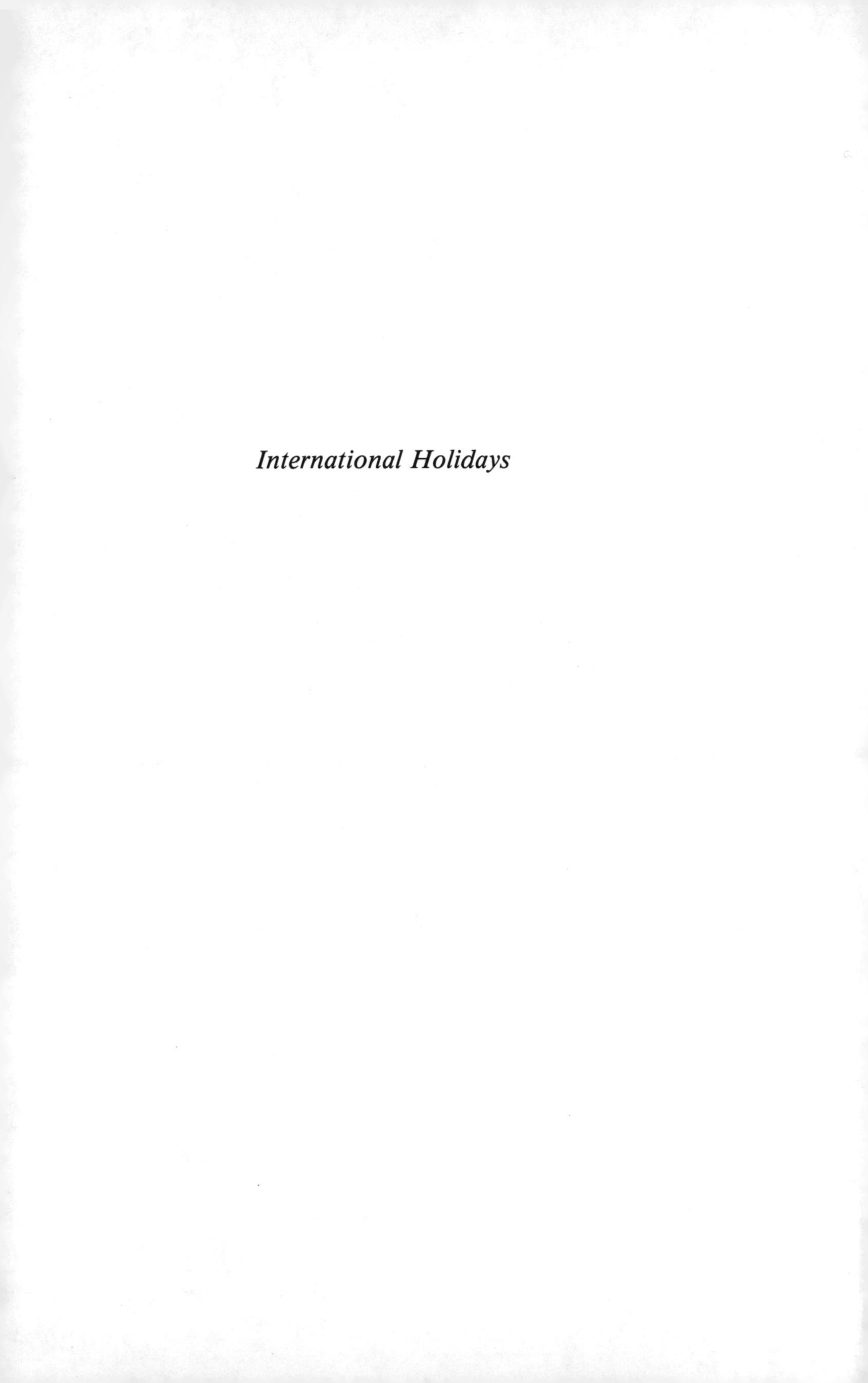

*International Holidays*

# International Holidays

## 204 Countries from 1994 through 2015

*with Tabular Appendices of Religious Holidays, 1900–2100*

*by* Robert S. Weaver

McFarland & Company, Inc., Publishers
*Jefferson, North Carolina, and London*

**British Cataloguing-in-Publication data are available**

**Library of Congress Cataloguing-in-Publication Data**

Weaver, Robert S., 1950–
International holidays : 204 countries from 1994 through 2015, with tabular appendices of religious holidays, 1900–2100 / by Robert S. Weaver.
p. cm.
Includes bibliographical references (p. ) and index.
ISBN 0-89950-953-3 (lib. bdg. : 50# alk. paper)
1. Holidays—Calendars. 2. Special days—Calendars. I. Title.
GT3930.W38 1995
394.2′6—dc20 94-19445
CIP



Manufactured in the United States of America

*McFarland & Company, Inc., Publishers*
*Box 611, Jefferson, North Carolina 28640*

to Sue Sincick

(because I said I would
a long time ago)

# Acknowledgments

In addition to my family and friends, who have airmailed books and photocopies from all parts of the globe, I must thank the many nameless clerical, embassy, airline, and library personnel whose assistance has made this book possible—and a friend of mine who recommended a totally different project, in a different medium, from which it sprang.

And my wife and kids, who have learned to ignore the table slapping and foreign language profanity at four in the morning, and found endless delight in bursting the reams of computer paper that emanated from "daddy, sir's" printer.

In any project as multifaceted as this one, there are bound to be sticking points. I had four of them—the Thai Buddhist holidays of Makha Bucha, Visakha Bucha, Asalaha Bucha, and Khao Phansa. All the more embarrassing, because Thailand is my adopted country.

In the end they fell—you'll find them on the calendars and a partial list of them in Appendix C—to a mixture of modern positional astronomy, old Thai astrology, ancient Buddhist practice, and mind-numbing numerology.

I cannot thank enough the many members of the Thai Cultural Commission, Department of Religious Affairs, Bank of Ayuddya, and *ah jahns* (professors) at Wat Rachapradit, all of whom provided a piece of the puzzle; nor the many Thais who pointed me in some direction I would never have thought of, provided translation, and made phone calls to set up appointments on my behalf.

Several Thais in particular get special mention; they are Professor Nibondh Saibejra, the director of the King Mongkut Memorial Park of Science and Technology, and Bangkok Planetarium, and his staff. Their patience (with my mangled Thai) and helpfulness (allowing me to photocopy out-of-print material in their personal collections) was outstanding. *Kahpun makh cahp* (Thank you very much, sir).

# Table of Contents

ACKNOWLEDGMENTS *vii*

INTRODUCTION *1*

**THE CALENDARS:**

| | page | | | | |
|---|---|---|---|---|---|
| 1994 | *10* | 2002 | *81* | 2010 | *152* |
| 1995 | *19* | 2003 | *90* | 2011 | *161* |
| 1996 | *28* | 2004 | *98* | 2012 | *169* |
| 1997 | *36* | 2005 | *107* | 2013 | *178* |
| 1998 | *45* | 2006 | *116* | 2014 | *187* |
| 1999 | *54* | 2007 | *125* | 2015 | *196* |
| 2000 | *63* | 2008 | *134* | | |
| 2001 | *72* | 2009 | *143* | | |

APPENDIX A: FIXED MULTINATIONAL HOLIDAYS

A1. New Year's Day (1 January) *207*

A2. Bank Holiday (1 January) *209*

A3. Epiphany (6 January) *209*

A4. Women's Day (8 March) *210*

A5. Saint Joseph's Day (19 March) *210*

A6. Tomb Sweeping Day (5 April) *210*

A7. Labor Day (1 May) *210*

A8. Africa Day (25 May) *212*

A9. Saint Paul's Day (29 June) *213*

A10. Bank Holiday (1 July) *213*

A11. Assumption (15 August) *213*
A12. Columbus Day (12 October) *214*
A13. All Saints' Day (1 November) *214*
A14. All Souls' Day (2 November) *215*
A15. Armistice Day (11 November) *215*
A16. Immaculate Conception (8 December) *216*
A17. Christmas Eve (24 December) *216*
A18. Christmas Day (25 December) *217*
A19. Boxing Day (26 December) *219*
A20. Bank Holiday (31 December) *219*
A21. New Year's Eve (31 December) *220*

APPENDIX B: ALGORITHMIC HOLIDAYS

***Asian***

B1. Chinese New Year Eve *221*
B2. Chinese New Year *221*
B3. 2nd Day of Chinese New Year *222*
B4. 3rd Day of Chinese New Year *222*
B5. Dragon Boat Festival *222*
B6. Ancestors' Day *222*

***Christian***

B7. Shrove Monday *223*
B8. Shrove Tuesday *223*
B9. Ash Wednesday *223*
B10. Palm Sunday *224*
B11. Maundy Thursday *224*
B12. Good Friday *224*
B13. Holy Saturday *226*
B14. Easter Sunday *226*
B15. Easter Monday *227*
B16. Ascension Thursday *228*
B17. Whitsunday *228*
B18. Whitmonday *228*
B19. Corpus Christi *229*

***Orthodox***

B20. Good Friday and Easter Monday *230*

*Hindu*

B21. Deepavali *230*

*Islamic*

B22. New Year *231*

B23. Ashura *231*

B24. Mohammed's Birthday *232*

B25. 1st Day of Ramadan *232*

B26. Eid al Fitr *233*

B27. Hari Raya Puasa *233*

B28. Eid al Adha *234*

B29. Hari Raya Haji *234*

B30. Isra a Majraj *235*

APPENDIX C: TABLE OF DATES FOR SELECTED ALGORITHMIC HOLIDAYS (1900 TO 2100)

C1. Chinese New Year *236*

C2. Christian *238*

C3. Orthodox *243*

C4. Hindu (Deepavali) *247*

C5. Islamic *249*

C6. Jewish *253*

C7. Theravada (Thai) Buddhist *258*

APPENDIX D: TABLES OF HOLIDAYS HONORED BY EACH COUNTRY

D1. Afghanistan *263*

D2. Albania *263*

D3. Algeria *264*

D4. Andorra *264*

D5. Angola *265*

D6. Antigua *265*

D7. Argentina *265*

D8. Armenia *266*

D9. Aruba *266*

D10. Australia *266*

D11. Austria *267*

D12. Azerbaijan *267*

D13. Bahamas *268*

D14. Bahrain *268*

D15. Bangladesh *269*

D16. Barbados *269*

D17. Belarus *269*

D18. Belgium *270*

D19. Belize *270*

D20. Benin *271*

D21. Bermuda *271*
D22. Bhutan *271*
D23. Bolivia *272*
D24. Bosnia and Herzegovina *272*
D25. Botswana *272*
D26. Brazil *273*
D27. Brunei *273*
D28. Bulgaria *274*
D29. Burkina Faso *274*
D30. Burma *275*
D31. Burundi *275*
D32. Cambodia *275*
D33. Cameroon *276*
D34. Canada *276*
D35. Cape Verde *276*
D36. Cayman Islands *277*
D37. Central African Republic *277*
D38. Chad *277*
D39. Chile *278*
D40. China *279*
D41. Colombia *279*
D42. Comoros *280*
D43. Congo *280*
D44. Costa Rica *280*
D45. Croatia *281*
D46. Cuba *281*
D47. Cyprus *282*
D48. Czech Republic *282*
D49. Denmark *282*
D50. Djibouti *283*
D51. Dominica *283*
D52. Dominican Republic *284*
D53. Ecuador *284*
D54. Egypt *285*
D55. El Salvador *285*
D56. England *286*
D57. Equatorial Guinea *286*
D58. Eritrea *286*
D59. Estonia *287*
D60. Ethiopia *287*
D61. Fiji *288*
D62. Finland *288*
D63. France *289*
D64. Gabon *289*
D65. Gambia *290*
D66. Georgia *290*
D67. Germany *291*
D68. Ghana *291*
D69. Gibraltar *291*
D70. Greece *292*
D71. Grenada *292*
D72. Guam *293*
D73. Guatemala *293*
D74. Guinea *294*
D75. Guinea-Bissau *294*
D76. Guyana *295*
D77. Haiti *295*
D78. Honduras *296*
D79. Hong Kong *296*
D80. Hungary *297*
D81. Iceland *297*
D82. India *297*
D83. Indonesia *298*
D84. Iran *298*
D85. Iraq *299*
D86. Ireland *299*
D87. Israel *299*
D88. Italy *300*
D89. Ivory Coast *300*
D90. Jamaica *301*

D91. Japan *301*
D92. Jordan *302*
D93. Kazakhstan *302*
D94. Kenya *303*
D95. Kiribati *303*
D96. Kuwait *303*
D97. Kyrgyzstan *304*
D98. Laos *304*
D99. Latvia *305*
D100. Lebanon *305*
D101. Lesotho *306*
D102. Liberia *306*
D103. Libya *306*
D104. Liechtenstein *307*
D105. Lithuania *307*
D106. Luxembourg *308*
D107. Macao *308*
D108. Madagascar *309*
D109. Malawi *310*
D110. Malaysia *310*
D111. Maldives *310*
D112. Mali *311*
D113. Malta *311*
D114. Marshall Islands *312*
D115. Mauritania *312*
D116. Mauritius *313*
D117. Mexico *313*
D118. Micronesia *314*
D119. Moldova *314*
D120. Monaco *314*
D121. Mongolia *315*
D122. Morocco *315*
D123. Mozambique *315*
D124. Namibia *316*
D125. Nauru *316*
D126. Nepal *316*
D127. Netherlands *317*
D128. New Guinea *317*
D129. New Zealand *317*
D130. Nicaragua *318*
D131. Niger *318*
D132. Nigeria *319*
D133. North Korea *319*
D134. Northern Ireland *320*
D135. Norway *320*
D136. Oman *320*
D137. Pakistan *321*
D138. Palau *321*
D139. Panama *321*
D140. Paraguay *322*
D141. Peru *323*
D142. Philippines *323*
D143. Poland *324*
D144. Portugal *324*
D145. Puerto Rico *325*
D146. Qatar *325*
D147. Romania *325*
D148. Russia *326*
D149. Rwanda *326*
D150. Saint Kitts *326*
D151. Saint Lucia *327*
D152. Saint Vincent *327*
D153. San Marino *327*
D154. São Tomé and Principe *328*
D155. Saudi Arabia *328*
D156. Scotland *328*
D157. Senegal *328*
D158. Seychelles *329*
D159. Sierra Leone *329*
D160. Singapore *330*
D161. Slovakia *330*

D162. Slovenia *331*
D163. Solomon Islands *331*
D164. Somalia *331*
D165. South Africa *332*
D166. South Korea *332*
D167. Spain *333*
D168. Sri Lanka *333*
D169. Sudan *334*
D170. Suriname *334*
D171. Swaziland *335*
D172. Sweden *335*
D173. Switzerland *336*
D174. Syria *336*
D175. Taiwan *337*
D176. Tajikistan *337*
D177. Tanzania *338*
D178. Thailand *338*
D179. Togo *339*
D180. Tonga *339*
D181. Trinidad and Tobago *339*
D182. Tunisia *340*
D183. Turkey *340*
D184. Turkmenistan *341*
D185. Tuvalu *341*
D186. Uganda *341*
D187. Ukraine *342*
D188. United Arab Emirates *342*
D189. United Kingdom *343*
D190. United States *343*
D191. Uruguay *343*
D192. Uzbekistan *344*
D193. Vanuatu *344*
D194. Vatican *345*
D195. Venezuela *345*
D196. Vietnam *346*
D197. Virgin Islands (U.S.) *346*
D198. Wales *347*
D199. Western Samoa *347*
D200. Yemeni Republic *347*
D201. Yugoslavia *348*
D202. Zaïre *348*
D203. Zambia *349*
D204. Zimbabwe *349*

INDEX AND HOLIDAY REGISTER (Subject access to appendices; dates for holidays) *351*

# Introduction

Did you have to cancel an important business meeting today and spend the whole day trying to count the holes in the Celotex ceiling of your hotel room—all because it's the king's birthday in the country? Or did you just discover in the small print of a travel brochure that the white-water rafting trip you planned today is not operated on the Afghani new year's day? If you are one of the few people who knows when the Afghani new year begins this year, count yourself among the very few people who now know when it will be next year—so you can reschedule that raft trip.

For 204 countries (listed in the Table of Contents on pages ix through xiv, and in Appendix D) you will find in this reference book all the secular and religious holidays observed.

The Index and Holiday Register at the back of the book guides the reader to all nations celebrant of a given holiday, whether it be individual countries (example: Igbal Day *Pakistan* 9 Nov.) or many countries (example: Maundy Thursday is listed in Appendix B11). The index also points to all appropriate appendices. Since the index provides the date for all fixed holidays, the reader may not need to look further for the information sought.

There are a few things that the reader might want to know. First, the Gregorian calendar is generally the one in use throughout the world for day-to-day time reckoning and forms the outline, the backbone, of this book. It is the well known "30 days hath September" one.*

If the year number is evenly divisible by 4 then it is a leap year, and February has not 28 but 29 days. There is an exception to the above procedure for determining leap year: The last year of a century (years ending in 00) must be divided by 400. If that comes out even it is a leap year. Otherwise it is not, even though evenly divisible by 4. By that rule, 1600, 2000, and 2400 *are* leap years.

**Quoted in Bartlett's* Familiar Quotations *as "Thirty days hath November,/ April, June, and September,/ February hath twenty-eight alone,/ And all the rest have thirty-one."*

Do not adopt the commonly held misconception that the 21st century starts with the year 2000. It does not, it starts with the year 2001. There was no year 0, the first century started with the year 1, and ran for one hundred years—through the year 100. Likewise, the 21st century will start in 2001 and run one hundred years—through the year 2100.

The Gregorian calendar may be the most widely used calendar in the world, but it is by no means the only one. It is viewed as a Christian calendar by the non-Christian world. It is tolerated by non-Christian countries as the calendar of business and international relations. You will find that many of these countries have even started to celebrate their secular holidays on Gregorian dates. The most common examples are New Year's Day (1 January), Labor Day (1 May) and Christmas Day (25 December)—the most popular of the multinational holidays listed in Appendix A.

Non-Christian religious holidays have their dates rooted in non-Gregorian calendars. Often these are lunar (moon based) or luni-solar (moon and sun based). These have been calculated according to the rules of the religion that dictates them, then translated to Gregorian dates for inclusion in this book.

The Gregorian calendar has been unchanged since 1582 when it was created at the behest of Pope Gregory. That is not true of the nations that use it nor their national holidays based on it. Holidays, like nations, are dynamic. Evacuation days tend to be celebrated for a few years, then forgotten; kings and queens die, abdicate, or are overthrown; governments establish algorithms for the dates of fixed holidays; etc. None of this is predictable.

The commonly accepted term Evacuation Day is used here for holidays in countries that celebrate the removal of foreign troops from their soil—in the absence of another better word for it.

Many countries were created while this book was going to press, with the collapse of the Soviet bloc, the break-up of Yugoslavia (you will still find Yugoslav holidays listed; the outcome of its troubles is still a matter for conjecture at the time of publication for this book), the partitioning of Czechoslovakia, and the creation of Eritrea. Holidays in those areas have not been settled yet. Indeed, the status of countries in those areas has not been settled in some cases. A best guess has been made about what the holidays in those countries will be, based on their history and religious make-up, and an asterisk (*) indicates that these holidays are "projected" here.

During the time period that this book covers, the leases on Hong Kong and Macao will expire (1997 and 1999 respectively) and they revert to Chinese rule. What that will do to the holidays there is uncertain.

Holidays are hardly the first priority of a nation in transition: time, politics, and religion all have their say. This book is as accurate as can be made with the information available at the time of publication. It is recommended to watch the papers or consult the local populace for updates.

Bank holidays (days the banks are closed) are included here as a help to the international businessperson. But there is a slow trend toward bank holidays' becoming national holidays. Refer to the local populace for up-to-the-minute information before scheduling important nonbanking business on a bank holiday.

There are two countries that are exceptions that prove the rule above—the United Kingdom and Ireland. Public holidays there are called bank holidays. All government offices, schools, and large businesses, not just the banks, close. To avoid the confusion this may cause among non–U.K. or non–Ireland residents, you will find them listed by name or as "public holidays" on the calendars herein.

It must be noted that all through the calendars in this book the nominal day of celebration is listed—even if that day were to fall on that country's day of rest. As a general rule, holidays that fall on Sunday are celebrated on the next day in the non–Islamic World, and those that fall on Friday are shifted to Saturday in Islamic countries that observe Friday as their scheduled day of rest.

Countries that observe Friday as the normal day of rest are: Afghanistan, Algeria, Bahrain, Egypt, Indonesia, Iraq, Iran, Jordan, Kuwait, Libya, Oman, Qatar, Saudi Arabia, Somalia, Sudan, Syria, Turkey, United Arab Emirates, and the Yemeni Republic.

Holidays that fall on Saturday are not as consistent. In those few countries that observe a two full day weekend, as do some in Europe and North America, the day can either be shifted to the preceding Friday, or the following Monday at local discretion. In countries observing Saturday as a half-day, the holiday is either observed on Saturday, making it a full rest day; or on Friday and Saturday, making them both full rest days.

But be warned: that is not always consistent. Should a country also celebrate a religious holiday during the same week, it may elect to celebrate both holidays concurrently, consecutively, or shift one to the following Monday.

The prudent businessperson will not schedule an important meeting on the Friday preceding, or the Monday following a national holiday scheduled for Saturday, especially if that country also celebrates a major religious holiday within the same period.

The local populace is the best guide.

Many countries are alliances of previously autonomous countries. And many countries have states, although they may not call them that. Countries may call their land divisions states, provinces, cantons, or something else. Canada, China, Greece, Italy, Malaysia, Switzerland, Tanzania, the United Arab Emirates, the United Kingdom, the United States, and Yugoslavia come to mind quickly. There are large countries with diverse religions, like India; and small countries with diverse religions, like Sri Lanka. What all these countries have in common is that states within them are usually allowed to add their own holidays to the national holidays. It is beyond the scope of this book to list states' holidays. There are thousands.

The exception again is the United Kingdom. Here you will find English, Northern Irish, Scottish, and Welsh holidays listed. (England and Wales celebrate the same holidays.) This in addition to United Kingdom holidays—which are nationwide. For example, you will find the United Kingdom listed among those countries that celebrate Boxing Day (26 December) in Appendix A, but only Northern Ireland listed as celebrating Saint Patrick's Day (17 March).

In a manner similar to the treatment of the United Kingdom, a dependency's unique holidays will be listed after the name of the dependency, but not listed if the parent country celebrates the same holiday. For instance you will see "Guam: Liberation Day" on the 21st of July, but no mention of it on the 4th of July. But you will see "United States: Independence Day" on the 4th of July, of course.

There are only two dependencies listed that do not celebrate their "parent" country's holidays concurrently with that parent: Gibraltar and Hong Kong. You will find those two dependencies with their holidays listed in full, as though they were sovereign countries.

## RELIGIOUS HOLIDAYS

Religious holidays on the whole are more tractable than secular ones. Nevertheless, what may be a religious festival this year, may be a religious holiday next. And vice versa. What may be a holiday to one person, may be a festival or ignored entirely by another. A religious holiday is listed if the secular part of a nation honors it: if the banks, government offices, schools, and large businesses honor it, it is a holiday, and is listed here.

Festivals are beyond the scope of this book—there are thousands of those too. A trip to your local bookstore or library is recommended. Books on festivals abound, many with pictures and full explanations. If you are looking for more information about the festivals in a particular country, try the travel guides, or contact the embassy for that country.

## Hinduism

To avoid cluttering the calendars, only the generally accepted nationwide holidays are reported for India and Sri Lanka. Be advised that these countries have a bewildering array of local and religious holidays too. Some are holidays, some are festivals. The dividing line between the two is often indistinct, or follows state lines or religious regions. To display them all would be tantamount to saying that every day is a holiday in India and Sri Lanka.

The cause can be found in Hinduism. It has almost as many sects as adherents. It, alone, among the world's major religions has no governing orthodoxy.

You will find "Hindu: Deepavali" in the calendars. A list of countries that celebrate it are in Appendix B21, and a 201 year list of dates for it in Appendix C4. Deepavali is the only Hindu holiday so treated, because of its multinational nature.

Sri Lanka has a maximum of 16 holidays reported on the calendars. Burma, with a maximum of 18, holds the record. Both Burma and Sri Lanka celebrate every full moon, so the number of holidays varies with the number of full moons in a year—12 or 13. This is about a third of the holidays you will encounter if you spend any appreciable time in Sri Lanka and move around in it.

People doing business in India and Sri Lanka cannot possibly avoid all the holidays by relying on a published report.

The name "Myanmar" for Burma does not yet have the acceptance of the Burmese. Perhaps, with time, this will change; but this book follows the current majority thinking and uses "Burma."

## Islam

The Islamic holidays listed here are based on the Islamic calendar of 354 days (355 in a leap year). Since that is a shorter year than that used by the non-Islamic world, there can be no one-to-one correlation to the Gregorian calendar; and it is possible to have two holidays of the same name in one Gregorian year. Both, if applicable, are shown on the calendars and in appendices B22–B30.

The Islamic calendar is a guide to only about when a holiday will be observed. For the Middle East and most of Islamic Africa, the actual holiday is based on observations of the moon from the observatory in Cairo and that is the date given as *Islamic* on the calendars.

As a general rule, Islamic holidays in the Far East are based on observations of the moon from the observer's country and as a result are observed later than the same holiday in the Middle East. That is the date given as *Far East Islamic* on the calendars.

Be it *Islamic* or *Far East Islamic* it is still only a guide. Religious authorities must proclaim the veracity of each observation. There is no way of knowing the outcome of that decision in advance.

The two Eid's, Eid al Fitr and Eid al Adha, are nominally four-day holidays, and are reported on the calendars as such, but each country makes its own decision about when to honor them, and for how long. They too are subject to review by local religious authorities.

Eid al Fitr and Eid al Adha are shorter, and are called by different names in the Far East—Hari Raya Puasa and Hari Raya Haji respectively.

The prudent businessperson will not do any tight scheduling in an Arab or Islamic country close to any Islamic holiday.

## Judaism

Only one date is displayed on the calendars and shown in Appendix C6 for the major Jewish holidays and the festival of Chanukah (Hanukkah). This is the date normally associated with the holiday, and celebrated by the only country that celebrates the Jewish holidays—Israel. Chanukah is the only true festival you'll find in this book—the Festival of Lights. Several holidays are, however, called festivals and many have a festive nature.

In fact, these dates are only the first day of longer periods given to feasting or fasting. Periods vary with different factions of Judaism, but are generally accepted as starting at dusk (6 P.M. local time is again generally accepted) on the day *prior* to the one shown on the calendars and tabulated in Appendix C6, and extending as follows: Rosh Hashanah, 2 days; Sukkot, 7 days; Chanukah, 8 days; Passover, 8 days; Pentecost (Shavout), 2 days.

## Theravada (Thai) Buddhism

Theravada Buddhism may be arguably the world's largest religion, being the predominant religion of the world's most populated hemisphere, but it is also the religion with the fewest holidays. Only Malaysia, Singapore, South Korea, and Thailand honor Buddhist holidays although a plethora of Buddhist festivals can be found throughout Asia.

All four countries honor the Buddha's birthday, which they call variously "Vesak Day, and Visakha Bucha"; and they calculate in different ways, using a variety of ancient calendars. Malaysia and Singapore calculate Vesak Day in the same way, so you will find only three different dates for the Buddha's birthday on the calendars, all associated with their honoring countries.

Thailand is unique in honoring more than just the Buddha's birthday, as Israel is unique in honoring the Jewish ones. But just as you will find adherents of Judaism beyond the borders of Israel , you will find adherents of Theravada Buddhism far beyond Thailand. Hence, both have their own listings in Appendix C7.

## SOFT HOLIDAYS

The "soft" holidays are Mother's Day, Valentine's Day, Palm Sunday, the starts and ends of daylight savings time, and the zodiac. These are not holidays at all. No nation in the world honors them as such. They are included here for information only.

### Zodiac

The cusp dates shown on the calendars are those for Greenwich, England, and will vary with a person's location. People born within a day of these dates are said to be born "on the cusp." People so affected need to know the latitude, longitude, and exact time of birth to know accurately which astronomical sign they were born under.

# The Calendars

# January 1994

**1 Sat.** *Cameroon:* Independence Day. *Cuba:* Liberation Day. *Haiti:* Independence Day. *Palau:* Independence Day. *Sudan:* Independence Day. *Taiwan:* Foundation Day (1st day of 2). *Western Samoa:* Independence Day. *Multinational:* Bank Holiday and New Year's Day (see App. A1 & A2).

**2 Sun.** *Japan:* Bank Holiday. *New Zealand:* New Year's Day (2nd day of 2). *South Korea:* New Year's Day (2nd day of 2). *Switzerland:* Berchtold's Day. *Taiwan:* Foundation Day (2nd day of 2).

**3 Mon.** *Burkina Faso:* Revolution Day. *Hong Kong:* New Year's Day. *Scotland:* New Year's Day (2nd day of 2).

**4 Tue.** *Burma:* Independence Day. *Zaïre:* Martyrs' Day.

**6 Thu.** *Iraq:* Army Day. *Uruguay:* Children's Day. *Christian:* Epiphany (see App. A3).

**7 Fri.** *Egypt:* Coptic Christmas. *Ethiopia:* Coptic Christmas.

**9 Sun.** *Islamic:* Isra a Majraj (see App. B30).

**11 Tue.** *Albania:* Republic Day. *Nepal:* Unification Day. *Puerto Rico:* Hostos Day.

**12 Wed.** *Tanzania:* Revolution Day.

**13 Thu.** *Togo:* Liberation Day.

**15 Sat.** *Japan:* Adult's Day. *Jordan:* Arbor Day.

**17 Mon.** *United States:* Martin Luther King's Birthday.

**19 Wed.** *Ethiopia:* Epiphany.

**20 Thu.** *Mali:* Award Day. *Zodiac Cusp:* Capricorn ends, Aquarius begins.

**21 Fri.** *Dominican Republic:* Altagracia Day.

**22 Sat.** *Saint Vincent:* Discovery Day.

**26 Wed.** *Burma:* Full Moon Day. *Dominican Republic:* Duarte Day. *India:* Republic Day. *Sri Lanka:* Full Moon Poya.

**27 Thu.** *Monaco:* Saint Devota's Day. *Vietnam:* Vietnam Day.

**28 Fri.** *Rwanda:* Democracy Day.

**31 Mon.** *Australia:* Australia Day. *Nauru:* Independence Day.

# February 1994

**2 Wed.** *Liechtenstein:* Candlemas.

**4 Fri.** *Sri Lanka:* Independence Day.

**5 Sat.** *Mexico:* Constitution Day.

**6 Sun.** *New Zealand:* Waitangi Day.

**7 Mon.** *Grenada:* Independence Day. *United States:* Lincoln's Birthday.

**8 Tue.** *Iraq:* Revolution Day.

**9 Wed.** *Lebanon:* Saint Marion's Day. *Asian:* Chinese New Year Eve (see App. B1).

**10 Thu.** *Malta:* Saint Paul's Day. *Vietnam:* Tet (1st day of 3). *Asian:* Chinese New Year (Year of the Dog) (see App. B2).

**11 Fri.** *Cameroon:* Youth Day. *Japan:* Foundation Day. *Liberia:* Armed Forces Day. *Vietnam:* Tet (2nd day of 3). *Asian:* 2nd Day of Chinese New Year (see App. B3). *Islamic:* 1st Day of Ramadan (see App. B25).

**12 Sat.** *Burma:* Union Day. *Vietnam:* Tet (3rd day of 3). *Asian:* 3rd Day of Chinese New Year (see App. B4).

**14 Mon.** *International:* Valentine's Day. *Christian:* Shrove Monday (see App. B7).

**15 Tue.** *Christian:* Shrove Tuesday (see App. B8).

**16 Wed.** *Christian:* Ash Wednesday (see App. B9).

**18 Fri.** *Gambia:* Independence Day.

**19 Sat.** *Nepal:* National Day. *Zodiac Cusp:* Aquarius ends, Pisces begins.
**21 Mon.** *Bangladesh:* Saheed Day. *United States:* Washington's Birthday.
**22 Tue.** *Saint Lucia:* Independence Day.
**23 Wed.** *Brunei:* National Day. *Guyana:* Republic Day.
**24 Thu.** *Burma:* Full Moon Day.
**25 Fri.** *Kuwait:* National Day. *Sri Lanka:* Full Moon Poya. *Thailand:* Makha Bucha Day. *Jewish:* Purim.
**27 Sun.** *Dominican Republic:* Independence Day.

# March 1994

**1 Tue.** *South Korea:* Independence Day.
**2 Wed.** *Ethiopia:* Victory of Aduwa Day. *Morocco:* Independence Day.
**3 Thu.** *Bulgaria:* Liberation Day. *Malawi:* Martyrs' Day. *Morocco:* National Day.
**6 Sun.** *Ghana:* Independence Day.
**7 Mon.** *Guam:* Discovery Day.
**8 Tue.** *Syria:* Revolution Day. *Multinational:* Women's Day (see App. A4).
**10 Thu.** *South Korea:* Labor Day.
**11 Fri.** *Lithuania:* National Day*.
**12 Sat.** *Lesotho:* Moshoeshoe's Day. *Mauritius:* Independence Day. *Zambia:* Youth Day.
**13 Sun.** *Grenada:* National Day. *Far East Islamic:* Hari Raya Puasa (see App. B27). *Islamic:* Eid al Fitr (1st day of 4) (see App. B26).
**14 Mon.** *Gibraltar:* Commonwealth Day. *Greece:* Shrove Monday. *Islamic:* Eid al Fitr (2nd day of 4) (see App. B26). *Orthodox:* Shrove Monday.
**15 Tue.** *Islamic:* Eid al Fitr (3rd day of 4) (see App. B26).
**16 Wed.** *Islamic:* Eid al Fitr (4th day of 4) (see App. B26).
**17 Thu.** *Ireland:* Saint Patrick's Day. *Northern Ireland:* Saint Patrick's Day.
**19 Sat.** *Christian:* Saint Joseph's Day (see App. A5).
**20 Sun.** *Iran:* New Year's Day. (Hegira: 1373). *Iraq:* New Year's Day. *Tunisia:* Independence Day. *Zodiac Cusp:* Pisces ends, Aries begins.
**21 Mon.** *Afghanistan:* New Year's Day (Shamsi: 1373). *Japan:* Vernal Equinox. *Mexico:* Juarez Day.
**22 Tue.** *Puerto Rico:* Abolition Day. *Zambia:* Africa Day.
**23 Wed.** *Pakistan:* Pakistan Day.
**25 Fri.** *Burma:* Full Moon Day. *Cyprus:* Greek Independence Day. *Greece:* Independence Day. *Liechtenstein:* Annunciation.
**26 Sat.** *Bangladesh:* Independence Day. *Sri Lanka:* Full Moon Poya.
**27 Sun.** *Angola:* Evacuation Day. *Burma:* Resistance Day. *Israel:* Passover. *Christian:* Palm Sunday. *Europe:* Daylight Savings Time starts (advance clocks 1 hour). *Jewish:* Passover.
**28 Mon.** *Virgin Islands (U.S.):* Transfer Day.
**29 Tue.** *Central African Republic:* Boganda Day. *Madagascar:* Memorial Day. *Taiwan:* Youth Day.
**31 Thu.** *Malta:* National Day. *Christian:* Maundy Thursday (see App. B11).

# April 1994

**1 Fri.** *Iran:* Republic Day. *San Marino:* National Day. *Sierra Leone:* Bank Holiday. *Christian:* Good Friday (see App. B12).
**2 Sat.** *Christian:* Holy Saturday (see App. B13).
**3 Sun.** *Canada and United States:* Daylight Savings Time starts (advance

clocks 1 hour). *Christian:* Easter Sunday (see App. B14).

**4 Mon.** *Hungary:* Liberation Day. *Senegal:* National Day. *Christian:* Easter Monday (see App. B15).

**5 Tue.** *South Korea:* Arbor Day. *Asian:* Tomb Sweeping Day (see App. A6).

**6 Wed.** *South Africa:* Founders' Day. *Thailand:* Chakri Day.

**9 Sat.** *Philippines:* Valour Day. *Tunisia:* Martyrs' Day.

**11 Mon.** *Costa Rica:* Heroes' Day. *Uganda:* Liberation Day.

**13 Wed.** *Chad:* National Day. *Thailand:* Songkrawn (1st day of 2).

**14 Thu.** *Honduras:* Pan American Day. *Thailand:* Songkrawn (2nd day of 2).

**15 Fri.** *Niger:* National Day.

**16 Sat.** *Burma:* New Year's Day (Burmese: 1356). *Cyprus:* Independence Day. *Israel:* Independence Day.

**17 Sun.** *Cambodia:* Independence Day. *Syria:* Independence Day.

**18 Mon.** *Zimbabwe:* Republic Day.

**19 Tue.** *Sierra Leone:* Republic Day. *Uruguay:* Patriots' Day. *Venezuela:* Independence Day.

**20 Wed.** *Zodiac Cusp:* Aries ends, Taurus begins.

**21 Thu.** *Brazil:* Tiradentes Day.

**23 Sat.** *Turkey:* Children's Day.

**24 Sun.** *Burma:* Full Moon Day.

**25 Mon.** *Australia:* ANZAC Day. *Egypt:* Sinai Day. *Iceland:* Children's Day. *Italy:* Liberation Day. *New Zealand:* ANZAC Day. *Portugal:* Liberation Day. *Sri Lanka:* Full Moon Poya. *Swaziland:* Flag Day.

**26 Tue.** *Tanzania:* Union Day.

**27 Wed.** *Afghanistan:* Independence Day. *Sierra Leone:* Independence Day. *Togo:* Independence Day.

**29 Fri.** *Denmark:* All Prayers' Day. *Japan:* Green Day. *Orthodox:* Good Friday (see App. B20).

**30 Sat.** *Finland:* Vappu Day. *Netherlands:* Queen's Birthday.

# May 1994

**1 Sun.** *Jordan:* Easter Sunday. *Multinational:* Labor Day (see App. A7). *Orthodox:* Easter Sunday.

**2 Mon.** *Lesotho:* King's Birthday. *United Kingdom:* Labour Day. *Zambia:* Labour Day. *Orthodox:* Easter Monday (see App. B20).

**3 Tue.** *Japan:* Constitution Day.

**4 Wed.** *Japan:* People's Day.

**5 Thu.** *Japan:* Children's Day. *Mexico:* Cinco de Mayo. *Netherlands:* Liberation Day. *South Korea:* Children's Day. *Thailand:* Coronation Day.

**6 Fri.** *Lebanon:* Martyrs' Day. *Philippines:* Corregidor Day.

**8 Sun.** *France:* Labour Day. *International:* Mother's Day.

**9 Mon.** *Czech Republic:* Liberation Day*. *Slovakia:* Liberation Day*.

**10 Tue.** *Micronesia:* Independence Day.

**12 Thu.** *Christian:* Ascension (see App. B16).

**14 Sat.** *Liberia:* Unification Day. *Malawi:* Kamuzu Day. *Paraguay:* Flag Day.

**15 Sun.** *Paraguay:* Independence Day.

**16 Mon.** *Israel:* Pentecost. *Jewish:* Pentecost.

**17 Tue.** *Cayman Islands:* Discovery Day. *Norway:* Constitution Day. *South Korea:* Vesak Day.

**18 Wed.** *Haiti:* Flag Day. *Uruguay:* Las Piedras Day.

**19 Thu.** *Finland:* Flag Day. *Turkey:* Youth Day.

**20 Fri.** *Cameroon:* Constitution Day. *Zaïre:* Popular Movement Day. *Islamic:* Eid al Adha (1st day of 4) (see App. B28).

**21 Sat.** *Chile:* Navy Day. *Far East*

*Islamic:* Hari Raya Haji (see App. B29). *Islamic:* Eid al Adha (2nd day of 4) (see App. B28). *Zodiac Cusp:* Taurus ends, Gemini begins.

**22 Sun.** *Haiti:* Sovereign Day. *Sri Lanka:* Heroes' Day. *Christian:* Whitsunday. *Islamic:* Eid al Adha (3rd day of 4) (see App. B28).

**23 Mon.** *Burma:* Full Moon Day. *Canada:* Victoria Day. *Jamaica:* Labour Day. *Christian:* Whitmonday (see App. B18). *Islamic:* Eid al Adha (4th day of 4) (see App. B28).

**24 Tue.** *Bulgaria:* Culture Day. *Ecuador:* Independence Battle Day. *Malaysia:* Vesak Day. *Singapore:* Vesak Day. *Sri Lanka:* Full Moon Poya. *Thailand:* Visakha Bucha Day.

**25 Wed.** *Argentina:* National Day. *Eritrea:* Independence Day*. *Jordan:* Independence Day. *Sudan:* Revolution Day. *Multinational:* Africa Day (see App. A8).

**26 Thu.** *Guyana:* Independence Day.

**27 Fri.** *Nigeria:* Children's Day.

**30 Mon.** *United Kingdom:* Spring Break. *United States:* Memorial Day.

**31 Tue.** *Brunei:* Regiment Day. *South Africa:* Republic Day.

# June 1994

**1 Wed.** *Kenya:* Madaraka Day. *Malaysia:* King's Birthday. *Tunisia:* National Day. *Western Samoa:* Independence Day.

**2 Thu.** *Italy:* Republic Day. *Tunisia:* Youth Day. *Christian:* Corpus Christi (see App. B19).

**4 Sat.** *Bahamas:* Labour Day. *Tonga:* Independence Day.

**5 Sun.** *Denmark:* Constitution Day. *Equatorial Guinea:* President's Birthday. *Seychelles:* Liberation Day.

**6 Mon.** *Ireland:* Public Holiday. *New Zealand:* Queen's Birthday. *South Korea:* Memorial Day. *Sweden:* Constitution Day.

**7 Tue.** *Chad:* Revolution Day.

**9 Thu.** *Argentina:* Independence Day. *Islamic:* New Year's Day (see App. B22). (Hegira: 1415).

**10 Fri.** *Macao:* Portugal Day. *Portugal:* Portugal Day. *Far East Islamic:* New Year's Day (Hegira: 1415).

**11 Sat.** *Hong Kong:* Queen's Birthday (1st day of 2). *Libya:* Evacuation Day.

**12 Sun.** *Philippines:* Independence Day.

**13 Mon.** *Australia:* Queen's Birthday. *Fiji:* Queen's Birthday. *Hong Kong:* Queen's Birthday (2nd day of 2). *New Guinea:* Queen's Birthday. *United Kingdom:* Queen's Birthday.

**15 Wed.** *Asian:* Dragon Boat Festival (see App. B5).

**17 Fri.** *Germany:* Unity Day. *Iceland:* Independence Day.

**18 Sat.** *Egypt:* Independence Day. *Islamic:* Ashura (see App. B23).

**19 Sun.** *Algeria:* Righting Day. *Kuwait:* Independence Day. *Uruguay:* Artigas Day. *Orthodox:* Pentecost Sunday.

**20 Mon.** *Argentina:* Flag Day. *Greece:* Pentecost Monday.

**21 Tue.** *Finland:* Midsummer Day (1st day of 2). *Sweden:* Midsummer Day (1st day of 2). *Zodiac Cusp:* Gemini ends, Cancer begins.

**22 Wed.** *Burma:* Full Moon Day. *Finland:* Midsummer Day (2nd day of 2). *Sri Lanka:* Full Moon Poya. *Sweden:* Midsummer Day (2nd day of 2).

**23 Thu.** *Luxembourg:* National Day.

**24 Fri.** *Andorra:* Saint John's Day. *Chile:* Bank Holiday. *Ecuador:* Bank Holiday. *El Salvador:* Bank Holiday. *Finland:* Bank Holiday. *Venezuela:* Carabobo Day. *Zaïre:* Constitution Day.

**25 Sat.** *Croatia:* Independence Day*.

*Finland:* Johannus Day. *Mozambique:* Independence Day. *Slovenia:* Independence Day*.

**26 Sun.** *Madagascar:* Independence Day. *Somalia:* Independence Day.

**27 Mon.** *Djibouti:* Independence Day.

**29 Wed.** *Seychelles:* Independence Day. *Christian:* Saint Paul's Day (see App. A9).

**30 Thu.** *Guatemala:* Army Day. *Sri Lanka:* Bank Holiday. *Zaïre:* Independence Day.

# July 1994

**1 Fri.** *Burundi:* Independence Day. *Canada:* Canada Day. *Ghana:* Republic Day. *Hong Kong:* Half Year Day. *Rwanda:* Independence Day. *Somalia:* Union Day. *Suriname:* Freedom Day. *Multinational:* Bank Holiday (see App. A10).

**4 Mon.** *Cayman Islands:* Constitution Day. *Lesotho:* Family Day. *Philippines:* United States Friendship Day. *United States:* Independence Day. *Yugoslavia:* Freedom Fighters' Day. *Zambia:* Heroes' Day.

**5 Tue.** *Algeria:* Independence Day. *Cape Verde:* Independence Day. *Rwanda:* Unity Day. *Venezuela:* Independence Day. *Zambia:* Unity Day.

**6 Wed.** *Comoros:* Independence Day. *Malawi:* Republic Day.

**7 Thu.** *Solomon Islands:* Independence Day. *Tanzania:* Farmers' Day. *Yugoslavia:* Serbian Day.

**10 Sun.** *Bahamas:* Independence Day.

**11 Mon.** *Mongolia:* Revolution Day.

**12 Tue.** *Kiribati:* Independence Day. *Northern Ireland:* Battle of the Boyne Day. *São Tomé:* National Day.

**14 Thu.** *France:* National Day. *Iraq:* Revolution Day.

**15 Fri.** *Brunei:* Sultan's Birthday.

**17 Sun.** *Iraq:* Revolution Day. *Israel:* Tisha Ab. *Puerto Rico:* Rivera Day. *Slovakia:* Independence Day*. *South Korea:* Constitution Day. *Jewish:* Tisha Ab.

**18 Mon.** *Botswana:* President's Day. *Uruguay:* Constitution Day.

**19 Tue.** *Burma:* Martyrs' Day. *Laos:* Independence Day. *Nicaragua:* Sandinista Day.

**20 Wed.** *Colombia:* Independence Day.

**21 Thu.** *Belgium:* National Day. *Burma:* Full Moon Day. *Guam:* Liberation Day.

**22 Fri.** *Poland:* Liberation Day. *Sri Lanka:* Full Moon Poya. *Thailand:* Asalaha Bucha Day.

**23 Sat.** *Egypt:* Revolution Day. *New Guinea:* Remembrance Day. *Thailand:* Khao Phansa Day. *Zodiac Cusp:* Cancer ends, Leo begins.

**24 Sun.** *Venezuela:* Bolivar Day.

**25 Mon.** *Costa Rica:* Guanacaste Day. *Cuba:* Revolution Day (1st day of 3). *Puerto Rico:* Constitution Day. *Spain:* Santiago Day. *Tunisia:* Republic Day. *Virgin Islands (U.S.):* Hurricane Supplication Day.

**26 Tue.** *Cuba:* Revolution Day (2nd day of 3). *Liberia:* Independence Day. *Maldives:* Independence Day.

**27 Wed.** *Cuba:* Revolution Day (3rd day of 3). *Puerto Rico:* Barbosa Day.

**28 Thu.** *Peru:* Independence Day (1st day of 2).

**29 Fri.** *Peru:* Independence Day (2nd day of 2).

**30 Sat.** *Vanuatu:* Independence Day.

# August 1994

**1 Mon.** *Bahamas:* Emancipation Day. *Barbados:* Emancipation Day. *Benin:* Independence Day. *Canada:* Civic Holiday. *Ireland:* Public Holiday. *Jamaica:* Independence Day. *Scotland:* Public Holiday. *Switzerland:* Confederation Day.

**2 Tue.** *Costa Rica:* Virgin of the Angels Day. *Guyana:* Freedom Day. *Trinidad:* Discovery Day.

**3 Wed.** *El Salvador:* Summer Day (1st day of 4). *Guinea-Bissau:* Martyrs' Day. *Niger:* Independence Day. *Tunisia:* President's Birthday. *Zambia:* Farmers' Day.

**4 Thu.** *Burkina Faso:* Independence Day (1st day of 2). *El Salvador:* Summer Day (2nd day of 4).

**5 Fri.** *Burkina Faso:* Independence Day (2nd day of 2). *El Salvador:* Summer Day (3rd day of 4).

**6 Sat.** *Bolivia:* Independence Day. *El Salvador:* Summer Day (4th day of 4). *United Arab Emirates:* Accession Day.

**7 Sun.** *Colombia:* Boyaca Day. *Ivory Coast:* Republic Day.

**9 Tue.** *Georgia:* Independence Day*. *Singapore:* National Day.

**10 Wed.** *Ecuador:* Independence Day.

**11 Thu.** *Chad:* Independence Day. *Jordan:* Accession Day. *Zimbabwe:* Heroes' Day (1st day of 2).

**12 Fri.** *Thailand:* Queen's Birthday. *Zimbabwe:* Heroes' Day (2nd day of 2).

**13 Sat.** *Central African Republic:* Independence Day. *Congo:* Independence Day (1st day of 2). *Tunisia:* Women's Day.

**14 Sun.** *Congo:* Independence Day (2nd day of 2). *Pakistan:* Independence Day.

**15 Mon.** *Congo:* Independence Day (3rd day of 3). *India:* Independence Day. *Liechtenstein:* National Day. *South Korea:* Republic Day. *Christian:* Assumption (see App. A11).

**16 Tue.** *Dominican Republic:* Republic Day.

**17 Wed.** *Argentina:* San Martin's Day. *Gabon:* Independence Day. *Indonesia:* Independence Day.

**18 Thu.** *Islamic:* Mohammed's Birthday (see App. B24).

**19 Fri.** *Burma:* Full Moon Day. *Far East Islamic:* Mohammed's Birthday.

**20 Sat.** *Hungary:* Constitution Day. *Senegal:* Independence Day. *Sri Lanka:* Full Moon Poya.

**21 Sun.** *Estonia:* Independence Day*. *Latvia:* Independence Day*. *Lithuania:* Independence Day*.

**23 Tue.** *Romania:* National Day (1st day of 2). *Zodiac Cusp:* Leo ends, Virgo begins.

**24 Wed.** *Kazakhstan:* National Day*. *Liberia:* Flag Day. *Romania:* National Day (2nd day of 2). *Russia:* Independence Day*. *Ukraine:* National Day*.

**25 Thu.** *Belarus:* Independence Day*. *Paraguay:* Constitution Day. *Uruguay:* Independence Day.

**27 Sat.** *Hong Kong:* Liberation Day (1st day of 2). *Moldova:* Independence Day*.

**29 Mon.** *England:* Summer Break. *Hong Kong:* Liberation Day (2nd day of 2). *Luxembourg:* Fair Day. *Northern Ireland:* Summer Break. *Uzbekistan:* Independence Day*. *Wales:* Summer Break.

**30 Tue.** *Afghanistan:* Children's Day. *Azerbaijan:* Independence Day*. *Peru:* Rose of Lima Day. *Turkey:* Victory Day.

**31 Wed.** *Afghanistan:* Pashtunistan Day. *Kyrgyzstan:* Independence Day*. *Malaysia:* National Day. *Trinidad:* Independence Day.

# September 1994

**1 Thu.** *Libya:* National Day. *Mexico:* President's Message Day. *Syria:* United Arab Republics Day.

**2 Fri.** *Vietnam:* Independence Day.

**3 Sat.** *Qatar:* National Day. *San Marino:* Saint Marinus' Day. *Tunisia:* Independence Movement Day.

**5 Mon.** *Canada:* Labour Day. *United States:* Labor Day.

**6 Tue.** *Israel:* New Year's Day. *Pakistan:* Defense Day. *Swaziland:* Independence Day. *Jewish:* Rosh Hashanah (Jewish: 5755).

**7 Wed.** *Brazil:* Independence Day.

**8 Thu.** *Andorra:* National Day. *Malta:* Our Lady of Victory Day.

**9 Fri.** *Bulgaria:* National Day (1st day of 2). *North Korea:* Independence Day. *Tajikistan:* Independence Day*.

**10 Sat.** *Belize:* National Day. *Bulgaria:* National Day (2nd day of 2).

**11 Sun.** *Chile:* Revolution Day. *Egypt:* New Year's Day (Coptic: 1712). *Ethiopia:* New Year's Day (Ethiopian: 1988). *Pakistan:* Anniversary of Quaid-e-Azam's Death.

**12 Mon.** *Ethiopia:* National Day.

**14 Wed.** *Guatemala:* San Jacinto Day. *Nicaragua:* San Jacinto Day.

**15 Thu.** *Costa Rica:* Independence Day. *El Salvador:* Independence Day. *Guatemala:* Independence Day. *Honduras:* Independence Day. *Israel:* Yom Kippur. *Japan:* Veneration Day. *Nicaragua:* Independence Day. *Jewish:* Yom Kippur.

**16 Fri.** *Mexico:* Independence Day. *New Guinea:* Independence Day.

**17 Sat.** *Angola:* Heroes' Day. *Marshall Islands:* Independence Day.

**18 Sun.** *Burma:* Full Moon Day. *Burundi:* Victory of Uprona Day. *Chile:* Independence Day.

**19 Mon.** *Chile:* Armed Forces Day. *Saint Kitts:* Independence Day. *Sri Lanka:* Full Moon Poya.

**20 Tue.** *Israel:* Sukkot. *Jewish:* Sukkot.

**21 Wed.** *Belize:* Independence Day. *Malta:* Independence Day.

**22 Thu.** *Mali:* Independence Day.

**23 Fri.** *Armenia:* Independence Day*. *Japan:* Autumnal Equinox. *Saudi Arabia:* National Day. *Zodiac Cusp:* Virgo ends, Libra begins.

**24 Sat.** *Dominican Republic:* Mercedes Day. *Guinea-Bissau:* Republic Day.

**25 Sun.** *Mozambique:* Liberation Day. *Rwanda:* Assembly Day. *Europe:* Daylight Savings Time ends (retard clocks 1 hour).

**26 Mon.** *Ethiopia:* True Cross Day.

**28 Wed.** *Taiwan:* Teachers' Day.

**29 Thu.** *Brunei:* Constitution Day. *Paraguay:* Boqueron Battle Day.

**30 Fri.** *Botswana:* Independence Day.

# October 1994

**1 Sat.** *Cameroon:* Unification Day. *China:* National Day (1st day of 2). *Nigeria:* Independence Day. *South Korea:* Armed Forces Day. (1st day of 2). *Tuvalu:* Independence Day.

**2 Sun.** *China:* National Day (2nd day of 2). *Guinea:* Independence Day. *India:* Ghandi Day. *South Korea:* Armed Forces Day (2nd day of 2).

**3 Mon.** *Barbados:* Bank Holiday. *Honduras:* Morazan Day. *South. Korea:* Foundation Day (1st day of 2).

**4 Tue.** *Lesotho:* Independence Day. *South Korea:* Foundation Day (2nd day of 2).

**5 Wed.** *Lesotho:* Sports Day. *Macao:* Portuguese Republic Day. *Portugal:* Republic Day.

**6 Thu.** *Egypt:* Armed Forces Day.

**9 Sun.** *Peru:* National Dignity Day. *South Korea:* Alphabet Day. *Uganda:* Independence Day.

**10 Mon.** *Canada:* Thanksgiving Day. *Fiji:* Cession Day. *Japan:* Health Day. *South Africa:* Kruger Day. *Taiwan:* National Day. *United States:* Bank Holiday. *Virgin Islands (U.S.):* Puerto Rican Friendship Day.

**11 Tue.** *Cuba:* Independence War. *Panama:* Revolution Day.

**12 Wed.** *Equatorial Guinea:* Independence Day. *Spain:* National Day. *Multinational:* Columbus Day (see App. A12).

**14 Fri.** *Zaïre:* Founders' Day. *Asian:* Ancestors' Day (see App. B6).

**15 Sat.** *Bosnia and Herzegovina:* Independence Day*. *Tunisia:* Evacuation Day.

**17 Mon.** *Haiti:* Dessalines Day. *Jamaica:* Heroes' Day. *Malawi:* Mother's Day.

**18 Tue.** *Burma:* Full Moon Day. *China:* Mid-autumn Day. *Sri Lanka:* Full Moon Poya. *Taiwan:* Mid-autumn Day.

**19 Wed.** *Hong Kong:* Mid-autumn Day. *Macao:* Mid-autumn Day.

**20 Thu.** *Guatemala:* Revolution Day. *Kenya:* Kenyatta Day.

**21 Fri.** *Honduras:* Army Day. *Somalia:* Revolution Day (1st day of 2).

**22 Sat.** *Somalia:* Revolution Day (2nd day of 2). *Vatican:* John Paul II Day.

**23 Sun.** *Hungary:* Revolution Day. *Thailand:* Chulalongkorn Day. *Zodiac Cusp:* Libra ends, Scorpio begins.

**24 Mon.** *Egypt:* Suez Victory Day. *Haiti:* United Nations Day. *Zambia:* Independence Day.

**25 Tue.** *Taiwan:* Restoration Day.

**26 Wed.** *Austria:* National Day. *Benin:* Revolution Day. *Rwanda:* Government Day.

**27 Thu.** *Saint Vincent:* Independence Day. *Turkmenistan:* Independence Day*. *Zaïre:* Naming Day.

**28 Fri.** *Greece:* Ohi! Day.

**29 Sat.** *Tanzania:* Naming Day. *Turkey:* Republic Day.

**30 Sun.** *Canada and United States:* Daylight Savings Time ends (retard clocks 1 hour).

**31 Mon.** *Ireland:* Public Holiday. *New Zealand:* Labour Day. *Taiwan:* Chiang Kai-shek's Birthday.

# November 1994

**1 Tue.** *Algeria:* Revolution Day. *Antigua:* Independence Day. *Christian:* All Saints' Day (see App. A13).

**2 Wed.** *Brazil:* Memorial Day. *Finland:* All Saints' Eve. *Sweden:* All Saints' Eve. *Christian:* All Souls' Day (see App. A14). *Hindu:* Deepavali (see App. B21).

**3 Thu.** *Dominica:* Independence Day. *Ecuador:* Cuenca Independence Day. *Japan:* Culture Day. *Liberia:* Thanksgiving Day. *Panama:* Independence Day.

**4 Fri.** *Andorra:* Saint Charles' Day. *Panama:* Flag Day. *Vatican:* John Paul II's Nameday.

**5 Sat.** *El Salvador:* Cry of Independence Day.

**7 Mon.** *Bangladesh:* Revolution Day. *Virgin Islands (U.S.):* Liberty Day.

**8 Tue.** *Nepal:* Queen's Birthday.

**9 Wed.** *Pakistan:* Iqbal Day.

**10 Thu.** *Panama:* Cry of Independence Day.

**11 Fri.** *Angola:* Independence Day. *Bhutan:* King's Birthday. *Maldives:* Republic Day. *Poland:* Independence Day. *Multinational:* Armistice Day (see App. A15).

**12 Sat.** *Taiwan:* Dr. Sun Yat-sen's Birthday.

**14 Mon.** *Jordan:* King's Birthday.

**15 Tue.** *Brazil:* Republic Day.

**16 Wed.** *Burma:* Full Moon Day. *Germany:* Repentance Day.

**17 Thu.** *Sri Lanka:* Full Moon Poya. *Zaïre:* Armed Forces Day.

**18 Fri.** *Haiti:* Vertieres' Day. *Morocco:* Independence Day. *Oman:* National Day.

**19 Sat.** *Belize:* Garifuna Day. *Mali:* Army Coup Day. *Monaco:* Prince Ranier's Day. *Puerto Rico:* Discovery Day.

**20 Sun.** *Mexico:* Revolution Day.

**21 Mon.** *Fiji:* Prince Charles' Birthday.

**22 Tue.** *Lebanon:* Independence Day. *Zodiac Cusp:* Scorpio ends, Sagittarius begins.

**23 Wed.** *Japan:* Labor Thanksgiving Day.

**24 Thu.** *United States:* Thanksgiving Day. *Zaïre:* New Regime Day.

**25 Fri.** *Argentina:* Bank Holiday. *Suriname:* Independence Day.

**28 Mon.** *Albania:* Independence Day. *Burundi:* Republic Day. *Chad:* Republic Day. *Mauritania:* Independence Day. *Panama:* Independence Day. *Jewish:* Chanukah.

**29 Tue.** *Albania:* Liberation Day. *Liberia:* Tubman's Birthday. *Yugoslavia:* Republic Day.

**30 Wed.** *Barbados:* Independence Day. *Benin:* National Day. *Philippines:* Heroes' Day.

# December 1994

**1 Thu.** *Central African Republic:* National Day. *Portugal:* Youth Day. *Ukraine:* Independence Day*.

**2 Fri.** *Laos:* Republic Day. *United Arab Emirates:* National Day.

**5 Mon.** *Haiti:* Discovery Day. *Thailand:* King's Birthday.

**6 Tue.** *Finland:* Independence Day.

**7 Wed.** *Ivory Coast:* Independence Day.

**8 Thu.** *Christian:* Immaculate Conception (see App. A16).

**9 Fri.** *Tanzania:* Independence Day.

**10 Sat.** *Angola:* MPLA Foundation Day. *Equatorial Guinea:* Human Rights Day. *Namibia:* Settlers' Day. *Thailand:* Constitution Day.

**11 Sun.** *Burkina Faso:* National Day.

**12 Mon.** *Kenya:* Independence Day. *Mexico:* Guadalupe Festival.

**13 Tue.** *Malta:* Republic Day.

**16 Fri.** *Bahrain:* National Day. *Bangladesh:* Victory Day. *Burma:* Full Moon Day. *Nepal:* Constitution Day. *South Africa:* Covenant Day.

**17 Sat.** *Bhutan:* National Day. *Sri Lanka:* Full Moon Poya.

**18 Sun.** *Niger:* Republic Day.

**21 Wed.** *Kazakhstan:* Independence Day*.

**22 Thu.** *Zodiac Cusp:* Sagittarius ends, Capricorn begins.

**23 Fri.** *Japan:* Emperor's Birthday.

**24 Sat.** *Multinational:* Christmas Eve (see App. A17).

**25 Sun.** *Angola:* Family Day. *Congo:* Children's Day. *Pakistan:* Quaid's Birthday. *Taiwan:* Constitution Day. *Multinational:* Christmas Day (see App. A18).

**26 Mon.** *South Africa:* Good Will Day. *Multinational:* Boxing Day (see App. A19).

**29 Thu.** *Islamic:* Isra a Majraj (see App. B20).

**30 Fri.** *Madagascar:* Republic Day. *Philippines:* Rizal Day (1st day of 2).

**31 Sat.** *Congo:* Republic Day. *Philippines:* Rizal Day (2nd day of 2). *Multinational:* Bank Holiday and New Year's Eve (see App. A20 & A21).

# January 1995

**1 Sun.** *Cameroon:* Independence Day. *Cuba:* Liberation Day. *Haiti:* Independence Day. *Palau:* Independence Day. *Sudan:* Independence Day. *Taiwan:* Foundation Day (1st day of 2). *Western Samoa:* Independence Day. *Multinational:* Bank Holiday and New Year's Day (see App. A1 & A2).

**2 Mon.** *Hong Kong:* New Year's Day. *Japan:* Bank Holiday. *New Zealand:* New Year's Day (2nd day of 2). *Scotland:* New Year's Day (2nd day of 2). *South Korea:* New Year's Day (2nd day of 2). *Switzerland:* Berchtold's Day. *Taiwan:* Foundation Day (2nd day of 2).

**3 Tue.** *Burkina Faso:* Revolution Day.

**4 Wed.** *Burma:* Independence Day. *Zaïre:* Martyrs' Day.

**6 Fri.** *Iraq:* Army Day. *Uruguay:* Children's Day. *Christian:* Epiphany (see App. A3).

**7 Sat.** *Egypt:* Coptic Christmas. *Ethiopia:* Coptic Christmas.

**11 Wed.** *Albania:* Republic Day. *Nepal:* Unification Day. *Puerto Rico:* Hostos Day.

**12 Thu.** *Tanzania:* Revolution Day.

**13 Fri.** *Togo:* Liberation Day.

**15 Sun.** *Burma:* Full Moon Day. *Japan:* Adult's Day. *Jordan:* Arbor Day.

**16 Mon.** *Sri Lanka:* Full Moon Poya. *United States:* Martin Luther King's Birthday.

**19 Thu.** *Ethiopia:* Epiphany.

**20 Fri.** *Mali:* Award Day. *Zodiac Cusp:* Capricorn ends, Aquarius begins.

**21 Sat.** *Dominican Republic:* Altagracia Day.

**22 Sun.** *Saint Vincent:* Discovery Day.

**26 Thu.** *Dominican Republic:* Duarte Day. *India:* Republic Day.

**27 Fri.** *Monaco:* Saint Devota's Day. *Vietnam:* Vietnam Day.

**28 Sat.** *Rwanda:* Democracy Day.

**30 Mon.** *Australia:* Australia Day. *Asian:* Chinese New Year Eve (see App. B1).

**31 Tue.** *Nauru:* Independence Day. *Vietnam:* Tet (1st day of 3). *Asian:* Chinese New Year (Year of the Pig) (see App. B2). *Islamic:* 1st Day of Ramadan (see App. B25).

# February 1995

**1 Wed.** *Vietnam:* Tet (2nd day of 3). *Asian:* 2nd Day of Chinese New Year (see App. B3).

**2 Thu.** *Liechtenstein:* Candlemas. *Vietnam:* Tet (3rd day of 3). *Asian:* 3rd Day of Chinese New Year (see App. B4).

**4 Sat.** *Sri Lanka:* Independence Day.

**5 Sun.** *Mexico:* Constitution Day.

**6 Mon.** *New Zealand:* Waitangi Day. *United States:* Lincoln's Birthday.

**7 Tue.** *Grenada:* Independence Day.

**8 Wed.** *Iraq:* Revolution Day.

**9 Thu.** *Lebanon:* Saint Marion's Day.

**10 Fri.** *Malta:* Saint Paul's Day.

**11 Sat.** *Cameroon:* Youth Day. *Japan:* Foundation Day. *Liberia:* Armed Forces Day.

**12 Sun.** *Burma:* Union Day.

**14 Tue.** *Burma:* Full Moon Day. *Sri Lanka:* Full Moon Poya. *Thailand:* Makha Bucha Day. *International:* Valentine's Day.

**18 Sat.** *Gambia:* Independence Day.

**19 Sun.** *Nepal:* National Day. *Zodiac Cusp:* Aquarius ends, Pisces begins.

**20 Mon.** *United States:* Washington's Birthday.

**21 Tue.** *Bangladesh:* Saheed Day.

**22 Wed.** *Saint Lucia:* Independence Day.

**23 Thu.** *Brunei:* National Day. *Guyana:* Republic Day.

**25 Sat.** *Kuwait:* National Day.

**27 Mon.** *Dominican Republic:* Independence Day. *Christian:* Shrove Monday (see App. B7).

**28 Tue.** *Christian:* Shrove Tuesday (see App. B8).

# March 1995

**1 Wed.** *South Korea:* Independence Day. *Christian:* Ash Wednesday (see App. B9). *Far East Islamic:* Hari Raya Puasa (see App. B27). *Islamic:* Eid al Fitr (1st day of 4) (see App. B26).

**2 Thu.** *Ethiopia:* Victory of Aduwa Day. *Morocco:* Independence Day. *Islamic:* Eid al Fitr (2nd day of 4) (see App. B26).

**3 Fri.** *Bulgaria:* Liberation Day. *Malawi:* Martyrs' Day. *Morocco:* National Day. *Islamic:* Eid al Fitr (3rd day of 4) (see App. B26).

**4 Sat.** *Islamic:* Eid al Fitr (4th day of 4) (see App. B26).

**6 Mon.** *Ghana:* Independence Day. *Greece:* Shrove Monday. *Guam:* Discovery Day. *Orthodox:* Shrove Monday.

**8 Wed.** *Syria:* Revolution Day. *Multinational:* Women's Day (see App. A4).

**10 Fri.** *South Korea:* Labor Day.

**11 Sat.** *Lithuania:* National Day*. *Zambia:* Youth Day.

**12 Sun.** *Lesotho:* Moshoeshoe's Day. *Mauritius:* Independence Day.

**13 Mon.** *Gibraltar:* Commonwealth Day. *Grenada:* National Day.

**15 Wed.** *Burma:* Full Moon Day.

**16 Thu.** *Sri Lanka:* Full Moon Poya. *Jewish:* Purim.

**17 Fri.** *Ireland:* Saint Patrick's Day. *Northern Ireland:* Saint Patrick's Day.

**19 Sun.** *Christian:* Saint Joseph's Day (see App. A5).

**20 Mon.** *Tunisia:* Independence Day.

**21 Tue.** *Afghanistan:* New Year's Day. (Shamsi: 1374). *Iran:* New Year's Day. (Hegira: 1374). *Iraq:* New Year's Day. *Japan:* Vernal Equinox. *Mexico:* Juarez Day. *Zodiac Cusp:* Pisces ends, Aries begins.

**22 Wed.** *Puerto Rico:* Abolition Day.

**23 Thu.** *Pakistan:* Pakistan Day.

**25 Sat.** *Cyprus:* Greek Independence Day. *Greece:* Independence Day. *Liechtenstein:* Annunciation.

**26 Sun.** *Bangladesh:* Independence Day. *Europe:* Daylight Savings Time starts (advance clocks 1 hour).

**27 Mon.** *Angola:* Evacuation Day. *Burma:* Resistance Day. *Virgin Islands (U.S.):* Transfer Day.

**28 Tue.** *Zambia:* Africa Day.

**29 Wed.** *Central African Republic:* Boganda Day. *Madagascar:* Memorial Day. *Taiwan:* Youth Day.

**31 Fri.** *Malta:* National Day.

# April 1995

**1 Sat.** *Iran:* Republic Day. *San Marino:* National Day.

**2 Sun.** *Canada and United States:* Daylight Savings Time starts (advance clocks 1 hour).

**4 Tue.** *Hungary:* Liberation Day. *Senegal:* National Day.

**5 Wed.** *South Korea:* Arbor Day. *Asian:* Tomb Sweeping Day (see App. A6).

**6 Thu.** *South Africa:* Founders' Day. *Thailand:* Chakri Day.

**7 Fri.** *Sierra Leone:* Bank Holiday.

**9 Sun.** *Philippines:* Valour Day. *Tunisia:* Martyrs' Day. *Christian:* Palm Sunday.

**11 Tue.** *Costa Rica:* Heroes' Day. *Uganda:* Liberation Day.

**13 Thu.** *Chad:* National Day. *Thailand:* Songkrawn (1st day of 2). *Christian:* Maundy Thursday (see App. B11).

**14 Fri.** *Burma:* Full Moon Day. *Honduras:* Pan American Day. *Sri Lanka:* Full Moon Poya. *Thailand:* Songkrawn (2nd day of 2). *Christian:* Good Friday (see App. B12).

**15 Sat.** *Israel:* Passover. *Niger:* National Day. *Christian:* Holy Saturday (see App. B13). *Jewish:* Passover.

**16 Sun.** *Burma:* New Year's Day (Burmese: 1357). *Cyprus:* Independence Day. *Christian:* Easter Sunday (see App. B14).

**17 Mon.** *Cambodia:* Independence Day. *Syria:* Independence Day. *Christian:* Easter Monday (see App. B15).

**18 Tue.** *Zimbabwe:* Republic Day.

**19 Wed.** *Sierra Leone:* Republic Day. *Uruguay:* Patriots' Day. *Venezuela:* Independence Day.

**20 Thu.** *Zodiac Cusp:* Aries ends, Taurus begins.

**21 Fri.** *Brazil:* Tiradentes Day. *Orthodox:* Good Friday (see App. B20).

**23 Sun.** *Jordan:* Easter Sunday. *Turkey:* Children's Day. *Orthodox:* Easter Sunday.

**24 Mon.** *Orthodox:* Easter Monday (see App. B20).

**25 Tue.** *Australia:* ANZAC Day. *Egypt:* Sinai Day. *Iceland:* Children's Day. *Italy:* Liberation Day. *New Zealand:* ANZAC Day. *Portugal:* Liberation Day. *Swaziland:* Flag Day.

**26 Wed.** *Tanzania:* Union Day.

**27 Thu.** *Afghanistan:* Independence Day. *Sierra Leone:* Independence Day. *Togo:* Independence Day.

**29 Sat.** *Japan:* Green Day.

**30 Sun.** *Finland:* Vappu Day. *Netherlands:* Queen's Birthday.

# May 1995

**1 Mon.** *United Kingdom:* Labour Day. *Zambia:* Labour Day. *Multinational:* Labor Day (see App. A7).

**2 Tue.** *Lesotho:* King's Birthday.

**3 Wed.** *Japan:* Constitution Day.

**4 Thu.** *Israel:* Independence Day. *Japan:* People's Day.

**5 Fri.** *Japan:* Children's Day. *Mexico:* Cinco de Mayo. *Netherlands:* Liberation Day. *South Korea:* Children's Day. *Thailand:* Coronation Day.

**6 Sat.** *Lebanon:* Martyrs' Day. *Philippines:* Corregidor Day. *South Korea:* Vesak Day.

**8 Mon.** *France:* Liberation Day. *Islamic:* Eid al Adha (1st day of 4) (see App. B28).

**9 Tue.** *Czech Republic:* Liberation Day*. *Slovakia:* Liberation Day*. *Far East Islamic:* Hari Raya Haji (see App. B29). *Islamic:* Eid al Adha (2nd day of 4) (see App. B28).

**10 Wed.** *Micronesia:* Independence Day. *Islamic:* Eid al Adha (3rd day of 4) (see App. B28).

**11 Thu.** *Islamic:* Eid al Adha (4th day of 4) (see App. B28).

**12 Fri.** *Denmark:* All Prayers' Day.

**13 Sat.** *Burma:* Full Moon Day. *Malaysia:* Vesak Day. *Singapore:* Vesak Day. *Thailand:* Visakha Bucha Day.

**14 Sun.** *Liberia:* Unification Day. *Malawi:* Kamuzu Day. *Paraguay:* Flag Day. *Sri Lanka:* Full Moon Poya. *International:* Mother's Day.

**15 Mon.** *Paraguay:* Independence Day.

**17 Wed.** *Cayman Islands:* Discovery Day. *Norway:* Constitution Day.

**18 Thu.** *Haiti:* Flag Day. *Uruguay:* Las Piedras Day.

**19 Fri.** *Finland:* Flag Day. *Turkey:* Youth Day.

**20 Sat.** *Cameroon:* Constitution Day. *Zaïre:* Popular Movement Day.

**21 Sun.** *Chile:* Navy Day. *Zodiac Cusp:* Taurus ends, Gemini begins.

**22 Mon.** *Canada:* Victoria Day. *Haiti:* Sovereign Day. *Sri Lanka:* Heroes' Day.

**23 Tue.** *Jamaica:* Labour Day.

**24 Wed.** *Bulgaria:* Culture Day. *Ecuador:* Independence Battle Day.

**25 Thu.** *Argentina:* National Day. *Eritrea:* Independence Day*. *Jordan:* Independence Day. *Sudan:* Revolution Day. *Christian:* Ascension (see App. B16). *Multinational:* Africa Day (see App. A8).

**26 Fri.** *Guyana:* Independence Day.

**27 Sat.** *Nigeria:* Children's Day.

**29 Mon.** *United Kingdom:* Spring Break. *United States:* Memorial Day. *Islamic:* New Year's Day. (Hegira: 1416) (see App. B22).

**30 Tue.** *Far East Islamic:* New Year's Day. (Hegira: 1416).

**31 Wed.** *Brunei:* Regiment Day. *South Africa:* Republic Day.

# June 1995

**1 Thu.** *Kenya:* Madaraka Day. *Tunisia:* National Day. *Western Samoa:* Independence Day.

**2 Fri.** *Italy:* Republic Day. *Tunisia:* Youth Day.

**4 Sun.** *Bahamas:* Labour Day. *Israel:* Pentecost. *Tonga:* Independence Day. *Asian:* Dragon Boat Festival (see App. B5). *Christian:* Whitsunday. *Jewish:* Pentecost.

**5 Mon.** *Denmark:* Constitution Day. *Equatorial Guinea:* President's Birthday. *Ireland:* Public Holiday. *New Zealand:* Queen's Birthday. *Seychelles:* Liberation Day. *Christian:* Whitmonday (see App. B18).

**6 Tue.** *South Korea:* Memorial Day. *Sweden:* Constitution Day.

**7 Wed.** *Chad:* Revolution Day. *Malaysia:* King's Birthday. *Islamic:* Ashura (see App. B23).

**9 Fri.** *Argentina:* Independence Day.

**10 Sat.** *Hong Kong:* Queen's Birthday (1st day of 2). *Macao:* Portugal Day. *Portugal:* Portugal Day.

**11 Sun.** *Burma:* Full Moon Day. *Libya:* Evacuation Day. *Orthodox:* Pentecost Sunday.

**12 Mon.** *Australia:* Queen's Birthday. *Fiji:* Queen's Birthday. *Greece:* Pentecost Monday. *Hong Kong:* Queen's Birthday (2nd day of 2). *New Guinea:* Queen's Birthday. *Philippines:* Independence Day. *Sri Lanka:* Full Moon Poya. *United Kingdom:* Queen's Birthday.

**15 Thu.** *Christian:* Corpus Christi (see App. B19).

**17 Sat.** *Germany:* Unity Day. *Iceland:* Independence Day.

**18 Sun.** *Egypt:* Independence Day.

**19 Mon.** *Algeria:* Righting Day. *Kuwait:* Independence Day. *Uruguay:* Artigas Day.

**20 Tue.** *Argentina:* Flag Day.

**21 Wed.** *Finland:* Midsummer Day (1st day of 2). *Sweden:* Midsummer Day (1st day of 2). *Zodiac Cusp:* Gemini ends, Cancer begins.

**22 Thu.** *Finland:* Midsummer Day (2nd day of 2). *Sweden:* Midsummer Day (2nd day of 2).

**23 Fri.** *Luxembourg:* National Day.

**24 Sat.** *Andorra:* Saint John's Day. *Finland:* Johannus Day. *Venezuela:* Carabobo Day. *Zaïre:* Constitution Day.

**25 Sun.** *Croatia:* Independence Day*. *Mozambique:* Independence Day. *Slovenia:* Independence Day*.

**26 Mon.** *Madagascar:* Independence Day. *Somalia:* Independence Day.

**27 Tue.** *Djibouti:* Independence Day.

**29 Thu.** *Seychelles:* Independence Day. *Christian:* Saint Paul's Day (see App. A9).

**30 Fri.** *Chile:* Bank Holiday. *Ecuador:* Bank Holiday. *El Salvador:* Bank Holiday. *Finland:* Bank Holiday. *Guatemala:* Army Day. *Sri Lanka:* Bank Holiday. *Zaïre:* Independence Day.

# July 1995

**1 Sat.** *Burundi:* Independence Day. *Canada:* Canada Day. *Ghana:* Republic Day. *Hong Kong:* Half Year Day. *Rwanda:* Independence Day. *Somalia:* Union Day. *Suriname:* Freedom Day. *Multinational:* Bank Holiday (see App. A10).

**3 Mon.** *Cayman Islands:* Constitution Day. *Lesotho:* Family Day. *Zambia:* Heroes' Day.

**4 Tue.** *Philippines:* United States Friendship Day. *United States:* Independence Day. *Yugoslavia:* Freedom Fighters' Day. *Zambia:* Unity Day.

**5 Wed.** *Algeria:* Independence Day. *Cape Verde:* Independence Day. *Rwanda:* Unity Day. *Venezuela:* Independence Day.

**6 Thu.** *Comoros:* Independence Day. *Malawi:* Republic Day.

**7 Fri.** *Solomon Islands:* Independence Day. *Tanzania:* Farmers' Day. *Yugoslavia:* Serbian Day.

**10 Mon.** *Bahamas:* Independence Day. *Burma:* Full Moon Day.

**11 Tue.** *Mongolia:* Revolution Day. *Sri Lanka:* Full Moon Poya.

**12 Wed.** *Kiribati:* Independence Day. *Northern Ireland:* Battle of the Boyne Day. *São Tomé:* National Day. *Thailand:* Asalaha Bucha Day.

**13 Thu.** *Thailand:* Khao Phansa Day.

**14 Fri.** *France:* National Day. *Iraq:* Revolution Day.

**15 Sat.** *Brunei:* Sultan's Birthday.

**17 Mon.** *Botswana:* President's Day. *Iraq:* Revolution Day. *Puerto Rico:* Rivera Day. *Slovakia:* Independence Day*. *South Korea:* Constitution Day.

**18 Tue.** *Uruguay:* Constitution Day.

**19 Wed.** *Burma:* Martyrs' Day. *Laos:* Independence Day. *Nicaragua:* Sandinista Day.

**20 Thu.** *Colombia:* Independence Day.

**21 Fri.** *Belgium:* National Day. *Guam:* Liberation Day.

**22 Sat.** *Poland:* Liberation Day.

**23 Sun.** *Egypt:* Revolution Day. *New Guinea:* Remembrance Day. *Zodiac Cusp:* Cancer ends, Leo begins.

**24 Mon.** *Virgin Islands (U.S.):* Hurricane Supplication Day. *Venezuela:* Bolivar Day.

**25 Tue.** *Costa Rica:* Guanacaste Day. *Cuba:* Revolution Day (1st day of 3). *Puerto Rico:* Constitution Day. *Spain:* Santiago Day. *Tunisia:* Republic Day.

**26 Wed.** *Cuba:* Revolution Day (2nd day of 3). *Liberia:* Independence Day. *Maldives:* Independence Day.

**27 Thu.** *Cuba:* Revolution Day (3rd day of 3). *Puerto Rico:* Barbosa Day.

**28 Fri.** *Peru:* Independence Day (1st day of 2).

**29 Sat.** *Peru:* Independence Day (2nd day of 2).

**30 Sun.** *Vanuatu:* Independence Day.

# August 1995

**1 Tue.** *Benin:* Independence Day. *Switzerland:* Confederation Day.

**2 Wed.** *Costa Rica:* Virgin of the Angels Day. *Guyana:* Freedom Day. *Trinidad:* Discovery Day. *Zambia:* Farmers' Day.

**3 Thu.** *El Salvador:* Summer Day (1st day of 4). *Guinea-Bissau:* Martyrs' Day. *Niger:* Independence Day. *Tunisia:* President's Birthday.

**4 Fri.** *Burkina Faso:* Independence Day (1st day of 2). *El Salvador:* Summer Day (2nd day of 4).

**5 Sat.** *Burkina Faso:* Independence Day (2nd day of 2). *El Salvador:* Summer Day (3rd day of 4).

**6 Sun.** *Bolivia:* Independence Day. *El Salvador:* Summer Day (4th day of 4). *Israel:* Tisha Ab. *United Arab Emirates:* Accession Day. *Jewish:* Tisha Ab.

**7 Mon.** *Bahamas:* Emancipation Day. *Barbados:* Emancipation Day. *Canada:* Civic Holiday. *Colombia:* Boyaca Day. *Ivory Coast:* Republic Day. *Ireland:* Public Holiday. *Jamaica:* Independence Day. *Scotland:* Public Holiday (see App. B24). *Islamic:* Mohammed's Birthday.

**8 Tue.** Far East Islamic: Mohammed's Birthday.

**9 Wed.** *Burma:* Full Moon Day. *Georgia:* Independence Day*. *Singapore:* National Day.

**10 Thu.** *Ecuador:* Independence Day. *Sri Lanka:* Full Moon Poya.

**11 Fri.** *Chad:* Independence Day. *Jordan:* Accession Day. *Zimbabwe:* Heroes' Day (1st day of 2).

**12 Sat.** *Thailand:* Queen's Birthday. *Zimbabwe:* Heroes' Day (2nd day of 2).

**13 Sun.** *Central African Republic:* Independence Day. *Congo:* Independence Day (1st day of 2). *Tunisia:* Women's Day.

**14 Mon.** *Congo:* Independence Day (2nd day of 2). *Pakistan:* Independence Day.

**15 Tue.** *Congo:* Independence Day (3rd day of 3). *India:* Independence Day. *Liechtenstein:* National Day. *South Korea:* Republic Day. *Christian:* Assumption (see App. A11).

**16 Wed.** *Dominican Republic:* Republic Day.

**17 Thu.** *Argentina:* San Martin's Day. *Gabon:* Independence Day. *Indonesia:* Independence Day.

**20 Sun.** *Hungary:* Constitution Day. *Senegal:* Independence Day.

**21 Mon.** *Estonia:* Independence Day*. *Latvia:* Independence Day*. *Lithuania:* Independence Day*.

**23 Wed.** *Romania:* National Day (1st day of 2). *Zodiac Cusp:* Leo ends, Virgo begins.

**24 Thu.** *Kazakhstan:* National Day*. *Liberia:* Flag Day. *Romania:* National Day (2nd day of 2). *Russia:* Independence Day*. *Ukraine:* National Day*.

**25 Fri.** *Belarus:* Independence Day*. *Paraguay:* Constitution Day. *Uruguay:* Independence Day.

**26 Sat.** *Hong Kong:* Liberation Day (1st day of 2).

**27 Sun.** *Moldova:* Independence Day*.

**28 Mon.** *England:* Summer Break. *Hong Kong:* Liberation Day (2nd day of 2). *Luxembourg:* Fair Day. *Northern Ireland:* Summer Break. *Wales:* Summer Break.

**29 Tue.** *Uzbekistan:* Independence Day*.

**30 Wed.** *Afghanistan:* Children's Day. *Azerbaijan:* Independence Day*. *Peru:* Rose of Lima Day. *Turkey:* Victory Day.

**31 Thu.** *Afghanistan:* Pashtunistan Day. *Kyrgyzstan:* Independence Day*. *Malaysia:* National Day. *Trinidad:* Independence Day.

# September 1995

**1 Fri.** *Libya:* National Day. *Mexico:* President's Message Day. *Syria:* United Arab Republics Day.

**2 Sat.** *Vietnam:* Independence Day.

**3 Sun.** *Qatar:* National Day. *San Marino:* Saint Marinus' Day. *Tunisia:* Independence Movement Day.

**4 Mon.** *Canada:* Labour Day. *United States:* Labor Day.

**6 Wed.** *Pakistan:* Defense Day. *Swaziland:* Independence Day.

**7 Thu.** *Brazil:* Independence Day. *Burma:* Full Moon Day.

**8 Fri.** *Andorra:* National Day. *Malta:* Our Lady of Victory Day. *Sri Lanka:* Full Moon Poya.

**9 Sat.** *Bulgaria:* National Day (1st day of 2). *North Korea:* Independence Day. *Tajikistan:* Independence Day*.

**10 Sun.** *Belize:* National Day. *Bulgaria:* National Day (2nd day of 2).

**11 Mon.** *Chile:* Revolution Day. *Pakistan:* Anniversary of Quaid-e-Azam's Death.

**12 Tue.** *Egypt:* New Year's Day (Coptic: 1713). *Ethiopia:* National Day and New Year's Day (Ethiopian: 1989).

**14 Thu.** *Guatemala:* San Jacinto Day. *Nicaragua:* San Jacinto Day.

**15 Fri.** *Costa Rica:* Independence Day. *El Salvador:* Independence Day. *Guatemala:* Independence Day. *Honduras:* Independence Day. *Japan:* Veneration Day. *Nicaragua:* Independence Day.

**16 Sat.** *Mexico:* Independence Day. *New Guinea:* Independence Day.

**17 Sun.** *Angola:* Heroes' Day. *Marshall Islands:* Independence Day.

**18 Mon.** *Burundi:* Victory of Uprona Day. *Chile:* Independence Day.

**19 Tue.** *Chile:* Armed Forces Day. *Saint Kitts:* Independence Day.

**21 Thu.** *Belize:* Independence Day. *Malta:* Independence Day.

**22 Fri.** *Mali:* Independence Day.

**23 Sat.** *Armenia:* Independence Day*. *Japan:* Autumnal Equinox *Saudi Arabia:* National Day. *Zodiac Cusp:* Virgo ends, Libra begins.

**24 Sun.** *Dominican Republic:* Mercedes Day. *Guinea-Bissau:* Republic Day. *Europe:* Daylight Savings Time ends (retard clocks 1 hour).

**25 Mon.** *Israel:* New Year's Day. *Mozambique:* Liberation Day. *Rwanda:* Assembly Day. *Jewish:* Rosh Hashanah (Jewish: 5756).

**27 Wed.** *Ethiopia:* True Cross Day.

**28 Thu.** *Taiwan:* Teachers' Day.

**29 Fri.** *Brunei:* Constitution Day. *Paraguay:* Boqueron Battle Day.

**30 Sat.** *Botswana:* Independence Day.

# October 1995

**1 Sun.** *Cameroon:* Unification Day. *China:* National Day (1st day of 2). *Nigeria:* Independence Day. *South Korea:* Armed Forces Day (1st day of 2). *Tuvalu:* Independence Day.

**2 Mon.** *Barbados:* Bank Holiday. *China:* National Day (2nd day of 2). *Guinea:* Independence Day. *India:* Ghandi Day. *South Korea:* Armed Force Day (2nd day of 2).

**3 Tue.** *Honduras:* Morazan Day. *South Korea:* Foundation Day (1st day of 2). *Asian:* Ancestors' Day (see App. B6).

**4 Wed.** *Israel:* Yom Kippur. *Lesotho:* Independence Day. *South Korea:* Foundation Day (2nd day of 2). *Jewish:* Yom Kippur.

**5 Thu.** *Lesotho:* Sports Day. *Macao:* Portuguese Republic Day. *Portugal:* Republic Day.

**6 Fri.** *Egypt:* Armed Forces Day.

**7 Sat.** *Burma:* Full Moon Day. *China:* Mid-autumn Day. *Taiwan:* Mid-autumn Day.

**8 Sun.** *Hong Kong:* Mid-autumn Day. *Macao:* Mid-autumn Day. *Sri Lanka:* Full Moon Poya.

**9 Mon.** *Canada:* Thanksgiving Day. *Fiji:* Cession Day. *Israel:* Sukkot. *Peru:* National Dignity Day. *South Korea:* Alphabet Day. *Uganda:* Independence Day. *United States:* Bank Holiday. *Virgin Islands (U.S.):* Puerto Rican Friendship Day. *Jewish:* Sukkot.

**10 Tue.** *Japan:* Health Day. *South Africa:* Kruger Day. *Taiwan:* National Day.

**11 Wed.** *Cuba:* Independence War. *Panama:* Revolution Day.

**12 Thu.** *Equatorial Guinea:* Independence Day. *Spain:* National Day. *Multinational:* Columbus Day (see App. A12).

**14 Sat.** *Zaïre:* Founders' Day.

**15 Sun.** *Bosnia and Herzegovina:* Independence Day*. *Tunisia:* Evacuation Day.

**16 Mon.** *Jamaica:* Heroes' Day.

**17 Tue.** *Haiti:* Dessalines Day. *Malawi:* Mother's Day.

**20 Fri.** *Guatemala:* Revolution Day. *Kenya:* Kenyatta Day.

**21 Sat.** *Honduras:* Armed Forces Day. *Somalia:* Revolution Day (1st day of 2).

**22 Sun.** *Somalia:* Revolution Day (2nd day of 2). *Vatican:* John Paul II Day.

**23 Mon.** *Hungary:* Revolution Day. *Thailand:* Chulalongkorn Day. *Hindu:* Deepavali (see App. B21). *Zodiac Cusp:* Libra ends, Scorpio begins.

**24 Tue.** *Egypt:* Suez Victory Day. *Haiti:* United Nations Day. *Zambia:* Independence Day.

**25 Wed.** *Taiwan:* Restoration Day.

**26 Thu.** *Austria:* National Day. *Benin:* Revolution Day. *Rwanda:* Government Day.

**27 Fri.** *Saint Vincent:* Independence Day. *Turkmenistan:* Independence Day*. *Zaïre:* Naming Day.

**28 Sat.** *Greece:* Ohi! Day.

**29 Sun.** *Tanzania:* Naming Day. *Turkey:* Republic Day. *Canada and United States:* Daylight Savings Time ends (retard clocks 1 hour).

**30 Mon.** *Ireland:* Public Holiday. *New Zealand:* Labour Day.

**31 Tue.** *Taiwan:* Chiang Kaishek's Birthday.

# November 1995

**1 Wed.** *Algeria:* Revolution Day. *Antigua:* Independence Day. *Christian:* All Saints' Day (see App. A13).

**2 Thu.** *Brazil:* Memorial Day. *Finland:* All Saints' Eve. *Liberia:* Thanksgiving Day. *Sweden:* All Saints' Eve. *Christian:* All Souls' Day (see App. A14).

**3 Fri.** *Dominica:* Independence Day. *Ecuador:* Cuenca Independence Day. *Japan:* Culture Day. *Panama:* Independence Day.

**4 Sat.** *Andorra:* Saint Charles' Day. *Panama:* Flag Day. *Vatican:* John Paul II's Nameday.

**5 Sun.** *Burma:* Full Moon Day. *El Salvador:* Cry of Independence Day.

**6 Mon.** *Sri Lanka:* Full Moon Poya. *Virgin Islands (U.S.):* Liberty Day.

**7 Tue.** *Bangladesh:* Revolution Day.

**8 Wed.** *Nepal:* Queen's Birthday.

**9 Thu.** *Pakistan:* Iqbal Day.

**10 Fri.** *Panama:* Cry of Independence Day.

**11 Sat.** *Angola:* Independence Day. *Bhutan:* King's Birthday. *Maldives:* Republic Day. *Poland:* Independence Day. *Multinational:* Armistice Day (see App. A15).

**12 Sun.** *Taiwan:* Dr. Sun Yatsen's Birthday.

**14 Tue.** *Jordan:* King's Birthday.

**15 Wed.** *Brazil:* Republic Day. *Germany:* Repentance Day.

**17 Fri.** *Zaïre:* Armed Forces Day.

**18 Sat.** *Haiti:* Vertieres' Day. *Morocco:* Independence Day. *Oman:* National Day.

**19 Sun.** *Belize:* Garifuna Day. *Mali:* Army Coup Day. *Monaco:* Prince Ranier's Day. *Puerto Rico:* Discovery Day.

**20 Mon.** *Fiji:* Prince Charles' Birthday. *Mexico:* Revolution Day.

**22 Wed.** *Lebanon:* Independence Day. *Zodiac Cusp:* Scorpio ends, Sagittarius begins.

**23 Thu.** *Japan:* Labor Thanksgiving Day. *United States:* Thanksgiving Day.

**24 Fri.** *Argentina:* Bank Holiday. *Zaïre:* New Regime Day.

**25 Sat.** *Suriname:* Independence Day.

**28 Tue.** *Albania:* Independence Day. *Burundi:* Republic Day. *Chad:* Republic Day. *Mauritania:* Independence Day. *Panama:* Independence Day.

**29 Wed.** *Albania:* Liberation Day. *Liberia:* Tubman's Birthday. *Yugoslavia:* Republic Day.

**30 Thu.** *Barbados:* Independence Day. *Benin:* National Day. *Philippines:* Heroes' Day.

# December 1995

**1 Fri.** *Central African Republic:* National Day. *Portugal:* Youth Day. *Ukraine:* Independence Day*.

**2 Sat.** *Laos:* Republic Day. *United Arab Emirates:* National Day.

**5 Tue.** *Burma:* Full Moon Day. *Haiti:* Discovery Day. *Thailand:* King's Birthday.

**6 Wed.** *Finland:* Independence Day. *Sri Lanka:* Full Moon Poya.

**7 Thu.** *Ivory Coast:* Independence Day.

**8 Fri.** *Christian:* Immaculate Conception (see App. A16).

**9 Sat.** *Tanzania:* Independence Day.

**10 Sun.** *Angola:* MPLA Foundation Day. *Equatorial Guinea:* Human Rights Day. *Namibia:* Settlers' Day. *Thailand:* Constitution Day.

**11 Mon.** *Burkina Faso:* National Day.

**12 Tue.** *Kenya:* Independence Day. *Mexico:* Guadalupe Festival.

**13 Wed.** *Malta:* Republic Day.

**16 Sat.** *Bahrain:* National Day. *Bangladesh:* Victory Day. *Nepal:* Constitution Day. *South Africa:* Covenant Day.

**17 Sun.** *Bhutan:* National Day. *Jewish:* Chanukah.

**18 Mon.** *Niger:* Republic Day.

**19 Tue.** *Islamic:* Isra a Majraj (see App. B30).

**21 Wed.** *Kazakhstan:* Independence Day*.

**22 Fri.** *Zodiac Cusp:* Sagittarius ends, Capricorn begins.

**23 Sat.** *Japan:* Emperor's Birthday.

**24 Sun.** *Multinational:* Christmas Eve (see App. A17).

**25 Mon.** *Angola:* Family Day. *Congo:* Children's Day. *Pakistan:* Quaid's Birthday. *Taiwan:* Constitution Day. *Multinational:* Christmas Day (see App. A18).

**26 Tue.** *South Africa:* Good Will Day. *Multinational:* Boxing Day (see App. A19).

**30 Sat.** *Madagascar:* Republic Day. *Philippines:* Rizal Day (1st day of 2).

**31 Sun.** *Congo:* Republic Day. *Philippines:* Rizal Day (2nd day of 2). *Multinational:* Bank Holiday and New Year's Eve (see App. A20 & A21).

# January 1996

**1 Mon.** *Cameroon:* Independence Day. *Cuba:* Liberation Day. *Haiti:* Independence Day. *Palau:* Independence Day. *Sudan:* Independence Day. *Taiwan:* Foundation Day (1st day of 2). *Western Samoa:* Independence Day. *Multinational:* Bank Holiday and New Year's Day (see App. A1 & A2).

**2 Tue.** *Japan:* Bank Holiday. *New Zealand:* New Year's Day (2nd day of 2). *Scotland:* New Year's Day (2nd day of 2). *South Korea:* New Year's Day (2nd day of 2). *Switzerland:* Berchtold's Day. *Taiwan:* Foundation Day (2nd day of 2).

**3 Wed.** *Burkina Faso:* Revolution Day.

**4 Thu.** *Burma:* Independence and Full Moon Day. *Zaïre:* Martyrs' Day.

**5 Fri.** *Sri Lanka:* Full Moon Poya.

**6 Sat.** *Iraq:* Army Day. *Uruguay:* Children's Day. *Christian:* Epiphany (see App. A3).

**7 Sun.** *Egypt:* Coptic Christmas. *Ethiopia:* Coptic Christmas.

**11 Thu.** *Albania:* Republic Day. *Nepal:* Unification Day. *Puerto Rico:* Hostos Day.

**12 Fri.** *Tanzania:* Revolution Day.

**13 Sat.** *Togo:* Liberation Day.

**15 Mon.** *Japan:* Adult's Day. *Jordan:* Arbor Day. *United States:* Martin Luther King's Birthday.

**19 Fri.** *Ethiopia:* Epiphany.

**20 Sat.** *Mali:* Award Day. *Zodiac Cusp:* Capricorn ends, Aquarius begins.

**21 Sun.** *Dominican Republic:* Altagracia Day. *Islamic:* 1st Day of Ramadan (see App. B25).

**22 Mon.** *Saint Vincent:* Discovery Day.

**26 Fri.** *Dominican Republic:* Duarte Day. *India:* Republic Day.

**27 Sat.** *Monaco:* Saint Devota's Day. *Vietnam:* Vietnam Day.

**28 Sun.** *Rwanda:* Democracy Day.

**29 Mon.** *Australia:* Australia Day.

**31 Wed.** *Nauru:* Independence Day.

# February 1996

**2 Fri.** *Liechtenstein:* Candlemas.

**3 Sat.** *Burma:* Full Moon Day.

**4 Sun.** *Sri Lanka:* Independence and Full Moon Poya.

**5 Mon.** *Mexico:* Constitution Day. *United States:* Lincoln's Birthday (see App. B27).

**6 Tue.** *New Zealand:* Waitangi Day.

**7 Wed.** *Grenada:* Independence Day.

**8 Thu.** *Iraq:* Revolution Day.

**9 Fri.** *Lebanon:* Saint Marion's Day.

**10 Sat.** *Malta:* Saint Paul's Day.

**11 Sun.** *Cameroon:* Youth Day. *Japan:* Foundation Day. *Liberia:* Armed Forces Day.

**12 Mon.** *Burma:* Union Day.

**14 Wed.** *International:* Valentine's Day.

**18 Sun.** *Gambia:* Independence Day. *Asian:* Chinese New Year Eve (see App. B1). *Zodiac Cusp:* Aquarius ends, Pisces begins.

**19 Mon.** *Nepal:* National Day. *United States:* Washington's Birthday. *Vietnam:* Tet (1st day of 3). *Asian:* Chinese New Year (Year of the Rat) (see App. B2). *Christian:* Shrove Monday (see App. B7).

**20 Tue.** *Vietnam:* Tet (2nd day of 3). *Asian:* 2nd Day of Chinese New Year (see App. B3). *Christian:* Shrove Tuesday (see App. B8). *Far East Islamic:* Hari Raya Puasa (see App. B27). *Islamic:* Eid al Fitr (1st day of 4) (see App. B26).

**21 Wed.** *Bangladesh:* Saheed Day.

*Vietnam:* Tet (3rd day of 3). *Asian:* 3rd Day of Chinese New Year (see App. B4). *Christian:* Ash Wednesday (see App. B9). *Islamic:* Eid al Fitr (2nd day of 4) (see App. B26).

**22 Thu.** *Saint Lucia:* Independence Day. *Islamic:* Eid al Fitr (3rd day of 4).

**23 Fri.** *Brunei:* National Day. *Guyana:* Republic Day. *Islamic:* Eid al Fitr (4th day of 4) (see App. B26).

**25 Sun.** *Kuwait:* National Day.

**26 Mon.** *Greece:* Shrove Monday. *Orthodox:* Shrove Monday.

**27 Tue.** *Dominican Republic:* Independence Day.

# March 1996

**1 Fri.** *South Korea:* Independence Day.

**2 Sat.** *Ethiopia:* Victory of Aduwa Day. *Morocco:* Independence Day.

**3 Sun.** *Bulgaria:* Liberation Day. *Burma:* Full Moon Day. *Malawi:* Martyrs' Day. *Morocco:* National Day.

**4 Mon.** *Guam:* Discovery Day. *Sri Lanka:* Full Moon Poya. *Thailand:* Makha Bucha Day.

**5 Tue.** Jewish: Purim.

**6 Wed.** *Ghana:* Independence Day.

**8 Fri.** *Syria:* Revolution Day. *Multinational:* Women's Day (see App. A4).

**9 Sat.** *Zambia:* Youth Day.

**10 Sun.** *South Korea:* Labor Day.

**11 Mon.** *Gibraltar:* Commonwealth Day. *Lithuania:* National Day*.

**12 Tue.** *Lesotho:* Moshoeshoe's Day. *Mauritius:* Independence Day.

**13 Wed.** *Grenada:* National Day.

**17 Sun.** *Ireland:* Saint Patrick's Day. *Northern Ireland:* Saint Patrick's Day.

**19 Tue.** *Christian:* Saint Joseph's Day (see App. A5).

**20 Wed.** *Afghanistan:* New Year's Day (Shamsi: 1375). *Iran:* New Year's Day (Hegira: 1375). *Iraq:* New Year's Day. *Japan:* Vernal Equinox. *Tunisia:* Independence Day. *Zodiac Cusp:* Pisces ends, Aries begins.

**21 Thu.** *Mexico:* Juarez Day.

**22 Fri.** *Puerto Rico:* Abolition Day.

**23 Sat.** *Pakistan:* Pakistan Day.

**25 Mon.** *Cyprus:* Greek Independence Day. *Greece:* Independence Day. *Liechtenstein:* Annunciation. *Virgin Islands (U.S.):* Transfer Day.

**26 Tue.** *Bangladesh:* Independence Day. *Zambia:* Africa Day.

**27 Wed.** *Angola:* Evacuation Day. *Burma:* Resistance Day.

**29 Fri.** *Central African Republic:* Boganda Day. *Madagascar:* Memorial Day. *Taiwan:* Youth Day.

**31 Sun.** *Malta:* National Day. *Christian:* Palm Sunday. *Europe:* Daylight Savings Time starts (advance clocks 1 hour).

# April 1996

**1 Mon.** *Iran:* Republic Day. *San Marino:* National Day.

**2 Tue.** *Burma:* Full Moon Day.

**3 Wed.** *Sri Lanka:* Full Moon Poya.

**4 Thu.** *Hungary:* Liberation Day. *Israel:* Passover. *Senegal:* National Day. *Christian:* Maundy Thursday (see App. B11). *Jewish:* Passover.

**5 Fri.** *Sierra Leone:* Bank Holiday. *South Korea:* Arbor Day. *Asian:* Tomb Sweeping Day (see App. A6). *Christian:* Good Friday (see App. B12).

**6 Sat.** *South Africa:* Founders' Day. *Thailand:* Chakri Day. *Christian:* Holy Saturday (see App. B13).

**7 Sun.** *Canada and United States:*

Daylight Savings Time starts (advance clocks 1 hour). *Christian:* Easter Sunday (see App. B14).

**8 Mon.** *Christian:* Easter Monday (see App. B15).

**9 Tue.** *Philippines:* Valour Day. *Tunisia:* Martyrs' Day.

**11 Thu.** *Costa Rica:* Heroes' Day. *Uganda:* Liberation Day.

**12 Fri.** *Orthodox:* Good Friday (see App. B20).

**13 Sat.** *Chad:* National Day. *Thailand:* Songkrawn (1st day of 2).

**14 Sun.** *Honduras:* Pan American Day. *Jordan:* Easter Sunday. *Thailand:* Songkrawn (2nd day of 2). *Orthodox:* Easter Sunday (see App. B20).

**15 Mon.** *Burma:* New Year's Day (Burmese: 1358). *Niger:* National Day. *Orthodox:* Easter Monday.

**16 Tue.** *Cyprus:* Independence Day.

**17 Wed.** *Cambodia:* Independence Day. *Syria:* Independence Day.

**18 Thu.** *Zimbabwe:* Republic Day.

**19 Fri.** *Sierra Leone:* Republic Day. *Uruguay:* Patriots' Day. *Venezuela:* Independence Day. *Zodiac Cusp:* Aries ends, Taurus begins.

**21 Sun.** *Brazil:* Tiradentes Day.

**23 Tue.** *Turkey:* Children's Day.

**24 Wed.** *Israel:* Independence Day.

**25 Thu.** *Australia:* ANZAC Day. *Egypt:* Sinai Day. *Iceland:* Children's Day. *Italy:* Liberation Day. *New Zealand:* ANZAC Day. *Portugal:* Liberation Day. *Swaziland:* Flag Day.

**26 Fri.** *Tanzania:* Union Day.

**27 Sat.** *Afghanistan:* Independence Day. *Sierra Leone:* Independence Day. *Togo:* Independence Day.

**28 Sun.** *Far East Islamic:* Hari Raya Haji (see App. B29). *Islamic:* Eid al Adha (1st day of 4) (see App. B28).

**29 Mon.** *Japan:* Green Day. *Islamic:* Eid al Adha (2nd day of 4) (see App. B28).

**30 Tue.** *Finland:* Vappu Day. *Netherlands:* Queen's Birthday. *Islamic:* Eid al Adha (3rd day of 4) (see App. B28).

# May 1996

**1 Wed.** *Islamic:* Eid al Adha (4th day of 4) (see App. B28). *Multinational:* Labor Day (see App. A7).

**2 Thu.** *Burma:* Full Moon Day. *Lesotho:* King's Birthday. *Sri Lanka:* Full Moon Poya.

**3 Fri.** *Denmark:* All Prayers' Day. *Japan:* Constitution Day.

**4 Sat.** *Japan:* People's Day.

**5 Sun.** *Japan:* Children's Day. *Mexico:* Cinco de Mayo. *Netherlands:* Liberation Day. *South Korea:* Children's Day. *Thailand:* Coronation Day.

**6 Mon.** *Lebanon:* Martyrs' Day. *Philippines:* Corregidor Day. *United Kingdom:* Labour Day. *Zambia:* Labour Day.

**8 Wed.** *France:* Liberation Day.

**9 Thu.** *Czech Republic:* Liberation Day*. *Slovakia:* Liberation Day*.

**10 Fri.** *Micronesia:* Independence Day.

**12 Sun.** *International:* Mother's Day.

**14 Tue.** *Liberia:* Unification Day. *Malawi:* Kamuzu Day. *Paraguay:* Flag Day.

**15 Wed.** *Paraguay:* Independence Day.

**16 Thu.** *Christian:* Ascension (see App. B16).

**17 Fri.** *Cayman Islands:* Discovery Day. *Norway:* Constitution Day. *Islamic:* New Year's Day (Hegira: 1417) (see App. B22).

**18 Sat.** *Haiti:* Flag Day. *Uruguay:* Las Piedras Day. *Far East Islamic:* New Year's Day (Hegira: 1417).

**19 Sun.** *Finland:* Flag Day. *Turkey:* Youth Day.

**20 Mon.** *Cameroon:* Constitution Day. *Canada:* Victoria Day. *Zaïre:*

Popular Movement Day. *Zodiac Cusp:* Taurus ends, Gemini begins.

**21 Tue.** *Chile:* Navy Day.

**22 Wed.** *Haiti:* Sovereign Day. *Sri Lanka:* Heroes' Day.

**23 Thu.** *Jamaica:* Labour Day.

**24 Fri.** *Bulgaria:* Culture Day. *Ecuador:* Independence Battle Day. *Israel:* Pentecost. *South Korea:* Vesak Day. *Jewish:* Pentecost.

**25 Sat.** *Argentina:* National Day. *Eritrea:* Independence Day*. *Jordan:* Independence Day. *Sudan:* Revolution Day. *Multinational:* Africa Day (see App. A8).

**26 Sun.** *Guyana:* Independence Day. *Christian:* Whitsunday. *Islamic:* Ashura (see App. B23).

**27 Mon.** *Nigeria:* Children's Day. *United Kingdom:* Spring Break. *United States:* Memorial Day. *Christian:* Whitmonday (see App. B18).

**31 Fri.** *Brunei:* Regiment Day. *Burma:* Full Moon Day. *Malaysia:* Vesak Day. *Singapore:* Vesak Day. *South Africa:* Republic Day.

# June 1996

**1 Sat.** *Kenya:* Madaraka Day. *Sri Lanka:* Full Moon Poya. *Thailand:* Visakha Bucha Day. *Tunisia:* National Day. *Western Samoa:* Independence Day.

**2 Sun.** *Italy:* Republic Day. *Tunisia:* Youth Day. *Orthodox:* Pentecost Sunday.

**3 Mon.** *Greece:* Pentecost Monday. *Ireland:* Public Holiday. *New Zealand:* Queen's Birthday.

**4 Tue.** *Bahamas:* Labour Day. *Tonga:* Independence Day.

**5 Wed.** *Denmark:* Constitution Day. *Equatorial Guinea:* President's Birthday. *Malaysia:* King's Birthday. *Seychelles:* Liberation Day.

**6 Thu.** *South Korea:* Memorial Day. *Sweden:* Constitution Day. *Christian:* Corpus Christi (see App. B19).

**7 Fri.** *Chad:* Revolution Day.

**8 Sat.** *Hong Kong:* Queen's Birthday (1st day of 2).

**9 Sun.** *Argentina:* Independence Day.

**10 Mon.** *Australia:* Queen's Birthday. *Fiji:* Queen's Birthday. *Hong Kong:* Queen's Birthday (2nd day of 2). *Macao:* Portugal Day. *New Guinea:* Queen's Birthday. *Portugal:* Portugal Day. *United Kingdom:* Queen's Birthday.

**11 Tue.** *Libya:* Evacuation Day.

**12 Wed.** *Philippines:* Independence Day.

**17 Mon.** *Germany:* Unity Day. *Iceland:* Independence Day.

**18 Tue.** *Egypt:* Independence Day.

**19 Wed.** *Algeria:* Righting Day. *Kuwait:* Independence Day. *Uruguay:* Artigas Day.

**20 Thu.** *Argentina:* Flag Day.

**21 Fri.** *Finland:* Midsummer Day (1st day of 2). *Sweden:* Midsummer Day (1st day of 2). *Zodiac Cusp:* Gemini ends, Cancer begins.

**22 Sat.** *Finland:* Johannus and Midsummer Day (2nd day of 2). *Sweden:* Midsummer Day (2nd day of 2). *Asian:* Dragon Boat Festival (see App. B5).

**23 Sun.** *Luxembourg:* National Day.

**24 Mon.** *Andorra:* Saint John's Day. *Venezuela:* Carabobo Day. *Zaïre:* Constitution Day.

**25 Tue.** *Croatia:* Independence Day*. *Mozambique:* Independence Day. *Slovenia:* Independence Day*.

**26 Wed.** *Madagascar:* Independence Day. *Somalia:* Independence Day.

**27 Thu.** *Djibouti:* Independence Day.

**28 Fri.** *Chile:* Bank Holiday. *Ecuador:* Bank Holiday. *El Salvador:* Bank Holiday. *Finland:* Bank Holiday.

**29 Sat.** *Burma:* Full Moon Day. *Seychelles:* Independence Day. *Christian:* Saint Paul's Day (see App. A9).

**30 Sun.** *Guatemala:* Army Day. *Sri Lanka:* Bank Holiday and Full Moon Poya. *Zaïre:* Independence Day.

# July 1996

**1 Mon.** *Burundi:* Independence Day. *Canada:* Canada Day. *Cayman Islands:* Constitution Day. *Ghana:* Republic Day. *Hong Kong:* Half Year Day. *Lesotho:* Family Day. *Rwanda:* Independence Day. *Somalia:* Union Day. *Suriname:* Freedom Day. *Zambia:* Heroes' Day. *Multinational:* Bank Holiday (see App. A10).

**2 Tue.** *Zambia:* Unity Day.

**4 Thu.** *Philippines:* United States Friendship Day. *United States:* Independence Day. *Yugoslavia:* Freedom Fighters' Day.

**5 Fri.** *Algeria:* Independence Day. *Cape Verde:* Independence Day. *Rwanda:* Unity Day. *Venezuela:* Independence Day.

**6 Sat.** *Comoros:* Independence Day. *Malawi:* Republic Day.

**7 Sun.** *Solomon Islands:* Independence Day. *Tanzania:* Farmers' Day. *Yugoslavia:* Serbian Day.

**10 Wed.** *Bahamas:* Independence Day.

**11 Thu.** *Mongolia:* Revolution Day.

**12 Fri.** *Kiribati:* Independence Day. *Northern Ireland:* Battle of the Boyne Day. *São Tomé:* National Day.

**14 Sun.** *France:* National Day. *Iraq:* Revolution Day.

**15 Mon.** *Botswana:* President's Day. *Brunei:* Sultan's Birthday.

**17 Wed.** *Iraq:* Revolution Day. *Puerto Rico:* Rivera Day. *Slovakia:* Independence Day*. *South Korea:* Constitution Day.

**18 Thu.** *Uruguay:* Constitution Day.

**19 Fri.** *Burma:* Martyrs' Day. *Laos:* Independence Day. *Nicaragua:* Sandinista Day.

**20 Sat.** *Colombia:* Independence Day.

**21 Sun.** *Belgium:* National Day. *Guam:* Liberation Day.

**22 Mon.** *Poland:* Liberation Day. *Virgin Islands (U.S.):* Hurricane Supplication Day. *Zodiac Cusp:* Cancer ends, Leo begins.

**23 Tue.** *Egypt:* Revolution Day. *New Guinea:* Remembrance Day.

**24 Wed.** *Venezuela:* Bolivar Day.

**25 Thu.** *Costa Rica:* Guanacaste Day. *Cuba:* Revolution Day (1st day of 3). *Israel:* Tisha Ab. *Puerto Rico:* Constitution Day. *Spain:* Santiago Day. *Tunisia:* Republic Day. *Jewish:* Tisha Ab.

**26 Fri.** *Cuba:* Revolution Day (2nd day of 3). *Liberia:* Independence Day. *Maldives:* Independence Day. *Islamic:* Mohammed's Birthday (see App. B24).

**27 Sat.** *Cuba:* Revolution Day (3rd day of 3). *Puerto Rico:* Barbosa Day. *Far East Islamic:* Mohammed's Birthday.

**28 Sun.** *Burma:* Full Moon Day. *Peru:* Independence Day (1st day of 2).

**29 Mon.** *Peru:* Independence Day (2nd day of 2). *Sri Lanka:* Full Moon Poya.

**30 Tue.** *Thailand:* Asalaha Bucha Day. *Vanuatu:* Independence Day.

**31 Wed.** *Thailand:* Khao Phansa Day.

# August 1996

**1 Thu.** *Benin:* Independence Day. *Switzerland:* Confederation Day.

**2 Fri.** *Costa Rica:* Virgin of the Angels Day. *Guyana:* Freedom Day.

*Trinidad:* Discovery Day.

**3 Sat.** *El Salvador:* Summer Day (1st day of 4). *Guinea-Bissau:* Martyrs' Day. *Niger:* Independence Day. *Tunisia:* President's Birthday.

**4 Sun.** *Burkina Faso:* Independence Day (1st day of 2). *El Salvador:* Summer Day (2nd day of 4).

**5 Mon.** *Bahamas:* Emancipation Day. *Barbados:* Emancipation Day. *Burkina Faso:* Independence Day (2nd day of 2). *Canada:* Civic Holiday. *El Salvador:* Summer Day (3rd day of 4). *Ireland:* Public Holiday. *Jamaica:* Independence Day. *Scotland:* Public Holiday.

**6 Tue.** *Bolivia:* Independence Day. *El Salvador:* Summer Day (4th day of 4). *United Arab Emirates:* Accession Day.

**7 Wed.** *Colombia:* Boyaca Day. *Ivory Coast:* Republic Day. *Zambia:* Farmers' Day.

**9 Fri.** *Georgia:* Independence Day*. *Singapore:* National Day.

**10 Sat.** *Ecuador:* Independence Day.

**11 Sun.** *Chad:* Independence Day. *Jordan:* Accession Day. *Zimbabwe:* Heroes' Day (1st day of 2).

**12 Mon.** *Thailand:* Queen's Birthday. *Zimbabwe:* Heroes' Day (2nd day of 2).

**13 Tue.** *Central African Republic:* Independence Day. *Congo:* Independence Day (1st day of 2). *Tunisia:* Women's Day.

**14 Wed.** *Congo:* Independence Day (2nd day of 2). *Pakistan:* Independence Day.

**15 Thu.** *Congo:* Independence Day (3rd day of 3). *India:* Independence Day. *Liechtenstein:* National Day. *South Korea:* Republic Day. *Christian:* Assumption (see App. A11).

**16 Fri.** *Dominican Republic:* Republic Day.

**17 Sat.** *Argentina:* San Martin's Day. *Gabon:* Independence Day. *Indonesia:* Independence Day.

**20 Tue.** *Hungary:* Constitution Day. *Senegal:* Independence Day.

**21 Wed.** *Estonia:* Independence Day*. *Latvia:* Independence Day*. *Lithuania:* Independence Day*.

**22 Thu.** *Zodiac Cusp:* Leo ends, Virgo begins.

**23 Fri.** *Romania:* National Day (1st day of 2).

**24 Sat.** *Hong Kong:* Liberation Day (1st day of 2). *Kazakhstan:* National Day*. *Liberia:* Flag Day. *Romania:* National Day (2nd day of 2). *Russia:* Independence Day*. *Ukraine:* National Day*.

**25 Sun.** *Belarus:* Independence Day*. *Paraguay:* Constitution Day. *Uruguay:* Independence Day.

**26 Mon.** *England:* Summer Break. *Hong Kong:* Liberation Day (2nd day of 2). *Northern Ireland:* Summer Break. *Wales:* Summer Break.

**27 Tue.** *Burma:* Full Moon Day. *Moldova:* Independence Day*.

**28 Wed.** *Sri Lanka:* Full Moon Poya.

**29 Thu.** *Uzbekistan:* Independence Day*.

**30 Fri.** *Afghanistan:* Children's Day. *Azerbaijan:* Independence Day*. *Peru:* Rose of Lima Day. *Turkey:* Victory Day.

**31 Sat.** *Afghanistan:* Pashtunistan Day. *Kyrgyzstan:* Independence Day*. *Malaysia:* National Day. *Trinidad:* Independence Day.

# September 1996

**1 Sun.** *Libya:* National Day. *Mexico:* President's Message Day. *Syria:* United Arab Republics Day.

**2 Mon.** *Canada:* Labour Day. *Luxembourg:* Fair Day. *United States:* Labor Day. *Vietnam:* Independence Day.

**3 Tue.** *Qatar:* National Day. *San*

*Marino:* Saint Marinus' Day. *Tunisia:* Independence Movement Day.

**6 Fri.** *Pakistan:* Defense Day. *Swaziland:* Independence Day.

**7 Sat.** *Brazil:* Independence Day.

**8 Sun.** *Andorra:* National Day. *Malta:* Our Lady of Victory Day.

**9 Mon.** *Bulgaria:* National Day (1st day of 2). *North Korea:* Independence Day. *Tajikistan:* Independence Day*.

**10 Tue.** *Belize:* National Day. *Bulgaria:* National Day (2nd day of 2).

**11 Wed.** *Chile:* Revolution Day. *Egypt:* New Year's Day (Coptic: 1714). *Ethiopia:* New Year's Day (Ethiopian: 1990). *Pakistan:* Anniversary of Quaid-e-Azam's Death.

**12 Thu.** *Ethiopia:* National Day.

**14 Sat.** *Guatemala:* San Jacinto Day. *Israel:* New Year's Day. *Nicaragua:* San Jacinto Day. *Jewish:* Rosh Hashanah (Jewish: 5757).

**15 Sun.** *Costa Rica:* Independence Day. *El Salvador:* Independence Day. *Guatemala:* Independence Day. *Honduras:* Independence Day. *Japan:* Veneration Day. *Nicaragua:* Independence Day.

**16 Mon.** *Mexico:* Independence Day. *New Guinea:* Independence Day.

**17 Tue.** *Angola:* Heroes' Day. *Marshall Islands:* Independence Day.

**18 Wed.** *Burundi:* Victory of Uprona Day. *Chile:* Independence Day.

**19 Thu.** *Chile:* Armed Forces Day. *Saint Kitts:* Independence Day.

**21 Sat.** *Belize:* Independence Day. *Malta:* Independence Day.

**22 Sun.** *Mali:* Independence Day. *Zodiac Cusp:* Virgo ends, Libra begins.

**23 Mon.** *Armenia:* Independence Day*. *Israel:* Yom Kippur. *Japan:* Autumnal Equinox. *Saudi Arabia:* National Day. *Jewish:* Yom Kippur.

**24 Tue.** *Dominican Republic:* Mercedes Day. *Guinea-Bissau:* Republic Day.

**25 Wed.** *Burma:* Full Moon Day. *Mozambique:* Liberation Day. *Rwanda:* Assembly Day.

**26 Thu.** *China:* Mid-autumn Day. *Ethiopia:* True Cross Day. *Sri Lanka:* Full Moon Poya. *Taiwan:* Mid-autumn Day.

**27 Fri.** *Hong Kong:* Mid-autumn Day. *Macao:* Mid-autumn Day.

**28 Sat.** *Israel:* Sukkot: Taiwan: Teachers' Day. *Jewish:* Sukkot.

**29 Sun.** *Brunei:* Constitution Day. *Paraguay:* Boqueron Battle Day. *Europe:* Daylight Savings Time ends (retard clocks 1 hour).

**30 Mon.** *Botswana:* Independence Day.

# October 1996

**1 Tue.** *Cameroon:* Unification Day. *China:* National Day (1st day of 2). *Nigeria:* Independence Day. *South Korea:* Armed Forces Day (1st day of 2). *Tuvalu:* Independence Day.

**2 Wed.** *China:* National Day (2nd day of 2). *Guinea:* Independence Day. *India:* Ghandi Day. *South Korea:* Armed Forces Day (2nd day of 2).

**3 Thu.** *Honduras:* Morazan Day. *South Korea:* Foundation Day (1st day of 2).

**4 Fri.** *Lesotho:* Independence Day. *South Korea:* Foundation Day (2nd day of 2).

**5 Sat.** *Lesotho:* Sports Day. *Macao:* Portuguese Republic Day. *Portugal:* Republic Day.

**6 Sun.** *Egypt:* Armed Forces Day.

**7 Mon.** *Barbados:* Bank Holiday.

**9 Wed.** *Peru:* National Dignity Day. *South Korea:* Alphabet Day. *Uganda:* Independence Day.

**10 Thu.** *Japan:* Health Day. *South Africa:* Kruger Day. *Taiwan:* National Day.

**11 Fri.** *Cuba:* Independence War. *Panama:* Revolution Day.

**12 Sat.** *Equatorial Guinea:* Independence Day. *Spain:* National Day. *Multinational:* Columbus Day (see App. A12).

**14 Mon.** *Canada:* Thanksgiving Day. *Fiji:* Cession Day. *United States:* Bank Holiday. *Virgin Islands (U.S.):* Puerto Rican Friendship Day. *Zaïre:* Founders' Day.

**15 Tue.** *Bosnia and Herzegovina:* Independence Day*. *Tunisia:* Evacuation Day.

**17 Thu.** *Haiti:* Dessalines Day. *Malawi:* Mother's Day.

**20 Sun.** *Guatemala:* Revolution Day. *Kenya:* Kenyatta Day.

**21 Mon.** *Honduras:* Army Day. *Jamaica:* Heroes' Day. *Somalia:* Revolution Day (1st day of 2). *Asian:* Ancestors' Day (see App. B6).

**22 Tue.** *Somalia:* Revolution Day (2nd day of 2). *Vatican:* John Paul II Day.

**23 Wed.** *Hungary:* Revolution Day. *Thailand:* Chulalongkorn Day. *Zodiac Cusp:* Libra ends, Scorpio begins.

**24 Thu.** *Egypt:* Suez Victory Day. *Haiti:* United Nations Day. *Zambia:* Independence Day.

**25 Fri.** *Burma:* Full Moon Day. *Taiwan:* Restoration Day.

**26 Sat.** *Austria:* National Day. *Benin:* Revolution Day. *Rwanda:* Government Day. *Sri Lanka:* Full Moon Poya.

**27 Sun.** *Saint Vincent:* Independence Day. *Turkmenistan:* Independence Day*. *Zaïre:* Naming Day. *Canada and United States:* Daylight Savings Time ends (retard clocks 1 hour).

**28 Mon.** *Greece:* Ohi! Day. *Ireland:* Public Holiday. *New Zealand:* Labour Day.

**29 Tue.** *Tanzania:* Naming Day. *Turkey:* Republic Day.

**31 Thu.** *Taiwan:* Chiang Kai-shek's Birthday.

# November 1996

**1 Fri.** *Algeria:* Revolution Day. *Antigua:* Independence Day. *Christian:* All Saints' Day (see App. A13).

**2 Sat.** *Brazil:* Memorial Day. *Finland:* All Saints' Eve. *Sweden:* All Saints' Eve. *Christian:* All Souls' Day (see App. A14).

**3 Sun.** *Dominica:* Independence Day. *Ecuador:* Cuenca Independence Day. *Japan:* Culture Day. *Panama:* Independence Day.

**4 Mon.** *Andorra:* Saint Charles' Day. *Panama:* Flag Day. *Virgin Islands (U.S.):* Liberty Day. *Vatican:* John Paul II's Nameday.

**5 Tue.** *El Salvador:* Cry of Independence Day.

**7 Thu.** *Bangladesh:* Revolution Day. *Liberia:* Thanksgiving Day.

**8 Fri.** *Nepal:* Queen's Birthday.

**9 Sat.** *Pakistan:* Iqbal Day.

**10 Sun.** *Panama:* Cry of Independence Day. *Hindu:* Deepavali (see App. B21).

**11 Mon.** *Angola:* Independence Day. *Bhutan:* King's Birthday. *Maldives:* Republic Day. *Poland:* Independence Day. *Multinational:* Armistice Day (see App. A15).

**12 Tue.** *Taiwan:* Dr. Sun Yat-sen's Birthday.

**14 Thu.** *Jordan:* King's Birthday.

**15 Fri.** *Brazil:* Republic Day.

**17 Sun.** *Zaïre:* Armed Forces Day.

**18 Mon.** *Fiji:* Prince Charles' Birthday. *Haiti:* Vertieres' Day. *Morocco:* Independence Day. *Oman:* National Day.

**19 Tue.** *Belize:* Garifuna Day. *Mali:* Army Coup Day. *Monaco:* Prince Ranier's Day. *Puerto Rico:* Discovery Day.

**20 Wed.** *Germany:* Repentance Day. *Mexico:* Revolution Day.

**22 Fri.** *Lebanon:* Independence Day. *Zodiac Cusp:* Scorpio ends, Sagittarius begins.

**23 Sat.** *Burma:* Full Moon Day. *Japan:* Labor Thanksgiving Day.

**24 Sun.** *Sri Lanka:* Full Moon Poya. *Zaïre:* New Regime Day.

**25 Mon.** *Suriname:* Independence Day.

**28 Thu.** *Albania:* Independence Day. *Burundi:* Republic Day. *Chad:* Republic Day. *Mauritania:* Independence Day. *Panama:* Independence Day. *United States:* Thanksgiving Day.

**29 Fri.** *Albania:* Liberation Day. *Argentina:* Bank Holiday. *Liberia:* Tubman's Birthday. *Yugoslavia:* Republic Day.

**30 Sat.** *Barbados:* Independence Day. *Benin:* National Day. *Philippines:* Heroes' Day.

# December 1996

**1 Sun.** *Central African Republic:* National Day. *Portugal:* Youth Day. *Ukraine:* Independence Day*.

**2 Mon.** *Laos:* Republic Day. *United Arab Emirates:* National Day.

**5 Thu.** *Haiti:* Discovery Day. *Thailand:* King's Birthday.

**6 Fri.** *Finland:* Independence Day.

**7 Sat.** *Ivory Coast:* Independence Day. *Islamic:* Isra a Majraj (see App. B30). *Jewish:* Chanukah.

**8 Sun.** *Christian:* Immaculate Conception (see App. A16).

**9 Mon.** *Tanzania:* Independence Day.

**10 Tue.** *Angola:* MPLA Foundation Day. *Equatorial Guinea:* Human Rights Day. *Namibia:* Settlers' Day. *Thailand:* Constitution Day.

**11 Wed.** *Burkina Faso:* National Day.

**12 Thu.** *Kenya:* Independence Day. *Mexico:* Guadalupe Festival.

**13 Fri.** *Malta:* Republic Day.

**16 Mon.** *Bahrain:* National Day. *Bangladesh:* Victory Day. *Nepal:* Constitution Day. *South Africa:* Covenant Day.

**17 Tue.** *Bhutan:* National Day.

**18 Wed.** *Niger:* Republic Day.

**21 Sat.** *Kazakhstan:* Independence Day*. *Zodiac Cusp:* Sagittarius ends, Capricorn begins.

**23 Mon.** *Burma:* Full Moon Day. *Japan:* Emperor's Birthday.

**24 Tue.** *Sri Lanka:* Full Moon Poya. *Multinational:* Christmas Eve (see App. A17).

**25 Wed.** *Angola:* Family Day. *Congo:* Children's Day. *Pakistan:* Quaid's Birthday. *Taiwan:* Constitution Day. *Multinational:* Christmas Day (see App. A18).

**26 Thu.** *South Africa:* Good Will Day. *Multinational:* Boxing Day (see App. A19).

**30 Mon.** *Madagascar:* Republic Day. *Philippines:* Rizal Day (1st day of 2).

**31 Tue.** *Congo:* Republic Day. *Philippines:* Rizal Day (2nd day of 2). *Multinational:* Bank Holiday and New Year's Eve (see App. A20 & A21).

# January 1997

**1 Wed.** *Cameroon:* Independence Day. *Cuba:* Liberation Day. *Haiti:* Independence Day. *Palau:* Independence Day. *Sudan:* Independence Day. *Taiwan:* Foundation Day (1st day of 2). *Western Samoa:* Independence Day.

*Multinational:* Bank Holiday and New Year's Day (see App. A1 & A2).

**2 Thu.** *Japan:* Bank Holiday. *New Zealand:* New Year's Day (2nd day of 2). *Scotland:* New Year's Day (2nd day of 2). *South Korea:* New Year's Day (2nd day of 2). *Switzerland:* Berchtold's Day. *Taiwan:* Foundation Day (2nd day of 2).

**3 Fri.** *Burkina Faso:* Revolution Day.

**4 Sat.** *Burma:* Independence Day. *Zaïre:* Martyrs' Day.

**6 Mon.** *Iraq:* Army Day. *Uruguay:* Children's Day. *Christian:* Epiphany (see App. A3).

**7 Tue.** *Egypt:* Coptic Christmas. *Ethiopia:* Coptic Christmas.

**9 Thu.** *Islamic:* 1st Day of Ramadan (see App. B25).

**11 Sat.** *Albania:* Republic Day. *Nepal:* Unification Day. *Puerto Rico:* Hostos Day.

**12 Sun.** *Tanzania:* Revolution Day.

**13 Mon.** *Togo:* Liberation Day.

**15 Wed.** *Japan:* Adult's Day. *Jordan:* Arbor Day.

**19 Sun.** *Ethiopia:* Epiphany.

**20 Mon.** *Mali:* Award Day. *United States:* Martin Luther King's Birthday. *Zodiac Cusp:* Capricorn ends, Aquarius begins.

**21 Tue.** *Dominican Republic:* Altagracia Day.

**22 Wed.** *Burma:* Full Moon Day. *Saint Vincent:* Discovery Day.

**23 Thu.** *Sri Lanka:* Full Moon Poya.

**26 Sun.** *Dominican Republic:* Duarte Day. *India:* Republic Day.

**27 Mon.** *Australia:* Australia Day. *Monaco:* Saint Devota's Day. *Vietnam:* Vietnam Day.

**28 Tue.** *Rwanda:* Democracy Day.

**31 Fri.** *Nauru:* Independence Day.

# February 1997

**2 Sun.** *Liechtenstein:* Candlemas.

**3 Mon.** *United States:* Lincoln's Birthday.

**4 Tue.** *Sri Lanka:* Independence Day.

**5 Wed.** *Mexico:* Constitution Day.

**6 Thu.** *New Zealand:* Waitangi Day. *Asian:* Chinese New Year Eve (see App. B1).

**7 Fri.** *Grenada:* Independence Day. *Vietnam:* Tet (1st day of 3). *Asian:* Chinese New Year (Year of the Ox) (see App. B2). *Far East Islamic:* Hari Raya Puasa (see App. B27). *Islamic:* Eid al Fitr (1st day of 4) (see App. B26).

**8 Sat.** *Iraq:* Revolution Day. *Vietnam:* Tet (2nd day of 3). *Asian:* 2nd Day of Chinese New Year (see App. B3). *Islamic:* Eid al Fitr (2nd day of 4) (see App. B26).

**9 Sun.** *Lebanon:* Saint Marion's Day. *Vietnam:* Tet (3rd day of 3). *Asian:* 3rd Day of Chinese New Year (see App. B4). *Islamic:* Eid al Fitr (3rd day of 4) (see App. B26).

**10 Mon.** *Malta:* Saint Paul's Day. *Christian:* Shrove Monday (see App. B7). *Islamic:* Eid al Fitr (4th day of 4) (see App. B26).

**11 Tue.** *Cameroon:* Youth Day. *Japan:* Foundation Day. *Liberia:* Armed Forces Day. *Christian:* Shrove Tuesday (see App. B8).

**12 Wed.** *Burma:* Union Day. *Christian:* Ash Wednesday (see App. B9).

**14 Fri.** *International:* Valentine's Day.

**17 Mon.** *United States:* Washington's Birthday.

**18 Tue.** *Gambia:* Independence Day. *Zodiac Cusp:* Aquarius ends, Pisces begins.

**19 Wed.** *Nepal:* National Day.

**20 Thu.** *Burma:* Full Moon Day.

**21 Fri.** *Bangladesh:* Saheed Day. *Sri Lanka:* Full Moon Poya.

**22 Sat.** *Saint Lucia:* Independence

Day. *Thailand:* Makha Bucha Day.

**23 Sun.** *Brunei:* National Day. *Guyana:* Republic Day.

**25 Tue.** *Kuwait:* National Day.

**27 Thu.** *Dominican Republic:* Independence Day.

# March 1997

**1 Sat.** *South Korea:* Independence Day.

**2 Sun.** *Ethiopia:* Victory of Aduwa Day. *Morocco:* Independence Day.

**3 Mon.** *Bulgaria:* Liberation Day. *Guam:* Discovery Day. *Malawi:* Martyrs' Day. *Morocco:* National Day.

**6 Thu.** *Ghana:* Independence Day.

**8 Sat.** *Syria:* Revolution Day. *Zambia:* Youth Day. *Multinational:* Women's Day (see App. A4).

**10 Mon.** *Gibraltar:* Commonwealth Day. *South Korea:* Labor Day.

**11 Tue.** *Lithuania:* National Day*.

**12 Wed.** *Lesotho:* Moshoeshoe's Day. *Mauritius:* Independence Day.

**13 Thu.** *Grenada:* National Day.

**17 Mon.** *Greece:* Shrove Monday. *Ireland:* Saint Patrick's Day. *Northern Ireland:* Saint Patrick's Day. *Orthodox:* Shrove Monday.

**19 Wed.** *Christian:* Saint Joseph's Day (see App. A5).

**20 Thu.** *Afghanistan:* New Year's Day (Shamsi: 1376). *Iran:* New Year's Day (Hegira: 1376). *Iraq:* New Year's Day. *Japan:* Vernal Equinox. *Tunisia:* Independence Day. *Zodiac Cusp:* Pisces ends, Aries begins.

**21 Fri.** *Mexico:* Juarez Day.

**22 Sat.** *Burma:* Full Moon Day. *Puerto Rico:* Abolition Day.

**23 Sun.** *Pakistan:* Pakistan Day. *Sri Lanka:* Full Moon Poya. *Christian:* Palm Sunday. *Jewish:* Purim.

**25 Tue.** *Cyprus:* Greek Independence Day. *Greece:* Independence Day. *Liechtenstein:* Annunciation. *Zambia:* Africa Day.

**26 Wed.** *Bangladesh:* Independence Day.

**27 Thu.** *Angola:* Evacuation Day. *Burma:* Resistance Day. *Christian:* Maundy Thursday (see App. B11).

**28 Fri.** *Christian:* Good Friday (see App. B12).

**29 Sat.** *Central African Republic:* Boganda Day. *Madagascar:* Memorial Day. *Taiwan:* Youth Day. *Christian:* Holy Saturday (see App. B13).

**30 Sun.** *Christian:* Easter Sunday (see App. B14). *Europe:* Daylight Savings Time starts (advance clocks 1 hour).

**31 Mon.** *Malta:* National Day. *Virgin Islands (U.S.):* Transfer Day. *Christian:* Easter Monday (see App. B15).

# April 1997

**1 Tue.** *Iran:* Republic Day. *San Marino:* National Day.

**4 Fri.** *Hungary:* Liberation Day. *Senegal:* National Day. *Sierra Leone:* Bank Holiday.

**5 Sat.** *South Korea:* Arbor Day. *Asian:* Tomb Sweeping Day (see App. A6).

**6 Sun.** *South Africa:* Founders' Day. *Thailand:* Chakri Day. Canada and United States: Daylight Savings Time starts (advance clocks 1 hour).

**9 Wed.** *Philippines:* Valour Day. *Tunisia:* Martyrs' Day.

**11 Fri.** *Costa Rica:* Heroes' Day. *Uganda:* Liberation Day.

**13 Sun.** *Chad:* National Day. *Thailand:* Songkrawn (1st day of 2).

**14 Mon.** *Honduras:* Pan American Day. *Thailand:* Songkrawn (2nd day of 2).

**15 Tue.** *Niger:* National Day.

**16 Wed.** *Burma:* New Year's Day (Burmese: 1359). *Cyprus:* Independence Day. *Islamic:* Eid al Adha (1st day of 4) (see App. B28).

**17 Thu.** *Cambodia:* Independence Day. *Syria:* Independence Day. *Far East Islamic:* Hari Raya Haji (see App. B29). *Islamic:* Eid al Adha (2nd day of 4) (see App. B28).

**18 Fri.** *Zimbabwe:* Republic Day. *Islamic:* Eid al Adha (3rd day of 4) (see App. B28).

**19 Sat.** *Sierra Leone:* Republic Day. *Uruguay:* Patriots' Day. *Venezuela:* Independence Day. *Islamic:* Eid al Adha (4th day of 4) (see App. B28).

**20 Sun.** *Zodiac Cusp:* Aries ends, Taurus begins.

**21 Mon.** *Brazil:* Tiradentes Day. *Burma:* Full Moon Day.

**22 Tue.** *Israel:* Passover. *Sri Lanka:* Full Moon Poya. *Jewish:* Passover.

**23 Wed.** *Turkey:* Children's Day.

**25 Fri.** *Australia:* ANZAC Day. *Denmark:* All Prayers' Day. *Egypt:* Sinai Day. *Iceland:* Children's Day. *Italy:* Liberation Day. *New Zealand:* ANZAC Day. *Portugal:* Liberation Day. *Swaziland:* Flag Day.

**26 Sat.** *Tanzania:* Union Day.

**27 Sun.** *Afghanistan:* Independence Day. *Sierra Leone:* Independence Day. *Togo:* Independence Day.

**29 Tue.** *Japan:* Green Day.

**30 Wed.** *Finland:* Vappu Day. *Netherlands:* Queen's Birthday.

# May 1997

**1 Thu.** *Multinational:* Labor Day (see App. A7).

**2 Fri.** *Lesotho:* King's Birthday. *Orthodox:* Good Friday (see App. B20).

**3 Sat.** *Japan:* Constitution Day.

**4 Sun.** *Japan:* People's Day. *Jordan:* Easter Sunday. *Orthodox:* Easter Sunday.

**5 Mon.** *Japan:* Children's Day. *Mexico: Cinco de Mayo Netherlands:* Liberation Day. *South Korea:* Children's Day. *Thailand:* Coronation Day. *United Kingdom:* Labour Day. *Zambia:* Labour Day. *Orthodox:* Easter Monday (see App. B20).

**6 Tue.** *Lebanon:* Martyrs' Day. *Philippines:* Corregidor Day. *Islamic:* New Year's Day (Hegira: 1418) (see App. B22).

**8 Thu.** *France:* Liberation Day. *Christian:* Ascension (see App. B16). *Far East Islamic:* New Year's Day (Hegira: 1418) (see App. B22).

**9 Fri.** *Czech Republic:* Liberation Day*. *Slovakia:* Liberation Day*.

**10 Sat.** *Micronesia:* Independence Day.

**11 Sun.** *International:* Mother's Day.

**12 Mon.** *Israel:* Independence Day.

**13 Tue.** *South Korea:* Vesak Day.

**14 Wed.** *Liberia:* Unification Day. *Malawi:* Kamuzu Day. *Paraguay:* Flag Day.

**15 Thu.** *Paraguay:* Independence Day. *Islamic:* Ashura (see App. B23).

**17 Sat.** *Cayman Islands:* Discovery Day. *Norway:* Constitution Day.

**18 Sun.** *Haiti:* Flag Day. *Uruguay:* Las Piedras Day. *Christian:* Whitsunday.

**19 Mon.** *Canada:* Victoria Day. *Finland:* Flag Day. *Turkey:* Youth Day. *Christian:* Whitmonday (see App. B18).

**20 Tue.** *Burma:* Full Moon Day. *Cameroon:* Constitution Day. *Malaysia:* Vesak Day. *Singapore:* Vesak Day. *Zaïre:* Popular Movement Day.

**21 Wed.** *Chile:* Navy Day. *Sri Lanka:* Full Moon Poya. *Thailand:* Visakha Bucha Day. *Zodiac Cusp:* Taurus ends, Gemini begins.

**22 Thu.** *Haiti:* Sovereign Day. *Sri Lanka:* Heroes' Day.

**23 Fri.** *Jamaica:* Labour Day.

**24 Sat.** *Bulgaria:* Culture Day. *Ecuador:* Independence Battle Day.

**25 Sun.** *Argentina:* National Day. *Eritrea:* Independence Day*. *Jordan:* Independence Day. *Sudan:* Revolution Day. *Multinational:* Africa Day (see App. A8).

**26 Mon.** *Guyana:* Independence Day. *United Kingdom:* Spring Break. *United States:* Memorial Day.

**27 Tue.** *Nigeria:* Children's Day.

**29 Thu.** *Christian:* Corpus Christi (see App. B19).

**31 Sat.** *Brunei:* Regiment Day. *South Africa:* Republic Day.

# June 1997

**1 Sun.** *Kenya:* Madaraka Day. *Tunisia:* National Day. *Western Samoa:* Independence Day.

**2 Mon.** *Ireland:* Public Holiday. *Italy:* Republic Day. *New Zealand:* Queen's Birthday. *Tunisia:* Youth Day.

**4 Wed.** *Bahamas:* Labour Day. *Malaysia:* King's Birthday. *Tonga:* Independence Day.

**5 Thu.** *Denmark:* Constitution Day. *Equatorial Guinea:* President's Birthday. *Seychelles:* Liberation Day.

**6 Fri.** *South Korea:* Memorial Day. *Sweden:* Constitution Day.

**7 Sat.** *Chad:* Revolution Day.

**9 Mon.** *Argentina:* Independence Day. *Australia:* Queen's Birthday. *Fiji:* Queen's Birthday. *New Guinea:* Queen's Birthday. *United Kingdom:* Queen's Birthday.

**10 Tue.** *Macao:* Portugal Day. *Portugal:* Portugal Day.

**11 Wed.** *Israel:* Pentecost. *Libya:* Evacuation Day. *Asian:* Dragon Boat Festival (see App. B5). *Jewish:* Pentecost.

**12 Thu.** *Philippines:* Independence Day.

**14 Sat.** *Hong Kong:* Queen's Birthday (1st day of 2).

**16 Mon.** *Hong Kong:* Queen's Birthday (2nd day of 2).

**17 Tue.** *Germany:* Unity Day. *Iceland:* Independence Day.

**18 Wed.** *Egypt:* Independence Day.

**19 Thu.** *Algeria:* Righting Day. *Burma:* Full Moon Day. *Kuwait:* Independence Day. *Uruguay:* Artigas Day.

**20 Fri.** *Argentina:* Flag Day. *Sri Lanka:* Full Moon Poya.

**21 Sat.** *Finland:* Johannus and Midsummer Day (1st day of 2). *Sweden:* Midsummer Day (1st day of 2). *Zodiac Cusp:* Gemini ends, Cancer begins.

**22 Sun.** *Finland:* Midsummer Day (2nd day of 2). *Sweden:* Midsummer Day (2nd day of 2). *Orthodox:* Pentecost Sunday.

**23 Mon.** *Greece:* Pentecost Monday. *Luxembourg:* National Day.

**24 Tue.** *Andorra:* Saint John's Day. *Venezuela:* Carabobo Day. *Zaïre:* Constitution Day.

**25 Wed.** *Croatia:* Independence Day*. *Mozambique:* Independence Day. *Slovenia:* Independence Day*.

**26 Thu.** *Madagascar:* Independence Day. *Somalia:* Independence Day.

**27 Fri.** *Chile:* Bank Holiday. *Djibouti:* Independence Day. *Ecuador:* Bank Holiday. *El Salvador:* Bank Holiday. *Finland:* Bank Holiday.

**29 Sun.** *Seychelles:* Independence Day. *Christian:* Saint Paul's Day (see App. A9).

**30 Mon.** *Guatemala:* Army Day. *Sri Lanka:* Bank Holiday. *Zaïre:* Independence Day.

# July 1997

**1 Tue.** *Burundi:* Independence Day. *Canada:* Canada Day. *Ghana:* Republic Day. *Hong Kong:* Half Year Day. *Rwanda:* Independence Day. *Somalia:* Union Day. *Suriname:* Freedom Day. *Zambia:* Unity Day. *Multinational:* Bank Holiday (see App. A10).

**4 Fri.** *Philippines:* United States Friendship Day. *United States:* Independence Day. *Yugoslavia:* Freedom Fighters' Day.

**5 Sat.** *Algeria:* Independence Day. *Cape Verde:* Independence Day. *Rwanda:* Unity Day. *Venezuela:* Independence Day.

**6 Sun.** *Comoros:* Independence Day. *Malawi:* Republic Day.

**7 Mon.** *Cayman Islands:* Constitution Day. *Lesotho:* Family Day. *Solomon Islands:* Independence Day. *Tanzania:* Farmers' Day. *Yugoslavia:* Serbian Day. *Zambia:* Heroes' Day.

**10 Thu.** *Bahamas:* Independence Day.

**11 Fri.** *Mongolia:* Revolution Day.

**12 Sat.** *Kiribati:* Independence Day. *Northern Ireland:* Battle of the Boyne Day. *São Tomé:* National Day.

**14 Mon.** *France:* National Day. *Iraq:* Revolution Day.

**15 Tue.** *Brunei:* Sultan's Birthday. *Islamic:* Mohammed's Birthday (see App. B24).

**16 Wed.** *Far East Islamic:* Mohammed's Birthday.

**17 Thu.** *Iraq:* Revolution Day. *Puerto Rico:* Rivera Day. *Slovakia:* Independence Day*. *South Korea:* Constitution Day.

**18 Fri.** *Burma:* Full Moon Day. *Uruguay:* Constitution Day.

**19 Sat.** *Burma:* Martyrs' Day. *Laos:* Independence Day. *Nicaragua:* Sandinista Day. *Sri Lanka:* Full Moon Poya. *Thailand:* Asalaha Bucha Day.

**20 Sun.** *Colombia:* Independence Day. *Thailand:* Khao Phansa Day.

**21 Mon.** *Belgium:* National Day. *Botswana:* President's Day. *Guam:* Liberation Day.

**22 Tue.** *Poland:* Liberation Day. *Zodiac Cusp:* Cancer ends, Leo begins.

**23 Wed.** *Egypt:* Revolution Day. *New Guinea:* Remembrance Day.

**24 Thu.** *Venezuela:* Bolivar Day.

**25 Fri.** *Costa Rica:* Guanacaste Day. *Cuba:* Revolution Day (1st day of 3). *Puerto Rico:* Constitution Day. *Spain:* Santiago Day. *Tunisia:* Republic Day.

**26 Sat.** *Cuba:* Revolution Day (2nd day of 3). *Liberia:* Independence Day. *Maldives:* Independence Day.

**27 Sun.** *Cuba:* Revolution Day (3rd day of 3). *Puerto Rico:* Barbosa Day.

**28 Mon.** *Peru:* Independence Day (1st day of 2). *Virgin Islands (U.S.):* Hurricane Supplication Day.

**29 Tue.** *Peru:* Independence Day (2nd day of 2).

**30 Wed.** *Vanuatu:* Independence Day.

# August 1997

**1 Fri.** *Benin:* Independence Day. *Switzerland:* Confederation Day.

**2 Sat.** *Costa Rica:* Virgin of the Angels Day. *Guyana:* Freedom Day. *Trinidad:* Discovery Day.

**3 Sun.** *El Salvador:* Summer Day (1st day of 4). *Guinea-Bissau:* Martyrs' Day. *Niger:* Independence Day. *Tunisia:* President's Birthday.

**4 Mon.** *Bahamas:* Emancipation Day. *Barbados:* Emancipation Day. *Burkina Faso:* Independence Day (1st day of 2). *Canada:* Civic Holiday. *El Salvador:* Summer Day (2nd day of 4).

*Ireland:* Public Holiday. *Jamaica:* Independence Day. *Scotland:* Public Holiday.

**5 Tue.** *Burkina Faso:* Independence Day (2nd day of 2). *El Salvador:* Summer Day (3rd day of 4).

**6 Wed.** *Bolivia:* Independence Day. *El Salvador:* Summer Day (4th day of 4). *United Arab Emirates:* Accession Day. *Zambia:* Farmers' Day.

**7 Thu.** *Colombia:* Boyaca Day. *Ivory Coast:* Republic Day.

**9 Sat.** *Georgia:* Independence Day*. *Singapore:* National Day.

**10 Sun.** *Ecuador:* Independence Day.

**11 Mon.** *Chad:* Independence Day. *Jordan:* Accession Day. *Zimbabwe:* Heroes' Day (1st day of 2).

**12 Tue.** *Israel:* Tisha Ab. *Thailand:* Queen's Birthday. *Zimbabwe:* Heroes' Day (2nd day of 2). *Jewish:* Tisha Ab.

**13 Wed.** *Central African Republic:* Independence Day. *Congo:* Independence Day (1st day of 2). *Tunisia:* Women's Day.

**14 Thu.** *Congo:* Independence Day (2nd day of 2). *Pakistan:* Independence Day.

**15 Fri.** *Congo:* Independence Day (3rd day of 3). *India:* Independence Day. *Liechtenstein:* National Day. *South Korea:* Republic Day. *Christian:* Assumption (see App. A11).

**16 Sat.** *Burma:* Full Moon Day. *Dominican Republic:* Republic Day.

**17 Sun.** *Argentina:* San Martin's Day. *Gabon:* Independence Day. *Indonesia:* Independence Day. *Sri Lanka:* Full Moon Poya.

**20 Wed.** *Hungary:* Constitution Day. *Senegal:* Independence Day.

**21 Thu.** *Estonia:* Independence Day*. *Latvia:* Independence Day*. *Lithuania:* Independence Day*.

**23 Sat.** *Hong Kong:* Liberation Day (1st day of 2). *Romania:* National Day (1st day of 2). *Zodiac Cusp:* Leo ends, Virgo begins.

**24 Sun.** *Kazakhstan:* National Day*. *Liberia:* Flag Day. *Romania:* National Day (2nd day of 2). *Russia:* Independence Day*. *Ukraine:* National Day*.

**25 Mon.** *Belarus:* Independence Day*. *England:* Summer Break. *Hong Kong:* Liberation Day (2nd day of 2). *Northern Ireland:* Summer Break. *Paraguay:* Constitution Day. *Uruguay:* Independence Day. *Wales:* Summer Break.

**27 Wed.** *Moldova:* Independence Day*.

**29 Fri.** *Uzbekistan:* Independence Day*.

**30 Sat.** *Afghanistan:* Children's Day. *Azerbaijan:* Independence Day*. *Peru:* Rose of Lima Day. *Turkey:* Victory Day.

**31 Sun.** *Afghanistan:* Pashtunistan Day. *Kyrgyzstan:* Independence Day*. *Malaysia:* National Day. *Trinidad:* Independence Day.

# September 1997

**1 Mon.** *Canada:* Labour Day. *Libya:* National Day. *Luxembourg:* Fair Day. *Mexico:* President's Message Day. *Syria:* United Arab Republics Day. *United States:* Labor Day.

**2 Tue.** *Vietnam:* Independence Day.

**3 Wed.** *Qatar:* National Day. *San Marino:* Saint Marinus' Day. *Tunisia:* Independence Movement Day.

**6 Sat.** *Pakistan:* Defense Day. *Swaziland:* Independence Day.

**7 Sun.** *Brazil:* Independence Day.

**8 Mon.** *Andorra:* National Day. *Malta:* Our Lady of Victory Day.

**9 Tue.** *Bulgaria:* National Day (1st day of 2). *North Korea:* Independence Day. *Tajikistan:* Independence Day*.

**10 Wed.** *Belize:* National Day. *Bulgaria:* National Day (2nd day of 2).

**11 Thu.** *Chile:* Revolution Day. *Egypt:* New Year's Day (Coptic: 1715). *Ethiopia:* New Year's Day (Ethiopian:

1991). *Pakistan:* Anniversary of Quaid-e-Azam's Death.

**12 Fri.** *Ethiopia:* National Day.

**14 Sun.** *Guatemala:* San Jacinto Day. *Nicaragua:* San Jacinto Day.

**15 Mon.** *Burma:* Full Moon Day. *Costa Rica:* Independence Day. *El Salvador:* Independence Day. *Guatemala:* Independence Day. *Honduras:* Independence Day. *Japan:* Veneration Day. *Nicaragua:* Independence Day.

**16 Tue.** *Mexico:* Independence Day. *New Guinea:* Independence Day. *Sri Lanka:* Full Moon Poya.

**17 Wed.** *Angola:* Heroes' Day. *Marshall Islands:* Independence Day.

**18 Thu.** *Burundi:* Victory of Uprona Day. *Chile:* Independence Day.

**19 Fri.** *Chile:* Armed Forces Day. *Saint Kitts:* Independence Day.

**21 Sun.** *Belize:* Independence Day. *Malta:* Independence Day.

**22 Mon.** *Mali:* Independence Day.

**23 Tue.** *Armenia:* Independence Day*. *Japan:* Autumnal Equinox. *Saudi Arabia:* National Day. *Zodiac Cusp:* Virgo ends, Libra begins.

**24 Wed.** *Dominican Republic:* Mercedes Day. *Guinea-Bissau:* Republic Day.

**25 Thu.** *Mozambique:* Liberation Day. *Rwanda:* Assembly Day.

**26 Fri.** *Ethiopia:* True Cross Day.

**28 Sun.** *Taiwan:* Teachers' Day. *Europe:* Daylight Savings Time ends (retard clocks 1 hour).

**29 Mon.** *Brunei:* Constitution Day. *Paraguay:* Boqueron Battle Day.

**30 Tue.** *Botswana:* Independence Day.

# October 1997

**1 Wed.** *Cameroon:* Unification Day. *China:* National Day (1st day of 2). *Nigeria:* Independence Day. *South Korea:* Armed Forces Day (1st day of 2). *Tuvalu:* Independence Day.

**2 Thu.** *China:* National Day (2nd day of 2). *Guinea:* Independence Day. *India:* Ghandi Day. *Israel:* New Year's Day. *South Korea:* Armed Forces Day (2nd day of 2). *Jewish:* Rosh Hashanah (Jewish: 5758).

**3 Fri.** *Honduras:* Morazan Day. *South Korea:* Foundation Day (1st day of 2).

**4 Sat.** *Lesotho:* Independence Day. *South Korea:* Foundation Day (2nd day of 2).

**5 Sun.** *Lesotho:* Sports Day. *Macao:* Portuguese Republic Day. *Portugal:* Republic Day.

**6 Mon.** *Barbados:* Bank Holiday. *Egypt:* Armed Forces Day.

**9 Thu.** *Peru:* National Dignity Day. *South Korea:* Alphabet Day. *Uganda:* Independence Day.

**10 Fri.** *Japan:* Health Day. *South Africa:* Kruger Day. *Taiwan:* National Day. *Asian:* Ancestors' Day (see App. B6).

**11 Sat.** *Cuba:* Independence War. *Israel:* Yom Kippur. *Panama:* Revolution Day. *Jewish:* Yom Kippur.

**12 Sun.** *Equatorial Guinea:* Independence Day. *Spain:* National Day. *Multinational:* Columbus Day (see App. A12).

**13 Mon.** *Canada:* Thanksgiving Day. *Fiji:* Cession Day. *United States:* Bank Holiday. *Virgin Islands (U.S.):* Puerto Rican Friendship Day.

**14 Tue.** *Burma:* Full Moon Day. *Zaïre:* Founders' Day.

**15 Wed.** *Bosnia and Herzegovina:* Independence Day*. *China:* Mid-autumn Day. *Sri Lanka:* Full Moon Poya. *Taiwan:* Mid-autumn Day. *Tunisia:* Evacuation Day.

**16 Thu.** *Hong Kong:* Mid-autumn Day. *Israel:* Sukkot. *Macao:* Mid-autumn Day. *Jewish:* Sukkot.

**17 Fri.** *Haiti:* Dessalines Day. *Malawi:* Mother's Day.

**20 Mon.** *Guatemala:* Revolution Day. *Jamaica:* Heroes' Day. *Kenya:* Kenyatta Day.

**21 Tue.** *Honduras:* Army Day. *Somalia:* Revolution Day (1st day of 2).

**22 Wed.** *Somalia:* Revolution Day (2nd day of 2). *Vatican:* John Paul II Day.

**23 Thu.** *Hungary:* Revolution Day. *Thailand:* Chulalongkorn Day. *Zodiac Cusp:* Libra ends, Scorpio begins.

**24 Fri.** *Egypt:* Suez Victory Day. *Haiti:* United Nations Day. *Zambia:* Independence Day.

**25 Sat.** *Taiwan:* Restoration Day.

**26 Sun.** *Austria:* National Day. *Benin:* Revolution Day. *Rwanda:* Government Day. *Canada and United States:* Daylight Savings Time ends (retard clocks 1 hour).

**27 Mon.** *Ireland:* Public Holiday. *New Zealand:* Labour Day. *Saint Vincent:* Independence Day. *Turkmenistan:* Independence Day*. *Zaïre:* Naming Day.

**28 Tue.** *Greece:* Ohi! Day.

**29 Wed.** *Tanzania:* Naming Day. *Turkey:* Republic Day.

**30 Thu.** *Hindu:* Deepavali (see App. B21).

**31 Fri.** *Taiwan:* Chiang Kai-shek's Birthday.

# November 1997

**1 Sat.** *Algeria:* Revolution Day. *Antigua:* Independence Day. *Christian:* All Saints' Day (see App. A13).

**2 Sun.** *Brazil:* Memorial Day. *Finland:* All Saints' Eve. *Sweden:* All Saints' Eve. *Christian:* All Souls' Day (see App. A14).

**3 Mon.** *Dominica:* Independence Day. *Ecuador:* Cuenca Independence Day. *Japan:* Culture Day. *Panama:* Independence Day. *Virgin Islands (U.S.):* Liberty Day.

**4 Tue.** *Andorra:* Saint Charles' Day. *Panama:* Flag Day. *Vatican:* John Paul II's Nameday.

**5 Wed.** *El Salvador:* Cry of Independence Day.

**6 Thu.** *Liberia:* Thanksgiving Day.

**7 Fri.** *Bangladesh:* Revolution Day.

**8 Sat.** *Nepal:* Queen's Birthday.

**9 Sun.** *Pakistan:* Iqbal Day.

**10 Mon.** *Panama:* Cry of Independence Day.

**11 Tue.** *Angola:* Independence Day. *Bhutan:* King's Birthday. *Maldives:* Republic Day. *Poland:* Independence Day. *Multinational:* Armistice Day (see App. A15).

**12 Wed.** *Taiwan:* Dr. Sun Yat-sen's Birthday.

**13 Thu.** *Burma:* Full Moon Day.

**14 Fri.** *Jordan:* King's Birthday. *Sri Lanka:* Full Moon Poya.

**15 Sat.** *Brazil:* Republic Day.

**17 Mon.** *Fiji:* Prince Charles' Birthday. *Zaïre:* Armed Forces Day.

**18 Tue.** *Haiti:* Vertieres' Day. *Morocco:* Independence Day. *Oman:* National Day.

**19 Wed.** *Belize:* Garifuna Day. *Germany:* Repentance Day. *Mali:* Army Coup Day. *Monaco:* Prince Ranier's Day. *Puerto Rico:* Discovery Day.

**20 Thu.** *Mexico:* Revolution Day.

**22 Sat.** *Lebanon:* Independence Day. *Zodiac Cusp:* Scorpio ends, Sagittarius begins.

**23 Sun.** *Japan:* Labor Thanksgiving Day.

**24 Mon.** *Zaïre:* New Regime Day.

**25 Tue.** *Suriname:* Independence Day.

**27 Thu.** *United States:* Thanksgiving Day. *Islamic:* Isra a Majraj (see App. B30).

**28 Fri.** *Albania:* Independence Day. *Argentina:* Bank Holiday. *Burundi:* Republic Day. *Chad:* Republic Day. *Mauritania:* Independence Day. *Panama:* Independence Day.

**29 Sat.** *Albania:* Liberation Day. *Liberia:* Tubman's Birthday. *Yugoslavia:* Republic Day.

**30 Sun.** *Barbados:* Independence Day. *Benin:* National Day. *Philippines:* Heroes' Day.

# December 1997

**1 Mon.** *Central African Republic:* National Day. *Portugal:* Youth Day. *Ukraine:* Independence Day*.

**2 Tue.** *Laos:* Republic Day. *United Arab Emirates:* National Day.

**5 Fri.** *Haiti:* Discovery Day. *Thailand:* King's Birthday.

**6 Sat.** *Finland:* Independence Day.

**7 Sun.** *Ivory Coast:* Independence Day.

**8 Mon.** *Christian:* Immaculate Conception (see App. A16).

**9 Tue.** *Tanzania:* Independence Day.

**10 Wed.** *Angola:* MPLA Foundation Day. *Equatorial Guinea:* Human Rights Day. *Namibia:* Settlers' Day. *Thailand:* Constitution Day.

**11 Thu.** *Burkina Faso:* National Day.

**12 Fri.** *Burma:* Full Moon Day. *Kenya:* Independence Day. *Mexico:* Guadalupe Festival.

**13 Sat.** *Malta:* Republic Day. *Sri Lanka:* Full Moon Poya.

**16 Tue.** *Bahrain:* National Day. *Bangladesh:* Victory Day. *Nepal:* Constitution Day. *South Africa:* Covenant Day.

**17 Wed.** *Bhutan:* National Day.

**18 Thu.** *Niger:* Republic Day.

**21 Sun.** *Kazakhstan:* Independence Day*. *Zodiac Cusp:* Sagittarius ends, Capricorn begins.

**23 Tue.** *Japan:* Emperor's Birthday.

**24 Wed.** *Jewish:* Chanukah *Multinational:* Christmas Eve (see App. A17).

**25 Thu.** *Angola:* Family Day. *Congo:* Children's Day. *Pakistan:* Quaid's Birthday. *Taiwan:* Constitution Day. *Multinational:* Christmas Day (see App. A18).

**26 Fri.** *South Africa:* Good Will Day. *Multinational:* Boxing Day (see App. A19).

**30 Tue.** *Madagascar:* Republic Day. *Philippines:* Rizal Day (1st day of 2). *Islamic:* 1st Day of Ramadan (see App. B25).

**31 Wed.** *Congo:* Republic Day. *Philippines:* Rizal Day (2nd day of 2). *Multinational:* Bank Holiday and New Year's Eve (see App. A20 & A21).

# January 1998

**1 Thu.** *Cameroon:* Independence Day. *Cuba:* Liberation Day. *Haiti:* Independence Day. *Palau:* Independence Day. *Sudan:* Independence Day. *Taiwan:* Foundation Day (1st day of 2). *Western Samoa:* Independence Day. *Multinational:* Bank Holiday and New Year's Day (see App. A1 & A2).

**2 Fri.** *Japan:* Bank Holiday. *New Zealand:* New Year's Day (2nd day of 2). *Scotland:* New Year's Day (2nd day of 2). *South Korea:* New Year's Day (2nd day of 2). *Switzerland:* Berchtold's Day. *Taiwan:* Foundation Day (2nd day of 2).

**3 Sat.** *Burkina Faso:* Revolution Day.

**4 Sun.** *Burma:* Independence Day. *Zaïre:* Martyrs' Day.

**6 Tue.** *Iraq:* Army Day. *Uruguay:* Children's Day. *Christian:* Epiphany (see App. A3).

7 **Wed.** *Egypt:* Coptic Christmas. *Ethiopia:* Coptic Christmas.

11 **Sun.** *Albania:* Republic Day. *Burma:* Full Moon Day. *Nepal:* Unification Day. *Puerto Rico:* Hostos Day.

12 **Mon.** *Sri Lanka:* Full Moon Poya. *Tanzania:* Revolution Day.

13 **Tue.** *Togo:* Liberation Day.

15 **Thu.** *Japan:* Adult's Day. *Jordan:* Arbor Day.

19 **Mon.** *Ethiopia:* Epiphany. *United States:* Martin Luther King's Birthday.

20 **Tue.** *Mali:* Award Day. *Zodiac Cusp:* Capricorn ends, Aquarius begins.

21 **Wed.** *Dominican Republic:* Altagracia Day.

22 **Thu.** *Saint Vincent:* Discovery Day.

26 **Mon.** *Australia:* Australia Day. *Dominican Republic:* Duarte Day. *India:* Republic Day.

27 **Tue.** *Monaco:* Saint Devota's Day. *Vietnam:* Vietnam Day. *Asian:* Chinese New Year Eve (see App. B1).

28 **Wed.** *Rwanda:* Democracy Day. *Vietnam:* Tet (1st day of 3). *Asian:* Chinese New Year (Year of the Tiger) (see App. B2).

29 **Thu.** *Vietnam:* Tet (2nd day of 3). *Asian:* 2nd Day of Chinese New Year (see App. B3). *Far East Islamic:* Hari Raya Puasa (see App. B27). *Islamic:* Eid al Fitr (1st day of 4) (see App. B26).

30 **Fri.** *Vietnam:* Tet (3rd day of 3). *Asian:* 3rd Day of Chinese New Year (see App. B4). *Islamic:* Eid al Fitr (2nd day of 4) (see App. B26).

31 **Sat.** *Nauru:* Independence Day. *Islamic:* Eid al Fitr (3rd day of 4) (see App. B26).

# February 1998

1 **Sun.** *Islamic:* Eid al Fitr (4th day of 4) (see App. B26).

2 **Mon.** *Liechtenstein:* Candlemas. *United States:* Lincoln's Birthday.

4 **Wed.** *Sri Lanka:* Independence Day.

5 **Thu.** *Mexico:* Constitution Day.

6 **Fri.** *New Zealand:* Waitangi Day.

7 **Sat.** *Grenada:* Independence Day.

8 **Sun.** *Iraq:* Revolution Day.

9 **Mon.** *Burma:* Full Moon Day. *Lebanon:* Saint Marion's Day.

10 **Tue.** *Malta:* Saint Paul's Day. *Sri Lanka:* Full Moon Poya.

11 **Wed.** *Cameroon:* Youth Day. *Japan:* Foundation Day. *Liberia:* Armed Forces Day. *Thailand:* Makha Bucha Day.

12 **Thu.** *Burma:* Union Day.

14 **Sat.** *International:* Valentine's Day.

16 **Mon.** *United States:* Washington's Birthday.

18 **Wed.** *Gambia:* Independence Day.

19 **Thu.** *Nepal:* National Day. *Zodiac Cusp:* Aquarius ends, Pisces begins.

21 **Sat.** *Bangladesh:* Saheed Day.

22 **Sun.** *Saint Lucia:* Independence Day.

23 **Mon.** *Brunei:* National Day. *Guyana:* Republic Day. *Christian:* Shrove Monday (see App. B7).

24 **Tue.** *Christian:* Shrove Tuesday (see App. B8).

25 **Wed.** *Kuwait:* National Day. *Christian:* Ash Wednesday (see App. B9).

27 **Fri.** *Dominican Republic:* Independence Day.

# March 1998

1 **Sun.** *South Korea:* Independence Day.

2 **Mon.** *Ethiopia:* Victory of Aduwa Day. *Greece:* Shrove Monday. *Guam:*

Discovery Day. *Morocco:* Independence Day. *Orthodox:* Shrove Monday.

**3 Tue.** *Bulgaria:* Liberation Day. *Malawi:* Martyrs' Day. *Morocco:* National Day.

**6 Fri.** *Ghana:* Independence Day.

**8 Sun.** *Syria:* Revolution Day. *Multinational:* Women's Day (see App. A4).

**9 Mon.** *Gibraltar:* Commonwealth Day.

**10 Tue.** *South Korea:* Labor Day.

**11 Wed.** *Burma:* Full Moon Day. *Lithuania:* National Day*.

**12 Thu.** *Lesotho:* Moshoeshoe's Day. *Mauritius:* Independence Day. *Sri Lanka:* Full Moon Poya. *Jewish:* Purim.

**13 Fri.** *Grenada:* National Day.

**14 Sat.** *Zambia:* Youth Day.

**17 Tue.** *Ireland:* Saint Patrick's Day. *Northern Ireland:* Saint Patrick's Day.

**19 Thu.** *Christian:* Saint Joseph's Day (see App. A5).

**20 Fri.** *Iran:* New Year's Day (Hegira: 1377). *Iraq:* New Year's Day. *Tunisia:* Independence Day. *Zodiac Cusp:* Pisces ends, Aries begins.

**21 Sat.** *Afghanistan:* New Year's Day (Shamsi: 1377). *Japan:* Vernal Equinox. *Mexico:* Juarez Day.

**22 Sun.** *Puerto Rico:* Abolition Day.

**23 Mon.** *Pakistan:* Pakistan Day.

**24 Tue.** *Zambia:* Africa Day.

**25 Wed.** *Cyprus:* Greek Independence Day. *Greece:* Independence Day. *Liechtenstein:* Annunciation.

**26 Thu.** *Bangladesh:* Independence Day.

**27 Fri.** *Angola:* Evacuation Day. *Burma:* Resistance Day.

**29 Sun.** *Central African Republic:* Boganda Day. *Madagascar:* Memorial. *Taiwan:* Youth Day. *Europe:* Daylight Savings Time starts (advance clocks 1 hour).

**30 Mon.** *Virgin Islands (U.S.):* Transfer Day.

**31 Tue.** *Malta:* National Day.

# April 1998

**1 Wed.** *Iran:* Republic Day. *San Marino:* National Day.

**3 Fri.** *Sierra Leone:* Bank Holiday.

**4 Sat.** *Hungary:* Liberation Day. *Senegal:* National Day.

**5 Sun.** *South Korea:* Arbor Day. *Asian:* Tomb Sweeping Day (see App. A6). *Canada and United States:* Daylight Savings Time starts (advance clocks 1 hour). *Christian:* Palm Sunday.

**6 Mon.** *South Africa:* Founders' Day. *Thailand:* Chakri Day.

**7 Tue.** *Far East Islamic:* Hari Raya Haji (see App. B29). *Islamic:* Eid al Adha (1st day of 4) (see App. B28).

**8 Wed.** *Islamic:* Eid al Adha (2nd day of 4) (see App. B28).

**9 Thu.** *Philippines:* Valour Day. *Tunisia:* Martyrs' Day. *Christian:* Maundy Thursday (see App. B11). *Islamic:* Eid al Adha (3rd day of 4) (see App. B28).

**10 Fri.** *Burma:* Full Moon Day. *Christian:* Good Friday (see App. B12). *Islamic:* Eid al Adha (4th day of 4) (see App. B28).

**11 Sat.** *Costa Rica:* Heroes' Day. *Israel:* Passover. *Sri Lanka:* Full Moon Poya. *Uganda:* Liberation Day. *Christian:* Holy Saturday (see App. B13). *Jewish:* Passover.

**12 Sun.** *Christian:* Easter Sunday (see App. B14).

**13 Mon.** *Chad:* National Day. *Thailand:* Songkrawn (1st day of 2). *Christian:* Easter Monday (see App. B15).

**14 Tue.** *Honduras:* Pan American Day. *Thailand:* Songkrawn (2nd day of 2).

**15 Wed.** *Niger:* National Day.

**16 Thu.** *Burma:* New Year's Day (Burmese: 1360). *Cyprus:* Independence Day.

**17 Fri.** *Cambodia:* Independence Day. *Syria:* Independence Day. *Orthodox:* Good Friday (see App. B20).

**18 Sat.** *Zimbabwe:* Republic Day.

**19 Sun.** *Jordan:* Easter Sunday. *Sierra Leone:* Republic Day. *Uruguay:* Patriots' Day. *Venezuela:* Independence Day. *Orthodox:* Easter Sunday.

**20 Mon.** *Orthodox:* Easter Monday (see App. B20). *Zodiac Cusp:* Aries ends, Taurus begins.

**21 Tue.** *Brazil:* Tiradentes Day.

**23 Thu.** *Turkey:* Children's Day.

**25 Sat.** *Australia:* ANZAC Day. *Egypt:* Sinai Day. *Iceland:* Children's Day. *Italy:* Liberation Day. *New Zealand:* ANZAC Day. *Portugal:* Liberation Day. *Swaziland:* Flag Day.

**26 Sun.** *Tanzania:* Union Day. *Islamic:* New Year's Day. (Hegira: 1419) (see App. B22).

**27 Mon.** *Afghanistan:* Independence Day. *Sierra Leone:* Independence Day. *Togo:* Independence Day. *Far East Islamic:* New Year's Day (Hegira: 1419).

**29 Wed.** *Japan:* Green Day.

**30 Thu.** *Finland:* Vappu Day. *Israel:* Independence Day. *Netherlands:* Queen's Birthday.

# May 1998

**1 Fri.** *Multinational:* Labor Day (see App. A7).

**2 Sat.** *Lesotho:* King's Birthday.

**3 Sun.** *Japan:* Constitution Day. *South Korea:* Vesak Day.

**4 Mon.** *Japan:* People's Day. *United Kingdom:* Labour Day. *Zambia:* Labour Day.

**5 Tue.** *Japan:* Children's Day. *Mexico:* Cinco de Mayo. *Netherlands:* Liberation Day. *South Korea:* Children's Day. *Thailand:* Coronation Day. *Islamic:* Ashura (see App. B23).

**6 Wed.** *Lebanon:* Martyrs' Day. *Philippines:* Corregidor Day.

**8 Fri.** *Denmark:* All Prayers' Day. *France:* Liberation Day.

**9 Sat.** *Czech Republic:* Liberation Day*. *Slovakia:* Liberation Day*.

**10 Sun.** *Burma:* Full Moon Day. *Malaysia:* Vesak Day. *Micronesia:* Independence Day. *Singapore:* Vesak Day. *Thailand:* Visakha Bucha Day. *International:* Mother's Day.

**11 Mon.** *Sri Lanka:* Full Moon Poya.

**14 Thu.** *Liberia:* Unification Day. *Malawi:* Kamuzu Day. *Paraguay:* Flag Day.

**15 Fri.** *Paraguay:* Independence Day.

**17 Sun.** *Cayman Islands:* Discovery Day. *Norway:* Constitution Day.

**18 Mon.** *Canada:* Victoria Day. *Haiti:* Flag Day. *Uruguay:* Las Piedras Day.

**19 Tue.** *Finland:* Flag Day. *Turkey:* Youth Day.

**20 Wed.** *Cameroon:* Constitution Day. *Zaïre:* Popular Movement Day.

**21 Thu.** *Chile:* Navy Day. *Christian:* Ascension (see App. B16). *Zodiac Cusp:* Taurus ends, Gemini begins.

**22 Fri.** *Haiti:* Sovereign Day. *Sri Lanka:* Heroes' Day.

**23 Sat.** *Jamaica:* Labour Day.

**24 Sun.** *Bulgaria:* Culture Day. *Ecuador:* Independence Battle Day.

**25 Mon.** *Argentina:* National Day. *Eritrea:* Independence Day*. *Jordan:* Independence Day. *Sudan:* Revolution Day. *United Kingdom:* Spring Break. *United States:* Memorial Day. *Multinational:* Africa Day (see App. A8).

**26 Tue.** *Guyana:* Independence Day.

**27 Wed.** *Nigeria:* Children's Day.

**31 Sun.** *Brunei:* Regiment Day. *Israel:* Pentecost. *South Africa:* Republic Day. *Asian:* Dragon Boat Festival (see App. B5). *Christian:* Whitsunday. *Jewish:* Pentecost.

# June 1998

**1 Mon.** *Ireland:* Public Holiday. *Kenya:* Madaraka Day. *New Zealand:* Queen's Birthday. *Tunisia:* National Day. *Western Samoa:* Independence Day. *Christian:* Whitmonday (see App. B18).

**2 Tue.** *Italy:* Republic Day. *Tunisia:* Youth Day.

**3 Wed.** *Malaysia:* King's Birthday.

**4 Thu.** *Bahamas:* Labour Day. *Tonga:* Independence Day.

**5 Fri.** *Denmark:* Constitution Day. *Equatorial Guinea:* President's Birthday. *Seychelles:* Liberation Day.

**6 Sat.** *South Korea:* Memorial Day. *Sweden:* Constitution Day.

**7 Sun.** *Chad:* Revolution Day. *Orthodox:* Pentecost Sunday.

**8 Mon.** *Australia:* Queen's Birthday. *Burma:* Full Moon Day. *Fiji:* Queen's Birthday. *Greece:* Pentecost Monday. *New Guinea:* Queen's Birthday. *United Kingdom:* Queen's Birthday.

**9 Tue.** *Argentina:* Independence Day. *Sri Lanka:* Full Moon Poya.

**10 Wed.** *Macao:* Portugal Day. *Portugal:* Portugal Day.

**11 Thu.** *Libya:* Evacuation Day. *Christian:* Corpus Christi (see App. B19).

**12 Fri.** *Philippines:* Independence Day.

**13 Sat.** *Hong Kong:* Queen's Birthday (1st day of 2).

**15 Mon.** *Hong Kong:* Queen's Birthday (2nd day of 2).

**17 Wed.** *Germany:* Unity Day. *Iceland:* Independence Day.

**18 Thu.** *Egypt:* Independence Day.

**19 Fri.** *Algeria:* Righting Day. *Kuwait:* Independence Day. *Uruguay:* Artigas Day.

**20 Sat.** *Argentina:* Flag Day.

**21 Sun.** *Finland:* Midsummer Day (1st day of 2). *Sweden:* Midsummer Day (1st day of 2). *Zodiac Cusp:* Gemini ends, Cancer begins.

**22 Mon.** *Finland:* Midsummer Day (2nd day of 2). *Sweden:* Midsummer Day (2nd day of 2).

**23 Tue.** *Luxembourg:* National Day.

**24 Wed.** *Andorra:* Saint John's Day. *Venezuela:* Carabobo Day. *Zaïre:* Constitution Day.

**25 Thu.** *Croatia:* Independence Day*. *Mozambique:* Independence Day. *Slovenia:* Independence Day*.

**26 Fri.** *Chile:* Bank Holiday. *Ecuador:* Bank Holiday. *El Salvador:* Bank Holiday. *Finland:* Bank Holiday. *Madagascar:* Independence Day. *Somalia:* Independence Day.

**27 Sat.** *Djibouti:* Independence Day. *Finland:* Johannus Day.

**29 Mon.** *Seychelles:* Independence Day. *Christian:* Saint Paul's Day (see App. A9).

**30 Tue.** *Guatemala:* Army Day. *Sri Lanka:* Bank Holiday. *Zaïre:* Independence Day.

# July 1998

**1 Wed.** *Burundi:* Independence Day. *Canada:* Canada Day. *Ghana:* Republic Day. *Hong Kong:* Half Year Day. *Rwanda:* Independence Day. *Somalia:* Union Day. *Suriname:* Freedom Day. *Multinational:* Bank Holiday (see App. A10).

**4 Sat.** *Philippines:* United States Friendship Day. *United States:* Independence Day. *Yugoslavia:* Freedom Fighters' Day.

**5 Sun.** *Algeria:* Independence Day. *Cape Verde:* Independence Day. *Rwanda:* Unity Day. *Venezuela:* Independence Day. *Far East Islamic:* Mohammed's Birthday. *Islamic:* Mohammed's Birthday (see App. B24).

**6 Mon.** *Cayman Islands:* Constitution Day. *Comoros:* Independence Day. *Lesotho:* Family Day. *Malawi:* Republic Day. *Zambia:* Heroes' Day.

**7 Tue.** *Solomon Islands:* Independence Day. *Tanzania:* Farmers' Day. *Yugoslavia:* Serbian Day. *Zambia:* Unity Day.

**8 Wed.** *Burma:* Full Moon Day. *Thailand:* Asalaha Bucha Day.

**9 Thu.** *Sri Lanka:* Full Moon Poya. *Thailand:* Khao Phansa Day.

**10 Fri.** *Bahamas:* Independence Day.

**11 Sat.** *Mongolia:* Revolution Day.

**12 Sun.** *Kiribati:* Independence Day. *Northern Ireland:* Battle of the Boyne Day. *São Tomé:* National Day.

**14 Tue.** *France:* National Day. *Iraq:* Revolution Day.

**15 Wed.** *Brunei:* Sultan's Birthday.

**17 Fri.** *Iraq:* Revolution Day. *Puerto Rico:* Rivera Day. *Slovakia:* Independence Day*. *South Korea:* Constitution Day.

**18 Sat.** *Uruguay:* Constitution Day.

**19 Sun.** *Burma:* Martyrs' Day. *Laos:* Independence Day. *Nicaragua:* Sandinista Day.

**20 Mon.** *Botswana:* President's Day. *Colombia:* Independence Day.

**21 Tue.** *Belgium:* National Day. *Guam:* Liberation Day.

**22 Wed.** *Poland:* Liberation Day.

**23 Thu.** *Egypt:* Revolution Day. *New Guinea:* Remembrance Day. *Zodiac Cusp:* Cancer ends, Leo begins.

**24 Fri.** *Venezuela:* Bolivar Day.

**25 Sat.** *Costa Rica:* Guanacaste Day. *Cuba:* Revolution Day (1st day of 3). *Puerto Rico:* Constitution Day. *Spain:* Santiago Day. *Tunisia:* Republic Day.

**26 Sun.** *Cuba:* Revolution Day (2nd day of 3). *Liberia:* Independence Day. *Maldives:* Independence Day.

**27 Mon.** *Cuba:* Revolution Day (3rd day of 3). *Puerto Rico:* Barbosa Day. *Virgin Islands (U.S.):* Hurricane Supplication Day.

**28 Tue.** *Peru:* Independence Day (1st day of 2).

**29 Wed.** *Peru:* Independence Day (2nd day of 2).

**30 Thu.** *Vanuatu:* Independence Day.

# August 1998

**1 Sat.** *Benin:* Independence Day. *Switzerland:* Confederation Day.

**2 Sun.** *Costa Rica:* Virgin of the Angels Day. *Guyana:* Freedom Day. *Israel:* Tisha Ab. *Trinidad:* Discovery Day. *Jewish:* Tisha Ab.

**3 Mon.** *Bahamas:* Emancipation Day. *Barbados:* Emancipation Day. *Canada:* Civic Holiday. *El Salvador:* Summer Day (1st day of 4). *Guinea-Bissau:* Martyrs' Day. *Ireland:* Public Holiday. *Jamaica:* Independence Day. *Niger:* Independence Day. *Scotland:* Public Holiday. *Tunisia:* President's Birthday.

**4 Tue.** *Burkina Faso:* Independence Day (1st day of 2). *El Salvador:* Summer Day (2nd day of 4).

**5 Wed.** *Burkina Faso:* Independence Day (2nd day of 2). *El Salvador:* Summer Day (3rd day of 4). *Zambia:* Farmers' Day.

**6 Thu.** *Bolivia:* Independence Day. *Burma:* Full Moon Day. *El Salvador:* Summer Day (4th day of 4). *United Arab Emirates:* Accession Day.

**7 Fri.** *Colombia:* Boyaca Day. *Ivory Coast:* Republic Day. *Sri Lanka:* Full Moon Poya.

**9 Sun.** *Georgia:* Independence Day*. *Singapore:* National Day.

**10 Mon.** *Ecuador:* Independence Day.

**11 Tue.** *Chad:* Independence Day. *Jordan:* Accession Day. *Zimbabwe:* Heroes' Day (1st day of 2).

**12 Wed.** *Thailand:* Queen's Birthday. *Zimbabwe:* Heroes' Day (2nd day of 2).

**13 Thu.** *Central African Republic:* Independence Day. *Congo:* Independence Day (1st day of 2). *Tunisia:* Women's Day.

**14 Fri.** *Congo:* Independence Day (2nd day of 2). *Pakistan:* Independence Day.

**15 Sat.** *Congo:* Independence Day (3rd day of 3). *India:* Independence Day. *Liechtenstein:* National Day. *South Korea:* Republic Day. *Christian:* Assumption (see App. A11).

**16 Sun.** *Dominican Republic:* Republic Day.

**17 Mon.** *Argentina:* San Martin's Day. *Gabon:* Independence Day. *Indonesia:* Independence Day.

**20 Thu.** *Hungary:* Constitution Day. *Senegal:* Independence Day.

**21 Fri.** *Estonia:* Independence Day*. *Latvia:* Independence Day*. *Lithuania:* Independence Day*.

**23 Sun.** *Romania:* National Day (1st day of 2). *Zodiac Cusp:* Leo ends, Virgo begins.

**24 Mon.** *Kazakhstan:* National Day*. *Liberia:* Flag Day. *Romania:* National Day (2nd day of 2). *Russia:* Independence Day*. *Ukraine:* National Day*.

**25 Tue.** *Belarus:* Independence Day*. *Paraguay:* Constitution Day. *Uruguay:* Independence Day.

**27 Thu.** *Moldova:* Independence Day*.

**29 Sat.** *Hong Kong:* Liberation Day (1st day of 2). *Uzbekistan:* Independence Day*.

**30 Sun.** *Afghanistan:* Children's Day. *Azerbaijan:* Independence Day*. *Peru:* Rose of Lima Day. *Turkey:* Victory Day.

**31 Mon.** *Afghanistan:* Pashtunistan Day. *England:* Summer Break. *Hong Kong:* Liberation Day (2nd day of 2). *Kyrgyzstan:* Independence Day*. *Luxembourg:* Fair Day. *Malaysia:* National Day. *Northern Ireland:* Summer Break. *Trinidad:* Independence Day. *Wales:* Summer Break.

# September 1998

**1 Tue.** *Libya:* National Day. *Mexico:* President's Message Day. *Syria:* United Arab Republics Day.

**2 Wed.** *Vietnam:* Independence Day.

**3 Thu.** *Qatar:* National Day. *San Marino:* Saint Marinus' Day. *Tunisia:* Independence Movement Day.

**4 Fri.** *Burma:* Full Moon Day.

**5 Sat.** *Sri Lanka:* Full Moon Poya.

**6 Sun.** *Pakistan:* Defense Day. *Swaziland:* Independence Day.

**7 Mon.** *Brazil:* Independence Day. *Canada:* Labour Day. *United States:* Labor Day.

**8 Tue.** *Andorra:* National Day. *Malta:* Our Lady of Victory Day.

**9 Wed.** *Bulgaria:* National Day (1st day of 2). *North Korea:* Independence Day. *Tajikistan:* Independence Day*.

**10 Thu.** *Belize:* National Day. *Bulgaria:* National Day (2nd day of 2).

**11 Fri.** *Chile:* Revolution Day. *Egypt:* New Year's Day (Coptic: 1716). *Ethiopia:* New Year's Day (Ethiopian: 1992). *Pakistan:* Anniversary of Quaid-e-Azam's Death.

**12 Sat.** *Ethiopia:* National Day.

**14 Mon.** *Guatemala:* San Jacinto Day. *Nicaragua:* San Jacinto Day.

**15 Tue.** *Costa Rica:* Independence Day. *El Salvador:* Independence Day. *Guatemala:* Independence Day. *Honduras:* Independence Day. *Japan:* Veneration Day. *Nicaragua:* Independence Day.

**16 Wed.** *Mexico:* Independence Day. *New Guinea:* Independence Day.

**17 Thu.** *Angola:* Heroes' Day. *Marshall Islands:* Independence Day.

**18 Fri.** *Burundi:* Victory of Uprona Day. *Chili:* Independence Day.

**19 Sat.** *Chile:* Armed Forces Day. *Saint Kitts:* Independence Day.

**21 Mon.** *Belize:* Independence Day. *Israel:* New Year's Day. *Malta:* Independence Day. *Jewish:* Rosh Hashanah (Jewish: 5759).

**22 Tue.** *Mali:* Independence Day.

**23 Wed.** *Armenia:* Independence Day*. *Japan:* Autumnal Equinox. *Saudi Arabia:* National Day. *Zodiac Cusp:* Virgo ends, Libra begins.

**24 Thu.** *Dominican Republic:* Mercedes Day. *Guinea-Bissau:* Republic Day.

**25 Fri.** *Mozambique:* Liberation Day. *Rwanda:* Assembly Day.

**26 Sat.** *Ethiopia:* True Cross Day. *Yemeni Republic:* National Day.

**27 Sun.** *Europe:* Daylight Savings Time ends (retard clocks 1 hour).

**28 Mon.** *Taiwan:* Teachers' Day.

**29 Tue.** *Brunei:* Constitution Day. *Paraguay:* Boqueron Battle Day. *Asian:* Ancestors' Day (see App. B6).

**30 Wed.** *Botswana:* Independence Day. *Israel:* Yom Kippur. *Jewish:* Yom Kippur.

# October 1998

**1 Thu.** *Cameroon:* Unification Day. *China:* National Day (1st day of 2). *Nigeria:* Independence Day. *South Korea:* Armed Forces Day (1st day of 2). *Tuvalu:* Independence Day.

**2 Fri.** *China:* National Day (2nd day of 2). *Guinea:* Independence Day. *India:* Ghandi Day. *South Korea:* Armed Forces Day (2nd day of 2).

**3 Sat.** *Honduras:* Morazan Day. *South Korea:* Foundation Day (1st day of 2).

**4 Sun.** *Burma:* Full Moon Day. *Lesotho:* Independence Day. *South Korea:* Foundation Day (2nd day of 2).

**5 Mon.** *Barbados:* Bank Holiday. *China:* Mid-autumn Day. *Israel:* Sukkot. *Lesotho:* Sports Day. *Macao:* Portuguese Republic Day. *Portugal:* Republic Day. *Sri Lanka:* Full Moon Poya. *Taiwan:* Mid-autumn Day. *Jewish:* Sukkot.

**6 Tue.** *Egypt:* Armed Forces Day. *Hong Kong:* Mid-autumn Day. *Macao:* Mid-autumn Day.

**9 Fri.** *Peru:* National Dignity Day. *South Korea:* Alphabet Day. *Uganda:* Independence Day.

**10 Sat.** *Japan:* Health Day. *South Africa:* Kruger Day. *Taiwan:* National Day.

**11 Sun.** *Cuba:* Independence War. *Panama:* Revolution Day.

**12 Mon.** *Canada:* Thanksgiving Day. *Equatorial Guinea:* Independence Day. *Fiji:* Cession Day. *Spain:* National Day. *United States:* Bank Holiday. *Virgin Islands (U.S.):* Puerto Rican Friendship Day. *Multinational:* Columbus Day (see App. A12).

**14 Wed.** *Zaïre:* Founders' Day.

**15 Thu.** *Bosnia and Herzegovina:* Independence Day*. *Tunisia:* Evacuation Day.

**17 Sat.** *Haiti:* Dessalines Day. *Malawi:* Mother's Day.

**19 Mon.** *Jamaica:* Heroes' Day. *Hindu:* Deepavali (see App. B21).

**20 Tue.** *Guatemala:* Revolution Day. *Kenya:* Kenyatta Day.

**21 Wed.** *Honduras:* Army Day. *Somalia:* Revolution Day (1st day of 2).

**22 Thu.** *Somalia:* Revolution Day (2nd day of 2). *Vatican:* John Paul II Day.

**23 Fri.** *Hungary:* Revolution Day. *Thailand:* Chulalongkorn Day. *Zodiac Cusp:* Libra ends, Scorpio begins.

**24 Sat.** *Egypt:* Suez Victory Day. *Haiti:* United Nations Day. *Zambia:* Independence Day.

**25 Sun.** *Taiwan:* Restoration Day.

*Canada and United States:* Daylight Savings Time ends (retard clocks 1 hour).

**26 Mon.** *Austria:* National Day. *Benin:* Revolution Day. *Ireland:* Public Holiday. *New Zealand:* Labour Day. *Rwanda:* Government Day.

**27 Tue.** *Saint Vincent:* Independence Day. *Turkmenistan:* Independence Day*. *Zaïre:* Naming Day.

**28 Wed.** *Greece:* Ohi! Day.

**29 Thu.** *Tanzania:* Naming Day. *Turkey:* Republic Day.

**31 Sat.** *Taiwan:* Chiang Kai-shek's Birthday.

# November 1998

**1 Sun.** *Algeria:* Revolution Day. *Antigua:* Independence Day. *Christian:* All Saints' Day (see App. A13).

**2 Mon.** *Brazil:* Memorial Day. *Burma:* Full Moon Day. *Finland:* All Saints' Eve. *Sweden:* All Saints' Eve. *Virgin Islands (U.S.):* Liberty Day. *Christian:* All Souls' Day (see App. A14).

**3 Tue.** *Dominica:* Independence Day. *Ecuador:* Cuenca Indcpendence Day. *Japan:* Culture Day. *Panama:* Independence Day. *Sri Lanka:* Full Moon Poya.

**4 Wed.** *Andorra:* Saint Charles' Day. *Panama:* Flag Day. *Vatican:* John Paul II's Nameday.

**5 Thu.** *El Salvador:* Cry of Independence Day. *Liberia:* Thanksgiving Day.

**7 Sat.** *Bangladesh:* Revolution Day.

**8 Sun.** *Nepal:* Queen's Birthday.

**9 Mon.** *Pakistan:* Iqbal Day.

**10 Tue.** *Panama:* Cry of Independence Day.

**11 Wed.** *Angola:* Independence Day. *Bhutan:* King's Birthday. *Maldives:* Republic Day. *Poland:* Independence Day. *Multinational:* Armistice Day (see App. A15).

**12 Thu.** *Taiwan:* Dr. Sun Yat-sen's Birthday.

**14 Sat.** *Jordan:* King's Birthday.

**15 Sun.** *Brazil:* Republic Day.

**16 Mon.** *Fiji:* Prince Charles' Birthday. *Islamic:* Isra a Majraj (see App. B30).

**17 Tue.** *Zaïre:* Armed Forces Day.

**18 Wed.** *Germany:* Repentance Day. *Haiti:* Vertieres' Day. *Morocco:* Independence Day. *Oman:* National Day.

**19 Thu.** *Belize:* Garifuna Day. *Mali:* Army Coup Day. *Monaco:* Prince Ranier's Day. *Puerto Rico:* Discovery Day.

**20 Fri.** *Mexico:* Revolution Day.

**22 Sun.** *Lebanon:* Independence Day. *Zodiac Cusp:* Scorpio ends, Sagittarius begins.

**23 Mon.** *Japan:* Labor Thanksgiving Day.

**24 Tue.** *Zaïre:* New Regime Day.

**25 Wed.** *Suriname:* Independence Day.

**26 Thu.** *United States:* Thanksgiving Day.

**27 Fri.** *Argentina:* Bank Holiday.

**28 Sat.** *Albania:* Independence Day. *Burundi:* Republic Day. *Chad:* Republic Day. *Mauritania:* Independence Day. *Panama:* Independence Day.

**29 Sun.** *Albania:* Liberation Day. *Liberia:* Tubman's Birthday. *Yugoslavia:* Republic Day.

**30 Mon.** *Barbados:* Independence Day. *Benin:* National Day. *Philippines:* Heroes' Day.

# December 1998

**1 Tue.** *Central African Republic:* National Day. *Portugal:* Youth Day. *Ukraine:* Independence Day*.

**2 Wed.** *Burma:* Full Moon Day. *Laos:* Republic Day. *United Arab Emirates:* National Day.

**3 Thu.** *Sri Lanka:* Full Moon Poya.

**5 Sat.** *Haiti:* Discovery Day. *Thailand:* King's Birthday.

**6 Sun.** *Finland:* Independence Day.

**7 Mon.** *Ivory Coast:* Independence Day.

**8 Tue.** *Christian:* Immaculate Conception (see App. A16).

**9 Wed.** *Tanzania:* Independence Day.

**10 Thu.** *Angola:* MPLA Foundation Day. *Equatorial Guinea:* Human Rights Day. *Namibia:* Settlers' Day. *Thailand:* Constitution Day.

**11 Fri.** *Burkina Faso:* National Day.

**12 Sat.** *Kenya:* Independence Day. *Mexico:* Guadalupe Festival.

**13 Sun.** *Malta:* Republic Day. *Jewish:* Chanukah.

**16 Wed.** *Bahrain:* National Day. *Bangladesh:* Victory Day. *Nepal:* Constitution Day. *South Africa:* Covenant Day.

**17 Thu.** *Bhutan:* National Day.

**18 Fri.** *Niger:* Republic Day.

**20 Sun.** *Islamic:* 1st Day of Ramadan (see App. B25).

**21 Mon.** *Kazakhstan:* Independence Day*.

**22 Tue.** *Zodiac Cusp:* Sagittarius ends, Capricorn begins.

**23 Wed.** *Japan:* Emperor's Birthday.

**24 Thu.** *Multinational:* Christmas Eve (see App. A17).

**25 Fri.** *Angola:* Family Day. *Congo:* Children's Day. *Pakistan:* Quaid's Birthday. *Taiwan:* Constitution Day. *Multinational:* Christmas Day (see App. A18).

**26 Sat.** *South Africa:* Good Will Day. *Multinational:* Boxing Day (see App. A19).

**28 Mon.** *Hong Kong:* Boxing Day.

**30 Wed.** *Madagascar:* Republic Day. *Philippines:* Rizal Day (1st day of 2).

**31 Thu.** *Burma:* Full Moon Day. *Congo:* Republic Day. *Philippines:* Rizal Day (2nd day of 2). *Multinational:* Bank Holiday and New Year's Eve (see App. A20 & A21).

# January 1999

**1 Fri.** *Cameroon:* Independence Day. *Cuba:* Liberation Day. *Haiti:* Independence Day. *Palau:* Independence Day. *Sri Lanka:* Full Moon Poya. *Sudan:* Independence Day. *Taiwan:* Foundation Day (1st day of 2). *Western Samoa:* Independence Day. *Multinational:* Bank Holiday and New Year's Day (see App. A1 & A2).

**2 Sat.** *Japan:* Bank Holiday. *New Zealand:* New Year's Day (2nd day of 2). *South Korea:* New Year's Day (2nd day of 2). *Switzerland:* Berchtold's Day. *Taiwan:* Foundation Day (2nd day of 2).

**3 Sun.** *Burkina Faso:* Revolution Day.

**4 Mon.** *Burma:* Independence Day. *Scotland:* New Year's Day (2nd day of 2). *Zaïre:* Martyrs' Day.

**6 Wed.** *Iraq:* Army Day. *Uruguay:* Children's Day. *Christian:* Epiphany (see App. A3).

**7 Thu.** *Egypt:* Coptic Christmas. *Ethiopia:* Coptic Christmas.

**11 Mon.** *Albania:* Republic Day. *Nepal:* Unification Day. *Puerto Rico:* Hostos Day.

**12 Tue.** *Tanzania:* Revolution Day.

**13 Wed.** *Togo:* Liberation Day.

**15 Fri.** *Japan:* Adult's Day. *Jordan:* Arbor Day.

**18 Mon.** *United States:* Martin Luther King's Birthday. *Far East Islamic:* Hari Raya Puasa (see App. B27). *Islamic:* Eid al Fitr (1st day of 4) (see App. B26).

**19 Tue.** *Ethiopia:* Epiphany *Islamic:* Eid al Fitr (2nd day of 4) (see App. B26).

**20 Wed.** *Mali:* Award Day. *Islamic:* Eid al Fitr (3rd day of 4) (see App. B26). *Zodiac Cusp:* Capricorn ends, Aquarius begins.

**21 Thu.** *Dominican Republic:* Altagracia Day. *Islamic:* Eid al Fitr (4th day of 4) (see App. B26).

**22 Fri.** *Saint Vincent:* Discovery Day.

**26 Tue.** *Dominican Republic:* Duarte Day. *India:* Republic Day.

**27 Wed.** *Monaco:* Saint Devota's Day. *Vietnam:* Vietnam Day.

**28 Thu.** *Rwanda:* Democracy Day.

**30 Sat.** *Burma:* Full Moon Day.

**31 Sun.** *Nauru:* Independence Day. *Sri Lanka:* Full Moon Poya.

# February 1999

**1 Mon.** *Australia:* Australia Day. *United States:* Lincoln's Birthday.

**2 Tue.** *Liechtenstein:* Candlemas.

**4 Thu.** *Sri Lanka:* Independence Day.

**5 Fri.** *Mexico:* Constitution Day.

**6 Sat.** *New Zealand:* Waitangi Day.

**7 Sun.** *Grenada:* Independence Day.

**8 Mon.** *Iraq:* Revolution Day.

**9 Tue.** *Lebanon:* Saint Marion's Day.

**10 Wed.** *Malta:* Saint Paul's Day.

**11 Thu.** *Cameroon:* Youth Day. *Japan:* Foundation Day. *Liberia:* Armed Forces Day.

**12 Fri.** *Burma:* Union Day.

**14 Sun.** *International:* Valentine's Day.

**15 Mon.** *United States:* Washington's Birthday. *Asian:* Chinese New Year Eve (see App. B1). *Christian:* Shrove Monday (see App. B7).

**16 Tue.** *Vietnam:* Tet (1st day of 3). *Asian:* Chinese New Year (Year of the Hare) (see App. B2). *Christian:* Shrove Tuesday (see App. B8).

**17 Wed.** *Vietnam:* Tet (2nd day of 3). *Asian:* 2nd Day of Chinese New Year (see App. B3). *Christian:* Ash Wednesday (see App. B9).

**18 Thu.** *Gambia:* Independence Day. *Vietnam:* Tet (3rd day of 3). *Asian:* 3rd Day of Chinese New Year (see App. B4).

**19 Fri.** *Nepal:* National Day. *Zodiac Cusp:* Aquarius ends, Pisces begins.

**21 Sun.** *Bangladesh:* Saheed Day.

**22 Mon.** *Greece:* Shrove Monday. *Saint Lucia:* Independence Day. *Orthodox:* Shrove Monday.

**23 Tue.** *Brunei:* National Day. *Guyana:* Republic Day.

**25 Thu.** *Kuwait:* National Day.

**27 Sat.** *Dominican Republic:* Independence Day.

**28 Sun.** *Burma:* Full Moon Day.

# March 1999

**1 Mon.** *Guam:* Discovery Day. *South Korea:* Independence Day. *Sri Lanka:* Full Moon Poya. *Thailand:* Makha Bucha Day.

**2 Tue.** *Ethiopia:* Victory of Aduwa Day. *Morocco:* Independence Day. *Jewish:* Purim.

**3 Wed.** *Bulgaria:* Liberation Day.

*Malawi:* Martyrs' Day. *Morocco:* National Day.

**6 Sat.** *Ghana:* Independence Day.

**8 Mon.** *Gibraltar:* Commonwealth Day. *Syria:* Revolution Day. *Multinational:* Women's Day (see App. A4).

**10 Wed.** *South Korea:* Labor Day.

**11 Thu.** *Lithuania:* National Day*.

**12 Fri.** *Lesotho:* Moshoeshoe's Day. *Mauritius:* Independence Day.

**13 Sat.** *Grenada:* National Day. *Zambia:* Youth Day.

**17 Wed.** *Ireland:* Saint Patrick's Day. *Northern Ireland:* Saint Patrick's Day.

**19 Fri.** *Christian:* Saint Joseph's Day (see App. A5).

**20 Sat.** *Tunisia:* Independence Day.

**21 Sun.** *Afghanistan:* New Year's Day (Shamsi: 1378). *Iran:* New Year's Day (Hegira: 1378). *Iraq:* New Year's Day. *Japan:* Vernal Equinox. *Mexico:* Juarez Day. *Zodiac Cusp:* Pisces ends, Aries begins.

**22 Mon.** *Puerto Rico:* Abolition Day.

**23 Tue.** *Pakistan:* Pakistan Day. *Zambia:* Africa Day.

**25 Thu.** *Cyprus:* Greek Independence Day. *Greece:* Independence Day. *Liechtenstein:* Annunciation.

**26 Fri.** *Bangladesh:* Independence Day.

**27 Sat.** *Angola:* Evacuation Day. *Burma:* Resistance Day. *Islamic:* Eid al Adha (1st day of 4) (see App. B28).

**28 Sun.** *Christian:* Palm Sunday. *Europe:* Daylight Savings Time starts (advance clocks 1 hour). *Far East Islamic:* Hari Raya Haji (see App. B29). *Islamic:* Eid al Adha (2nd day of 4) (see App. B28).

**29 Mon.** *Central African Republic:* Boganda Day. *Madagascar:* Memorial Day. *Taiwan:* Youth Day. *Virgin Islands (U.S.):* Transfer Day. *Islamic:* Eid al Adha (3rd day of 4) (see App. B28).

**30 Tue.** *Burma:* Full Moon Day. *Islamic:* Eid al Adha (4th day of 4) (see App. B28).

**31 Wed.** *Malta:* National Day. *Sri Lanka:* Full Moon Poya.

# April 1999

**1 Thu.** *Iran:* Republic Day. *Israel:* Passover. *San Marino:* National Day. *Christian:* Maundy Thursday (see App. B11). *Jewish:* Passover.

**2 Fri.** *Sierra Leone:* Bank Holiday *Christian:* Good Friday (see App. B12).

**3 Sat.** *Christian:* Holy Saturday (see App. B13).

**4 Sun.** *Hungary:* Liberation Day. *Senegal:* National Day. *Canada and United States:* Daylight Savings Time starts (advance clocks 1 hour). *Christian:* Easter Sunday (see App. B14).

**5 Mon.** *South Korea:* Arbor Day. *Asian:* Tomb Sweeping Day (see App. A6). *Christian:* Easter Monday (see App. B15).

**6 Tue.** *South Africa:* Founders' Day. *Thailand:* Chakri Day.

**9 Fri.** *Philippines:* Valour Day. *Tunisia:* Martyrs' Day. *Orthodox:* Good Friday (see App. B20).

**11 Sun.** *Costa Rica:* Heroes' Day. *Jordan:* Easter Sunday. *Uganda:* Liberation Day. *Orthodox:* Easter Sunday.

**12 Mon.** *Orthodox:* Easter Monday (see App. B20).

**13 Tue.** *Chad:* National Day. *Thailand:* Songkrawn (1st day of 2).

**14 Wed.** *Honduras:* Pan American Day. *Thailand:* Songkrawn (2nd day of 2).

**15 Thu.** *Niger:* National Day.

**16 Fri.** *Burma:* New Year's Day (Burmese: 1361). *Cyprus:* Independence Day. *Islamic:* New Year's Day (Hegira: 1420) (see App. B22).

**17 Sat.** *Cambodia:* Independence Day. *Syria:* Independence Day. *Far*

*East Islamic:* New Year's Day (Hegira: 1420).

**18 Sun.** *Zimbabwe:* Republic Day.

**19 Mon.** *Sierra Leone:* Republic Day. *Uruguay:* Patriots' Day. *Venezuela:* Independence Day.

**20 Tue.** *Zodiac Cusp:* Aries ends, Taurus begins.

**21 Wed.** *Brazil:* Tiradentes Day. *Israel:* Independence Day.

**23 Fri.** *Turkey:* Children's Day.

**25 Sun.** *Australia:* ANZAC Day. *Egypt:* Sinai Day. *Iceland:* Children's Day. *Italy:* Liberation Day. *New Zealand:* ANZAC Day. *Portugal:* Liberation Day. *Swaziland:* Flag Day. *Islamic:* Ashura (see App. B23).

**26 Mon.** *Tanzania:* Union Day.

**27 Tue.** *Afghanistan:* Independence Day. *Sierra Leone:* Independence Day. *Togo:* Independence Day.

**29 Thu.** *Burma:* Full Moon Day. *Japan:* Green Day.

**30 Fri.** *Denmark:* All Prayers' Day. *Finland:* Vappu Day. *Netherlands:* Queen's Birthday. *Sri Lanka:* Full Moon Poya.

# May 1999

**1 Sat.** *Multinational:* Labor Day (see App. A7).

**2 Sun.** *Lesotho:* King's Birthday.

**3 Mon.** *Japan:* Constitution Day. *United Kingdom:* Labour Day. *Zambia:* Labour Day.

**4 Tue.** *Japan:* People's Day.

**5 Wed.** *Japan:* Children's Day. *Mexico:* Cinco de Mayo. *Netherlands:* Liberation Day. *South Korea:* Children's Day. *Thailand:* Coronation Day.

**6 Thu.** *Lebanon:* Martyrs' Day. *Philippines:* Corregidor Day.

**8 Sat.** *France:* Liberation Day.

**9 Sun.** *Czech Republic:* Liberation Day*. *Slovakia:* Liberation Day*. *International:* Mother's Day.

**10 Mon.** *Micronesia:* Independence Day.

**13 Thu.** *Christian:* Ascension (see App. B16).

**14 Fri.** *Liberia:* Unification Day. *Malawi:* Kamuzu Day. *Paraguay:* Flag Day.

**15 Sat.** *Paraguay:* Independence Day.

**17 Mon.** *Cayman Islands:* Discovery Day. *Norway:* Constitution Day.

**18 Tue.** *Haiti:* Flag Day. *Uruguay:* Las Piedras Day.

**19 Wed.** *Finland:* Flag Day. *Turkey:* Youth Day.

**20 Thu.** *Cameroon:* Constitution Day. *Zaïre:* Popular Movement Day.

**21 Fri.** *Chile:* Navy Day. *Israel:* Pentecost. *Jewish:* Pentecost. *Zodiac Cusp:* Taurus ends, Gemini begins.

**22 Sat.** *Haiti:* Sovereign Day. *South Korea:* Vesak Day. *Sri Lanka:* Heroes' Day.

**23 Sun.** *Jamaica:* Labour Day. *Christian:* Whitsunday.

**24 Mon.** *Bulgaria:* Culture Day. *Canada:* Victoria Day. *Ecuador:* Independence Battle Day. *Christian:* Whitmonday (see App. B18).

**25 Tue.** *Argentina:* National Day. *Eritrea:* Independence Day*. *Jordan:* Independence Day. *Sudan:* Revolution Day. *Multinational:* Africa Day (see App. A8).

**26 Wed.** *Guyana:* Independence Day.

**27 Thu.** *Nigeria:* Children's Day.

**28 Fri.** *Burma:* Full Moon Day.

**29 Sat.** *Malaysia:* Vesak Day. *Singapore:* Vesak Day. *Sri Lanka:* Full Moon Poya. *Thailand:* Visakha Bucha Day.

**30 Sun.** *Orthodox:* Pentecost Sunday.

**31 Mon.** *Brunei:* Regiment Day. *Greece:* Pentecost Monday. *South Africa:* Republic Day. *United Kingdom:* Spring Break. *United States:* Memorial Day.

# June 1999

**1 Tue.** *Kenya:* Madaraka Day. *Tunisia:* National Day. *Western Samoa:* Independence Day.

**2 Wed.** *Italy:* Republic Day. *Malaysia:* King's Birthday. *Tunisia:* Youth Day.

**3 Thu.** *Christian:* Corpus Christi (see App. B19).

**4 Fri.** *Bahamas:* Labour Day. *Tonga:* Independence Day.

**5 Sat.** *Denmark:* Constitution Day. *Equatorial Guinea:* President's Birthday. *Seychelles:* Liberation Day.

**6 Sun.** *South Korea:* Memorial Day. *Sweden:* Constitution Day.

**7 Mon.** *Chad:* Revolution Day. *Ireland:* Public Holiday. *New Zealand:* Queen's Birthday.

**9 Wed.** *Argentina:* Independence Day.

**10 Thu.** *Macao:* Portugal Day. *Portugal:* Portugal Day.

**11 Fri.** *Libya:* Evacuation Day.

**12 Sat.** *Hong Kong:* Queen's Birthday (1st day of 2). *Philippines:* Independence Day.

**14 Mon.** *Australia:* Queen's Birthday. *Fiji:* Queen's Birthday. *Hong Kong:* Queen's Birthday (2nd day of 2). *New Guinea:* Queen's Birthday. *United Kingdom:* Queen's Birthday.

**17 Thu.** *Germany:* Unity Day. *Iceland:* Independence Day.

**18 Fri.** *Egypt:* Independence Day.

**19 Sat.** *Algeria:* Righting Day. *Kuwait:* Independence Day. *Uruguay:* Artigas Day. *Asian:* Dragon Boat Festival (see App. B5).

**20 Sun.** *Argentina:* Flag Day.

**21 Mon.** *Finland:* Midsummer Day (1st day of 2). *Sweden:* Midsummer Day (1st day of 2). *Zodiac Cusp:* Gemini ends, Cancer begins.

**22 Tue.** *Finland:* Midsummer Day (2nd day of 2). *Sweden:* Midsummer Day (2nd day of 2).

**23 Wed.** *Luxembourg:* National Day.

**24 Thu.** *Andorra:* Saint John's Day. *Venezuela:* Carabobo Day. *Zaïre:* Constitution Day. *Islamic:* Mohammed's Birthday (see App. B24).

**25 Fri.** *Chile:* Bank Holiday. *Croatia:* Independence Day*. *Ecuador:* Bank Holiday. *El Salvador:* Bank Holiday. *Finland:* Bank Holiday. *Mozambique:* Independence Day. *Slovenia:* Independence Day*. *Far East Islamic:* Mohammed's Birthday.

**26 Sat.** *Finland:* Johannus Day. *Madagascar:* Independence Day. *Somalia:* Independence Day.

**27 Sun.** *Burma:* Full Moon Day. *Djibouti:* Independence Day.

**28 Mon.** *Sri Lanka:* Full Moon Poya.

**29 Tue.** *Seychelles:* Independence Day. *Christian:* Saint Paul's Day (see App. A9).

**30 Wed.** *Guatemala:* Army Day. *Sri Lanka:* Bank Holiday. *Zaïre:* Independence Day.

# July 1999

**1 Thu.** *Burundi:* Independence Day. *Canada:* Canada Day. *Ghana:* Republic Day. *Hong Kong:* Half Year Day. *Rwanda:* Independence Day. *Somalia:* Union Day. *Suriname:* Freedom Day. *Multinational:* Bank Holiday (see App. A10).

**4 Sun.** *Philippines:* United States Friendship Day. *United States:* Independence Day. *Yugoslavia:* Freedom Fighters' Day.

**5 Mon.** *Algeria:* Independence Day. *Cape Verde:* Independence Day. *Cayman Islands:* Constitution Day. *Le-*

*sotho:* Family Day. *Rwanda:* Unity Day. *Venezuela:* Independence Day. *Zambia:* Heroes' Day.

**6 Tue.** *Comoros:* Independence Day. *Malawi:* Republic Day. *Zambia:* Unity Day.

**7 Wed.** *Solomon Islands:* Independence Day. *Tanzania:* Farmers' Day. *Yugoslavia:* Serbian Day.

**10 Sat.** *Bahamas:* Independence Day.

**11 Sun.** *Mongolia:* Revolution Day.

**12 Mon.** *Kiribati:* Independence Day. *Northern Ireland:* Battle of the Boyne Day. *São Tomé:* National Day.

**14 Wed.** *France:* National Day. *Iraq:* Revolution Day.

**15 Thu.** *Brunei:* Sultan's Birthday.

**17 Sat.** *Iraq:* Revolution Day. *Puerto Rico:* Rivera Day. *Slovakia:* Independence Day*. *South Korea:* Constitution Day.

**18 Sun.** *Uruguay:* Constitution Day.

**19 Mon.** *Botswana:* President's Day. *Burma:* Martyrs' Day. *Laos:* Independence Day. *Nicaragua:* Sandinista Day.

**20 Tue.** *Colombia:* Independence Day.

**21 Wed.** *Belgium:* National Day. *Guam:* Liberation Day.

**22 Thu.** *Israel:* Tisha Ab. *Poland:* Liberation Day. *Jewish:* Tisha Ab.

**23 Fri.** *Egypt:* Revolution Day. *New Guinea:* Remembrance Day. *Zodiac Cusp:* Cancer ends, Leo begins.

**24 Sat.** *Venezuela:* Bolivar Day.

**25 Sun.** *Costa Rica:* Guanacaste Day. *Cuba:* Revolution Day (1st day of 3). *Puerto Rico:* Constitution Day. *Spain:* Santiago Day. *Tunisia:* Republic Day.

**26 Mon.** *Burma:* Full Moon Day. *Cuba:* Revolution Day (2nd day of 3). *Liberia:* Independence Day. *Maldives:* Independence Day. *Virgin Islands (U.S.):* Hurricane Supplication Day.

**27 Tue.** *Cuba:* Revolution Day (3rd day of 3). *Puerto Rico:* Barbosa Day. *Sri Lanka:* Full Moon Poya. *Thailand:* Asalaha Bucha Day.

**28 Wed.** *Peru:* Independence Day (1st day of 2). *Thailand:* Khao Phansa Day.

**29 Thu.** *Peru:* Independence Day (2nd day of 2).

**30 Fri.** *Vanuatu:* Independence Day.

# August 1999

**1 Sun.** *Benin:* Independence Day. *Switzerland:* Confederation Day.

**2 Mon.** *Bahamas:* Emancipation Day. *Barbados:* Emancipation Day. *Canada:* Civic Holiday. *Costa Rica:* Virgin of the Angels Day. *Guyana:* Freedom Day. *Ireland:* Public Holiday. *Jamaica:* Independence Day. *Scotland:* Public Holiday. *Trinidad:* Discovery Day.

**3 Tue.** *El Salvador:* Summer Day (1st day of 4). *Guinea-Bissau:* Martyrs' Day. *Niger:* Independence Day. *Tunisia:* President's Birthday.

**4 Wed.** *Burkina Faso:* Independence Day (1st day of 2). *El Salvador:* Summer Day (2nd day of 4). *Zambia:* Farmers' Day.

**5 Thu.** *Burkina Faso:* Independence Day (2nd day of 2). *El Salvador:* Summer Day (3rd day of 4).

**6 Fri.** *Bolivia:* Independence Day. *El Salvador:* Summer Day (4th day of 4). *United Arab Emirates:* Accession Day.

**7 Sat.** *Colombia:* Boyaca Day. *Ivory Coast:* Republic Day.

**9 Mon.** *Georgia:* Independence Day*. *Singapore:* National Day.

**10 Tue.** *Ecuador:* Independence Day.

**11 Wed.** *Chad:* Independence Day. *Jordan:* Accession Day. *Zimbabwe:* Heroes' Day (1st day of 2).

**12 Thu.** *Thailand:* Queen's Birthday. *Zimbabwe:* Heroes' Day (2nd day of 2).

**13 Fri.** *Central African Republic:*

Independence Day. *Congo:* Independence Day (1st day of 2). *Tunisia:* Women's Day.

**14 Sat.** *Congo:* Independence Day (2nd day of 2). *Pakistan:* Independence Day.

**15 Sun.** *Congo:* Independence Day (3rd day of 3). *India:* Independence Day. *Liechtenstein:* National Day. *South Korea:* Republic Day. *Christian:* Assumption (see App. A11).

**16 Mon.** *Dominican Republic:* Republic Day.

**17 Tue.** *Argentina:* San Martin's Day. *Gabon:* Independence Day. *Indonesia:* Independence Day.

**20 Fri.** *Hungary:* Constitution Day. *Senegal:* Independence Day.

**21 Sat.** *Estonia:* Independence Day*. *Latvia:* Independence Day*. *Lithuania:* Independence Day*.

**23 Mon.** *Romania:* National Day (1st day of 2). *Zodiac Cusp:* Leo ends, Virgo begins.

**24 Tue.** *Kazakhstan:* National Day*. *Liberia:* Flag Day. *Romania:* National Day (2nd day of 2). *Russia:* Independence Day*. *Ukraine:* National Day*.

**25 Wed.** *Belarus:* Independence Day*. *Burma:* Full Moon Day. *Paraguay:* Constitution Day. *Uruguay:* Independence Day.

**26 Thu.** *Sri Lanka:* Full Moon Poya.

**27 Fri.** *Moldova:* Independence Day*.

**28 Sat.** *Hong Kong:* Liberation Day (1st day of 2).

**29 Sun.** *Uzbekistan:* Independence Day*.

**30 Mon.** *Afghanistan:* Children's Day. *Azerbaijan:* Independence Day*. *England:* Summer Break. *Hong Kong:* Liberation Day (2nd day of 2). *Luxembourg:* Fair Day. *Northern Ireland:* Summer Break. *Peru:* Rose of Lima Day. *Turkey:* Victory Day. *Wales:* Summer Break.

**31 Tue.** *Afghanistan:* Pashtunistan Day. *Kyrgyzstan:* Independence Day*. *Malaysia:* National Day. *Trinidad:* Independence Day.

# September 1999

**1 Wed.** *Libya:* National Day. *Mexico:* President's Message Day. *Syria:* United Arab Republics Day.

**2 Thu.** *Vietnam:* Independence Day.

**3 Fri.** *Qatar:* National Day. *San Marino:* Saint Marinus' Day. *Tunisia:* Independence Movement Day.

**6 Mon.** *Canada:* Labour Day. *Pakistan:* Defense Day. *Swaziland:* Independence Day. *United States:* Labor Day.

**7 Tue.** *Brazil:* Independence Day.

**8 Wed.** *Andorra:* National Day. *Malta:* Our Lady of Victory Day.

**9 Thu.** *Bulgaria:* National Day (1st day of 2). *North Korea:* Independence Day. *Tajikistan:* Independence Day*.

**10 Fri.** *Belize:* National Day. *Bulgaria:* National Day (2nd day of 2).

**11 Sat.** *Chile:* Revolution Day. *Israel:* New Year's Day. *Pakistan:* Anniversary of Quaid-e-Azam's Death. *Jewish:* Rosh Hashanah (Jewish: 5760).

**12 Sun.** *Egypt:* New Year's Day (Coptic: 1717). *Ethiopia:* National Day and New Year's Day (Ethiopian: 1993).

**14 Tue.** *Guatemala:* San Jacinto Day. *Nicaragua:* San Jacinto Day.

**15 Wed.** *Costa Rica:* Independence Day. *El Salvador:* Independence Day. *Guatemala:* Independence Day. *Honduras:* Independence Day. *Japan:* Veneration Day. *Nicaragua:* Independence Day.

**16 Thu.** *Mexico:* Independence Day. *New Guinea:* Independence Day.

**17 Fri.** *Angola:* Heroes' Day. *Marshall Islands:* Independence Day.

**18 Sat.** *Burundi:* Victory of Uprona Day. *Chile:* Independence Day.

**19 Sun.** *Chile:* Armed Forces Day. *Saint Kitts:* Independence Day.

**20 Mon.** *Israel:* Yom Kippur. *Jewish:* Yom Kippur.

**21 Tue.** *Belize:* Independence Day. *Malta:* Independence Day.

**22 Wed.** *Mali:* Independence Day.

**23 Thu.** *Armenia:* Independence Day*. *Burma:* Full Moon Day. *Japan:* Autumnal Equinox. *Saudi Arabia:* National Day. *Zodiac Cusp:* Virgo ends, Libra begins.

**24 Fri.** *China:* Mid-autumn Day. *Dominican Republic:* Mercedes Day. *Guinea-Bissau:* Republic Day. *Sri Lanka:* Full Moon Poya. *Taiwan:* Mid-autumn Day.

**25 Sat.** *Hong Kong:* Mid-autumn Day. *Israel:* Sukkot. *Mozambique:* Liberation Day. *Macao:* Mid-autumn Day. *Rwanda:* Assembly Day. *Jewish:* Sukkot.

**26 Sun.** *Europe:* Daylight Savings Time ends (retard clocks 1 hour).

**27 Mon.** *Ethiopia:* True Cross Day.

**28 Tue.** *Taiwan:* Teachers' Day.

**29 Wed.** *Brunei:* Constitution Day. *Paraguay:* Boqueron Battle Day.

**30 Thu.** *Botswana:* Independence Day.

# October 1999

**1 Fri.** *Cameroon:* Unification Day. *China:* National Day (1st day of 2). *Nigeria:* Independence Day. *South Korea:* Armed Forces Day (1st day of 2). *Tuvalu:* Independence Day.

**2 Sat.** *China:* National Day (2nd day of 2). *Guinea:* Independence Day. *India:* Ghandi Day. *South Korea:* Armed Forces Day (2nd day of 2).

**3 Sun.** *Honduras:* Morazan Day. *South Korea:* Foundation Day (1st day of 2).

**4 Mon.** *Barbados:* Bank Holiday. *Lesotho:* Independence Day. *South Korea:* Foundation Day (2nd day of 2).

**5 Tue.** *Lesotho:* Sports Day. *Macao:* Portuguese Republic Day. *Portugal:* Republic Day.

**6 Wed.** *Egypt:* Armed Forces Day.

**9 Sat.** *Peru:* National Dignity Day. *South Korea:* Alphabet Day. *Uganda:* Independence Day.

**10 Sun.** *Japan:* Health Day. *South Africa:* Kruger Day. *Taiwan:* National Day.

**11 Mon.** *Canada:* Thanksgiving Day. *Cuba:* Independence War. *Fiji:* Cession Day. *Panama:* Revolution Day. *United States:* Bank Holiday. *Virgin Islands (U.S.):* Puerto Rican Friendship Day.

**12 Tue.** *Equatorial Guinea:* Independence Day. *Spain:* National Day. *Multinational:* Columbus Day (see App. A12).

**14 Thu.** *Zaïre:* Founders' Day.

**15 Fri.** *Bosnia and Herzegovina:* Independence Day*. *Tunisia:* Evacuation Day.

**17 Sun.** *Haiti:* Dessalines Day. *Malawi:* Mother's Day.

**18 Mon.** *Jamaica:* Heroes' Day. *Asian:* Ancestors' Day (see App. B6).

**20 Wed.** *Guatemala:* Revolution Day. *Kenya:* Kenyatta Day.

**21 Thu.** *Honduras:* Army Day. *Somalia:* Revolution Day (1st day of 2).

**22 Fri.** *Somalia:* Revolution Day (2nd day of 2). *Vatican:* John Paul II Day.

**23 Sat.** *Burma:* Full Moon Day. *Hungary:* Revolution Day. *Thailand:* Chulalongkorn Day. *Zodiac Cusp:* Libra ends, Scorpio begins.

**24 Sun.** *Egypt:* Suez Victory Day. *Haiti:* United Nations Day. *Sri Lanka:* Full Moon Poya. *Zambia:* Independence Day.

**25 Mon.** *Ireland:* Public Holiday. *New Zealand:* Labour Day. *Taiwan:* Restoration Day.

**26 Tue.** *Austria:* National Day. *Benin:* Revolution Day. *Rwanda:* Government Day.

**27 Wed.** *Saint Vincent:* Independence Day. *Turkmenistan:* Independence Day*. *Zaïre:* Naming Day.

**28 Thu.** *Greece:* Ohi! Day.

**29 Fri.** *Tanzania:* Naming Day. *Turkey:* Republic Day.

**31 Sun.** *Taiwan:* Chiang Kai-shek's Birthday. *Canada and United States:* Daylight Savings Time ends (retard clocks 1 hour).

# November 1999

**1 Mon.** *Algeria:* Revolution Day. *Antigua:* Independence Day. *Virgin Islands (U.S.):* Liberty Day. *Christian:* All Saints' Day (see App. A13).

**2 Tue.** *Brazil:* Memorial Day. *Finland:* All Saints' Eve. *Sweden:* All Saints' Eve. *Christian:* All Souls' Day (see App. A14).

**3 Wed.** *Dominica:* Independence Day. *Ecuador:* Cuenca Independence Day. *Japan:* Culture Day. *Panama:* Independence Day.

**4 Thu.** *Andorra:* Saint Charles' Day. *Liberia:* Thanksgiving Day. *Panama:* Flag Day. *Vatican:* John Paul II's Nameday.

**5 Fri.** *El Salvador:* Cry of Independence Day. *Islamic:* Isra a Majraj (see App. B30).

**7 Sun.** *Bangladesh:* Revolution Day. *Hindu:* Deepavali (see App. B21).

**8 Mon.** *Nepal:* Queen's Birthday.

**9 Tue.** *Pakistan:* Iqbal Day.

**10 Wed.** *Panama:* Cry of Independence Day.

**11 Thu.** *Angola:* Independence Day. *Bhutan:* King's Birthday. *Maldives:* Republic Day. *Poland:* Independence Day. *Multinational:* Armistice Day (see App. A15).

**12 Fri.** *Taiwan:* Dr. Sun Yat-sen's Birthday.

**14 Sun.** *Jordan:* King's Birthday.

**15 Mon.** *Brazil:* Republic Day. *Fiji:* Prince Charles' Birthday.

**17 Wed.** *Germany:* Repentance Day. *Zaïre:* Armed Forces Day.

**18 Thu.** *Haiti:* Vertieres' Day. *Morocco:* Independence Day. *Oman:* National Day.

**19 Fri.** *Belize:* Garifuna Day. *Mali:* Army Coup Day. *Monaco:* Prince Ranier's Day. *Puerto Rico:* Discovery Day.

**20 Sat.** *Mexico:* Revolution Day.

**21 Sun.** *Burma:* Full Moon Day.

**22 Mon.** *Lebanon:* Independence Day. *Sri Lanka:* Full Moon Poya. *Zodiac Cusp:* Scorpio ends, Sagittarius begins.

**23 Tue.** *Japan:* Labor Thanksgiving Day.

**24 Wed.** *Zaïre:* New Regime Day.

**25 Thu.** *Suriname:* Independence Day. *United States:* Thanksgiving Day.

**26 Fri.** *Argentina:* Bank Holiday.

**28 Sun.** *Albania:* Independence Day. *Burundi:* Republic Day. *Chad:* Republic Day. *Mauritania:* Independence Day. *Panama:* Independence Day.

**29 Mon.** *Albania:* Liberation Day. *Liberia:* Tubman's Birthday. *Yugoslavia:* Republic Day.

**30 Tue.** *Barbados:* Independence Day. *Benin* National Day. *Philippines:* Heroes' Day: Independence Day.

# December 1999

**1 Wed.** *Central African Republic:* National Day. *Portugal:* Youth Day. *Ukraine:* Independence Day*.

**2 Thu.** *Laos:* Republic Day. *United Arab Emirates:* National Day.

**4 Sat.** *Jewish:* Chanukah.

**5 Sun.** *Haiti:* Discovery Day. *Thailand:* King's Birthday.

**6 Mon.** *Finland:* Independence Day.

**7 Tue.** *Ivory Coast:* Independence Day.

**8 Wed.** *Christian:* Immaculate Conception (see App. A16).

**9 Thu.** *Tanzania:* Independence Day. *Islamic:* 1st Day of Ramadan.

**10 Fri.** *Angola:* MPLA Foundation Day. *Equatorial Guinea:* Human Rights Day. *Namibia:* Settlers' Day. *Thailand:* Constitution Day.

**11 Sat.** *Burkina Faso:* National Day.

**12 Sun.** *Kenya:* Independence Day. *Mexico:* Guadalupe Festival.

**13 Mon.** *Malta:* Republic Day.

**16 Thu.** *Bahrain:* National Day. *Bangladesh:* Victory Day. *Nepal:* Constitution Day. *South Africa:* Covenant Day.

**17 Fri.** *Bhutan:* National Day.

**18 Sat.** *Niger:* Republic Day.

**21 Tue.** *Burma:* Full Moon Day. *Kazakhstan:* Independence Day*.

**22 Wed.** *Sri Lanka:* Full Moon Poya. *Zodiac Cusp:* Sagittarius ends, Capricorn begins.

**23 Thu.** *Japan:* Emperor's Birthday.

**24 Fri.** *Multinational:* Christmas Eve (see App. A17).

**25 Sat.** *Angola:* Family Day. *Congo:* Children's Day. *Pakistan:* Quaid's Birthday. *Taiwan:* Constitution Day. *Multinational:* Christmas Day (see App. A18).

**26 Sun.** *South Africa:* Good Will Day. *Multinational:* Boxing Day (see App. A19).

**27 Mon.** *Hong Kong:* Boxing Day.

**30 Thu.** *Madagascar:* Republic Day. *Philippines:* Rizal Day (1st day of 2).

**31 Fri.** *Congo:* Republic Day. *Philippines:* Rizal Day (2nd day of 2). *Multinational:* Bank Holiday and New Year's Eve (see App. A20 & A21).

# January 2000

**1 Sat.** *Cameroon:* Independence Day. *Cuba:* Liberation Day. *Haiti:* Independence Day. *Palau:* Independence Day. *Sudan:* Independence Day. *Taiwan:* Foundation Day (1st day of 2). *Western Samoa:* Independence Day. *Multinational:* Bank Holiday and New Year's Day (see App. A1 & A2).

**2 Sun.** *Japan:* Bank Holiday. *New Zealand:* New Year's Day (2nd day of 2). *South Korea:* New Year's Day (2nd day of 2). *Switzerland:* Berchtold's Day. *Taiwan:* Foundation Day (2nd day of 2).

**3 Mon.** *Burkina Faso:* Revolution Day. *Hong Kong:* New Year's Day. *Scotland:* New Year's Day (2nd day of 2).

**4 Tue.** *Burma:* Independence Day. *Zaïre:* Martyrs' Day.

**6 Thu.** *Iraq:* Army Day. *Uruguay:* Children's Day. *Christian:* Epiphany (see App. A3). *Islamic:* Eid al Fitr (1st day of 4) (see App. B26).

**7 Fri.** *Egypt:* Coptic Christmas. *Ethiopia:* Coptic Christmas. *Far East Islamic:* Hari Raya Puasa (see App. B27). *Islamic:* Eid al Fitr (2nd day of 4) (see App. B26).

**8 Sat.** *Islamic:* Eid al Fitr (3rd day of 4) (see App. B26).

**9 Sun.** *Islamic:* Eid al Fitr (4th day of 4) (see App. B26).

**11 Tue.** *Albania:* Republic Day. *Nepal:* Unification Day. *Puerto Rico:* Hostos Day.

**12 Wed.** *Tanzania:* Revolution Day.

**13 Thu.** *Togo:* Liberation Day.

**15 Sat.** *Japan:* Adult's Day. *Jordan:* Arbor Day.

**17 Mon.** *United States:* Martin Luther King's Birthday.

**19 Wed.** *Burma:* Full Moon Day. *Ethiopia:* Epiphany. *Zodiac Cusp:* Capricorn ends, Aquarius begins.

**20 Thu.** *Mali:* Award Day. *Sri Lanka:* Full Moon Poya.

**21 Fri.** *Dominican Republic:* Altagracia Day.

**22 Sat.** *Saint Vincent:* Discovery Day.

**26 Wed.** *Dominican Republic:* Duarte Day. *India:* Republic Day.

**27 Thu.** *Monaco:* Saint Devota's Day. *Vietnam:* Vietnam Day.

**28 Fri.** *Rwanda:* Democracy Day.

**31 Mon.** *Australia:* Australia Day. *Nauru:* Independence Day.

# February 2000

**2 Wed.** *Liechtenstein:* Candlemas.

**4 Fri.** *Sri Lanka:* Independence Day. *Asian:* Chinese New Year Eve (see App. B1).

**5 Sat.** *Mexico:* Constitution Day. *Vietnam:* Tet (1st day of 3). *Asian:* Chinese New Year (Year of the Dragon) (see App. B2).

**6 Sun.** *New Zealand:* Waitangi Day. *Vietnam:* Tet (2nd day of 3). *Asian:* 2nd Day of Chinese New Year (see App. B3).

**7 Mon.** *Grenada:* Independence Day. *United States:* Lincoln's Birthday. *Vietnam:* Tet (3rd day of 3). *Asian:* 3rd Day of Chinese New Year (see App. B4).

**8 Tue.** *Iraq:* Revolution Day.

**9 Wed.** *Lebanon:* Saint Marion's Day.

**10 Thu.** *Malta:* Saint Paul's Day.

**11 Fri.** *Cameroon:* Youth Day. *Japan:* Foundation Day. *Liberia:* Armed Forces Day.

**12 Sat.** *Burma:* Union Day.

**14 Mon.** *International:* Valentine's Day.

**18 Fri.** *Burma:* Full Moon Day. *Gambia:* Independence Day. *Zodiac Cusp:* Aquarius ends, Pisces begins.

**19 Sat.** *Nepal:* National Day. *Sri Lanka:* Full Moon Poya. *Thailand:* Makha Bucha Day.

**21 Mon.** *Bangladesh:* Saheed Day. *United States:* Washington's Birthday.

**22 Tue.** *Saint Lucia:* Independence Day.

**23 Wed.** *Brunei:* National Day. *Guyana:* Republic Day.

**25 Fri.** *Kuwait:* National Day.

**27 Sun.** *Dominican Republic:* Independence Day.

# March 2000

**1 Wed.** *South Korea:* Independence Day.

**2 Thu.** *Ethiopia:* Victory of Aduwa Day. *Morocco:* Independence Day.

**3 Fri.** *Bulgaria:* Liberation Day. *Malawi:* Martyrs' Day. *Morocco:* National Day.

**6 Mon.** *Ghana:* Independence Day. *Guam:* Discovery Day. *Christian:* Shrove Monday (see App. B7).

**7 Tue.** *Christian:* Shrove Tuesday (see App. B8).

**8 Wed.** *Syria:* Revolution Day. *Christian:* Ash Wednesday (see App. B9). *Multinational:* Women's Day (see App. A4).

**10 Fri.** *South Korea:* Labor Day.

**11 Sat.** *Lithuania:* National Day*. *Zambia:* Youth Day.

**12 Sun.** *Lesotho:* Moshoeshoe's Day. *Mauritius:* Independence Day.

**13 Mon.** *Gibraltar:* Commonwealth Day. *Greece:* Shrove Monday. *Grenada:* National Day. *Orthodox:* Shrove Monday.

**15 Wed.** *Islamic:* Eid al Adha (1st day of 4) (see App. B28).

**16 Thu.** *Far East Islamic:* Hari Raya Haji (see App. B29). *Islamic:* Eid al Adha (2nd day of 4) (see App. B28).

**17 Fri.** *Ireland:* Saint Patrick's Day. *Northern Ireland:* Saint Patrick's Day.

*Islamic:* Eid al Adha (3rd day of 4) (see App. B28).

**18 Sat.** *Burma:* Full Moon Day. *Islamic:* Eid al Adha (4th day of 4) (see App. B28).

**19 Sun.** *Sri Lanka:* Full Moon Poya *Christian:* Saint Joseph's Day (see App. A5).

**20 Mon.** *Afghanistan:* New Year's Day (Shamsi: 1379). *Iran:* New Year's Day (Hegira: 1379). *Iraq:* New Year's Day. *Japan:* Vernal Equinox. *Tunisia:* Independence Day. *Zodiac Cusp:* Pisces ends, Aries begins.

**21 Tue.** *Mexico:* Juarez Day. *Jewish:* Purim.

**22 Wed.** *Puerto Rico:* Abolition Day.

**23 Thu.** *Pakistan:* Pakistan Day.

**25 Sat.** *Cyprus:* Greek Independence Day. *Greece:* Independence Day. *Liechtenstein:* Annunciation.

**26 Sun.** *Bangladesh:* Independence Day. *Europe:* Daylight Savings Time starts (advance clocks 1 hour).

**27 Mon.** *Angola:* Evacuation Day. *Burma:* Resistance Day. *Virgin Islands (U.S.):* Transfer Day.

**28 Tue.** *Zambia:* Africa Day.

**29 Wed.** *Central African Republic:* Boganda Day. *Madagascar:* Memorial Day. *Taiwan:* Youth Day.

**31 Fri.** *Malta:* National Day.

# April 2000

**1 Sat.** *Iran:* Republic Day. *San Marino:* National Day.

**2 Sun.** *Canada and United States:* Daylight Savings Time starts (advance clocks 1 hour).

**4 Tue.** *Hungary:* Liberation Day. *Senegal:* National Day. *Islamic:* New Year's Day (Hegira: 1421) (see App. B22).

**5 Wed.** *South Korea:* Arbor Day. *Asian:* Tomb Sweeping Day (see App. A6).

**6 Thu.** *South Africa:* Founders' Day. *Thailand:* Chakri Day. *Far East Islamic:* New Year's Day (Hegira: 1421).

**7 Fri.** *Sierra Leone:* Bank Holiday.

**9 Sun.** *Philippines:* Valour Day. *Tunisia:* Martyrs' Day.

**11 Tue.** *Costa Rica:* Heroes' Day. *Uganda:* Liberation Day.

**13 Thu.** *Chad:* National Day. *Thailand:* Songkrawn (1st day of 2). *Islamic:* Ashura (see App. B23).

**14 Fri.** *Honduras:* Pan American Day. *Thailand:* Songkrawn (2nd day of 2).

**15 Sat.** *Burma:* New Year's Day (Burmese: 1362). *Niger:* National Day.

**16 Sun.** *Cyprus:* Independence Day. Christian: Palm Sunday.

**17 Mon.** *Burma:* Full Moon Day. *Cambodia:* Independence Day. *Syria:* Independence Day.

**18 Tue.** *Sri Lanka:* Full Moon Poya. *Zimbabwe:* Republic Day.

**19 Wed.** *Sierra Leone:* Republic Day. *Uruguay:* Patriots' Day. *Venezuela:* Independence Day. *Zodiac Cusp:* Aries ends, Taurus begins.

**20 Thu.** *Israel:* Passover *Christian:* Maundy Thursday (see App. B11). *Jewish:* Passover.

**21 Fri.** *Brazil:* Tiradentes Day. *Christian:* Good Friday (see App. B12).

**22 Sat.** *Christian:* Holy Saturday (see App. B13).

**23 Sun.** *Turkey:* Children's Day. *Christian:* Easter Sunday (see App. B14).

**24 Mon.** *Christian:* Easter Monday (see App. B15).

**25 Tue.** *Australia:* ANZAC Day. *Egypt:* Sinai Day. *Iceland:* Children's Day. *Italy:* Liberation Day. *New Zealand:* ANZAC Day. *Portugal:* Liberation Day. *Swaziland:* Flag Day.

**26 Wed.** *Tanzania:* Union Day.

**27 Thu.** *Afghanistan:* Independence Day. *Sierra Leone:* Independence Day. *Togo:* Independence Day.

**28 Fri.** *Orthodox:* Good Friday (see App. B20).
**29 Sat.** *Japan:* Green Day.
**30 Sun.** *Finland:* Vappu Day. *Jordan:* Easter Sunday. *Netherlands:* Queen's Birthday. *Orthodox:* Easter Sunday.

# May 2000

**1 Mon.** *United Kingdom:* Labour Day. *Zambia:* Labour Day. *Orthodox:* Easter Monday (see App. B20). *Multinational:* Labor Day (see App. A7).
**2 Tue.** *Lesotho:* King's Birthday.
**3 Wed.** *Japan:* Constitution Day.
**4 Thu.** *Japan:* People's Day.
**5 Fri.** *Japan:* Children's Day. *Mexico:* Cinco de Mayo. *Netherlands:* Liberation Day. *South Korea:* Children's Day. *Thailand:* Coronation Day.
**6 Sat.** *Lebanon:* Martyrs' Day. *Philippines:* Corregidor Day.
**8 Mon.** *France:* Liberation Day.
**9 Tue.** *Czech Republic:* Liberation Day*. *Slovakia:* Liberation Day*.
**10 Wed.** *Israel:* Independence Day. *Micronesia:* Independence Day.
**11 Thu.** *South Korea:* Vesak Day.
**14 Sun.** *Liberia:* Unification Day. *Malawi:* Kamuzu Day. *Paraguay:* Flag Day. *International:* Mother's Day.
**15 Mon.** *Paraguay:* Independence Day.
**16 Tue.** *Burma:* Full Moon Day.
**17 Wed.** *Cayman Islands:* Discovery Day. *Norway:* Constitution Day. *Sri Lanka:* Full Moon Poya. *Thailand:* Visakha Bucha Day.
**18 Thu.** *Haiti:* Flag Day. *Malaysia:* Vesak Day. *Singapore:* Vesak Day. *Uruguay:* Las Piedras Day.
**19 Fri.** *Denmark:* All Prayers' Day. *Finland:* Flag Day. *Turkey:* Youth Day.
**20 Sat.** *Cameroon:* Constitution Day. *Zaïre:* Popular Movement Day. *Zodiac Cusp:* Taurus ends, Gemini begins.
**21 Sun.** *Chile:* Navy Day.
**22 Mon.** *Canada:* Victoria Day. *Haiti:* Sovereign Day. *Sri Lanka:* Heroes' Day.
**23 Tue.** *Jamaica:* Labour Day.
**24 Wed.** *Bulgaria:* Culture Day. *Ecuador:* Independence Battle Day.
**25 Thu.** *Argentina:* National Day. *Eritrea:* Independence Day*. *Jordan:* Independence Day. *Sudan:* Revolution Day. *Multinational:* Africa Day (see App. A8).
**26 Fri.** *Guyana:* Independence Day.
**27 Sat.** *Nigeria:* Children's Day.
**29 Mon.** *United Kingdom:* Spring Break. *United States:* Memorial Day.
**31 Wed.** *Brunei:* Regiment Day. *South Africa:* Republic Day.

# June 2000

**1 Thu.** *Kenya:* Madaraka Day. *Tunisia:* National Day. *Western Samoa:* Independence Day. *Christian:* Ascension (see App. B16).
**2 Fri.** *Italy:* Republic Day. *Tunisia:* Youth Day.
**4 Sun.** *Bahamas:* Labour Day. *Tonga:* Independence Day.
**5 Mon.** *Denmark:* Constitution Day. *Equatorial Guinea:* President's Birthday. *Ireland:* Public Holiday. *New Zealand:* Queen's Birthday. *Seychelles:* Liberation Day.
**6 Tue.** *South Korea:* Memorial Day. *Sweden:* Constitution Day.
**7 Wed.** *Chad:* Revolution Day.

*Malaysia:* King's Birthday.

**8 Thu.** *Asian:* Dragon Boat Festival (see App. B5).

**9 Fri.** *Argentina:* Independence Day. *Israel:* Pentecost. *Jewish:* Pentecost.

**10 Sat.** *Hong Kong:* Queen's Birthday (1st day of 2). *Macao:* Portugal Day. *Portugal:* Portugal Day.

**11 Sun.** *Libya:* Evacuation Day. Christian: Whitsunday.

**12 Mon.** *Australia:* Queen's Birthday. *Fiji:* Queen's Birthday. *Hong Kong:* Queen's Birthday (2nd day of 2). *New Guinea:* Queen's Birthday. *Philippines:* Independence Day. *United Kingdom:* Queen's Birthday. *Christian:* Whitmonday (see App. B18).

**13 Tue.** *Islamic:* Mohammed's Birthday (see App. B24).

**14 Wed.** *Far East Islamic:* Mohammed's Birthday.

**15 Thu.** *Burma:* Full Moon Day.

**16 Fri.** *Sri Lanka:* Full Moon Poya.

**17 Sat.** *Germany:* Unity Day. *Iceland:* Independence Day.

**18 Sun.** *Egypt:* Independence Day. *Orthodox:* Pentecost Sunday.

**19 Mon.** *Algeria:* Righting Day. *Greece:* Pentecost Monday. *Kuwait:* Independence Day. *Uruguay:* Artigas Day.

**20 Tue.** *Argentina:* Flag Day.

**21 Wed.** *Finland:* Midsummer Day (1st day of 2). *Sweden:* Midsummer Day (1st day of 2). *Zodiac Cusp:* Gemini ends, Cancer begins.

**22 Thu.** *Finland:* Midsummer Day (2nd day of 2). *Sweden:* Midsummer Day (2nd day of 2). *Christian:* Corpus Christi (see App. B19).

**23 Fri.** *Luxembourg:* National Day.

**24 Sat.** *Andorra:* Saint John's Day. *Finland:* Johannus Day. *Venezuela:* Carabobo Day. *Zaïre:* Constitution Day.

**25 Sun.** *Croatia:* Independence Day*. *Mozambique:* Independence Day. *Slovenia:* Independence Day*.

**26 Mon.** *Madagascar:* Independence Day. *Somalia:* Independence Day.

**27 Tue.** *Djibouti:* Independence Day.

**29 Thu.** *Seychelles:* Independence Day. *Christian:* Saint Paul's Day (see App. A9).

**30 Fri.** *Chile:* Bank Holiday. *Ecuador:* Bank Holiday. *El Salvador:* Bank Holiday. *Finland:* Bank Holiday. *Guatemala:* Army Day. *Sri Lanka:* Bank Holiday. *Zaïre:* Independence Day.

# July 2000

**1 Sat.** *Burundi:* Independence Day. *Canada:* Canada Day. *Ghana:* Republic Day. *Hong Kong:* Half Year Day. *Rwanda:* Independence Day. *Somalia:* Union Day. *Suriname:* Freedom Day. *Multinational:* Bank Holiday (see App. A10).

**3 Mon.** *Cayman Islands:* Constitution Day. *Lesotho:* Family Day. *Zambia:* Heroes' Day.

**4 Tue.** *Philippines:* United States Friendship Day. *United States:* Independence Day. *Yugoslavia:* Freedom Fighters' Day. *Zambia:* Unity Day.

**5 Wed.** *Algeria:* Independence Day. *Cape Verde:* Independence Day. *Rwanda:* Unity Day. *Venezuela:* Independence Day.

**6 Thu.** *Comoros:* Independence Day. *Malawi:* Republic Day.

**7 Fri.** *Solomon Islands:* Independence Day. *Tanzania:* Farmers' Day. *Yugoslavia:* Serbian Day.

**10 Mon.** *Bahamas:* Independence Day.

**11 Tue.** *Mongolia:* Revolution Day.

**12 Wed.** *Kiribati:* Independence Day. *Northern Ireland:* Battle of the Boyne Day. *São Tomé:* National Day.

**14 Fri.** *France:* National Day. *Iraq:* Revolution Day.

**15 Sat.** *Brunei:* Sultan's Birthday. *Burma:* Full Moon Day.

**16 Sun.** *Sri Lanka:* Full Moon Poya. *Thailand:* Asalaha Bucha Day.

**17 Mon.** *Botswana:* President's Day. *Iraq:* Revolution Day. *Puerto Rico:* Rivera Day. *Slovakia:* Independence Day*. *South Korea:* Constitution Day. *Thailand:* Khao Phansa Day.

**18 Tue.** *Uruguay:* Constitution Day.

**19 Wed.** *Burma:* Martyrs' Day. *Laos:* Independence Day. *Nicaragua:* Sandinista Day.

**20 Thu.** *Colombia:* Independence Day.

**21 Fri.** *Belgium:* National Day. *Guam:* Liberation Day.

**22 Sat.** *Poland:* Liberation Day. *Zodiac Cusp:* Cancer ends, Leo begins.

**23 Sun.** *Egypt:* Revolution Day. *New Guinea:* Remembrance Day.

**24 Mon.** *Virgin Islands (U.S.):* Hurricane Supplication Day. *Venezuela:* Bolivar Day.

**25 Tue.** *Costa Rica:* Guanacaste Day. *Cuba:* Revolution Day (1st day of 3). *Puerto Rico:* Constitution Day. *Spain:* Santiago Day. *Tunisia:* Republic Day.

**26 Wed.** *Cuba:* Revolution Day (2nd day of 3). *Liberia:* Independence Day. *Maldives:* Independence Day.

**27 Thu.** *Cuba:* Revolution Day (3rd day of 3). *Puerto Rico:* Barbosa Day.

**28 Fri.** *Peru:* Independence Day (1st day of 2).

**29 Sat.** *Peru:* Independence Day (2nd day of 2).

**30 Sun.** *Vanuatu:* Independence Day.

# August 2000

**1 Tue.** *Benin:* Independence Day. *Switzerland:* Confederation Day.

**2 Wed.** *Costa Rica:* Virgin of the Angels Day. *Guyana:* Freedom Day. *Trinidad:* Discovery Day. *Zambia:* Farmers' Day.

**3 Thu.** *El Salvador:* Summer Day (1st day of 4). *Guinea-Bissau:* Martyrs' Day. *Niger:* Independence Day. *Tunisia:* President's Birthday.

**4 Fri.** *Burkina Faso:* Independence Day (1st day of 2). *El Salvador:* Summer Day (2nd day of 4).

**5 Sat.** *Burkina Faso:* Independence Day (2nd day of 2). *El Salvador:* Summer Day (3rd day of 4).

**6 Sun.** *Bolivia:* Independence Day. *El Salvador:* Summer Day (4th day of 4). *United Arab Emirates:* Accession Day.

**7 Mon.** *Bahamas:* Emancipation Day. *Barbados:* Emancipation Day. *Canada:* Civic Holiday. *Colombia:* Boyaca Day. *Ivory Coast:* Republic Day. *Ireland:* Public Holiday. *Jamaica:* Independence Day. *Scotland:* Public Holiday.

**9 Wed.** *Georgia:* Independence Day*. *Singapore:* National Day.

**10 Thu.** *Ecuador:* Independence Day. *Israel:* Tisha Ab. *Jewish:* Tisha Ab.

**11 Fri.** *Chad:* Independence Day. *Jordan:* Accession Day. *Zimbabwe:* Heroes' Day (1st day of 2).

**12 Sat.** *Thailand:* Queen's Birthday. *Zimbabwe:* Heroes' Day (2nd day of 2).

**13 Sun.** *Burma:* Full Moon Day. *Central African Republic:* Independence Day. *Congo:* Independence Day (1st day of 2). *Tunisia:* Women's Day.

**14 Mon.** *Congo:* Independence Day (2nd day of 2). *Pakistan:* Independence Day. *Sri Lanka:* Full Moon Poya.

**15 Tue.** *Congo:* Independence Day (3rd day of 3). *India:* Independence Day. *Liechtenstein:* National Day. *South Korea:* Republic Day. *Christian:* Assumption (see App. A11).

**16 Wed.** *Dominican Republic:* Republic Day.

**17 Thu.** *Argentina:* San Martin's Day. *Gabon:* Independence Day. *Indonesia:* Independence Day.

**20 Sun.** *Hungary:* Constitution Day. *Senegal:* Independence Day.

**21 Mon.** *Estonia:* Independence Day*. *Latvia:* Independence Day*. *Lithuania:* Independence Day*.

**22 Tue.** *Zodiac Cusp:* Leo ends, Virgo begins.

**23 Wed.** *Romania:* National Day (1st day of 2).

**24 Thu.** *Kazakhstan:* National Day*. *Liberia:* Flag Day. *Romania:* National Day (2nd day of 2). *Russia:* Independence Day*. *Ukraine:* National Day*.

**25 Fri.** *Belarus:* Independence Day*. *Paraguay:* Constitution Day. *Uruguay:* Independence Day.

**26 Sat.** *Hong Kong:* Liberation Day (1st day of 2).

**27 Sun.** *Moldova:* Independence Day*.

**28 Mon.** *England:* Summer Break. *Hong Kong:* Liberation Day (2nd day of 2). *Luxembourg:* Fair Day. *Northern Ireland:* Summer Break. *Wales:* Summer Break.

**29 Tue.** *Uzbekistan:* Independence Day*.

**30 Wed.** *Afghanistan:* Children's Day. *Azerbaijan:* Independence Day*. *Peru:* Rose of Lima Day. *Turkey:* Victory Day.

**31 Thu.** *Afghanistan:* Pashtunistan Day. *Kyrgyzstan:* Independence Day*. *Malaysia:* National Day. *Trinidad:* Independence Day.

# September 2000

**1 Fri.** *Libya:* National Day. *Mexico:* President's Message Day. *Syria:* United Arab Republics Day.

**2 Sat.** *Vietnam:* Independence Day.

**3 Sun.** *Qatar:* National Day. *San Marino:* Saint Marinus' Day. *Tunisia:* Independence Movement Day.

**4 Mon.** *Canada:* Labour Day. *United States:* Labor Day.

**6 Wed.** *Pakistan:* Defense Day. *Swaziland:* Independence Day.

**7 Thu.** *Brazil:* Independence Day.

**8 Fri.** *Andorra:* National Day. *Malta:* Our Lady of Victory Day.

**9 Sat.** *Bulgaria:* National Day (1st day of 2). *North Korea:* Independence Day. *Tajikistan:* Independence Day*.

**10 Sun.** *Belize:* National Day. *Bulgaria:* National Day (2nd day of 2).

**11 Mon.** *Chile:* Revolution Day. *Egypt:* New Year's Day (Coptic: 1718). *Ethiopia:* New Year's Day (Ethiopian: 1994). *Pakistan:* Anniversary of Quaid-e-Azam's Death.

**12 Tue.** *Burma:* Full Moon Day. *Ethiopia:* National Day.

**13 Wed.** *Sri Lanka:* Full Moon Poya.

**14 Thu.** *Guatemala:* San Jacinto Day. *Nicaragua:* San Jacinto Day.

**15 Fri.** *Costa Rica:* Independence Day. *El Salvador:* Independence Day. *Guatemala:* Independence Day. *Honduras:* Independence Day. *Japan:* Veneration Day. *Nicaragua:* Independence Day.

**16 Sat.** *Mexico:* Independence Day. *New Guinea:* Independence Day.

**17 Sun.** *Angola:* Heroes' Day. *Marshall Islands:* Independence Day.

**18 Mon.** *Burundi:* Victory of Uprona Day. *Chile:* Independence Day.

**19 Tue.** *Chile:* Armed Forces Day. *Saint Kitts:* Independence Day.

**21 Thu.** *Belize:* Independence Day. *Malta:* Independence Day.

**22 Fri.** *Mali:* Independence Day. *Zodiac Cusp:* Virgo ends, Libra begins.

**23 Sat.** *Armenia:* Independence Day*. *Japan:* Autumnal Equinox. *Saudi Arabia:* National Day.

**24 Sun.** *Dominican Republic:* Mercedes Day. *Guinea-Bissau:* Republic Day. *Europe:* Daylight Savings Time ends (retard clocks 1 hour).

**25 Mon.** *Mozambique:* Liberation Day. *Rwanda:* Assembly Day.

**26 Tue.** *Ethiopia:* True Cross Day. *Yemeni Republic:* National Day.

**28 Thu.** *Taiwan:* Teachers' Day.

**29 Fri.** *Brunei:* Constitution Day. *Paraguay:* Boqueron Battle Day.

**30 Sat.** *Botswana:* Independence Day. *Israel:* New Year's Day. *Jewish:* Rosh Hashanah (Jewish: 5761).

# October 2000

**1 Sun.** *Cameroon:* Unification Day. *China:* National Day (1st day of 2). *Nigeria:* Independence Day. *South Korea:* Armed Forces Day (1st day of 2). *Tuvalu:* Independence Day.

**2 Mon.** *Barbados:* Bank Holiday. *China:* National Day (2nd day of 2). *Guinea:* Independence Day. *India:* Ghandi Day. *South Korea:* Armed Forces Day (2nd day of 2).

**3 Tue.** *Honduras:* Morazan Day. *South Korea:* Foundation Day (1st day of 2).

**4 Wed.** *Lesotho:* Independence Day. *South Korea:* Foundation Day. (2nd day of 2).

**5 Thu.** *Lesotho:* Sports Day. *Macao:* Portuguese Republic Day. *Portugal:* Republic Day.

**6 Fri.** *Egypt:* Armed Forces Day. *Asian:* Ancestors' Day (see App. B6).

**9 Mon.** *Canada:* Thanksgiving Day. *Fiji:* Cession Day. *Israel:* Yom Kippur. *Peru:* National Dignity Day. *South Korea:* Alphabet Day. *Uganda:* Independence Day. *United States:* Bank Holiday. *Virgin Islands (U.S.):* Puerto Rican Friendship Day. *Jewish:* Yom Kippur.

**10 Tue.** *Japan:* Health Day. *South Africa:* Kruger Day. *Taiwan:* National Day.

**11 Wed.** *Burma:* Full Moon Day. *Cuba:* Independence War. *Panama:* Revolution Day.

**12 Thu.** *China:* Mid-autumn Day. *Equatorial Guinea:* Independence Day. *Spain:* National Day. *Sri Lanka:* Full Moon Poya. *Taiwan:* Mid-autumn Day. *Multinational:* Columbus Day (see App. A12).

**13 Fri.** *Hong Kong:* Mid-autumn Day. *Macao:* Mid-autumn Day.

**14 Sat.** *Israel:* Sukkot. *Zaïre:* Founders' Day. *Jewish:* Sukkot.

**15 Sun.** *Bosnia and Herzegovina:* Independence Day*. *Tunisia:* Evacuation Day.

**16 Mon.** *Jamaica:* Heroes' Day.

**17 Tue.** *Haiti:* Dessalines Day. *Malawi:* Mother's Day.

**20 Fri.** *Guatemala:* Revolution Day. *Kenya:* Kenyatta Day.

**21 Sat.** *Honduras:* Armed Forces Day. *Somalia:* Revolution Day. (1st day of 2).

**22 Sun.** *Somalia:* Revolution Day (2nd day of 2). *Vatican:* John Paul II Day.

**23 Mon.** *Hungary:* Revolution Day. *Thailand:* Chulalongkorn Day. *Zodiac Cusp:* Libra ends, Scorpio begins.

**24 Tue.** *Egypt:* Suez Victory Day. *Haiti:* United Nations Day. *Zambia:* Independence Day. *Islamic:* Isra a Majraj (see App. B30).

**25 Wed.** *Taiwan:* Restoration Day.

**26 Thu.** *Austria:* National Day. *Benin:* Revolution Day. *Rwanda:* Government Day. *Hindu:* Deepavali (see App. B21).

**27 Fri.** *Saint Vincent:* Independence Day. *Turkmenistan:* Independence Day*. *Zaïre:* Naming Day.

**28 Sat.** *Greece:* Ohi! Day.

**29 Sun.** *Tanzania:* Naming Day. *Turkey:* Republic Day. *Canada and United States:* Daylight Savings Time ends (retard clocks 1 hour).

**30 Mon.** *Ireland:* Public Holiday. *New Zealand:* Labour Day.

**31 Tue.** *Taiwan:* Chiang Kai-shek's Birthday.

# November 2000

**1 Wed.** *Algeria:* Revolution Day. *Antigua:* Independence Day. *Christian:* All Saints' Day (see App. A13).

**2 Thu.** *Brazil:* Memorial Day. *Finland:* All Saints' Eve. *Liberia:* Thanksgiving Day. *Sweden:* All Saints' Eve. *Christian:* All Souls' Day (see App. A14).

**3 Fri.** *Dominica:* Independence Day. *Ecuador:* Cuenca Independence Day. *Japan:* Culture Day. *Panama:* Independence Day.

**4 Sat.** *Andorra:* Saint Charles' Day. *Panama:* Flag Day. *Vatican:* John Paul II's Nameday.

**5 Sun.** *El Salvador:* Cry of Independence Day.

**6 Mon.** *Virgin Islands (U.S.):* Liberty Day.

**7 Tue.** *Bangladesh:* Revolution Day.

**8 Wed.** *Nepal:* Queen's Birthday.

**9 Thu.** *Pakistan:* Iqbal Day.

**10 Fri.** *Burma:* Full Moon Day. *Panama:* Cry of Independence Day.

**11 Sat.** *Angola:* Independence Day. *Bhutan:* King's Birthday. *Maldives:* Republic Day. *Poland:* Independence Day. *Sri Lanka:* Full Moon Poya *Multinational:* Armistice Day (see App. A15).

**12 Sun.** *Taiwan:* Dr. Sun Yat-sen's Birthday.

**14 Tue.** *Jordan:* King's Birthday.

**15 Wed.** *Brazil:* Republic Day. *Germany:* Repentance Day.

**17 Fri.** *Zaïre:* Armed Forces Day.

**18 Sat.** *Haiti:* Vertieres' Day. *Morocco:* Independence Day. *Oman:* National Day.

**19 Sun.** *Belize:* Garifuna Day. *Mali:* Army Coup Day. *Monaco:* Prince Ranier's Day. *Puerto Rico:* Discovery Day.

**20 Mon.** *Fiji:* Prince Charles' Birthday. *Mexico:* Revolution Day.

**21 Tue.** *Zodiac Cusp:* Scorpio ends, Sagittarius begins.

**22 Wed.** *Lebanon:* Independence Day.

**23 Thu.** *Japan:* Labor Thanksgiving Day. *United States:* Thanksgiving Day.

**24 Fri.** *Argentina:* Bank Holiday. *Zaïre:* New Regime Day.

**25 Sat.** *Suriname:* Independence Day.

**27 Mon.** *Islamic:* 1st Day of Ramadan (see App. B25).

**28 Tue.** *Albania:* Independence Day. *Burundi:* Republic Day. *Chad:* Republic Day. *Mauritania:* Independence Day. *Panama:* Independence Day.

**29 Wed.** *Albania:* Liberation Day. *Liberia:* Tubman's Birthday. *Yugoslavia:* Republic Day.

**30 Thu.** *Barbados:* Independence Day. *Benin:* National Day. *Philippines:* Heroes' Day.

# December 2000

**1 Fri.** *Central African Republic:* National Day. *Portugal:* Youth Day. *Ukraine:* Independence Day*.

**2 Sat.** *Laos:* Republic Day. *United Arab Emirates:* National Day.

**5 Tue.** *Haiti:* Discovery Day. *Thailand:* King's Birthday.

**6 Wed.** *Finland:* Independence Day.

**7 Thu.** *Ivory Coast:* Independence Day.

**8 Fri.** *Christian:* Immaculate Conception (see App. A16).

**9 Sat.** *Burma:* Full Moon Day. *Tanzania:* Independence Day.

**10 Sun.** *Angola:* MPLA Foundation Day. *Equatorial Guinea:* Human Rights

Day. *Namibia:* Settlers' Day. *Sri Lanka:* Full Moon Poya. *Thailand:* Constitution Day.

**11 Mon.** *Burkina Faso:* National Day.

**12 Tue.** *Kenya:* Independence Day. *Mexico:* Guadalupe Festival.

**13 Wed.** *Malta:* Republic Day.

**16 Sat.** *Bahrain:* National Day. *Bangladesh:* Victory Day. *Nepal:* Constitution Day. *South Africa:* Covenant Day.

**17 Sun.** *Bhutan:* National Day.

**18 Mon.** *Niger:* Republic Day.

**21 Thu.** *Kazakhstan:* Independence Day*. *Zodiac Cusp:* Sagittarius ends, Capricorn begins.

**23 Sat.** *Japan:* Emperor's Birthday. *Jewish:* Chanukah.

**24 Sun.** *Multinational:* Christmas Eve (see App. A17).

**25 Mon.** *Angola:* Family Day. *Congo:* Children's Day. *Pakistan:* Quaid's Birthday. *Taiwan:* Constitution Day. *Multinational:* Christmas Day (see App. A18).

**26 Tue.** *South Africa:* Good Will Day. *Islamic:* Eid al Fitr (1st day of 4) (see App. B26). *Multinational:* Boxing Day (see App. A19).

**27 Wed.** *Far East Islamic:* Hari Raya Puasa (see App. B27). *Islamic:* Eid al Fitr (2nd day of 4) (see App. B26).

**28 Thu.** *Islamic:* Eid al Fitr (3rd day of 4) (see App. B26).

**29 Fri.** *Islamic:* Eid al Fitr (4th day of 4) (see App. B26).

**30 Sat.** *Madagascar:* Republic Day. *Philippines:* Rizal Day (1st day of 2).

**31 Sun.** *Congo:* Republic Day. *Philippines:* Rizal Day (2nd day of 2). *Multinational:* Bank Holiday and New Year's Eve (see App. A20 & A21).

# January 2001

**1 Mon.** *Cameroon:* Independence Day. *Cuba:* Liberation Day. *Haiti:* Independence Day. *Palau:* Independence Day. *Sudan:* Independence Day. *Taiwan:* Foundation Day (1st day of 2). *Western Samoa:* Independence Day. *Multinational:* Bank Holiday and New Year's Day (see App. A1 & A2).

**2 Tue.** *Japan:* Bank Holiday. *New Zealand:* New Year's Day (2nd day of 2). *Scotland:* New Year's Day (2nd day of 2). *South Korea:* New Year's Day (2nd day of 2). *Switzerland:* Berchtold's Day. *Taiwan:* Foundation Day (2nd day of 2).

**3 Wed.** *Burkina Faso:* Revolution Day.

**4 Thu.** *Burma:* Independence Day. *Zaïre:* Martyrs' Day.

**6 Sat.** *Iraq:* Army Day. *Uruguay:* Children's Day. *Christian:* Epiphany (see App. A3).

**7 Sun.** *Egypt:* Coptic Christmas. *Ethiopia:* Coptic Christmas.

**8 Mon.** *Burma:* Full Moon Day.

**9 Tue.** *Sri Lanka:* Full Moon Poya.

**11 Thu.** *Albania:* Republic Day. *Nepal:* Unification Day. *Puerto Rico:* Hostos Day.

**12 Fri.** *Tanzania:* Revolution Day.

**13 Sat.** *Togo:* Liberation Day.

**15 Mon.** *Japan:* Adult's Day. *Jordan:* Arbor Day. *United States:* Martin Luther King's Birthday.

**19 Fri.** *Ethiopia:* Epiphany.

**20 Sat.** *Mali:* Award Day. *Zodiac Cusp:* Capricorn ends, Aquarius begins.

**21 Sun.** *Dominican Republic:* Altagracia Day.

**22 Mon.** *Saint Vincent:* Discovery Day.

**23 Tue.** *Asian:* Chinese New Year Eve (see App. B1).

**24 Wed.** *Vietnam:* Tet (1st day of 3). *Asian:* Chinese New Year (Year of the Snake) (see App. B2).

**25 Thu.** *Vietnam:* Tet (2nd day of 3).

*Asian:* 2nd Day of Chinese New Year (see App. B3).

**26 Fri.** *Dominican Republic:* Duarte Day. *India:* Republic Day. *Vietnam:* Tet (3rd day of 3). *Asian:* 3rd Day of Chinese New Year (see App. B4).

**27 Sat.** *Monaco:* Saint Devota's Day. *Vietnam:* Vietnam Day.

**28 Sun.** *Rwanda:* Democracy Day.

**29 Mon.** *Australia:* Australia Day.

**31 Wed.** *Nauru:* Independence Day.

# February 2001

**2 Fri.** *Liechtenstein:* Candlemas.

**4 Sun.** *Sri Lanka:* Independence Day.

**5 Mon.** *Mexico:* Constitution Day. *United States:* Lincoln's Birthday.

**6 Tue.** *Burma:* Full Moon Day. *New Zealand:* Waitangi Day.

**7 Wed.** *Grenada:* Independence Day. *Sri Lanka:* Full Moon Poya.

**8 Thu.** *Iraq:* Revolution Day. *Thailand:* Makha Bucha Day.

**9 Fri.** *Lebanon:* Saint Marion's Day.

**10 Sat.** *Malta:* Saint Paul's Day.

**11 Sun.** *Cameroon:* Youth Day. *Japan:* Foundation Day. *Liberia:* Armed Forces Day.

**12 Mon.** *Burma:* Union Day.

**14 Wed.** *International:* Valentine's Day.

**18 Sun.** *Gambia:* Independence Day. *Zodiac Cusp:* Aquarius ends, Pisces begins.

**19 Mon.** *Nepal:* National Day. *United States:* Washington's Birthday.

**21 Wed.** *Bangladesh:* Saheed Day.

**22 Thu.** *Saint Lucia:* Independence Day.

**23 Fri.** *Brunei:* National Day. *Guyana:* Republic Day.

**25 Sun.** *Kuwait:* National Day.

**26 Mon.** *Greece:* Shrove Monday. *Christian:* Shrove Monday (see App. B7). *Orthodox:* Shrove Monday.

**27 Tue.** *Dominican Republic:* Independence Day. *Christian:* Shrove Tuesday (see App. B8).

**28 Wed.** *Christian:* Ash Wednesday (see App. B9).

# March 2001

**1 Thu.** *South Korea:* Independence Day.

**2 Fri.** *Ethiopia:* Victory of Aduwa Day. *Morocco:* Independence Day.

**3 Sat.** *Bulgaria:* Liberation Day. *Malawi:* Martyrs' Day. *Morocco:* National Day.

**5 Mon.** *Guam:* Discovery Day. *Islamic:* Eid al Adha (1st day of 4) (see App. B28).

**6 Tue.** *Ghana:* Independence Day. *Far East Islamic:* Hari Raya Haji (see App. B29). *Islamic:* Eid al Adha (2nd day of 4).

**7 Wed.** *Islamic:* Eid al Adha (3rd day of 4) (see App. B28).

**8 Thu.** *Burma:* Full Moon Day. *Syria:* Revolution Day. *Islamic:* Eid al Adha (4th day of 4). *Multinational:* Women's Day (see App. A4).

**9 Fri.** *Sri Lanka:* Full Moon Poya. *Jewish:* Purim.

**10 Sat.** *South Korea:* Labor Day. *Zambia:* Youth Day.

**11 Sun.** *Lithuania:* National Day*.

**12 Mon.** *Gibraltar:* Commonwealth Day. *Lesotho:* Moshoeshoe's Day. *Mauritius:* Independence Day.

**13 Tue.** *Grenada:* National Day.

**17 Sat.** *Ireland:* Saint Patrick's Day. *Northern Ireland:* Saint Patrick's Day.

**19 Mon.** *Christian:* Saint Joseph's Day (see App. A5).

**20 Tue.** *Afghanistan:* New Year's Day (Shamsi: 1380). *Iran:* New Year's Day (Hegira: 1380). *Iraq:* New Year's Day. *Japan:* Vernal Equinox. *Tunisia:* Independence Day. *Zodiac Cusp:* Pisces ends, Aries begins.

**21 Wed.** *Mexico:* Juarez Day.

**22 Thu.** *Puerto Rico:* Abolition Day.

**23 Fri.** *Pakistan:* Pakistan Day.

**25 Sun.** *Cyprus:* Greek Independence Day. *Greece:* Independence Day. *Liechtenstein:* Annunciation. *Europe:* Daylight Savings Time starts (advance clocks 1 hour). *Islamic:* New Year's Day (Hegira: 1422) (see App. B22).

**26 Mon.** *Bangladesh:* Independence Day. *Virgin Islands (U.S.):* Transfer Day. *Far East Islamic:* New Year's Day (Hegira: 1422).

**27 Tue.** *Angola:* Evacuation Day. *Burma:* Resistance Day. *Zambia:* Africa Day.

**29 Thu.** *Central African Republic:* Boganda Day. *Madagascar:* Memorial Day. *Taiwan:* Youth Day.

**31 Sat.** *Malta:* National Day.

# April 2001

**1 Sun.** *Iran:* Republic Day. *San Marino:* National Day. *Canada and United States:* Daylight Savings Time starts (advance clocks 1 hour).

**3 Tue.** *Islamic:* Ashura (see App. B23).

**4 Wed.** *Hungary:* Liberation Day. *Senegal:* National Day.

**5 Thu.** *South Korea:* Arbor Day. *Asian:* Tomb Sweeping Day (see App. A6).

**6 Fri.** *Burma:* Full Moon Day. *Sierra Leone:* Bank Holiday. *South Africa:* Founders' Day. *Thailand:* Chakri Day.

**7 Sat.** *Sri Lanka:* Full Moon Poya.

**8 Sun.** *Israel:* Passover. *Christian:* Palm Sunday. *Jewish:* Passover.

**9 Mon.** *Philippines:* Valour Day. *Tunisia:* Martyrs' Day.

**11 Wed.** *Costa Rica:* Heroes' Day. *Uganda:* Liberation Day.

**12 Thu.** *Christian:* Maundy Thursday (see App. B11).

**13 Fri.** *Chad:* Independence Day. *Thailand:* Songkrawn (1st day of 2). *Christian:* Good Friday (see App. B12). *Orthodox:* Good Friday (see App. B20).

**14 Sat.** *Honduras:* Pan American Day. *Thailand:* Songkrawn (2nd day of 2). *Christian:* Holy Saturday (see App. B13).

**15 Sun.** *Jordan:* Easter Sunday. *Niger:* National Day. *Christian:* Easter Sunday (see App. B14). *Orthodox:* Easter Sunday.

**16 Mon.** *Burma:* New Year's Day (Burmese: 1363). *Cyprus:* Independence Day. *Christian:* Easter Monday (see App. B15). *Orthodox:* Easter Monday (see App. B20).

**17 Tue.** *Cambodia:* Independence Day. *Syria:* Independence Day.

**18 Wed.** *Zimbabwe:* Republic Day.

**19 Thu.** *Sierra Leone:* Republic Day. *Uruguay:* Patriots' Day. *Venezuela:* Independence Day.

**20 Fri.** *Zodiac Cusp:* Aries ends, Taurus begins.

**21 Sat.** *Brazil:* Tiradentes Day.

**23 Mon.** *Turkey:* Children's Day.

**25 Wed.** *Australia:* ANZAC Day. *Egypt:* Sinai Day. *Iceland:* Children's Day. *Italy:* Liberation Day. *New Zealand:* ANZAC Day. *Portugal:* Liberation Day. *Swaziland:* Flag Day.

**26 Thu.** *Tanzania:* Union Day.

**27 Fri.** *Afghanistan:* Independence Day. *Sierra Leone:* Independence Day. *Togo:* Independence Day.

**28 Sat.** *Israel:* Independence Day.

**29 Sun.** *Japan:* Green Day.

**30 Mon.** *Finland:* Vappu Day. *Netherlands:* Queen's Birthday. *South Korea:* Vesak Day.

# May 2001

**1 Tue.** *Multinational:* Labor Day (see App. A7).

**2 Wed.** *Lesotho:* King's Birthday.

**3 Thu.** *Japan:* Constitution Day.

**4 Fri.** *Japan:* People's Day.

**5 Sat.** *Japan:* Children's Day. *Mexico:* Cinco de Mayo. *Netherlands:* Liberation Day. *South Korea:* Children's Day. *Thailand:* Coronation Day.

**6 Sun.** *Burma:* Full Moon Day. *Lebanon:* Martyrs' Day. *Philippines:* Corregidor Day.

**7 Mon.** *Malaysia:* Vesak Day. *Singapore:* Vesak Day. *Sri Lanka:* Full Moon Poya. *Thailand:* Visakha Bucha Day. *United Kingdom:* Labour Day. *Zambia:* Labour Day.

**8 Tue.** *France:* Liberation Day.

**9 Wed.** *Czech Republic:* Liberation Day*. *Slovakia:* Liberation Day*.

**10 Thu.** *Micronesia:* Independence Day.

**11 Fri.** *Denmark:* All Prayers' Day.

**13 Sun.** *International:* Mother's Day.

**14 Mon.** *Liberia:* Unification Day. *Malawi:* Kamuzu Day. *Paraguay:* Flag Day.

**15 Tue.** *Paraguay:* Independence Day.

**17 Thu.** *Cayman Islands:* Discovery Day. *Norway:* Constitution Day.

**18 Fri.** *Haiti:* Flag Day. *Uruguay:* Las Piedras Day.

**19 Sat.** *Finland:* Flag Day. *Turkey:* Youth Day.

**20 Sun.** *Cameroon:* Constitution Day. *Zaïre:* Popular Movement Day.

**21 Mon.** *Canada:* Victoria Day. *Chile:* Navy Day. *Zodiac Cusp:* Taurus ends, Gemini begins.

**22 Tue.** *Haiti:* Sovereign Day. *Sri Lanka:* Heroes' Day.

**23 Wed.** *Jamaica:* Labour Day.

**24 Thu.** *Bulgaria:* Culture Day. *Ecuador:* Independence Battle Day. *Christian:* Ascension (see App. B16).

**25 Fri.** *Argentina:* National Day. *Eritrea:* Independence Day*. *Jordan:* Independence Day. *Sudan:* Revolution Day. *Multinational:* Africa Day (see App. A8).

**26 Sat.** *Guyana:* Independence Day.

**27 Sun.** *Nigeria:* Children's Day.

**28 Mon.** *Israel:* Pentecost. *United Kingdom:* Spring Break. *United States:* Memorial Day. *Jewish:* Pentecost.

**29 Tue.** *Asian:* Dragon Boat Festival (see App. B5).

**31 Thu.** *Brunei:* Regiment Day. *South Africa:* Republic Day.

# June 2001

**1 Fri.** *Kenya:* Madaraka Day. *Tunisia:* National Day. *Western Samoa:* Independence Day.

**2 Sat.** *Italy:* Republic Day. *Tunisia:* Youth Day.

**3 Sun.** *Christian:* Whitsunday. *Far East Islamic:* Mohammed's Birthday. *Islamic:* Mohammed's Birthday (see App. B24). *Orthodox:* Pentecost Sunday.

**4 Mon.** *Bahamas:* Labour Day. *Burma:* Full Moon Day. *Greece:* Pentecost Monday. *Ireland:* Public Holiday. *New Zealand:* Queen's Birthday. *Tonga:* Independence Day. *Christian:* Whitmonday (see App. B18).

**5 Tue.** *Denmark:* Constitution Day. *Equatorial Guinea:* President's Birthday. *Sri Lanka:* Full Moon Poya. *Seychelles:* Liberation Day.

**6 Wed.** *Malaysia:* King's Birthday. *South Korea:* Memorial Day. *Sweden:* Constitution Day.

**7 Thu.** *Chad:* Revolution Day.

**9 Sat.** *Argentina:* Independence Day. *Hong Kong:* Queen's Birthday (1st day of 2).

**10 Sun.** *Macao:* Portugal Day. *Portugal:* Portugal Day.

**11 Mon.** *Australia:* Queen's Birthday. *Fiji:* Queen's Birthday. *Hong Kong:* Queen's Birthday (2nd day of 2). *Libya:* Evacuation Day. *New Guinea:* Queen's Birthday. *United Kingdom:* Queen's Birthday.

**12 Tue.** *Philippines:* Independence Day.

**14 Thu.** *Christian:* Corpus Christi (see App. B19).

**17 Sun.** *Germany:* Unity Day. *Iceland:* Independence Day.

**18 Mon.** *Egypt:* Independence Day.

**19 Tue.** *Algeria:* Righting Day. *Kuwait:* Independence Day. *Uruguay:* Artigas Day.

**20 Wed.** *Argentina:* Flag Day.

**21 Thu.** *Finland:* Midsummer Day (1st day of 2). *Sweden:* Midsummer Day (1st day of 2). *Zodiac Cusp:* Gemini ends, Cancer begins.

**22 Fri.** *Finland:* Midsummer Day (2nd day of 2). *Sweden:* Midsummer Day (2nd day of 2).

**23 Sat.** *Finland:* Johannus Day. *Luxembourg:* National Day.

**24 Sun.** *Andorra:* Saint John's Day. *Venezuela:* Carabobo Day. *Zaïre:* Constitution Day.

**25 Mon.** *Croatia:* Independence Day*. *Mozambique:* Independence Day. *Slovenia:* Independence Day*.

**26 Tue.** *Madagascar:* Independence Day. *Somalia:* Independence Day.

**27 Wed.** *Djibouti:* Independence Day.

**29 Fri.** *Chile:* Bank Holiday. *Ecuador:* Bank Holiday. *El Salvador:* Bank Holiday. *Finland:* Bank Holiday. *Seychelles:* Independence Day. *Christian:* Saint Paul's Day (see App. A9).

**30 Sat.** *Guatemala:* Army Day. *Sri Lanka:* Bank Holiday. *Zaïre:* Independence Day.

# July 2001

**1 Sun.** *Burundi:* Independence Day. *Canada:* Canada Day. *Ghana:* Republic Day. *Hong Kong:* Half Year Day. *Rwanda:* Independence Day. *Somalia:* Union Day. *Suriname:* Freedom Day. *Multinational:* Bank Holiday (see App. A10).

**2 Mon.** *Cayman Islands:* Constitution Day. *Lesotho:* Family Day. *Zambia:* Heroes' Day.

**3 Tue.** *Zambia:* Unity Day.

**4 Wed.** *Burma:* Full Moon Day. *Philippines:* United States Friendship Day. *United States:* Independence Day. *Yugoslavia:* Freedom Fighters' Day.

**5 Thu.** *Algeria:* Independence Day. *Cape Verde:* Independence Day. *Rwanda:* Unity Day. *Sri Lanka:* Full Moon Poya. *Thailand:* Asalaha Bucha Day. *Venezuela:* Independence Day.

**6 Fri.** *Comoros:* Independence Day. *Malawi:* Republic Day. *Thailand:* Khao Phansa Day.

**7 Sat.** *Solomon Islands:* Independence Day. *Tanzania:* Farmers' Day. *Yugoslavia:* Serbian Day.

**10 Tue.** *Bahamas:* Independence Day.

**11 Wed.** *Mongolia:* Revolution Day.

**12 Thu.** *Kiribati:* Independence Day. *Northern Ireland:* Battle of the Boyne Day. *São Tomé:* National Day.

**14 Sat.** *France:* National Day. *Iraq:* Revolution Day.

**15 Sun.** *Brunei:* Sultan's Birthday.

**16 Mon.** *Botswana:* President's Day.

**17 Tue.** *Iraq:* Revolution Day. *Puerto Rico:* Rivera Day. *Slovakia:* Independence Day*. *South Korea:* Constitution Day.

**18 Wed.** *Uruguay:* Constitution Day.

**19 Thu.** *Burma:* Martyrs' Day. *Laos:* Independence Day. *Nicaragua:* Sandinista Day.

**20 Fri.** *Colombia:* Independence Day.

**21 Sat.** *Belgium:* National Day. *Guam:* Liberation Day.

**22 Sun.** *Poland:* Liberation Day. *Zodiac Cusp:* Cancer ends, Leo begins.

**23 Mon.** *Egypt:* Revolution Day. *New Guinea:* Remembrance Day. *Virgin Islands (U.S.):* Hurricane Supplication Day.

**24 Tue.** *Venezuela:* Bolivar Day.

**25 Wed.** *Costa Rica:* Guanacaste Day. *Cuba:* Revolution Day (1st day of 3). *Puerto Rico:* Constitution Day. *Spain:* Santiago Day. *Tunisia:* Republic Day.

**26 Thu.** *Cuba:* Revolution Day (2nd day of 3). *Liberia:* Independence Day. *Maldives:* Independence Day.

**27 Fri.** *Cuba:* Revolution Day (3rd day of 3). *Puerto Rico:* Barbosa Day.

**28 Sat.** *Peru:* Independence Day (1st day of 2).

**29 Sun.** *Israel:* Tisha Ab. *Peru:* Independence Day (2nd day of 2). *Jewish:* Tisha Ab.

**30 Mon.** *Vanuatu:* Independence Day.

# August 2001

**1 Wed.** *Benin:* Independence Day. *Switzerland:* Confederation Day. *Zambia:* Farmers' Day.

**2 Thu.** *Burma:* Full Moon Day. *Costa Rica:* Virgin of the Angels Day. *Guyana:* Freedom Day. *Trinidad:* Discovery Day.

**3 Fri.** *El Salvador:* Summer Day (1st day of 4). *Guinea-Bissau:* Martyrs' Day. *Niger:* Independence Day. *Sri Lanka:* Full Moon Poya. *Tunisia:* President's Birthday.

**4 Sat.** *Burkina Faso:* Independence Day (1st day of 2). *El Salvador:* Summer Day (2nd day of 4).

**5 Sun.** *Burkina Faso:* Independence Day (2nd day of 2). *El Salvador:* Summer Day (3rd day of 4).

**6 Mon.** *Bahamas:* Emancipation Day. *Barbados:* Emancipation Day. *Bolivia:* Independence Day. *Canada:* Civic Holiday. *El Salvador:* Summer Day (4th day of 4). *Ireland:* Public Holiday. *Jamaica:* Independence Day. *Scotland:* Public Holiday. *United Arab Emirates:* Accession Day.

**7 Tue.** *Colombia:* Boyaca Day. *Ivory Coast:* Republic Day.

**9 Thu.** *Georgia:* Independence Day*. *Singapore:* National Day.

**10 Fri.** *Ecuador:* Independence Day.

**11 Sat.** *Chad:* Independence Day. *Jordan:* Accession Day. *Zimbabwe:* Heroes' Day (1st day of 2).

**12 Sun.** *Thailand:* Queen's Birthday. *Zimbabwe:* Heroes' Day (2nd day of 2).

**13 Mon.** *Central African Republic:* Independence Day. *Congo:* Independence Day (1st day of 2). *Tunisia:* Women's Day.

**14 Tue.** *Congo:* Independence Day (2nd day of 2). *Pakistan:* Independence Day.

**15 Wed.** *Congo:* Independence Day (3rd day of 3). *India:* Independence Day. *Liechtenstein:* National Day. *South Korea:* Republic Day. *Christian:* Assumption (see App. A11).

**16 Thu.** *Dominican Republic:* Republic Day.

**17 Fri.** *Argentina:* San Martin's Day. *Gabon:* Independence Day. *Indonesia:* Independence Day.

**20 Mon.** *Hungary:* Constitution Day. *Senegal:* Independence Day.

**21 Tue.** *Estonia:* Independence Day*. *Latvia:* Independence Day*. *Lithuania:* Independence Day*.

**23 Thu.** *Romania:* National Day (1st day of 2). *Zodiac Cusp:* Leo ends, Virgo begins.

**24 Fri.** *Kazakhstan:* National Day*. *Liberia:* Flag Day. *Romania:* National Day (2nd day of 2). *Russia:* Independence Day*. *Ukraine:* National Day*.

**25 Sat.** *Belarus:* Independence Day*.

*Hong Kong:* Liberation Day (1st day of 2). *Paraguay:* Constitution Day. *Uruguay:* Independence Day.

**27 Mon.** *England:* Summer Break. *Hong Kong:* Liberation Day (2nd day of 2). *Moldova:* Independence Day*. *Northern Ireland:* Summer Break. *Wales:* Summer Break.

**29 Wed.** *Uzbekistan:* Independence Day*.

**30 Thu.** *Afghanistan:* Children's Day. *Azerbaijan:* Independence Day*. *Peru:* Rose of Lima Day. *Turkey:* Victory Day.

**31 Fri.** *Afghanistan:* Pashtunistan Day. *Kyrgyzstan:* Independence Day*. *Malaysia:* National Day. *Trinidad:* Independence Day.

# September 2001

**1 Sat.** *Burma:* Full Moon Day. *Libya:* National Day. *Mexico:* President's Message Day. *Syria:* United Arab Republics Day.

**2 Sun.** *Sri Lanka:* Full Moon Poya. *Vietnam:* Independence Day.

**3 Mon.** *Canada:* Labour Day. *Luxembourg:* Fair Day. *Qatar:* National Day. *San Marino:* Saint Marinus' Day. *Tunisia:* Independence Movement Day. *United States:* Labor Day.

**6 Thu.** *Pakistan:* Defense Day. *Swaziland:* Independence Day.

**7 Fri.** *Brazil:* Independence Day.

**8 Sat.** *Andorra:* National Day. *Malta:* Our Lady of Victory Day.

**9 Sun.** *Bulgaria:* National Day (1st day of 2). *Tajikistan:* Independence Day*. *North Korea:* Independence Day.

**10 Mon.** *Belize:* National Day. *Bulgaria:* National Day (2nd day of 2).

**11 Tue.** *Chile:* Revolution Day. *Egypt:* New Year's Day (Coptic: 1719). *Ethiopia:* New Year's Day (Ethiopian: 1995). *Pakistan:* Anniversary of Quaid-e-Azam's Death.

**12 Wed.** *Ethiopia:* National Day.

**14 Fri.** *Guatemala:* San Jacinto Day. *Nicaragua:* San Jacinto Day.

**15 Sat.** *Costa Rica:* Independence Day. *El Salvador:* Independence Day. *Guatemala:* Independence Day. *Honduras:* Independence Day. *Japan:* Veneration Day. *Nicaragua:* Independence Day.

**16 Sun.** *Mexico:* Independence Day. *New Guinea:* Independence Day.

**17 Mon.** *Angola:* Heroes' Day. *Marshall Islands:* Independence Day.

**18 Tue.** *Burundi:* Victory of Uprona Day. *Chile:* Independence Day. *Israel:* New Year's Day. *Jewish:* Rosh Hashanah (Jewish: 5762).

**19 Wed.** *Chile:* Armed Forces Day. *Saint Kitts:* Independence Day.

**21 Fri.** *Belize:* Independence Day. *Malta:* Independence Day.

**22 Sat.** *Mali:* Independence Day. *Zodiac Cusp:* Virgo ends, Libra begins.

**23 Sun.** *Armenia:* Independence Day*. *Japan:* Autumnal Equinox. *Saudi Arabia:* National Day.

**24 Mon.** *Dominican Republic:* Mercedes Day. *Guinea-Bissau:* Republic Day.

**25 Tue.** *Mozambique:* Liberation Day. *Rwanda:* Assembly Day.

**26 Wed.** *Ethiopia:* True Cross Day. *Asian:* Ancestors' Day (see App. B6).

**27 Thu.** *Israel:* Yom Kippur. *Jewish:* Yom Kippur.

**28 Fri.** *Taiwan:* Teachers' Day.

**29 Sat.** *Brunei:* Constitution Day. *Paraguay:* Boqueron Battle Day.

**30 Sun.** *Botswana:* Independence Day. *Europe:* Daylight Savings Time ends (retard clocks 1 hour).

# October 2001

**1 Mon.** *Barbados:* Bank Holiday. *Burma:* Full Moon Day. *Cameroon:* Unification Day. *China:* Mid-autumn and National Day (1st day of 2). *Nigeria:* Independence Day. *South Korea:* Armed Forces Day (1st day of 2). *Sri Lanka:* Full Moon Poya. *Taiwan:* Mid-autumn Day. *Tuvalu:* Independence Day.

**2 Tue.** *China:* National Day (2nd day of 2). *Guinea:* Independence Day. *Hong Kong:* Mid-autumn Day. *India:* Ghandi Day. *Israel:* Sukkot. *Macao:* Mid-autumn Day. *South Korea:* Armed Forces Day (2nd day of 2). *Jewish:* Sukkot.

**3 Wed.** *Honduras:* Morazan Day. *South Korea:* Foundation Day (1st day of 2).

**4 Thu.** *Lesotho:* Independence Day. *South Korea:* Foundation Day (2nd day of 2).

**5 Fri.** *Lesotho:* Sports Day. *Macao:* Portuguese Republic Day. *Portugal:* Republic Day.

**6 Sat.** *Egypt:* Armed Forces Day.

**8 Mon.** *Canada:* Thanksgiving Day. *Fiji:* Cession Day. *United States:* Bank Holiday. *Virgin Islands (U.S.):* Puerto Rican Friendship Day.

**9 Tue.** *Peru:* National Dignity Day. *South Korea:* Alphabet Day. *Uganda:* Independence Day.

**10 Wed.** *Japan:* Health Day. *South Africa:* Kruger Day. *Taiwan:* National Day.

**11 Thu.** *Cuba:* Independence War. *Panama:* Revolution Day.

**12 Fri.** *Equatorial Guinea:* Independence Day. *Spain:* National Day. *Multinational:* Columbus Day (see App. A12).

**13 Sat.** *Islamic:* Isra a Majraj (see App. B30).

**14 Sun.** *Zaïre:* Founders' Day.

**15 Mon.** *Bosnia and Herzegovina:* Independence Day*. *Jamaica:* Heroes' Day. *Tunisia:* Evacuation Day. *Hindu:* Deepavali (see App. B21).

**17 Wed.** *Haiti:* Dessalines Day. *Malawi:* Mother's Day.

**20 Sat.** *Guatemala:* Revolution Day. *Kenya:* Kenyatta Day.

**21 Sun.** *Honduras:* Army Day. *Somalia:* Revolution Day (1st day of 2).

**22 Mon.** *Somalia:* Revolution Day (2nd day of 2). *Vatican:* John Paul II Day.

**23 Tue.** *Hungary:* Revolution Day. *Thailand:* Chulalongkorn Day. *Zodiac Cusp:* Libra ends, Scorpio begins.

**24 Wed.** *Egypt:* Suez Victory Day. *Haiti:* United Nations Day. *Zambia:* Independence Day.

**25 Thu.** *Taiwan:* Restoration Day.

**26 Fri.** *Austria:* National Day. *Benin:* Revolution Day. *Rwanda:* Government Day.

**27 Sat.** *Saint Vincent:* Independence Day. *Turkmenistan:* Independence Day*. *Zaïre:* Naming Day.

**28 Sun.** *Greece:* Ohi! Day. *Canada and United States:* Daylight Savings Time ends (retard clocks 1 hour).

**29 Mon.** *Ireland:* Public Holiday. *New Zealand:* Labour Day. *Tanzania:* Naming Day. *Turkey:* Republic Day.

**30 Tue.** *Burma:* Full Moon Day.

**31 Wed.** *Sri Lanka:* Full Moon Poya. *Taiwan:* Chiang Kai-shek's Birthday.

# November 2001

**1 Thu.** *Algeria:* Revolution Day. *Antigua:* Independence Day. *Liberia:* Thanksgiving Day. *Christian:* All Saints' Day (see App. A13).

**2 Fri.** *Brazil:* Memorial Day. *Finland:* All Saints' Eve. *Sweden:* All Saints' Eve. *Christian:* All Souls' Day (see App. A14).

**3 Sat.** *Dominica:* Independence Day. *Ecuador:* Cuenca Independence Day. *Japan:* Culture Day. *Panama:* Independence Day.

**4 Sun.** *Andorra:* Saint Charles' Day. *Panama:* Flag Day. *Vatican:* John Paul II's Nameday.

**5 Mon.** *El Salvador:* Cry of Independence Day. *Virgin Islands (U.S.):* Liberty Day.

**7 Wed.** *Bangladesh:* Revolution Day.

**8 Thu.** *Nepal:* Queen's Birthday.

**9 Fri.** *Pakistan:* Iqbal Day.

**10 Sat.** *Panama:* Cry of Independence Day.

**11 Sun.** *Angola:* Independence Day. *Bhutan:* King's Birthday. *Maldives:* Republic Day. *Poland:* Independence Day. *Multinational:* Armistice Day (see App. A15).

**12 Mon.** *Taiwan:* Dr. Sun Yat-sen's Birthday.

**14 Wed.** *Jordan:* King's Birthday.

**15 Thu.** *Brazil:* Republic Day.

**16 Fri.** *Islamic:* 1st Day of Ramadan (see App. B25).

**17 Sat.** *Zaïre:* Armed Forces Day.

**18 Sun.** *Haiti:* Vertieres' Day. *Morocco:* Independence Day. *Oman:* National Day.

**19 Mon.** *Belize:* Garifuna Day. *Fiji:* Prince Charles' Birthday. *Mali:* Army Coup Day. *Monaco:* Prince Ranier's Day. *Puerto Rico:* Discovery Day.

**20 Tue.** *Mexico:* Revolution Day.

**21 Wed.** *Germany:* Repentance Day.

**22 Thu.** *Lebanon:* Independence Day. *United States:* Thanksgiving Day. *Zodiac Cusp:* Scorpio ends, Sagittarius begins.

**23 Fri.** *Japan:* Labor Thanksgiving Day.

**24 Sat.** *Zaïre:* New Regime Day.

**25 Sun.** *Suriname:* Independence Day.

**28 Wed.** *Albania:* Independence Day. *Burundi:* Republic Day. *Chad:* Republic Day. *Mauritania:* Independence Day. *Panama:* Independence Day.

**29 Thu.** *Albania:* Liberation Day. *Burma:* Full Moon Day. *Liberia:* Tubman's Birthday. *Yugoslavia:* Republic Day.

**30 Fri.** *Argentina:* Bank Holiday. *Barbados:* Independence Day. *Benin:* National Day. *Philippines:* Heroes' Day. *Sri Lanka:* Full Moon Poya.

# December 2001

**1 Sat.** *Central African Republic:* National Day. *Portugal:* Youth Day. *Ukraine:* Independence Day*.

**2 Sun.** *Laos:* Republic Day. *United Arab Emirates:* National Day.

**5 Wed.** *Haiti:* Discovery Day. *Thailand:* King's Birthday.

**6 Thu.** *Finland:* Independence Day.

**7 Fri.** *Ivory Coast:* Independence Day.

**8 Sat.** *Christian:* Immaculate Conception (see App. A16).

**9 Sun.** *Tanzania:* Independence Day.

**10 Mon.** *Angola:* MPLA Foundation Day. *Equatorial Guinea:* Human Rights Day. *Namibia:* Settlers' Day. *Thailand:* Constitution Day. *Jewish:* Chanukah.

**11 Tue.** *Burkina Faso:* National Day.

**12 Wed.** *Kenya:* Independence Day. *Mexico:* Guadalupe Festival.

**13 Thu.** *Malta:* Republic Day.

**15 Sat.** *Islamic:* Eid al Fitr (1st day of 4) (see App. B26).

**16 Sun.** *Bahrain:* National Day. *Bangladesh:* Victory Day. *Nepal:* Constitution Day. *South Africa:* Covenant Day. *Far East Islamic:* Hari Raya Puasa (see App. B27). *Islamic:* Eid al Fitr (2nd day of 4) (see App. B26).

**17 Mon.** *Bhutan:* National Day. *Islamic:* Eid al Fitr (3rd day of 4) (see App. B26).

**18 Tue.** *Niger:* Republic Day. *Islamic:* Eid al Fitr (4th day of 4) (see App. B26).

**21 Fri.** *Kazakhstan:* Independence Day*. *Zodiac Cusp:* Sagittarius ends, Capricorn begins.

**23 Sun.** *Japan:* Emperor's Birthday.

**24 Mon.** *Multinational:* Christmas Eve (see App. A17).

**25 Tue.** *Angola:* Family Day. *Congo:* Children's Day. *Pakistan:* Quaid's Birthday. *Taiwan:* Constitution Day. *Multinational:* Christmas Day (see App. A18).

**26 Wed.** *South Africa:* Good Will Day. *Multinational:* Boxing Day (see App. A19).

**28 Fri.** *Burma:* Full Moon Day.

**29 Sat.** *Sri Lanka:* Full Moon Poya.

**30 Sun.** *Madagascar:* Republic Day. *Philippines:* Rizal Day (1st day of 2).

**31 Mon.** *Congo:* Republic Day. *Philippines:* Rizal Day (2nd day of 2). *Multinational:* Bank Holiday and New Year's Eve (see App. A20 & A21).

# January 2002

**1 Tue.** *Cameroon:* Independence Day. *Cuba:* Liberation Day. *Haiti:* Independence Day. *Palau:* Independence Day. *Sudan:* Independence Day. *Taiwan:* Foundation Day (1st day of 2). *Western Samoa:* Independence Day. *Multinational:* Bank Holiday and New Year's Day (see App. A1 & A2).

**2 Wed.** *Japan:* Bank Holiday. *New Zealand:* New Year's Day (2nd day of 2). *Scotland:* New Year's Day (2nd day of 2). *South Korea:* New Year's Day (2nd day of 2). *Switzerland:* Berchtold's Day. *Taiwan:* Foundation Day (2nd day of 2).

**3 Thu.** *Burkina Faso:* Revolution Day.

**4 Fri.** *Burma:* Independence Day. *Zaïre:* Martyrs' Day.

**6 Sun.** *Iraq:* Army Day. *Uruguay:* Children's Day. *Christian:* Epiphany (see App. A3).

**7 Mon.** *Egypt:* Coptic Christmas. *Ethiopia:* Coptic Christmas.

**11 Fri.** *Albania:* Republic Day. *Nepal:* Unification Day. *Puerto Rico:* Hostos Day.

**12 Sat.** *Tanzania:* Revolution Day.

**13 Sun.** *Togo:* Liberation Day.

**15 Tue.** *Japan:* Adult's Day. *Jordan:* Arbor Day.

**19 Sat.** *Ethiopia:* Epiphany.

**20 Sun.** *Mali:* Award Day. *Zodiac Cusp:* Capricorn ends, Aquarius begins.

**21 Mon.** *Dominican Republic:* Altagracia Day. *United States:* Martin Luther King's Birthday.

**22 Tue.** *Saint Vincent:* Discovery Day.

**26 Sat.** *Dominican Republic:* Duarte Day. *India:* Republic Day.

**27 Sun.** *Burma:* Full Moon Day. *Monaco:* Saint Devota's Day. *Vietnam:* Vietnam Day.

**28 Mon.** *Australia:* Australia Day. *Rwanda:* Democracy Day. *Sri Lanka:* Full Moon Poya.

**31 Thu.** *Nauru:* Independence Day.

# February 2002

**2 Sat.** *Liechtenstein:* Candlemas.

**4 Mon.** *Sri Lanka:* Independence Day. *United States:* Lincoln's Birthday.

**5 Tue.** *Mexico:* Constitution Day.

**6 Wed.** *New Zealand:* Waitangi Day.

**7 Thu.** *Grenada:* Independence Day.

**8 Fri.** *Iraq:* Revolution Day.
**9 Sat.** *Lebanon:* Saint Marion's Day.
**10 Sun.** *Malta:* Saint Paul's Day.
**11 Mon.** *Cameroon:* Youth Day. *Japan:* Foundation Day. *Liberia:* Armed Forces Day. *Asian:* Chinese New Year Eve (see App. B1). *Christian:* Shrove Monday (see App. B7).
**12 Tue.** *Burma:* Union Day. *Vietnam:* Tet (1st day of 3). *Asian:* Chinese New Year (Year of the Horse) (see App. B2). *Christian:* Shrove Tuesday (see App. B8).
**13 Wed.** *Vietnam:* Tet (2nd day of 3). *Asian:* 2nd Day of Chinese New Year (see App. B3). *Christian:* Ash Wednesday (see App. B9).
**14 Thu.** *Vietnam:* Tet (3rd day of 3). *Asian:* 3rd Day of Chinese New Year (see App. B4). *International:* Valentine's Day.
**18 Mon.** *Gambia:* Independence Day. *United States:* Washington's Birthday.
**19 Tue.** *Nepal:* National Day. *Zodiac Cusp:* Aquarius ends, Pisces begins.
**21 Thu.** *Bangladesh:* Saheed Day.
**22 Fri.** *Saint Lucia:* Independence Day. *Islamic:* Eid al Adha (1st day of 4) (see App. B28).
**23 Sat.** *Brunei:* National Day. *Guyana:* Republic Day. *Far East Islamic:* Hari Raya Haji (see App. B29). *Islamic:* Eid al Adha (2nd day of 4) (see App. B28).
**24 Sun.** *Islamic:* Eid al Adha (3rd day of 4) (see App. B28).
**25 Mon.** *Burma:* Full Moon Day. *Kuwait:* National Day. *Islamic:* Eid al Adha (4th day of 4) (see App. B28).
**26 Tue.** *Sri Lanka:* Full Moon Poya. *Thailand:* Makha Bucha Day. *Jewish:* Purim.
**27 Wed.** *Dominican Republic:* Independence Day.

# March 2002

**1 Fri.** *South Korea:* Independence Day.
**2 Sat.** *Ethiopia:* Victory of Aduwa Day. *Morocco:* Independence Day.
**3 Sun.** *Bulgaria:* Liberation Day. *Malawi:* Martyrs' Day. *Morocco:* National Day.
**4 Mon.** *Guam:* Discovery Day.
**6 Wed.** *Ghana:* Independence Day.
**8 Fri.** *Syria:* Revolution Day. *Multinational:* Women's Day (see App. A4).
**9 Sat.** *Zambia:* Youth Day.
**10 Sun.** *South Korea:* Labor Day.
**11 Mon.** *Gibraltar:* Commonwealth Day. *Lithuania:* National Day*.
**12 Tue.** *Lesotho:* Moshoeshoe's Day. *Mauritius:* Independence Day.
**13 Wed.** *Grenada:* National Day.
**14 Thu.** *Islamic:* New Year's Day (Hegira: 1423) (see App. B22).
**15 Fri.** *Far East Islamic:* New Year's Day (Hegira: 1423).
**17 Sun.** *Ireland:* Saint Patrick's Day. *Northern Ireland:* Saint Patrick's Day.
**18 Mon.** *Greece:* Shrove Monday. *Orthodox:* Shrove Monday.
**19 Tue.** *Christian:* Saint Joseph's Day (see App. A5).
**20 Wed.** *Afghanistan:* New Year's Day (Shamsi: 1381). *Iran:* New Year's Day (Hegira: 1381). *Iraq:* New Year's Day. *Tunisia:* Independence Day. *Zodiac Cusp:* Pisces ends, Aries begins.
**21 Thu.** *Japan:* Vernal Equinox. *Mexico:* Juarez Day.
**22 Fri.** *Puerto Rico:* Abolition Day.
**23 Sat.** *Pakistan:* Pakistan Day. *Islamic:* Ashura (see App. B23).
**24 Sun.** *Christian:* Palm Sunday.
**25 Mon.** *Cyprus:* Greek Independence Day. *Greece:* Independence Day. *Liechtenstein:* Annunciation. *Virgin Islands (U.S.):* Transfer Day.
**26 Tue.** *Bangladesh:* Independence Day. *Zambia:* Africa Day.
**27 Wed.** *Angola:* Evacuation Day. *Burma:* Resistance and Full Moon Day.

**28 Thu.** *Israel:* Passover. *Sri Lanka:* Full Moon Poya. *Christian:* Maundy Thursday (see App. B11). *Jewish:* Passover.

**29 Fri.** *Central African Republic:* Boganda Day. *Madagascar:* Memorial Day. *Taiwan:* Youth Day. *Christian:* Good Friday (see App. B12).

**30 Sat.** *Christian:* Holy Saturday (see App. B13).

**31 Sun.** *Malta:* National Day. *Christian:* Easter Sunday (see App. B14). *Europe:* Daylight Savings Time starts (advance clocks 1 hour).

# April 2002

**1 Mon.** *Iran:* Republic Day. *San Marino:* National Day. *Christian:* Easter Monday (see App. B15).

**4 Thu.** *Hungary:* Liberation Day. *Senegal:* National Day.

**5 Fri.** *Sierra Leone:* Bank Holiday. *South Korea:* Arbor Day. *Asian:* Tomb Sweeping Day (see App. A6).

**6 Sat.** *South Africa:* Founders' Day. *Thailand:* Chakri Day.

**7 Sun.** *Canada and United States:* Daylight Savings Time starts (advance clocks 1 hour).

**9 Tue.** *Philippines:* Valour Day. *Tunisia:* Martyrs' Day.

**11 Thu.** *Costa Rica:* Heroes' Day. *Uganda:* Liberation Day.

**13 Sat.** *Chad:* National Day. *Thailand:* Songkrawn (1st day of 2).

**14 Sun.** *Honduras:* Pan American Day. *Thailand:* Songkrawn (2nd day of 2).

**15 Mon.** *Niger:* National Day.

**16 Tue.** *Burma:* New Year's Day (Burmese: 1364). *Cyprus:* Independence Day.

**17 Wed.** *Cambodia:* Independence Day. *Israel:* Independence Day. *Syria:* Independence Day.

**18 Thu.** *Zimbabwe:* Republic Day.

**19 Fri.** *Sierra Leone:* Republic Day. *Uruguay:* Patriots' Day. *Venezuela:* Independence Day.

**20 Sat.** *Zodiac Cusp:* Aries ends, Taurus begins.

**21 Sun.** *Brazil:* Tiradentes Day.

**23 Tue.** *Turkey:* Children's Day.

**25 Thu.** *Australia:* ANZAC. *Burma:* Full Moon Day. *Egypt:* Sinai Day. *Iceland:* Children's Day. *Italy:* Liberation Day. *New Zealand:* ANZAC Day. *Portugal:* Liberation Day. *Swaziland:* Flag Day.

**26 Fri.** *Denmark:* All Prayers' Day. *Sri Lanka:* Full Moon Poya. *Tanzania:* Union Day.

**27 Sat.** *Afghanistan:* Independence Day. *Sierra Leone:* Independence Day. *Togo:* Independence Day.

**29 Mon.** *Japan:* Green Day.

**30 Tue.** *Finland:* Vappu Day. *Netherlands:* Queen's Birthday.

# May 2002

**1 Wed.** *Multinational:* Labor Day (see App. A7).

**2 Thu.** *Lesotho:* King's Birthday.

**3 Fri.** *Japan:* Constitution Day. *Orthodox:* Good Friday (see App. B20).

**4 Sat.** *Japan:* People's Day.

**5 Sun.** *Japan:* Children's Day. *Jordan:* Easter Sunday. *Mexico:* Cinco de Mayo. *Netherlands:* Liberation Day. *South Korea:* Children's Day. *Thailand:* Coronation Day. *Orthodox:* Easter Sunday.

**6 Mon.** *Lebanon:* Martyrs' Day. *Philippines:* Corregidor Day. *United Kingdom:* Labour Day. *Zambia:* Labour

Day. *Orthodox:* Easter Monday (see App. B20).

**8 Wed.** *France:* Liberation Day.

**9 Thu.** *Czech Republic:* Liberation Day*. *Slovakia:* Liberation Day. *Christian:* Ascension (see App. B16).

**10 Fri.** *Micronesia:* Independence Day.

**12 Sun.** *International:* Mother's Day.

**14 Tue.** *Liberia:* Unification Day. *Malawi:* Kamuzu Day. *Paraguay:* Flag Day.

**15 Wed.** *Paraguay:* Independence Day.

**17 Fri.** *Cayman Islands:* Discovery Day. *Israel:* Pentecost. *Norway:* Constitution Day. *Jewish:* Pentecost.

**18 Sat.** *Haiti:* Flag Day. *Uruguay:* Las Piedras Day.

**19 Sun.** *Finland:* Flag Day. *South Korea:* Vesak Day. *Turkey:* Youth Day. *Christian:* Whitsunday.

**20 Mon.** *Cameroon:* Constitution Day. *Canada:* Victoria Day. *Zaïre:* Popular Movement Day. *Christian:* Whitmonday (see App. B18).

**21 Tue.** *Chile:* Navy Day. *Zodiac Cusp:* Taurus ends, Gemini begins.

**22 Wed.** *Haiti:* Sovereign Day. *Sri Lanka:* Heroes' Day.

**23 Thu.** *Jamaica:* Labour Day. *Islamic:* Mohammed's Birthday (see App. B24).

**24 Fri.** *Bulgaria:* Culture Day. *Ecuador:* Independence Battle Day. *Far East Islamic:* Mohammed's Birthday.

**25 Sat.** *Argentina:* National Day. *Burma:* Full Moon Day. *Eritrea:* Independence Day*. *Jordan:* Independence Day. *Sri Lanka:* Full Moon Poya. *Sudan:* Revolution Day. *Multinational:* Africa Day (see App. A8).

**26 Sun.** *Guyana:* Independence Day. *Malaysia:* Vesak Day. *Singapore:* Vesak Day. *Thailand:* Visakha Bucha Day.

**27 Mon.** *Nigeria:* Children's Day. *United Kingdom:* Spring Break. *United States:* Memorial Day.

**30 Thu.** *Christian:* Corpus Christi (see App. B19).

**31 Fri.** *Brunei:* Regiment Day. *South Africa:* Republic Day.

# June 2002

**1 Sat.** *Kenya:* Madaraka Day. *Tunisia:* National Day. *Western Samoa:* Independence Day.

**2 Sun.** *Italy:* Republic Day. *Tunisia:* Youth Day.

**3 Mon.** *Ireland:* Public Holiday. *New Zealand:* Queen's Birthday.

**4 Tue.** *Bahamas:* Labour Day. *Tonga:* Independence Day.

**5 Wed.** *Denmark:* Constitution Day. *Equatorial Guinea:* President's Birthday. *Malaysia:* King's Birthday. *Seychelles:* Liberation Day.

**6 Thu.** *South Korea:* Memorial Day. *Sweden:* Constitution Day.

**7 Fri.** *Chad:* Revolution Day.

**8 Sat.** *Hong Kong:* Queen's Birthday (1st day of 2).

**9 Sun.** *Argentina:* Independence Day.

**10 Mon.** *Australia:* Queen's Birthday. *Fiji:* Queen's Birthday. *Hong Kong:* Queen's Birthday (2nd day of 2). *Macao:* Portugal Day. *New Guinea:* Queen's Birthday. *Portugal:* Portugal Day. *United Kingdom:* Queen's Birthday.

**11 Tue.** *Libya:* Evacuation Day.

**12 Wed.** *Philippines:* Independence Day.

**16 Sun.** *Asian:* Dragon Boat Festival (see App. B5).

**17 Mon.** *Germany:* Unity Day. *Iceland:* Independence Day.

**18 Tue.** *Egypt:* Independence Day.

**19 Wed.** *Algeria:* Righting Day. *Kuwait:* Independence Day. *Uruguay:* Artigas Day.

**20 Thu.** *Argentina:* Flag Day.

**21 Fri.** *Finland:* Midsummer Day (1st day of 2). *Sweden:* Midsummer Day (1st day of 2). *Zodiac Cusp:* Gemini ends, Cancer begins.

**22 Sat.** *Finland:* Johannus and Midsummer Day (2nd day of 2). *Sweden:* Midsummer Day (2nd day of 2).

**23 Sun.** *Burma:* Full Moon Day. *Luxembourg:* National Day. *Orthodox:* Pentecost Sunday.

**24 Mon.** *Andorra:* Saint John's Day. *Greece:* Pentecost Monday. *Sri Lanka:* Full Moon Poya. *Venezuela:* Carabobo Day. *Zaïre:* Constitution Day.

**25 Tue.** *Croatia:* Independence Day*. *Mozambique:* Independence Day. *Slovenia:* Independence Day*.

**26 Wed.** *Madagascar:* Independence Day. *Somalia:* Independence Day.

**27 Thu.** *Djibouti:* Independence Day.

**28 Fri.** *Chile:* Bank Holiday. *Ecuador:* Bank Holiday. *El Salvador:* Bank Holiday. *Finland:* Bank Holiday.

**29 Sat.** *Seychelles:* Independence Day. *Christian:* Saint Paul's Day (see App. A9).

**30 Sun.** *Guatemala:* Army Day. *Sri Lanka:* Bank Holiday. *Zaïre:* Independence Day.

# July 2002

**1 Mon.** *Burundi:* Independence Day. *Canada:* Canada Day. *Cayman Islands:* Constitution Day. *Ghana:* Republic Day. *Hong Kong:* Half Year Day. *Lesotho:* Family Day. *Rwanda:* Independence Day. *Somalia:* Union Day. *Suriname:* Freedom Day. *Zambia:* Heroes' Day. *Multinational:* Bank Holiday (see App. A10).

**2 Tue.** *Zambia:* Unity Day.

**4 Thu.** *Philippines:* United States Friendship Day. *United States:* Independence Day. *Yugoslavia:* Freedom Fighters' Day.

**5 Fri.** *Algeria:* Independence Day. *Cape Verde:* Independence Day. *Rwanda:* Unity Day. *Venezuela:* Independence Day.

**6 Sat.** *Comoros:* Independence Day. *Malawi:* Republic Day.

**7 Sun.** *Solomon Islands:* Independence Day. *Tanzania:* Farmers' Day. *Yugoslavia:* Serbian Day.

**10 Wed.** *Bahamas:* Independence Day.

**11 Thu.** *Mongolia:* Revolution Day.

**12 Fri.** *Kiribati:* Independence Day. *Northern Ireland:* Battle of the Boyne Day. *São Tomé:* National Day.

**14 Sun.** *France:* National Day. *Iraq:* Revolution Day.

**15 Mon.** *Botswana:* President's Day. *Brunei:* Sultan's Birthday.

**17 Wed.** *Iraq:* Revolution Day. *Puerto Rico:* Rivera Day. *Slovakia:* Independence Day*. *South Korea:* Constitution Day.

**18 Thu.** *Israel:* Tisha Ab. *Uruguay:* Constitution Day. *Jewish:* Tisha Ab.

**19 Fri.** *Burma:* Martyrs' Day. *Laos:* Independence Day. *Nicaragua:* Sandinista Day.

**20 Sat.** *Colombia:* Independence Day.

**21 Sun.** *Belgium:* National Day. *Guam:* Liberation Day.

**22 Mon.** *Burma:* Full Moon Day. *Poland:* Liberation Day. *Virgin Islands (U.S.):* Hurricane Supplication Day.

**23 Tue.** *Egypt:* Revolution Day. *New Guinea:* Remembrance Day. *Sri Lanka:* Full Moon Poya. *Zodiac Cusp:* Cancer ends, Leo begins.

**24 Wed.** *Thailand:* Asalaha Bucha Day. *Venezuela:* Bolivar Day.

**25 Thu.** *Costa Rica:* Guanacaste Day. *Cuba:* Revolution Day (1st day of 3). *Puerto Rico:* Constitution Day. *Spain:* Santiago Day. *Thailand:* Khao Phansa Day. *Tunisia:* Republic Day.

**26 Fri.** *Cuba:* Revolution Day (2nd

day of 3). *Liberia:* Independence Day. *Maldives:* Independence Day.

**27 Sat.** *Cuba:* Revolution Day (3rd day of 3). *Puerto Rico:* Barbosa Day.

**28 Sun.** *Peru:* Independence Day (1st day of 2).

**29 Mon.** *Peru:* Independence Day (2nd day of 2).

**30 Tue.** *Vanuatu:* Independence Day.

# August 2002

**1 Thu.** *Benin:* Independence Day. *Switzerland:* Confederation Day.

**2 Fri.** *Costa Rica:* Virgin of the Angels Day. *Guyana:* Freedom Day. *Trinidad:* Discovery Day.

**3 Sat.** *El Salvador:* Summer Day (1st day of 4). *Guinea-Bissau:* Martyrs' Day. *Niger:* Independence Day. *Tunisia:* President's Birthday.

**4 Sun.** *Burkina Faso:* Independence Day (1st day of 2). *El Salvador:* Summer Day (2nd day of 4).

**5 Mon.** *Bahamas:* Emancipation Day. *Barbados:* Emancipation Day. *Burkina Faso:* Independence Day (2nd day of 2). *Canada:* Civic Holiday. *El Salvador:* Summer Day (3rd day of 4). *Ireland:* Public Holiday. *Jamaica:* Independence Day. *Scotland:* Public Holiday.

**6 Tue.** *Bolivia:* Independence Day. *El Salvador:* Summer Day (4th day of 4). *United Arab Emirates:* Accession Day.

**7 Wed.** *Colombia:* Boyaca Day. *Ivory Coast:* Republic Day. *Zambia:* Farmers' Day.

**9 Fri.** *Georgia:* Independence Day*. *Singapore:* National Day.

**10 Sat.** *Ecuador:* Independence Day.

**11 Sun.** *Chad:* Independence Day. *Jordan:* Accession Day. *Zimbabwe:* Heroes' Day (1st day of 2).

**12 Mon.** *Thailand:* Queen's Birthday. *Zimbabwe:* Heroes' Day (2nd day of 2).

**13 Tue.** *Central African Republic:* Independence Day. *Congo:* Independence Day (1st day of 2). *Tunisia:* Women's Day.

**14 Wed.** *Congo:* Independence Day (2nd day of 2). *Pakistan:* Independence Day.

**15 Thu.** *Congo:* Independence Day (3rd day of 3). *India:* Independence Day. *Liechtenstein:* National Day. *South Korea:* Republic Day. *Christian:* Assumption (see App. A11).

**16 Fri.** *Dominican Republic:* Republic Day.

**17 Sat.** *Argentina:* San Martin's Day. *Gabon:* Independence Day. *Indonesia:* Independence Day.

**20 Tue.** *Hungary:* Constitution Day. *Senegal:* Independence Day.

**21 Wed.** *Burma:* Full Moon Day. *Estonia:* Independence Day*. *Latvia:* Independence Day*. *Lithuania:* Independence Day*.

**22 Thu.** *Sri Lanka:* Full Moon Poya.

**23 Fri.** *Romania:* National Day (1st day of 2). *Zodiac Cusp:* Leo ends, Virgo begins.

**24 Sat.** *Hong Kong:* Liberation Day (1st day of 2). *Kazakhstan:* National Day*. *Liberia:* Flag Day. *Romania:* National Day (2nd day of 2). *Russia:* Independence Day*. *Ukraine:* National Day*.

**25 Sun.** *Belarus:* Independence Day*. *Paraguay:* Constitution Day. *Uruguay:* Independence Day.

**26 Mon.** *England:* Summer Break. *Hong Kong:* Liberation Day (2nd day of 2). *Northern Ireland:* Summer Break. *Wales:* Summer Break.

**27 Tue.** *Moldova:* Independence Day*.

**29 Thu.** *Uzbekistan:* Independence Day*.

**30 Fri.** *Afghanistan:* Children's Day.

*Azerbaijan:* Independence Day*. *Peru:* Rose of Lima Day. *Turkey:* Victory Day.

**31 Sat.** *Afghanistan:* Pashtunistan Day. *Kyrgyzstan:* Independence Day*. *Malaysia:* National Day. *Trinidad:* Independence Day.

# September 2002

**1 Sun.** *Libya:* National Day. *Mexico:* President's Message Day. *Syria:* United Arab Republics Day.

**2 Mon.** *Canada:* Labour Day. *Luxembourg:* Fair Day. *United States:* Labor Day. *Vietnam:* Independence Day.

**3 Tue.** *Qatar:* National Day. *San Marino:* Saint Marinus' Day. *Tunisia:* Independence Movement Day.

**6 Fri.** *Pakistan:* Defense Day. *Swaziland:* Independence Day.

**7 Sat.** *Brazil:* Independence Day. *Israel:* New Year's Day. *Jewish:* Rosh Hashanah (Jewish: 5763).

**8 Sun.** *Andorra:* National Day. *Malta:* Our Lady of Victory Day.

**9 Mon.** *Bulgaria:* National Day (1st day of 2). *North Korea:* Independence Day. *Tajikistan:* Independence Day*.

**10 Tue.** *Belize:* National Day. *Bulgaria:* National Day (2nd day of 2).

**11 Wed.** *Chile:* Revolution Day. *Egypt:* New Year's Day (Coptic: 1720). *Ethiopia:* New Year's Day (Ethiopian: 1996). *Pakistan:* Anniversary of Quaid-e-Azam's Death.

**12 Thu.** *Ethiopia:* National Day.

**14 Sat.** *Guatemala:* San Jacinto Day. *Nicaragua:* San Jacinto Day.

**15 Sun.** *Costa Rica:* Independence Day. *El Salvador:* Independence Day. *Guatemala:* Independence Day. *Honduras:* Independence Day. *Japan:* Veneration Day. *Nicaragua:* Independence Day.

**16 Mon.** *Israel:* Yom Kippur. *Mexico:* Independence Day. *New Guinea:* Independence Day. *Jewish:* Yom Kippur.

**17 Tue.** *Angola:* Heroes' Day. *Marshall Islands:* Independence Day.

**18 Wed.** *Burundi:* Victory of Uprona Day. *Chile:* Independence Day.

**19 Thu.** *Chile:* Armed Forces Day. *Saint Kitts:* Independence Day.

**20 Fri.** *Burma:* Full Moon Day.

**21 Sat.** *Belize:* Independence Day. *Israel:* Sukkot. *Malta:* Independence Day. *Sri Lanka:* Full Moon Poya. *Jewish:* Sukkot.

**22 Sun.** *Mali:* Independence Day.

**23 Mon.** *Armenia:* Independence Day*. *Japan:* Autumnal Equinox. *Saudi Arabia:* National Day. *Zodiac Cusp:* Virgo ends, Libra begins.

**24 Tue.** *Dominican Republic:* Mercedes Day. *Guinea-Bissau:* Republic Day.

**25 Wed.** *Mozambique:* Liberation Day. *Rwanda:* Assembly Day.

**26 Thu.** *Ethiopia:* True Cross Day.

**28 Sat.** *Taiwan:* Teachers' Day.

**29 Sun.** *Brunei:* Constitution Day. *Paraguay:* Boqueron Battle Day. Europe: Daylight Savings Time ends (retard clocks 1 hour).

**30 Mon.** *Botswana:* Independence Day.

# October 2002

**1 Tue.** *Cameroon:* Unification Day. *China:* National Day (1st day of 2). *Nigeria:* Independence Day. *South Korea:* Armed Forces Day (1st day of 2). *Tuvalu:* Independence Day.

**2 Wed.** *China:* National Day (2nd

day of 2). *Guinea:* Independence Day. *India:* Ghandi Day. *South Korea:* Armed Forces Day. (2nd day of 2).

**3 Thu.** *Honduras:* Morazan Day. *South Korea:* Foundation Day (1st day of 2). *Islamic:* Isra a Majraj (see App. B30).

**4 Fri.** *Lesotho:* Independence Day. *South Korea:* Foundation Day (2nd day of 2).

**5 Sat.** *Lesotho:* Sports Day. *Macao:* Portuguese Republic Day. *Portugal:* Republic Day.

**6 Sun.** *Egypt:* Armed Forces Day.

**7 Mon.** *Barbados:* Bank Holiday.

**9 Wed.** *Peru:* National Dignity Day. *South Korea:* Alphabet Day. *Uganda:* Independence Day.

**10 Thu.** *Japan:* Health Day. *South Africa:* Kruger Day. *Taiwan:* National Day.

**11 Fri.** *Cuba:* Independence War. *Panama:* Revolution Day.

**12 Sat.** *Equatorial Guinea:* Independence Day. *Spain:* National Day. *Multinational:* Columbus Day (see App. A12).

**14 Mon.** *Canada:* Thanksgiving Day. *Fiji:* Cession Day. *United States:* Bank Holiday. *Virgin Islands (U.S.):* Puerto Rican Friendship Day. *Zaïre:* Founders' Day.

**15 Tue.** *Bosnia and Herzegovina:* Independence Day*. *Tunisia:* Evacuation Day. *Asian:* Ancestors' Day (see App. B6).

**17 Thu.** *Haiti:* Dessalines Day. *Malawi:* Mother's Day.

**19 Sat.** *Burma:* Full Moon Day.

**20 Sun.** *China:* Mid-autumn Day. *Guatemala:* Revolution Day. *Kenya:* Kenyatta Day. *Sri Lanka:* Full Moon Poya. *Taiwan:* Mid-autumn Day.

**21 Mon.** *Hong Kong:* Mid-autumn Day. *Honduras:* Army Day. *Jamaica:* Heroes' Day. *Macao:* Mid-autumn Day. *Somalia:* Revolution Day (1st day of 2).

**22 Tue.** *Somalia:* Revolution Day (2nd day of 2). *Vatican:* John Paul II Day.

**23 Wed.** *Hungary:* Revolution Day. *Thailand:* Chulalongkorn Day. *Zodiac Cusp:* Libra ends, Scorpio begins.

**24 Thu.** *Egypt:* Suez Victory Day. *Haiti:* United Nations Day. *Zambia:* Independence Day.

**25 Fri.** *Taiwan:* Restoration Day.

**26 Sat.** *Austria:* National Day. *Benin:* Revolution Day. *Rwanda:* Government Day.

**27 Sun.** *Saint Vincent:* Independence Day. *Turkmenistan:* Independence Day*. *Zaïre:* Naming Day. *Canada and United States:* Daylight Savings Time ends (retard clocks 1 hour).

**28 Mon.** *Greece:* Ohi! Day. *Ireland:* Public Holiday. *New Zealand:* Labour Day.

**29 Tue.** *Tanzania:* Naming Day. *Turkey:* Republic Day.

**31 Thu.** *Taiwan:* Chiang Kai-shek's Birthday.

# November 2002

**1 Fri.** *Algeria:* Revolution Day. *Antigua:* Independence Day. *Christian:* All Saints' Day (see App. A13).

**2 Sat.** *Brazil:* Memorial Day. *Finland:* All Saints' Eve. *Sweden:* All Saints' Eve. *Christian:* All Souls' Day (see App. A14).

**3 Sun.** *Dominica:* Independence Day. *Ecuador:* Cuenca Independence Day. *Japan:* Culture Day. *Panama:* Independence Day. *Hindu:* Deepavali (see App. B21).

**4 Mon.** *Andorra:* Saint Charles' Day. *Panama:* Flag Day. *Virgin Islands (U.S.):* Liberty Day. *Vatican:* John Paul II's Nameday.

**5 Tue.** *El Salvador:* Cry of Independence Day.

**6 Wed.** *Islamic:* 1st Day of Ramadan (see App. B25).

**7 Thu.** *Bangladesh:* Revolution Day. *Liberia:* Thanksgiving Day.

**8 Fri.** *Nepal:* Queen's Birthday.

**9 Sat.** *Pakistan:* Iqbal Day.

**10 Sun.** *Panama:* Cry of Independence Day.

**11 Mon.** *Angola:* Independence Day. *Bhutan:* King's Birthday. *Maldives:* Republic Day. *Poland:* Independence Day. *Multinational:* Armistice Day (see App. A15).

**12 Tue.** *Taiwan:* Dr. Sun Yat-sen's Birthday.

**14 Thu.** *Jordan:* King's Birthday.

**15 Fri.** *Brazil:* Republic Day.

**17 Sun.** *Zaïre:* Armed Forces Day.

**18 Mon.** *Burma:* Full Moon Day. *Fiji:* Prince Charles' Birthday. *Haiti:* Vertieres' Day. *Morocco:* Independence Day. *Oman:* National Day.

**19 Tue.** *Belize:* Garifuna Day. *Mali:* Army Coup Day. *Monaco:* Prince Ranier's Day. *Puerto Rico:* Discovery Day. *Sri Lanka:* Full Moon Poya.

**20 Wed.** *Germany:* Repentance Day. *Mexico:* Revolution Day.

**22 Fri.** *Lebanon:* Independence Day. *Zodiac Cusp:* Scorpio ends, Sagittarius begins.

**23 Sat.** *Japan:* Labor Thanksgiving Day.

**24 Sun.** *Zaïre:* New Regime Day.

**25 Mon.** *Suriname:* Independence Day.

**28 Thu.** *Albania:* Independence Day. *Burundi:* Republic Day. *Chad:* Republic Day. *Mauritania:* Independence Day. *Panama:* Independence Day. *United States:* Thanksgiving Day.

**29 Fri.** *Albania:* Liberation Day. *Argentina:* Bank Holiday. *Liberia:* Tubman's Birthday. *Yugoslavia:* Republic Day.

**30 Sat.** *Barbados:* Independence Day. *Benin:* National Day. *Philippines:* Heroes' Day. *Jewish:* Chanukah.

# December 2002

**1 Sun.** *Central African Republic:* National Day. *Portugal:* Youth Day. *Ukraine:* Independence Day*.

**2 Mon.** *Laos:* Republic Day. *United Arab Emirates:* National Day.

**5 Thu.** *Haiti:* Discovery Day. *Thailand:* King's Birthday. *Far East Islamic:* Hari Raya Puasa (see App. B27). *Islamic:* Eid al Fitr (1st day of 4) (see App. B26).

**6 Fri.** *Finland:* Independence Day. *Islamic:* Eid al Fitr (2nd day of 4) (see App. B26).

**7 Sat.** *Ivory Coast:* Independence Day. *Islamic:* Eid al Fitr (3rd day of 4) (see App. B26).

**8 Sun.** *Christian:* Immaculate Conception (see App. A16). *Islamic:* Eid al Fitr (4th day of 4) (see App. B26).

**9 Mon.** *Tanzania:* Independence Day.

**10 Tue.** *Angola:* MPLA Foundation Day. *Equatorial Guinea:* Human Rights Day. *Namibia:* Settlers' Day. *Thailand:* Constitution Day.

**11 Wed.** *Burkina Faso:* National Day.

**12 Thu.** *Kenya:* Independence Day. *Mexico:* Guadalupe Festival.

**13 Fri.** *Malta:* Republic Day.

**16 Mon.** *Bahrain:* National Day. *Bangladesh:* Victory Day. *Nepal:* Constitution Day. *South Africa:* Covenant Day.

**17 Tue.** *Bhutan:* National Day.

**18 Wed.** *Burma:* Full Moon Day. *Niger:* Republic Day.

**19 Thu.** *Sri Lanka:* Full Moon Poya.

**21 Sat.** *Kazakhstan:* Independence Day*.

**22 Sun.** *Zodiac Cusp:* Sagittarius ends, Capricorn begins.

**23 Mon.** *Japan:* Emperor's Birthday.

**24 Tue.** *Multinational:* Christmas Eve (see App. A17).

**25 Wed.** *Angola:* Family Day. *Congo:* Children's Day. *Pakistan:* Quaid's Birthday. *Taiwan:* Constitution Day. *Multinational:* Christmas Day (see App. A18).

**26 Thu.** *South Africa:* Good Will Day. *Multinational:* Boxing Day (see App. A19).

**30 Mon.** *Madagascar:* Republic Day. *Philippines:* Rizal Day (1st day of 2).

**31 Tue.** *Congo:* Republic Day. *Philippines:* Rizal Day (2nd day of 2). *Multinational:* Bank Holiday and New Year's Eve (see App. A20 & A21).

# January 2003

**1 Wed.** *Cameroon:* Independence Day. *Cuba:* Liberation Day. *Haiti:* Independence Day. *Palau:* Independence Day. *Sudan:* Independence Day. *Taiwan:* Foundation Day (1st day of 2). *Western Samoa:* Independence Day. *Multinational:* Bank Holiday and New Year's Day (see App. A1 & A2).

**2 Thu.** *Japan:* Bank Holiday. *New Zealand:* New Year's Day (2nd day of 2). *Scotland:* New Year's Day (2nd day of 2). *South Korea:* New Year's Day (2nd day of 2). *Switzerland:* Berchtold's Day. *Taiwan:* Foundation Day (2nd day of 2).

**3 Fri.** *Burkina Faso:* Revolution Day.

**4 Sat.** *Burma:* Independence Day. *Zaïre:* Martyrs' Day.

**6 Mon.** *Iraq:* Army Day. *Uruguay:* Children's Day. *Christian:* Epiphany (see App. A3).

**7 Tue.** *Egypt:* Coptic Christmas. *Ethiopia:* Coptic Christmas.

**11 Sat.** *Albania:* Republic Day. *Nepal:* Unification Day. *Puerto Rico:* Hostos Day.

**12 Sun.** *Tanzania:* Revolution Day.

**13 Mon.** *Togo:* Liberation Day.

**15 Wed.** *Japan:* Adult's Day. *Jordan:* Arbor Day.

**16 Thu.** *Burma:* Full Moon Day.

**17 Fri.** *Sri Lanka:* Full Moon Poya.

**19 Sun.** *Ethiopia:* Epiphany.

**20 Mon.** *Mali:* Award Day. *United States:* Martin Luther King's Birthday. *Zodiac Cusp:* Capricorn ends, Aquarius begins.

**21 Tue.** *Dominican Republic:* Altagracia Day.

**22 Wed.** *Saint Vincent:* Discovery Day.

**26 Sun.** *Dominican Republic:* Duarte Day. *India:* Republic Day.

**27 Mon.** *Australia:* Australia Day. *Monaco:* Saint Devota's Day. *Vietnam:* Vietnam Day.

**28 Tue.** *Rwanda:* Democracy Day.

**31 Fri.** *Nauru:* Independence Day. *Asian:* Chinese New Year Eve (see App. B1).

# February 2003

**1 Sat.** *Vietnam:* Tet (1st day of 3). *Asian:* Chinese New Year (Year of the Sheep) (see App. B2).

**2 Sun.** *Liechtenstein:* Candlemas. *Vietnam:* Tet (2nd day of 3). *Asian:* 2nd Day of Chinese New Year (see App. B3).

**3 Mon.** *United States:* Lincoln's Birthday. *Vietnam:* Tet (3rd day of 3). *Asian:* 3rd Day of Chinese New Year (see App. B4).

**4 Tue.** *Sri Lanka:* Independence Day.

**5 Wed.** *Mexico:* Constitution Day.

**6 Thu.** *New Zealand:* Waitangi Day.

**7 Fri.** *Grenada:* Independence Day.

**8 Sat.** *Iraq:* Revolution Day.

**9 Sun.** *Lebanon:* Saint Marion's Day.

**10 Mon.** *Malta:* Saint Paul's Day. *Islamic:* Eid al Adha (1st day of 4) (see App. B28).

**11 Tue.** *Cameroon:* Youth Day. *Japan:* Foundation Day. *Liberia:* Armed Forces Day. *Far East Islamic:* Hari Raya Haji (see App. B29). *Islamic:* Eid al Adha (2nd day of 4) (see App. B28).

**12 Wed.** *Burma:* Union Day. *Islamic:* Eid al Adha (3rd day of 4) (see App. B28).

**13 Thu.** *Islamic:* Eid al Adha (4th day of 4) (see App. B28).

**14 Fri.** *International:* Valentine's Day.

**15 Sat.** *Burma:* Full Moon Day.

**16 Sun.** *Sri Lanka:* Full Moon Poya. *Thailand:* Makha Bucha Day.

**17 Mon.** *United States:* Washington's Birthday.

**18 Tue.** *Gambia:* Independence Day.

**19 Wed.** *Nepal:* National Day. *Zodiac Cusp:* Aquarius ends, Pisces begins.

**21 Fri.** *Bangladesh:* Saheed Day.

**22 Sat.** *Saint Lucia:* Independence Day.

**23 Sun.** *Brunei:* National Day. *Guyana:* Republic Day.

**25 Tue.** *Kuwait:* National Day.

**27 Thu.** *Dominican Republic:* Independence Day.

# March 2003

**1 Sat.** *South Korea:* Independence Day.

**2 Sun.** *Ethiopia:* Victory of Aduwa Day. *Morocco:* Independence Day.

**3 Mon.** *Bulgaria:* Liberation Day. *Guam:* Discovery Day. *Malawi:* Martyrs' Day. *Morocco:* National Day. *Christian:* Shrove Monday (see App. B7). *Islamic:* New Year's Day (Hegira: 1424) (see App. B22).

**4 Tue.** *Christian:* Shrove Tuesday (see App. B8). *Far East Islamic:* New Year's Day (Hegira: 1424).

**5 Wed.** *Christian:* Ash Wednesday (see App. B9).

**6 Thu.** *Ghana:* Independence Day.

**8 Sat.** *Syria:* Revolution Day. *Zambia:* Youth Day. *Multinational:* Women's Day (see App. A4).

**10 Mon.** *Gibraltar:* Commonwealth Day. *Greece:* Shrove Monday. *South Korea:* Labor Day. *Orthodox:* Shrove Monday.

**11 Tue.** *Lithuania:* National Day*.

**12 Wed.** *Lesotho:* Moshoeshoe's Day. *Mauritius:* Independence Day. *Islamic:* Ashura (see App. B23).

**13 Thu.** *Grenada:* National Day.

**16 Sun.** *Burma:* Full Moon Day.

**17 Mon.** *Ireland:* Saint Patrick's Day. *Northern Ireland:* Saint Patrick's Day. *Sri Lanka:* Full Moon Poya.

**18 Tue.** *Jewish:* Purim.

**19 Wed.** *Christian:* Saint Joseph's Day (see App. A5).

**20 Thu.** *Tunisia:* Independence Day.

**21 Fri.** *Afghanistan:* New Year's Day (Shamsi: 1382). *Iran:* New Year's Day (Hegira: 1382). *Iraq:* New Year's Day. *Japan:* Vernal Equinox. *Mexico:* Juarez Day. *Zodiac Cusp:* Pisces ends, Aries begins.

**22 Sat.** *Puerto Rico:* Abolition Day.

**23 Sun.** *Pakistan:* Pakistan Day.

**25 Tue.** *Cyprus:* Greek Independence Day. *Greece:* Independence Day. *Liechtenstein:* Annunciation. *Zambia:* Africa Day.

**26 Wed.** *Bangladesh:* Independence Day.

**27 Thu.** *Angola:* Evacuation Day. *Burma:* Resistance Day.

**29 Sat.** *Central African Republic:* Boganda Day. *Madagascar:* Memorial Day. *Taiwan:* Youth Day.

**30 Sun.** *Europe:* Daylight Savings Time starts (advance clocks 1 hour).

**31 Mon.** *Malta:* National Day. *Virgin Islands (U.S.):* Transfer Day.

# April 2003

**1 Tue.** *Iran:* Republic Day. *San Marino:* National Day.

**4 Fri.** *Hungary:* Liberation Day. *Senegal:* National Day. *Sierra Leone:* Bank Holiday.

**5 Sat.** *South Korea:* Arbor Day. *Asian:* Tomb Sweeping Day (see App. A6).

**6 Sun.** *South Africa:* Founders' Day. *Thailand:* Chakri Day. *Canada and United States:* Daylight Savings Time starts (advance clocks 1 hour).

**9 Wed.** *Philippines:* Valour Day. *Tunisia:* Martyrs' Day.

**11 Fri.** *Costa Rica:* Heroes' Day. *Uganda:* Liberation Day.

**13 Sun.** *Chad:* National Day. *Thailand:* Songkrawn (1st day of 2). *Christian:* Palm Sunday.

**14 Mon.** *Honduras:* Pan American Day. *Thailand:* Songkrawn (2nd day of 2).

**15 Tue.** *Burma:* Full Moon Day. *Niger:* National Day.

**16 Wed.** *Burma:* New Year's Day (Burmese: 1365). *Cyprus:* Independence Day. *Sri Lanka:* Full Moon Poya.

**17 Thu.** *Cambodia:* Independence Day. *Israel:* Passover. *Syria:* Independence Day. *Christian:* Maundy Thursday (see App. B11). *Jewish:* Passover.

**18 Fri.** *Zimbabwe:* Republic Day. *Christian:* Good Friday (see App. B12).

**19 Sat.** *Sierra Leone:* Republic Day. *Uruguay:* Patriots' Day. *Venezuela:* Independence Day. *Christian:* Holy Saturday (see App. B13).

**20 Sun.** *Christian:* Easter Sunday (see App. B14). *Zodiac Cusp:* Aries ends, Taurus begins.

**21 Mon.** *Brazil:* Tiradentes Day. *Christian:* Easter Monday (see App. B15).

**23 Wed.** *Turkey:* Children's Day.

**25 Fri.** *Australia:* ANZAC Day. *Egypt:* Sinai Day. *Iceland:* Children's Day. *Italy:* Liberation Day. *New Zealand:* ANZAC Day. *Portugal:* Liberation Day. *Swaziland:* Flag Day. *Orthodox:* Good Friday (see App. B20).

**26 Sat.** *Tanzania:* Union Day.

**27 Sun.** *Afghanistan:* Independence Day. *Jordan:* Easter Sunday Sierra Leone: Independence Day. *Togo:* Independence Day. *Orthodox:* Easter Sunday.

**28 Mon.** *Orthodox:* Easter Monday (see App. B20).

**29 Tue.** *Japan:* Green Day.

**30 Wed.** *Finland:* Vappu Day. *Netherlands:* Queen's Birthday.

# May 2003

**1 Thu.** *Multinational:* Labor Day (see App. A7).

**2 Fri.** *Lesotho:* King's Birthday.

**3 Sat.** *Japan:* Constitution Day.

**4 Sun.** *Japan:* People's Day.

**5 Mon.** *Japan:* Children's Day. *Mexico:* Cinco de Mayo. *Netherlands:* Liberation Day. *South Korea:* Children's Day. *Thailand:* Coronation Day. *United Kingdom:* Labour Day. *Zambia:* Labour Day.

**6 Tue.** *Lebanon:* Martyrs' Day. *Philippines:* Corregidor Day.

**7 Wed.** *Israel:* Independence Day.

**8 Thu.** *France:* Liberation Day. *South Korea:* Vesak Day.

**9 Fri.** *Czech Republic:* Liberation Day*. *Slovakia:* Liberation Day*.

**10 Sat.** *Micronesia:* Independence Day.

**11 Sun.** *International:* Mother's Day.

**12 Mon.** *Islamic:* Mohammed's Birthday (see App. B24).

**13 Tue.** *Far East Islamic:* Mohammed's Birthday.

**14 Wed.** *Burma:* Full Moon Day. *Liberia:* Unification Day. *Malawi:* Kamuzu Day. *Paraguay:* Flag Day.

**15 Thu.** *Malaysia:* Independence Day. *Paraguay:* Independence Day. *Singapore:* Vesak Day. *Sri Lanka:* Full Moon Poya. *Thailand:* Visakha Bucha Day.

**16 Fri.** *Denmark:* All Prayers' Day.

**17 Sat.** *Cayman Islands:* Discovery Day. *Norway:* Constitution Day.

**18 Sun.** *Haiti:* Flag Day. *Uruguay:* Las Piedras Day.

**19 Mon.** *Canada:* Victoria Day. *Finland:* Flag Day. *Turkey:* Youth Day.

**20 Tue.** *Cameroon:* Constitution Day. *Zaïre:* Popular Movement Day.

**21 Wed.** *Chile:* Navy Day. *Zodiac Cusp:* Taurus ends, Gemini begins.

**22 Thu.** *Haiti:* Sovereign Day. *Sri Lanka:* Heroes' Day.

**23 Fri.** *Jamaica:* Labour Day.

**24 Sat.** *Bulgaria:* Culture Day. *Ecuador:* Independence Battle Day.

**25 Sun.** *Argentina:* National Day. *Eritrea:* Independence Day*. *Jordan:* Independence Day. *Sudan:* Revolution Day. *Multinational:* Africa Day (see App. A8).

**26 Mon.** *Guyana:* Independence Day. *United Kingdom:* Spring Break. *United States:* Memorial Day.

**27 Tue.** *Nigeria:* Children's Day.

**29 Thu.** *Christian:* Ascension (see App. B16).

**31 Sat.** *Brunei:* Regiment Day. *South Africa:* Republic Day.

# June 2003

**1 Sun.** *Kenya:* Madaraka Day. *Tunisia:* National Day. *Western Samoa:* Independence Day.

**2 Mon.** *Ireland:* Public Holiday. *Italy:* Republic Day. *New Zealand:* Queen's Birthday. *Tunisia:* Youth Day.

**4 Wed.** *Bahamas:* Labour Day. *Malaysia:* King's Birthday. *Tonga:* Independence Day.

**5 Thu.** *Denmark:* Constitution Day. *Equatorial Guinea:* President's Birthday. *Seychelles:* Liberation Day.

**6 Fri.** *Israel:* Pentecost. *South Korea:* Memorial Day. *Sweden:* Constitution Day. *Asian:* Dragon Boat Festival (see App. B5). *Jewish:* Pentecost.

**7 Sat.** *Chad:* Revolution Day.

**8 Sun.** *Christian:* Whitsunday.

**9 Mon.** *Argentina:* Independence Day. *Australia:* Queen's Birthday. *Fiji:* Queen's Birthday. *New Guinea:* Queen's Birthday. *United Kingdom:* Queen's Birthday. *Christian:* Whitmonday (see App. B18).

**10 Tue.** *Macao:* Portugal Day. *Portugal:* Portugal Day.

**11 Wed.** *Libya:* Evacuation Day.

**12 Thu.** *Burma:* Full Moon Day. *Philippines:* Independence Day.

**13 Fri.** *Sri Lanka:* Full Moon Poya.

**14 Sat.** *Hong Kong:* Queen's Birthday (1st day of 2).

**15 Sun.** *Orthodox:* Pentecost Sunday.

**16 Mon.** *Greece:* Pentecost Monday. *Hong Kong:* Queen's Birthday (2nd day of 2).

**17 Tue.** *Germany:* Unity Day. *Iceland:* Independence Day.

**18 Wed.** *Egypt:* Independence Day.

**19 Thu.** *Algeria:* Righting Day. *Kuwait:* Independence Day. *Uruguay:* Artigas Day. *Christian:* Corpus Christi (see App. B19).

**20 Fri.** *Argentina:* Flag Day.

**21 Sat.** *Finland:* Johannus and Midsummer Day (1st day of 2). *Sweden:* Midsummer Day (1st day of 2). *Zodiac Cusp:* Gemini ends, Cancer begins.

**22 Sun.** *Finland:* Midsummer Day (2nd day of 2). *Sweden:* Midsummer Day (2nd day of 2).

**23 Mon.** *Luxembourg:* National Day.

**24 Tue.** *Andorra:* Saint John's Day. *Venezuela:* Carabobo Day. *Zaïre:* Constitution Day.

**25 Wed.** *Croatia:* Independence Day*. *Mozambique:* Independence Day. *Slovenia:* Independence Day*.

**26 Thu.** *Madagascar:* Independence Day. *Somalia:* Independence Day.

**27 Fri.** *Chile:* Bank Holiday. *Djibouti:* Independence Day. *Ecuador:* Bank Holiday. *El Salvador:* Bank Holiday. *Finland:* Bank Holiday.

**29 Sun.** *Seychelles:* Independence Day. *Christian:* Saint Paul's Day (see App. A9).

**30 Mon.** *Guatemala:* Army Day. *Sri Lanka:* Bank Holiday. *Zaïre:* Independence Day.

# July 2003

**1 Tue.** *Burundi:* Independence Day. *Canada:* Canada Day. *Ghana:* Republic Day. *Hong Kong:* Half Year Day. *Rwanda:* Independence Day. *Somalia:* Union Day. *Suriname:* Freedom Day. *Zambia:* Unity Day. *Multinational:* Bank Holiday (see App. A10).

**4 Fri.** *Philippines:* United States Friendship Day. *United States:* Independence Day. *Yugoslavia:* Freedom Fighters' Day.

**5 Sat.** *Algeria:* Independence Day. *Cape Verde:* Independence Day. *Rwanda:* Unity Day. *Venezuela:* Independence Day.

**6 Sun.** *Comoros:* Independence Day. *Malawi:* Republic Day.

**7 Mon.** *Cayman Islands:* Constitution Day. *Lesotho:* Family Day. *Solomon Islands:* Independence Day. *Tanzania:* Farmers' Day. *Yugoslavia:* Serbian Day. *Zambia:* Heroes' Day.

**10 Thu.** *Bahamas:* Independence Day.

**11 Fri.** *Mongolia:* Revolution Day.

**12 Sat.** *Burma:* Full Moon Day. *Kiribati:* Independence Day. *Northern Ireland:* Battle of the Boyne Day. *São Tomé:* National Day.

**13 Sun.** *Sri Lanka:* Full Moon Poya. *Thailand:* Asalaha Bucha Day.

**14 Mon.** *France:* National Day. *Iraq:* Revolution Day. *Thailand:* Khao Phansa Day.

**15 Tue.** *Brunei:* Sultan's Birthday.

**17 Thu.** *Iraq:* Revolution Day. *Puerto Rico:* Rivera Day. *Slovakia:* Independence Day*. *South Korea:* Constitution Day.

**18 Fri.** *Uruguay:* Constitution Day.

**19 Sat.** *Burma:* Martyrs' Day. *Laos:* Independence Day. *Nicaragua:* Sandinista Day.

**20 Sun.** *Colombia:* Independence Day.

**21 Mon.** *Belgium:* National Day. *Botswana:* President's Day. *Guam:* Liberation Day.

**22 Tue.** *Poland:* Liberation Day.

**23 Wed.** *Egypt:* Revolution Day. *New Guinea:* Remembrance Day. *Zodiac Cusp:* Cancer ends, Leo begins.

**24 Thu.** *Venezuela:* Bolivar Day.

**25 Fri.** *Costa Rica:* Guanacaste Day. *Cuba:* Revolution Day (1st day of 3). *Puerto Rico:* Constitution Day. *Spain:* Santiago Day. *Tunisia:* Republic Day.

**26 Sat.** *Cuba:* Revolution Day (2nd day of 3). *Liberia:* Independence Day. *Maldives:* Independence Day.

**27 Sun.** *Cuba:* Revolution Day (3rd day of 3). *Puerto Rico:* Barbosa Day.

**28 Mon.** *Peru:* Independence Day (1st day of 2). *Virgin Islands (U.S.):* Hurricane Supplication Day.

**29 Tue.** *Peru:* Independence Day (2nd day of 2).

**30 Wed.** *Vanuatu:* Independence Day.

# August 2003

**1 Fri.** *Benin:* Independence Day. *Switzerland:* Confederation Day.

**2 Sat.** *Costa Rica:* Virgin of the Angels Day. *Guyana:* Freedom Day. *Trinidad:* Discovery Day.

**3 Sun.** *El Salvador:* Summer Day (1st day of 4). *Guinea-Bissau:* Martyrs' Day. *Niger:* Independence Day. *Tunisia:* President's Birthday.

**4 Mon.** *Bahamas:* Emancipation Day. *Barbados:* Emancipation Day. *Burkina Faso:* Independence Day (1st day of 2). *Canada:* Civic Holiday. *El Salvador:* Summer Day (2nd day of 4). *Ireland:* Public Holiday. *Jamaica:* Independence Day. *Scotland:* Public Holiday.

**5 Tue.** *Burkina Faso:* Independence Day (2nd day of 2). *El Salvador:* Summer Day (3rd day of 4).

**6 Wed.** *Bolivia:* Independence Day. *El Salvador:* Summer Day (4th day of 4). *United Arab Emirates:* Accession Day. *Zambia:* Farmers' Day.

**7 Thu.** *Colombia:* Boyaca Day. *Israel:* Tisha Ab. *Ivory Coast:* Republic Day. *Jewish:* Tisha Ab.

**9 Sat.** *Georgia:* Independence Day*. *Singapore:* National Day.

**10 Sun.** *Burma:* Full Moon Day. *Ecuador:* Independence Day.

**11 Mon.** *Chad:* Independence Day. *Jordan:* Accession Day. *Sri Lanka:* Full Moon Poya. *Zimbabwe:* Heroes' Day (1st day of 2).

**12 Tue.** *Thailand:* Queen's Birthday. *Zimbabwe:* Heroes' Day (2nd day of 2).

**13 Wed.** *Central African Republic:* Independence Day. *Congo:* Independence Day (1st day of 2). *Tunisia:* Women's Day.

**14 Thu.** *Congo:* Independence Day (2nd day of 2). *Pakistan:* Independence Day.

**15 Fri.** *Congo:* Independence Day (3rd day of 3). *India:* Independence Day. *Liechtenstein:* National Day. *South Korea:* Republic Day. *Christian:* Assumption (see App. A11).

**16 Sat.** *Dominican Republic:* Republic Day.

**17 Sun.** *Argentina:* San Martin's Day. *Gabon:* Independence Day. *Indonesia:* Independence Day.

**20 Wed.** *Hungary:* Constitution Day. *Senegal:* Independence Day.

**21 Thu.** *Estonia:* Independence Day*. *Latvia:* Independence Day*. *Lithuania:* Independence Day*.

**23 Sat.** *Hong Kong:* Liberation Day (1st day of 2). *Romania:* National Day (1st day of 2). *Zodiac Cusp:* Leo ends, Virgo begins.

**24 Sun.** *Kazakhstan:* National Day*. *Liberia:* Flag Day. *Romania:* National Day (2nd day of 2). *Russia:* Independence Day*. *Ukraine:* National Day*.

**25 Mon.** *Belarus:* Independence Day*. *England:* Summer Break. *Hong Kong:* Liberation Day (2nd day of 2). *Northern Ireland:* Summer Break. *Paraguay:* Constitution Day. *Uruguay:* Independence Day. *Wales:* Summer Break.

**27 Wed.** *Moldova:* Independence Day*.

**29 Fri.** *Uzbekistan:* Independence Day*.

**30 Sat.** *Afghanistan:* Children's Day. *Azerbaijan:* Independence Day*. *Peru:* Rose of Lima Day. *Turkey:* Victory Day.

**31 Sun.** *Afghanistan:* Pashtunistan Day. *Kyrgyzstan:* Independence Day*. *Malaysia:* National Day. *Trinidad:* Independence Day.

# September 2003

**1 Mon.** *Canada:* Labour Day. *Libya:* National Day. *Luxembourg:* Fair Day. *Mexico:* President's Message Day. *Syria:* United Arab Republics Day. *United States:* Labor Day.

**2 Tue.** *Vietnam:* Independence Day.

**3 Wed.** *Qatar:* National Day. *San Marino:* Saint Marinus' Day. *Tunisia:* Independence Movement Day.

**6 Sat.** *Pakistan:* Defense Day. *Swaziland:* Independence Day.

**7 Sun.** *Brazil:* Independence Day.

**8 Mon.** *Andorra:* National Day. *Malta:* Our Lady of Victory Day.

**9 Tue.** *Bulgaria:* National Day (1st day of 2). *Burma:* Full Moon Day. *North Korea:* Independence Day. *Tajikistan:* Independence Day*.

**10 Wed.** *Belize:* National Day. *Bulgaria:* National Day (2nd day of 2). *Sri Lanka:* Full Moon Poya.

**11 Thu.** *Chile:* Revolution Day. *Pakistan:* Anniversary of Quaid-e-Azam's Death.

**12 Fri.** *Egypt:* New Year's Day (Coptic: 1721). *Ethiopia:* National Day and New Year's Day (Ethiopian: 1997).

**14 Sun.** *Guatemala:* San Jacinto Day. *Nicaragua:* San Jacinto Day.

**15 Mon.** *Costa Rica:* Independence Day. *El Salvador:* Independence Day. *Guatemala:* Independence Day. *Honduras:* Independence Day. *Japan:* Veneration Day. *Nicaragua:* Independence Day.

**16 Tue.** *Mexico:* Independence Day. *New Guinea:* Independence Day.

**17 Wed.** *Angola:* Heroes' Day. *Marshall Islands:* Independence Day.

**18 Thu.** *Burundi:* Victory of Uprona Day. *Chile:* Independence Day.

**19 Fri.** *Chile:* Armed Forces Day. *Saint Kitts:* Independence Day.

**21 Sun.** *Belize:* Independence Day. *Malta:* Independence Day.

**22 Mon.** *Mali:* Independence Day.

**23 Tue.** *Armenia:* Independence Day*. *Japan:* Autumnal Equinox. *Saudi Arabia:* National Day. *Islamic:* Isra a Majraj (see App. B30). *Zodiac Cusp:* Virgo ends, Libra begins.

**24 Wed.** *Dominican Republic:* Mercedes Day. *Guinea-Bissau:* Republic Day.

**25 Thu.** *Mozambique:* Liberation Day. *Rwanda:* Assembly Day.

**27 Sat.** *Ethiopia:* True Cross Day. *Israel:* New Year's Day. *Jewish:* Rosh Hashanah (Jewish: 5764).

**28 Sun.** *Taiwan:* Teachers' Day. *Europe:* Daylight Savings Time ends (retard clocks 1 hour).

**29 Mon.** *Brunei:* Constitution Day. *Paraguay:* Boqueron Battle Day.

**30 Tue.** *Botswana:* Independence Day.

# October 2003

**1 Wed.** *Cameroon:* Unification Day. *China:* National Day (1st day of 2). *Nigeria:* Independence Day. *South Korea:* Armed Forces Day (1st day of 2). *Tuvalu:* Independence Day.

**2 Thu.** *China:* National Day (2nd day of 2). *Guinea:* Independence Day. *India:* Ghandi Day. *South Korea:* Armed Forces Day (2nd day of 2).

**3 Fri.** *Honduras:* Morazan Day. *South Korea:* Foundation Day (1st day of 2).

**4 Sat.** *Lesotho:* Independence Day. *South Korea:* Foundation Day (2nd day of 2).

**5 Sun.** *Lesotho:* Sports Day. *Macao:* Portuguese Republic Day. *Portugal:* Republic Day. *Asian:* Ancestors' Day (see App. B6).

**6 Mon.** *Barbados:* Bank Holiday. *Egypt:* Armed Forces Day. *Israel:* Yom Kippur. *Jewish:* Yom Kippur.

**8 Wed.** *Burma:* Full Moon Day.

**9 Thu.** *China:* Mid-autumn Day. *Peru:* National Dignity Day. *South Korea:* Alphabet Day. *Sri Lanka:* Full Moon Poya. *Taiwan:* Mid-autumn Day. *Uganda:* Independence Day.

**10 Fri.** *Hong Kong:* Mid-autumn Day. *Japan:* Health Day. *Macao:* Mid-autumn Day. *South Africa:* Kruger Day. *Taiwan:* National Day.

**11 Sat.** *Cuba:* Independence War. *Israel:* Sukkot. *Panama:* Revolution Day. *Jewish:* Sukkot.

**12 Sun.** *Equatorial Guinea:* Independence Day. *Spain:* National Day. *Multinational:* Columbus Day (see App. A12).

**13 Mon.** *Canada:* Thanksgiving Day. *Fiji:* Cession Day. *United States:* Bank Holiday. *Virgin Islands (U.S.):* Puerto Rican Friendship Day.

**14 Tue.** *Zaïre:* Founders' Day.

**15 Wed.** *Bosnia and Herzegovina:* Independence Day*. *Tunisia:* Evacuation Day.

**17 Fri.** *Haiti:* Dessalines Day. *Malawi:* Mother's Day.

**20 Mon.** *Guatemala:* Revolution Day. *Jamaica:* Heroes' Day. *Kenya:* Kenyatta Day.

**21 Tue.** *Honduras:* Army Day. *Somalia:* Revolution Day (1st day of 2).

**22 Wed.** *Somalia:* Revolution Day (2nd day of 2). *Vatican:* John Paul II Day.

**23 Thu.** *Hungary:* Revolution Day. *Thailand:* Chulalongkorn Day. *Zodiac Cusp:* Libra ends, Scorpio begins.

**24 Fri.** *Egypt:* Suez Victory Day. *Haiti:* United Nations Day. *Zambia:* Independence Day. *Hindu:* Deepavali (see App. B21).

**25 Sat.** *Taiwan:* Restoration Day.

**26 Sun.** *Austria:* National Day. *Benin:* Revolution Day. *Rwanda:* Government Day. *Canada and United States:* Daylight Savings Time ends (retard clocks 1 hour). *Islamic:* 1st Day of Ramadan (see App. B25).

**27 Mon.** *Ireland:* Public Holiday. *New Zealand:* Labour Day. *Saint Vincent:* Independence Day. *Turkmenistan:* Independence Day*. *Zaïre:* Naming Day.

**28 Tue.** *Greece:* Ohi! Day.

**29 Wed.** *Tanzania:* Naming Day. *Turkey:* Republic Day.

**31 Fri.** *Taiwan:* Chiang Kai-shek's Birthday.

# November 2003

**1 Sat.** *Algeria:* Revolution Day. *Antigua:* Independence Day. *Christian:* All Saints' Day (see App. A13).

**2 Sun.** *Brazil:* Memorial Day. *Finland:* All Saints' Eve. *Sweden:* All Saints' Eve. *Christian:* All Souls' Day (see App. A14).

**3 Mon.** *Dominica:* Independence Day. *Ecuador:* Cuenca Independence Day. *Japan:* Culture Day. *Panama:* Independence Day. *Virgin Islands (U.S.):* Liberty Day.

**4 Tue.** *Andorra:* Saint Charles' Day. *Panama:* Flag Day. *Vatican:* John Paul II's Nameday.

**5 Wed.** *El Salvador:* Cry of Independence Day.

**6 Thu.** *Liberia:* Thanksgiving Day.

**7 Fri.** *Bangladesh:* Revolution Day. *Burma:* Full Moon Day.

**8 Sat.** *Nepal:* Queen's Birthday. *Sri Lanka:* Full Moon Poya.

**9 Sun.** *Pakistan:* Iqbal Day.

**10 Mon.** *Panama:* Cry of Independence Day.

**11 Tue.** *Angola:* Independence Day. *Bhutan:* King's Birthday. *Maldives:* Republic Day. *Poland:* Independence Day. *Multinational:* Armistice Day (see App. A15).

**12 Wed.** *Taiwan:* Dr. Sun Yat-sen's Birthday.

**14 Fri.** *Jordan:* King's Birthday.

**15 Sat.** *Brazil:* Republic Day.

**17 Mon.** *Fiji:* Prince Charles' Birthday. *Zaïre:* Armed Forces Day.

**18 Tue.** *Haiti:* Vertieres' Day. *Morocco:* Independence Day. *Oman:* National Day.

**19 Wed.** *Belize:* Garifuna Day. *Germany:* Repentance Day. *Mali:* Army Coup Day. *Monaco:* Prince Ranier's Day. *Puerto Rico:* Discovery Day.

**20 Thu.** *Mexico:* Revolution Day.

**22 Sat.** *Lebanon:* Independence Day. *Zodiac Cusp:* Scorpio ends, Sagittarius begins.

**23 Sun.** *Japan:* Labor Thanksgiving Day.

**24 Mon.** *Zaïre:* New Regime Day.

**25 Tue.** *Suriname:* Independence Day. *Far East Islamic:* Hari Raya Puasa (see App. B27). *Islamic:* Eid al Fitr (1st day of 4) (see App. B26).

**26 Wed.** *Islamic:* Eid al Fitr (2nd day of 4) (see App. B26).

**27 Thu.** *United States:* Thanksgiving Day. *Islamic:* Eid al Fitr (3rd day of 4) (see App. B26).

**28 Fri.** *Albania:* Independence Day. *Argentina:* Bank Holiday. *Burundi:* Republic Day. *Chad:* Republic Day. *Panama:* Independence Day. *Panama:* Independence Day. *Islamic:* Eid al Fitr (4th day of 4) (see App. B26).

**29 Sat.** *Albania:* Liberation Day. *Liberia:* Tubman's Birthday. *Yugoslavia:* Republic Day.

**30 Sun.** *Barbados:* Independence Day. *Benin:* National Day. *Philippines:* Heroes' Day.

# December 2003

**1 Mon.** *Central African Republic:* National Day. *Portugal:* Youth Day. *Ukraine:* Independence Day*.

**2 Tue.** *Laos:* Republic Day. *United Arab Emirates:* National Day.

**5 Fri.** *Haiti:* Discovery Day. *Thailand:* King's Birthday.

**6 Sat.** *Finland:* Independence Day.

**7 Sun.** *Burma:* Full Moon Day. *Ivory Coast:* Independence Day.

**8 Mon.** *Sri Lanka:* Full Moon Poya. *Christian:* Immaculate Conception (see App. A16).

**9 Tue.** *Tanzania:* Independence Day.

**10 Wed.** *Angola:* MPLA Foundation Day. *Equatorial Guinea:* Human Rights Day. *Namibia:* Settlers' Day. *Thailand:* Constitution Day.

**11 Thu.** *Burkina Faso:* National Day.

**12 Fri.** *Kenya:* Independence Day. *Mexico:* Guadalupe Festival.

**13 Sat.** *Malta:* Republic Day.

**16 Tue.** *Bahrain:* National Day. *Bangladesh:* Victory Day. *Nepal:* Constitution Day. *South Africa:* Covenant Day.

**17 Wed.** *Bhutan:* National Day.

**18 Thu.** *Niger:* Republic Day.

**20 Sat.** *Jewish:* Chanukah.

**21 Sun.** *Kazakhstan:* Independence Day*.

**22 Mon.** *Zodiac Cusp:* Sagittarius ends, Capricorn begins.

**23 Tue.** *Japan:* Emperor's Birthday.

**24 Wed.** *Multinational:* Christmas Eve (see App. A17).

**25 Thu.** *Angola:* Family Day. *Congo:* Children's Day. *Pakistan:* Quaid's Birthday. *Taiwan:* Constitution Day. *Multinational:* Christmas Day (see App. A18).

**26 Fri.** *South Africa:* Good Will Day. *Multinational:* Boxing Day (see App. A19).

**30 Tue.** *Madagascar:* Republic Day. *Philippines:* Rizal Day (1st day of 2).

**31 Wed.** *Congo:* Republic Day. *Philippines:* Rizal Day (2nd day of 2). *Multinational:* Bank Holiday and New Year's Eve (see App. A20 & A21).

# January 2004

**1 Thu.** *Cameroon:* Independence Day. *Cuba:* Liberation Day. *Haiti:* Independence Day. *Palau:* Independence Day. *Sudan:* Independence Day. *Tai-*

*wan:* Foundation Day (1st day of 2). *Western Samoa:* Independence Day. *Multinational:* Bank Holiday and New Year's Day (see App. A1 & A2).

**2 Fri.** *Japan:* Bank Holiday. *New Zealand:* New Year's Day (2nd day of 2). *Scotland:* New Year's Day (2nd day of 2). *South Korea:* New Year's Day (2nd day of 2). *Switzerland:* Berchtold's Day. *Taiwan:* Foundation Day (2nd day of 2).

**3 Sat.** *Burkina Faso:* Revolution Day.

**4 Sun.** *Burma:* Independence Day. *Zaïre:* Martyrs' Day.

**6 Tue.** *Burma:* Full Moon Day. *Iraq:* Army Day. *Uruguay:* Children's Day. *Christian:* Epiphany (see App. A3).

**7 Wed.** *Egypt:* Coptic Christmas. *Ethiopia:* Coptic Christmas. *Sri Lanka:* Full Moon Poya.

**11 Sun.** *Albania:* Republic Day. *Nepal:* Unification Day. *Puerto Rico:* Hostos Day.

**12 Mon.** *Tanzania:* Revolution Day.

**13 Tue.** *Togo:* Liberation Day.

**15 Thu.** *Japan:* Adult's Day. *Jordan:* Arbor Day.

**19 Mon.** *Ethiopia:* Epiphany. *United States:* Martin Luther King's Birthday. *Zodiac Cusp:* Capricorn ends, Aquarius begins.

**20 Tue.** *Mali:* Award Day.

**21 Wed.** *Dominican Republic:* Altagracia Day.

**22 Thu.** *Saint Vincent:* Discovery Day.

**26 Mon.** *Australia:* Australia Day. *Dominican Republic:* Duarte Day. *India:* Republic Day.

**27 Tue.** *Monaco:* Saint Devota's Day. *Vietnam:* Vietnam Day.

**28 Wed.** *Rwanda:* Democracy Day.

**31 Sat.** *Nauru:* Independence Day. *Islamic:* Eid al Adha (1st day of 4) (see App. B28).

# February 2004

**1 Sun.** *Far East Islamic:* Hari Raya Haji (see App. B29). *Islamic:* Eid al Adha (2nd day of 4) (see App. B28).

**2 Mon.** *Liechtenstein:* Candlemas. *United States:* Lincoln's Birthday. *Islamic:* Eid al Adha (3rd day of 4) (see App. B28).

**3 Tue.** *Islamic:* Eid al Adha (4th day of 4) (see App. B28).

**4 Wed.** *Burma:* Full Moon Day. *Sri Lanka:* Independence Day.

**5 Thu.** *Mexico:* Constitution Day. *Sri Lanka:* Full Moon Poya.

**6 Fri.** *New Zealand:* Waitangi Day.

**7 Sat.** *Grenada:* Independence Day.

**8 Sun.** *Iraq:* Revolution Day.

**9 Mon.** *Lebanon:* Saint Marion's Day.

**10 Tue.** *Malta:* Saint Paul's Day.

**11 Wed.** *Cameroon:* Youth Day. *Japan:* Foundation Day. *Liberia:* Armed Forces Day.

**12 Thu.** *Burma:* Union Day.

**14 Sat.** *International:* Valentine's Day.

**16 Mon.** *United States:* Washington's Birthday.

**18 Wed.** *Gambia:* Independence Day. *Zodiac Cusp:* Aquarius ends, Pisces begins.

**19 Thu.** *Nepal:* National Day. *Asian:* Chinese New Year Eve (see App. B1).

**20 Fri.** *Vietnam:* Tet (1st day of 3). *Asian:* Chinese New Year (Year of the Monkey) (see App. B2). *Islamic:* New Year's Day (Hegira: 1425) (see App. B22).

**21 Sat.** *Bangladesh:* Saheed Day. *Vietnam:* Tet (2nd day of 3). *Asian:* 2nd Day of Chinese New Year (see App. B3). *Far East Islamic:* New Year's Day (Hegira: 1425).

**22 Sun.** *Saint Lucia:* Independence Day. *Vietnam:* Tet (3rd day of 3). *Asian:* 3rd Day of Chinese New Year.

**23 Mon.** *Brunei:* National Day.

*Greece:* Shrove Monday. *Guyana:* Republic Day. *Christian:* Shrove Monday (see App. B7). *Orthodox:* Shrove Monday.

**24 Tue.** *Christian:* Shrove Tuesday (see App. B8).

**25 Wed.** *Kuwait:* National Day. *Christian:* Ash Wednesday (see App. B9).

**27 Fri.** *Dominican Republic:* Independence Day.

**29 Sun.** *Islamic:* Ashura (see App. B23).

# March 2004

**1 Mon.** *Guam:* Discovery Day. *South Korea:* Independence Day.

**2 Tue.** *Ethiopia:* Victory of Aduwa Day. *Morocco:* Independence Day.

**3 Wed.** *Bulgaria:* Liberation Day. *Malawi:* Martyrs' Day. *Morocco:* National Day.

**5 Fri.** *Burma:* Full Moon Day. *Thailand:* Makha Bucha Day.

**6 Sat.** *Ghana:* Independence Day. *Sri Lanka:* Full Moon Poya.

**7 Sun.** *Jewish:* Purim.

**8 Mon.** *Gibraltar:* Commonwealth Day. *Syria:* Revolution Day. *Multinational:* Women's Day (see App. A4).

**10 Wed.** *South Korea:* Labor Day.

**11 Thu.** *Lithuania:* National Day*.

**12 Fri.** *Lesotho:* Moshoeshoe's Day. *Mauritius:* Independence Day.

**13 Sat.** *Grenada:* National Day. *Zambia:* Youth Day.

**17 Wed.** *Ireland:* Saint Patrick's Day. *Northern Ireland:* Saint Patrick's Day.

**19 Fri.** *Christian:* Saint Joseph's Day (see App. A5).

**20 Sat.** *Afghanistan:* New Year's Day (Shamsi: 1383). *Iran:* New Year's Day (Hegira: 1383). *Iraq:* New Year's Day. *Japan:* Vernal Equinox. *Tunisia:* Independence Day. *Zodiac Cusp:* Pisces ends, Aries begins.

**21 Sun.** *Mexico:* Juarez Day.

**22 Mon.** *Puerto Rico:* Abolition Day.

**23 Tue.** *Pakistan:* Pakistan Day. *Zambia:* Africa Day.

**25 Thu.** *Cyprus:* Greek Independence Day. *Greece:* Independence Day. *Liechtenstein:* Annunciation.

**26 Fri.** *Bangladesh:* Independence Day.

**27 Sat.** *Angola:* Evacuation Day. *Burma:* Resistance Day.

**28 Sun.** *Europe:* Daylight Savings Time starts (advance clocks 1 hour).

**29 Mon.** *Central African Republic:* Boganda Day. *Madagascar:* Memorial Day. *Taiwan:* Youth Day. *Virgin Islands (U.S.):* Transfer Day.

**31 Wed.** *Malta:* National Day.

# April 2004

**1 Thu.** *Iran:* Republic Day. *San Marino:* National Day.

**2 Fri.** *Sierra Leone:* Bank Holiday.

**3 Sat.** *Burma:* Full Moon Day.

**4 Sun.** *Hungary:* Liberation Day. *Sri Lanka:* Full Moon Poya. *Senegal:* National Day. *Canada and United States:* Daylight Savings Time starts (advance clocks 1 hour). *Christian:* Palm Sunday.

**5 Mon.** *South Korea:* Arbor Day. *Asian:* Tomb Sweeping Day (see App. A6).

**6 Tue.** *Israel:* Passover. *South Africa:* Founders' Day. *Thailand:* Chakri Day. *Jewish:* Passover.

**8 Thu.** *Christian:* Maundy Thursday (see App. B11).

**9 Fri.** *Philippines:* Valour Day. *Tunisia:* Martyrs' Day. *Christian:*

Good Friday (see App. B12). *Orthodox:* Good Friday (see App. B20).

**10 Sat.** *Christian:* Holy Saturday (see App. B13).

**11 Sun.** *Costa Rica:* Heroes' Day. *Jordan:* Easter Sunday. *Uganda:* Liberation Day. *Christian:* Easter Sunday (see App. B14). *Orthodox:* Easter Sunday.

**12 Mon.** *Christian:* Easter Monday (see App. B15). *Orthodox:* Easter Monday (see App. B20).

**13 Tue.** *Chad:* National Day. *Thailand:* Songkrawn (1st day of 2).

**14 Wed.** *Honduras:* Pan American Day. *Thailand:* Songkrawn (2nd day of 2).

**15 Thu.** *Niger:* National Day.

**16 Fri.** *Burma:* New Year's Day (Burmese: 1366). *Cyprus:* Independence Day.

**17 Sat.** *Cambodia:* Independence Day. *Syria:* Independence Day.

**18 Sun.** *Zimbabwe:* Republic Day.

**19 Mon.** *Sierra Leone:* Republic Day. *Uruguay:* Patriots' Day. *Venezuela:* Independence Day. *Zodiac Cusp:* Aries ends, Taurus begins.

**21 Wed.** *Brazil:* Tiradentes Day.

**23 Fri.** *Turkey:* Children's Day.

**25 Sun.** *Australia:* ANZAC Day. *Egypt:* Sinai Day. *Iceland:* Children's Day. *Italy:* Liberation Day. *New Zealand:* ANZAC Day. *Portugal:* Liberation Day. *Swaziland:* Flag Day.

**26 Mon.** *Israel:* Independence Day. *Tanzania:* Union Day.

**27 Tue.** *Afghanistan:* Independence Day. *Sierra Leone:* Independence Day. *Togo:* Independence Day.

**29 Thu.** *Japan:* Green Day.

**30 Fri.** *Finland:* Vappu Day. *Netherlands:* Queen's Birthday. *Islamic:* Mohammed's Birthday (see App. B24).

# May 2004

**1 Sat.** *Far East Islamic:* Mohammed's Birthday. *Multinational:* Labor Day (see App. A7).

**2 Sun.** *Lesotho:* King's Birthday.

**3 Mon.** *Burma:* Full Moon Day. *Japan:* Constitution Day. *United Kingdom:* Labour Day. *Zambia:* Labour Day.

**4 Tue.** *Japan:* People's Day. *Sri Lanka:* Full Moon Poya.

**5 Wed.** *Japan:* Children's Day. *Mexico:* Cinco de Mayo. *Netherlands:* Liberation Day. *South Korea:* Children's Day. *Thailand:* Coronation Day.

**6 Thu.** *Lebanon:* Martyrs' Day. *Philippines:* Corregidor Day.

**7 Fri.** *Denmark:* All Prayers' Day.

**8 Sat.** *France:* Liberation Day.

**9 Sun.** *Czech Republic:* Liberation Day*. *Slovakia:* Liberation Day*. *International:* Mother's Day.

**10 Mon.** *Micronesia:* Independence Day.

**14 Fri.** *Liberia:* Unification Day. *Malawi:* Kamuzu Day. *Paraguay:* Flag Day.

**15 Sat.** *Paraguay:* Independence Day.

**17 Mon.** *Cayman Islands:* Discovery Day. *Norway:* Constitution Day.

**18 Tue.** *Haiti:* Flag Day. *Uruguay:* Las Piedras Day.

**19 Wed.** *Finland:* Flag Day. *Turkey:* Youth Day.

**20 Thu.** *Cameroon:* Constitution Day. *Zaïre:* Popular Movement Day. *Christian:* Ascension (see App. B16). *Zodiac Cusp:* Taurus ends, Gemini begins.

**21 Fri.** *Chile:* Navy Day.

**22 Sat.** *Haiti:* Sovereign Day. *Sri Lanka:* Heroes' Day.

**23 Sun.** *Jamaica:* Labour Day.

**24 Mon.** *Bulgaria:* Culture Day. *Canada:* Victoria Day. *Ecuador:* Independence Battle Day.

**25 Tue.** *Argentina:* National Day. *Eritrea:* Independence Day*. *Jordan:* Independence Day. *Sudan:* Revolution

Day. *Multinational:* Africa Day (see App. A8).

**26 Wed.** *Guyana:* Independence Day. *Israel:* Pentecost. *South Korea:* Vesak Day. *Jewish:* Pentecost.

**27 Thu.** *Nigeria:* Children's Day.

**30 Sun.** *Christian:* Whitsunday. *Orthodox:* Pentecost Sunday.

**31 Mon.** *Brunei:* Regiment Day. *Greece:* Pentecost Monday. *South Africa:* Republic Day. *United Kingdom:* Spring Break. *United States:* Memorial Day. *Christian:* Whitmonday (see App. B18).

# June 2004

**1 Tue.** *Burma:* Full Moon Day. *Kenya:* Madaraka Day. *Tunisia:* National Day. *Western Samoa:* Independence Day.

**2 Wed.** *Italy:* Republic Day. *Malaysia:* King's Birthday and Vesak Day. *Singapore:* Vesak Day. *Sri Lanka:* Full Moon Poya. *Thailand:* Visakha Bucha Day. *Tunisia:* Youth Day.

**4 Fri.** *Bahamas:* Labour Day. *Tonga:* Independence Day.

**5 Sat.** *Denmark:* Constitution Day. *Equatorial Guinea:* President's Birthday. *Seychelles:* Liberation Day.

**6 Sun.** *South Korea:* Memorial Day. *Sweden:* Constitution Day.

**7 Mon.** *Chad:* Revolution Day. *Ireland:* Public Holiday. *New Zealand:* Queen's Birthday.

**9 Wed.** *Argentina:* Independence Day.

**10 Thu.** *Macao:* Portugal Day. *Portugal:* Portugal Day. *Christian:* Corpus Christi (see App. B19).

**11 Fri.** *Libya:* Evacuation Day.

**12 Sat.** *Hong Kong:* Queen's Birthday (1st day of 2). *Philippines:* Independence Day.

**14 Mon.** *Australia:* Queen's Birthday. *Fiji:* Queen's Birthday. *Hong Kong:* Queen's Birthday (2nd day of 2). *New Guinea:* Queen's Birthday. *United Kingdom:* Queen's Birthday.

**17 Thu.** *Germany:* Unity Day. *Iceland:* Independence Day.

**18 Fri.** *Egypt:* Independence Day.

**19 Sat.** *Algeria:* Righting Day. *Kuwait:* Independence Day. *Uruguay:* Artigas Day.

**20 Sun.** *Argentina:* Flag Day.

**21 Mon.** *Finland:* Midsummer Day (1st day of 2). *Sweden:* Midsummer Day (1st day of 2). *Zodiac Cusp:* Gemini ends, Cancer begins.

**22 Tue.** *Finland:* Midsummer Day (2nd day of 2). *Sweden:* Midsummer Day (2nd day of 2).

**23 Wed.** *Luxembourg:* National Day. *Asian:* Dragon Boat Festival (see App. B5).

**24 Thu.** *Andorra:* Saint John's Day. *Venezuela:* Carabobo Day. *Zaïre:* Constitution Day.

**25 Fri.** *Chile:* Bank Holiday. *Croatia:* Independence Day*. *Ecuador:* Bank Holiday. *El Salvador:* Bank Holiday. *Finland:* Bank Holiday. *Mozambique:* Independence Day. *Slovenia:* Independence Day*.

**26 Sat.** *Finland:* Johannus Day. *Madagascar:* Independence Day. *Somalia:* Independence Day.

**27 Sun.** *Djibouti:* Independence Day.

**29 Tue.** *Seychelles:* Independence Day. *Christian:* Saint Paul's Day (see App. A9).

**30 Wed.** *Burma:* Full Moon Day. *Guatemala:* Army Day. *Sri Lanka:* Bank Holiday. *Zaïre:* Independence Day.

# July 2004

**1 Thu.** *Burundi:* Independence Day. *Canada:* Canada Day. *Ghana:* Republic Day. *Hong Kong:* Half Year Day. *Rwanda:* Independence Day. *Somalia:* Union Day. *Sri Lanka:* Full Moon Poya. *Suriname:* Freedom Day. *Multinational:* Bank Holiday (see App. A10).

**4 Sun.** *Philippines:* United States Friendship Day. *United States:* Independence Day. *Yugoslavia:* Freedom Fighters' Day.

**5 Mon.** *Algeria:* Independence Day. *Cape Verde:* Independence Day. *Cayman Islands:* Constitution Day. *Lesotho:* Family Day. *Rwanda:* Unity Day. *Venezuela:* Independence Day. *Zambia:* Heroes' Day.

**6 Tue.** *Comoros:* Independence Day. *Malawi:* Republic Day. *Zambia:* Unity Day.

**7 Wed.** *Solomon Islands:* Independence Day. *Tanzania:* Farmers' Day. *Yugoslavia:* Serbian Day.

**10 Sat.** *Bahamas:* Independence Day.

**11 Sun.** *Mongolia:* Revolution Day.

**12 Mon.** *Kiribati:* Independence Day. *Northern Ireland:* Battle of the Boyne Day. *São Tomé:* National Day.

**14 Wed.** *France:* National Day. *Iraq:* Revolution Day.

**15 Thu.** *Brunei:* Sultan's Birthday.

**17 Sat.** *Iraq:* Revolution Day. *Puerto Rico:* Rivera Day. *Slovakia:* Independence Day*. *South Korea:* Constitution Day.

**18 Sun.** *Uruguay:* Constitution Day.

**19 Mon.** *Botswana:* President's Day. *Burma:* Martyrs' Day. *Laos:* Independence Day. *Nicaragua:* Sandinista Day.

**20 Tue.** *Colombia:* Independence Day.

**21 Wed.** *Belgium:* National Day. *Guam:* Liberation Day.

**22 Thu.** *Poland:* Liberation Day. *Zodiac Cusp:* Cancer ends, Leo begins.

**23 Fri.** *Egypt:* Revolution Day. *New Guinea:* Remembrance Day.

**24 Sat.** *Venezuela:* Bolivar Day.

**25 Sun.** *Costa Rica:* Guanacaste Day. *Cuba:* Revolution Day (1st day of 3). *Puerto Rico:* Constitution Day. *Spain:* Santiago Day. *Tunisia:* Republic Day.

**26 Mon.** *Cuba:* Revolution Day (2nd day of 3). *Liberia:* Independence Day. *Maldives:* Independence Day. *Virgin Islands (U.S.):* Hurricane Supplication Day.

**27 Tue.** *Cuba:* Revolution Day (3rd day of 3). *Israel:* Tisha Ab. *Puerto Rico:* Barbosa Day. *Jewish:* Tisha Ab.

**28 Wed.** *Peru:* Independence Day (1st day of 2).

**29 Thu.** *Peru:* Independence Day (2nd day of 2).

**30 Fri.** *Burma:* Full Moon Day. *Vanuatu:* Independence Day.

**31 Sat.** *Sri Lanka:* Full Moon Poya. *Thailand:* Asalaha Bucha Day.

# August 2004

**1 Sun.** *Benin:* Independence Day. *Switzerland:* Confederation Day. *Thailand:* Khao Phansa Day.

**2 Mon.** *Bahamas:* Emancipation Day. *Barbados:* Emancipation Day. Canada: Civic Holiday. *Costa Rica:* Virgin of the Angels Day. *Guyana:* Freedom Day. *Ireland:* Public Holiday. *Jamaica:* Independence Day. *Scotland:* Public Holiday. *Trinidad:* Discovery Day.

**3 Tue.** *El Salvador:* Summer Day (1st day of 4). *Guinea-Bissau:* Martyrs' Day. *Niger:* Independence Day. *Tunisia:* President's Birthday.

**4 Wed.** *Burkina Faso:* Independence

Day (1st day of 2). *El Salvador:* Summer Day (2nd day of 4). *Zambia:* Farmers' Day.

**5 Thu.** *Burkina Faso:* Independence Day (2nd day of 2). *El Salvador:* Summer Day (3rd day of 4).

**6 Fri.** *Bolivia:* Independence Day. *El Salvador:* Summer Day (4th day of 4). *United Arab Emirates:* Accession Day.

**7 Sat.** *Colombia:* Boyaca Day. *Ivory Coast:* Republic Day.

**9 Mon.** *Georgia:* Independence Day*. *Singapore:* National Day.

**10 Tue.** *Ecuador:* Independence Day.

**11 Wed.** *Chad:* Independence Day. *Jordan:* Accession Day. *Zimbabwe:* Heroes' Day (1st day of 2).

**12 Thu.** *Thailand:* Queen's Birthday. *Zimbabwe:* Heroes' Day (2nd day of 2).

**13 Fri.** *Central African Republic:* Independence Day. *Congo:* Independence Day (1st day of 2). *Tunisia:* Women's Day.

**14 Sat.** *Congo:* Independence Day (2nd day of 2). *Pakistan:* Independence Day.

**15 Sun.** *Congo:* Independence Day (3rd day of 3). *India:* Independence Day. *Liechtenstein:* National Day. *South Korea:* Republic Day. *Christian:* Assumption (see App. A11).

**16 Mon.** *Dominican Republic:* Republic Day.

**17 Tue.** *Argentina:* San Martin's Day. *Gabon:* Independence Day. *Indonesia:* Independence Day.

**20 Fri.** *Hungary:* Constitution Day. *Senegal:* Independence Day.

**21 Sat.** *Estonia:* Independence Day*. *Latvia:* Independence Day*. *Lithuania:* Independence Day*.

**22 Sun.** *Zodiac Cusp:* Leo ends, Virgo begins.

**23 Mon.** *Romania:* National Day (1st day of 2).

**24 Tue.** *Kazakhstan:* National Day*. *Liberia:* Flag Day. *Romania:* National Day (2nd day of 2). *Russia:* Independence Day*. *Ukraine:* National Day*.

**25 Wed.** *Belarus:* Independence Day*. *Paraguay:* Constitution Day. *Uruguay:* Independence Day.

**27 Fri.** *Moldova:* Independence Day*.

**28 Sat.** *Burma:* Full Moon Day. *Hong Kong:* Liberation Day (1st day of 2).

**29 Sun.** *Sri Lanka:* Full Moon Poya. *Uzbekistan:* Independence Day*.

**30 Mon.** *Afghanistan:* Children's Day. *Azerbaijan:* Independence Day*. *England:* Summer Break. *Hong Kong:* Liberation Day (2nd day of 2). *Luxembourg:* Fair Day. *Northern Ireland:* Summer Break. *Peru:* Rose of Lima Day. *Turkey:* Victory Day. *Wales:* Summer Break.

**31 Tue.** *Afghanistan:* Pashtunistan Day. *Kyrgyzstan:* Independence Day*. *Malaysia:* National Day. *Trinidad:* Independence Day.

# September 2004

**1 Wed.** *Libya:* National Day. *Mexico:* President's Message Day. *Syria:* United Arab Republics Day.

**2 Thu.** *Vietnam:* Independence Day.

**3 Fri.** *Qatar:* National Day. *San Marino:* Saint Marinus' Day. *Tunisia:* Independence Movement Day.

**6 Mon.** *Canada:* Labour Day. *Pakistan:* Defense Day. *Swaziland:* Independence Day. *United States:* Labor Day.

**7 Tue.** *Brazil:* Independence Day.

**8 Wed.** *Andorra:* National Day. *Malta:* Our Lady of Victory Day.

**9 Thu.** *Bulgaria:* National Day (1st day of 2). *North Korea:* Independence Day. *Tajikistan:* Independence Day*.

**10 Fri.** *Belize:* National Day. *Bulgaria:* National Day (2nd day of 2).

**11 Sat.** *Chile:* Revolution Day. *Egypt:* New Year's Day (Coptic: 1722).

*Ethiopia:* New Year's Day (Ethiopian: 1998). *Pakistan:* Anniversary of Quaid-e-Azam's Death. *Islamic:* Isra a Majraj (see App. B30).

**12 Sun.** *Ethiopia:* National Day.

**14 Tue.** *Guatemala:* San Jacinto Day. *Nicaragua:* San Jacinto Day.

**15 Wed.** *Costa Rica:* Independence Day. *El Salvador:* Independence Day. *Guatemala:* Independence Day. *Honduras:* Independence Day. *Japan:* Veneration Day. *Nicaragua:* Independence Day.

**16 Thu.** *Israel:* New Year's Day. *Mexico:* Independence Day. *New Guinea:* Independence Day. *Jewish:* Rosh Hashanah (Jewish: 5765).

**17 Fri.** *Angola:* Heroes' Day. *Marshall Islands:* Independence Day.

**18 Sat.** *Burundi:* Victory of Uprona Day. *Chile:* Independence Day.

**19 Sun.** *Chile:* Armed Forces Day. *Saint Kitts:* Independence Day.

**21 Tue.** *Belize:* Independence Day. *Malta:* Independence Day.

**22 Wed.** *Mali:* Independence Day. *Zodiac Cusp:* Virgo ends, Libra begins.

**23 Thu.** *Armenia:* Independence Day*. *Japan:* Autumnal Equinox. *Saudi Arabia:* National Day.

**24 Fri.** *Dominican Republic:* Mercedes Day. *Guinea-Bissau:* Republic Day.

**25 Sat.** *Israel:* Yom Kippur. *Mozambique:* Liberation Day. *Rwanda:* Assembly Day. *Jewish:* Yom Kippur.

**26 Sun.** *Ethiopia:* True Cross Day. *Europe:* Daylight Savings Time ends (retard clocks 1 hour).

**27 Mon.** *Burma:* Full Moon Day. *China:* Mid-autumn Day. *Sri Lanka:* Full Moon Poya. *Taiwan:* Mid-autumn Day.

**28 Tue.** *Hong Kong:* Mid-autumn Day. *Macao:* Mid-autumn Day. *Taiwan:* Teachers' Day.

**29 Wed.** *Brunei:* Constitution Day. *Paraguay:* Boqueron Battle Day.

**30 Thu.** *Botswana:* Independence Day. *Israel:* Sukkot. *Jewish:* Sukkot.

# October 2004

**1 Fri.** *Cameroon:* Unification Day. *China:* National Day (1st day of 2). *Nigeria:* Independence Day. *South Korea:* Armed Forces Day (1st day of 2). *Tuvalu:* Independence Day.

**2 Sat.** *China:* National Day (2nd day of 2). *Guinea:* Independence Day. *India:* Ghandi Day. *South Korea:* Armed Forces Day (2nd day of 2).

**3 Sun.** *Honduras:* Morazan Day. *South Korea:* Foundation Day (1st day of 2).

**4 Mon.** *Barbados:* Bank Holiday. *Lesotho:* Independence Day. *South Korea:* Foundation Day (2nd day of 2).

**5 Tue.** *Lesotho:* Sports Day. *Macao:* Portuguese Republic Day. *Portugal:* Republic Day.

**6 Wed.** *Egypt:* Armed Forces Day.

**9 Sat.** *Peru:* National Dignity Day. *South Korea:* Alphabet Day. *Uganda:* Independence Day.

**10 Sun.** *Japan:* Health Day. *South Africa:* Kruger Day. *Taiwan:* National Day.

**11 Mon.** *Canada:* Thanksgiving Day. *Cuba:* Independence War. *Fiji:* Cession Day. *Panama:* Revolution Day. *United States:* Bank Holiday. *Virgin Islands (U.S.):* Puerto Rican Friendship Day.

**12 Tue.** *Equatorial Guinea:* Independence Day. *Spain:* National Day. *Multinational:* Columbus Day (see App. A12).

**14 Thu.** *Zaïre:* Founders' Day.

**15 Fri.** *Bosnia and Herzegovina:* Independence Day*. *Tunisia:* Evacuation Day. *Islamic:* 1st Day of Ramadan (see App. B25).

**17 Sun.** *Haiti:* Dessalines Day. *Malawi:* Mother's Day.

**18 Mon.** *Jamaica:* Heroes' Day.

**20 Wed.** *Guatemala:* Revolution Day. *Kenya:* Kenyatta Day.

**21 Thu.** *Honduras:* Army Day. *Somalia:* Revolution Day (1st day of 2).

**22 Fri.** *Somalia:* Revolution Day (2nd day of 2). *Vatican:* John Paul II Day.

**23 Sat.** *Hungary:* Revolution Day. *Thailand:* Chulalongkorn Day. *Asian:* Ancestors' Day (see App. B6). *Zodiac Cusp:* Libra ends, Scorpio begins.

**24 Sun.** *Egypt:* Suez Victory Day. *Haiti:* United Nations Day. *Zambia:* Independence Day.

**25 Mon.** *Ireland:* Public Holiday. *New Zealand:* Labour Day. *Taiwan:* Restoration Day.

**26 Tue.** *Austria:* National Day. *Benin:* Revolution Day. *Burma:* Full Moon Day. *Rwanda:* Government Day.

**27 Wed.** *Saint Vincent:* Independence Day. *Sri Lanka:* Full Moon Poya. *Turkmenistan:* Independence Day*. *Zaïre:* Naming Day.

**28 Thu.** *Greece:* Ohi! Day.

**29 Fri.** *Tanzania:* Naming Day. *Turkey:* Republic Day.

**31 Sun.** *Taiwan:* Chiang Kai-shek's Birthday. *Canada and United States:* Daylight Savings Time ends (retard clocks 1 hour).

# November 2004

**1 Mon.** *Algeria:* Revolution Day. *Antigua:* Independence Day. *Virgin Islands (U.S.):* Liberty Day. *Christian:* All Saints' Day (see App. A13).

**2 Tue.** *Brazil:* Memorial Day. *Finland:* All Saints' Eve. *Sweden:* All Saints' Eve. *Christian:* All Souls' Day (see App. A14).

**3 Wed.** *Dominica:* Independence Day. *Ecuador:* Cuenca Independence Day. *Japan:* Culture Day. *Panama:* Independence Day.

**4 Thu.** *Andorra:* Saint Charles' Day. *Liberia:* Thanksgiving Day. *Panama:* Flag Day. *Vatican:* John Paul II's Nameday.

**5 Fri.** *El Salvador:* Cry of Independence Day.

**7 Sun.** *Bangladesh:* Revolution Day.

**8 Mon.** *Nepal:* Queen's Birthday.

**9 Tue.** *Pakistan:* Iqbal Day.

**10 Wed.** *Panama:* Cry of Independence Day.

**11 Thu.** *Angola:* Independence Day. *Bhutan:* King's Birthday. *Maldives:* Republic Day. *Poland:* Independence Day. *Hindu:* Deepavali (see App. B21). *Multinational:* Armistice Day (see App. A15).

**12 Fri.** *Taiwan:* Dr. Sun Yat-sen's Birthday.

**13 Sat.** *Far East Islamic:* Hari Raya Puasa (see App. B27). *Islamic:* Eid al Fitr (1st day of 4) (see App. B26).

**14 Sun.** *Jordan:* King's Birthday. *Islamic:* Eid al Fitr (2nd day of 4) (see App. B26).

**15 Mon.** *Brazil:* Republic Day. *Fiji:* Prince Charles' Birthday. *Islamic:* Eid al Fitr (3rd day of 4) (see App. B26).

**16 Tue.** *Islamic:* Eid al Fitr (4th day of 4) (see App. B26).

**17 Wed.** *Germany:* Repentance Day. *Zaïre:* Armed Forces Day.

**18 Thu.** *Haiti:* Vertieres' Day. *Morocco:* Independence Day. *Oman:* National Day.

**19 Fri.** *Belize:* Garifuna Day. *Mali:* Army Coup Day. *Monaco:* Prince Ranier's Day. *Puerto Rico:* Discovery Day.

**20 Sat.** *Mexico:* Revolution Day.

**21 Sun.** *Zodiac Cusp:* Scorpio ends, Sagittarius begins.

**22 Mon.** *Lebanon:* Independence Day.

**23 Tue.** *Japan:* Labor Thanksgiving Day.

**24 Wed.** *Zaïre:* New Regime Day.

**25 Thu.** *Burma:* Full Moon Day. *Suriname:* Independence Day. *United States:* Thanksgiving Day.

**26 Fri.** *Argentina:* Bank Holiday. *Sri Lanka:* Full Moon Poya.

**28 Sun.** *Albania:* Independence Day. *Burundi:* Republic Day. *Chad:* Republic Day. *Mauritania:* Independence Day. *Panama:* Independence Day.

**29 Mon.** *Albania:* Liberation Day. *Liberia:* Tubman's Birthday. *Yugoslavia:* Republic Day.

**30 Tue.** *Barbados:* Independence Day. *Benin:* National Day. *Philippines:* Heroes' Day.

# December 2004

**1 Wed.** *Central African Republic:* National Day. *Portugal:* Youth Day. *Ukraine:* Independence Day*.

**2 Thu.** *Laos:* Republic Day. *United Arab Emirates:* National Day.

**5 Sun.** *Haiti:* Discovery Day. *Thailand:* King's Birthday.

**6 Mon.** *Finland:* Independence Day.

**7 Tue.** *Ivory Coast:* Independence Day.

**8 Wed.** *Christian:* Immaculate Conception (see App. A16). *Jewish:* Chanukah.

**9 Thu.** *Tanzania:* Independence Day.

**10 Fri.** *Angola:* MPLA Foundation Day. *Equatorial Guinea:* Human Rights Day. *Namibia:* Settlers' Day. *Thailand:* Constitution Day.

**11 Sat.** *Burkina Faso:* National Day.

**12 Sun.** *Kenya:* Independence Day. *Mexico:* Guadalupe Festival.

**13 Mon.** *Malta:* Republic Day.

**16 Thu.** *Bahrain:* National Day. *Bangladesh:* Victory Day. *Nepal:* Constitution Day. *South Africa:* Covenant Day.

**17 Fri.** *Bhutan:* National Day.

**18 Sat.** *Niger:* Republic Day.

**21 Tue.** *Kazakhstan:* Independence Day*. *Zodiac Cusp:* Sagittarius ends, Capricorn begins.

**23 Thu.** *Japan:* Emperor's Birthday.

**24 Fri.** *Multinational:* Christmas Eve (see App. A17).

**25 Sat.** *Angola:* Family Day. *Burma:* Full Moon Day. *Congo:* Children's Day. *Pakistan:* Quaid's Birthday. *Taiwan:* Constitution Day. *Multinational:* Christmas Day (see App. A18).

**26 Sun.** *South Africa:* Good Will Day. *Sri Lanka:* Full Moon Poya. *Multinational:* Boxing Day (see App. A19).

**27 Mon.** *Hong Kong:* Boxing Day.

**30 Thu.** *Madagascar:* Republic Day. *Philippines:* Rizal Day (1st day of 2).

**31 Fri.** *Congo:* Republic Day. *Philippines:* Rizal Day (2nd day of 2). *Multinational:* Bank Holiday and New Year's Eve (see App. A20 & A21).

# January 2005

**1 Sat.** *Cameroon:* Independence Day. *Cuba:* Liberation Day. *Haiti:* Independence Day. *Palau:* Independence Day. *Sudan:* Independence Day. *Taiwan:* Foundation Day (1st day of 2). *Western Samoa:* Independence Day. *Multinational:* Bank Holiday and New Year's Day (see App. A1 & A2).

**2 Sun.** *Japan:* Bank Holiday. *New Zealand:* New Year's Day (2nd day of 2). *South Korea:* New Year's Day (2nd day of 2). *Switzerland:* Berchtold's

Day. *Taiwan:* Foundation Day (2nd day of 2).

**3 Mon.** *Burkina Faso:* Revolution Day. *Hong Kong:* New Year's Day. *Scotland:* New Year's Day (2nd day of 2).

**4 Tue.** *Burma:* Independence Day. *Zaïre:* Martyrs' Day.

**6 Thu.** *Iraq:* Army Day. *Uruguay:* Children's Day. *Christian:* Epiphany (see App. A3).

**7 Fri.** *Egypt:* Coptic Christmas. *Ethiopia:* Coptic Christmas.

**11 Tue.** *Albania:* Republic Day. *Nepal:* Unification Day. *Puerto Rico:* Hostos Day.

**12 Wed.** *Tanzania:* Revolution Day.

**13 Thu.** *Togo:* Liberation Day.

**15 Sat.** *Japan:* Adult's Day. *Jordan:* Arbor Day.

**17 Mon.** *United States:* Martin Luther King's Birthday.

**19 Wed.** *Ethiopia:* Epiphany.

**20 Thu.** *Mali:* Award Day. *Islamic:* Eid al Adha (1st day of 4) (see App. B28). *Zodiac Cusp:* Capricorn ends, Aquarius begins.

**21 Fri.** *Dominican Republic:* Altagracia Day. *Far East Islamic:* Hari Raya Haji (see App. B29). *Islamic:* Eid al Adha (2nd day of 4) (see App. B28).

**22 Sat.** *Saint Vincent:* Discovery Day. *Islamic:* Eid al Adha (3rd day of 4) (see App. B28).

**23 Sun.** *Burma:* Full Moon Day. *Islamic:* Eid al Adha (4th day of 4) (see App. B28).

**24 Mon.** *Sri Lanka:* Full Moon Poya.

**26 Wed.** *Dominican Republic:* Duarte Day. *India:* Republic Day.

**27 Thu.** *Monaco:* Saint Devota's Day. *Vietnam:* Vietnam Day.

**28 Fri.** *Rwanda:* Democracy Day.

**31 Mon.** *Australia:* Australia Day. *Nauru:* Independence Day.

# February 2005

**2 Wed.** *Liechtenstein:* Candlemas.

**4 Fri.** *Sri Lanka:* Independence Day.

**5 Sat.** *Mexico:* Constitution Day.

**6 Sun.** *New Zealand:* Waitangi Day.

**7 Mon.** *Grenada:* Independence Day. *United States:* Lincoln's Birthday. *Christian:* Shrove Monday (see App. B7).

**8 Tue.** *Iraq:* Revolution Day. *Asian:* Chinese New Year Eve (see App. B1). *Christian:* Shrove Tuesday (see App. B8).

**9 Wed.** *Lebanon:* Saint Marion's Day. *Vietnam:* Tet (1st day of 3). *Asian:* Chinese New Year (Year of the Rooster) (see App. B2). *Christian:* Ash Wednesday (see App. B9). *Islamic:* New Year's Day (Hegira: 1426) (see App. B22).

**10 Thu.** *Malta:* Saint Paul's Day. *Vietnam:* Tet (2nd day of 3). *Asian:* 2nd Day of Chinese New Year (see App. B3). *Far East Islamic:* New Year's Day (Hegira: 1426).

**11 Fri.** *Cameroon:* Youth Day. *Japan:* Foundation Day. *Liberia:* Armed Forces Day. *Vietnam:* Tet (3rd day of 3). *Asian:* 3rd Day of Chinese New Year (see App. B4).

**12 Sat.** *Burma:* Union Day.

**14 Mon.** *International:* Valentine's Day.

**18 Fri.** *Gambia:* Independence Day. *Islamic:* Ashura (see App. B23). *Zodiac Cusp:* Aquarius ends, Pisces begins.

**19 Sat.** *Nepal:* National Day.

**21 Mon.** *Bangladesh:* Saheed Day. *United States:* Washington's Birthday.

**22 Tue.** *Burma:* Full Moon Day. *Saint Lucia:* Independence Day.

**23 Wed.** *Brunei:* National Day. *Guyana:* Republic Day. *Sri Lanka:* Full Moon Poya. *Thailand:* Makha Bucha Day.

**25 Fri.** *Kuwait:* National Day.

**27 Sun.** *Dominican Republic:* Independence Day.

# March 2005

**1 Tue.** *South Korea:* Independence Day.

**2 Wed.** *Ethiopia:* Victory of Aduwa Day. *Morocco:* Independence Day.

**3 Thu.** *Bulgaria:* Liberation Day. *Malawi:* Martyrs' Day. *Morocco:* National Day.

**6 Sun.** *Ghana:* Independence Day.

**7 Mon.** *Guam:* Discovery Day.

**8 Tue.** *Syria:* Revolution Day. *Multinational:* Women's Day (see App. A4).

**10 Thu.** *South Korea:* Labor Day.

**11 Fri.** *Lithuania:* National Day*.

**12 Sat.** *Lesotho:* Moshoeshoe's Day. *Mauritius:* Independence Day. *Zambia:* Youth Day.

**13 Sun.** *Grenada:* National Day.

**14 Mon.** *Gibraltar:* Commonwealth Day. *Greece:* Shrove Monday. *Orthodox:* Shrove Monday.

**17 Thu.** *Ireland:* Saint Patrick's Day. *Northern Ireland:* Saint Patrick's Day.

**19 Sat.** *Christian:* Saint Joseph's Day (see App. A5).

**20 Sun.** *Afghanistan:* New Year's Day (Shamsi: 1384). *Iran:* New Year's Day (Hegira: 1384). *Iraq:* New Year's Day. *Japan:* Vernal Equinox. *Tunisia:* Independence Day. *Christian:* Palm Sunday. *Zodiac Cusp:* Pisces ends, Aries begins.

**21 Mon.** *Mexico:* Juarez Day.

**22 Tue.** *Puerto Rico:* Abolition Day. *Zambia:* Africa Day.

**23 Wed.** *Pakistan:* Pakistan Day.

**24 Thu.** *Burma:* Full Moon Day. *Christian:* Maundy Thursday (see App. B11).

**25 Fri.** *Cyprus:* Greek Independence Day. *Greece:* Independence Day. *Liechtenstein:* Annunciation. *Sri Lanka:* Full Moon Poya. *Christian:* Good Friday (see App. B12). *Jewish:* Purim.

**26 Sat.** *Bangladesh:* Independence Day. *Christian:* Easter Saturday (see App. B13).

**27 Sun.** *Angola:* Evacuation Day. *Burma:* Resistance Day. *Christian:* Easter Sunday (see App. B14). *Europe:* Daylight Savings Time starts (advance clocks 1 hour).

**28 Mon.** *Virgin Islands (U.S.):* Transfer Day. *Christian:* Easter Monday (see App. B15).

**29 Tue.** *Central African Republic:* Boganda Day. *Madagascar:* Memorial Day. *Taiwan:* Youth Day.

**31 Thu.** *Malta:* National Day.

# April 2005

**1 Fri.** *Iran:* Republic Day. *San Marino:* National Day. *Sierra Leone:* Bank Holiday.

**3 Sun.** *Canada and United States:* Daylight Savings Time starts (advance clocks 1 hour).

**4 Mon.** *Hungary:* Liberation Day. *Senegal:* National Day.

**5 Tue.** *South Korea:* Arbor Day. *Asian:* Tomb Sweeping Day (see App. A6).

**6 Wed.** *South Africa:* Founders' Day. *Thailand:* Chakri Day.

**9 Sat.** *Philippines:* Valour Day. *Tunisia:* Martyrs' Day.

**11 Mon.** *Costa Rica:* Heroes' Day. *Uganda:* Liberation Day.

**13 Wed.** *Chad:* National Day. *Thailand:* Songkrawn (1st day of 2).

**14 Thu.** *Honduras:* Pan American Day. *Thailand:* Songkrawn (2nd day of 2).

**15 Fri.** *Niger:* National Day.

**16 Sat.** *Burma:* New Year's Day (Burmese: 1367). *Cyprus:* Independence Day.

**17 Sun.** *Cambodia:* Independence Day. *Syria:* Independence Day.

**18 Mon.** *Zimbabwe:* Republic Day.

**19 Tue.** *Sierra Leone:* Republic Day. *Uruguay:* Patriots' Day. *Venezuela:* Independence Day. *Islamic:* Mohammed's Birthday (see App. B24). *Zodiac Cusp:* Aries ends, Taurus begins.

**20 Wed.** *Far East Islamic:* Mohammed's Birthday.

**21 Thu.** *Brazil:* Tiradentes Day.

**22 Fri.** *Burma:* Full Moon Day. *Denmark:* All Prayers' Day.

**23 Sat.** *Sri Lanka:* Full Moon Poya. *Turkey:* Children's Day.

**24 Sun.** *Israel:* Passover. *Jewish:* Passover.

**25 Mon.** *Australia:* ANZAC Day. *Egypt:* Sinai Day. *Iceland:* Children's Day. *Italy:* Liberation Day. *New Zealand:* ANZAC Day. *Portugal:* Liberation Day. *Swaziland:* Flag Day.

**26 Tue.** *Tanzania:* Union Day.

**27 Wed.** *Afghanistan:* Independence Day. *Sierra Leone:* Independence Day. *Togo:* Independence Day.

**29 Fri.** *Japan:* Green Day. *Orthodox:* Good Friday (see App. B20).

**30 Sat.** *Finland:* Vappu Day. *Netherlands:* Queen's Birthday.

# May 2005

**1 Sun.** *Jordan:* Easter Sunday. *Multinational:* Labor Day (see App. A7). *Orthodox:* Easter Sunday.

**2 Mon.** *Lesotho:* King's Birthday. *United Kingdom:* Labour Day. *Zambia:* Labour Day. *Orthodox:* Easter Monday (see App. B20).

**3 Tue.** *Japan:* Constitution Day.

**4 Wed.** *Japan:* People's Day.

**5 Thu.** *Japan:* Children's Day. *Mexico:* Cinco de Mayo. *Netherlands:* Liberation Day. *South Korea:* Children's Day. *Thailand:* Coronation Day. *Christian:* Ascension (see App. B16).

**6 Fri.** *Lebanon:* Martyrs' Day. *Philippines:* Corregidor Day.

**8 Sun.** *France:* Labour Day. *International:* Mother's Day.

**9 Mon.** *Czech Republic:* Liberation Day*. *Slovakia:* Liberation Day*.

**10 Tue.** *Micronesia:* Independence Day.

**14 Sat.** *Israel:* Independence Day. *Liberia:* Unification Day. *Malawi:* Kamuzu Day. *Paraguay:* Flag Day.

**15 Sun.** *South Korea:* Vesak Day. *Paraguay:* Independence Day. *Christian:* Whitsunday.

**16 Mon.** *Christian:* Whitmonday (see App. B18).

**17 Tue.** *Cayman Islands:* Discovery Day. *Norway:* Constitution Day.

**18 Wed.** *Haiti:* Flag Day. *Uruguay:* Las Piedras Day.

**19 Thu.** *Finland:* Flag Day. *Turkey:* Youth Day.

**20 Fri.** *Cameroon:* Constitution Day. *Zaïre:* Popular Movement Day. *Zodiac Cusp:* Taurus ends, Gemini begins.

**21 Sat.** *Chile:* Navy Day.

**22 Sun.** *Burma:* Full Moon Day. *Haiti:* Sovereign Day. *Malaysia:* Vesak Day. *Singapore:* Vesak Day. *Sri Lanka:* Heroes' Day. *Thailand:* Visakha Bucha Day.

**23 Mon.** *Canada:* Victoria Day. *Jamaica:* Labour Day. *Sri Lanka:* Full Moon Poya.

**24 Tue.** *Bulgaria:* Culture Day. *Ecuador:* Independence Battle Day.

**25 Wed.** *Argentina:* National Day. *Eritrea:* Independence Day*. *Jordan:* Independence Day. *Sudan:* Revolution Day. *Multinational:*. Africa Day (see App. A8).

**26 Thu.** *Guyana:* Independence Day. *Christian:* Corpus Christi (see App. B19).

**27 Fri.** *Nigeria:* Children's Day.

**30 Mon.** *United Kingdom:* Spring Break. *United States:* Memorial Day.

**31 Tue.** *Brunei:* Regiment Day. *South Africa:* Republic Day.

# June 2005

**1 Wed.** *Kenya:* Madaraka Day. *Malaysia:* King's Birthday. *Tunisia:* National Day. *Western Samoa:* Independence Day.

**2 Thu.** *Italy:* Republic Day. *Tunisia:* Youth Day.

**4 Sat.** *Bahamas:* Labour Day. *Tonga:* Independence Day.

**5 Sun.** *Denmark:* Constitution Day. *Equatorial Guinea:* President's Birthday. *Seychelles:* Liberation Day.

**6 Mon.** *Ireland:* Public Holiday. *New Zealand:* Queen's Birthday. *South Korea:* Memorial Day. *Sweden:* Constitution Day.

**7 Tue.** *Chad:* Revolution Day.

**9 Thu.** *Argentina:* Independence Day.

**10 Fri.** *Macao:* Portugal Day. *Portugal:* Portugal Day.

**11 Sat.** *Hong Kong:* Queen's Birthday (1st day of 2). *Libya:* Evacuation Day.

**12 Sun.** *Philippines:* Independence Day. *Asian:* Dragon Boat Festival (see App. B5).

**13 Mon.** *Australia:* Queen's Birthday. *Fiji:* Queen's Birthday. *Hong Kong:* Queen's Birthday (2nd day of 2). *Israel:* Pentecost. *New Guinea:* Queen's Birthday. *United Kingdom:* Queen's Birthday. *Jewish:* Pentecost.

**17 Fri.** *Germany:* Unity Day. *Iceland:* Independence Day.

**18 Sat.** *Egypt:* Independence Day.

**19 Sun.** *Algeria:* Righting Day. *Kuwait:* Independence Day. *Uruguay:* Artigas Day. *Orthodox:* Pentecost Sunday.

**20 Mon.** *Argentina:* Flag Day. *Burma:* Full Moon Day. *Greece:* Pentecost Monday.

**21 Tue.** *Finland:* Midsummer Day (1st day of 2). *Sri Lanka:* Full Moon Poya. *Sweden:* Midsummer Day (1st day of 2). *Zodiac Cusp:* Gemini ends, Cancer begins.

**22 Wed.** *Finland:* Midsummer Day (2nd day of 2). *Sweden:* Midsummer Day (2nd day of 2).

**23 Thu.** *Luxembourg:* National Day.

**24 Fri.** *Andorra:* Saint John's Day. *Chile:* Bank Holiday. *Ecuador:* Bank Holiday. *El Salvador:* Bank Holiday. *Finland:* Bank Holiday. *Venezuela:* Carabobo Day. *Zaïre:* Constitution Day.

**25 Sat.** *Croatia:* Independence Day*. *Finland:* Johannus Day. *Mozambique:* Independence Day. *Slovenia:* Independence Day*.

**26 Sun.** *Madagascar:* Independence Day. *Somalia:* Independence Day.

**27 Mon.** *Djibouti:* Independence Day.

**29 Wed.** *Seychelles:* Independence Day. *Christian:* Saint Paul's Day (see App. A9).

**30 Thu.** *Guatemala:* Army Day. *Sri Lanka:* Bank Holiday. *Zaïre:* Independence Day.

# July 2005

**1 Fri.** *Burundi:* Independence Day. *Canada:* Canada Day. *Ghana:* Republic Day. *Hong Kong:* Half Year Day. *Rwanda:* Independence Day. *Somalia:* Union Day. *Suriname:* Freedom Day. *Multinational:* Bank Holiday (see App. A10).

**4 Mon.** *Cayman Islands:* Constitution Day. *Lesotho:* Family Day. *Philippines:* United States Friendship Day. *United States:* Independence Day. *Yugoslavia:* Freedom Fighters' Day. *Zambia:* Heroes' Day.

**5 Tue.** *Algeria:* Independence Day. *Cape Verde:* Independence Day. *Rwanda:* Unity Day. *Venezuela:* Independence Day. *Zambia:* Unity Day.

**6 Wed.** *Comoros:* Independence Day. *Malawi:* Republic Day.

**7 Thu.** *Solomon Islands:* Independence Day. *Tanzania:* Farmers' Day. *Yugoslavia:* Serbian Day.

**10 Sun.** *Bahamas:* Independence Day.

**11 Mon.** *Mongolia:* Revolution Day.

**12 Tue.** *Kiribati:* Independence Day. *Northern Ireland:* Battle of the Boyne Day. *São Tomé:* National Day.

**14 Thu.** *France:* National Day. *Iraq:* Revolution Day.

**15 Fri.** *Brunei:* Sultan's Birthday.

**17 Sun.** *Iraq:* Revolution Day. *Puerto Rico:* Rivera Day. *Slovakia:* Independence Day*. *South Korea:* Constitution Day.

**18 Mon.** *Botswana:* President's Day. *Uruguay:* Constitution Day.

**19 Tue.** *Burma:* Full Moon and Martyrs' Day. *Laos:* Independence Day. *Nicaragua:* Sandinista Day.

**20 Wed.** *Colombia:* Independence Day. *Sri Lanka:* Full Moon Poya.

**21 Thu.** *Belgium:* National Day. *Guam:* Liberation Day. *Thailand:* Asalaha Bucha Day.

**22 Fri.** *Poland:* Liberation Day. *Thailand:* Khao Phansa Day. *Zodiac Cusp:* Cancer ends, Leo begins.

**23 Sat.** *Egypt:* Revolution Day. *New Guinea:* Remembrance Day.

**24 Sun.** *Venezuela:* Bolivar Day.

**25 Mon.** *Costa Rica:* Guanacaste Day. *Cuba:* Revolution Day (1st day of 3). *Puerto Rico:* Constitution Day. *Spain:* Santiago Day. *Tunisia:* Republic Day. *Virgin Islands (U.S.):* Hurricane Supplication Day.

**26 Tue.** *Cuba:* Revolution Day (2nd day of 3). *Liberia:* Independence Day. *Maldives:* Independence Day.

**27 Wed.** *Cuba:* Revolution Day (3rd day of 3). *Puerto Rico:* Barbosa Day.

**28 Thu.** *Peru:* Independence Day (1st day of 2).

**29 Fri.** *Peru:* Independence Day (2nd day of 2).

**30 Sat.** *Vanuatu:* Independence Day.

# August 2005

**1 Mon.** *Bahamas:* Emancipation Day. *Barbados:* Emancipation Day. *Benin:* Independence Day. *Canada:* Civic Holiday. *Ireland:* Public Holiday. *Jamaica:* Independence Day. *Scotland:* Public Holiday. *Switzerland:* Confederation Day.

**2 Tue.** *Costa Rica:* Virgin of the Angels Day. *Guyana:* Freedom Day. *Trinidad:* Discovery Day.

**3 Wed.** *El Salvador:* Summer Day (1st day of 4). *Guinea-Bissau:* Martyrs' Day. *Niger:* Independence Day. *Tunisia:* President's Birthday. *Zambia:* Farmers' Day.

**4 Thu.** *Burkina Faso:* Independence Day (1st day of 2). *El Salvador:* Summer Day (2nd day of 4).

**5 Fri.** *Burkina Faso:* Independence Day (2nd day of 2). *El Salvador:* Summer Day (3rd day of 4).

**6 Sat.** *Bolivia:* Independence Day. *El Salvador:* Summer Day (4th day of 4). *United Arab Emirates:* Accession Day.

**7 Sun.** *Colombia:* Boyaca Day. *Ivory Coast:* Republic Day.

**9 Tue.** *Georgia:* Independence Day*. *Singapore:* National Day.

**10 Wed.** *Ecuador:* Independence Day.

**11 Thu.** *Chad:* Independence Day.

*Jordan:* Accession Day. *Zimbabwe:* Heroes' Day (1st day of 2).

**12 Fri.** *Thailand:* Queen's Birthday. *Zimbabwe:* Heroes' Day (2nd day of 2).

**13 Sat.** *Central African Republic:* Independence Day. *Congo:* Independence Day (1st day of 2). *Tunisia:* Women's Day.

**14 Sun.** *Congo:* Independence Day (2nd day of 2). *Israel:* Tisha Ab. *Pakistan:* Independence Day. *Jewish:* Tisha Ab.

**15 Mon.** *Congo:* Independence Day (3rd day of 3). *India:* Independence Day. *Liechtenstein:* National Day. *South Korea:* Republic Day. *Christian:* Assumption (see App. A11).

**16 Tue.** *Dominican Republic:* Republic Day.

**17 Wed.** *Argentina:* San Martin's Day. *Gabon:* Independence Day. *Indonesia:* Independence Day.

**18 Thu.** *Burma:* Full Moon Day.

**19 Fri.** *Sri Lanka:* Full Moon Poya.

**20 Sat.** *Hungary:* Constitution Day. *Senegal:* Independence Day.

**21 Sun.** *Estonia:* Independence Day*. *Latvia:* Independence Day*. *Lithuania:* Independence Day*.

**23 Tue.** *Romania:* National Day (1st day of 2). *Zodiac Cusp:* Leo ends, Virgo begins.

**24 Wed.** *Kazakhstan:* National Day*. *Liberia:* Flag Day. *Romania:* National Day (2nd day of 2). *Russia:* Independence Day*. *Ukraine:* National Day*.

**25 Thu.** *Belarus:* Independence Day*. *Paraguay:* Constitution Day. *Uruguay:* Independence Day.

**27 Sat.** *Hong Kong:* Liberation Day (1st day of 2). *Moldova:* Independence Day*.

**29 Mon.** *England:* Summer Break. *Hong Kong:* Liberation Day (2nd day of 2). *Luxembourg:* Fair Day. *Northern Ireland:* Summer Break. *Uzbekistan:* Independence Day*. *Wales:* Summer Break.

**30 Tue.** *Afghanistan:* Children's Day. *Azerbaijan:* Independence Day*. *Peru:* Rose of Lima Day. *Turkey:* Victory Day.

**31 Wed.** *Afghanistan:* Pashtunistan Day. *Kyrgyzstan:* Independence Day*. *Malaysia:* National Day. *Trinidad:* Independence Day. *Islamic:* Isra a Majraj (see App. B30).

# September 2005

**1 Thu.** *Libya:* National Day. *Mexico:* President's Message Day. *Syria:* United Arab Republics Day.

**2 Fri.** *Vietnam:* Independence Day.

**3 Sat.** *Qatar:* National Day. *San Marino:* Saint Marinus' Day. *Tunisia:* Independence Movement Day.

**5 Mon.** *Canada:* Labour Day. *United States:* Labor Day.

**6 Tue.** *Pakistan:* Defense Day. *Swaziland:* Independence Day.

**7 Wed.** *Brazil:* Independence Day.

**8 Thu.** *Andorra:* National Day. *Malta:* Our Lady of Victory Day.

**9 Fri.** *Bulgaria:* National Day (1st day of 2). *North Korea:* Independence Day. *Tajikistan:* Independence Day*.

**10 Sat.** *Belize:* National Day. *Bulgaria:* National Day (2nd day of 2).

**11 Sun.** *Chile:* Revolution Day. *Egypt:* New Year's Day (Coptic: 1723). *Ethiopia:* New Year's Day (Ethiopian: 1999). *Pakistan:* Anniversary of Quaid-e-Azam's Death.

**12 Mon.** *Ethiopia:* National Day.

**14 Wed.** *Guatemala:* San Jacinto Day. *Nicaragua:* San Jacinto Day.

**15 Thu.** *Costa Rica:* Independence Day. *El Salvador:* Independence Day. *Guatemala:* Independence Day. *Honduras:* Independence Day. *Japan:* Veneration Day. *Nicaragua:* Independence Day.

**16 Fri.** *Burma:* Full Moon Day.

*Mexico:* Independence Day. *New. Guinea:* Independence Day.

**17 Sat.** *Angola:* Heroes' Day. *Marshall Islands:* Independence Day. *Sri Lanka:* Full Moon Poya.

**18 Sun.** *Burundi:* Victory of Uprona Day. *Chile:* Independence Day.

**19 Mon.** *Chile:* Armed Forces Day. *Saint Kitts:* Independence Day.

**21 Wed.** *Belize:* Independence Day. *Malta:* Independence Day.

**22 Thu.** *Mali:* Independence Day. *Zodiac Cusp:* Virgo ends, Libra begins.

**23 Fri.** *Armenia:* Independence Day*. *Japan:* Autumnal Equinox. *Saudi Arabia:* National Day.

**24 Sat.** *Dominican Republic:* Mercedes Day. *Guinea-Bissau:* Republic Day.

**25 Sun.** *Mozambique:* Liberation Day. *Rwanda:* Assembly Day. *Europe:* Daylight Savings Time ends (retard clocks 1 hour).

**26 Mon.** *Ethiopia:* True Cross Day. *Yemeni Republic:* National Day.

**28 Wed.** *Taiwan:* Teachers' Day.

**29 Thu.** *Brunei:* Constitution Day. *Paraguay:* Boqueron Battle Day.

**30 Fri.** *Botswana:* Independence Day.

# October 2005

**1 Sat.** *Cameroon:* Unification Day. *China:* National Day (1st day of 2). *Nigeria:* Independence Day. *South Korea:* Armed Forces Day. (1st day of 2). *Tuvalu:* Independence Day.

**2 Sun.** *China:* National Day (2nd day of 2). *Guinea:* Independence Day. *India:* Ghandi Day. *South Korea:* Armed Forces Day (2nd day of 2).

**3 Mon.** *Barbados:* Bank Holiday. *Honduras:* Morazan Day. *South Korea:* Foundation Day (1st day of 2).

**4 Tue.** *Israel:* New Year's Day. *Lesotho:* Independence Day. *South Korea:* Foundation Day (2nd day of 2). *Islamic:* 1st Day of Ramadan (see App. B25). *Jewish:* Rosh Hashanah (Jewish: 5766).

**5 Wed.** *Lesotho:* Sports Day. *Macao:* Portuguese Republic Day. *Portugal:* Republic Day.

**6 Thu.** *Egypt:* Armed Forces Day.

**9 Sun.** *Peru:* National Dignity Day. *South Korea:* Alphabet Day. *Uganda:* Independence Day.

**10 Mon.** *Canada:* Thanksgiving Day. *Fiji:* Cession Day. *Japan:* Health Day. *South Africa:* Kruger Day. *Taiwan:* National Day. *United States:* Bank Holiday. *Virgin Islands (U.S.):* Puerto Rican Friendship Day.

**11 Tue.** *Cuba:* Independence War. *Panama:* Revolution Day.

**12 Wed.** *Equatorial Guinea:* Independence Day. *Spain:* National Day. *Asian:* Ancestors' Day (see App. B6). *Multinational:* Columbus Day (see App. A12).

**13 Thu.** *Israel:* Yom Kippur. *Jewish:* Yom Kippur.

**14 Fri.** *Zaïre:* Founders' Day.

**15 Sat.** *Bosnia and Herzegovina:* Independence Day*. *Tunisia:* Evacuation Day.

**16 Sun.** *Burma:* Full Moon Day. *China:* Mid-autumn Day. *Sri Lanka:* Full Moon Poya. *Taiwan:* Mid-autumn Day.

**17 Mon.** *Hong Kong:* Mid-autumn Day. *Haiti:* Dessalines Day. *Jamaica:* Heroes' Day. *Macao:* Mid-autumn Day. *Malawi:* Mother's Day.

**18 Tue.** *Israel:* Sukkot. *Jewish:* Sukkot.

**20 Thu.** *Guatemala:* Revolution Day. *Kenya:* Kenyatta Day.

**21 Fri.** *Honduras:* Army Day. *Somalia:* Revolution Day (1st day of 2).

**22 Sat.** *Somalia:* Revolution Day (2nd day of 2). *Vatican:* John Paul II Day.

**23 Sun.** *Hungary:* Revolution Day.

*Thailand:* Chulalongkorn Day. *Zodiac Cusp:* Libra ends, Scorpio begins.

**24 Mon.** *Egypt:* Suez Victory Day. *Haiti:* United Nations Day. *Zambia:* Independence Day.

**25 Tue.** *Taiwan:* Restoration Day.

**26 Wed.** *Austria:* National Day. *Benin:* Revolution Day. *Rwanda:* Government Day.

**27 Thu.** *Saint Vincent:* Independence Day. *Turkmenistan:* Independence Day*. *Zaïre:* Naming Day.

**28 Fri.** *Greece:* Ohi! Day.

**29 Sat.** *Tanzania:* Naming Day. *Turkey:* Republic Day.

**30 Sun.** *Canada and United States:* Daylight Savings Time ends (retard clocks 1 hour).

**31 Mon.** *Ireland:* Public Holiday. *New Zealand:* Labour Day. *Taiwan:* Chiang Kai-shek's Birthday.

# November 2005

**1 Tue.** *Algeria:* Revolution Day. *Antigua:* Independence Day. *Christian:* All Saints' Day (see App. A13). *Hindu:* Deepavali (see App. B21).

**2 Wed.** *Brazil:* Memorial Day. *Finland:* All Saints' Eve. *Sweden:* All Saints' Eve. *Christian:* All Souls' Day (see App. A14).

**3 Thu.** *Dominica:* Independence Day. *Ecuador:* Cuenca Independence Day. *Panama:* Independence Day. *Liberia:* Thanksgiving Day. *Panama:* Independence Day. *Far East Islamic:* Hari Raya Puasa (see App. B27). *Islamic:* Eid al Fitr (1st day of 4) (see App. B26).

**4 Fri.** *Andorra:* Saint Charles' Day. *Panama:* Flag Day. *Vatican:* John Paul II's Nameday *Islamic:* Eid al Fitr (2nd day of 4) (see App. B26).

**5 Sat.** *El Salvador:* Cry of Independence Day. *Islamic:* Eid al Fitr (3rd day of 4) (see App. B26).

**6 Sun.** *Islamic:* Eid al Fitr (4th day of 4) (see App. B26).

**7 Mon.** *Bangladesh:* Revolution Day. *Virgin Islands (U.S.):* Liberty Day.

**8 Tue.** *Nepal:* Queen's Birthday.

**9 Wed.** *Pakistan:* Iqbal Day.

**10 Thu.** *Panama:* Cry of Independence Day.

**11 Fri.** *Angola:* Independence Day. *Bhutan:* King's Birthday. *Maldives:* Republic Day. *Poland:* Independence Day. *Multinational:* Armistice Day (see App. A15).

**12 Sat.** *Taiwan:* Dr. Sun Yat-sen's Birthday.

**14 Mon.** *Burma:* Full Moon Day. *Jordan:* King's Birthday.

**15 Tue.** *Brazil:* Republic Day. *Sri Lanka:* Full Moon Poya.

**16 Wed.** *Germany:* Repentance Day.

**17 Thu.** *Zaïre:* Armed Forces Day.

**18 Fri.** *Haiti:* Vertieres' Day. *Morocco:* Independence Day. *Oman:* National Day.

**19 Sat.** *Belize:* Garifuna Day. *Mali:* Army Coup Day. *Monaco:* Prince Ranier's Day. *Puerto Rico:* Discovery Day.

**20 Sun.** *Mexico:* Revolution Day.

**21 Mon.** *Fiji:* Prince Charles' Birthday.

**22 Tue.** *Lebanon:* Independence Day. *Zodiac Cusp:* Scorpio ends, Sagittarius begins.

**23 Wed.** *Japan:* Labor Thanksgiving Day.

**24 Thu.** *United States:* Thanksgiving Day. *Zaïre:* New Regime Day.

**25 Fri.** *Argentina:* Bank Holiday. *Suriname:* Independence Day.

**28 Mon.** *Albania:* Independence Day. *Burundi:* Republic Day. *Chad:* Republic Day. *Mauritania:* Independence Day. *Panama:* Independence Day.

**29 Tue.** *Albania:* Liberation Day.

*Liberia:* Tubman's Birthday. *Yugoslavia:* Republic Day.

**30 Wed.** *Barbados:* Independence Day. *Benin:* National Day. *Philippines:* Heroes' Day.

# December 2005

**1 Thu.** *Central African Republic:* National Day. *Portugal:* Youth Day. *Ukraine:* Independence Day*.

**2 Fri.** *Laos:* Republic Day. *United Arab Emirates:* National Day.

**5 Mon.** *Haiti:* Discovery Day. *Thailand:* King's Birthday.

**6 Tue.** *Finland:* Independence Day.

**7 Wed.** *Ivory Coast:* Independence Day.

**8 Thu.** *Christian:* Immaculate Conception (see App. A16).

**9 Fri.** *Tanzania:* Independence Day.

**10 Sat.** *Angola:* MPLA Foundation Day. *Equatorial Guinea:* Human Rights Day. *Namibia:* Settlers' Day. *Thailand:* Constitution Day.

**11 Sun.** *Burkina Faso:* National Day.

**12 Mon.** *Kenya:* Independence Day. *Mexico:* Guadalupe Festival.

**13 Tue.** *Malta:* Republic Day.

**14 Wed.** *Burma:* Full Moon Day.

**15 Thu.** *Sri Lanka:* Full Moon Poya.

**16 Fri.** *Bahrain:* National Day. *Bangladesh:* Victory Day. *Nepal:* Constitution Day. *South Africa:* Covenant Day.

**17 Sat.** *Bhutan:* National Day.

**18 Sun.** *Niger:* Republic Day.

**21 Wed.** *Kazakhstan:* Independence Day*. *Zodiac Cusp:* Sagittarius ends, Capricorn begins.

**23 Fri.** *Japan:* Emperor's Birthday.

**24 Sat.** *Multinational:* Christmas Eve.

**25 Sun.** *Angola:* Family Day. *Congo:* Children's Day. *Pakistan:* Quaid's Birthday. *Taiwan:* Constitution Day. *Multinational:* Christmas Day.

**26 Mon.** *South Africa:* Good Will Day. *Jewish:* Chanukah. *Multinational:* Boxing Day.

**30 Fri.** *Madagascar:* Republic Day. *Philippines:* Rizal Day (1st day of 2).

**31 Sat.** *Congo:* Republic Day. *Philippines:* Rizal Day (2nd day of 2). *Multinational:* Bank Holiday and New Year's Eve.

# January 2006

**1 Sun.** *Cameroon:* Independence Day. *Cuba:* Liberation Day. *Haiti:* Independence Day. *Palau:* Independence Day. *Sudan:* Independence Day. *Taiwan:* Foundation Day (1st day of 2). *Western Samoa:* Independence Day. *Multinational:* Bank Holiday and New Year's Day (see App. A1 & A2).

**2 Mon.** *Hong Kong:* New Year's Day. *Japan:* Bank Holiday. *New Zealand:* New Year's Day (2nd day of 2). *Scotland:* New Year's Day (2nd day of 2). *South Korea:* New Year's Day (2nd day of 2). *Switzerland:* Berchtold's Day. *Taiwan:* Foundation Day (2nd day of 2).

**3 Tue.** *Burkina Faso:* Revolution Day.

**4 Wed.** *Burma:* Independence Day. *Zaïre:* Martyrs' Day.

**6 Fri.** *Iraq:* Army Day. *Uruguay:* Children's Day. *Christian:* Epiphany (see App. A3).

**7 Sat.** *Egypt:* Coptic Christmas. *Ethiopia:* Coptic Christmas.

**9 Mon.** *Far East Islamic:* Hari Raya

Haji (see App. B29). *Islamic:* Eid al Adha (1st day of 4) (see App. B28).

**10 Tue.** *Islamic:* Eid al Adha (2nd day of 4) (see App. B28).

**11 Wed.** *Albania:* Republic Day. *Nepal:* Unification Day. *Puerto Rico:* Hostos Day. *Islamic:* Eid al Adha (3rd day of 4) (see App. B28).

**12 Thu.** *Burma:* Full Moon Day. *Tanzania:* Revolution Day. *Islamic:* Eid al Adha (4th day of 4) (see App. B28).

**13 Fri.** *Sri Lanka:* Full Moon Poya. *Togo:* Liberation Day.

**15 Sun.** *Japan:* Adult's Day. *Jordan:* Arbor Day.

**16 Mon.** *United States:* Martin Luther King's Birthday.

**19 Thu.** *Ethiopia:* Epiphany.

**20 Fri.** *Mali:* Award Day. *Zodiac Cusp:* Capricorn ends, Aquarius begins.

**21 Sat.** *Dominican Republic:* Altagracia Day.

**22 Sun.** *Saint Vincent:* Discovery Day.

**26 Thu.** *Dominican Republic:* Duarte Day. *India:* Republic Day.

**27 Fri.** *Monaco:* Saint Devota's Day. *Vietnam:* Vietnam Day.

**28 Sat.** *Rwanda:* Democracy Day. *Asian:* Chinese New Year Eve (see App. B1).

**29 Sun.** *Vietnam:* Tet (1st day of 3). *Asian:* Chinese New Year (Year of the Dog) (see App. B2). *Islamic:* New Year's Day (Hegira: 1427) (see App. B22).

**30 Mon.** *Australia:* Australia Day. *Vietnam:* Tet (2nd day of 3). *Asian:* 2nd Day of Chinese New Year (see App. B3). *Far East Islamic:* New Year's Day (Hegira: 1427).

**31 Tue.** *Nauru:* Independence Day. *Vietnam:* Tet (3rd day of 3). *Asian:* 3rd Day of Chinese New Year (see App. B4).

# February 2006

**2 Thu.** *Liechtenstein:* Candlemas.

**4 Sat.** *Sri Lanka:* Independence Day.

**5 Sun.** *Mexico:* Constitution Day.

**6 Mon.** *New Zealand:* Waitangi Day. *United States:* Lincoln's Birthday.

**7 Tue.** *Grenada:* Independence Day. *Islamic:* Ashura (see App. B23).

**8 Wed.** *Iraq:* Revolution Day.

**9 Thu.** *Lebanon:* Saint Marion's Day.

**10 Fri.** *Malta:* Saint Paul's Day.

**11 Sat.** *Burma:* Full Moon Day. *Cameroon:* Youth Day. *Japan:* Foundation Day. *Liberia:* Armed Forces Day.

**12 Sun.** *Burma:* Union Day. *Sri Lanka:* Full Moon Poya.

**13 Mon.** *Thailand:* Makha Bucha Day.

**14 Tue.** *International:* Valentine's Day.

**18 Sat.** *Gambia:* Independence Day.

**19 Sun.** *Nepal:* National Day. *Zodiac Cusp:* Aquarius ends, Pisces begins.

**20 Mon.** *United States:* Washington's Birthday.

**21 Tue.** *Bangladesh:* Saheed Day.

**22 Wed.** *Saint Lucia:* Independence Day.

**23 Thu.** *Brunei:* National Day. *Guyana:* Republic Day.

**25 Sat.** *Kuwait:* National Day.

**27 Mon.** *Dominican Republic:* Independence Day. *Christian:* Shrove Monday (see App. B7).

**28 Tue.** *Christian:* Shrove Tuesday (see App. B8).

# March 2006

**1 Wed.** *South Korea:* Independence Day. *Christian:* Ash Wednesday (see App. B9).

**2 Thu.** *Ethiopia:* Victory of Aduwa Day. *Morocco:* Independence Day.

**3 Fri.** *Bulgaria:* Liberation Day. *Malawi:* Martyrs' Day. *Morocco:* National Day.

**6 Mon.** *Ghana:* Independence Day. *Greece:* Shrove Monday. *Guam:* Discovery Day. *Orthodox:* Shrove Monday.

**8 Wed.** *Syria:* Revolution Day. *Multinational:* Women's Day (see App. A4).

**10 Fri.** *South Korea:* Labor Day.

**11 Sat.** *Lithuania:* National Day*. *Zambia:* Youth Day.

**12 Sun.** *Lesotho:* Moshoeshoe's Day. *Mauritius:* Independence Day.

**13 Mon.** *Burma:* Full Moon Day. *Gibraltar:* Commonwealth Day. *Grenada:* National Day.

**14 Tue.** *Sri Lanka:* Full Moon Poya. *Jewish:* Purim.

**17 Fri.** *Ireland:* Saint Patrick's Day. *Northern Ireland:* Saint Patrick's Day.

**19 Sun.** *Christian:* Saint Joseph's Day (see App. A5).

**20 Mon.** *Afghanistan:* New Year's Day (Shamsi: 1385). *Iran:* New Year's Day (Hegira: 1385). *Iraq:* New Year's Day. *Tunisia:* Independence Day. *Zodiac Cusp:* Pisces ends, Aries begins.

**21 Tue.** *Japan:* Vernal Equinox. *Mexico:* Juarez Day.

**22 Wed.** *Puerto Rico:* Abolition Day.

**23 Thu.** *Pakistan:* Pakistan Day.

**25 Sat.** *Cyprus:* Greek Independence Day. *Greece:* Independence Day. *Liechtenstein:* Annunciation.

**26 Sun.** *Bangladesh:* Independence Day. *Europe:* Daylight Savings Time starts (advance clocks 1 hour).

**27 Mon.** *Angola:* Evacuation Day. *Burma:* Resistance Day. *Virgin Islands (U.S.):* Transfer Day.

**28 Tue.** *Zambia:* Africa Day.

**29 Wed.** *Central African Republic:* Boganda Day. *Madagascar:* Memorial Day. *Taiwan:* Youth Day.

**31 Fri.** *Malta:* National Day.

# April 2006

**1 Sat.** *Iran:* Republic Day. *San Marino:* National Day.

**2 Sun.** *Canada and United States:* Daylight Savings Time starts (advance clocks 1 hour).

**4 Tue.** *Hungary:* Liberation Day. *Senegal:* National Day.

**5 Wed.** *South Korea:* Arbor Day. *Asian:* Tomb Sweeping Day (see App. A6).

**6 Thu.** *South Africa:* Founders' Day. *Thailand:* Chakri Day.

**7 Fri.** *Sierra Leone:* Bank Holiday.

**9 Sun.** *Philippines:* Valour Day. *Tunisia:* Martyrs' Day. *Christian:* Palm Sunday. *Islamic:* Mohammed's Birthday (see App. B24).

**10 Mon.** *Far East Islamic:* Mohammed's Birthday.

**11 Tue.** *Costa Rica:* Heroes' Day. *Uganda:* Liberation Day.

**12 Wed.** *Burma:* Full Moon Day.

**13 Thu.** *Chad:* National Day. *Israel:* Passover. *Sri Lanka:* Full Moon Poya. *Thailand:* Songkrawn (1st day of 2). *Christian:* Maundy Thursday (see App. B11). *Jewish:* Passover.

**14 Fri.** *Honduras:* Pan American Day. *Thailand:* Songkrawn (2nd day of 2). *Christian:* Good Friday (see App. B12).

**15 Sat.** *Niger:* National Day. *Christian:* Holy Saturday (see App. B13).

**16 Sun.** *Burma:* New Year's Day

(Burmese: 1368). *Cyprus:* Independence Day. *Christian:* Easter Sunday (see App. B14).

**17 Mon.** *Cambodia:* Independence Day. *Syria:* Independence Day. *Christian:* Easter Monday (see App. B15).

**18 Tue.** *Zimbabwe:* Republic Day.

**19 Wed.** *Sierra Leone:* Republic Day. *Uruguay:* Patriots' Day. *Venezuela:* Independence Day.

**20 Thu.** *Zodiac Cusp:* Aries ends, Taurus begins.

**21 Fri.** *Brazil:* Tiradentes Day. *Orthodox:* Good Friday (see App. B20).

**23 Sun.** *Jordan:* Easter Sunday. *Turkey:* Children's Day. *Orthodox:* Easter Sunday.

**24 Mon.** *Orthodox:* Easter Monday (see App. B20).

**25 Tue.** *Australia:* ANZAC Day. *Egypt:* Sinai Day. *Iceland:* Children's Day. *Italy:* Liberation Day. *New Zealand:* ANZAC Day. *Portugal:* Liberation Day. *Swaziland:* Flag Day.

**26 Wed.** *Tanzania:* Union Day.

**27 Thu.** *Afghanistan:* Independence Day. *Sierra Leone:* Independence Day. *Togo:* Independence Day.

**29 Sat.** *Japan:* Green Day.

**30 Sun.** *Finland:* Vappu Day. *Netherlands:* Queen's Birthday.

# May 2006

**1 Mon.** *United Kingdom:* Labour Day. *Zambia:* Labour Day. *Multinational:* Labor Day (see App. A7).

**2 Tue.** *Lesotho:* King's Birthday.

**3 Wed.** *Israel:* Independence Day. *Japan:* Constitution Day.

**4 Thu.** *Japan:* People's Day. *South Korea:* Vesak Day.

**5 Fri.** *Japan:* Children's Day. *Mexico:* Cinco de Mayo. *Netherlands:* Liberation Day. *South Korea:* Children's Day. *Thailand:* Coronation Day.

**6 Sat.** *Lebanon:* Martyrs' Day. *Philippines:* Corregidor Day.

**8 Mon.** *France:* Liberation Day.

**9 Tue.** *Czech Republic:* Liberation Day*. *Slovakia:* Liberation Day*.

**10 Wed.** *Micronesia:* Independence Day.

**11 Thu.** *Burma:* Full Moon Day. *Malaysia:* Vesak Day. *Singapore:* Vesak Day.

**12 Fri.** *Denmark:* All Prayers' Day. *Sri Lanka:* Full Moon Poya. *Thailand:* Visakha Bucha Day.

**14 Sun.** *Liberia:* Unification Day. *Malawi:* Kamuzu Day. *Paraguay:* Flag Day. *International:* Mother's Day.

**15 Mon.** *Paraguay:* Independence Day.

**17 Wed.** *Cayman Islands:* Discovery Day. *Norway:* Constitution Day.

**18 Thu.** *Haiti:* Flag Day. *Uruguay:* Las Piedras Day.

**19 Fri.** *Finland:* Flag Day. *Turkey:* Youth Day.

**20 Sat.** *Cameroon:* Constitution Day. *Zaïre:* Popular Movement Day.

**21 Sun.** *Chile:* Navy Day. *Zodiac Cusp:* Taurus ends, Gemini begins.

**22 Mon.** *Canada:* Victoria Day. *Haiti:* Sovereign Day. *Sri Lanka:* Heroes' Day.

**23 Tue.** *Jamaica:* Labour Day.

**24 Wed.** *Bulgaria:* Culture Day. *Ecuador:* Independence Battle Day.

**25 Thu.** *Argentina:* National Day. *Eritrea:* Independence Day*. *Jordan:* Independence Day. *Sudan:* Revolution Day. *Christian:* Ascension (see App. B16). *Multinational:* Africa Day (see App. A8).

**26 Fri.** *Guyana:* Independence Day.

**27 Sat.** *Nigeria:* Children's Day.

**29 Mon.** *United Kingdom:* Spring Break. *United States:* Memorial Day.

**31 Wed.** *Brunei:* Regiment Day. *South Africa:* Republic Day.

# June 2006

**1 Thu.** *Kenya:* Madaraka Day. *Tunisia:* National Day. *Western Samoa:* Independence Day.

**2 Fri.** *Israel:* Pentecost. *Italy:* Republic Day. *Tunisia:* Youth Day. *Asian:* Dragon Boat Festival (see App. B5). *Jewish:* Pentecost.

**4 Sun.** *Bahamas:* Labour Day. *Tonga:* Independence Day. *Christian:* Whitsunday.

**5 Mon.** *Denmark:* Constitution Day. *Equatorial Guinea:* President's Birthday. *Ireland:* Public Holiday. *New Zealand:* Queen's Birthday. *Seychelles:* Liberation Day. *Christian:* Whitmonday (see App. B18).

**6 Tue.** *South Korea:* Memorial Day. *Sweden:* Constitution Day.

**7 Wed.** *Chad:* Revolution Day. *Malaysia:* King's Birthday.

**9 Fri.** *Argentina:* Independence Day.

**10 Sat.** *Burma:* Full Moon Day. *Hong Kong:* Queen's Birthday (1st day of 2). *Macao:* Portugal Day. *Portugal:* Portugal Day.

**11 Sun.** *Libya:* Evacuation Day. *Sri Lanka:* Full Moon Poya. *Orthodox:* Pentecost Sunday.

**12 Mon.** *Australia:* Queen's Birthday. *Fiji:* Queen's Birthday. *Greece:* Pentecost Monday. *Hong Kong:* Queen's Birthday (2nd day of 2). *New Guinea:* Queen's Birthday. *Philippines:* Independence Day. *United Kingdom:* Queen's Birthday.

**15 Thu.** *Christian:* Corpus Christi (see App. B19).

**17 Sat.** *Germany:* Unity Day. *Iceland:* Independence Day.

**18 Sun.** *Egypt:* Independence Day.

**19 Mon.** *Algeria:* Righting Day. *Kuwait:* Independence Day. *Uruguay:* Artigas Day.

**20 Tue.** *Argentina:* Flag Day.

**21 Wed.** *Finland:* Midsummer Day (1st day of 2). *Sweden:* Midsummer Day (1st day of 2). *Zodiac Cusp:* Gemini ends, Cancer begins.

**22 Thu.** *Finland:* Midsummer Day (2nd day of 2). *Sweden:* Midsummer Day (2nd day of 2).

**23 Fri.** *Luxembourg:* National Day.

**24 Sat.** *Andorra:* Saint John's Day. *Finland:* Johannus Day. *Venezuela:* Carabobo Day. *Zaïre:* Constitution Day.

**25 Sun.** *Croatia:* Independence Day*. *Mozambique:* Independence Day. *Slovenia:* Independence Day*.

**26 Mon.** *Madagascar:* Independence Day. *Somalia:* Independence Day.

**27 Tue.** *Djibouti:* Independence Day.

**29 Thu.** *Seychelles:* Independence Day. *Christian:* Saint Paul's Day (see App. A9).

**30 Fri.** *Chile:* Bank Holiday. *Ecuador:* Bank Holiday. *El Salvador:* Bank Holiday. *Finland:* Bank Holiday. *Guatemala:* Army Day. *Sri Lanka:* Bank Holiday. *Zaïre:* Independence Day.

# July 2006

**1 Sat.** *Burundi:* Independence Day. *Canada:* Canada Day. *Ghana:* Republic Day. *Hong Kong:* Half Year Day. *Rwanda:* Independence Day. *Somalia:* Union Day. *Suriname:* Freedom Day. *Multinational:* Bank Holiday (see App. A10).

**3 Mon.** *Cayman Islands:* Constitution Day. *Lesotho:* Family Day. *Zambia:* Heroes' Day.

**4 Tue.** *Philippines:* United States Friendship Day. *United States:* Independence Day. *Yugoslavia:* Freedom Fighters' Day. *Zambia:* Unity Day.

**5 Wed.** *Algeria:* Independence Day. *Cape Verde:* Independence Day. *Rwanda:* Unity Day. *Venezuela:* Independence Day.

**6 Thu.** *Comoros:* Independence Day. *Malawi:* Republic Day.

**7 Fri.** *Solomon Islands:* Independence Day. *Tanzania:* Farmers' Day. *Yugoslavia:* Serbian Day.

**9 Sun.** *Burma:* Full Moon Day.

**10 Mon.** *Bahamas:* Independence Day. *Sri Lanka:* Full Moon Poya. *Thailand:* Asalaha Bucha Day.

**11 Tue.** *Mongolia:* Revolution Day. *Thailand:* Khao Phansa Day.

**12 Wed.** *Kiribati:* Independence Day. *Northern Ireland:* Battle of the Boyne Day. *São Tomé:* National Day.

**14 Fri.** *France:* National Day. *Iraq:* Revolution Day.

**15 Sat.** *Brunei:* Sultan's Birthday.

**17 Mon.** *Botswana:* President's Day. *Iraq:* Revolution Day. *Puerto Rico:* Rivera Day. *Slovakia:* Independence Day*. *South Korea:* Constitution Day.

**18 Tue.** *Uruguay:* Constitution Day.

**19 Wed.** *Burma:* Martyrs' Day. *Laos:* Independence Day. *Nicaragua:* Sandinista Day.

**20 Thu.** *Colombia:* Independence Day.

**21 Fri.** *Belgium:* National Day. *Guam:* Liberation Day.

**22 Sat.** *Poland:* Liberation Day.

**23 Sun.** *Egypt:* Revolution Day. *New Guinea:* Remembrance Day. *Zodiac Cusp:* Cancer ends, Leo begins.

**24 Mon.** *Virgin Islands (U.S.):* Hurricane Supplication Day. *Venezuela:* Bolivar Day.

**25 Tue.** *Costa Rica:* Guanacaste Day. *Cuba:* Revolution Day (1st day of 3). *Puerto Rico:* Constitution Day. *Spain:* Santiago Day. *Tunisia:* Republic Day.

**26 Wed.** *Cuba:* Revolution Day (2nd day of 3). *Liberia:* Independence Day. *Maldives:* Independence Day.

**27 Thu.** *Cuba:* Revolution Day (3rd day of 3). *Puerto Rico:* Barbosa Day.

**28 Fri.** *Peru:* Independence Day (1st day of 2).

**29 Sat.** *Peru:* Independence Day (2nd day of 2).

**30 Sun.** *Vanuatu:* Independence Day.

# August 2006

**1 Tue.** *Benin:* Independence Day. *Switzerland:* Confederation Day.

**2 Wed.** *Costa Rica:* Virgin of the Angels Day. *Guyana:* Freedom Day. *Trinidad:* Discovery Day. *Zambia:* Farmers' Day.

**3 Thu.** *El Salvador:* Summer Day (1st day of 4). *Guinea-Bissau:* Martyrs' Day. *Israel:* Tisha Ab. *Niger:* Independence Day. *Tunisia:* President's Birthday. *Jewish:* Tisha Ab.

**4 Fri.** *Burkina Faso:* Independence Day (1st day of 2). *El Salvador:* Summer Day (2nd day of 4).

**5 Sat.** *Burkina Faso:* Independence Day (2nd day of 2). *El Salvador:* Summer Day (3rd day of 4).

**6 Sun.** *Bolivia:* Independence Day. *El Salvador:* Summer Day (4th day of 4). *United Arab Emirates:* Accession Day.

**7 Mon.** *Bahamas:* Emancipation Day. *Barbados:* Emancipation Day. *Burma:* Full Moon Day. *Canada:* Civic Holiday. *Colombia:* Boyaca Day. *Ivory Coast:* Independence Day. *Ireland:* Public Holiday. *Jamaica:* Independence Day. *Scotland:* Public Holiday.

**8 Tue.** *Sri Lanka:* Full Moon Poya.

**9 Wed.** *Georgia:* Independence Day*. *Singapore:* National Day.

**10 Thu.** *Ecuador:* Independence Day.

**11 Fri.** *Chad:* Independence Day. *Jordan:* Accession Day. *Zimbabwe:* Heroes' Day (1st day of 2).

**12 Sat.** *Thailand:* Queen's Birthday.

*Zimbabwe:* Heroes' Day (2nd day of 2).

**13 Sun.** *Central African Republic:* Independence Day. *Congo:* Independence Day (1st day of 2). *Tunisia:* Women's Day.

**14 Mon.** *Congo:* Independence Day (2nd day of 2). *Pakistan:* Independence Day.

**15 Tue.** *Congo:* Independence Day (3rd day of 3). *India:* Independence Day. *Liechtenstein:* National Day. *South Korea:* Republic Day. *Christian:* Assumption (see App. A11).

**16 Wed.** *Dominican Republic:* Republic Day.

**17 Thu.** *Argentina:* San Martin's Day. *Gabon:* Independence Day. *Indonesia:* Independence Day.

**20 Sun.** *Hungary:* Constitution Day. *Senegal:* Independence Day. *Islamic:* Isra a Majraj (see App. B30).

**21 Mon.** *Estonia:* Independence Day*. *Latvia:* Independence Day*. *Lithuania:* Independence Day*.

**23 Wed.** *Romania:* National Day (1st day of 2). *Zodiac Cusp:* Leo ends, Virgo begins.

**24 Thu.** *Kazakhstan:* National Day*. *Liberia:* Flag Day. *Romania:* National Day (2nd day of 2). *Russia:* Independence Day*. *Ukraine:* National Day*.

**25 Fri.** *Belarus:* Independence Day*. *Paraguay:* Constitution Day. *Uruguay:* Independence Day.

**26 Sat.** *Hong Kong:* Liberation Day (1st day of 2).

**27 Sun.** *Moldova:* Independence Day*.

**28 Mon.** *England:* Summer Break. *Hong Kong:* Liberation Day (2nd day of 2). *Luxembourg:* Fair Day. *Northern Ireland:* Summer Break. *Wales:* Summer Break.

**29 Tue.** *Uzbekistan:* Independence Day*.

**30 Wed.** *Afghanistan:* Children's Day. *Azerbaijan:* Independence Day*. *Peru:* Rose of Lima Day. *Turkey:* Victory Day.

**31 Thu.** *Afghanistan:* Pashtunistan Day. *Kyrgyzstan:* Independence Day*. *Malaysia:* National Day. *Trinidad:* Independence Day.

# September 2006

**1 Fri.** *Libya:* National Day. *Mexico:* President's Message Day. *Syria:* United Arab Republics Day.

**2 Sat.** *Vietnam:* Independence Day.

**3 Sun.** *Qatar:* National Day. *San Marino:* Saint Marinus' Day. *Tunisia:* Independence Movement Day.

**4 Mon.** *Canada:* Labour Day. *United States:* Labor Day.

**6 Wed.** *Burma:* Full Moon Day. *Pakistan:* Defense Day. *Swaziland:* Independence Day.

**7 Thu.** *Brazil:* Independence Day. *Sri Lanka:* Full Moon Poya.

**8 Fri.** *Andorra:* National Day. *Malta:* Our Lady of Victory Day.

**9 Sat.** *Bulgaria:* National Day (1st day of 2). *North Korea:* Independence Day. *Tajikistan:* Independence Day*.

**10 Sun.** *Belize:* National Day. *Bulgaria:* National Day (2nd day of 2).

**11 Mon.** *Chile:* Revolution Day. *Egypt:* New Year's Day (Coptic: 1724). *Ethiopia:* New Year's Day (Ethiopian: 2000). *Pakistan:* Anniversary of Quaid-e-Azam's Death.

**12 Tue.** *Ethiopia:* National Day.

**14 Thu.** *Guatemala:* San Jacinto Day. *Nicaragua:* San Jacinto Day.

**15 Fri.** *Costa Rica:* Independence Day. *El Salvador:* Independence Day. *Guatemala:* Independence Day. *Honduras:* Independence Day. *Japan:* Veneration Day. *Nicaragua:* Independence Day.

**16 Sat.** *Mexico:* Independence Day. *New Guinea:* Independence Day.

**17 Sun.** *Angola:* Heroes' Day. *Marshall Islands:* Independence Day.

**18 Mon.** *Burundi:* Victory of Uprona Day. *Chile:* Independence Day.

**19 Tue.** *Chile:* Armed Forces Day. *Saint Kitts:* Independence Day.

**21 Thu.** *Belize:* Independence Day. *Malta:* Independence Day.

**22 Fri.** *Mali:* Independence Day.

**23 Sat.** *Armenia:* Independence Day*. *Israel:* New Year's Day. *Japan:* Autumnal Equinox. *Saudi Arabia:* National Day. *Islamic:* 1st Day of Ramadan (see App. B25). *Jewish:* Rosh Hashanah (Jewish: 5767). *Zodiac Cusp:* Virgo ends, Libra begins.

**24 Sun.** *Dominican Republic:* Mercedes Day. *Guinea-Bissau:* Republic Day. *Europe:* Daylight Savings Time ends (retard clocks 1 hour).

**25 Mon.** *Mozambique:* Liberation Day. *Rwanda:* Assembly Day.

**26 Tue.** *Ethiopia:* True Cross Day.

**28 Thu.** *Taiwan:* Teachers' Day.

**29 Fri.** *Brunei:* Constitution Day. *Paraguay:* Boqueron Battle Day.

**30 Sat.** *Botswana:* Independence Day.

# October 2006

**1 Sun.** *Cameroon:* Unification Day. *China:* National Day (1st day of 2). *Nigeria:* Independence Day. *South Korea:* Armed Forces Day (1st day of 2). *Tuvalu:* Independence Day. *Asian:* Ancestors' Day (see App. B6).

**2 Mon.** *Barbados:* Bank Holiday. *China:* National Day (2nd day of 2). *Guinea:* Independence Day. *India:*: Ghandi Day. *Israel:* Yom Kippur. *South Korea:* Armed Forces Day (2nd day of 2). Jewish: Yom Kippur.

**3 Tue.** *Honduras:* Morazan Day. *South Korea:* Foundation Day (1st day of 2).

**4 Wed.** *Lesotho:* Independence Day. *South Korea:* Foundation Day (2nd day of 2).

**5 Thu.** *Burma:* Full Moon Day. *Lesotho:* Sports Day. *Macao:* Portuguese Republic Day. *Portugal:* Republic Day.

**6 Fri.** *China:* Mid-autumn Day. *Egypt:* Armed Forces Day. *Sri Lanka:* Full Moon Poya. *Taiwan:* Mid-autumn Day.

**7 Sat.** *Hong Kong:* Mid-autumn Day. *Israel:* Sukkot. *Macao:* Mid-autumn Day. *Jewish:* Sukkot.

**9 Mon.** *Canada:* Thanksgiving Day. *Fiji:* Cession Day. *Peru:* National Dignity Day. *South Korea:* Alphabet Day. *Uganda:* Independence Day. *United States:* Bank Holiday. *Virgin Islands (U.S.):* Puerto Rican Friendship Day.

**10 Tue.** *Japan:* Health Day. *South Africa:* Kruger Day. *Taiwan:* National Day.

**11 Wed.** *Cuba:* Independence War. *Panama:* Revolution Day.

**12 Thu.** *Equatorial Guinea:* Independence Day. *Spain:* National Day. *Multinational:* Columbus Day (see App. A12).

**14 Sat.** *Zaïre:* Founders' Day.

**15 Sun.** *Bosnia and Herzegovina:* Independence Day*. *Tunisia:* Evacuation Day.

**16 Mon.** *Jamaica:* Heroes' Day.

**17 Tue.** *Haiti:* Dessalines Day. *Malawi:* Mother's Day.

**20 Fri.** *Guatemala:* Revolution Day. *Kenya:* Kenyatta Day.

**21 Sat.** *Honduras:* Armed Forces Day. *Somalia:* Revolution Day (1st day of 2). *Hindu:* Deepavali (see App. B21).

**22 Sun.** *Somalia:* Revolution Day (2nd day of 2). *Vatican:* John Paul II Day.

**23 Mon.** *Hungary:* Revolution Day. *Thailand:* Chulalongkorn Day. *Far East Islamic:* Hari Raya Puasa (see App. B27). *Islamic:* Eid al Fitr (1st day of 4) (see App. B26). *Zodiac Cusp:* Libra ends, Scorpio begins.

**24 Tue.** *Egypt:* Suez Victory Day. *Haiti:* United Nations Day. *Zambia:* Independence Day. *Islamic:* Eid al Fitr (2nd day of 4) (see App. B26).

**25 Wed.** *Taiwan:* Restoration Day. *Islamic:* Eid al Fitr (3rd day of 4) (see App. B26).

**26 Thu.** *Austria:* National Day. *Benin:* Revolution Day. *Rwanda:* Government Day. *Islamic:* Eid al Fitr (4th day of 4) (see App. B26).

**27 Fri.** *Saint Vincent:* Independence Day. *Turkmenistan:* Independence Day*. *Zaïre:* Naming Day.

**28 Sat.** *Greece:* Ohi! Day.

**29 Sun.** *Tanzania:* Naming Day. *Turkey:* Republic Day. *Canada and United States:* Daylight Savings Time ends (retard clocks 1 hour).

**30 Mon.** *Ireland:* Public Holiday. *New Zealand:* Labour Day.

**31 Tue.** *Taiwan:* Chiang Kai-shek's Birthday.

# November 2006

**1 Wed.** *Algeria:* Revolution Day. *Antigua:* Independence Day. *Christian:* All Saints' Day (see App. A13).

**2 Thu.** *Brazil:* Memorial Day. *Finland:* All Saints' Eve. *Liberia:* Thanksgiving Day. *Sweden:* All Saints' Eve. *Christian:* All Souls' Day (see App. A14).

**3 Fri.** *Dominica:* Independence Day. *Ecuador:* Cuenca Independence Day. *Japan:* Culture Day. *Panama:* Independence Day.

**4 Sat.** *Andorra:* Saint Charles' Day. *Burma:* Full Moon Day. *Panama:* Flag Day. *Sri Lanka:* Full Moon Poya. *Vatican:* John Paul II's Nameday.

**5 Sun.** *El Salvador:* Cry of Independence Day.

**6 Mon.** *Virgin Islands (U.S.):* Liberty Day.

**7 Tue.** *Bangladesh:* Revolution Day.

**8 Wed.** *Nepal:* Queen's Birthday.

**9 Thu.** *Pakistan:* Iqbal Day.

**10 Fri.** *Panama:* Cry of Independence Day.

**11 Sat.** *Angola:* Independence Day. *Bhutan:* King's Birthday. *Maldives:* Republic Day. *Poland:* Independence Day. *Multinational:* Armistice Day (see App. A15).

**12 Sun.** *Taiwan:* Dr. Sun Yat-sen's Birthday.

**14 Tue.** *Jordan:* King's Birthday.

**15 Wed.** *Brazil:* Republic Day. *Germany:* Repentance Day.

**17 Fri.** *Zaïre:* Armed Forces Day.

**18 Sat.** *Haiti:* Vertieres' Day. *Morocco:* Independence Day. *Oman:* National Day.

**19 Sun.** *Belize:* Garifuna Day. *Mali:* Army Coup Day. *Monaco:* Prince Ranier's Day. *Puerto Rico:* Discovery Day.

**20 Mon.** *Fiji:* Prince Charles' Birthday. *Mexico:* Revolution Day.

**22 Wed.** *Lebanon:* Independence Day. *Zodiac Cusp:* Scorpio ends, Sagittarius begins.

**23 Thu.** *Japan:* Labor Thanksgiving Day. *United States:* Thanksgiving Day.

**24 Fri.** *Argentina:* Bank Holiday. *Zaïre:* New Regime Day.

**25 Sat.** *Suriname:* Independence Day.

**28 Tue.** *Albania:* Independence Day. *Burundi:* Republic Day. *Chad:* Republic Day. *Mauritania:* Independence Day. *Panama:* Independence Day.

**29 Wed.** *Albania:* Liberation Day. *Liberia:* Tubman's Birthday. *Yugoslavia:* Republic Day.

**30 Thu.** *Barbados:* Independence Day. *Benin:* National Day. *Philippines:* Heroes' Day.

# December 2006

**1 Fri.** *Central African Republic:* National Day. *Portugal:* Youth Day. *Ukraine:* Independence Day*.

**2 Sat.** *Laos:* Republic Day. *United Arab Emirates:* National Day.

**3 Sun.** *Burma:* Full Moon Day.

**4 Mon.** *Sri Lanka:* Full Moon Poya.

**5 Tue.** *Haiti:* Discovery Day. *Thailand:* King's Birthday.

**6 Wed.** *Finland:* Independence Day.

**7 Thu.** *Ivory Coast:* Independence Day.

**8 Fri.** *Christian:* Immaculate Conception (see App. A16).

**9 Sat.** *Tanzania:* Independence Day.

**10 Sun.** *Angola:* MPLA Foundation Day. *Equatorial Guinea:* Human Rights Day. *Namibia:* Settlers' Day. *Thailand:* Constitution Day.

**11 Mon.** *Burkina Faso:* National Day.

**12 Tue.** *Kenya:* Independence Day. *Mexico:* Guadalupe Festival.

**13 Wed.** *Malta:* Republic Day.

**16 Sat.** *Bahrain:* National Day. *Bangladesh:* Victory Day. *Nepal:* Constitution Day. *South Africa:* Covenant Day. *Jewish:* Chanukah.

**17 Sun.** *Bhutan:* National Day.

**18 Mon.** *Niger:* Republic Day.

**21 Thu.** *Kazakhstan:* Independence Day*. *Zodiac Cusp:* Sagittarius ends, Capricorn begins.

**23 Sat.** *Japan:* Emperor's Birthday.

**24 Sun.** *Multinational:* Christmas Eve (see App. A17).

**25 Mon.** *Angola:* Family Day. *Congo:* Children's Day. *Pakistan:* Quaid's Birthday. *Taiwan:* Constitution Day. *Multinational:* Christmas Day (see App. A18).

**26 Tue.** *South Africa:* Good Will Day. *Multinational:* Boxing Day (see App. A19).

**30 Sat.** *Madagascar:* Republic Day. *Philippines:* Rizal Day (1st day of 2). *Islamic:* Eid al Adha (1st day of 4) (see App. B28).

**31 Sun.** *Congo:* Republic Day. *Philippines:* Rizal Day (2nd day of 2). *Far East Islamic:* Hari Raya Haji (see App. B29). *Islamic:* Eid al Adha (2nd day of 4) (see App. B28). *Multinational:* Bank Holiday and New Year's Eve (see App. A20 & A21).

# January 2007

**1 Mon.** *Cameroon:* Independence Day. *Cuba:* Liberation Day. *Haiti:* Independence Day. *Palau:* Independence Day. *Sudan:* Independence Day. *Taiwan:* Foundation Day (1st day of 2). *Western Samoa:* Independence Day. *Islamic:* Eid al Adha (3rd day of 4) (see App. B28). *Multinational:* Bank Holiday and New Year's Day (see App. A1 & A2).

**2 Tue.** *Burma:* Full Moon Day. *Japan:* Bank Holiday. *New Zealand:* New Year's Day (2nd day of 2). *Scotland:* New Year's Day. (2nd day of 2). *South Korea:* New Year's Day (2nd day of 2). *Switzerland:* Berchtold's Day. *Taiwan:* Foundation Day (2nd day of 2). *Islamic:* Eid al Adha (4th day of 4) (see App. B28).

**3 Wed.** *Burkina Faso:* Revolution Day. *Sri Lanka:* Full Moon Poya.

**4 Thu.** *Burma:* Independence Day. *Zaïre:* Martyrs' Day.

**6 Sat.** *Iraq:* Army Day. *Uruguay:* Children's Day. *Christian:* Epiphany (see App. A3).

**7 Sun.** *Egypt:* Coptic Christmas. *Ethiopia:* Coptic Christmas.

**11 Thu.** *Albania:* Republic Day. *Nepal:* Unification Day. *Puerto Rico:* Hostos Day.

**12 Fri.** *Tanzania:* Revolution Day.

**13 Sat.** *Togo:* Liberation Day.

**15 Mon.** *Japan:* Adult's Day. *Jordan:* Arbor Day. *United States:* Martin Luther King's Birthday.

**19 Fri.** *Ethiopia:* Epiphany. *Islamic:* New Year's Day (Hegira: 1428) (see App. B22).

**20 Sat.** *Mali:* Award Day. *Far East Islamic:* New Year's Day (Hegira: 1428). *Zodiac Cusp:* Capricorn ends, Aquarius begins.

**21 Sun.** *Dominican Republic:* Altagracia Day.

**22 Mon.** *Saint Vincent:* Discovery Day.

**26 Fri.** *Dominican Republic:* Duarte Day. *India:* Republic Day.

**27 Sat.** *Monaco:* Saint Devota's Day. *Vietnam:* Vietnam Day.

**28 Sun.** *Rwanda:* Democracy Day. *Islamic:* Ashura (see App. B23).

**29 Mon.** *Australia:* Australia Day.

**31 Wed.** *Burma:* Full Moon Day. *Nauru:* Independence Day.

# February 2007

**1 Thu.** *Sri Lanka:* Full Moon Poya.

**2 Fri.** *Liechtenstein:* Candlemas.

**4 Sun.** *Sri Lanka:* Independence Day.

**5 Mon.** *Mexico:* Constitution Day. *United States:* Lincoln's Birthday.

**6 Tue.** *New Zealand:* Waitangi Day.

**7 Wed.** *Grenada:* Independence Day.

**8 Thu.** *Iraq:* Revolution Day.

**9 Fri.** *Lebanon:* Saint Marion's Day.

**10 Sat.** *Malta:* Saint Paul's Day.

**11 Sun.** *Cameroon:* Youth Day. *Japan:* Foundation Day. *Liberia:* Armed Forces Day.

**12 Mon.** *Burma:* Union Day.

**14 Wed.** *International:* Valentine's Day.

**17 Sat.** *Asian:* Chinese New Year Eve (see App. B1).

**18 Sun.** *Gambia:* Independence Day. *Vietnam:* Tet (1st day of 3). *Asian:* Chinese New Year (Year of the Pig) (see App. B2).

**19 Mon.** *Greece:* Shrove Monday. *Nepal:* National Day. *United States:* Washington's Birthday. *Vietnam:* Tet (2nd day of 3). *Asian:* 2nd Day of Chinese New Year (see App. B3). *Christian:* Shrove Monday (see App. B7). *Orthodox:* Shrove Monday. *Zodiac Cusp:* Aquarius ends, Pisces Begins.

**20 Tue.** *Vietnam:* Tet (3rd day of 3). *Asian:* 3rd Day of Chinese New Year (see App. B4). *Christian:* Shrove Tuesday (see App. B8).

**21 Wed.** *Bangladesh:* Saheed Day. *Christian:* Ash Wednesday (see App. B9).

**22 Thu.** *Saint Lucia:* Independence Day.

**23 Fri.** *Brunei:* National Day. *Guyana:* Republic Day.

**25 Sun.** *Kuwait:* National Day.

**27 Tue.** *Dominican Republic:* Independence Day.

# March 2007

**1 Thu.** *South Korea:* Independence Day.

**2 Fri.** *Burma:* Full Moon Day. *Ethiopia:* Victory of Aduwa Day. *Morocco:* Independence Day.

**3 Sat.** *Bulgaria:* Liberation Day. *Malawi:* Martyrs' Day. *Morocco:* National Day. *Sri Lanka:* Full Moon Poya. *Thailand:* Makha Bucha Day.

**4 Sun.** *Jewish:* Purim.

**5 Mon.** *Guam:* Discovery Day.

**6 Tue.** *Ghana:* Independence Day.

**8 Thu.** *Syria:* Revolution Day. *Multinational:* Women's Day (see App. A4).

**10 Sat.** *South Korea:* Labor Day. *Zambia:* Youth Day.

**11 Sun.** *Lithuania:* National Day*.

**12 Mon.** *Gibraltar:* Commonwealth Day. *Lesotho:* Moshoeshoe's Day. *Mauritius:* Independence Day.

**13 Tue.** *Grenada:* National Day.

**17 Sat.** *Ireland:* Saint Patrick's Day. *Northern Ireland:* Saint Patrick's Day.

**19 Mon.** *Christian:* Saint Joseph's Day (see App. A5).

**20 Tue.** *Tunisia:* Independence Day.

**21 Wed.** *Afghanistan:* New Year's Day (Shamsi: 1386). *Iran:* New Year's Day (Hegira: 1386). *Iraq:* New Year's Day. *Japan:* Vernal Equinox. *Mexico:* Juarez Day. *Zodiac Cusp:* Pisces ends, Aries begins.

**22 Thu.** *Puerto Rico:* Abolition Day.

**23 Fri.** *Pakistan:* Pakistan Day.

**25 Sun.** *Cyprus:* Greek Independence Day. *Greece:* Independence Day. *Liechtenstein:* Annunciation. *Europe:* Daylight Savings Time starts (advance clocks 1 hour).

**26 Mon.** *Bangladesh:* Independence Day. *Virgin Islands (U.S.):* Transfer Day.

**27 Tue.** *Angola:* Evacuation Day. *Burma:* Resistance Day. *Zambia:* Africa Day.

**29 Thu.** *Central African Republic:* Boganda Day. *Madagascar:* Memorial Day. *Taiwan:* Youth Day.

**30 Fri.** *Far East Islamic:* Mohammed's Birthday. *Islamic:* Mohammed's Birthday (see App. B24).

**31 Sat.** *Malta:* National Day.

# April 2007

**1 Sun.** *Burma:* Full Moon Day. *Iran:* Republic Day. *San Marino:* National Day. *Canada and United States:* Daylight Savings Time starts (advance clocks 1 hour). *Christian:* Palm Sunday.

**2 Mon.** *Sri Lanka:* Full Moon Poya.

**3 Tue.** *Israel:* Passover. *Jewish:* Passover.

**4 Wed.** *Hungary:* Liberation Day. *Senegal:* National Day.

**5 Thu.** *South Korea:* Arbor Day. *Asian:* Tomb Sweeping Day (see App. A6). *Christian:* Maundy Thursday (see App. B11).

**6 Fri.** *Sierra Leone:* Bank Holiday. *South Africa:* Founders' Day. *Thailand:* Chakri Day. *Christian:* Good Friday (see App. B12). *Orthodox:* Good Friday (see App. B20).

**7 Sat.** *Christian:* Holy Saturday (see App. B13).

**8 Sun.** *Jordan:* Easter Sunday. *Christian:* Easter Sunday (see App. B14). *Orthodox:* Easter Sunday.

**9 Mon.** *Philippines:* Valour Day. *Tunisia:* Martyrs' Day. *Christian:* Easter Monday (see App. B15). *Orthodox:* Easter Monday (see App. B20).

**11 Wed.** *Costa Rica:* Heroes' Day. *Uganda:* Liberation Day.

**13 Fri.** *Chad:* National Day. *Thailand:* Songkrawn (1st day of 2).

**14 Sat.** *Honduras:* Pan American Day. *Thailand:* Songkrawn (2nd day of 2).

**15 Sun.** *Niger:* National Day.

**16 Mon.** *Burma:* New Year's Day (Burmese: 1369). *Cyprus:* Independence Day.

**17 Tue.** *Cambodia:* Independence Day. *Syria:* Independence Day.

**18 Wed.** *Zimbabwe:* Republic Day.

**19 Thu.** *Sierra Leone:* Republic Day. *Uruguay:* Patriots' Day. *Venezuela:* Independence Day.

**20 Fri.** *Zodiac Cusp:* Aries ends, Taurus begins.

**21 Sat.** *Brazil:* Tiradentes Day.

**23 Mon.** *Israel:* Independence Day. *Turkey:* Children's Day.

**25 Wed.** *Australia:* ANZAC Day. *Egypt:* Sinai Day. *Iceland:* Children's Day. *Italy:* Liberation Day. *New Zealand:* ANZAC Day. *Portugal:* Liberation Day. *Swaziland:* Flag Day.

**26 Thu.** *Tanzania:* Union Day.

**27 Fri.** *Afghanistan:* Independence Day. *Sierra Leone:* Independence Day. *Togo:* Independence Day.

**29 Sun.** *Japan:* Green Day.

**30 Mon.** *Burma:* Full Moon Day. *Finland:* Vappu Day. *Netherlands:* Queen's Birthday.

# May 2007

**1 Tue.** *Sri Lanka:* Full Moon Poya. *Multinational:* Labor Day (see App. A7).

**2 Wed.** *Lesotho:* King's Birthday.

**3 Thu.** *Japan:* Constitution Day.

**4 Fri.** *Denmark:* All Prayers' Day. *Japan:* People's Day.

**5 Sat.** *Japan:* Children's Day. *Mexico:* Cinco de Mayo. *Netherlands:* Liberation Day. *South Korea:* Children's Day. *Thailand:* Coronation Day.

**6 Sun.** *Lebanon:* Martyrs' Day. *Philippines:* Corregidor Day.

**7 Mon.** *United Kingdom:* Labour Day. *Zambia:* Labour Day.

**8 Tue.** *France:* Liberation Day.

**9 Wed.** *Czech Republic:* Liberation Day*. *Slovakia:* Liberation Day*.

**10 Thu.** *Micronesia:* Independence Day.

**13 Sun.** *International:* Mother's Day.

**14 Mon.** *Liberia:* Unification Day. *Malawi:* Kamuzu Day. *Paraguay:* Flag Day.

**15 Tue.** *Paraguay:* Independence Day.

**17 Thu.** *Cayman Islands:* Discovery Day. *Norway:* Constitution Day. *Christian:* Ascension (see App. B16).

**18 Fri.** *Haiti:* Flag Day. *Uruguay:* Las Piedras Day.

**19 Sat.** *Finland:* Flag Day. *Turkey:* Youth Day.

**20 Sun.** *Cameroon:* Constitution Day. *Zaïre:* Popular Movement Day.

**21 Mon.** *Canada:* Victoria Day. *Chile:* Navy Day. *Zodiac Cusp:* Taurus ends, Gemini begins.

**22 Tue.** *Haiti:* Sovereign Day. *Sri Lanka:* Heroes' Day.

**23 Wed.** *Israel:* Pentecost. *Jamaica:* Labour Day. *South Korea:* Vesak Day. *Jewish:* Pentecost.

**24 Thu.** *Bulgaria:* Culture Day. *Ecuador:* Independence Battle Day.

**25 Fri.** *Argentina:* National Day. *Eritrea:* Independence Day*. *Jordan:* Independence Day. *Sudan:* Revolution Day. *Multinational:* Africa Day (see App. A8).

**26 Sat.** *Guyana:* Independence Day.

**27 Sun.** *Nigeria:* Children's Day. *Christian:* Whitsunday. *Orthodox:* Pentecost Sunday.

**28 Mon.** *Greece:* Pentecost Monday. *United Kingdom:* Spring Break. *United States:* Memorial Day. *Christian:* Whitmonday (see App. B18).

**30 Wed.** *Burma:* Full Moon Day. *Malaysia:* Vesak Day. *Singapore:* Vesak Day.

**31 Thu.** *Brunei:* Regiment Day. *South Africa:* Republic Day. *Sri Lanka:* Full Moon Poya. *Thailand:* Visakha Bucha Day.

# June 2007

**1 Fri.** *Kenya:* Madaraka Day. *Tunisia:* National Day. *Western Samoa:* Independence Day.

**2 Sat.** *Italy:* Republic Day. *Tunisia:* Youth Day.

**4 Mon.** *Bahamas:* Labour Day.

*Ireland:* Public Holiday. *New Zealand:* Queen's Birthday. *Tonga:* Independence Day.

**5 Tue.** *Denmark:* Constitution Day. *Equatorial Guinea:* President's Birthday. *Seychelles:* Liberation Day.

**6 Wed.** *Malaysia:* King's Birthday. *South Korea:* Memorial Day. *Sweden:* Constitution Day.

**7 Thu.** *Chad:* Revolution Day. *Christian:* Corpus Christi (see App. B19).

**9 Sat.** *Argentina:* Independence Day. *Hong Kong:* Queen's Birthday (1st day of 2).

**10 Sun.** *Macao:* Portugal Day. *Portugal:* Portugal Day.

**11 Mon.** *Australia:* Queen's Birthday. *Fiji:* Queen's Birthday. *Hong Kong:* Queen's Birthday (2nd day of 2). *Libya:* Evacuation Day. *New Guinea:* Queen's Birthday. *United Kingdom:* Queen's Birthday.

**12 Tue.** *Philippines:* Independence Day.

**17 Sun.** *Germany:* Unity Day. *Iceland:* Independence Day.

**18 Mon.** *Egypt:* Independence Day.

**19 Tue.** *Algeria:* Righting Day. *Kuwait:* Independence Day. *Uruguay:* Artigas Day.

**20 Wed.** *Argentina:* Flag Day.

**21 Thu.** *Finland:* Midsummer Day (1st day of 2). *Sweden:* Midsummer Day (1st day of 2). *Asian:* Dragon Boat Festival (see App. B5). *Zodiac Cusp:* Gemini ends, Cancer begins.

**22 Fri.** *Finland:* Midsummer Day (2nd day of 2). *Sweden:* Midsummer Day (2nd day of 2).

**23 Sat.** *Finland:* Johannus Day. *Luxembourg:* National Day.

**24 Sun.** *Andorra:* Saint John's Day. *Venezuela:* Carabobo Day. *Zaïre:* Constitution Day.

**25 Mon.** *Croatia:* Independence Day*. *Mozambique:* Independence Day. *Slovenia:* Independence Day*.

**26 Tue.** *Madagascar:* Independence Day. *Somalia:* Independence Day.

**27 Wed.** *Djibouti:* Independence Day.

**29 Fri.** *Burma:* Full Moon Day. *Chile:* Bank Holiday. *Ecuador:* Bank Holiday. *El Salvador:* Bank Holiday. *Finland:* Bank Holiday. *Seychelles:* Independence Day. *Sri Lanka:* Full Moon Poya. *Christian:* Saint Paul's Day (see App. A9).

**30 Sat.** *Guatemala:* Army Day. *Sri Lanka:* Bank Holiday. *Zaïre:* Independence Day.

# July 2007

**1 Sun.** *Burundi:* Independence Day. *Canada:* Canada Day. *Ghana:* Republic Day. *Hong Kong:* Half Year Day. *Rwanda:* Independence Day. *Somalia:* Union Day. *Suriname:* Freedom Day. *Multinational:* Bank Holiday (see App. A10).

**2 Mon.** *Cayman Islands:* Constitution Day. *Lesotho:* Family Day. *Zambia:* Heroes' Day.

**3 Tue.** *Zambia:* Unity Day.

**4 Wed.** *Philippines:* United States Friendship Day. *United States:* Independence Day. *Yugoslavia:* Freedom Fighters' Day.

**5 Thu.** *Algeria:* Independence Day. *Cape Verde:* Independence Day. *Rwanda:* Unity Day. *Venezuela:* Independence Day.

**6 Fri.** *Comoros:* Independence Day. *Malawi:* Republic Day.

**7 Sat.** *Solomon Islands:* Independence Day. *Tanzania:* Farmers' Day. *Yugoslavia:* Serbian Day.

**10 Tue.** *Bahamas:* Independence Day.

**11 Wed.** *Mongolia:* Revolution Day.

**12 Thu.** *Kiribati:* Independence Day. *Northern Ireland:* Battle of the Boyne Day. *São Tomé:* National Day.

**14 Sat.** *France:* National Day. *Iraq:* Revolution Day.

**15 Sun.** *Brunei:* Sultan's Birthday.

**16 Mon.** *Botswana:* President's Day.

**17 Tue.** *Iraq:* Revolution Day. *Puerto Rico:* Rivera Day. *Slovakia:* Independence Day*. *South Korea:* Constitution Day.

**18 Wed.** *Uruguay:* Constitution Day.

**19 Thu.** *Burma:* Martyrs' Day. *Laos:* Independence Day. *Nicaragua:* Sandinista Day.

**20 Fri.** *Colombia:* Independence Day.

**21 Sat.** *Belgium:* National Day. *Guam:* Liberation Day.

**22 Sun.** *Poland:* Liberation Day.

**23 Mon.** *Egypt:* Revolution Day. *New Guinea:* Remembrance Day. *Virgin Islands (U.S.):* Hurricane Supplication Day. *Zodiac Cusp:* Cancer ends, Leo begins.

**24 Tue.** *Israel:* Tisha Ab. *Venezuela:* Bolivar Day. *Jewish:* Tisha Ab.

**25 Wed.** *Costa Rica:* Guanacaste Day. *Cuba:* Revolution Day (1st day of 3). *Puerto Rico:* Constitution Day. *Spain:* Santiago Day. *Tunisia:* Republic Day.

**26 Thu.** *Cuba:* Revolution Day (2nd day of 3). *Liberia:* Independence Day. *Maldives:* Independence Day.

**27 Fri.** *Cuba:* Revolution Day (3rd day of 3). *Puerto Rico:* Barbosa Day.

**28 Sat.** *Burma:* Full Moon Day. *Peru:* Independence Day (1st day of 2).

**29 Sun.** *Peru:* Independence Day (2nd day of 2). *Sri Lanka:* Full Moon Poya. *Thailand:* Asalaha Bucha Day.

**30 Mon.** *Vanuatu:* Independence Day. *Thailand:* Khao Phansa Day.

# August 2007

**1 Wed.** *Benin:* Independence Day. *Switzerland:* Confederation Day. *Zambia:* Farmers' Day.

**2 Thu.** *Costa Rica:* Virgin of the Angels Day. *Guyana:* Freedom Day. *Trinidad:* Discovery Day.

**3 Fri.** *El Salvador:* Summer Day (1st day of 4). *Guinea-Bissau:* Martyrs' Day. *Niger:* Independence Day. *Tunisia:* President's Birthday.

**4 Sat.** *Burkina Faso:* Independence Day (1st day of 2). *El Salvador:* Summer Day (2nd day of 4).

**5 Sun.** *Burkina Faso:* Independence Day (2nd day of 2). *El Salvador:* Summer Day (3rd day of 4).

**6 Mon.** *Bahamas:* Emancipation Day. *Barbados:* Emancipation Day. *Bolivia:* Independence Day. *Canada:* Civic Holiday. *El Salvador:* Summer Day (4th day of 4). *Ireland:* Public Holiday. *Jamaica:* Independence Day. *Scotland:* Public Holiday. *United Arab Emirates:* Accession Day.

**7 Tue.** *Colombia:* Boyaca Day. *Ivory Coast:* Republic Day.

**9 Thu.** *Georgia:* Independence Day*. *Singapore:* National Day.

**10 Fri.** *Ecuador:* Independence Day. *Islamic:* Isra a Majraj (see App. B30).

**11 Sat.** *Chad:* Independence Day. *Jordan:* Accession Day. *Zimbabwe:* Heroes' Day (1st day of 2).

**12 Sun.** *Thailand:* Queen's Birthday. *Zimbabwe:* Heroes' Day (2nd day of 2).

**13 Mon.** *Central African Republic:* Independence Day. *Congo:* Independence Day (1st day of 2). *Tunisia:* Women's Day.

**14 Tue.** *Congo:* Independence Day (2nd day of 2). *Pakistan:* Independence Day.

**15 Wed.** *Congo:* Independence Day (3rd day of 3). *India:* Independence Day. *Liechtenstein:* National Day. *South Korea:* Republic Day. *Christian:* Assumption (see App. A11).

**16 Thu.** *Dominican Republic:* Republic Day.

**17 Fri.** *Argentina:* San Martin's Day. *Gabon:* Independence Day. *Indonesia:* Independence Day.

**20 Mon.** *Hungary:* Constitution Day. *Senegal:* Independence Day.

**21 Tue.** *Estonia:* Independence Day*. *Latvia:* Independence Day*. *Lithuania:* Independence Day*.

**23 Thu.** *Romania:* National Day (1st day of 2). *Zodiac Cusp:* Leo ends, Virgo begins.

**24 Fri.** *Kazakhstan:* National Day*. *Liberia:* Flag Day. *Romania:* National Day (2nd day of 2). *Russia:* Independence Day*. *Ukraine:* National Day*.

**25 Sat.** *Belarus:* Independence Day*. *Hong Kong:* Liberation Day. (1st day of 2). *Paraguay:* Constitution Day. *Uruguay:* Independence Day.

**26 Sun.** *Burma:* Full Moon Day.

**27 Mon.** *England:* Summer Break. *Hong Kong:* Liberation Day (2nd day of 2). *Moldova:* Independence Day*. *Northern Ireland:* Public Holiday. *Sri Lanka:* Full Moon Poya. *Wales:* Summer Break.

**29 Wed.** *Uzbekistan:* Independence Day*.

**30 Thu.** *Afghanistan:* Children's Day. *Azerbaijan:* Independence Day*. *Peru:* Rose of Lima Day. *Turkey:* Victory Day.

**31 Fri.** *Afghanistan:* Pashtunistan Day. *Kyrgyzstan:* Independence Day*. *Malaysia:* National Day. *Trinidad:* Independence Day.

# September 2007

**1 Sat.** *Libya:* National Day. *Mexico:* President's Message Day. *Syria:* United Arab Republics Day.

**2 Sun.** *Vietnam:* Independence Day.

**3 Mon.** *Canada:* Labour Day. *Luxembourg:* Fair Day. *Qatar:* National Day. *San Marino:* Saint Marinus' Day. *Tunisia:* Independence Movement Day. *United States:* Labor Day.

**6 Thu.** *Pakistan:* Defense Day. *Swaziland:* Independence Day.

**7 Fri.** *Brazil:* Independence Day.

**8 Sat.** *Andorra:* National Day. *Malta:* Our Lady of Victory Day.

**9 Sun.** *Bulgaria:* National Day (1st day of 2). *North Korea:* Independence Day. *Tajikistan:* Independence Day*.

**10 Mon.** *Belize:* National Day. *Bulgaria:* National Day (2nd day of 2).

**11 Tue.** *Chile:* Revolution Day. *Pakistan:* Anniversary of Quaid-e-Azam's Death.

**12 Wed.** *Egypt:* New Year's Day (Coptic: 1725). *Ethiopia:* National Day and New Year's Day (Ethiopian: 2001). *Islamic:* 1st Day of Ramadan (see App. B25).

**13 Thu.** *Israel:* New Year's Day. *Jewish:* Rosh Hashanah (Jewish: 5768).

**14 Fri.** *Guatemala:* San Jacinto Day. *Nicaragua:* San Jacinto Day.

**15 Sat.** *Costa Rica:* Independence Day. *El Salvador:* Independence Day. *Guatemala:* Independence Day. *Honduras:* Independence Day. *Japan:* Veneration Day. *Nicaragua:* Independence Day.

**16 Sun.** *Mexico:* Independence Day. *New Guinea:* Independence Day.

**17 Mon.** *Angola:* Heroes' Day. *Marshall Islands:* Independence Day.

**18 Tue.** *Burundi:* Victory of Uprona Day. *Chile:* Independence Day.

**19 Wed.** *Chile:* Armed Forces Day. *Saint Kitts:* Independence Day.

**21 Fri.** *Belize:* Independence Day. *Malta:* Independence Day.

**22 Sat.** *Israel:* Yom Kippur. *Mali:* Independence Day. *Jewish:* Yom Kippur.

**23 Sun.** *Armenia:* Independence Day*. *Japan:* Autumnal Equinox. *Saudi Arabia:* National Day. *Zodiac Cusp:* Virgo ends, Libra begins.

**24 Mon.** *Dominican Republic:* Mercedes Day. *Guinea-Bissau:* Republic Day.

**25 Tue.** *Burma:* Full Moon Day. *Mo-*

*zambique:* Liberation Day. *Rwanda:* Assembly Day.

**26 Wed.** *China:* Mid-autumn Day. *Sri Lanka:* Full Moon Poya. *Taiwan:* Mid-autumn Day.

**27 Thu.** *Ethiopia:* True Cross Day. *Hong Kong:* Mid-autumn Day. *Israel:* Sukkot. *Macao:* Mid-autumn Day. *Jewish:* Sukkot.

**28 Fri.** *Taiwan:* Teachers' Day.

**29 Sat.** *Brunei:* Constitution Day. *Paraguay:* Boqueron Battle Day.

**30 Sun.** *Botswana:* Independence Day. *Europe:* Daylight Savings Time ends (retard clocks 1 hour).

# October 2007

**1 Mon.** *Barbados:* Bank Holiday. *Cameroon:* Unification Day. *China:* National Day (1st day of 2). *Nigeria:* Independence Day. *South Korea:* Armed Forces Day (1st day of 2). *Tuvalu:* Independence Day.

**2 Tue.** *China:* National Day (2nd day of 2). *Guinea:* Independence Day. *India:* Ghandi Day. *South Korea:* Armed Forces Day. (2nd day of 2).

**3 Wed.** *Honduras:* Morazan Day. *South Korea:* Foundation Day (1st day of 2).

**4 Thu.** *Lesotho:* Independence Day. *South Korea:* Foundation Day. (2nd day of 2).

**5 Fri.** *Lesotho:* Sports Day. *Macao:* Portuguese Republic Day. *Portugal:* Republic Day.

**6 Sat.** *Egypt:* Armed Forces Day.

**8 Mon.** *Canada:* Thanksgiving Day. *Fiji:* Cession Day. *United States:* Bank Holiday. *Virgin Islands (U.S.):* Puerto Rican Friendship Day.

**9 Tue.** *Peru:* National Dignity Day. *South Korea:* Alphabet Day. *Uganda:* Independence Day.

**10 Wed.** *Japan:* Health Day. *South Africa:* Kruger Day. *Taiwan:* National Day.

**11 Thu.** *Cuba:* Independence War. *Panama:* Revolution Day.

**12 Fri.** *Equatorial Guinea:* Independence Day. *Spain:* National Day. *Far East Islamic:* Hari Raya Puasa (see App. B27). *Islamic:* Eid al Fitr (1st day of 4) (see App. B26). *Multinational:* Columbus Day (see App. A12).

**13 Sat.** *Islamic:* Eid al Fitr (2nd day of 4) (see App. B26).

**14 Sun.** *Zaïre:* Founders' Day. *Islamic:* Eid al Fitr (3rd day of 4) (see App. B26).

**15 Mon.** *Bosnia and Herzegovina:* Independence Day*. *Jamaica:* Heroes' Day. *Tunisia:* Evacuation Day. *Islamic:* Eid al Fitr (4th day of 4) (see App. B26).

**17 Wed.** *Haiti:* Dessalines Day. *Malawi:* Mother's Day.

**20 Sat.** *Guatemala:* Revolution Day. *Kenya:* Kenyatta Day. *Asian:* Ancestors' Day (see App. B6).

**21 Sun.** *Honduras:* Army Day. *Somalia:* Revolution Day (1st day of 2).

**22 Mon.** *Somalia:* Revolution Day (2nd day of 2). *Vatican:* John Paul II Day.

**23 Tue.** *Hungary:* Revolution Day. *Thailand:* Chulalongkorn Day. *Zodiac Cusp:* Libra ends, Scorpio begins.

**24 Wed.** *Burma:* Full Moon Day. *Egypt:* Suez Victory Day. *Haiti:* United Nations Day. *Zambia:* Independence Day.

**25 Thu.** *Sri Lanka:* Full Moon Poya. *Taiwan:* Restoration Day.

**26 Fri.** *Austria:* National Day. *Benin:* Revolution Day. *Rwanda:* Government Day.

**27 Sat.** *Saint Vincent:* Independence Day. *Turkmenistan:* Independence Day*. *Zaïre:* Naming Day.

**28 Sun.** *Greece:* Ohi! Day. *Canada and United States:* Daylight Savings Time ends (retard clocks 1 hour).

**29 Mon.** *Ireland:* Public Holiday. *New Zealand:* Labour Day. *Tanzania:* Naming Day. *Turkey:* Republic Day.

**31 Wed.** *Taiwan:* Chiang Kai-shek's Birthday.

# November 2007

**1 Thu.** *Algeria:* Revolution Day. *Antigua:* Independence Day. *Liberia:* Thanksgiving Day. *Christian:* All Saints' Day (see App. A13).

**2 Fri.** *Brazil:* Memorial Day. *Finland:* All Saints' Eve. *Sweden:* All Saints' Eve. *Christian:* All Souls' Day (see App. A14).

**3 Sat.** *Dominica:* Independence Day. *Ecuador:* Cuenca Independence Day. *Japan:* Culture Day. *Panama:* Independence Day.

**4 Sun.** *Andorra:* Saint Charles' Day. *Panama:* Flag Day. *Vatican:* John Paul II's Nameday.

**5 Mon.** *El Salvador:* Cry of Independence Day. *Virgin Islands (U.S.):* Liberty Day.

**7 Wed.** *Bangladesh:* Revolution Day.

**8 Thu.** *Nepal:* Queen's Birthday. *Hindu:* Deepavali (see App. B21).

**9 Fri.** *Pakistan:* Iqbal Day.

**10 Sat.** *Panama:* Cry of Independence Day.

**11 Sun.** *Angola:* Independence Day. *Bhutan:* King's Birthday. *Maldives:* Republic Day. *Poland:* Independence Day. *Multinational:* Armistice Day (see App. A15).

**12 Mon.** *Taiwan:* Dr. Sun Yat-sen's Birthday.

**14 Wed.** *Jordan:* King's Birthday.

**15 Thu.** *Brazil:* Republic Day.

**17 Sat.** *Zaïre:* Armed Forces Day.

**18 Sun.** *Haiti:* Vertieres' Day. *Morocco:* Independence Day. *Oman:* National Day.

**19 Mon.** *Belize:* Garifuna Day. *Fiji:* Prince Charles' Birthday. *Mali:* Army Coup Day. *Monaco:* Prince Ranier's Day. *Puerto Rico:* Discovery Day.

**20 Tue.** *Mexico:* Revolution Day.

**21 Wed.** *Germany:* Repentance Day.

**22 Thu.** *Lebanon:* Independence Day. *United States:* Thanksgiving Day. *Zodiac Cusp:* Scorpio ends, Sagittarius begins.

**23 Fri.** *Burma:* Full Moon Day. *Japan:* Labor Thanksgiving Day.

**24 Sat.** *Sri Lanka:* Full Moon Poya. *Zaïre:* New Regime Day.

**25 Sun.** *Suriname:* Independence Day.

**28 Wed.** *Albania:* Independence Day. *Burundi:* Republic Day. *Chad:* Republic Day. *Mauritania:* Independence Day. *Panama:* Independence Day.

**29 Thu.** *Albania:* Liberation Day. *Liberia:* Tubman's Birthday. *Yugoslavia:* Republic Day.

**30 Fri.** *Argentina:* Bank Holiday. *Barbados:* Independence Day. *Benin:* National Day. *Philippines:* Heroes' Day.

# December 2007

**1 Sat.** *Central African Republic:* National Day. *Portugal:* Youth Day. *Ukraine:* Independence Day*.

**2 Sun.** *Laos:* Republic Day. *United Arab Emirates:* National Day.

**5 Wed.** *Haiti:* Discovery Day. *Thailand:* King's Birthday. *Jewish:* Chanukah.

**6 Thu.** *Finland:* Independence Day.

**7 Fri.** *Ivory Coast:* Independence Day.

**8 Sat.** *Christian:* Immaculate Conception (see App. A16).

**9 Sun.** *Tanzania:* Independence Day.

**10 Mon.** *Angola:* MPLA Foundation Day. *Equatorial Guinea:* Human Rights Day. *Namibia:* Settlers' Day. *Thailand:* Constitution Day.

**11 Tue.** *Burkina Faso:* National Day.

**12 Wed.** *Kenya:* Independence Day. *Mexico:* Guadalupe Festival.

**13 Thu.** *Malta:* Republic Day.

**16 Sun.** *Bahrain:* National Day. *Bangladesh:* Victory Day. *Nepal:* Constitution Day. *South Africa:* Covenant Day.

**17 Mon.** *Bhutan:* National Day.

**18 Tue.** *Niger:* Republic Day.

**19 Wed.** *Islamic:* Eid al Adha (1st day of 4) (see App. B28).

**20 Thu.** *Far East Islamic:* Hari Raya Haji (see App. B29). *Islamic:* Eid al Adha (2nd day of 4) (see App. B28).

**21 Fri.** *Kazakhstan:* Independence Day*. *Islamic:* Eid al Adha (3rd day of 4) (see App. B28).

**22 Sat.** *Burma:* Full Moon Day. *Islamic:* Eid al Adha (4th day of 4) (see App. B28). *Zodiac Cusp:* Sagittarius ends, Capricorn begins.

**23 Sun.** *Japan:* Emperor's Birthday. *Sri Lanka:* Full Moon Poya.

**24 Mon.** *Multinational:* Christmas Eve (see App. A17).

**25 Tue.** *Angola:* Family Day. *Congo:* Children's Day. *Pakistan:* Quaid's Birthday. *Taiwan:* Constitution Day. *Multinational:* Christmas Day (see App. A18).

**26 Wed.** *South Africa:* Good Will Day. *Multinational:* Boxing Day (see App. A19).

**30 Sun.** *Madagascar:* Republic Day. *Philippines:* Rizal Day (1st day of 2).

**31 Mon.** *Congo:* Republic Day. *Philippines:* Rizal Day (2nd day of 2). *Multinational:* Bank Holiday and New Year's Eve (see App. A20 & A21).

# January 2008

**1 Tue.** *Cameroon:* Independence Day. *Cuba:* Liberation Day. *Haiti:* Independence Day. *Palau:* Independence Day. *Sudan:* Independence Day. *Taiwan:* Foundation Day (1st day of 2). *Western Samoa:* Independence Day. *Multinational:* Bank Holiday and New Year's Day (see App. A1 & A2).

**2 Wed.** *Japan:* Bank Holiday. *New Zealand:* New Year's Day (2nd day of 2). *Scotland:* New Year's Day (2nd day of 2). *South Korea:* New Year's Day (2nd day of 2). *Switzerland:* Berchtold's Day. *Taiwan:* Foundation Day (2nd day of 2).

**3 Thu.** *Burkina Faso:* Revolution Day.

**4 Fri.** *Burma:* Independence Day. *Zaïre:* Martyrs' Day.

**6 Sun.** *Iraq:* Army Day. *Uruguay:* Children's Day. *Christian:* Epiphany (see App. A3).

**7 Mon.** *Egypt:* Coptic Christmas. *Ethiopia:* Coptic Christmas.

**8 Tue.** *Islamic:* New Year's Day (Hegira: 1429) (see App. B22).

**9 Wed.** *Far East Islamic:* New Year's Day (Hegira: 1429).

**11 Fri.** *Albania:* Republic Day. *Nepal:* Unification Day. *Puerto Rico:* Hostos Day.

**12 Sat.** *Tanzania:* Revolution Day.

**13 Sun.** *Togo:* Liberation Day.

**15 Tue.** *Japan:* Adult's Day. *Jordan:* Arbor Day.

**17 Thu.** *Islamic:* Ashura (see App. B23).

**19 Sat.** *Ethiopia:* Epiphany. *Zodiac Cusp:* Capricorn ends, Aquarius begins.

**20 Sun.** *Mali:* Award Day.

**21 Mon.** *Burma:* Full Moon Day. *Dominican Republic:* Altagracia Day. *Sri Lanka:* Full Moon Poya. *United States:* Martin Luther King's Birthday.

**22 Tue.** *Saint Vincent:* Discovery Day.

**26 Sat.** *Dominican Republic:* Duarte Day. *India:* Republic Day.

**27 Sun.** *Monaco:* Saint Devota's Day. *Vietnam:* Vietnam Day.

**28 Mon.** *Australia:* Australia Day. *Rwanda:* Democracy Day.

**31 Thu.** *Nauru:* Independence Day.

# February 2008

**2 Sat.** *Liechtenstein:* Candlemas.

**4 Mon.** *Sri Lanka:* Independence Day. *United States:* Lincoln's Birthday. *Christian:* Shrove Monday (see App. B7).

**5 Tue.** *Mexico:* Constitution Day. *Christian:* Shrove Tuesday (see App. B8).

**6 Wed.** *New Zealand:* Waitangi Day. *Asian:* Chinese New Year Eve (see App. B1). *Christian:* Ash Wednesday (see App. B9).

**7 Thu.** *Grenada:* Independence Day. *Vietnam:* Tet (1st day of 3). *Asian:* Chinese New Year (Year of the Rat) (see App. B2).

**8 Fri.** *Iraq:* Revolution Day. *Vietnam:* Tet (2nd day of 3). *Asian:* 2nd Day of Chinese New Year (see App. B3).

**9 Sat.** *Lebanon:* Saint Marion's Day. *Vietnam:* Tet (3rd day of 3). *Asian:* 3rd Day of Chinese New Year (see App. B4).

**10 Sun.** *Malta:* Saint Paul's Day.

**11 Mon.** *Cameroon:* Youth Day. *Japan:* Foundation Day. *Liberia:* Armed Forces Day.

**12 Tue.** *Burma:* Union Day.

**14 Thu.** *International:* Valentine's Day.

**18 Mon.** *Gambia:* Independence Day. *United States:* Washington's Birthday. *Zodiac Cusp:* Aquarius ends, Pisces begins.

**19 Tue.** *Burma:* Full Moon Day. *Nepal:* National Day.

**20 Wed.** *Sri Lanka:* Full Moon Poya.

**21 Thu.** *Bangladesh:* Saheed Day. *Thailand:* Makha Bucha Day.

**22 Fri.** *Saint Lucia:* Independence Day.

**23 Sat.** *Brunei:* National Day. *Guyana:* Republic Day.

**25 Mon.** *Kuwait:* National Day.

**27 Wed.** *Dominican Republic:* Independence Day.

# March 2008

**1 Sat.** *South Korea:* Independence Day.

**2 Sun.** *Ethiopia:* Victory of Aduwa Day. *Morocco:* Independence Day.

**3 Mon.** *Bulgaria:* Liberation Day. *Guam:* Discovery Day. *Malawi:* Martyrs' Day. *Morocco:* National Day.

**6 Thu.** *Ghana:* Independence Day.

**8 Sat.** *Syria:* Revolution Day. *Zambia:* Youth Day. *Multinational:* Women's Day (see App. A4).

**10 Mon.** *Gibraltar:* Commonwealth Day. *Greece:* Shrove Monday. *South Korea:* Labor Day. *Orthodox:* Shrove Monday.

**11 Tue.** *Lithuania:* National Day*.

**12 Wed.** *Lesotho:* Moshoeshoe's Day. *Mauritius:* Independence Day.

**13 Thu.** *Grenada:* National Day.

**16 Sun.** *Christian:* Palm Sunday.

**17 Mon.** *Ireland:* Saint Patrick's Day. *Northern Ireland:* Saint Patrick's Day.

**18 Tue.** *Islamic:* Mohammed's Birthday (see App. B24).

**19 Wed.** *Christian:* Saint Joseph's

Day (see App. A5). *Far East Islamic:* Mohammed's Birthday.

**20 Thu.** *Afghanistan:* New Year's Day (Shamsi: 1387). *Burma:* Full Moon Day. *Iran:* New Year's Day (Hegira: 1387). *Iraq:* New Year's Day. *Japan:* Vernal Equinox. *Tunisia:* Independence Day. *Christian:* Maundy Thursday (see App. B11). *Zodiac Cusp:* Pisces ends, Aries begins.

**21 Fri.** *Mexico:* Juarez Day. *Sri Lanka:* Full Moon Poya. *Christian:* Good Friday (see App. B12). *Jewish:* Purim.

**22 Sat.** *Puerto Rico:* Abolition Day. *Christian:* Holy Saturday (see App. B13).

**23 Sun.** *Pakistan:* Pakistan Day. *Christian:* Easter Sunday (see App. B14).

**24 Mon.** *Christian:* Easter Monday (see App. B15).

**25 Tue.** *Cyprus:* Greek Independence Day. *Greece:* Independence Day. *Liechtenstein:* Annunciation. *Zambia:* Africa Day.

**26 Wed.** *Bangladesh:* Independence Day.

**27 Thu.** *Angola:* Evacuation Day. *Burma:* Resistance Day.

**29 Sat.** *Central African Republic:* Boganda Day. *Madagascar:* Memorial Day. *Taiwan:* Youth Day.

**30 Sun.** *Europe:* Daylight Savings Time starts (advance clocks 1 hour).

**31 Mon.** *Malta:* National Day. *Virgin Islands (U.S.):* Transfer Day.

# April 2008

**1 Tue.** *Iran:* Republic Day. *San Marino:* National Day.

**4 Fri.** *Hungary:* Liberation Day. *Senegal:* National Day. *Sierra Leone:* Bank Holiday.

**5 Sat.** *South Korea:* Arbor Day. *Asian:* Tomb Sweeping Day (see App. A6).

**6 Sun.** *South Africa:* Founders' Day. *Thailand:* Chakri Day. *Canada and United States:* Daylight Savings Time starts (advance clocks 1 hour).

**9 Wed.** *Philippines:* Valour Day. *Tunisia:* Martyrs' Day.

**11 Fri.** *Costa Rica:* Heroes' Day. *Uganda:* Liberation Day.

**13 Sun.** *Chad:* National Day. *Thailand:* Songkrawn (1st day of 2).

**14 Mon.** *Honduras:* Pan American Day. *Thailand:* Songkrawn (2nd day of 2).

**15 Tue.** *Niger:* National Day.

**16 Wed.** *Burma:* New Year's Day (Burmese: 1370). *Cyprus:* Independence Day.

**17 Thu.** *Cambodia:* Independence Day. *Syria:* Independence Day.

**18 Fri.** *Burma:* Full Moon Day. *Denmark:* All Prayers' Day. *Zimbabwe:* Republic Day.

**19 Sat.** *Sierra Leone:* Republic Day. *Sri Lanka:* Full Moon Poya. *Uruguay:* Patriots' Day. *Venezuela:* Independence Day. *Zodiac Cusp:* Aries ends, Taurus begins.

**20 Sun.** *Israel:* Passover. *Jewish:* Passover.

**21 Mon.** *Brazil:* Tiradentes Day.

**23 Wed.** *Turkey:* Children's Day.

**25 Fri.** *Australia:* ANZAC Day. *Egypt:* Sinai Day. *Iceland:* Children's Day. *Italy:* Liberation Day. *New Zealand:* ANZAC Day. *Portugal:* Liberation Day. *Swaziland:* Flag Day. *Orthodox:* Good Friday (see App. B20).

**26 Sat.** *Tanzania:* Union Day.

**27 Sun.** *Afghanistan:* Independence Day. *Jordan:* Easter Sunday. *Sierra Leone:* Independence Day. *Togo:* Independence Day. *Orthodox:* Easter Sunday.

**28 Mon.** *Orthodox:* Easter Monday (see App. B20).

**29 Tue.** *Japan:* Green Day.

**30 Wed.** *Finland:* Vappu Day. *Netherlands:* Queen's Birthday.

# May 2008

**1 Thu.** *Christian:* Ascension (see App. B16). *Multinational:* Labor Day (see App. A7).

**2 Fri.** *Lesotho:* King's Birthday.

**3 Sat.** *Japan:* Constitution Day.

**4 Sun.** *Japan:* People's Day.

**5 Mon.** *Japan:* Children's Day. *Mexico:* Cinco de Mayo. *Netherlands:* Liberation Day. *South Korea:* Children's Day. *Thailand:* Coronation Day. *United Kingdom:* Labour Day. *Zambia:* Labour Day.

**6 Tue.** *Lebanon:* Martyrs' Day. *Philippines:* Corregidor Day.

**8 Thu.** *France:* Liberation Day.

**9 Fri.** *Czech Republic:* Liberation Day*. *Slovakia:* Liberation Day*.

**10 Sat.** *Israel:* Independence Day. *Micronesia:* Independence Day.

**11 Sun.** *International:* Mother's Day. *Christian:* Whitsunday.

**12 Mon.** *South Korea:* Vesak Day. *Christian:* Whitmonday (see App. B18).

**14 Wed.** *Liberia:* Unification Day. *Malawi:* Kamuzu Day. *Paraguay:* Flag Day.

**15 Thu.** *Paraguay:* Independence Day.

**17 Sat.** *Cayman Islands:* Discovery Day. *Norway:* Constitution Day.

**18 Sun.** *Burma:* Full Moon Day. *Haiti:* Flag Day. *Uruguay:* Las Piedras Day.

**19 Mon.** *Canada:* Victoria Day. *Finland:* Flag Day. *Malaysia:* Vesak Day. *Singapore:* Vesak Day. *Sri Lanka:* Full Moon Poya. *Thailand:* Visakha Bucha Day. *Turkey:* Youth Day.

**20 Tue.** *Cameroon:* Constitution Day. *Zaïre:* Popular Movement Day. *Zodiac Cusp:* Taurus ends, Gemini begins.

**21 Wed.** *Chile:* Navy Day.

**22 Thu.** *Haiti:* Sovereign Day. *Sri Lanka:* Heroes' Day. *Christian:* Corpus Christi (see App. B19).

**23 Fri.** *Jamaica:* Labour Day.

**24 Sat.** *Bulgaria:* Culture Day. *Ecuador:* Independence Battle Day.

**25 Sun.** *Argentina:* National Day. *Eritrea:* Independence Day*. *Jordan:* Independence Day. *Sudan:* Revolution Day. *Multinational:* Africa Day (see App. A8).

**26 Mon.** *Guyana:* Independence Day. *United Kingdom:* Spring Break. *United States:* Memorial Day.

**27 Tue.** *Nigeria:* Children's Day.

**31 Sat.** *Brunei:* Regiment Day. *South Africa:* Republic Day.

# June 2008

**1 Sun.** *Kenya:* Madaraka Day. *Tunisia:* National Day. *Western Samoa:* Independence Day.

**2 Mon.** *Ireland:* Public Holiday. *Italy:* Republic Day. *New Zealand:* Queen's Birthday. *Tunisia:* Youth Day.

**4 Wed.** *Bahamas:* Labour Day. *Malaysia:* King's Birthday. *Tonga:* Independence Day.

**5 Thu.** *Denmark:* Constitution Day. *Equatorial Guinea:* President's Birthday. *Seychelles:* Liberation Day.

**6 Fri.** *South Korea:* Memorial Day. *Sweden:* Constitution Day.

**7 Sat.** *Chad:* Revolution Day.

**9 Mon.** *Argentina:* Independence Day. *Australia:* Queen's Birthday. *Fiji:* Queen's Birthday. *Israel:* Pentecost. *New Guinea:* Queen's Birthday. *United Kingdom:* Queen's Birthday. *Asian:* Dragon Boat Festival (see App. B5). *Jewish:* Pentecost.

**10 Tue.** *Macao:* Portugal Day. *Portugal:* Portugal Day.

**11 Wed.** *Libya:* Evacuation Day.

**12 Thu.** *Philippines:* Independence Day.

**14 Sat.** *Hong Kong:* Queen's Birthday (1st day of 2).

**15 Sun.** *Orthodox:* Pentecost Sunday.

**16 Mon.** *Greece:* Pentecost Monday. *Hong Kong:* Queen's Birthday (2nd day of 2).

**17 Tue.** *Burma:* Full Moon Day. *Germany:* Unity Day. *Iceland:* Independence Day.

**18 Wed.** *Egypt:* Independence Day. *Sri Lanka:* Full Moon Poya.

**19 Thu.** *Algeria:* Righting Day. *Kuwait:* Independence Day. *Uruguay:* Artigas Day.

**20 Fri.** *Argentina:* Flag Day.

**21 Sat.** *Finland:* Johannus and Midsummer Day (1st day of 2). *Sweden:* Midsummer Day (1st day of 2). *Zodiac Cusp:* Gemini ends, Cancer begins.

**22 Sun.** *Finland:* Midsummer Day (2nd day of 2). *Sweden:* Midsummer Day (2nd day of 2).

**23 Mon.** *Luxembourg:* National Day.

**24 Tue.** *Andorra:* Saint John's Day. *Venezuela:* Carabobo Day. *Zaïre:* Constitution Day.

**25 Wed.** *Croatia:* Independence Day*. *Mozambique:* Independence Day. *Slovenia:* Independence Day*.

**26 Thu.** *Madagascar:* Independence Day. *Somalia:* Independence Day.

**27 Fri.** *Chile:* Bank Holiday. *Djibouti:* Independence Day. *Ecuador:* Bank Holiday. *El Salvador:* Bank Holiday. *Finland:* Bank Holiday.

**29 Sun.** *Seychelles:* Independence Day. *Christian:* Saint Paul's Day (see App. A9).

**30 Mon.** *Guatemala:* Army Day. *Sri Lanka:* Bank Holiday. *Zaïre:* Independence Day.

# July 2008

**1 Tue.** *Burundi:* Independence Day. *Canada:* Canada Day. *Ghana:* Republic Day. *Hong Kong:* Half Year Day. *Rwanda:* Independence Day. *Somalia:* Union Day. *Suriname:* Freedom Day. *Zambia:* Unity Day. *Multinational:* Bank Holiday (see App. A10).

**4 Fri.** *Philippines:* United States Friendship Day. *United States:* Independence Day. *Yugoslavia:* Freedom Fighters' Day.

**5 Sat.** *Algeria:* Independence Day. *Cape Verde:* Independence Day. *Rwanda:* Unity Day. *Venezuela:* Independence Day.

**6 Sun.** *Comoros:* Independence Day. *Malawi:* Republic Day.

**7 Mon.** *Cayman Islands:* Constitution Day. *Lesotho:* Family Day. *Solomon Islands:* Independence Day. *Tanzania:* Farmers' Day. *Yugoslavia:* Serbian Day. *Zambia:* Heroes' Day.

**10 Thu.** *Bahamas:* Independence Day.

**11 Fri.** *Mongolia:* Revolution Day.

**12 Sat.** *Kiribati:* Independence Day. *Northern Ireland:* Battle of the Boyne Day. *São Tomé:* National Day.

**14 Mon.** *France:* National Day. *Iraq:* Revolution Day.

**15 Tue.** *Brunei:* Sultan's Birthday.

**16 Wed.** *Burma:* Full Moon Day.

**17 Thu.** *Iraq:* Revolution Day. *Puerto Rico:* Rivera Day. *Slovakia:* Independence Day*. *South Korea:* Constitution Day. *Sri Lanka:* Full Moon Poya. *Thailand:* Asalaha Bucha Day.

**18 Fri.** *Thailand:* Khao Phansa Day. *Uruguay:* Constitution Day.

**19 Sat.** *Burma:* Martyrs' Day. *Laos:* Independence Day. *Nicaragua:* Sandinista Day.

**20 Sun.** *Colombia:* Independence Day.

**21 Mon.** *Belgium:* National Day. *Botswana:* President's Day. *Guam:* Liberation Day.

**22 Tue.** *Poland:* Liberation Day. *Zodiac Cusp:* Cancer ends, Leo begins.

**23 Wed.** *Egypt:* Revolution Day. *New Guinea:* Remembrance Day.

**24 Thu.** *Venezuela:* Bolivar Day.

**25 Fri.** *Costa Rica:* Guanacaste Day. *Cuba:* Revolution Day (1st day of 3). *Puerto Rico:* Constitution Day. *Spain:* Santiago Day. *Tunisia:* Republic Day.

**26 Sat.** *Cuba:* Revolution Day (2nd day of 3). *Liberia:* Independence Day. *Maldives:* Independence Day.

**27 Sun.** *Cuba:* Revolution Day (3rd day of 3). *Puerto Rico:* Barbosa Day.

**28 Mon.** *Peru:* Independence Day (1st day of 2). *Virgin Islands (U.S.):* Hurricane Supplication Day.

**29 Tue.** *Peru:* Independence Day (2nd day of 2). *Islamic:* Isra a Majraj (see App. B30).

**30 Wed.** *Vanuatu:* Independence Day.

# August 2008

**1 Fri.** *Benin:* Independence Day. *Switzerland:* Confederation Day.

**2 Sat.** *Costa Rica:* Virgin of the Angels Day. *Guyana:* Freedom Day. *Trinidad:* Discovery Day.

**3 Sun.** *El Salvador:* Summer Day (1st day of 4). *Guinea-Bissau:* Martyrs' Day. *Niger:* Independence Day. *Tunisia:* President's Birthday.

**4 Mon.** *Bahamas:* Emancipation Day. *Barbados:* Emancipation Day. *Burkina Faso:* Independence Day (1st day of 2). *Canada:* Civic Holiday. *El Salvador:* Summer Day (2nd day of 4). *Ireland:* Public Holiday. *Jamaica:* Independence Day. *Scotland:* Public Holiday.

**5 Tue.** *Burkina Faso:* Independence Day (2nd day of 2). *El Salvador:* Summer Day (3rd day of 4).

**6 Wed.** *Bolivia:* Independence Day. *El Salvador:* Summer Day (4th day of 4). *United Arab Emirates:* Accession Day. *Zambia:* Farmers' Day.

**7 Thu.** *Colombia:* Boyaca Day. *Ivory Coast:* Republic Day.

**9 Sat.** *Georgia:* Independence Day*. *Singapore:* National Day.

**10 Sun.** *Ecuador:* Independence Day. *Israel:* Tisha Ab. *Jewish:* Tisha Ab.

**11 Mon.** *Chad:* Independence Day. *Jordan:* Accession Day. *Zimbabwe:* Heroes' Day (1st day of 2).

**12 Tue.** *Thailand:* Queen's Birthday. *Zimbabwe:* Heroes' Day (2nd day of 2).

**13 Wed.** *Central African Republic:* Independence Day. *Congo:* Independence Day (1st day of 2). *Tunisia:* Women's Day.

**14 Thu.** *Congo:* Independence Day (2nd day of 2). *Pakistan:* Independence Day.

**15 Fri.** *Burma:* Full Moon Day. *Congo:* Independence Day (3rd day of 3). *India:* Independence Day. *Liechtenstein:* National Day. *South Korea:* Republic Day. *Christian:* Assumption (see App. A11).

**16 Sat.** *Dominican Republic:* Republic Day. *Sri Lanka:* Full Moon Poya.

**17 Sun.** *Argentina:* San Martin's Day. *Gabon:* Independence Day. *Indonesia:* Independence Day.

**20 Wed.** *Hungary:* Constitution Day. *Senegal:* Independence Day.

**21 Thu.** *Estonia:* Independence Day*. *Latvia:* Independence Day*. *Lithuania:* Independence Day*.

**22 Fri.** *Zodiac Cusp:* Leo ends, Virgo begins.

**23 Sat.** *Hong Kong:* Liberation Day (1st day of 2). *Romania:* National Day (1st day of 2).

**24 Sun.** *Kazakhstan:* National Day*. *Liberia:* Flag Day. *Romania:* National Day (2nd day of 2). *Russia:* Independence Day*. *Ukraine:* National Day*.

**25 Mon.** *Belarus:* Independence Day*. *England:* Summer Break. *Hong Kong:* Liberation Day (2nd day of 2). *Northern Ireland:* Summer Break. *Paraguay:* Constitution Day. *Uruguay:* Independence Day. *Wales:* Summer Break.

**27 Wed.** *Moldova:* Independence Day*.

**29 Fri.** *Uzbekistan:* Independence Day*.

**30 Sat.** *Afghanistan:* Children's Day. *Azerbaijan:* Independence Day*. *Peru:* Rose of Lima Day. *Turkey:* Victory Day.

**31 Sun.** *Afghanistan:* Pashtunistan Day. *Kyrgyzstan:* Independence Day*. *Malaysia:* National Day. *Trinidad:* Independence Day.

# September 2008

**1 Mon.** *Canada:* Labour Day. *Libya:* National Day. *Luxembourg:* Fair Day. *Mexico:* President's Message Day. *Syria:* United Arab Republics Day. *United States:* Labor Day. *Islamic:* 1st Day of Ramadan (see App. B25).

**2 Tue.** *Vietnam:* Independence Day.

**3 Wed.** *Qatar:* National Day. *San Marino:* Saint Marinus' Day. *Tunisia:* Independence Movement Day.

**6 Sat.** *Pakistan:* Defense Day. *Swaziland:* Independence Day.

**7 Sun.** *Brazil:* Independence Day.

**8 Mon.** *Andorra:* National Day. *Malta:* Our Lady of Victory Day.

**9 Tue.** *Bulgaria:* National Day (1st day of 2). *North Korea:* Independence Day. *Tajikistan:* Independence Day*.

**10 Wed.** *Belize:* National Day. *Bulgaria:* National Day (2nd day of 2).

**11 Thu.** *Chile:* Revolution Day. *Egypt:* New Year's Day (Coptic: 1726). *Ethiopia:* New Year's Day (Ethiopian: 2002). *Pakistan:* Anniversary of Quaid-e-Azam's Death.

**12 Fri.** *Ethiopia:* National Day.

**13 Sat.** *Burma:* Full Moon Day.

**14 Sun.** *Guatemala:* San Jacinto Day. *Nicaragua:* San Jacinto Day. *Sri Lanka:* Full Moon Poya.

**15 Mon.** *Costa Rica:* Independence Day. *El Salvador:* Independence Day. *Guatemala:* Independence Day. *Honduras:* Independence Day. *Japan:* Veneration Day. *Nicaragua:* Independence Day.

**16 Tue.** *Mexico:* Independence Day. *New Guinea:* Independence Day.

**17 Wed.** *Angola:* Heroes' Day. *Marshall Islands:* Independence Day.

**18 Thu.** *Burundi:* Victory of Uprona Day. *Chile:* Independence Day.

**19 Fri.** *Chile:* Armed Forces Day. *Saint Kitts:* Independence Day.

**21 Sun.** *Belize:* Independence Day. *Malta:* Independence Day.

**22 Mon.** *Mali:* Independence Day. *Zodiac Cusp:* Virgo ends, Libra begins.

**23 Tue.** *Armenia:* Independence Day*. *Japan:* Autumnal Equinox. *Saudi Arabia:* National Day.

**24 Wed.** *Dominican Republic:* Mercedes Day. *Guinea-Bissau:* Republic Day.

**25 Thu.** *Mozambique:* Liberation Day. *Rwanda:* Assembly Day.

**26 Fri.** *Ethiopia:* True Cross Day.

**28 Sun.** *Taiwan:* Teachers' Day. *Europe:* Daylight Savings Time ends (retard clocks 1 hour).

**29 Mon.** *Brunei:* Constitution Day. *Paraguay:* Boqueron Battle Day.

**30 Tue.** *Botswana:* Independence Day. *Israel:* New Year's Day. *Far East Islamic:* Hari Raya Puasa (see App. B27). *Islamic:* Eid al Fitr (1st day of 4) (see App. B26). *Jewish:* Rosh Hashanah (Jewish: 5769).

# October 2008

**1 Wed.** *Cameroon:* Unification Day. *China:* National Day (1st day of 2). *Nigeria:* Independence Day. *South Korea:* Armed Forces Day (1st day of 2). *Tuvalu:* Independence Day. *Islamic:* Eid al Fitr (2nd day of 4) (see App. B26).

**2 Thu.** *China:* National Day (2nd day of 2). *Guinea:* Independence Day. *India:* Ghandi Day. *South Korea:* Armed Forces Day (2nd day of 2). *Islamic:* Eid al Fitr (3rd day of 4) (see App. B26).

**3 Fri.** *Honduras:* Morazan Day. *South Korea:* Foundation Day (1st day of 2). *Islamic:* Eid al Fitr (4th day of 4) (see App. B26).

**4 Sat.** *Lesotho:* Independence Day. *South Korea:* Foundation Day (2nd day of 2).

**5 Sun.** *Lesotho:* Sports Day. *Macao:* Portuguese Republic Day. *Portugal:* Republic Day.

**6 Mon.** *Barbados:* Bank Holiday. *Egypt:* Armed Forces Day.

**8 Wed.** *Asian:* Ancestors' Day (see App. B6).

**9 Thu.** *Israel:* Yom Kippur. *Peru:* National Dignity Day. *South Korea:* Alphabet Day. *Uganda:* Independence Day. *Jewish:* Yom Kippur.

**10 Fri.** *Japan:* Health Day. *South Africa:* Kruger Day. *Taiwan:* National Day.

**11 Sat.** *Cuba:* Independence War. *Panama:* Revolution Day.

**12 Sun.** *Equatorial Guinea:* Independence Day. *Spain:* National Day. *Multinational:* Columbus Day (see App. A12).

**13 Mon.** *Burma:* Full Moon Day. *Canada:* Thanksgiving Day. *Fiji:* Cession Day. *United States:* Bank Holiday. *Virgin Islands (U.S.):* Puerto Rican Friendship Day.

**14 Tue.** *China:* Mid-autumn Day. *Israel:* Sukkot. *Sri Lanka:* Full Moon Poya. *Taiwan:* Mid-autumn Day. *Zaïre:* Founders' Day. *Jewish:* Sukkot.

**15 Wed.** *Bosnia and Herzegovina:* Independence Day*. *Hong Kong:* Mid-autumn Day. *Macao:* Mid-autumn Day. *Tunisia:* Evacuation Day.

**17 Fri.** *Haiti:* Dessalines Day. *Malawi:* Mother's Day.

**20 Mon.** *Guatemala:* Revolution Day. *Jamaica:* Heroes' Day. *Kenya:* Kenyatta Day.

**21 Tue.** *Honduras:* Army Day. *Somalia:* Revolution Day (1st day of 2).

**22 Wed.** *Somalia:* Revolution Day (2nd day of 2). *Vatican:* John Paul II Day.

**23 Thu.** *Hungary:* Revolution Day. *Thailand:* Chulalongkorn Day. *Zodiac Cusp:* Libra ends, Scorpio begins.

**24 Fri.** *Egypt:* Suez Victory Day. *Haiti:* United Nations Day. *Zambia:* Independence Day.

**25 Sat.** *Taiwan:* Restoration Day.

**26 Sun.** *Austria:* National Day. *Benin:* Revolution Day. *Rwanda:* Government Day. *Canada and United States:* Daylight Savings Time ends (retard clocks 1 hour).

**27 Mon.** *Ireland:* Public Holiday. *New Zealand:* Labour Day. *Saint Vincent:* Independence Day. *Turkmenistan:* Independence Day*. *Zaïre:* Naming Day. *Hindu:* Deepavali (see App. B21).

**28 Tue.** *Greece:* Ohi! Day.

**29 Wed.** *Tanzania:* Naming Day. *Turkey:* Republic Day.

**31 Fri.** *Taiwan:* Chiang Kai-shek's Birthday.

# November 2008

**1 Sat.** *Algeria:* Revolution Day. *Antigua:* Independence Day. *Christian:* All Saints' Day (see App. A13).

**2 Sun.** *Brazil:* Memorial Day.

*Finland:* All Saints' Eve. *Sweden:* All Saints' Eve. *Christian:* All Souls' Day (see App. A14).

**3 Mon.** *Dominica:* Independence Day. *Ecuador:* Cuenca Independence Day. *Japan:* Culture Day. *Panama:* Independence Day. *Virgin Islands (U.S.):* Liberty Day.

**4 Tue.** *Andorra:* Saint Charles' Day. *Panama:* Flag Day. *Vatican:* John Paul II's Nameday.

**5 Wed.** *El Salvador:* Cry of Independence Day.

**6 Thu.** *Liberia:* Thanksgiving Day.

**7 Fri.** *Bangladesh:* Revolution Day.

**8 Sat.** *Nepal:* Queen's Birthday.

**9 Sun.** *Pakistan:* Iqbal Day.

**10 Mon.** *Panama:* Cry of Independence Day.

**11 Tue.** *Angola:* Independence Day. *Bhutan:* King's Birthday. *Burma:* Full Moon Day. *Maldives:* Republic Day. *Poland:* Independence Day. *Multinational:* Armistice Day (see App. A15).

**12 Wed.** *Sri Lanka:* Full Moon Poya. *Taiwan:* Dr. Sun Yat-sen's Birthday.

**14 Fri.** *Jordan:* King's Birthday.

**15 Sat.** *Brazil:* Republic Day.

**17 Mon.** *Fiji:* Prince Charles' Birthday. *Zaïre:* Armed Forces Day.

**18 Tue.** *Haiti:* Vertieres' Day. *Morocco:* Independence Day. *Oman:* National Day.

**19 Wed.** *Belize:* Garifuna Day. *Germany:* Repentance Day. *Mali:* Army Coup Day. *Monaco:* Prince Ranier's Day. *Puerto Rico:* Discovery Day.

**20 Thu.** *Mexico:* Revolution Day.

**21 Fri.** *Zodiac Cusp:* Scorpio ends, Sagittarius begins.

**22 Sat.** *Lebanon:* Independence Day.

**23 Sun.** *Japan:* Labor Thanksgiving Day.

**24 Mon.** *Zaïre:* New Regime Day.

**25 Tue.** *Suriname:* Independence Day.

**27 Thu.** *United States:* Thanksgiving Day.

**28 Fri.** *Albania:* Independence Day. *Argentina:* Bank Holiday. *Burundi:* Republic Day. *Chad:* Republic Day. *Mauritania:* Independence Day. *Panama:* Independence Day.

**29 Sat.** *Albania:* Liberation Day. *Liberia:* Tubman's Birthday. *Yugoslavia:* Republic Day.

**30 Sun.** *Barbados:* Independence Day. *Benin:* National Day. *Philippines:* Heroes' Day.

# December 2008

**1 Mon.** *Central African Republic:* National Day. *Portugal:* Youth Day. *Ukraine:* Independence Day*.

**2 Tue.** *Laos:* Republic Day. *United Arab Emirates:* National Day.

**5 Fri.** *Haiti:* Discovery Day. *Thailand:* King's Birthday.

**6 Sat.** *Finland:* Independence Day.

**7 Sun.** *Ivory Coast:* Independence Day. *Islamic:* Eid al Adha (1st day of 4) (see App. B28).

**8 Mon.** *Christian:* Immaculate Conception (see App. A16). *Far East Islamic:* Hari Raya Haji (see App. B29). *Islamic:* Eid al Adha (2nd day of 4) (see App. B28).

**9 Tue.** *Tanzania:* Independence Day. *Islamic:* Eid al Adha (3rd day of 4) (see App. B28).

**10 Wed.** *Angola:* MPLA Foundation Day. *Equatorial Guinea:* Human Rights Day. *Namibia:* Settlers' Day. *Thailand:* Constitution Day. *Islamic:* Eid al Adha (4th day of 4) (see App. B28).

**11 Thu.** *Burkina Faso:* National Day. *Burma:* Full Moon Day.

**12 Fri.** *Kenya:* Independence Day. *Mexico:* Guadalupe Festival. *Sri Lanka:* Full Moon Poya.

**13 Sat.** *Malta:* Republic Day.

**16 Tue.** *Bahrain:* National Day.

*Bangladesh:* Victory Day. *Nepal:* Constitution Day. *South Africa:* Covenant Day.

**17 Wed.** *Bhutan:* National Day.

**18 Thu.** *Niger:* Republic Day.

**21 Sun.** *Kazakhstan:* Independence Day*. *Zodiac Cusp:* Sagittarius ends, Capricorn begins.

**22 Mon.** *Jewish:* Chanukah.

**23 Tue.** *Japan:* Emperor's Birthday.

**24 Wed.** *Multinational:* Christmas Eve (see App. A17).

**25 Thu.** *Angola:* Family Day. *Congo:* Children's Day. *Pakistan:* Quaid's Birthday. *Taiwan:* Constitution Day. *Multinational:* Christmas Day (see App. A18).

**26 Fri.** *South Africa:* Good Will Day. *Multinational:* Boxing Day (see App. A19).

**27 Sat.** *Islamic:* New Year's Day (Hegira: 1430) (see App. B22).

**28 Sun.** *Far East Islamic:* New Year's Day (Hegira: 1430).

**30 Tue.** *Madagascar:* Republic Day. *Philippines:* Rizal Day (1st day of 2).

**31 Wed.** *Congo:* Republic Day. *Philippines:* Rizal Day (2nd day of 2). *Multinational:* Bank Holiday and New Year's Eve (see App. A20 & A21).

# January 2009

**1 Thu.** *Cameroon:* Independence Day. *Cuba:* Liberation Day. *Haiti:* Independence Day. *Palau:* Independence Day. *Sudan:* Independence Day. *Taiwan:* Foundation Day (1st day of 2). *Western Samoa:* Independence Day. *Multinational:* Bank Holiday and New Year's Day (see App. A1 & A2).

**2 Fri.** *Japan:* Bank Holiday. *New Zealand:* New Year's Day (2nd day of 2). *Scotland:* New Year's Day (2nd day of 2). *South Korea:* New Year's Day (2nd day of 2). *Switzerland:* Berchtold's Day. *Taiwan:* Foundation Day (2nd day of 2).

**3 Sat.** *Burkina Faso:* Revolution Day.

**4 Sun.** *Burma:* Independence Day. *Zaïre:* Martyrs' Day.

**5 Mon.** *Islamic:* Ashura (see App. B23).

**6 Tue.** *Iraq:* Army Day. *Uruguay:* Children's Day. *Christian:* Epiphany (see App. A3).

**7 Wed.** *Egypt:* Coptic Christmas. *Ethiopia:* Coptic Christmas.

**9 Fri.** *Burma:* Full Moon Day.

**10 Sat.** *Sri Lanka:* Full Moon Poya.

**11 Sun.** *Albania:* Republic Day. *Nepal:* Unification Day. *Puerto Rico:* Hostos Day.

**12 Mon.** *Tanzania:* Revolution Day.

**13 Tue.** *Togo:* Liberation Day.

**15 Thu.** *Japan:* Adult's Day. *Jordan:* Arbor Day.

**19 Mon.** *Ethiopia:* Epiphany. *United States:* Martin Luther King's Birthday.

**20 Tue.** *Mali:* Award Day. *Zodiac Cusp:* Capricorn ends, Aquarius begins.

**21 Wed.** *Dominican Republic:* Altagracia Day.

**22 Thu.** *Saint Vincent:* Discovery Day.

**25 Sun.** *Asian:* Chinese New Year Eve (see App. B1).

**26 Mon.** *Australia:* Australia Day. *Dominican Republic:* Duarte Day. *India:* Republic Day. *Vietnam:* Tet (1st day of 3). *Asian:* Chinese New Year (Year of the Ox) (see App. B2).

**27 Tue.** *Monaco:* Saint Devota's Day. *Vietnam:* Vietnam Day and Tet (2nd day of 3). *Asian:* 2nd Day of Chinese New Year (see App. B3).

**28 Wed.** *Rwanda:* Democracy Day. *Vietnam:* Tet (3rd day of 3). *Asian:* 3rd Day of Chinese New Year (see App. B4).

**31 Sat.** *Nauru:* Independence Day.

# February 2009

2 **Mon.** *Liechtenstein:* Candlemas. *United States:* Lincoln's Birthday.

4 **Wed.** *Sri Lanka:* Independence Day.

5 **Thu.** *Mexico:* Constitution Day.

6 **Fri.** *New Zealand:* Waitangi Day.

7 **Sat.** *Grenada:* Independence Day.

8 **Sun.** *Burma:* Full Moon Day. *Iraq:* Revolution Day.

9 **Mon.** *Lebanon:* Saint Marion's Day. *Sri Lanka:* Full Moon Poya. *Thailand:* Makha Bucha Day.

10 **Tue.** *Malta:* Saint Paul's Day.

11 **Wed.** *Cameroon:* Youth Day. *Japan:* Foundation Day. *Liberia:* Armed Forces Day.

12 **Thu.** *Burma:* Union Day.

14 **Sat.** *International:* Valentine's Day.

16 **Mon.** *United States:* Washington's Birthday.

18 **Wed.** *Gambia:* Independence Day. *Zodiac Cusp:* Aquarius ends, Pisces begins.

19 **Thu.** *Nepal:* National Day.

21 **Sat.** *Bangladesh:* Saheed Day.

22 **Sun.** *Saint Lucia:* Independence Day.

23 **Mon.** *Brunei:* National Day. *Guyana:* Republic Day. *Christian:* Shrove Monday (see App. B7).

24 **Tue.** *Christian:* Shrove Tuesday (see App. B8).

25 **Wed.** *Kuwait:* National Day. *Christian:* Ash Wednesday (see App. B9).

27 **Fri.** *Dominican Republic:* Independence Day.

# March 2009

1 **Sun.** *South Korea:* Independence Day.

2 **Mon.** *Ethiopia:* Victory of Aduwa Day. *Greece:* Shrove Monday. *Guam:* Discovery Day. *Morocco:* Independence Day. *Orthodox:* Shrove Monday.

3 **Tue.** *Bulgaria:* Liberation Day. *Malawi:* Martyrs' Day. *Morocco:* National Day.

6 **Fri.** *Ghana:* Independence Day.

8 **Sun.** *Syria:* Revolution Day. *Far East Islamic:* Mohammed's Birthday. *Islamic:* Mohammed's Birthday (see App. B24). *Multinational:* Women's Day (see App. A4).

9 **Mon.** *Burma:* Full Moon Day. *Gibraltar:* Commonwealth Day.

10 **Tue.** *South Korea:* Labor Day. *Sri Lanka:* Full Moon Poya. *Jewish:* Purim.

11 **Wed.** *Lithuania:* National Day*.

12 **Thu.** *Lesotho:* Moshoeshoe's Day. *Mauritius:* Independence Day.

13 **Fri.** *Grenada:* National Day.

14 **Sat.** *Zambia:* Youth Day.

17 **Tue.** *Ireland:* Saint Patrick's Day. *Northern Ireland:* Saint Patrick's Day.

19 **Thu.** *Christian:* Saint Joseph's Day (see App. A5).

20 **Fri.** *Afghanistan:* New Year's Day (Shamsi:1388). *Iran:* New Year's Day (Hegira: 1388). *Iraq:* New Year's Day. *Japan:* Vernal Equinox. *Tunisia:* Independence Day. *Zodiac Cusp:* Pisces ends, Aries begins.

21 **Sat.** *Mexico:* Juarez Day.

22 **Sun.** *Puerto Rico:* Abolition Day.

23 **Mon.** *Pakistan:* Pakistan Day.

24 **Tue.** *Zambia:* Africa Day.

25 **Wed.** *Cyprus:* Greek Independence Day. *Greece:* Independence Day. *Liechtenstein:* Annunciation.

26 **Thu.** *Bangladesh:* Independence Day.

27 **Fri.** *Angola:* Evacuation Day. *Burma:* Resistance Day.

29 **Sun.** *Central African Republic:*

Boganda Day. *Madagascar:* Memorial. *Taiwan:* Youth Day. *Europe:* Daylight Savings Time starts (advance clocks 1 hour).

**30 Mon.** *Virgin Islands (U.S.):* Transfer Day.

**31 Tue.** *Malta:* National Day.

# April 2009

**1 Wed.** *Iran:* Republic Day. *San Marino:* National Day.

**3 Fri.** *Sierra Leone:* Bank Holiday.

**4 Sat.** *Hungary:* Liberation Day. *Senegal:* National Day.

**5 Sun.** *South Korea:* Arbor Day. *Asian:* Tomb Sweeping Day (see App. A6). Canada and United States: Daylight Savings Time starts (advance clocks 1 hour). *Christian:* Palm Sunday.

**6 Mon.** *South Africa:* Founders' Day. *Thailand:* Chakri Day.

**8 Wed.** *Burma:* Full Moon Day.

**9 Thu.** *Israel:* Passover. *Philippines:* Valour Day. *Sri Lanka:* Full Moon Poya. *Tunisia:* Martyrs' Day. *Christian:* Maundy Thursday (see App. B11). *Jewish:* Passover.

**10 Fri.** *Christian:* Good Friday (see App. B12).

**11 Sat.** *Costa Rica:* Heroes' Day. *Uganda:* Liberation Day. *Christian:* Holy Saturday (see App. B13).

**12 Sun.** *Christian:* Easter Sunday (see App. B14).

**13 Mon.** *Chad:* National Day. *Thailand:* Songkrawn (1st day of 2). *Christian:* Easter Monday (see App. B15).

**14 Tue.** *Honduras:* Pan American Day. *Thailand:* Songkrawn (2nd day of 2).

**15 Wed.** *Niger:* National Day.

**16 Thu.** *Burma:* New Year's Day (Burmese: 1371). *Cyprus:* Independence Day.

**17 Fri.** *Cambodia:* Independence Day. *Syria:* Independence Day. *Orthodox:* Good Friday (see App. B20).

**18 Sat.** *Zimbabwe:* Republic Day.

**19 Sun.** *Jordan:* Easter Sunday. *Sierra Leone:* Republic Day. *Uruguay:* Patriots' Day. *Venezuela:* Independence Day. *Orthodox:* Easter Sunday. *Zodiac Cusp:* Aries ends, Taurus begins.

**20 Mon.** *Orthodox:* Easter Monday (see App. B20).

**21 Tue.** *Brazil:* Tiradentes Day.

**23 Thu.** *Turkey:* Children's Day.

**25 Sat.** *Australia:* ANZAC Day. *Egypt:* Sinai Day. *Iceland:* Children's Day. *Italy:* Liberation Day. *New Zealand:* ANZAC Day. *Portugal:* Liberation Day. *Swaziland:* Flag Day.

**26 Sun.** *Tanzania:* Union Day.

**27 Mon.** *Afghanistan:* Independence Day. *Sierra Leone:* Independence Day. *Togo:* Independence Day.

**29 Wed.** *Israel:* Independence Day. *Japan:* Green Day.

**30 Thu.** *Finland:* Vappu Day. *Netherlands:* Queen's Birthday.

# May 2009

**1 Fri.** *Multinational:* Labor Day (see App. A7).

**2 Sat.** *South Korea:* Vesak Day. *Lesotho:* King's Birthday.

**3 Sun.** *Japan:* Constitution Day.

**4 Mon.** *Japan:* People's Day. *United Kingdom:* Labour Day. *Zambia:* Labour Day.

**5 Tue.** *Japan:* Children's Day. *Mexico:* Cinco de Mayo. *Netherlands:* Liberation Day. *South Korea:* Children's Day. *Thailand:* Coronation Day.

**6 Wed.** *Lebanon:* Martyrs' Day. *Philippines:* Corregidor Day.

**7 Thu.** *Burma:* Full Moon Day.

**8 Fri.** *Denmark:* All Prayers' Day. *France:* Liberation Day. *Sri Lanka:* Full Moon Poya. *Thailand:* Visakha Bucha Day.

**9 Sat.** *Czech Republic:* Liberation Day*. *Malaysia:* Vesak Day. *Singapore:* Vesak Day. *Slovakia:* Liberation Day*.

**10 Sun.** *Micronesia:* Independence Day. *International:* Mother's Day.

**14 Thu.** *Liberia:* Unification Day. *Malawi:* Kamuzu Day. *Paraguay:* Flag Day.

**15 Fri.** *Paraguay:* Independence Day.

**17 Sun.** *Cayman Islands:* Discovery Day. *Norway:* Constitution Day.

**18 Mon.** *Canada:* Victoria Day. *Haiti:* Flag Day. *Uruguay:* Las Piedras Day.

**19 Tue.** *Finland:* Flag Day. *Turkey:* Youth Day.

**20 Wed.** *Cameroon:* Constitution Day. *Zaïre:* Popular Movement Day. *Zodiac Cusp:* Taurus ends, Gemini begins.

**21 Thu.** *Chile:* Navy Day. *Christian:* Ascension (see App. B16).

**22 Fri.** *Haiti:* Sovereign Day. *Sri Lanka:* Heroes' Day.

**23 Sat.** *Jamaica:* Labour Day.

**24 Sun.** *Bulgaria:* Culture Day. *Ecuador:* Independence Battle Day.

**25 Mon.** *Argentina:* National Day. *Eritrea:* Independence Day*. *Jordan:* Independence Day. *Sudan:* Revolution Day. *United Kingdom:* Spring Break. *United States:* Memorial Day. *Multinational:* Africa Day (see App. A8).

**26 Tue.** *Guyana:* Independence Day.

**27 Wed.** *Nigeria:* Children's Day.

**29 Fri.** *Israel:* Pentecost. *Jewish:* Pentecost.

**30 Sat.** *Asian:* Dragon Boat Festival (see App. B5).

**31 Sun.** *Brunei:* Regiment Day. *South Africa:* Republic Day. *Christian:* Whitsunday.

# June 2009

**1 Mon.** *Ireland:* Public Holiday. *Kenya:* Madaraka Day. *New Zealand:* Queen's Birthday. *Tunisia:* National Day. *Western Samoa:* Independence Day. *Christian:* Whitmonday (see App. B18).

**2 Tue.** *Italy:* Republic Day. *Tunisia:* Youth Day.

**3 Wed.** *Malaysia:* King's Birthday.

**4 Thu.** *Bahamas:* Labour Day. *Tonga:* Independence Day.

**5 Fri.** *Denmark:* Constitution Day. *Equatorial Guinea:* President's Birthday. *Seychelles:* Liberation Day.

**6 Sat.** *Burma:* Full Moon Day. *South Korea:* Memorial Day. *Sweden:* Constitution Day.

**7 Sun.** *Chad:* Revolution Day. *Sri Lanka:* Full Moon Poya. *Orthodox:* Pentecost Sunday.

**8 Mon.** *Australia:* Queen's Birthday. *Fiji:* Queen's Birthday. *Greece:* Pentecost Monday. *New Guinea:* Queen's Birthday. *United Kingdom:* Queen's Birthday.

**9 Tue.** *Argentina:* Independence Day.

**10 Wed.** *Macao:* Portugal Day. *Portugal:* Portugal Day.

**11 Thu.** *Libya:* Evacuation Day. *Christian:* Corpus Christi (see App. B19).

**12 Fri.** *Philippines:* Independence Day.

**13 Sat.** *Hong Kong:* Queen's Birthday (1st day of 2).

**15 Mon.** *Hong Kong:* Queen's Birthday (2nd day of 2).

**17 Wed.** *Germany:* Unity Day. *Iceland:* Independence Day.

**18 Thu.** *Egypt:* Independence Day.

**19 Fri.** *Algeria:* Righting Day.

*Kuwait:* Independence Day. *Uruguay:* Artigas Day.

**20 Sat.** *Argentina:* Flag Day.

**21 Sun.** *Finland:* Midsummer Day (1st day of 2). *Sweden:* Midsummer Day (1st day of 2). *Zodiac Cusp:* Gemini ends, Cancer begins.

**22 Mon.** *Finland:* Midsummer Day (2nd day of 2). *Sweden:* Midsummer Day (2nd day of 2).

**23 Tue.** *Luxembourg:* National Day.

**24 Wed.** *Andorra:* Saint John's Day. *Venezuela:* Carabobo Day. *Zaïre:* Constitution Day.

**25 Thu.** *Croatia:* Independence Day*. *Mozambique:* Independence Day. *Slovenia:* Independence Day*.

**26 Fri.** *Chile:* Bank Holiday. *Ecuador:* Bank Holiday. *El Salvador:* Bank Holiday. *Finland:* Bank Holiday. *Madagascar:* Independence Day. *Somalia:* Independence Day.

**27 Sat.** *Djibouti:* Independence Day. *Finland:* Johannus Day.

**29 Mon.** *Seychelles:* Independence Day. *Christian:* Saint Paul's Day (see App. A9).

**30 Tue.** *Guatemala:* Army Day. *Sri Lanka:* Bank Holiday. *Zaïre:* Independence Day.

# July 2009

**1 Wed.** *Burundi:* Independence Day. *Canada:* Canada Day. *Ghana:* Republic Day. *Hong Kong:* Half Year Day. *Rwanda:* Independence Day. *Somalia:* Union Day. *Suriname:* Freedom Day. *Multinational:* Bank Holiday (see App. A10).

**4 Sat.** *Philippines:* United States Friendship Day. *United States:* Independence Day. *Yugoslavia:* Freedom Fighters' Day.

**5 Sun.** *Algeria:* Independence Day. *Burma:* Full Moon Day. *Cape Verde:* Independence Day. *Rwanda:* Unity Day. *Venezuela:* Independence Day.

**6 Mon.** *Cayman Islands:* Constitution Day. *Comoros:* Independence Day. *Lesotho:* Family Day. *Malawi:* Republic Day. *Sri Lanka:* Full Moon Poya. *Zambia:* Heroes' Day.

**7 Tue.** *Solomon Islands:* Independence Day. *Tanzania:* Farmers' Day. *Thailand:* Asalaha Bucha Day. *Yugoslavia:* Serbian Day. *Zambia:* Unity Day.

**8 Wed.** *Thailand:* Khao Phansa Day.

**10 Fri.** *Bahamas:* Independence Day.

**11 Sat.** *Mongolia:* Revolution Day.

**12 Sun.** *Kiribati:* Independence Day. *Northern Ireland:* Battle of the Boyne Day. *São Tomé:* National Day.

**14 Tue.** *France:* National Day. *Iraq:* Revolution Day.

**15 Wed.** *Brunei:* Sultan's Birthday.

**17 Fri.** *Iraq:* Revolution Day. *Puerto Rico:* Rivera Day. *Slovakia:* Independence Day*. *South Korea:* Constitution Day.

**18 Sat.** *Uruguay:* Constitution Day.

**19 Sun.** *Burma:* Martyrs' Day. *Laos:* Independence Day. *Nicaragua:* Sandinista Day. *Islamic:* Isra a Majraj (see App. B30).

**20 Mon.** *Botswana:* President's Day. *Colombia:* Independence Day.

**21 Tue.** *Belgium:* National Day. *Guam:* Liberation Day.

**22 Wed.** *Poland:* Liberation Day. *Zodiac Cusp:* Cancer ends, Leo begins.

**23 Thu.** *Egypt:* Revolution Day. *New Guinea:* Remembrance Day.

**24 Fri.** *Venezuela:* Bolivar Day.

**25 Sat.** *Costa Rica:* Guanacaste Day. *Cuba:* Revolution Day (1st day of 3). *Puerto Rico:* Constitution Day. *Spain:* Santiago Day. *Tunisia:* Republic Day.

**26 Sun.** *Cuba:* Revolution Day (2nd day of 3). *Liberia:* Independence Day. *Maldives:* Independence Day.

**27 Mon.** *Cuba:* Revolution Day (3rd day of 3). *Puerto Rico:* Barbosa Day.

*Virgin Islands (U.S.):* Hurricane Supplication Day.

**28 Tue.** *Peru:* Independence Day (1st day of 2).

**29 Wed.** *Peru:* Independence Day (2nd day of 2).

**30 Thu.** *Israel:* Tisha Ab. *Vanuatu:* Independence Day. *Jewish:* Tisha Ab.

# August 2009

**1 Sat.** *Benin:* Independence Day. *Switzerland:* Confederation Day.

**2 Sun.** *Costa Rica:* Virgin of the Angels Day. *Guyana:* Freedom Day. *Trinidad:* Discovery Day.

**3 Mon.** *Bahamas:* Emancipation Day. *Barbados:* Emancipation Day. *Canada:* Civic Holiday. *El Salvador:* Summer Day (1st day of 4). *Guinea-Bissau:* Martyrs' Day. *Ireland:* Public Holiday. *Jamaica:* Independence Day. *Niger:* Independence Day. *Scotland:* Public Holiday. *Tunisia:* President's Birthday.

**4 Tue.** *Burkina Faso:* Independence Day (1st day of 2). *Burma:* Full Moon Day. *El Salvador:* Summer Day (2nd day of 4).

**5 Wed.** *Burkina Faso:* Independence Day (2nd day of 2). *El Salvador:* Summer Day (3rd day of 4). *Sri Lanka:* Full Moon Poya. *Zambia:* Farmers' Day.

**6 Thu.** *Bolivia:* Independence Day. *El Salvador:* Summer Day (4th day of 4). *United Arab Emirates:* Accession Day.

**7 Fri.** *Colombia:* Boyaca Day. *Ivory Coast:* Republic Day.

**9 Sun.** *Georgia:* Independence Day*. *Singapore:* National Day.

**10 Mon.** *Ecuador:* Independence Day.

**11 Tue.** *Chad:* Independence Day. *Jordan:* Accession Day. *Zimbabwe:* Heroes' Day (1st day of 2).

**12 Wed.** *Thailand:* Queen's Birthday. *Zimbabwe:* Heroes' Day (2nd day of 2).

**13 Thu.** *Central African Republic:* Independence Day. *Congo:* Independence Day (1st day of 2). *Tunisia:* Women's Day.

**14 Fri.** *Congo:* Independence Day (2nd day of 2). *Pakistan:* Independence Day.

**15 Sat.** *Congo:* Independence Day (3rd day of 3). *India:* Independence Day. *Liechtenstein:* National Day. *South Korea:* Republic Day. *Christian:* Assumption (see App. A11).

**16 Sun.** *Dominican Republic:* Republic Day.

**17 Mon.** *Argentina:* San Martin's Day. *Gabon:* Independence Day. *Indonesia:* Independence Day.

**20 Thu.** *Hungary:* Constitution Day. *Senegal:* Independence Day.

**21 Fri.** *Estonia:* Independence Day*. *Latvia:* Independence Day*. *Lithuania:* Independence Day*. *Islamic:* 1st Day of Ramadan (see App. B25).

**23 Sun.** *Romania:* National Day (1st day of 2). *Zodiac Cusp:* Leo ends, Virgo begins.

**24 Mon.** *Kazakhstan:* National Day*. *Liberia:* Flag Day. *Romania:* National Day (2nd day of 2). *Russia:* Independence Day*. *Ukraine:* National Day*.

**25 Tue.** *Belarus:* Independence Day*. *Paraguay:* Constitution Day. *Uruguay:* Independence Day.

**27 Wed.** *Moldova:* Independence Day*.

**29 Sat.** *Hong Kong:* Liberation Day (1st day of 2). *Uzbekistan:* Independence Day*.

**30 Sun.** *Afghanistan:* Children's Day. *Azerbaijan:* Independence Day*. *Peru:* Rose of Lima Day. *Turkey:* Victory Day.

**31 Mon.** *Afghanistan:* Pashtunistan Day. *England:* Summer Break. *Hong Kong:* Liberation Day (2nd day of 2).

*Kyrgyzstan:* Independence Day*. *Luxembourg:* Fair Day. *Malaysia:* National Day. *Northern Ireland:* Summer Break. *Trinidad:* Independence Day. *Wales:* Summer Break.

# September 2009

**1 Tue.** *Libya:* National Day. *Mexico:* President's Message Day. *Syria:* United Arab Republics Day.

**2 Wed.** *Vietnam:* Independence Day.

**3 Thu.** *Burma:* Full Moon Day. *Qatar:* National Day. *San Marino:* Saint Marinus' Day. *Tunisia:* Independence Movement Day.

**4 Fri.** *Sri Lanka:* Full Moon Poya.

**6 Sun.** *Pakistan:* Defense Day. *Swaziland:* Independence Day.

**7 Mon.** *Brazil:* Independence Day. *Canada:* Labour Day. *United States:* Labor Day.

**8 Tue.** *Andorra:* National Day. *Malta:* Our Lady of Victory Day.

**9 Wed.** *Bulgaria:* National Day (1st day of 2). *North Korea:* Independence Day. *Tajikistan:* Independence Day*.

**10 Thu.** *Belize:* National Day. *Bulgaria:* National Day (2nd day of 2).

**11 Fri.** *Chile:* Revolution Day. *Egypt:* New Year's Day (Coptic: 1727). *Ethiopia:* New Year's Day (Ethiopian: 2003). *Pakistan:* Anniversary of Quaid-e-Azam's Death.

**12 Sat.** *Ethiopia:* National Day.

**14 Mon.** *Guatemala:* San Jacinto Day. *Nicaragua:* San Jacinto Day.

**15 Tue.** *Costa Rica:* Independence Day. *El Salvador:* Independence Day. *Guatemala:* Independence Day. *Honduras:* Independence Day. *Japan:* Veneration Day. *Nicaragua:* Independence Day.

**16 Wed.** *Mexico:* Independence Day. *New Guinea:* Independence Day.

**17 Thu.** *Angola:* Heroes' Day. *Marshall Islands:* Independence Day.

**18 Fri.** *Burundi:* Victory of Uprona Day. *Chile:* Independence Day.

**19 Sat.** *Chile:* Armed Forces Day. *Israel:* New Year's Day. *Saint Kitts:* Independence Day. *Islamic:* Eid al Fitr (1st day of 4) (see App. B26). *Jewish:* Rosh Hashanah (Jewish: 5770).

**20 Sun.** *Far East Islamic:* Hari Raya Puasa (see App. B27). *Islamic:* Eid al Fitr (2nd day of 4) (see App. B26).

**21 Mon.** *Belize:* Independence Day. *Malta:* Independence Day. *Islamic:* Eid al Fitr (3rd day of 4) (see App. B26).

**22 Tue.** *Mali:* Independence Day. *Islamic:* Eid al Fitr (4th day of 4) (see App. B26). *Zodiac Cusp:* Virgo ends, Libra begins.

**23 Wed.** *Armenia:* Independence Day*. *Japan:* Autumnal Equinox. *Saudi Arabia:* National Day.

**24 Thu.** *Dominican Republic:* Mercedes Day. *Guinea-Bissau:* Republic Day.

**25 Fri.** *Mozambique:* Liberation Day. *Rwanda:* Assembly Day.

**26 Sat.** *Ethiopia:* True Cross Day.

**27 Sun.** *Asian:* Ancestors' Day (see App. B6). *Europe:* Daylight Savings Time ends (retard clocks 1 hour).

**28 Mon.** *Israel:* Yom Kippur. *Taiwan:* Teachers' Day. *Jewish:* Yom Kippur.

**29 Tue.** *Brunei:* Constitution Day. *Paraguay:* Boqueron Battle Day.

**30 Wed.** *Botswana:* Independence Day.

# October 2009

**1 Thu.** *Cameroon:* Unification Day. *China:* National Day (1st day of 2). *Nigeria:* Independence Day. *South Korea:* Armed Forces Day (1st day of

2). *Tuvalu:* Independence Day.

**2 Fri.** *Burma:* Full Moon Day. *China:* National Day (2nd day of 2). *Guinea:* Independence Day. *India:* Ghandi Day. *South Korea:* Armed Forces Day (2nd day of 2).

**3 Sat.** *China:* Mid-autumn Day. *Honduras:* Morazan Day. *Israel:* Sukkot. *South Korea:* Foundation Day (1st day of 2). *Sri Lanka:* Full Moon Poya. *Taiwan:* Mid-autumn Day. *Jewish:* Sukkot.

**4 Sun.** *Hong Kong:* Mid-autumn Day. *Lesotho:* Independence Day. *Macao:* Mid-autumn Day. *South Korea:* Foundation Day (2nd day of 2).

**5 Mon.** *Barbados:* Bank Holiday. *Lesotho:* Sports Day. *Macao:* Portuguese Republic Day. *Portugal:* Republic Day.

**6 Tue.** *Egypt:* Armed Forces Day.

**9 Fri.** *Peru:* National Dignity Day. *South Korea:* Alphabet Day. *Uganda:* Independence Day.

**10 Sat.** *Japan:* Health Day. *South Africa:* Kruger Day. *Taiwan:* National Day.

**11 Sun.** *Cuba:* Independence War. *Panama:* Revolution Day.

**12 Mon.** *Canada:* Thanksgiving Day. *Equatorial Guinea:* Independence Day. *Fiji:* Cession Day. *Spain:* National Day. *United States:* Bank Holiday. *Virgin Islands (U.S.):* Puerto Rican Friendship Day. *Multinational:* Columbus Day (see App. A12).

**14 Wed.** *Zaïre:* Founders' Day.

**15 Thu.** *Bosnia and Herzegovina:* Independence Day*. *Tunisia:* Evacuation Day.

**17 Sat.** *Haiti:* Dessalines Day. *Malawi:* Mother's Day. *Hindu:* Deepavali (see App. B21).

**19 Mon.** *Jamaica:* Heroes' Day.

**20 Tue.** *Guatemala:* Revolution Day. *Kenya:* Kenyatta Day.

**21 Wed.** *Honduras:* Army Day. *Somalia:* Revolution Day (1st day of 2).

**22 Thu.** *Somalia:* Revolution Day (2nd day of 2). *Vatican:* John Paul II Day.

**23 Fri.** *Hungary:* Revolution Day. *Thailand:* Chulalongkorn Day. *Zodiac Cusp:* Libra ends, Scorpio begins.

**24 Sat.** *Egypt:* Suez Victory Day. *Haiti:* United Nations Day. *Zambia:* Independence Day.

**25 Sun.** *Taiwan:* Restoration Day. *Canada and United States:* Daylight Savings Time ends (retard clocks 1 hour).

**26 Mon.** *Austria:* National Day. *Benin:* Revolution Day. *Ireland:* Public Holiday. *New Zealand:* Labour Day. *Rwanda:* Government Day.

**27 Tue.** *Saint Vincent:* Independence Day. *Turkmenistan:* Independence Day*. *Zaïre:* Naming Day.

**28 Wed.** *Greece:* Ohi! Day.

**29 Thu.** *Tanzania:* Naming Day. *Turkey:* Republic Day.

**31 Sat.** *Taiwan:* Chiang Kai-shek's Birthday.

# November 2009

**1 Sun.** *Algeria:* Revolution Day. *Antigua:* Independence Day. *Burma:* Full Moon Day. *Christian:* All Saints' Day (see App. A13).

**2 Mon.** *Brazil:* Memorial Day. *Finland:* All Saints' Eve. *Sri Lanka:* Full Moon Poya. *Sweden:* All Saints' Eve. *Virgin Islands (U.S.):* Liberty Day. *Christian:* All Souls' Day (see App. A14).

**3 Tue.** *Dominica:* Independence Day. *Ecuador:* Cuenca Independence Day. *Japan:* Culture Day. *Panama:* Independence Day.

**4 Wed.** *Andorra:* Saint Charles' Day. *Panama:* Flag Day. *Vatican:* John Paul II's Nameday.

**5 Thu.** *El Salvador:* Cry of Independence Day. *Liberia:* Thanksgiving Day.

**7 Sat.** *Bangladesh:* Revolution Day.

**8 Sun.** *Nepal:* Queen's Birthday.

**9 Mon.** *Pakistan:* Iqbal Day.

**10 Tue.** *Panama:* Cry of Independence Day.

**11 Wed.** *Angola:* Independence Day. *Bhutan:* King's Birthday. *Maldives:* Republic Day. *Poland:* Independence Day. *Multinational:* Armistice Day (see App. A15).

**12 Thu.** *Taiwan:* Dr. Sun Yat-sen's Birthday.

**14 Sat.** *Jordan:* King's Birthday.

**15 Sun.** *Brazil:* Republic Day.

**16 Mon.** *Fiji:* Prince Charles' Birthday.

**17 Tue.** *Zaïre:* Armed Forces Day.

**18 Wed.** *Germany:* Repentance Day. *Haiti:* Vertieres' Day. *Morocco:* Independence Day. *Oman:* National Day.

**19 Thu.** *Belize:* Garifuna Day. *Mali:* Army Coup Day. *Monaco:* Prince Ranier's Day. *Puerto Rico:* Discovery Day.

**20 Fri.** *Mexico:* Revolution Day.

**22 Sun.** *Lebanon:* Independence Day. *Zodiac Cusp:* Scorpio ends, Sagittarius begins.

**23 Mon.** *Japan:* Labor Thanksgiving Day.

**24 Tue.** *Zaïre:* New Regime Day.

**25 Wed.** *Suriname:* Independence Day.

**26 Thu.** *United States:* Thanksgiving Day. *Islamic:* Eid al Adha (1st day of 4) (see App. B28).

**27 Fri.** *Argentina:* Bank Holiday. *Far East Islamic:* Hari Raya Haji (see App. B29). *Islamic:* Eid al Adha (2nd day of 4) (see App. B28).

**28 Sat.** *Albania:* Independence Day. *Burundi:* Republic Day. *Chad:* Republic Day. *Mauritania:* Independence Day. *Panama:* Independence Day. *Islamic:* Eid al Adha (3rd day of 4) (see App. B28).

**29 Sun.** *Albania:* Liberation Day. *Liberia:* Tubman's Birthday. *Yugoslavia:* Republic Day. *Islamic:* Eid al Adha (4th day of 4) (see App. B28).

**30 Mon.** *Barbados:* Independence Day. *Benin:* National Day. *Philippines:* Heroes' Day.

# December 2009

**1 Tue.** *Central African Republic:* National Day. *Portugal:* Youth Day. *Sri Lanka:* Full Moon Poya. *Ukraine:* Independence Day*.

**2 Wed.** *Laos:* Republic Day. *United Arab Emirates:* National Day.

**5 Sat.** *Haiti:* Discovery Day. *Thailand:* King's Birthday.

**6 Sun.** *Finland:* Independence Day.

**7 Mon.** *Ivory Coast:* Independence Day.

**8 Tue.** *Christian:* Immaculate Conception (see App. A16).

**9 Wed.** *Tanzania:* Independence Day.

**10 Thu.** *Angola:* MPLA Foundation Day. *Equatorial Guinea:* Human Rights Day. *Namibia:* Settlers' Day. *Thailand:* Constitution Day.

**11 Fri.** *Burkina Faso:* National Day.

**12 Sat.** *Kenya:* Independence Day. *Mexico:* Guadalupe Festival. *Jewish:* Chanukah.

**13 Sun.** *Malta:* Republic Day.

**16 Wed.** *Bahrain:* National Day. *Bangladesh:* Victory Day. *Nepal:* Constitution Day. *South Africa:* Covenant Day. *Islamic:* New Year's Day (Hegira: 1431) (see App. B22).

**17 Thu.** *Bhutan:* National Day. *Far East Islamic:* New Year's Day (Hegira: 1431).

**18 Fri.** *Niger:* Republic Day.

**21 Mon.** *Kazakhstan:* Independence Day*. *Zodiac Cusp:* Sagittarius ends, Capricorn begins.

**23 Wed.** *Japan:* Emperor's Birthday.

**24 Thu.** *Multinational:* Christmas Eve (see App. A17).

**25 Fri.** *Angola:* Family Day. *Congo:* Children's Day. *Pakistan:* Quaid's Birthday. *Taiwan:* Constitution Day. *Islamic:* Ashura (see App. B23). *Multinational:* Christmas Day (see App. A18).

**26 Sat.** *South Africa:* Good Will Day. *Multinational:* Boxing Day (see App. A19).

**28 Mon.** *Hong Kong:* Boxing Day.

**30 Wed.** *Burma:* Full Moon Day. *Madagascar:* Republic Day. *Philippines:* Rizal Day (1st day of 2).

**31 Thu.** *Congo:* Republic Day. *Philippines:* Rizal Day (2nd day of 2). *Sri Lanka:* Full Moon Poya. *Multinational:* Bank Holiday and New Year's Eve (see App. A20 & A21).

# January 2010

**1 Fri.** *Cameroon:* Independence Day. *Cuba:* Liberation Day. *Haiti:* Independence Day. *Palau:* Independence Day. *Sudan:* Independence Day. *Taiwan:* Foundation Day (1st day of 2). *Western Samoa:* Independence Day. *Multinational:* Bank Holiday and New Year's Day (see App. A1 & A2).

**2 Sat.** *Japan:* Bank Holiday. *New Zealand:* New Year's Day (2nd day of 2). *South Korea:* New Year's Day (2nd day of 2). *Switzerland:* Berchtold's Day. *Taiwan:* Foundation Day (2nd day of 2).

**3 Sun.** *Burkina Faso:* Revolution Day.

**4 Mon.** *Burma:* Independence Day. *Scotland:* New Year's Day (2nd day of 2). *Zaïre:* Martyrs' Day.

**6 Wed.** *Iraq:* Army Day. *Uruguay:* Children's Day. *Christian:* Epiphany (see App. A3).

**7 Thu.** *Egypt:* Coptic Christmas. *Ethiopia:* Coptic Christmas.

**11 Mon.** *Albania:* Republic Day. *Nepal:* Unification Day. *Puerto Rico:* Hostos Day.

**12 Tue.** *Tanzania:* Revolution Day.

**13 Wed.** *Togo:* Liberation Day.

**15 Fri.** *Japan:* Adult's Day. *Jordan:* Arbor Day.

**18 Mon.** *United States:* Martin Luther King's Birthday.

**19 Tue.** *Ethiopia:* Epiphany.

**20 Wed.** *Mali:* Award Day. *Zodiac Cusp:* Capricorn ends, Aquarius begins.

**21 Thu.** *Dominican Republic:* Altagracia Day.

**22 Fri.** *Saint Vincent:* Discovery Day.

**26 Tue.** *Dominican Republic:* Duarte Day. *India:* Republic Day.

**27 Wed.** *Monaco:* Saint Devota's Day. *Vietnam:* Vietnam Day.

**28 Thu.** *Burma:* Full Moon Day. *Rwanda:* Democracy Day.

**29 Fri.** *Sri Lanka:* Full Moon Poya.

**31 Sun.** *Nauru:* Independence Day.

# February 2010

**1 Mon.** *Australia:* Australia Day. *United States:* Lincoln's Birthday.

**2 Tue.** *Liechtenstein:* Candlemas.

**4 Thu.** *Sri Lanka:* Independence Day.

**5 Fri.** *Mexico:* Constitution Day.

**6 Sat.** *New Zealand:* Waitangi Day.

**7 Sun.** *Grenada:* Independence Day.

**8 Mon.** *Iraq:* Revolution Day.

**9 Tue.** *Lebanon:* Saint Marion's Day.

**10 Wed.** *Malta:* Saint Paul's Day.

**11 Thu.** *Cameroon:* Youth Day. *Japan:* Foundation Day. *Liberia:* Armed Forces Day.

**12 Fri.** *Burma:* Union Day.

**13 Sat.** *Asian:* Chinese New Year Eve (see App. B1).

**14 Sun.** *Vietnam:* Tet (1st day of 3). *International:* Valentine's Day. *Asian:* Chinese New Year (Year of the Tiger) (see App. B2).

**15 Mon.** *Greece:* Shrove Monday. *United States:* Washington's Birthday. *Vietnam:* Tet (2nd day of 3). *Asian:* 2nd Day of Chinese New Year (see App. B3). *Christian:* Shrove Monday (see App. B7). *Orthodox:* Shrove Monday.

**16 Tue.** *Vietnam:* Tet (3rd day of 3). *Asian:* 3rd Day of Chinese New Year (see App. B4). *Christian:* Shrove Tuesday (see App. B8).

**17 Wed.** *Christian:* Ash Wednesday (see App. B9).

**18 Thu.** *Gambia:* Independence Day.

**19 Fri.** *Nepal:* National Day. *Zodiac Cusp:* Aquarius ends, Pisces begins.

**21 Sun.** *Bangladesh:* Saheed Day.

**22 Mon.** *Saint Lucia:* Independence Day.

**23 Tue.** *Brunei:* National Day. *Guyana:* Republic Day.

**24 Wed.** *Far East Islamic:* Mohammed's Birthday. *Islamic:* Mohammed's Birthday (see App. B24).

**25 Thu.** *Kuwait:* National Day.

**27 Sat.** *Burma:* Full Moon Day. *Dominican Republic:* Independence Day.

**28 Sun.** *Sri Lanka:* Full Moon Poya. *Thailand:* Makha Bucha Day. *Jewish:* Purim.

# March 2010

**1 Mon.** *Guam:* Discovery Day. *South Korea:* Independence Day.

**2 Tue.** *Ethiopia:* Victory of Aduwa Day. *Morocco:* Independence Day.

**3 Wed.** *Bulgaria:* Liberation Day. *Malawi:* Martyrs' Day. *Morocco:* National Day.

**6 Sat.** *Ghana:* Independence Day.

**8 Mon.** *Gibraltar:* Commonwealth Day. *Syria:* Revolution Day. *Multinational:* Women's Day (see App. A4).

**10 Wed.** *South Korea:* Labor Day.

**11 Thu.** *Lithuania:* National Day*.

**12 Fri.** *Lesotho:* Moshoeshoe's Day. *Mauritius:* Independence Day.

**13 Sat.** *Grenada:* National Day. *Zambia:* Youth Day.

**17 Wed.** *Ireland:* Saint Patrick's Day. *Northern Ireland:* Saint Patrick's Day.

**19 Fri.** *Christian:* Saint Joseph's Day (see App. A5).

**20 Sat.** *Afghanistan:* New Year's Day (Shamsi: 1389). *Iran:* New Year's Day (Hegira: 1389). *Iraq:* New Year's Day. *Tunisia:* Independence Day. *Zodiac Cusp:* Pisces ends, Aries begins.

**21 Sun.** *Japan:* Vernal Equinox. *Mexico:* Juarez Day.

**22 Mon.** *Puerto Rico:* Abolition Day.

**23 Tue.** *Pakistan:* Pakistan Day. *Zambia:* Africa Day.

**25 Thu.** *Cyprus:* Greek Independence Day. *Greece:* Independence Day. *Liechtenstein:* Annunciation.

**26 Fri.** *Bangladesh:* Independence Day.

**27 Sat.** *Angola:* Evacuation Day. *Burma:* Resistance Day.

**28 Sun.** *Burma:* Full Moon Day. *Christian:* Palm Sunday. *Europe:* Daylight Savings Time starts (advance clocks 1 hour).

**29 Mon.** *Central African Republic:* Boganda Day. *Madagascar:* Memorial Day. *Sri Lanka:* Full Moon Poya. *Taiwan:* Youth Day. *Virgin Islands (U.S.):* Transfer Day.

**30 Tue.** *Israel:* Passover. *Jewish:* Passover.

**31 Wed.** *Malta:* National Day.

# April 2010

**1 Thu.** *Iran:* Republic Day. *San Marino:* National Day. *Christian:* Maundy Thursday (see App. B11).

**2 Fri.** *Sierra Leone:* Bank Holiday. *Christian:* Good Friday (see App. B12). *Orthodox:* Good Friday (see App. B20).

**3 Sat.** *Christian:* Holy Saturday (see App. B13).

**4 Sun.** *Hungary:* Liberation Day. *Jordan:* Easter Sunday. *Senegal:* National Day. *Canada and United States:* Daylight Savings Time starts (advance clocks 1 hour). *Christian:* Easter Sunday (see App. B14). *Orthodox:* Easter Sunday.

**5 Mon.** *South Korea:* Arbor Day. *Asian:* Tomb Sweeping Day (see App. A6). *Christian:* Easter Monday (see App. B15). *Orthodox:* Easter Monday (see App. B20).

**6 Tue.** *South Africa:* Founders' Day. *Thailand:* Chakri Day.

**9 Fri.** *Philippines:* Valour Day. *Tunisia:* Martyrs' Day.

**11 Sun.** *Costa Rica:* Heroes' Day. *Uganda:* Liberation Day.

**13 Tue.** *Chad:* National Day. *Thailand:* Songkrawn (1st day of 2).

**14 Wed.** *Honduras:* Pan American Day. *Thailand:* Songkrawn (2nd day of 2).

**15 Thu.** *Niger:* National Day.

**16 Fri.** *Burma:* New Year's Day (Burmese: 1372). *Cyprus:* Independence Day.

**17 Sat.** *Cambodia:* Independence Day. *Syria:* Independence Day.

**18 Sun.** *Zimbabwe:* Republic Day.

**19 Mon.** *Israel:* Independence Day. *Sierra Leone:* Republic Day. *Uruguay:* Patriots' Day. *Venezuela:* Independence Day.

**20 Tue.** *Zodiac Cusp:* Aries ends, Taurus begins.

**21 Wed.** *Brazil:* Tiradentes Day.

**23 Fri.** *Turkey:* Children's Day.

**25 Sun.** *Australia:* ANZAC Day. *Egypt:* Sinai Day. *Iceland:* Children's Day. *Italy:* Liberation Day. *New Zealand:* ANZAC Day. *Portugal:* Liberation Day. *Swaziland:* Flag Day.

**26 Mon.** *Tanzania:* Union Day.

**27 Tue.** *Afghanistan:* Independence Day. *Burma:* Full Moon Day. *Sri Lanka:* Full Moon Poya. *Sierra Leone:* Independence Day. *Togo:* Independence Day.

**29 Thu.** *Japan:* Green Day.

**30 Fri.** *Denmark:* All Prayers' Day. *Finland:* Vappu Day. *Netherlands:* Queen's Birthday.

# May 2010

**1 Sat.** *Multinational:* Labor Day (see App. A7).

**2 Sun.** *Lesotho:* King's Birthday.

**3 Mon.** *Japan:* Constitution Day. *United Kingdom:* Labour Day. *Zambia:* Labour Day.

**4 Tue.** *Japan:* People's Day.

**5 Wed.** *Japan:* Children's Day. *Mexico:* Cinco de Mayo. *Netherlands:* Liberation Day. *South Korea:* Children's Day. *Thailand:* Coronation Day.

**6 Thu.** *Lebanon:* Martyrs' Day. *Philippines:* Corregidor Day.

**8 Sat.** *France:* Liberation Day.

**9 Sun.** *Czech Republic:* Liberation Day*. *Slovakia:* Liberation Day*. *International:* Mother's Day.

**10 Mon.** *Micronesia:* Independence Day.

**13 Thu.** *Christian:* Ascension (see App. B16).

**14 Fri.** *Liberia:* Unification Day. *Malawi:* Kamuzu Day. *Paraguay:* Flag Day.

**15 Sat.** *Paraguay:* Independence Day.

**17 Mon.** *Cayman Islands:* Discovery Day. *Norway:* Constitution Day.

**18 Tue.** *Haiti:* Flag Day. *Uruguay:* Las Piedras Day.

**19 Wed.** *Finland:* Flag Day. *Israel:* Pentecost. *Turkey:* Youth Day. *Jewish:* Pentecost.

**20 Thu.** *Cameroon:* Constitution Day. *Zaïre:* Popular Movement Day.

**21 Fri.** *Chile:* Navy Day. *South Korea:* Vesak Day. *Zodiac Cusp:* Taurus ends, Gemini begins.

**22 Sat.** *Haiti:* Sovereign Day. *Sri Lanka:* Heroes' Day.

**23 Sun.** *Jamaica:* Labour Day. *Christian:* Whitsunday. *Orthodox:* Pentecost Sunday.

**24 Mon.** *Bulgaria:* Culture Day. *Canada:* Victoria Day. *Ecuador:* Independence Battle Day. *Greece:* Pentecost Monday. *Christian:* Whitmonday (see App. B18).

**25 Tue.** *Argentina:* National Day. *Eritrea:* Independence Day*. *Jordan:* Independence Day. *Sudan:* Revolution Day. *Multinational:* Africa Day (see App. A8).

**26 Wed.** *Burma:* Full Moon Day. *Guyana:* Independence Day.

**27 Thu.** *Nigeria:* Children's Day. *Sri Lanka:* Full Moon Poya.

**28 Fri.** *Malaysia:* Vesak Day. *Singapore:* Vesak Day. *Thailand:* Visakha Bucha Day.

**31 Mon.** *Brunei:* Regiment Day. *South Africa:* Republic Day. *United Kingdom:* Spring Break. *United States:* Memorial Day.

# June 2010

**1 Tue.** *Kenya:* Madaraka Day. *Tunisia:* National Day. *Western Samoa:* Independence Day.

**2 Wed.** *Italy:* Republic Day. *Malaysia:* King's Birthday. *Tunisia:* Youth Day.

**3 Thu.** *Christian:* Corpus Christi (see App. B19).

**4 Fri.** *Bahamas:* Labour Day. *Tonga:* Independence Day.

**5 Sat.** *Denmark:* Constitution Day. *Equatorial Guinea:* President's Birthday. *Seychelles:* Liberation Day.

**6 Sun.** *South Korea:* Memorial Day. *Sweden:* Constitution Day.

**7 Mon.** *Chad:* Revolution Day. *Ireland:* Public Holiday. *New Zealand:* Queen's Birthday.

**9 Wed.** *Argentina:* Independence Day.

**10 Thu.** *Macao:* Portugal Day. *Portugal:* Portugal Day.

**11 Fri.** *Libya:* Evacuation Day.

**12 Sat.** *Hong Kong:* Queen's Birthday (1st day of 2). *Philippines:* Independence Day.

**14 Mon.** *Australia:* Queen's Birthday. *Fiji:* Queen's Birthday. *Hong Kong:* Queen's Birthday (2nd day of 2). *New Guinea:* Queen's Birthday. *United Kingdom:* Queen's Birthday.

**17 Thu.** *Germany:* Unity Day. *Iceland:* Independence Day.

**18 Fri.** *Egypt:* Independence Day. *Asian:* Dragon Boat Festival (see App. B5).

**19 Sat.** *Algeria:* Righting Day. *Kuwait:* Independence Day. *Uruguay:* Artigas Day.

**20 Sun.** *Argentina:* Flag Day.

**21 Mon.** *Finland:* Midsummer Day (1st day of 2). *Sweden:* Midsummer Day (1st day of 2). *Zodiac Cusp:* Gemini ends, Cancer begins.

**22 Tue.** *Finland:* Midsummer Day (2nd day of 2). *Sweden:* Midsummer Day (2nd day of 2).

**23 Wed.** *Luxembourg:* National Day.

**24 Thu.** *Andorra:* Saint John's Day. *Venezuela:* Carabobo Day. *Zaïre:* Constitution Day.

**25 Fri.** *Burma:* Full Moon Day. *Chile:* Bank Holiday. *Croatia:* Independence Day*. *Ecuador:* Bank Holiday. *El Salvador:* Bank Holiday. *Finland:* Bank Holiday. *Mozambique:* Independence Day. *Slovenia:* Independence Day*. *Sri Lanka:* Full Moon Poya.

**26 Sat.** *Finland:* Johannus Day. *Madagascar:* Independence Day. *Somalia:* Independence Day.

**27 Sun.** *Djibouti:* Independence Day.

**29 Tue.** *Seychelles:* Independence Day. *Christian:* Saint Paul's Day (see App. A9).

**30 Wed.** *Guatemala:* Army Day. *Sri Lanka:* Bank Holiday. *Zaïre:* Independence Day.

# July 2010

**1 Thu.** *Burundi:* Independence Day. *Canada:* Canada Day. *Ghana:* Republic Day. *Hong Kong:* Half Year Day. *Rwanda:* Independence Day. *Somalia:* Union Day. *Suriname:* Freedom Day. *Multinational:* Bank Holiday (see App. A10).

**4 Sun.** *Philippines:* United States Friendship Day. *United States:* Independence Day. *Yugoslavia:* Freedom Fighters' Day.

**5 Mon.** *Algeria:* Independence Day. *Cape Verde:* Independence Day. *Cayman Islands:* Constitution Day. *Lesotho:* Family Day. *Rwanda:* Unity Day. *Venezuela:* Independence Day. *Zambia:* Heroes' Day.

**6 Tue.** *Comoros:* Independence Day. *Malawi:* Republic Day. *Zambia:* Unity Day.

**7 Wed.** *Solomon Islands:* Independence Day. *Tanzania:* Farmers' Day. *Yugoslavia:* Serbian Day. *Islamic:* Isra a Majraj (see App. B30).

**10 Sat.** *Bahamas:* Independence Day.

**11 Sun.** *Mongolia:* Revolution Day.

**12 Mon.** *Kiribati:* Independence Day. *Northern Ireland:* Battle of the Boyne Day. *São Tomé:* National Day.

**14 Wed.** *France:* National Day. *Iraq:* Revolution Day.

**15 Thu.** *Brunei:* Sultan's Birthday.

**17 Sat.** *Iraq:* Revolution Day. *Puerto Rico:* Rivera Day. *Slovakia:* Independence Day*. *South Korea:* Constitution Day.

**18 Sun.** *Uruguay:* Constitution Day.

**19 Mon.** *Botswana:* President's Day. *Burma:* Martyrs' Day. *Laos:* Independence Day. *Nicaragua:* Sandinista Day.

**20 Tue.** *Colombia:* Independence Day. *Israel:* Tisha Ab. *Jewish:* Tisha Ab.

**21 Wed.** *Belgium:* National Day. *Guam:* Liberation Day.

**22 Thu.** *Poland:* Liberation Day. *Zodiac Cusp:* Cancer ends, Leo begins.

**23 Fri.** *Egypt:* Revolution Day. *New Guinea:* Remembrance Day.

**24 Sat.** *Burma:* Full Moon Day. *Venezuela:* Bolivar Day.

**25 Sun.** *Costa Rica:* Guanacaste Day. *Cuba:* Revolution Day (1st day of 3). *Puerto Rico:* Constitution Day. *Spain:* Santiago Day. *Sri Lanka:* Full Moon Poya. *Tunisia:* Republic Day.

**26 Mon.** *Cuba:* Revolution Day (2nd day of 3). *Liberia:* Independence Day. *Maldives:* Independence Day. *Thailand:* Asalaha Bucha Day. *Virgin Islands (U.S.):* Hurricane Supplication Day.

**27 Tue.** *Cuba:* Revolution Day (3rd day of 3). *Puerto Rico:* Barbosa Day. *Thailand:* Khao Phansa Day.

**28 Wed.** *Peru:* Independence Day (1st day of 2).

**29 Thu.** *Peru:* Independence Day (2nd day of 2).

**30 Fri.** *Vanuatu:* Independence Day.

# August 2010

**1 Sun.** *Benin:* Independence Day. *Switzerland:* Confederation Day.

**2 Mon.** *Bahamas:* Emancipation Day. *Barbados:* Emancipation Day. *Canada:* Civic Holiday. *Costa Rica:* Virgin of the Angels Day. *Guyana:* Freedom Day. *Ireland:* Public Holiday. *Jamaica:* Independence Day. *Scotland:* Public Holiday. *Trinidad:* Discovery Day.

**3 Tue.** *El Salvador:* Summer Day (1st day of 4). *Guinea-Bissau:* Martyrs' Day. *Niger:* Independence Day. *Tunisia:* President's Birthday.

**4 Wed.** *Burkina Faso:* Independence Day (1st day of 2). *El Salvador:* Summer Day (2nd day of 4). *Zambia:* Farmers' Day.

**5 Thu.** *Burkina Faso:* Independence Day (2nd day of 2). *El Salvador:* Summer Day (3rd day of 4).

**6 Fri.** *Bolivia:* Independence Day. *El Salvador:* Summer Day (4th day of 4). *United Arab Emirates:* Accession Day.

**7 Sat.** *Colombia:* Boyaca Day. *Ivory Coast:* Republic Day.

**9 Mon.** *Georgia:* Independence Day*. *Singapore:* National Day.

**10 Tue.** *Ecuador:* Independence Day. *Islamic:* 1st Day of Ramadan (see App. B25).

**11 Wed.** *Chad:* Independence Day. *Jordan:* Accession Day. *Zimbabwe:* Heroes' Day (1st day of 2).

**12 Thu.** *Thailand:* Queen's Birthday. *Zimbabwe:* Heroes' Day (2nd day of 2).

**13 Fri.** *Central African Republic:* Independence Day. *Congo:* Independence Day (1st day of 2). *Tunisia:* Women's Day.

**14 Sat.** *Congo:* Independence Day (2nd day of 2). *Pakistan:* Independence Day.

**15 Sun.** *Congo:* Independence Day (3rd day of 3). *India:* Independence Day. *Liechtenstein:* National Day. *South Korea:* Republic Day. *Christian:* Assumption (see App. A11).

**16 Mon.** *Dominican Republic:* Republic Day.

**17 Tue.** *Argentina:* San Martin's Day. *Gabon:* Independence Day. *Indonesia:* Independence Day.

**20 Fri.** *Hungary:* Constitution Day. *Senegal:* Independence Day.

**21 Sat.** *Estonia:* Independence Day*. *Latvia:* Independence Day*. *Lithuania:* Independence Day*.

**23 Mon.** *Burma:* Full Moon Day. *Romania:* National Day (1st day of 2). *Zodiac Cusp:* Leo ends, Virgo begins.

**24 Tue.** *Kazakhstan:* National Day*. *Liberia:* Flag Day. *Romania:* National Day (2nd day of 2). *Russia:* Independence Day*. *Sri Lanka:* Full Moon Poya. *Ukraine:* National Day*.

**25 Wed.** *Belarus:* Independence Day*. *Paraguay:* Constitution Day. *Uruguay:* Independence Day.

**27 Fri.** *Moldova:* Independence Day*.

**28 Sat.** *Hong Kong:* Liberation Day (1st day of 2).

**29 Sun.** *Uzbekistan:* Independence Day*.

**30 Mon.** *Afghanistan:* Children's Day. *Azerbaijan:* Independence Day*. *England:* Summer Break. *Hong Kong:* Liberation Day (2nd day of 2). *Luxembourg:* Fair Day. *Northern Ireland:* Summer Break. *Peru:* Rose of Lima Day. *Turkey:* Victory Day. *Wales:* Summer Break.

**31 Tue.** *Afghanistan:* Pashtunistan Day. *Kyrgyzstan:* Independence Day*. *Malaysia:* National Day. *Trinidad:* Independence Day.

# September 2010

**1 Wed.** *Libya:* National Day. *Mexico:* President's Message Day. *Syria:* United Arab Republics Day.

**2 Thu.** *Vietnam:* Independence Day.

**3 Fri.** *Qatar:* National Day. *San Marino:* Saint Marinus' Day. *Tunisia:* Independence Movement Day.

**6 Mon.** *Canada:* Labour Day. *Pakistan:* Defense Day. *Swaziland:* Independence Day. *United States:* Labor Day.

**7 Tue.** *Brazil:* Independence Day.

**8 Wed.** *Andorra:* National Day. *Malta:* Our Lady of Victory Day. *Far East Islamic:* Hari Raya Puasa (see App. B27). *Islamic:* Eid al Fitr (1st day of 4) (see App. B26).

**9 Thu.** *Bulgaria:* National Day (1st day of 2). *Israel:* New Year's Day. *North Korea:* Independence Day. *Tajikistan:* Independence Day*. *Islamic:* Eid al Fitr (2nd day of 4) (see App. B26). *Jewish:* Rosh Hashanah (Jewish: 5771).

**10 Fri.** *Belize:* National Day. *Bulgaria:* National Day (2nd day of 2). *Islamic:* Eid al Fitr (3rd day of 4) (see App. B26).

**11 Sat.** *Chile:* Revolution Day. *Egypt:* New Year's Day (Coptic: 1728). *Ethiopia:* New Year's Day (Ethiopian: 2004). *Pakistan:* Anniversary of Quaid-e-Azam's Death. *Islamic:* Eid al Fitr (4th day of 4) (see App. B26).

**12 Sun.** *Ethiopia:* National Day.

**14 Tue.** *Guatemala:* San Jacinto Day. *Nicaragua:* San Jacinto Day.

**15 Wed.** *Costa Rica:* Independence Day. *El Salvador:* Independence Day. *Guatemala:* Independence Day. *Honduras:* Independence Day. *Japan:* Veneration Day. *Nicaragua:* Independence Day.

**16 Thu.** *Mexico:* Independence Day. *New Guinea:* Independence Day.

**17 Fri.** *Angola:* Heroes' Day. *Marshall Islands:* Independence Day.

**18 Sat.** *Burundi:* Victory of Uprona Day. *Chile:* Independence Day. *Israel:* Yom Kippur. *Jewish:* Yom Kippur.

**19 Sun.** *Chile:* Armed Forces Day. *Saint Kitts:* Independence Day.

**21 Tue.** *Belize:* Independence Day. *Burma:* Full Moon Day. *Malta:* Independence Day.

**22 Wed.** *China:* Mid-autumn Day. *Mali:* Independence Day. *Sri Lanka:* Full Moon Poya. *Taiwan:* Mid-autumn Day.

**23 Thu.** *Armenia:* Independence Day*. *Hong Kong:* Mid-autumn Day. *Israel:* Sukkot. *Japan:* Autumnal Equinox. *Macao:* Mid-autumn Day. *Saudi Arabia:* National Day. *Jewish:* Sukkot. *Zodiac Cusp:* Virgo ends, Libra begins.

**24 Fri.** *Dominican Republic:* Mercedes Day. *Guinea-Bissau:* Republic Day.

**25 Sat.** *Mozambique:* Liberation Day. *Rwanda:* Assembly Day.

**26 Sun.** *Ethiopia:* True Cross Day. *Europe:* Daylight Savings Time ends (retard clocks 1 hour).

**28 Tue.** *Taiwan:* Teachers' Day.

**29 Wed.** *Brunei:* Constitution Day. *Paraguay:* Boqueron Battle Day.

**30 Thu.** *Botswana:* Independence Day.

# October 2010

**1 Fri.** *Cameroon:* Unification Day. *China:* National Day (1st day of 2). *Nigeria:* Independence Day. *South Korea:* Armed Forces Day (1st day of 2). *Tuvalu:* Independence Day.

**2 Sat.** *China:* National Day (2nd day of 2). *Guinea:* Independence Day. *India:* Ghandi Day. *South Korea:* Armed Forces Day (2nd day of 2).

**3 Sun.** *Honduras:* Morazan Day. *South Korea:* Foundation Day (1st day of 2).

**4 Mon.** *Barbados:* Bank Holiday. *Lesotho:* Independence Day. *South Korea:* Foundation Day (2nd day of 2).

**5 Tue.** *Lesotho:* Sports Day. *Macao:* Portuguese Republic Day. *Portugal:* Republic Day.

**6 Wed.** *Egypt:* Armed Forces Day.

**9 Sat.** *Peru:* National Dignity Day. *South Korea:* Alphabet Day. *Uganda:* Independence Day.

**10 Sun.** *Japan:* Health Day. *South Africa:* Kruger Day. *Taiwan:* National Day.

**11 Mon.** *Canada:* Thanksgiving Day. *Cuba:* Independence War. *Fiji:* Cession Day. *Panama:* Revolution Day. *United States:* Bank Holiday. *Virgin Islands (U.S.):* Puerto Rican Friendship Day.

**12 Tue.** *Equatorial Guinea:* Independence Day. *Spain:* National Day. *Multinational:* Columbus Day (see App. A12).

**14 Thu.** *Zaïre:* Founders' Day.

**15 Fri.** *Bosnia and Herzegovina:* Independence Day*. *Tunisia:* Evacuation Day.

**16 Sat.** *Asian:* Ancestors' Day (see App. B6).

**17 Sun.** *Haiti:* Dessalines Day. *Malawi:* Mother's Day.

**18 Mon.** *Jamaica:* Heroes' Day.

**20 Wed.** *Guatemala:* Revolution Day. *Kenya:* Kenyatta Day.

**21 Thu.** *Burma:* Full Moon Day. *Honduras:* Army Day. *Somalia:* Revolution Day (1st day of 2).

**22 Fri.** *Somalia:* Revolution Day (2nd day of 2). *Sri Lanka:* Full Moon Poya. *Vatican:* John Paul II Day.

**23 Sat.** *Hungary:* Revolution Day. *Thailand:* Chulalongkorn Day. *Zodiac Cusp:* Libra ends, Scorpio begins.

**24 Sun.** *Egypt:* Suez Victory Day. *Haiti:* United Nations Day. *Zambia:* Independence Day.

**25 Mon.** *Ireland:* Public Holiday. *New Zealand:* Labour Day. *Taiwan:* Restoration Day.

**26 Tue.** *Austria:* National Day. *Benin:* Revolution Day. *Rwanda:* Government Day.

**27 Wed.** *Saint Vincent:* Independence Day. *Turkmenistan:* Independence Day*. *Zaïre:* Naming Day.

**28 Thu.** *Greece:* Ohi! Day.

**29 Fri.** *Tanzania:* Naming Day. *Turkey:* Republic Day.

**31 Sun.** *Taiwan:* Chiang Kai-shek's Birthday. *Canada and United States:* Daylight Savings Time ends (retard clocks 1 hour).

# November 2010

**1 Mon.** *Algeria:* Revolution Day. *Antigua:* Independence Day. *Virgin Islands (U.S.):* Liberty Day. *Christian:* All Saints' Day (see App. A13).

**2 Tue.** *Brazil:* Memorial Day. *Finland:* All Saints' Eve. *Sweden:* All Saints' Eve. *Christian:* All Souls' Day (see App. A14).

**3 Wed.** *Dominica:* Independence Day. *Ecuador:* Cuenca Independence Day. *Japan:* Culture Day. *Panama:* Independence Day.

**4 Thu.** *Andorra:* Saint Charles' Day. *Liberia:* Thanksgiving Day. *Panama:* Flag Day. *Vatican:* John Paul II's Nameday.

**5 Fri.** *El Salvador:* Cry of Independence Day. *Hindu:* Deepavali (see App. B21).

**7 Sun.** *Bangladesh:* Revolution Day.

**8 Mon.** *Nepal:* Queen's Birthday.

**9 Tue.** *Pakistan:* Iqbal Day.

**10 Wed.** *Panama:* Cry of Independence Day.

**11 Thu.** *Angola:* Independence Day. *Bhutan:* King's Birthday. *Maldives:* Republic Day. *Poland:* Independence Day. *Multinational:* Armistice Day (see App. A15).

**12 Fri.** *Taiwan:* Dr. Sun Yat-sen's Birthday.

**14 Sun.** *Jordan:* King's Birthday.

**15 Mon.** *Brazil:* Republic Day. *Fiji:* Prince Charles' Birthday. *Far East

*Islamic:* Hari Raya Haji (see App. B29). *Islamic:* Eid al Adha (1st day of 4) (see App. B28).

**16 Tue.** *Islamic:* Eid al Adha (2nd day of 4) (see App. B28).

**17 Wed.** *Germany:* Repentance Day. *Zaïre:* Armed Forces Day. *Islamic:* Eid al Adha (3rd day of 4) (see App. B28).

**18 Thu.** *Haiti:* Vertieres' Day. *Morocco:* Independence Day. *Oman:* National Day. *Islamic:* Eid al Adha (4th day of 4) (see App. B28).

**19 Fri.** *Belize:* Garifuna Day. *Mali:* Army Coup Day. *Monaco:* Prince Ranier's Day. *Puerto Rico:* Discovery Day.

**20 Sat.** *Burma:* Full Moon Day. *Mexico:* Revolution Day.

**21 Sun.** *Sri Lanka:* Full Moon Poya.

**22 Mon.** *Lebanon:* Independence Day. *Zodiac Cusp:* Scorpio ends, Sagittarius begins.

**23 Tue.** *Japan:* Labor Thanksgiving Day.

**24 Wed.** *Zaïre:* New Regime Day.

**25 Thu.** *Suriname:* Independence Day. *United States:* Thanksgiving Day.

**26 Fri.** *Argentina:* Bank Holiday.

**28 Sun.** *Albania:* Independence Day. *Burundi:* Republic Day. *Chad:* Republic Day. *Mauritania:* Independence Day. *Panama:* Independence Day.

**29 Mon.** *Albania:* Liberation Day. *Liberia:* Tubman's Birthday. *Yugoslavia:* Republic Day.

**30 Tue.** *Barbados:* Independence Day. *Benin:* National Day. *Philippines:* Heroes' Day.

# December 2010

**1 Wed.** *Central African Republic:* National Day. *Portugal:* Youth Day. *Ukraine:* Independence Day*. *Jewish:* Chanukah.

**2 Thu.** *Laos:* Republic Day. *United Arab Emirates:* National Day.

**5 Sun.** *Haiti:* Discovery Day. *Thailand:* King's Birthday. *Islamic:* New Year's Day (Hegira: 1432) (see App. B22).

**6 Mon.** *Finland:* Independence Day.

**7 Tue.** *Ivory Coast:* Independence Day. *Far East Islamic:* New Year's Day (Hegira: 1432).

**8 Wed.** *Christian:* Immaculate Conception (see App. A16).

**9 Thu.** *Tanzania:* Independence Day.

**10 Fri.** *Angola:* MPLA Foundation Day. *Equatorial Guinea:* Human Rights Day. *Namibia:* Settlers' Day. *Thailand:* Constitution Day.

**11 Sat.** *Burkina Faso:* National Day.

**12 Sun.** *Kenya:* Independence Day. *Mexico:* Guadalupe Festival.

**13 Mon.** *Malta:* Republic Day.

**14 Tue.** *Islamic:* Ashura (see App. B23).

**16 Thu.** *Bahrain:* National Day. *Bangladesh:* Victory Day. *Nepal:* Constitution Day. *South Africa:* Covenant Day.

**17 Fri.** *Bhutan:* National Day.

**18 Sat.** *Niger:* Republic Day.

**19 Sun.** *Burma:* Full Moon Day.

**20 Mon.** *Sri Lanka:* Full Moon Poya.

**21 Tue.** *Kazakhstan:* Independence Day* *Zodiac Cusp:* Sagittarius ends, Capricorn begins.

**23 Thu.** *Japan:* Emperor's Birthday.

**24 Fri.** *Multinational:* Christmas Eve (see App. A17).

**25 Sat.** *Angola:* Family Day. *Congo:* Children's Day. *Pakistan:* Quaid's Birthday. *Taiwan:* Constitution Day. *Multinational:* Christmas Day (see App. A18).

**26 Sun.** *South Africa:* Good Will Day. *Multinational:* Boxing Day (see App. A19).

**27 Mon.** *Hong Kong:* Boxing Day.

**30 Thu.** *Madagascar:* Republic Day. *Philippines:* Rizal Day (1st day of 2).

**31 Fri.** *Congo:* Republic Day. *Philippines:* Rizal Day (2nd day of 2). *Multinational:* Bank Holiday and New Year's Eve (see App. A20 & A21).

# January 2011

**1 Sat.** *Cameroon:* Independence Day. *Cuba:* Liberation Day. *Haiti:* Independence Day. *Palau:* Independence Day. *Sudan:* Independence Day. *Taiwan:* Foundation Day (1st day of 2). *Western Samoa:* Independence Day. *Multinational:* Bank Holiday and New Year's Day (see App. A1 & A2).

**2 Sun.** *Japan:* Bank Holiday. *New Zealand:* New Year's Day (2nd day of 2). *South Korea:* New Year's Day (2nd day of 2). *Switzerland:* Berchtold's Day. *Taiwan:* Foundation Day (2nd day of 2).

**3 Mon.** *Burkina Faso:* Revolution Day. *Hong Kong:* New Year's Day. *Scotland:* New Year's Day (2nd day of 2).

**4 Tue.** *Burma:* Independence Day. *Zaïre:* Martyrs' Day.

**6 Thu.** *Iraq:* Army Day. *Uruguay:* Children's Day. *Christian:* Epiphany (see App. A3).

**7 Fri.** *Egypt:* Coptic Christmas. *Ethiopia:* Coptic Christmas.

**11 Tue.** *Albania:* Republic Day. *Nepal:* Unification Day. *Puerto Rico:* Hostos Day.

**12 Wed.** *Tanzania:* Revolution Day.

**13 Thu.** *Togo:* Liberation Day.

**15 Sat.** *Japan:* Adult's Day. *Jordan:* Arbor Day.

**17 Mon.** *United States:* Martin Luther King's Birthday.

**18 Tue.** *Burma:* Full Moon Day.

**19 Wed.** *Ethiopia:* Epiphany. *Sri Lanka:* Full Moon Poya.

**20 Thu.** *Mali:* Award Day. *Zodiac Cusp:* Capricorn ends, Aquarius begins.

**21 Fri.** *Dominican Republic:* Altagracia Day.

**22 Sat.** *Saint Vincent:* Discovery Day.

**26 Wed.** *Dominican Republic:* Duarte Day. *India:* Republic Day.

**27 Thu.** *Monaco:* Saint Devota's Day. *Vietnam:* Vietnam Day.

**28 Fri.** *Rwanda:* Democracy Day.

**31 Mon.** *Australia:* Australia Day. *Nauru:* Independence Day.

# February 2011

**2 Wed.** *Liechtenstein:* Candlemas. *Asian:* Chinese New Year Eve (see App. B1).

**3 Thu.** *Vietnam:* Tet (1st day of 3). *Asian:* Chinese New Year (Year of the Hare) (see App. B2).

**4 Fri.** *Sri Lanka:* Independence Day. *Vietnam:* Tet (2nd day of 3). *Asian:* 2nd Day of Chinese New Year (see App. B2).

**5 Sat.** *Mexico:* Constitution Day. *Vietnam:* Tet (3rd day of 3). *Asian:* 3rd Day of Chinese New Year (see App. B4).

**6 Sun.** *New Zealand:* Waitangi Day.

**7 Mon.** *Grenada:* Independence Day. *United States:* Lincoln's Birthday.

**8 Tue.** *Iraq:* Revolution Day.

**9 Wed.** *Lebanon:* Saint Marion's Day.

**10 Thu.** *Malta:* Saint Paul's Day.

**11 Fri.** *Cameroon:* Youth Day. *Japan:* Foundation Day. *Liberia:* Armed Forces Day.

**12 Sat.** *Burma:* Union Day.

**14 Mon.** *Far East Islamic:* Mohammed's Birthday. *International:* Valentine's Day. *Islamic:* Mohammed's Birthday (see App. B24).

**16 Wed.** *Burma:* Full Moon Day.

**17 Thu.** *Sri Lanka:* Full Moon Poya.

**18 Fri.** *Gambia:* Independence Day. *Thailand:* Makha Bucha Day.

**19 Sat.** *Nepal:* National Day. *Zodiac Cusp:* Aquarius ends, Pisces begins.

**21 Mon.** *Bangladesh:* Saheed Day. *United States:* Washington's Birthday.

**22 Tue.** *Saint Lucia:* Independence Day.

**23 Wed.** *Brunei:* National Day. *Guyana:* Republic Day.

**25 Fri.** *Kuwait:* National Day.

**27 Sun.** *Dominican Republic:* Independence Day.

# March 2011

**1 Tue.** *South Korea:* Independence Day.

**2 Wed.** *Ethiopia:* Victory of Aduwa Day. *Morocco:* Independence Day.

**3 Thu.** *Bulgaria:* Liberation Day. *Malawi:* Martyrs' Day. *Morocco:* National Day.

**6 Sun.** *Ghana:* Independence Day.

**7 Mon.** *Greece:* Shrove Monday. *Guam:* Discovery Day. *Christian:* Shrove Monday (see App. B7). *Orthodox:* Shrove Monday.

**8 Tue.** *Syria:* Revolution Day. *Christian:* Shrove Tuesday (see App. B8). *Multinational:* Women's Day (see App. A4).

**9 Wed.** *Christian:* Ash Wednesday (see App. B9).

**10 Thu.** *South Korea:* Labor Day.

**11 Fri.** *Lithuania:* National Day*.

**12 Sat.** *Lesotho:* Moshoeshoe's Day. *Mauritius:* Independence Day. *Zambia:* Youth Day.

**13 Sun.** *Grenada:* National Day.

**14 Mon.** *Gibraltar:* Commonwealth Day.

**17 Thu.** *Ireland:* Saint Patrick's Day. *Northern Ireland:* Saint Patrick's Day.

**18 Fri.** *Burma:* Full Moon Day.

**19 Sat.** *Sri Lanka:* Full Moon Poya. *Christian:* Saint Joseph's Day (see App. A5).

**20 Sun.** *Tunisia:* Independence Day. *Jewish:* Purim. *Zodiac Cusp:* Pisces ends, Aries begins.

**21 Mon.** *Afghanistan:* New Year's Day (Shamsi: 1390). *Iran:* New Year's Day (Hegira: 1390). *Iraq:* New Year's Day. *Japan:* Vernal Equinox. *Mexico:* Juarez Day.

**22 Tue.** *Puerto Rico:* Abolition Day. *Zambia:* Africa Day.

**23 Wed.** *Pakistan:* Pakistan Day.

**25 Fri.** *Cyprus:* Greek Independence Day. *Greece:* Independence Day. *Liechtenstein:* Annunciation.

**26 Sat.** *Bangladesh:* Independence Day.

**27 Sun.** *Angola:* Evacuation Day. *Burma:* Resistance Day. *Europe:* Daylight Savings Time starts (advance clocks 1 hour).

**28 Mon.** *Virgin Islands (U.S.):* Transfer Day.

**29 Tue.** *Central African Republic:* Boganda Day. *Madagascar:* Memorial Day. *Taiwan:* Youth Day.

**31 Thu.** *Malta:* National Day.

# April 2011

**1 Fri.** *Iran:* Republic Day. *San Marino:* National Day. *Sierra Leone:* Bank Holiday.

**3 Sun.** *Canada and United States:* Daylight Savings Time starts (advance clocks 1 hour).

**4 Mon.** *Hungary:* Liberation Day. *Senegal:* National Day.

**5 Tue.** *South Korea:* Arbor Day. *Asian:* Tomb Sweeping Day (see App. A6).

**6 Wed.** *South Africa:* Founders'

Day. *Thailand:* Chakri Day.

**9 Sat.** *Philippines:* Valour Day. *Tunisia:* Martyrs' Day.

**11 Mon.** *Costa Rica:* Heroes' Day. *Uganda:* Liberation Day.

**13 Wed.** *Chad:* National Day. *Thailand:* Songkrawn (1st day of 2).

**14 Thu.** *Honduras:* Pan American Day. *Thailand:* Songkrawn (2nd day of 2).

**15 Fri.** *Niger:* National Day.

**16 Sat.** *Burma:* Full Moon and New Year's Day (Burmese: 1373). *Cyprus:* Independence Day.

**17 Sun.** *Cambodia:* Independence Day. *Sri Lanka:* Full Moon Poya. *Syria:* Independence Day. *Christian:* Palm Sunday.

**18 Mon.** *Zimbabwe:* Republic Day.

**19 Tue.** *Israel:* Passover. *Sierra Leone:* Republic Day. *Uruguay:* Patriots' Day. *Venezuela:* Independence Day. *Jewish:* Passover.

**20 Wed.** *Zodiac Cusp:* Aries ends, Taurus begins.

**21 Thu.** *Brazil:* Tiradentes Day. *Christian:* Maundy Thursday (see App. B11).

**22 Fri.** *Christian:* Good Friday (see App. B12). *Orthodox:* Good Friday (see App. B20).

**23 Sat.** *Turkey:* Children's Day. *Christian:* Holy Saturday (see App. B13).

**24 Sun.** *Jordan:* Easter Sunday. *Christian:* Easter Sunday (see App. B14). *Orthodox:* Easter Sunday.

**25 Mon.** *Australia:* ANZAC Day. *Egypt:* Sinai Day. *Iceland:* Children's Day. *Italy:* Liberation Day. *New Zealand:* ANZAC Day. *Portugal:* Liberation Day. *Swaziland:* Flag Day. *Christian:* Easter Monday (see App. B15). *Orthodox:* Easter Monday (see App. B20).

**26 Tue.** *Tanzania:* Union Day.

**27 Wed.** *Afghanistan:* Independence Day. *Sierra Leone:* Independence Day. *Togo:* Independence Day.

**29 Fri.** *Japan:* Green Day.

**30 Sat.** *Finland:* Vappu Day. *Netherlands:* Queen's Birthday.

# May 2011

**1 Sun.** *Multinational:* Labor Day (see App. A7).

**2 Mon.** *Lesotho:* King's Birthday. *United Kingdom:* Labour Day. *Zambia:* Labour Day.

**3 Tue.** *Japan:* Constitution Day.

**4 Wed.** *Japan:* People's Day.

**5 Thu.** *Japan:* Children's Day. *Mexico:* Cinco de Mayo. *Netherlands:* Liberation Day. *South Korea:* Children's Day. *Thailand:* Coronation Day.

**6 Fri.** *Lebanon:* Martyrs' Day. *Philippines:* Corregidor Day.

**8 Sun.** *France:* Labour Day. *International:* Mother's Day.

**9 Mon.** *Czech Republic:* Liberation Day*. *Israel:* Independence Day. *Slovakia:* Liberation Day*.

**10 Tue.** *Micronesia:* Independence Day. *South Korea:* Vesak Day.

**14 Sat.** *Liberia:* Unification Day. *Malawi:* Kamuzu Day. *Paraguay:* Flag Day.

**15 Sun.** *Burma:* Full Moon Day. *Paraguay:* Independence Day.

**16 Mon.** *Sri Lanka:* Full Moon Poya.

**17 Tue.** *Cayman Islands:* Discovery Day. *Malaysia:* Vesak Day. *Norway:* Constitution Day. *Singapore:* Vesak Day. *Thailand:* Visakha Bucha Day.

**18 Wed.** *Haiti:* Flag Day. *Uruguay:* Las Piedras Day.

**19 Thu.** *Finland:* Flag Day. *Turkey:* Youth Day.

**20 Fri.** *Cameroon:* Constitution Day. *Denmark:* All Prayers' Day. *Zaïre:* Popular Movement Day.

**21 Sat.** *Chile:* Navy Day. *Zodiac Cusp:* Taurus ends, Gemini begins.

**22 Sun.** *Haiti:* Sovereign Day. *Sri Lanka:* Heroes' Day.

**23 Mon.** *Canada:* Victoria Day. *Jamaica:* Labour Day.

**24 Tue.** *Bulgaria:* Culture Day. *Ecuador:* Independence Battle Day.

**25 Wed.** *Argentina:* National Day. *Eritrea:* Independence Day*. *Jordan:* Independence Day. *Sudan:* Revolution Day. *Multinational:* Africa Day (see App. A8).

**26 Thu.** *Guyana:* Independence Day.

**27 Fri.** *Nigeria:* Children's Day.

**30 Mon.** *United Kingdom:* Spring Break. *United States:* Memorial Day.

**31 Tue.** *Brunei:* Regiment Day. *South Africa:* Republic Day.

# June 2011

**1 Wed.** *Kenya:* Madaraka Day. *Malaysia:* King's Birthday. *Tunisia:* National Day. *Western Samoa:* Independence Day.

**2 Thu.** *Italy:* Republic Day. *Tunisia:* Youth Day. *Christian:* Ascension (see App. B16).

**4 Sat.** *Bahamas:* Labour Day. *Tonga:* Independence Day.

**5 Sun.** *Denmark:* Constitution Day. *Equatorial Guinea:* President's Birthday. *Seychelles:* Liberation Day.

**6 Mon.** *Ireland:* Public Holiday. *New Zealand:* Queen's Birthday. *South Korea:* Memorial Day. *Sweden:* Constitution Day.

**7 Tue.** *Chad:* Revolution Day. *Asian:* Dragon Boat Festival (see App. B5).

**8 Wed.** *Israel:* Pentecost. *Jewish:* Pentecost.

**9 Thu.** *Argentina:* Independence Day.

**10 Fri.** *Macao:* Portugal Day. *Portugal:* Portugal Day.

**11 Sat.** *Hong Kong:* Queen's Birthday (1st day of 2). *Libya:* Evacuation Day.

**12 Sun.** *Philippines:* Independence Day. *Christian:* Whitsunday. *Orthodox:* Pentecost Sunday.

**13 Mon.** *Australia:* Queen's Birthday. *Fiji:* Queen's Birthday. *Greece:* Pentecost Monday. *Hong Kong:* Queen's Birthday (2nd day of 2). *New Guinea:* Queen's Birthday. *United Kingdom:* Queen's Birthday. *Christian:* Whitmonday (see App. B18).

**14 Tue.** *Burma:* Full Moon Day.

**15 Wed.** *Sri Lanka:* Full Moon Poya.

**17 Fri.** *Germany:* Unity Day. *Iceland:* Independence Day.

**18 Sat.** *Egypt:* Independence Day.

**19 Sun.** *Algeria:* Righting Day. *Kuwait:* Independence Day. *Uruguay:* Artigas Day.

**20 Mon.** *Argentina:* Flag Day.

**21 Tue.** *Finland:* Midsummer Day (1st day of 2). *Sweden:* Midsummer Day (1st day of 2). *Zodiac Cusp:* Gemini ends, Cancer begins.

**22 Wed.** *Finland:* Midsummer Day (2nd day of 2). *Sweden:* Midsummer Day (2nd day of 2).

**23 Thu.** *Luxembourg:* National Day. *Christian:* Corpus Christi (see App. B19).

**24 Fri.** *Andorra:* Saint John's Day. *Chile:* Bank Holiday. *Ecuador:* Bank Holiday. *El Salvador:* Bank Holiday. *Finland:* Bank Holiday. *Venezuela:* Carabobo Day. *Zaïre:* Constitution Day.

**25 Sat.** *Croatia:* Independence Day*. *Finland:* Johannus Day. *Mozambique:* Independence Day. *Slovenia:* Independence Day*.

**26 Sun.** *Madagascar:* Independence Day. *Somalia:* Independence Day.

**27 Mon.** *Djibouti:* Independence Day.

**28 Tue.** *Islamic:* Isra a Majraj (see App. B30).

**29 Wed.** *Seychelles:* Independence Day. *Christian:* Saint Paul's Day (see App. A9).

**30 Thu.** *Guatemala:* Army Day. *Sri Lanka:* Bank Holiday. *Zaïre:* Independence Day.

# July 2011

**1 Fri.** *Burundi:* Independence Day. *Canada:* Canada Day. *Ghana:* Republic Day. *Hong Kong:* Half Year Day. *Rwanda:* Independence Day. *Somalia:* Union Day. *Suriname:* Freedom Day. *Multinational:* Bank Holiday (see App. A10).

**4 Mon.** *Cayman Islands:* Constitution Day. *Lesotho:* Family Day. *Philippines:* United States Friendship Day. *United States:* Independence Day. *Yugoslavia:* Freedom Fighters' Day. *Zambia:* Heroes' Day.

**5 Tue.** *Algeria:* Independence Day. *Cape Verde:* Independence Day. *Rwanda:* Unity Day. *Venezuela:* Independence Day. *Zambia:* Unity Day.

**6 Wed.** *Comoros:* Independence Day. *Malawi:* Republic Day.

**7 Thu.** *Solomon Islands:* Independence Day. *Tanzania:* Farmers' Day. *Yugoslavia:* Serbian Day.

**10 Sun.** *Bahamas:* Independence Day.

**11 Mon.** *Mongolia:* Revolution Day.

**12 Tue.** *Kiribati:* Independence Day. *Northern Ireland:* Battle of the Boyne Day. *São Tomé:* National Day.

**13 Wed.** *Burma:* Full Moon Day.

**14 Thu.** *France:* National Day. *Iraq:* Revolution Day. *Sri Lanka:* Full Moon Poya.

**15 Fri.** *Brunei:* Sultan's Birthday. *Thailand:* Asalaha Bucha Day.

**16 Sat.** *Thailand:* Khao Phansa Day.

**17 Sun.** *Iraq:* Revolution Day. *Puerto Rico:* Rivera Day. *Slovakia:* Independence Day*. *South Korea:* Constitution Day.

**18 Mon.** *Botswana:* President's Day. *Uruguay:* Constitution Day.

**19 Tue.** *Burma:* Martyrs' Day. *Laos:* Independence Day. *Nicaragua:* Sandinista Day.

**20 Wed.** *Colombia:* Independence Day.

**21 Thu.** *Belgium:* National Day. *Guam:* Liberation Day.

**22 Fri.** *Poland:* Liberation Day.

**23 Sat.** *Egypt:* Revolution Day. *New Guinea:* Remembrance Day. *Zodiac Cusp:* Cancer ends, Leo begins.

**24 Sun.** *Venezuela:* Bolivar Day.

**25 Mon.** *Costa Rica:* Guanacaste Day. *Cuba:* Revolution Day (1st day of 3). *Puerto Rico:* Constitution Day. *Spain:* Santiago Day. *Tunisia:* Republic Day. *Virgin Islands (U.S.):* Hurricane Supplication Day.

**26 Tue.** *Cuba:* Revolution Day (2nd day of 3). *Liberia:* Independence Day. *Maldives:* Independence Day.

**27 Wed.** *Cuba:* Revolution Day (3rd day of 3). *Puerto Rico:* Barbosa Day.

**28 Thu.** *Peru:* Independence Day (1st day of 2).

**29 Fri.** *Peru:* Independence Day (2nd day of 2).

**30 Sat.** *Vanuatu:* Independence Day.

**31 Sun.** *Islamic:* 1st Day of Ramadan (see App. B25).

# August 2011

**1 Mon.** *Bahamas:* Emancipation Day. *Barbados:* Emancipation Day. *Benin:* Independence Day. *Canada:* Civic Holiday. *Ireland:* Public Holiday. *Jamaica:* Independence Day. *Scotland:* Public Holiday. *Switzerland:* Confederation Day.

**2 Tue.** *Costa Rica:* Virgin of the Angels Day. *Guyana:* Freedom Day. *Trinidad:* Discovery Day.

**3 Wed.** *El Salvador:* Summer Day (1st day of 4). *Guinea-Bissau:* Martyrs' Day. *Niger:* Independence Day. *Tunisia:* President's Birthday. *Zambia:* Farmers' Day.

**4 Thu.** *Burkina Faso:* Independence

Day (1st day of 2). *El Salvador:* Summer Day (2nd day of 4).

**5 Fri.** *Burkina Faso:* Independence Day (2nd day of 2). *El Salvador:* Summer Day (3rd day of 4).

**6 Sat.** *Bolivia:* Independence Day. *El Salvador:* Summer Day (4th day of 4). *United Arab Emirates:* Accession Day.

**7 Sun.** *Colombia:* Boyaca Day. *Ivory Coast:* Republic Day.

**9 Tue.** *Georgia:* Independence Day*. *Israel:* Tisha Ab. *Singapore:* National Day. *Jewish:* Tisha Ab.

**10 Wed.** *Ecuador:* Independence Day.

**11 Thu.** *Chad:* Independence Day. *Jordan:* Accession Day. *Zimbabwe:* Heroes' Day (1st day of 2).

**12 Fri.** *Burma:* Full Moon Day. *Thailand:* Queen's Birthday. *Zimbabwe:* Heroes' Day (2nd day of 2).

**13 Sat.** *Central African Republic:* Independence Day. *Congo:* Independence Day (1st day of 2). *Sri Lanka:* Full Moon Poya. *Tunisia:* Women's Day.

**14 Sun.** *Congo:* Independence Day (2nd day of 2). *Pakistan:* Independence Day.

**15 Mon.** *Congo:* Independence Day (3rd day of 3). *India:* Independence Day. *Liechtenstein:* National Day. *South Korea:* Republic Day. *Christian:* Assumption (see App. A11).

**16 Tue.** *Dominican Republic:* Republic Day.

**17 Wed.** *Argentina:* San Martin's Day. *Gabon:* Independence Day. *Indonesia:* Independence Day.

**20 Sat.** *Hungary:* Constitution Day. *Senegal:* Independence Day.

**21 Sun.** *Estonia:* Independence Day*. *Latvia:* Independence Day*. *Lithuania:* Independence Day*.

**23 Tue.** *Romania:* National Day (1st day of 2). *Zodiac Cusp:* Leo ends, Virgo begins.

**24 Wed.** *Kazakhstan:* National Day*. *Liberia:* Flag Day. *Romania:* National Day (2nd day of 2). *Russia:* Independence Day*. *Ukraine:* National Day*.

**25 Thu.** *Belarus:* Independence Day*. *Paraguay:* Constitution Day. *Uruguay:* Independence Day.

**27 Sat.** *Hong Kong:* Liberation Day (1st day of 2). *Moldova:* Independence Day*.

**29 Mon.** *England:* Summer Break. *Hong Kong:* Liberation Day (2nd day of 2). *Luxembourg:* Fair Day. *Northern Ireland:* Summer Break. *Uzbekistan:* Independence Day*. *Wales:* Summer Break.

**30 Tue.** *Afghanistan:* Children's Day. *Azerbaijan:* Independence Day*. *Peru:* Rose of Lima Day. *Turkey:* Victory Day. *Far East Islamic:* Hari Raya Puasa (see App. B27). *Islamic:* Eid al Fitr (1st day of 4) (see App. B26).

**31 Wed.** *Afghanistan:* Pashtunistan Day. *Kyrgyzstan:* Independence Day*. *Malaysia:* National Day. *Trinidad:* Independence Day. *Islamic:* Eid al Fitr (2nd day of 4) (see App. B26).

# September 2011

**1 Thu.** *Libya:* National Day. *Mexico:* President's Message Day. *Syria:* United Arab Republics Day. *Islamic:* Eid al Fitr (3rd day of 4) (see App. B26).

**2 Fri.** *Vietnam:* Independence Day. *Islamic:* Eid al Fitr (4th day of 4) (see App. B26).

**3 Sat.** *Qatar:* National Day. *San Marino:* Saint Marinus' Day. *Tunisia:* Independence Movement Day.

**5 Mon.** *Canada:* Labour Day. *United States:* Labor Day.

**6 Tue.** *Pakistan:* Defense Day. *Swaziland:* Independence Day.

**7 Wed.** *Brazil:* Independence Day.

**8 Thu.** *Andorra:* National Day. *Malta:* Our Lady of Victory Day.

**9 Fri.** *Bulgaria:* National Day (1st day of 2). *North Korea:* Independence Day. *Tajikistan:* Independence Day*.

**10 Sat.** *Belize:* National Day. *Bulgaria:* National Day (2nd day of 2). *Burma:* Full Moon Day.

**11 Sun.** *Chile:* Revolution Day. *Pakistan:* Anniversary of Quaid-e-Azam's Death. *Sri Lanka:* Full Moon Poya.

**12 Mon.** *Egypt:* New Year's Day (Coptic: 1729). *Ethiopia:* National Day and New Year's Day (Ethiopian: 2005).

**14 Wed.** *Guatemala:* San Jacinto Day. *Nicaragua:* San Jacinto Day.

**15 Thu.** *Costa Rica:* Independence Day. *El Salvador:* Independence Day. *Guatemala:* Independence Day. *Honduras:* Independence Day. *Japan:* Veneration Day. *Nicaragua:* Independence Day.

**16 Fri.** *Mexico:* Independence Day. *New Guinea:* Independence Day.

**17 Sat.** *Angola:* Heroes' Day. *Marshall Islands:* Independence Day.

**18 Sun.** *Burundi:* Victory of Uprona Day. *Chile:* Independence Day.

**19 Mon.** *Chile:* Armed Forces Day. *Saint Kitts:* Independence Day.

**21 Wed.** *Belize:* Independence Day. *Malta:* Independence Day.

**22 Thu.** *Mali:* Independence Day.

**23 Fri.** *Armenia:* Independence Day*. *Japan:* Autumnal Equinox. *Saudi Arabia:* National Day. *Zodiac Cusp:* Virgo ends, Libra begins.

**24 Sat.** *Dominican Republic:* Mercedes Day. *Guinea-Bissau:* Republic Day.

**25 Sun.** *Mozambique:* Liberation Day. *Rwanda:* Assembly Day. *Europe:* Daylight Savings Time ends (retard clocks 1 hour).

**27 Tue.** *Ethiopia:* True Cross Day.

**28 Wed.** *Taiwan:* Teachers' Day.

**29 Thu.** *Brunei:* Constitution Day. *Israel:* New Year's Day. *Paraguay:* Boqueron Battle Day. *Jewish:* Rosh Hashanah (Jewish: 5772).

**30 Fri.** *Botswana:* Independence Day.

# October 2011

**1 Sat.** *Cameroon:* Unification Day. *China:* National Day (1st day of 2). *Nigeria:* Independence Day. *South Korea:* Armed Forces Day. (1st day of 2). *Tuvalu:* Independence Day.

**2 Sun.** *China:* National Day (2nd day of 2). *Guinea:* Independence Day. *India:* Ghandi Day. *South Korea:* Armed Forces Day. (2nd day of 2).

**3 Mon.** *Barbados:* Bank Holiday. *Honduras:* Morazan Day. *South Korea:* Foundation Day (1st day of 2).

**4 Tue.** *Lesotho:* Independence Day. *South Korea:* Foundation Day. (2nd day of 2).

**5 Wed.** *Lesotho:* Sports Day. *Macao:* Portuguese Republic Day. *Portugal:* Republic Day.

**6 Thu.** *Egypt:* Armed Forces Day. *Asian:* Ancestors' Day (see App. B6).

**8 Sat.** *Israel:* Yom Kippur. *Jewish:* Yom Kippur.

**9 Sun.** *Peru:* National Dignity Day. *South Korea:* Alphabet Day. *Uganda:* Independence Day.

**10 Mon.** *Burma:* Full Moon Day. *Canada:* Thanksgiving Day. *Fiji:* Cession Day. *Japan:* Health Day. *South Africa:* Kruger Day. *Taiwan:* National Day. *United States:* Bank Holiday. *Virgin Islands (U.S.):* Puerto Rican Friendship Day.

**11 Tue.** *China:* Mid-autumn Day. *Cuba:* Independence War. *Panama:* Revolution Day. *Sri Lanka:* Full Moon Poya. *Taiwan:* Mid-autumn Day.

**12 Wed.** *Equatorial Guinea:* Independence Day. *Hong Kong:* Mid-autumn Day. *Macao:* Mid-autumn Day. *Spain:* National Day. *Multinational:* Columbus Day (see App. A12).

**13 Thu.** *Israel:* Sukkot. *Jewish:* Sukkot.

**14 Fri.** *Zaïre:* Founders' Day.

**15 Sat.** *Bosnia and Herzegovina:* Independence Day*. *Tunisia:* Evacuation Day.

**17 Mon.** *Haiti:* Dessalines Day. *Jamaica:* Heroes' Day. *Malawi:* Mother's Day.

**20 Thu.** *Guatemala:* Revolution Day. *Kenya:* Kenyatta Day.

**21 Fri.** *Honduras:* Army Day. *Somalia:* Revolution Day (1st day of 2).

**22 Sat.** *Somalia:* Revolution Day (2nd day of 2). *Vatican:* John Paul II Day.

**23 Sun.** *Hungary:* Revolution Day. *Thailand:* Chulalongkorn Day. *Zodiac Cusp:* Libra ends, Scorpio begins.

**24 Mon.** *Egypt:* Suez Victory Day. *Haiti:* United Nations Day. *Zambia:* Independence Day.

**25 Tue.** *Taiwan:* Restoration Day. *Hindu:* Deepavali (see App. B21).

**26 Wed.** *Austria:* National Day. *Benin:* Revolution Day. *Rwanda:* Government Day.

**27 Thu.** *Saint Vincent:* Independence Day. *Turkmenistan:* Independence Day*. *Zaïre:* Naming Day.

**28 Fri.** *Greece:* Ohi! Day.

**29 Sat.** *Tanzania:* Naming Day. *Turkey:* Republic Day.

**30 Sun.** *Canada and United States:* Daylight Savings Time ends (retard clocks 1 hour).

**31 Mon.** *Ireland:* Public Holiday. *New Zealand:* Labour Day. *Taiwan:* Chiang Kai-shek's Birthday.

# November 2011

**1 Tue.** *Algeria:* Revolution Day. *Antigua:* Independence Day. *Christian:* All Saints' Day (see App. A13).

**2 Wed.** *Brazil:* Memorial Day. *Finland:* All Saints' Eve. *Sweden:* All Saints' Eve. *Christian:* All Souls' Day (see App. A14).

**3 Thu.** *Dominica:* Independence Day. *Ecuador:* Cuenca Independence Day. *Japan:* Culture Day. *Liberia:* Thanksgiving Day. *Panama:* Independence Day.

**4 Fri.** *Andorra:* Saint Charles' Day. *Panama:* Flag Day. *Vatican:* John Paul II's Nameday.

**5 Sat.** *El Salvador:* Cry of Independence Day. *Islamic:* Eid al Adha (1st day of 4) (see App. B28).

**6 Sun.** *Far East Islamic:* Hari Raya Haji (see App. B29). *Islamic:* Eid al Adha (2nd day of 4) (see App. B28).

**7 Mon.** *Bangladesh:* Revolution Day. *Virgin Islands (U.S.):* Liberty Day. *Islamic:* Eid al Adha (3rd day of 4) (see App. B28).

**8 Tue.** *Nepal:* Queen's Birthday. *Islamic:* Eid al Adha (4th day of 4) (see App. B28).

**9 Wed.** *Burma:* Full Moon Day. *Pakistan:* Iqbal Day.

**10 Thu.** *Panama:* Cry of Independence Day. *Sri Lanka:* Full Moon Poya.

**11 Fri.** *Angola:* Independence Day. *Bhutan:* King's Birthday. *Maldives:* Republic Day. *Poland:* Independence Day. *Multinational:* Armistice Day (see App. A15).

**12 Sat.** *Taiwan:* Dr. Sun Yat-sen's Birthday.

**14 Mon.** *Jordan:* King's Birthday.

**15 Tue.** *Brazil:* Republic Day.

**16 Wed.** *Germany:* Repentance Day.

**17 Thu.** *Zaïre:* Armed Forces Day.

**18 Fri.** *Haiti:* Vertieres' Day. *Morocco:* Independence Day. *Oman:* National Day.

**19 Sat.** *Belize:* Garifuna Day. *Mali:* Army Coup Day. *Monaco:* Prince Ranier's Day. *Puerto Rico:* Discovery Day.

**20 Sun.** *Mexico:* Revolution Day.

**21 Mon.** *Fiji:* Prince Charles' Birthday.

**22 Tue.** *Lebanon:* Independence Day. *Zodiac Cusp:* Scorpio ends, Sagittarius begins.

**23 Wed.** *Japan:* Labor Thanksgiving Day.

**24 Thu.** *United States:* Thanksgiving Day. *Zaïre:* New Regime Day.

**25 Fri.** *Argentina:* Bank Holiday. *Suriname:* Independence Day. *Islamic:* New Year's Day (Hegira: 1433) (see App. B22).

**26 Sat.** *Far East Islamic:* New Year's Day (Hegira: 1433).

**28 Mon.** *Albania:* Independence Day. *Burundi:* Republic Day. *Chad:* Republic Day. *Mauritania:* Independence Day. *Panama:* Independence Day.

**29 Tue.** *Albania:* Liberation Day. *Liberia:* Tubman's Birthday. *Yugoslavia:* Republic Day.

**30 Wed.** *Barbados:* Independence Day. *Benin:* National Day. *Philippines:* Heroes' Day.

# December 2011

**1 Thu.** *Central African Republic:* National Day. *Portugal:* Youth Day. *Ukraine:* Independence Day*.

**2 Fri.** *Laos:* Republic Day. *United Arab Emirates:* National Day.

**4 Sun.** *Islamic:* Ashura (see App. B23).

**5 Mon.** *Haiti:* Discovery Day. *Thailand:* King's Birthday.

**6 Tue.** *Finland:* Independence Day.

**7 Wed.** *Ivory Coast:* Independence Day.

**8 Thu.** *Christian:* Immaculate Conception (see App. A16).

**9 Fri.** *Burma:* Full Moon Day. *Tanzania:* Independence Day.

**10 Sat.** *Angola:* MPLA Foundation Day. *Equatorial Guinea:* Human Rights Day. *Namibia:* Settlers' Day. *Sri Lanka:* Full Moon Poya. *Thailand:* Constitution Day.

**11 Sun.** *Burkina Faso:* National Day.

**12 Mon.** *Kenya:* Independence Day. *Mexico:* Guadalupe Festival.

**13 Tue.** *Malta:* Republic Day.

**16 Fri.** *Bahrain:* National Day. *Bangladesh:* Victory Day. *Nepal:* Constitution Day. *South Africa:* Covenant Day.

**17 Sat.** *Bhutan:* National Day.

**18 Sun.** *Niger:* Republic Day.

**21 Wed.** *Kazakhstan:* Independence Day*. *Jewish:* Chanukah.

**22 Thu.** *Zodiac Cusp:* Sagittarius ends, Capricorn begins.

**23 Fri.** *Japan:* Emperor's Birthday.

**24 Sat.** *Multinational:* Christmas Eve (see App. A17).

**25 Sun.** *Angola:* Family Day. *Congo:* Children's Day. *Pakistan:* Quaid's Birthday. *Taiwan:* Constitution Day. *Multinational:* Christmas Day (see App. A18).

**26 Mon.** *South Africa:* Good Will Day. *Multinational:* Boxing Day (see App. A19).

**30 Fri.** *Madagascar:* Republic Day. *Philippines:* Rizal Day (1st day of 2).

**31 Sat.** *Congo:* Republic Day. *Philippines:* Rizal Day (2nd day of 2). *Multinational:* Bank Holiday and New Year's Eve (see App. A20 & A21).

# January 2012

**1 Sun.** *Cameroon:* Independence Day. *Cuba:* Liberation Day. *Haiti:* Independence Day. *Palau:* Independence Day. *Sudan:* Independence Day. *Tai-

*wan:* Foundation Day (1st day of 2). *Western Samoa:* Independence Day. *Multinational:* Bank Holiday and New Year's Day (see App. A1 & A2).

**2 Mon.** *Hong Kong:* New Year's Day. *Japan:* Bank Holiday. *New Zealand:* New Year's Day (2nd day of 2). *Scotland:* New Year's Day (2nd day of 2). *South Korea:* New Year's Day (2nd day of 2). *Switzerland:* Berchtold's Day. *Taiwan:* Foundation Day (2nd day of 2).

**3 Tue.** *Burkina Faso:* Revolution Day.

**4 Wed.** *Burma:* Independence Day. *Zaïre:* Martyrs' Day.

**6 Fri.** *Iraq:* Army Day. *Uruguay:* Children's Day. *Christian:* Epiphany (see App. A3).

**7 Sat.** *Burma:* Full Moon Day. *Egypt:* Coptic Christmas. *Ethiopia:* Coptic Christmas.

**8 Sun.** *Sri Lanka:* Full Moon Poya.

**11 Wed.** *Albania:* Republic Day. *Nepal:* Unification Day. *Puerto Rico:* Hostos Day.

**12 Thu.** *Tanzania:* Revolution Day.

**13 Fri.** *Togo:* Liberation Day.

**15 Sun.** *Japan:* Adult's Day. *Jordan:* Arbor Day.

**16 Mon.** *United States:* Martin Luther King's Birthday.

**19 Thu.** *Ethiopia:* Epiphany. *Zodiac Cusp:* Capricorn ends, Aquarius begins.

**20 Fri.** *Mali:* Award Day.

**21 Sat.** *Dominican Republic:* Altagracia Day.

**22 Sun.** *Saint Vincent:* Discovery Day. *Asian:* Chinese New Year Eve (see App. B1).

**23 Mon.** *Vietnam:* Tet (1st day of 3). *Asian:* Chinese New Year (Year of the Dragon) (see App. B2).

**24 Tue.** *Vietnam:* Tet (2nd day of 3). *Asian:* 2nd Day of Chinese New Year (see App. B3).

**25 Wed.** *Vietnam:* Tet (3rd day of 3). *Asian:* 3rd Day of Chinese New Year (see App. B4).

**26 Thu.** *Dominican Republic:* Duarte Day. *India:* Republic Day.

**27 Fri.** *Monaco:* Saint Devota's Day. *Vietnam:* Vietnam Day.

**28 Sat.** *Rwanda:* Democracy Day.

**30 Mon.** *Australia:* Australia Day.

**31 Tue.** *Nauru:* Independence Day.

# February 2012

**2 Thu.** *Liechtenstein:* Candlemas.

**3 Fri.** *Islamic:* Mohammed's Birthday (see App. B24).

**4 Sat.** *Sri Lanka:* Independence Day. *Far East Islamic:* Mohammed's Birthday.

**5 Sun.** *Mexico:* Constitution Day.

**6 Mon.** *Burma:* Full Moon Day. *New Zealand:* Waitangi Day. *United States:* Lincoln's Birthday.

**7 Tue.** *Grenada:* Independence Day. *Sri Lanka:* Full Moon Poya.

**8 Wed.** *Iraq:* Revolution Day.

**9 Thu.** *Lebanon:* Saint Marion's Day.

**10 Fri.** *Malta:* Saint Paul's Day.

**11 Sat.** *Cameroon:* Youth Day. *Japan:* Foundation Day. *Liberia:* Armed Forces Day.

**12 Sun.** *Burma:* Union Day.

**14 Tue.** *International:* Valentine's Day.

**18 Sat.** *Gambia:* Independence Day. *Zodiac Cusp:* Aquarius ends, Pisces begins.

**19 Sun.** *Nepal:* National Day.

**20 Mon.** *United States:* Washington's Birthday. *Christian:* Shrove Monday (see App. B7).

**21 Tue.** *Bangladesh:* Saheed Day. *Christian:* Shrove Tuesday (see App. B8).

**22 Wed.** *Saint Lucia:* Independence Day. *Christian:* Ash Wednesday (see App. B9).

**23 Thu.** *Brunei:* National Day. *Guyana:* Republic Day.

**25 Sat.** *Kuwait:* National Day.

**27 Mon.** *Dominican Republic:* Independence Day. *Greece:* Shrove Monday. *Orthodox:* Shrove Monday.

# March 2012

**1 Thu.** *South Korea:* Independence Day.

**2 Fri.** *Ethiopia:* Victory of Aduwa Day. *Morocco:* Independence Day.

**3 Sat.** *Bulgaria:* Liberation Day. *Malawi:* Martyrs' Day. *Morocco:* National Day.

**5 Mon.** *Guam:* Discovery Day.

**6 Tue.** *Burma:* Full Moon Day. *Ghana:* Independence Day.

**7 Wed.** *Sri Lanka:* Full Moon Poya. *Thailand:* Makha Bucha Day.

**8 Thu.** *Syria:* Revolution Day. *Jewish:* Purim. *Multinational:* Women's Day (see App. A4).

**10 Sat.** *South Korea:* Labor Day. *Zambia:* Youth Day.

**11 Sun.** *Lithuania:* National Day*.

**12 Mon.** *Gibraltar:* Commonwealth Day. *Lesotho:* Moshoeshoe's Day. *Mauritius:* Independence Day.

**13 Tue.** *Grenada:* National Day.

**17 Sat.** *Ireland:* Saint Patrick's Day. *Northern Ireland:* Saint Patrick's Day.

**19 Mon.** *Christian:* Saint Joseph's Day (see App. A5).

**20 Tue.** *Afghanistan:* New Year's Day (Shamsi: 1391). *Iran:* New Year's Day (Hegira: 1391). *Iraq:* New Year's Day. *Japan:* Vernal Equinox. *Tunisia:* Independence Day. *Zodiac Cusp:* Pisces ends, Aries begins.

**21 Wed.** *Mexico:* Juarez Day.

**22 Thu.** *Puerto Rico:* Abolition Day.

**23 Fri.** *Pakistan:* Pakistan Day.

**25 Sun.** *Cyprus:* Greek Independence Day. *Greece:* Independence Day. *Liechtenstein:* Annunciation. *Europe:* Daylight Savings Time starts (advance clocks 1 hour).

**26 Mon.** *Bangladesh:* Independence Day. *Virgin Islands (U.S.):* Transfer Day.

**27 Tue.** *Angola:* Evacuation Day. *Burma:* Resistance Day. *Zambia:* Africa Day.

**29 Thu.** *Central African Republic:* Boganda Day. *Madagascar:* Memorial Day. *Taiwan:* Youth Day.

**31 Sat.** *Malta:* National Day.

# April 2012

**1 Sun.** *Iran:* Republic Day. *San Marino:* National Day. *Canada and United States:* Daylight Savings Time starts (advance clocks 1 hour). *Christian:* Palm Sunday.

**4 Wed.** *Hungary:* Liberation Day. *Senegal:* National Day.

**5 Thu.** *Burma:* Full Moon Day. *South Korea:* Arbor Day. *Asian:* Tomb Sweeping Day (see App. A6). *Christian:* Maundy Thursday (see App. B11).

**6 Fri.** *Sierra Leone:* Bank Holiday. *South Africa:* Founders' Day. *Sri Lanka:* Full Moon Poya. *Thailand:* Chakri Day. *Christian:* Good Friday (see App. B12).

**7 Sat.** *Israel:* Passover *Christian:* Holy Saturday (see App. B13). *Jewish:* Passover.

**8 Sun.** *Christian:* Easter Sunday (see App. B14).

**9 Mon.** *Philippines:* Valour Day. *Tunisia:* Martyrs' Day. *Christian:* Easter Monday (see App. B15).

**11 Wed.** *Costa Rica:* Heroes' Day. *Uganda:* Liberation Day.

**13 Fri.** *Chad:* National Day. *Thailand:* Songkrawn (1st day of 2).

*Orthodox:* Good Friday (see App. B20).

**14 Sat.** *Honduras:* Pan American Day. *Thailand:* Songkrawn (2nd day of 2).

**15 Sun.** *Jordan:* Easter Sunday. *Niger:* National Day. *Orthodox:* Easter Sunday.

**16 Mon.** *Burma:* New Year's Day (Burmese: 1374). *Cyprus:* Independence Day. *Orthodox:* Easter Monday (see App. B20).

**17 Tue.** *Cambodia:* Independence Day. *Syria:* Independence Day.

**18 Wed.** *Zimbabwe:* Republic Day.

**19 Thu.** *Sierra Leone:* Republic Day. *Uruguay:* Patriots' Day. *Venezuela:* Independence Day. *Zodiac Cusp:* Aries ends, Taurus begins.

**21 Sat.** *Brazil:* Tiradentes Day.

**23 Mon.** *Turkey:* Children's Day.

**25 Wed.** *Australia:* ANZAC Day. *Egypt:* Sinai Day. *Iceland:* Children's Day. *Italy:* Liberation Day. *New Zealand:* ANZAC Day. *Portugal:* Liberation Day. *Swaziland:* Flag Day.

**26 Thu.** *Israel:* Independence Day. *Tanzania:* Union Day.

**27 Fri.** *Afghanistan:* Independence Day. *Sierra Leone:* Independence Day. *Togo:* Independence Day.

**28 Sat.** *South Korea:* Vesak Day.

**29 Sun.** *Japan:* Green Day.

**30 Mon.** *Finland:* Vappu Day. *Netherlands:* Queen's Birthday.

# May 2012

**1 Tue.** *Multinational:* Labor Day (see App. A7).

**2 Wed.** *Lesotho:* King's Birthday.

**3 Thu.** *Japan:* Constitution Day.

**4 Fri.** *Burma:* Full Moon Day. *Denmark:* All Prayers' Day. *Japan:* People's Day.

**5 Sat.** *Japan:* Children's Day. *Malaysia:* Vesak Day. *Mexico:* Cinco de Mayo. *Netherlands:* Liberation Day. *Singapore:* Vesak Day. *Sri Lanka:* Full Moon Poya. *South Korea:* Children's Day. *Thailand:* Coronation Day.

**6 Sun.** *Lebanon:* Martyrs' Day. *Philippines:* Corregidor Day.

**7 Mon.** *United Kingdom:* Labour Day. *Zambia:* Labour Day.

**8 Tue.** *France:* Liberation Day.

**9 Wed.** *Czech Republic:* Liberation Day*. *Slovakia:* Liberation Day*.

**10 Thu.** *Micronesia:* Independence Day.

**13 Sun.** *International:* Mother's Day.

**14 Mon.** *Liberia:* Unification Day. *Malawi:* Kamuzu Day. *Paraguay:* Flag Day.

**15 Tue.** *Paraguay:* Independence Day.

**17 Thu.** *Cayman Islands:* Discovery Day. *Norway:* Constitution Day. *Christian:* Ascension (see App. B16).

**18 Fri.** *Haiti:* Flag Day. *Uruguay:* Las Piedras Day.

**19 Sat.** *Finland:* Flag Day. *Turkey:* Youth Day.

**20 Sun.** *Cameroon:* Constitution Day. *Zaïre:* Popular Movement Day. *Zodiac Cusp:* Taurus ends, Gemini begins.

**21 Mon.** *Canada:* Victoria Day. *Chile:* Navy Day.

**22 Tue.** *Haiti:* Sovereign Day. *Sri Lanka:* Heroes' Day.

**23 Wed.** *Jamaica:* Labour Day.

**24 Thu.** *Bulgaria:* Culture Day. *Ecuador:* Independence Battle Day.

**25 Fri.** *Argentina:* National Day. *Eritrea:* Independence Day*. *Jordan:* Independence Day. *Sudan:* Revolution Day. *Multinational:* Africa Day (see App. A8).

**26 Sat.** *Guyana:* Independence Day. *Asian:* Dragon Boat Festival (see App. B5).

**27 Sun.** *Israel:* Pentecost. *Nigeria:* Children's Day. *Christian:* Whitsunday. *Jewish:* Pentecost.

**28 Mon.** *United Kingdom:* Spring Break. *United States:* Memorial Day. *Christian:* Whitmonday (see App. B18).

**31 Thu.** *Brunei:* Regiment Day. *South Africa:* Republic Day.

# June 2012

**1 Fri.** *Kenya:* Madaraka Day. *Tunisia:* National Day. *Western Samoa:* Independence Day.

**2 Sat.** *Burma:* Full Moon Day. *Italy:* Republic Day. *Tunisia:* Youth Day.

**3 Sun.** *Sri Lanka:* Full Moon Poya. *Orthodox:* Pentecost Sunday.

**4 Mon.** *Bahamas:* Labour Day. *Greece:* Pentecost Monday. *Ireland:* Public Holiday. *New Zealand:* Queen's Birthday. *Thailand:* Visakha Bucha Day. *Tonga:* Independence Day.

**5 Tue.** *Denmark:* Constitution Day. *Equatorial Guinea:* President's Birthday. *Seychelles:* Liberation Day.

**6 Wed.** *Malaysia:* King's Birthday. *South Korea:* Memorial Day. *Sweden:* Constitution Day.

**7 Thu.** *Chad:* Revolution Day. *Christian:* Corpus Christi (see App. B19).

**9 Sat.** *Argentina:* Independence Day. *Hong Kong:* Queen's Birthday (1st day of 2).

**10 Sun.** *Macao:* Portugal Day. *Portugal:* Portugal Day.

**11 Mon.** *Australia:* Queen's Birthday. *Fiji:* Queen's Birthday. *Hong Kong:* Queen's Birthday (2nd day of 2). *Libya:* Evacuation Day. *New Guinea:* Queen's Birthday. *United Kingdom:* Queen's Birthday.

**12 Tue.** *Philippines:* Independence Day.

**16 Sat.** *Islamic:* Isra a Majraj (see App. B30).

**17 Sun.** *Germany:* Unity Day. *Iceland:* Independence Day.

**18 Mon.** *Egypt:* Independence Day.

**19 Tue.** *Algeria:* Righting Day. *Kuwait:* Independence Day. *Uruguay:* Artigas Day.

**20 Wed.** *Argentina:* Flag Day.

**21 Thu.** *Finland:* Midsummer Day (1st day of 2). *Sweden:* Midsummer Day (1st day of 2). *Zodiac Cusp:* Gemini ends, Cancer begins.

**22 Fri.** *Finland:* Midsummer Day (2nd day of 2). *Sweden:* Midsummer Day (2nd day of 2).

**23 Sat.** *Finland:* Johannus Day. *Luxembourg:* National Day.

**24 Sun.** *Andorra:* Saint John's Day. *Venezuela:* Carabobo Day. *Zaïre:* Constitution Day.

**25 Mon.** *Croatia:* Independence Day*. *Mozambique:* Independence Day. *Slovenia:* Independence Day*.

**26 Tue.** *Madagascar:* Independence Day. *Somalia:* Independence Day.

**27 Wed.** *Djibouti:* Independence Day.

**29 Fri.** *Chile:* Bank Holiday. *Ecuador:* Bank Holiday. *El Salvador:* Bank Holiday. *Finland:* Bank Holiday. *Seychelles:* Independence Day. *Christian:* Saint Paul's Day (see App. A9).

**30 Sat.** *Guatemala:* Army Day. *Sri Lanka:* Bank Holiday. *Zaïre:* Independence Day.

# July 2012

**1 Sun.** *Burundi:* Independence Day. *Canada:* Canada Day. *Ghana:* Republic Day. *Hong Kong:* Half Year Day. *Rwanda:* Independence Day. *Somalia:*

Union Day. *Suriname:* Freedom Day. *Multinational:* Bank Holiday (see App. A10).

**2 Mon.** *Burma:* Full Moon Day. *Cayman Islands:* Constitution Day. *Lesotho:* Family Day. *Zambia:* Heroes' Day.

**3 Tue.** *Sri Lanka:* Full Moon Poya. *Zambia:* Unity Day.

**4 Wed.** *Philippines:* United States Friendship Day. *United States:* Independence Day. *Yugoslavia:* Freedom Fighters' Day.

**5 Thu.** *Algeria:* Independence Day. *Cape Verde:* Independence Day. *Rwanda:* Unity Day. *Venezuela:* Independence Day.

**6 Fri.** *Comoros:* Independence Day. *Malawi:* Republic Day.

**7 Sat.** *Solomon Islands:* Independence Day. *Tanzania:* Farmers' Day. *Yugoslavia:* Serbian Day.

**10 Tue.** *Bahamas:* Independence Day.

**11 Wed.** *Mongolia:* Revolution Day.

**12 Thu.** *Kiribati:* Independence Day. *Northern Ireland:* Battle of the Boyne Day. *São Tomé:* National Day.

**14 Sat.** *France:* National Day. *Iraq:* Revolution Day.

**15 Sun.** *Brunei:* Sultan's Birthday.

**16 Mon.** *Botswana:* President's Day.

**17 Tue.** *Iraq:* Revolution Day. *Puerto Rico:* Rivera Day. *Slovakia:* Independence Day*. *South Korea:* Constitution Day.

**18 Wed.** *Uruguay:* Constitution Day.

**19 Thu.** *Burma:* Martyrs' Day. *Laos:* Independence Day. *Nicaragua:* Sandinista Day.

**20 Fri.** *Colombia:* Independence Day. *Islamic:* 1st Day of Ramadan (see App. B25).

**21 Sat.** *Belgium:* National Day. *Guam:* Liberation Day.

**22 Sun.** *Poland:* Liberation Day. *Zodiac Cusp:* Cancer ends, Leo begins.

**23 Mon.** *Egypt:* Revolution Day. *New Guinea:* Remembrance Day. *Virgin Islands (U.S.):* Hurricane Supplication Day.

**24 Tue.** *Venezuela:* Bolivar Day.

**25 Wed.** *Costa Rica:* Guanacaste Day. *Cuba:* Revolution Day (1st day of 3). *Puerto Rico:* Constitution Day. *Spain:* Santiago Day. *Tunisia:* Republic Day.

**26 Thu.** *Cuba:* Revolution Day (2nd day of 3). *Liberia:* Independence Day. *Maldives:* Independence Day.

**27 Fri.** *Cuba:* Revolution Day (3rd day of 3). *Puerto Rico:* Barbosa Day.

**28 Sat.** *Peru:* Independence Day (1st day of 2).

**29 Sun.** *Israel:* Tisha Ab. *Peru:* Independence Day (2nd day of 2). *Jewish:* Tisha Ab.

**30 Mon.** *Vanuatu:* Independence Day.

**31 Tue.** *Burma:* Full Moon Day.

# August 2012

**1 Wed.** *Benin:* Independence Day. *Sri Lanka:* Full Moon Poya. *Switzerland:* Confederation Day. *Zambia:* Farmers' Day.

**2 Thu.** *Costa Rica:* Virgin of the Angels Day. *Guyana:* Freedom Day. *Thailand:* Asalaha Bucha Day. *Trinidad:* Discovery Day.

**3 Fri.** *El Salvador:* Summer Day (1st day of 4). *Guinea-Bissau:* Martyrs' Day. *Niger:* Independence Day. *Thailand:* Khao Phansa Day. *Tunisia:* President's Birthday.

**4 Sat.** *Burkina Faso:* Independence Day (1st day of 2). *El Salvador:* Summer Day (2nd day of 4).

**5 Sun.** *Burkina Faso:* Independence Day (2nd day of 2). *El Salvador:* Summer Day (3rd day of 4).

**6 Mon.** *Bahamas:* Emancipation Day. *Barbados:* Emancipation Day. *Bolivia:* Independence Day. *Canada:*

Civic Holiday. *El Salvador:* Summer Day (4th day of 4). *Ireland:* Public Holiday. *Jamaica:* Independence Day. *Scotland:* Public Holiday. *United Arab Emirates:* Accession Day.

**7 Tue.** *Colombia:* Boyaca Day. *Ivory Coast:* Republic Day.

**9 Thu.** *Georgia:* Independence Day*. *Singapore:* National Day.

**10 Fri.** *Ecuador:* Independence Day.

**11 Sat.** *Chad:* Independence Day. *Jordan:* Accession Day. *Zimbabwe:* Heroes' Day (1st day of 2).

**12 Sun.** *Thailand:* Queen's Birthday. *Zimbabwe:* Heroes' Day (2nd day of 2).

**13 Mon.** *Central African Republic:* Independence Day. *Congo:* Independence Day (1st day of 2). *Tunisia:* Women's Day.

**14 Tue.** *Congo:* Independence Day (2nd day of 2). *Pakistan:* Independence Day.

**15 Wed.** *Congo:* Independence Day (3rd day of 3). *India:* Independence Day. *Liechtenstein:* National Day. *South Korea:* Republic Day. *Christian:* Assumption (see App. A11).

**16 Thu.** *Dominican Republic:* Republic Day.

**17 Fri.** *Argentina:* San Martin's Day. *Gabon:* Independence Day. *Indonesia:* Independence Day.

**18 Sat.** *Far East Islamic:* Hari Raya Puasa (see App. B27). *Islamic:* Eid al Fitr (1st day of 4) (see App. B26).

**19 Sun.** *Islamic:* Eid al Fitr (2nd day of 4) (see App. B26).

**20 Mon.** *Hungary:* Constitution Day. *Senegal:* Independence Day. *Islamic:* Eid al Fitr (3rd day of 4) (see App. B26).

**21 Tue.** *Estonia:* Independence Day*. *Latvia:* Independence Day*. *Lithuania:* Independence Day*. *Islamic:* Eid al Fitr (4th day of 4) (see App. B26).

**22 Wed.** *Zodiac Cusp:* Leo ends, Virgo begins.

**23 Thu.** *Romania:* National Day (1st day of 2).

**24 Fri.** *Kazakhstan:* National Day*. *Liberia:* Flag Day. *Romania:* National Day (2nd day of 2). *Russia:* Independence Day*. *Ukraine:* National Day*.

**25 Sat.** *Belarus:* Independence Day*. *Hong Kong:* Liberation Day (1st day of 2). *Paraguay:* Constitution Day. *Uruguay:* Independence Day.

**27 Mon.** *England:* Summer Break. *Hong Kong:* Liberation Day (2nd day of 2). *Moldova:* Independence Day*. *Northern Ireland:* Summer Break. *Wales:* Summer Break.

**29 Wed.** *Uzbekistan:* Independence Day*.

**30 Thu.** *Afghanistan:* Children's Day. *Azerbaijan:* Independence Day*. *Burma:* Full Moon Day. *Peru:* Rose of Lima Day. *Turkey:* Victory Day.

**31 Fri.** *Afghanistan:* Pashtunistan Day. *Kyrgyzstan:* Independence Day*. *Malaysia:* National Day. *Sri Lanka:* Full Moon Poya. *Trinidad:* Independence Day.

# September 2012

**1 Sat.** *Libya:* National Day. *Mexico:* President's Message Day. *Syria:* United Arab Republics Day.

**2 Sun.** *Vietnam:* Independence Day.

**3 Mon.** *Canada:* Labour Day. *Luxembourg:* Fair Day. *Qatar:* National Day. *San Marino:* Saint Marinus' Day. *Tunisia:* Independence Movement Day. *United States:* Labor Day.

**6 Thu.** *Pakistan:* Defense Day. *Swaziland:* Independence Day.

**7 Fri.** *Brazil:* Independence Day.

**8 Sat.** *Andorra:* National Day. *Malta:* Our Lady of Victory Day.

**9 Sun.** *Bulgaria:* National Day (1st day of 2). *North Korea:* Independence Day. *Tajikistan:* Independence Day*.

**10 Mon.** *Belize:* National Day. *Bulgaria:* National Day (2nd day of 2).

**11 Tue.** *Chile:* Revolution Day. *Egypt:* New Year's Day (Coptic: 1730). *Ethiopia:* New Year's Day (Ethiopian: 2006). *Pakistan:* Anniversary of Quaid-e-Azam's Death.

**12 Wed.** *Ethiopia:* National Day.

**14 Fri.** *Guatemala:* San Jacinto Day. *Nicaragua:* San Jacinto Day.

**15 Sat.** *Costa Rica:* Independence Day. *El Salvador:* Independence Day. *Guatemala:* Independence Day. *Honduras:* Independence Day. *Japan:* Veneration Day. *Nicaragua:* Independence Day.

**16 Sun.** *Mexico:* Independence Day. *New Guinea:* Independence Day.

**17 Mon.** *Angola:* Heroes' Day. *Israel:* New Year's Day. *Marshall Islands:* Independence Day. *Jewish:* Rosh Hashanah (Jewish: 5773).

**18 Tue.** *Burundi:* Victory of Uprona Day. *Chile:* Independence Day.

**19 Wed.** *Chile:* Armed Forces Day. *Saint Kitts:* Independence Day.

**21 Fri.** *Belize:* Independence Day. *Malta:* Independence Day.

**22 Sat.** *Mali:* Independence Day. *Zodiac Cusp:* Virgo ends, Libra begins.

**23 Sun.** *Armenia:* Independence Day*. *Japan:* Autumnal Equinox. *Saudi Arabia:* National Day.

**24 Mon.** *Dominican Republic:* Mercedes Day. *Guinea-Bissau:* Republic Day.

**25 Tue.** *Mozambique:* Liberation Day. *Rwanda:* Assembly Day. *Asian:* Ancestors' Day (see App. B6).

**26 Wed.** *Ethiopia:* True Cross Day. *Israel:* Yom Kippur. *Jewish:* Yom Kippur.

**28 Fri.** *Burma:* Full Moon Day. *Taiwan:* Teachers' Day.

**29 Sat.** *Brunei:* Constitution Day. *China:* Mid-autumn Day. *Paraguay:* Boqueron Battle Day. *Sri Lanka:* Full Moon Poya. *Taiwan:* Mid-autumn Day.

**30 Sun.** *Botswana:* Independence Day. *Hong Kong:* Mid-autumn Day. *Macao:* Mid-autumn Day. *Europe:* Daylight Savings Time ends (retard clocks 1 hour).

# October 2012

**1 Mon.** *China:* National Day (1st day of 2). *Israel:* Sukkot. *Nigeria:* Independence Day. *South Korea:* Armed Forces Day (1st day of 2). *Tuvalu:* Independence Day. *Jewish:* Sukkot.

**2 Tue.** *China:* National Day (2nd day of 2). *Guinea:* Independence Day. *India:* Ghandi Day. *South Korea:* Armed Forces Day (2nd day of 2).

**3 Wed.** *Honduras:* Morazan Day. *South Korea:* Foundation Day (1st day of 2).

**4 Thu.** *Lesotho:* Independence Day. *South Korea:* Foundation Day (2nd day of 2).

**5 Fri.** *Lesotho:* Sports Day. *Macao:* Portuguese Republic Day. *Portugal:* Republic Day.

**6 Sat.** *Egypt:* Armed Forces Day.

**8 Mon.** *Canada:* Thanksgiving Day. *Fiji:* Cession Day. *United States:* Bank Holiday. *Virgin Islands (U.S.):* Puerto Rican Friendship Day.

**9 Tue.** *Peru:* National Dignity Day. *South Korea:* Alphabet Day. *Uganda:* Independence Day.

**10 Wed.** *Japan:* Health Day. *South Africa:* Kruger Day. *Taiwan:* National Day.

**11 Thu.** *Cuba:* Independence War. *Panama:* Revolution Day.

**12 Fri.** *Equatorial Guinea:* Independence Day. *Spain:* National Day. *Multinational:* Columbus Day (see App. A12).

**14 Sun.** *Zaïre:* Founders' Day. *Hindu:* Deepavali (see App. B21).

**15 Mon.** *Bosnia and Herzegovina:* Independence Day*. *Jamaica:* Heroes' Day. *Tunisia:* Evacuation Day.

**17 Wed.** *Haiti:* Dessalines Day. *Malawi:* Mother's Day.

**20 Sat.** *Guatemala:* Revolution Day. *Kenya:* Kenyatta Day.

**21 Sun.** *Honduras:* Army Day. *Somalia:* Revolution Day (1st day of 2).

**22 Mon.** *Somalia:* Revolution Day (2nd day of 2). *Vatican:* John Paul II Day.

**23 Tue.** *Hungary:* Revolution Day. *Thailand:* Chulalongkorn Day. *Zodiac Cusp:* Libra ends, Scorpio begins.

**24 Wed.** *Egypt:* Suez Victory Day. *Haiti:* United Nations Day. *Zambia:* Independence Day.

**25 Thu.** *Taiwan:* Restoration Day. *Islamic:* Eid al Adha (1st day of 4) (see App. B28).

**26 Fri.** *Austria:* National Day. *Benin:* Revolution Day. *Rwanda:* Government Day. *Far East Islamic:* Hari Raya Haji (see App. B29). *Islamic:* Eid al Adha (2nd day of 4) (see App. B28).

**27 Sat.** *Saint Vincent:* Independence Day. *Turkmenistan:* Independence Day*. *Zaïre:* Naming Day. *Islamic:* Eid al Adha (3rd day of 4) (see App. B28).

**28 Sun.** *Burma:* Full Moon Day. *Greece:* Ohi! Day. *Canada and United States:* Daylight Savings Time ends (retard clocks 1 hour). *Islamic:* Eid al Adha (4th day of 4) (see App. B28).

**29 Mon.** *Ireland:* Public Holiday. *New Zealand:* Labour Day. *Sri Lanka:* Full Moon Poya. *Tanzania:* Naming Day. *Turkey:* Republic Day.

**31 Wed.** *Taiwan:* Chiang Kai-shek's Birthday.

# November 2012

**1 Thu.** *Algeria:* Revolution Day. *Antigua:* Independence Day. *Liberia:* Thanksgiving Day. *Christian:* All Saints' Day (see App. A13).

**2 Fri.** *Brazil:* Memorial Day. *Finland:* All Saints' Eve. *Sweden:* All Saints' Eve. *Christian:* All Souls' Day (see App. A14).

**3 Sat.** *Dominica:* Independence Day. *Ecuador:* Cuenca Independence Day. *Japan:* Culture Day. *Panama:* Independence Day.

**4 Sun.** *Andorra:* Saint Charles' Day. *Panama:* Flag Day. *Vatican:* John Paul II's Nameday.

**5 Mon.** *El Salvador:* Cry of Independence Day. *Virgin Islands (U.S.):* Liberty Day.

**7 Wed.** *Bangladesh:* Revolution Day.

**8 Thu.** *Nepal:* Queen's Birthday.

**9 Fri.** *Pakistan:* Iqbal Day.

**10 Sat.** *Panama:* Cry of Independence Day.

**11 Sun.** *Angola:* Independence Day. *Bhutan:* King's Birthday. *Maldives:* Republic Day. *Poland:* Independence Day. *Multinational:* Armistice Day (see App. A15).

**12 Mon.** *Taiwan:* Dr. Sun Yat-sen's Birthday.

**14 Wed.** *Jordan:* King's Birthday. *Islamic:* New Year's Day (Hegira: 1434) (see App. B22).

**15 Thu.** *Brazil:* Republic Day. *Far East Islamic:* New Year's Day (Hegira: 1434).

**17 Sat.** *Zaïre:* Armed Forces Day.

**18 Sun.** *Haiti:* Vertieres' Day. *Morocco:* Independence Day. *Oman:* National Day.

**19 Mon.** *Belize:* Garifuna Day. *Fiji:* Prince Charles' Birthday. *Mali:* Army Coup Day. *Monaco:* Prince Ranier's Day. *Puerto Rico:* Discovery Day.

**20 Tue.** *Mexico:* Revolution Day.

**21 Wed.** *Germany:* Repentance Day. *Zodiac Cusp:* Scorpio ends, Sagittarius begins.

**22 Thu.** *Lebanon:* Independence Day. *United States:* Thanksgiving Day.

**23 Fri.** *Japan:* Labor Thanksgiving Day. *Islamic:* Ashura (see App. B23).

**24 Sat.** *Zaïre:* New Regime Day.

**25 Sun.** *Suriname:* Independence Day.

**27 Tue.** *Burma:* Full Moon Day.

**28 Wed.** *Albania:* Independence Day. *Burundi:* Republic Day. *Chad:* Republic Day. *Mauritania:* Independence Day. *Panama:* Independence Day. *Sri Lanka:* Full Moon Poya.

**29 Thu.** *Albania:* Liberation Day. *Liberia:* Tubman's Birthday. *Yugoslavia:* Republic Day.

**30 Fri.** *Argentina:* Bank Holiday. *Barbados:* Independence Day. *Benin:* National Day. *Philippines:* Heroes' Day.

# December 2012

**1 Sat.** *Central African Republic:* National Day. *Portugal:* Youth Day. *Ukraine:* Independence Day*.

**2 Sun.** *Laos:* Republic Day. *United Arab Emirates:* National Day.

**5 Wed.** *Haiti:* Discovery Day. *Thailand:* King's Birthday.

**6 Thu.** *Finland:* Independence Day.

**7 Fri.** *Ivory Coast:* Independence Day.

**8 Sat.** *Christian:* Immaculate Conception (see App. A16).

**9 Sun.** *Tanzania:* Independence Day. *Jewish:* Chanukah.

**10 Mon.** *Angola:* MPLA Foundation Day. *Equatorial Guinea:* Human Rights Day. *Namibia:* Settlers' Day. *Thailand:* Constitution Day.

**11 Tue.** *Burkina Faso:* National Day.

**12 Wed.** *Kenya:* Independence Day. *Mexico:* Guadalupe Festival.

**13 Thu.** *Malta:* Republic Day.

**16 Sun.** *Bahrain:* National Day. *Bangladesh:* Victory Day. *Nepal:* Constitution Day. *South Africa:* Covenant Day.

**17 Mon.** *Bhutan:* National Day.

**18 Tue.** *Niger:* Republic Day.

**21 Fri.** *Kazakhstan:* Independence Day*. *Zodiac Cusp:* Sagittarius ends, Capricorn begins.

**23 Sun.** *Japan:* Emperor's Birthday.

**24 Mon.** *Multinational:* Christmas Eve (see App. A17).

**25 Tue.** *Angola:* Family Day. *Congo:* Children's Day. *Pakistan:* Quaid's Birthday. *Taiwan:* Constitution Day. *Multinational:* Christmas Day (see App. A18).

**26 Wed.** *Burma:* Full Moon Day. *South Africa:* Good Will Day. *Multinational:* Boxing Day (see App. A19).

**27 Thu.** *Sri Lanka:* Full Moon Poya.

**30 Sun.** *Madagascar:* Republic Day. *Philippines:* Rizal Day (1st day of 2).

**31 Mon.** *Congo:* Republic Day. *Philippines:* Rizal Day (2nd day of 2). *Multinational:* Bank Holiday and New Year's Eve (see App. A20 & A21).

# January 2013

**1 Tue.** *Cameroon:* Independence Day. *Cuba:* Liberation Day. *Haiti:* Independence Day. *Palau:* Independence Day. *Sudan:* Independence Day. *Taiwan:* Foundation Day (1st day of 2). *Western Samoa:* Independence Day. *Multinational:* Bank Holiday and New Year's Day (see App. A1 & A2).

**2 Wed.** *Japan:* Bank Holiday. *New Zealand:* New Year's Day (2nd day of 2). *Scotland:* New Year's Day (2nd day of 2). *South Korea:* New Year's Day

(2nd day of 2). *Switzerland:* Berchtold's Day. *Taiwan:* Foundation Day (2nd day of 2).

**3 Thu.** *Burkina Faso:* Revolution Day.

**4 Fri.** *Burma:* Independence Day. *Zaïre:* Martyrs' Day.

**6 Sun.** *Iraq:* Army Day. *Uruguay:* Children's Day. *Christian:* Epiphany (see App. A3).

**7 Mon.** *Egypt:* Coptic Christmas. *Ethiopia:* Coptic Christmas.

**11 Fri.** *Albania:* Republic Day. *Nepal:* Unification Day. *Puerto Rico:* Hostos Day.

**12 Sat.** *Tanzania:* Revolution Day.

**13 Sun.** *Togo:* Liberation Day.

**15 Tue.** *Japan:* Adult's Day. *Jordan:* Arbor Day.

**19 Sat.** *Ethiopia:* Epiphany.

**20 Sun.** *Mali:* Award Day. *Zodiac Cusp:* Capricorn ends, Aquarius begins.

**21 Mon.** *Dominican Republic:* Altagracia Day. *United States:* Martin Luther King's Birthday. *Islamic:* Mohammed's Birthday (see App. B24).

**22 Tue.** *Saint Vincent:* Discovery Day. *Far East Islamic:* Mohammed's Birthday.

**25 Fri.** *Burma:* Full Moon Day.

**26 Sat.** *Dominican Republic:* Duarte Day. *India:* Republic Day. *Sri Lanka:* Full Moon Poya.

**27 Sun.** *Monaco:* Saint Devota's Day. *Vietnam:* Vietnam Day.

**28 Mon.** *Australia:* Australia Day. *Rwanda:* Democracy Day.

**31 Thu.** *Nauru:* Independence Day.

# February 2013

**2 Sat.** *Liechtenstein:* Candlemas.

**4 Mon.** *Sri Lanka:* Independence Day. *United States:* Lincoln's Birthday.

**5 Tue.** *Mexico:* Constitution Day.

**6 Wed.** *New Zealand:* Waitangi Day.

**7 Thu.** *Grenada:* Independence Day.

**8 Fri.** *Iraq:* Revolution Day.

**9 Sat.** *Lebanon:* Saint Marion's Day. *Asian:* Chinese New Year Eve (see App. B1).

**10 Sun.** *Malta:* Saint Paul's Day. *Vietnam:* Tet (1st day of 3). *Asian:* Chinese New Year (Year of the Snake) (see App. B2).

**11 Mon.** *Cameroon:* Youth Day. *Japan:* Foundation Day. *Liberia:* Armed Forces Day. *Vietnam:* Tet (2nd day of 3). *Asian:* 2nd Day of Chinese New Year (see App. B3). *Christian:* Shrove Monday (see App. B7).

**12 Tue.** *Burma:* Union Day. *Vietnam:* Tet (3rd day of 3). *Asian:* 3rd Day of Chinese New Year (see App. B4). *Christian:* Shrove Tuesday (see App. B8).

**13 Wed.** *Christian:* Ash Wednesday (see App. B9).

**14 Thu.** *International:* Valentine's Day.

**18 Mon.** *Gambia:* Independence Day. *United States:* Washington's Birthday. *Zodiac Cusp:* Aquarius ends, Pisces begins.

**19 Tue.** *Nepal:* National Day.

**21 Thu.** *Bangladesh:* Saheed Day.

**22 Fri.** *Saint Lucia:* Independence Day.

**23 Sat.** *Brunei:* National Day. *Guyana:* Republic Day.

**24 Sun.** *Burma:* Full Moon Day. *Jewish:* Purim.

**25 Mon.** *Kuwait:* National Day. *Sri Lanka:* Full Moon Poya. *Thailand:* Makha Bucha Day.

**27 Wed.** *Dominican Republic:* Independence Day.

# March 2013

**1 Fri.** *South Korea:* Independence Day.

**2 Sat.** *Ethiopia:* Victory of Aduwa Day. *Morocco:* Independence Day.

**3 Sun.** *Bulgaria:* Liberation Day. *Malawi:* Martyrs' Day. *Morocco:* National Day.

**4 Mon.** *Guam:* Discovery Day.

**6 Wed.** *Ghana:* Independence Day.

**8 Fri.** *Syria:* Revolution Day. *Multinational:* Women's Day (see App. A4).

**9 Sat.** *Zambia:* Youth Day.

**10 Sun.** *South Korea:* Labor Day.

**11 Mon.** *Gibraltar:* Commonwealth Day. *Lithuania:* National Day*.

**12 Tue.** *Lesotho:* Moshoeshoe's Day. *Mauritius:* Independence Day.

**13 Wed.** *Grenada:* National Day.

**17 Sun.** *Ireland:* Saint Patrick's Day. *Northern Ireland:* Saint Patrick's Day.

**18 Mon.** *Greece:* Shrove Monday. *Orthodox:* Shrove Monday.

**19 Tue.** *Christian:* Saint Joseph's Day (see App. A5).

**20 Wed.** *Afghanistan:* New Year's Day (Shamsi: 1392). *Iran:* New Year's Day (Hegira: 1392). *Iraq:* New Year's Day. *Japan:* Vernal Equinox. *Tunisia:* Independence Day. *Zodiac Cusp:* Pisces ends, Aries begins.

**21 Thu.** *Mexico:* Juarez Day.

**22 Fri.** *Puerto Rico:* Abolition Day.

**23 Sat.** *Pakistan:* Pakistan Day.

**24 Sun.** *Christian:* Palm Sunday.

**25 Mon.** *Burma:* Full Moon Day. *Cyprus:* Greek Independence Day. *Greece:* Independence Day. *Liechtenstein:* Annunciation. *Virgin Islands (U.S.):* Transfer Day.

**26 Tue.** *Bangladesh:* Independence Day. *Israel:* Passover. *Sri Lanka:* Full Moon Poya. *Zambia:* Africa Day. *Jewish:* Passover.

**27 Wed.** *Angola:* Evacuation Day. *Burma:* Resistance Day.

**28 Thu.** *Christian:* Maundy Thursday (see App. B11).

**29 Fri.** *Central African Republic:* Boganda Day. *Madagascar:* Memorial Day. *Taiwan:* Youth Day. *Christian:* Good Friday (see App. B12).

**30 Sat.** *Christian:* Holy Saturday (see App. B13).

**31 Sun.** *Malta:* National Day. *Christian:* Easter Sunday (see App. B14). *Europe:* Daylight Savings Time starts (advance clocks 1 hour).

# April 2013

**1 Mon.** *Iran:* Republic Day. *San Marino:* National Day. *Christian:* Easter Monday (see App. B15).

**4 Thu.** *Hungary:* Liberation Day. *Senegal:* National Day.

**5 Fri.** *Sierra Leone:* Bank Holiday. *South Korea:* Arbor Day. *Asian:* Tomb Sweeping Day (see App. A6).

**6 Sat.** *South Africa:* Founders' Day. *Thailand:* Chakri Day.

**7 Sun.** *Canada and United States:* Daylight Savings Time starts (advance clocks 1 hour).

**9 Tue.** *Philippines:* Valour Day. *Tunisia:* Martyrs' Day.

**11 Thu.** *Costa Rica:* Heroes' Day. *Uganda:* Liberation Day.

**13 Sat.** *Chad:* National Day. *Thailand:* Songkrawn (1st day of 2).

**14 Sun.** *Honduras:* Pan American Day. *Thailand:* Songkrawn (2nd day of 2).

**15 Mon.** *Israel:* Independence Day. *Niger:* National Day.

**16 Tue.** *Burma:* New Year's Day (Burmese: 1375). *Cyprus:* Independence Day.

**17 Wed.** *Cambodia:* Independence Day. *Syria:* Independence Day.
**18 Thu.** *Zimbabwe:* Republic Day.
**19 Fri.** *Sierra Leone:* Republic Day. *Uruguay:* Patriots' Day. *Venezuela:* Independence Day. *Zodiac Cusp:* Aries ends, Taurus begins.
**21 Sun.** *Brazil:* Tiradentes Day.
**23 Tue.** *Turkey:* Children's Day.
**24 Wed.** *Burma:* Full Moon Day.
**25 Thu.** *Australia:* ANZAC Day. *Egypt:* Sinai Day. *Iceland:* Children's Day. *Italy:* Liberation Day. *New Zealand:* ANZAC Day. *Portugal:* Liberation Day. *Sri Lanka:* Full Moon Poya. *Swaziland:* Flag Day.
**26 Fri.** *Denmark:* All Prayers' Day. *Tanzania:* Union Day.
**27 Sat.** *Afghanistan:* Independence Day. *Sierra Leone:* Independence Day. *Togo:* Independence Day.
**29 Mon.** *Japan:* Green Day.
**30 Tue.** *Finland:* Vappu Day. *Netherlands:* Queen's Birthday.

# May 2013

**1 Wed.** *Multinational:* Labor Day (see App. A7).
**2 Thu.** *Lesotho:* King's Birthday.
**3 Fri.** *Japan:* Constitution Day. *Orthodox:* Good Friday (see App. B20).
**4 Sat.** *Japan:* People's Day.
**5 Sun.** *Japan:* Children's Day. *Jordan:* Easter Sunday. *Mexico:* Cinco de Mayo. *Netherlands:* Liberation Day. *South Korea:* Children's Day. *Thailand:* Coronation Day. *Orthodox:* Easter Sunday.
**6 Mon.** *Lebanon:* Martyrs' Day. *Philippines:* Corregidor Day. *United Kingdom:* Labour Day. *Zambia:* Labour Day. *Orthodox:* Easter Monday (see App. B20).
**8 Wed.** *France:* Liberation Day.
**9 Thu.** *Czech Republic:* Liberation Day*. *Slovakia:* Liberation Day*. *Christian:* Ascension (see App. B16).
**10 Fri.** *Micronesia:* Independence Day.
**12 Sun.** *International:* Mother's Day.
**14 Tue.** *Liberia:* Unification Day. *Malawi:* Kamuzu Day. *Paraguay:* Flag Day.
**15 Wed.** *Israel:* Pentecost. *Paraguay:* Independence Day. *Jewish:* Pentecost.
**17 Fri.** *Cayman Islands:* Discovery Day. *Norway:* Constitution Day. *South Korea:* Vesak Day.
**18 Sat.** *Haiti:* Flag Day. *Uruguay:* Las Piedras Day.
**19 Sun.** *Finland:* Flag Day. *Turkey:* Youth Day. *Christian:* Whitsunday.
**20 Mon.** *Cameroon:* Constitution Day. *Canada:* Victoria Day. *Zaïre:* Popular Movement Day. *Christian:* Whitmonday (see App. B18). *Zodiac Cusp:* Taurus ends, Gemini begins.
**21 Tue.** *Chile:* Navy Day.
**22 Wed.** *Haiti:* Sovereign Day. *Sri Lanka:* Heroes' Day.
**23 Thu.** *Burma:* Full Moon Day. *Jamaica:* Labour Day.
**24 Fri.** *Bulgaria:* Culture Day. *Ecuador:* Independence Battle Day. *Malaysia:* Vesak Day. *Singapore:* Vesak Day. *Sri Lanka:* Full Moon Poya. *Thailand:* Visakha Bucha Day.
**25 Sat.** *Argentina:* National Day. *Eritrea:* Independence Day*. *Jordan:* Independence Day. *Sudan:* Revolution Day. *Multinational:* Africa Day (see App. A8).
**26 Sun.** *Guyana:* Independence Day.
**27 Mon.** *Nigeria:* Children's Day. *United Kingdom:* Spring Break. *United States:* Memorial Day.
**30 Thu.** *Christian:* Corpus Christi (see App. B19).
**31 Fri.** *Brunei:* Regiment Day. *South Africa:* Republic Day.

# June 2013

**1 Sat.** *Kenya:* Madaraka Day. *Tunisia:* National Day. *Western Samoa:* Independence Day.

**2 Sun.** *Italy:* Republic Day. *Tunisia:* Youth Day.

**3 Mon.** *Ireland:* Public Holiday. *New Zealand:* Queen's Birthday.

**4 Tue.** *Bahamas:* Labour Day. *Tonga:* Independence Day. *Islamic:* Isra a Majraj (see App. B30).

**5 Wed.** *Denmark:* Constitution Day. *Equatorial Guinea:* President's Birthday. *Malaysia:* King's Birthday. *Seychelles:* Liberation Day.

**6 Thu.** *South Korea:* Memorial Day. *Sweden:* Constitution Day.

**7 Fri.** *Chad:* Revolution Day.

**8 Sat.** *Hong Kong:* Queen's Birthday (1st day of 2).

**9 Sun.** *Argentina:* Independence Day.

**10 Mon.** *Australia:* Queen's Birthday. *Fiji:* Queen's Birthday. *Hong Kong:* Queen's Birthday (2nd day of 2). *Macao:* Portugal Day. *New Guinea:* Queen's Birthday. *Portugal:* Portugal Day. *United Kingdom:* Queen's Birthday.

**11 Tue.** *Libya:* Evacuation Day.

**12 Wed.** *Philippines:* Independence Day.

**14 Fri.** *Asian:* Dragon Boat Festival (see App. B5).

**17 Mon.** *Germany:* Unity Day. *Iceland:* Independence Day.

**18 Tue.** *Egypt:* Independence Day.

**19 Wed.** *Algeria:* Righting Day. *Kuwait:* Independence Day. *Uruguay:* Artigas Day.

**20 Thu.** *Argentina:* Flag Day.

**21 Fri.** *Finland:* Midsummer Day (1st day of 2). *Sweden:* Midsummer Day (1st day of 2). *Zodiac Cusp:* Gemini ends, Cancer begins.

**22 Sat.** *Burma:* Full Moon Day. *Finland:* Johannus and Midsummer Day (2nd day of 2). *Sri Lanka:* Full Moon Poya. *Sweden:* Midsummer Day (2nd day of 2).

**23 Sun.** *Luxembourg:* National Day. *Orthodox:* Pentecost Sunday.

**24 Mon.** *Andorra:* Saint John's Day. *Greece:* Pentecost Monday. *Venezuela:* Carabobo Day. *Zaïre:* Constitution Day.

**25 Tue.** *Croatia:* Independence Day*. *Mozambique:* Independence Day. *Slovenia:* Independence Day*.

**26 Wed.** *Madagascar:* Independence Day. *Somalia:* Independence Day.

**27 Thu.** *Djibouti:* Independence Day.

**28 Fri.** *Chile:* Bank Holiday. *Ecuador:* Bank Holiday. *El Salvador:* Bank Holiday. *Finland:* Bank Holiday.

**29 Sat.** *Seychelles:* Independence Day. *Christian:* Saint Paul's Day (see App. A9).

**30 Sun.** *Guatemala:* Army Day. *Sri Lanka:* Bank Holiday. *Zaïre:* Independence Day.

# July 2013

**1 Mon.** *Burundi:* Independence Day. *Canada:* Canada Day. *Cayman Islands:* Constitution Day. *Ghana:* Republic Day. *Hong Kong:* Half Year Day. *Lesotho:* Family Day. *Rwanda:* Independence Day. *Somalia:* Union Day. *Suriname:* Freedom Day. *Zambia:* Heroes' Day. *Multinational:* Bank Holiday (see App. A10).

**2 Tue.** *Zambia:* Unity Day.

**4 Thu.** *Philippines:* United States Friendship Day. *United States:* Independence Day. *Yugoslavia:* Freedom Fighters' Day.

**5 Fri.** *Algeria:* Independence Day. *Cape Verde:* Independence Day. *Rwanda:* Unity Day. *Venezuela:* Independence Day.

**6 Sat.** *Comoros:* Independence Day. *Malawi:* Republic Day.

**7 Sun.** *Solomon Islands:* Independence Day. *Tanzania:* Farmers' Day. *Yugoslavia:* Serbian Day.

**8 Mon.** *Islamic:* 1st Day of Ramadan (see App. B25).

**10 Wed.** *Bahamas:* Independence Day.

**11 Thu.** *Mongolia:* Revolution Day.

**12 Fri.** *Kiribati:* Independence Day. *Northern Ireland:* Battle of the Boyne Day. *São Tomé:* National Day.

**14 Sun.** *France:* National Day. *Iraq:* Revolution Day.

**15 Mon.** *Botswana:* President's Day. *Brunei:* Sultan's Birthday.

**16 Tue.** *Israel:* Tisha Ab. *Jewish:* Tisha Ab.

**17 Wed.** *Iraq:* Revolution Day. *Puerto Rico:* Rivera Day. *Slovakia:* Independence Day*. *South Korea:* Constitution Day.

**18 Thu.** *Uruguay:* Constitution Day.

**19 Fri.** *Burma:* Martyrs' Day. *Laos:* Independence Day. *Nicaragua:* Sandinista Day.

**20 Sat.** *Colombia:* Independence Day.

**21 Sun.** *Belgium:* National Day. *Burma:* Full Moon Day. *Guam:* Liberation Day.

**22 Mon.** *Poland:* Liberation Day. *Sri Lanka:* Full Moon Poya. *Thailand:* Asalaha Bucha Day. *Virgin Islands (U.S.):* Hurricane Supplication Day. *Zodiac Cusp:* Cancer ends, Leo begins.

**23 Tue.** *Egypt:* Revolution Day. *New Guinea:* Remembrance Day. *Thailand:* Khao Phansa Day.

**24 Wed.** *Venezuela:* Bolivar Day.

**25 Thu.** *Costa Rica:* Guanacaste Day. *Cuba:* Revolution Day (1st day of 3). *Puerto Rico:* Constitution Day. *Spain:* Santiago Day. *Tunisia:* Republic Day.

**26 Fri.** *Cuba:* Revolution Day (2nd day of 3). *Liberia:* Independence Day. *Maldives:* Independence Day.

**27 Sat.** *Cuba:* Revolution Day (3rd day of 3). *Puerto Rico:* Barbosa Day.

**28 Sun.** *Peru:* Independence Day (1st day of 2).

**29 Mon.** *Peru:* Independence Day (2nd day of 2).

**30 Tue.** *Vanuatu:* Independence Day.

# August 2013

**1 Thu.** *Benin:* Independence Day. *Switzerland:* Confederation Day.

**2 Fri.** *Costa Rica:* Virgin of the Angels Day. *Guyana:* Freedom Day. *Trinidad:* Discovery Day.

**3 Sat.** *El Salvador:* Summer Day (1st day of 4). *Guinea-Bissau:* Martyrs' Day. *Niger:* Independence Day. *Tunisia:* President's Birthday.

**4 Sun.** *Burkina Faso:* Independence Day (1st day of 2). *El Salvador:* Summer Day (2nd day of 4).

**5 Mon.** *Bahamas:* Emancipation Day. *Barbados:* Emancipation Day. *Burkina Faso:* Independence Day (2nd day of 2). *Canada:* Civic Holiday. *El Salvador:* Summer Day (3rd day of 4). *Ireland:* Public Holiday. *Jamaica:* Independence Day. *Scotland:* Public Holiday.

**6 Tue.** *Bolivia:* Independence Day. *El Salvador:* Summer Day (4th day of 4). *United Arab Emirates:* Accession Day. *Islamic:* Eid al Fitr (1st day of 4) (see App. B26).

**7 Wed.** *Colombia:* Boyaca Day. *Ivory Coast:* Republic Day. *Zambia:* Farmers' Day. *Far East Islamic:* Hari Raya Puasa (see App. B27). *Islamic:* Eid al Fitr (2nd day of 4) (see App. B26).

**8 Thu.** *Islamic:* Eid al Fitr (3rd day of 4) (see App. B26).

**9 Fri.** *Georgia:* Independence Day*. *Singapore:* National Day. *Islamic:* Eid al Fitr (4th day of 4) (see App. B26).

**10 Sat.** *Ecuador:* Independence Day.

**11 Sun.** *Chad:* Independence Day. *Jordan:* Accession Day. *Zimbabwe:* Heroes' Day (1st day of 2).

**12 Mon.** *Thailand:* Queen's Birthday. *Zimbabwe:* Heroes' Day (2nd day of 2).

**13 Tue.** *Central African Republic:* Independence Day. *Congo:* Independence Day (1st day of 2). *Tunisia:* Women's Day.

**14 Wed.** *Congo:* Independence Day (2nd day of 2). *Pakistan:* Independence Day.

**15 Thu.** *Congo:* Independence Day (3rd day of 3). *India:* Independence Day. *Liechtenstein:* National Day. *South Korea:* Republic Day. *Christian:* Assumption (see App. A11).

**16 Fri.** *Dominican Republic:* Republic Day.

**17 Sat.** *Argentina:* San Martin's Day. *Gabon:* Independence Day. *Indonesia:* Independence Day.

**19 Mon.** *Burma:* Full Moon Day.

**20 Tue.** *Hungary:* Constitution Day. *Senegal:* Independence Day. *Sri Lanka:* Full Moon Poya.

**21 Wed.** *Estonia:* Independence Day*. *Latvia:* Independence Day*. *Lithuania:* Independence Day*.

**22 Thu.** *Zodiac Cusp:* Leo ends, Virgo begins.

**23 Fri.** *Romania:* National Day (1st day of 2).

**24 Sat.** *Hong Kong:* Liberation Day (1st day of 2). *Kazakhstan:* National Day*. *Liberia:* Flag Day. *Romania:* National Day (2nd day of 2). *Russia:* Independence Day*. *Ukraine:* National Day*.

**25 Sun.** *Belarus:* Independence Day*. *Paraguay:* Constitution Day. *Uruguay:* Independence Day.

**26 Mon.** *England:* Summer Break. *Hong Kong:* Liberation Day (2nd day of 2). *Northern Ireland:* Summer Break. *Wales:* Summer Break.

**27 Tue.** *Moldova:* Independence Day*.

**29 Thu.** *Uzbekistan:* Independence Day*.

**30 Fri.** *Afghanistan:* Children's Day. *Azerbaijan:* Independence Day*. *Peru:* Rose of Lima Day. *Turkey:* Victory Day.

**31 Sat.** *Afghanistan:* Pashtunistan Day. *Kyrgyzstan:* Independence Day*. *Malaysia:* National Day. *Trinidad:* Independence Day.

# September 2013

**1 Sun.** *Libya:* National Day. *Mexico:* President's Message Day. *Syria:* United Arab Republics Day.

**2 Mon.** *Canada:* Labour Day. *Luxembourg:* Fair Day. *United States:* Labor Day. *Vietnam:* Independence Day.

**3 Tue.** *Qatar:* National Day. *San Marino:* Saint Marinus' Day. *Tunisia:* Independence Movement Day.

**5 Thu.** *Israel:* New Year's Day. *Jewish:* Rosh Hashanah (Jewish: 5774).

**6 Fri.** *Pakistan:* Defense Day. *Swaziland:* Independence Day.

**7 Sat.** *Brazil:* Independence Day.

**8 Sun.** *Andorra:* National Day. *Malta:* Our Lady of Victory Day.

**9 Mon.** *Bulgaria:* National Day (1st day of 2). *North Korea:* Independence Day. *Tajikistan:* Independence Day*.

**10 Tue.** *Belize:* National Day. *Bulgaria:* National Day (2nd day of 2).

**11 Wed.** *Chile:* Revolution Day. *Egypt:* New Year's Day (Coptic: 1731). *Ethiopia:* New Year's Day (Ethiopian: 2007). *Pakistan:* Anniversary of Quaid-e-Azam's Death.

**12 Thu.** *Ethiopia:* National Day.

**14 Sat.** *Guatemala:* San Jacinto Day. *Israel:* Yom Kippur. *Nicaragua:* San Jacinto Day. *Jewish:* Yom Kippur.

**15 Sun.** *Costa Rica:* Independence Day. *El Salvador:* Independence Day. *Guatemala:* Independence Day. *Hon-*

*duras:* Independence Day. *Japan:* Veneration Day. *Nicaragua:* Independence Day.

**16 Mon.** *Mexico:* Independence Day. *New Guinea:* Independence Day.

**17 Tue.** *Angola:* Heroes' Day. *Burma:* Full Moon Day. *Marshall Islands:* Independence Day.

**18 Wed.** *Burundi:* Victory of Uprona Day. *Chile:* Independence Day. *Sri Lanka:* Full Moon Poya.

**19 Thu.** *Chile:* Armed Forces Day. *Israel:* Sukkot. *Saint Kitts:* Independence Day. *Jewish:* Sukkot.

**21 Sat.** *Belize:* Independence Day. *Malta:* Independence Day.

**22 Sun.** *Mali:* Independence Day. *Zodiac Cusp:* Virgo ends, Libra begins.

**23 Mon.** *Armenia:* Independence Day*. *Japan:* Autumnal Equinox. *Saudi Arabia:* National Day.

**24 Tue.** *Dominican Republic:* Mercedes Day. *Guinea-Bissau:* Republic Day.

**25 Wed.** *Mozambique:* Liberation Day. *Rwanda:* Assembly Day.

**26 Thu.** *Ethiopia:* True Cross Day.

**28 Sat.** *Taiwan:* Teachers' Day.

**29 Sun.** *Brunei:* Constitution Day. *Paraguay:* Boqueron Battle Day. *Europe:* Daylight Savings Time ends (retard clocks 1 hour).

**30 Mon.** *Botswana:* Independence Day.

# October 2013

**1 Tue.** *Cameroon:* Unification Day. *China:* National Day (1st day of 2). *Nigeria:* Independence Day. *South Korea:* Armed Forces Day (1st day of 2). *Tuvalu:* Independence Day.

**2 Wed.** *China:* National Day (2nd day of 2). *Guinea:* Independence Day. *India:* Ghandi Day. *South Korea:* Armed Forces Day (2nd day of 2).

**3 Thu.** *Honduras:* Morazan Day. *South Korea:* Foundation Day (1st day of 2).

**4 Fri.** *Lesotho:* Independence Day. *South Korea:* Foundation Day (2nd day of 2).

**5 Sat.** *Lesotho:* Sports Day. *Macao:* Portuguese Republic Day. *Portugal:* Republic Day.

**6 Sun.** *Egypt:* Armed Forces Day.

**7 Mon.** *Barbados:* Bank Holiday.

**9 Wed.** *Peru:* National Dignity Day. *South Korea:* Alphabet Day. *Uganda:* Independence Day.

**10 Thu.** *Japan:* Health Day. *South Africa:* Kruger Day. *Taiwan:* National Day.

**11 Fri.** *Cuba:* Independence War. *Panama:* Revolution Day.

**12 Sat.** *Equatorial Guinea:* Independence Day. *Spain:* National Day. *Multinational:* Columbus Day (see App. A12).

**14 Mon.** *Canada:* Thanksgiving Day. *Fiji:* Cession Day. *United States:* Bank Holiday. *Virgin Islands (U.S.):* Puerto Rican Friendship Day. *Zaïre:* Founders' Day. *Asian:* Ancestors' Day (see App. B6). *Far East Islamic:* Hari Raya Haji (see App. B29). *Islamic:* Eid al Adha (1st day of 4) (see App. B28).

**15 Tue.** *Bosnia and Herzegovina:* Independence Day*. *Tunisia:* Evacuation Day. *Islamic:* Eid al Adha (2nd day of 4) (see App. B28).

**16 Wed.** *Islamic:* Eid al Adha (3rd day of 4) (see App. B28).

**17 Thu.** *Burma:* Full Moon Day. *Haiti:* Dessalines Day. *Malawi:* Mother's Day. *Islamic:* Eid al Adha (4th day of 4) (see App. B28).

**18 Fri.** *China:* Mid-autumn Day. *Sri Lanka:* Full Moon Poya. *Taiwan:* Mid-autumn Day.

**19 Sat.** *Hong Kong:* Mid-autumn Day. *Macao:* Mid-autumn Day.

**20 Sun.** *Guatemala:* Revolution Day. *Kenya:* Kenyatta Day.

**21 Mon.** *Honduras:* Army Day.

*Jamaica:* Heroes' Day. *Somalia:* Revolution Day (1st day of 2).

**22 Tue.** *Somalia:* Revolution Day (2nd day of 2). *Vatican:* John Paul II Day.

**23 Wed.** *Hungary:* Revolution Day. *Thailand:* Chulalongkorn Day. *Zodiac Cusp:* Libra ends, Scorpio begins.

**24 Thu.** *Egypt:* Suez Victory Day. *Haiti:* United Nations Day. *Zambia:* Independence Day.

**25 Fri.** *Taiwan:* Restoration Day.

**26 Sat.** *Austria:* National Day. *Benin:* Revolution Day. *Rwanda:* Government Day.

**27 Sun.** *Saint Vincent:* Independence Day. *Turkmenistan:* Independence Day*. *Zaïre:* Naming Day. *Canada and United States:* Daylight Savings Time ends (retard clocks 1 hour).

**28 Mon.** *Greece:* Ohi! Day. *Ireland:* Public Holiday. *New. Zealand:* Labour Day.

**29 Tue.** *Tanzania:* Naming Day. *Turkey:* Republic Day.

**31 Thu.** *Taiwan:* Chiang Kai-shek's Birthday.

# November 2013

**1 Fri.** *Algeria:* Revolution Day. *Antigua:* Independence Day. *Christian:* All Saints' Day (see App. A13).

**2 Sat.** *Brazil:* Memorial Day. *Finland:* All Saints' Eve. *Sweden:* All Saints' Eve. *Christian:* All Souls' Day (see App. A14). *Hindu:* Deepavali (see App. B21).

**3 Sun.** *Dominica:* Independence Day. *Ecuador:* Cuenca Independence Day. *Japan:* Culture Day. *Panama:* Independence Day. *Islamic:* New Year's Day (Hegira: 1435) (see App. B22).

**4 Mon.** *Andorra:* Saint Charles' Day. *Panama:* Flag Day. *Virgin Islands (U.S.):* Liberty Day. *Vatican:* John Paul II's Nameday. *Far East Islamic:* New Year's Day (Hegira: 1435).

**5 Tue.** *El Salvador:* Cry of Independence Day.

**7 Thu.** *Bangladesh:* Revolution Day. *Liberia:* Thanksgiving Day.

**8 Fri.** *Nepal:* Queen's Birthday.

**9 Sat.** *Pakistan:* Iqbal Day.

**10 Sun.** *Panama:* Cry of Independence Day.

**11 Mon.** *Angola:* Independence Day. *Bhutan:* King's Birthday. *Maldives:* Republic Day. *Poland:* Independence Day. *Multinational:* Armistice Day (see App. A15).

**12 Tue.** *Taiwan:* Dr. Sun Yat-sen's Birthday. *Islamic:* Ashura (see App. B23).

**14 Thu.** *Jordan:* King's Birthday.

**15 Fri.** *Brazil:* Republic Day.

**16 Sat.** *Burma:* Full Moon Day.

**17 Sun.** *Sri Lanka:* Full Moon Poya. *Zaïre:* Armed Forces Day.

**18 Mon.** *Fiji:* Prince Charles' Birthday. *Haiti:* Vertieres' Day. *Morocco:* Independence Day. *Oman:* National Day.

**19 Tue.** *Belize:* Garifuna Day. *Mali:* Army Coup Day. *Monaco:* Prince Ranier's Day. *Puerto Rico:* Discovery Day.

**20 Wed.** *Germany:* Repentance Day. *Mexico:* Revolution Day.

**22 Fri.** *Lebanon:* Independence Day. *Zodiac Cusp:* Scorpio ends, Sagittarius begins.

**23 Sat.** *Japan:* Labor Thanksgiving Day.

**24 Sun.** *Zaïre:* New Regime Day.

**25 Mon.** *Suriname:* Independence Day.

**27 Wed.** *Jewish:* Chanukah.

**28 Thu.** *Albania:* Independence Day. *Burundi:* Republic Day. *Chad:* Republic Day. *Mauritania:* Independence Day. *Panama:* Independence Day. *United States:* Thanksgiving Day.

**29 Fri.** *Albania:* Liberation Day. *Argentina:* Bank Holiday. *Liberia:* Tubman's Birthday. *Yugoslavia:* Republic Day.

**30 Sat.** *Barbados:* Independence Day. *Benin:* National Day. *Philippines:* Heroes' Day.

# December 2013

**1 Sun.** *Central African Republic:* National Day. *Portugal:* Youth Day. *Ukraine:* Independence Day*.

**2 Mon.** *Laos:* Republic Day. *United Arab Emirates:* National Day.

**5 Thu.** *Haiti:* Discovery Day. *Thailand:* King's Birthday.

**6 Fri.** *Finland:* Independence Day.

**7 Sat.** *Ivory Coast:* Independence Day.

**8 Sun.** *Christian:* Immaculate Conception (see App. A16).

**9 Mon.** *Tanzania:* Independence Day.

**10 Tue.** *Angola:* MPLA Foundation Day. *Equatorial Guinea:* Human Rights Day. *Namibia:* Settlers' Day. *Thailand:* Constitution Day.

**11 Wed.** *Burkina Faso:* National Day.

**12 Thu.** *Kenya:* Independence Day. *Mexico:* Guadalupe Festival.

**13 Fri.** *Malta:* Republic Day.

**15 Sun.** *Burma:* Full Moon Day.

**16 Mon.** *Bahrain:* National Day. *Bangladesh:* Victory Day. *Nepal:* Constitution Day. *South Africa:* Covenant Day. *Sri Lanka:* Full Moon Poya.

**17 Tue.** *Bhutan:* National Day.

**18 Wed.** *Niger:* Republic Day.

**21 Sat.** *Kazakhstan:* Independence Day*. *Zodiac Cusp:* Sagittarius ends, Capricorn begins.

**23 Mon.** *Japan:* Emperor's Birthday.

**24 Tue.** *Multinational:* Christmas Eve (see App. A17).

**25 Wed.** *Angola:* Family Day. *Congo:* Children's Day. *Pakistan:* Quaid's Birthday. *Taiwan:* Constitution Day. *Multinational:* Christmas Day (see App. A18).

**26 Thu.** *South Africa:* Good Will Day. *Multinational:* Boxing Day (see App. A19).

**30 Mon.** *Madagascar:* Republic Day. *Philippines:* Rizal Day (1st day of 2).

**31 Tue.** *Congo:* Republic Day. *Philippines:* Rizal Day (2nd day of 2). *Multinational:* Bank Holiday and New Year's Eve (see App. A20 & A21).

# January 2014

**1 Wed.** *Cameroon:* Independence Day. *Cuba:* Liberation Day. *Haiti:* Independence Day. *Palau:* Independence Day. *Sudan:* Independence Day. *Taiwan:* Foundation Day (1st day of 2). *Western Samoa:* Independence Day. *Multinational:* Bank Holiday and New Year's Day (see App. A1 & A2).

**2 Thu.** *Japan:* Bank Holiday. *New Zealand:* New Year's Day (2nd day of 2). *Scotland:* New Year's Day (2nd day of 2). *South Korea:* New Year's Day (2nd day of 2). *Switzerland:* Berchtold's Day. *Taiwan:* Foundation Day (2nd day of 2).

**3 Fri.** *Burkina Faso:* Revolution Day.

**4 Sat.** *Burma:* Independence Day. *Zaïre:* Martyrs' Day.

**6 Mon.** *Iraq:* Army Day. *Uruguay:* Children's Day. *Christian:* Epiphany (see App. A3).

**7 Tue.** *Egypt:* Coptic Christmas. *Ethiopia:* Coptic Christmas.

**11 Sat.** *Albania:* Republic Day. *Nepal:* Unification Day. *Puerto Rico:* Hostos Day.

**12 Sun.** *Tanzania:* Revolution Day. *Islamic:* Mohammed's Birthday (see App. B24).

**13 Mon.** *Togo:* Liberation Day. *Far East Islamic:* Mohammed's Birthday.

**14 Tue.** *Burma:* Full Moon Day.

**15 Wed.** *Japan:* Adult's Day. *Jordan:* Arbor Day. *Sri Lanka:* Full Moon Poya.

**19 Sun.** *Ethiopia:* Epiphany.

**20 Mon.** *Mali:* Award Day. *United States:* Martin Luther King's Birthday. *Zodiac Cusp:* Capricorn ends, Aquarius begins.

**21 Tue.** *Dominican Republic:* Altagracia Day.

**22 Wed.** *Saint Vincent:* Discovery Day.

**26 Sun.** *Dominican Republic:* Duarte Day. *India:* Republic Day.

**27 Mon.** *Australia:* Australia Day. *Monaco:* Saint Devota's Day. *Vietnam:* Vietnam Day.

**28 Tue.** *Rwanda:* Democracy Day.

**30 Thu.** *Asian:* Chinese New Year Eve (see App. B1).

**31 Fri.** *Nauru:* Independence Day. *Vietnam:* Tet (1st day of 3). *Asian:* Chinese New Year (Year of the Horse) (see App. B2).

# February 2014

**1 Sat.** *Vietnam:* Tet (2nd day of 3). *Asian:* 2nd Day of Chinese New Year (see App. B3).

**2 Sun.** *Liechtenstein:* Candlemas. *Vietnam:* Tet (3rd day of 3). *Asian:* 3rd Day of Chinese New Year (see App. B4).

**3 Mon.** *United States:* Lincoln's Birthday.

**4 Tue.** *Sri Lanka:* Independence Day.

**5 Wed.** *Mexico:* Constitution Day.

**6 Thu.** *New Zealand:* Waitangi Day.

**7 Fri.** *Grenada:* Independence Day.

**8 Sat.** *Iraq:* Revolution Day.

**9 Sun.** *Lebanon:* Saint Marion's Day.

**10 Mon.** *Malta:* Saint Paul's Day.

**11 Tue.** *Cameroon:* Youth Day. *Japan:* Foundation Day. *Liberia:* Armed Forces Day.

**12 Wed.** *Burma:* Union Day.

**13 Thu.** *Burma:* Full Moon Day.

**14 Fri.** *Sri Lanka:* Full Moon Poya. *Thailand:* Makha Bucha Day. *International:* Valentine's Day.

**17 Mon.** *United States:* Washington's Birthday.

**18 Tue.** *Gambia:* Independence Day. *Zodiac Cusp:* Aquarius ends, Pisces begins.

**19 Wed.** *Nepal:* National Day.

**21 Fri.** *Bangladesh:* Saheed Day.

**22 Sat.** *Saint Lucia:* Independence Day.

**23 Sun.** *Brunei:* National Day. *Guyana:* Republic Day.

**25 Tue.** *Kuwait:* National Day.

**27 Thu.** *Dominican Republic:* Independence Day.

# March 2014

**1 Sat.** *South Korea:* Independence Day.

**2 Sun.** *Ethiopia:* Victory of Aduwa Day. *Morocco:* Independence Day.

**3 Mon.** *Bulgaria:* Liberation Day. *Guam:* Discovery Day. *Malawi:* Martyrs' Day. *Morocco:* National Day. *Christian:* Shrove Monday (see App. B7).

**4 Tue.** *Christian:* Shrove Tuesday (see App. B8).

**5 Wed.** *Christian:* Ash Wednesday (see App. B9).

**6 Thu.** *Ghana:* Independence Day.

**8 Sat.** *Syria:* Revolution Day. *Zambia:* Youth Day. *Multinational:* Women's Day (see App. A4).

**10 Mon.** *Gibraltar:* Commonwealth Day. *Greece:* Shrove Monday. *South Korea:* Labor Day. *Orthodox:* Shrove Monday.

**11 Tue.** *Lithuania:* National Day*.

**12 Wed.** *Lesotho:* Moshoeshoe's Day. *Mauritius:* Independence Day.

**13 Thu.** *Grenada:* National Day.

**15 Sat.** *Burma:* Full Moon Day.

**16 Sun.** *Sri Lanka:* Full Moon Poy. *Jewish:* Purim.

**17 Mon.** *Ireland:* Saint Patrick's Day. *Northern Ireland:* Saint Patrick's Day.

**19 Wed.** *Christian:* Saint Joseph's Day (see App. A5).

**20 Thu.** *Afghanistan:* New Year's Day (Shamsi: 1393). *Iran:* New Year's Day (Hegira: 1393). *Iraq:* New Year's Day. *Tunisia:* Independence Day. *Zodiac Cusp:* Pisces ends, Aries begins.

**21 Fri.** *Japan:* Vernal Equinox. *Mexico:* Juarez Day.

**22 Sat.** *Puerto Rico:* Abolition Day.

**23 Sun.** *Pakistan:* Pakistan Day.

**25 Tue.** *Cyprus:* Greek Independence Day. *Greece:* Independence Day. *Liechtenstein:* Annunciation. *Zambia:* Africa Day.

**26 Wed.** *Bangladesh:* Independence Day.

**27 Thu.** *Angola:* Evacuation Day. *Burma:* Resistance Day.

**29 Sat.** *Central African Republic:* Boganda Day. *Madagascar:* Memorial Day. *Taiwan:* Youth Day.

**30 Sun.** *Europe:* Daylight Savings Time starts (advance clocks 1 hour).

**31 Mon.** *Malta:* National Day. *Virgin Islands (U.S.):* Transfer Day.

# April 2014

**1 Tue.** *Iran:* Republic Day. *San Marino:* National Day.

**4 Fri.** *Hungary:* Liberation Day. *Senegal:* National Day. *Sierra Leone:* Bank Holiday.

**5 Sat.** *South Korea:* Arbor Day. *Asian:* Tomb Sweeping Day (see App. A6).

**6 Sun.** *South Africa:* Founders' Day. *Thailand:* Chakri Day. *Canada and United States:* Daylight Savings Time starts (advance clocks 1 hour).

**9 Wed.** *Philippines:* Valour Day. *Tunisia:* Martyrs' Day.

**11 Fri.** *Costa Rica:* Heroes' Day. *Uganda:* Liberation Day.

**13 Sun.** *Burma:* Full Moon Day. *Chad:* National Day. *Thailand:* Songkrawn (1st day of 2). *Christian:* Palm Sunday.

**14 Mon.** *Honduras:* Pan American Day. *Sri Lanka:* Full Moon Poya. *Thailand:* Songkrawn (2nd day of 2).

**15 Tue.** *Israel:* Passover. *Niger:* National Day. *Jewish:* Passover.

**16 Wed.** *Burma:* New Year's Day (Burmese: 1376). *Cyprus:* Independence Day.

**17 Thu.** *Cambodia:* Independence Day. *Syria:* Independence Day. *Christian:* Maundy Thursday (see App. B11).

**18 Fri.** *Zimbabwe:* Republic Day. *Christian:* Good Friday (see App. B12).

**19 Sat.** *Sierra Leone:* Republic Day. *Uruguay:* Patriots' Day. *Venezuela:* Independence Day. *Christian:* Holy Saturday (see App. B13).

**20 Sun.** *Christian:* Easter Sunday (see App. B14). *Zodiac Cusp:* Aries ends, Taurus begins.

**21 Mon.** *Brazil:* Tiradentes Day. *Christian:* Easter Monday (see App. B15).

**23 Wed.** *Turkey:* Children's Day.

**25 Fri.** *Australia:* ANZAC Day. *Egypt:* Sinai Day. *Iceland:* Children's

Day. *Italy:* Liberation Day. *New Zealand:* ANZAC Day. *Portugal:* Liberation Day. *Swaziland:* Flag Day. *Orthodox:* Good Friday (see App. B20).

**26 Sat.** *Tanzania:* Union Day.

**27 Sun.** *Afghanistan:* Independence Day. *Jordan:* Easter Sunday. *Sierra Leone:* Independence Day. *Togo:* Independence Day. *Orthodox:* Easter Sunday.

**28 Mon.** *Orthodox:* Easter Monday (see App. B20).

**29 Tue.** *Japan:* Green Day.

**30 Wed.** *Finland:* Vappu Day. *Netherlands:* Queen's Birthday.

# May 2014

**1 Thu.** *Multinational:* Labor Day (see App. A7).

**2 Fri.** *Lesotho:* King's Birthday.

**3 Sat.** *Japan:* Constitution Day.

**4 Sun.** *Japan:* People's Day.

**5 Mon.** *Israel:* Independence Day. *Japan:* Children's Day. *Mexico:* Cinco de Mayo. *Netherlands:* Liberation Day. *South Korea:* Children's Day. *Thailand:* Coronation Day. *United Kingdom:* Labour Day. *Zambia:* Labour Day.

**6 Tue.** *South Korea:* Vesak Day. *Lebanon:* Martyrs' Day. *Philippines:* Corregidor Day.

**8 Thu.** *France:* Liberation Day.

**9 Fri.** *Czech Republic:* Liberation Day*. *Slovakia:* Liberation Day*.

**10 Sat.** *Micronesia:* Independence Day.

**11 Sun.** *International:* Mother's Day.

**13 Tue.** *Burma:* Full Moon Day. *Malaysia:* Vesak Day. *Singapore:* Vesak Day. *Thailand:* Visakha Bucha Day.

**14 Wed.** *Liberia:* Unification Day. *Malawi:* Kamuzu Day. *Paraguay:* Flag Day. *Sri Lanka:* Full Moon Poya.

**15 Thu.** *Paraguay:* Independence Day.

**16 Fri.** *Denmark:* All Prayers' Day.

**17 Sat.** *Cayman Islands:* Discovery Day. *Norway:* Constitution Day.

**18 Sun.** *Haiti:* Flag Day. *Uruguay:* Las Piedras Day.

**19 Mon.** *Canada:* Victoria Day. *Finland:* Flag Day. *Turkey:* Youth Day.

**20 Tue.** *Cameroon:* Constitution Day. *Zaïre:* Popular Movement Day.

**21 Wed.** *Chile:* Navy Day. *Zodiac Cusp:* Taurus ends, Gemini begins.

**22 Thu.** *Haiti:* Sovereign Day. *Sri Lanka:* Heroes' Day.

**23 Fri.** *Jamaica:* Labour Day.

**24 Sat.** *Bulgaria:* Culture Day. *Ecuador:* Independence Battle Day.

**25 Sun.** *Argentina:* National Day. *Eritrea:* Independence Day*. *Jordan:* Independence Day. *Sudan:* Revolution Day. *Islamic:* Isra a Majraj (see App. B30). *Multinational:* Africa Day (see App. A8).

**26 Mon.** *Guyana:* Independence Day. *United Kingdom:* Spring Break. *United States:* Memorial Day.

**27 Tue.** *Nigeria:* Children's Day.

**29 Thu.** *Christian:* Ascension (see App. B16).

**31 Sat.** *Brunei:* Regiment Day. *South Africa:* Republic Day.

# June 2014

**1 Sun.** *Kenya:* Madaraka Day. *Tunisia:* National Day. *Western Samoa:* Independence Day.

**2 Mon.** *Ireland:* Public Holiday. *Italy:* Republic Day. *New Zealand:* Queen's Birthday. *Tunisia:* Youth Day.

**3 Tue.** *Asian:* Dragon Boat Festival (see App. B5).

**4 Wed.** *Bahamas:* Labour Day. *Israel:* Pentecost. *Malaysia:* King's Birthday. *Tonga:* Independence Day. *Jewish:* Pentecost.

**5 Thu.** *Denmark:* Constitution Day. *Equatorial Guinea:* President's Birthday. *Seychelles:* Liberation Day.

**6 Fri.** *South Korea:* Memorial Day. *Sweden:* Constitution Day.

**7 Sat.** *Chad:* Revolution Day.

**8 Sun.** *Christian:* Whitsunday.

**9 Mon.** *Argentina:* Independence Day. *Australia:* Queen's Birthday. *Fiji:* Queen's Birthday. *New Guinea:* Queen's Birthday. *United Kingdom:* Queen's Birthday. *Christian:* Whitmonday (see App. B18).

**10 Tue.** *Macao:* Portugal Day. *Portugal:* Portugal Day.

**11 Wed.** *Burma:* Full Moon Day. *Libya:* Evacuation Day.

**12 Thu.** *Philippines:* Independence Day. *Sri Lanka:* Full Moon Poya.

**14 Sat.** *Hong Kong:* Queen's Birthday (1st day of 2).

**15 Sun.** *Orthodox:* Pentecost Sunday.

**16 Mon.** *Greece:* Pentecost Monday. *Hong Kong:* Queen's Birthday (2nd day of 2).

**17 Tue.** *Germany:* Unity Day. *Iceland:* Independence Day.

**18 Wed.** *Egypt:* Independence Day.

**19 Thu.** *Algeria:* Righting Day. *Kuwait:* Independence Day. *Uruguay:* Artigas Day. *Christian:* Corpus Christi (see App. B19).

**20 Fri.** *Argentina:* Flag Day.

**21 Sat.** *Finland:* Johannus and Midsummer Day (1st day of 2). *Sweden:* Midsummer Day (1st day of 2). *Zodiac Cusp:* Gemini ends, Cancer begins.

**22 Sun.** *Finland:* Midsummer Day (2nd day of 2). *Sweden:* Midsummer Day (2nd day of 2).

**23 Mon.** *Luxembourg:* National Day.

**24 Tue.** *Andorra:* Saint John's Day. *Venezuela:* Carabobo Day. *Zaïre:* Constitution Day.

**25 Wed.** *Croatia:* Independence Day*. *Mozambique:* Independence Day. *Slovenia:* Independence Day*.

**26 Thu.** *Madagascar:* Independence Day. *Somalia:* Independence Day.

**27 Fri.** *Chile:* Bank Holiday. *Djibouti:* Independence Day. *Ecuador:* Bank Holiday. *El Salvador:* Bank Holiday. *Finland:* Bank Holiday.

**28 Sat.** *Islamic:* 1st Day of Ramadan (see App. B25).

**29 Sun.** *Seychelles:* Independence Day. *Christian:* Saint Paul's Day (see App. A9).

**30 Mon.** *Guatemala:* Army Day. *Sri Lanka:* Bank Holiday. *Zaïre:* Independence Day.

# July 2014

**1 Tue.** *Burundi:* Independence Day. *Canada:* Canada Day. *Ghana:* Republic Day. *Hong Kong:* Half Year Day. *Rwanda:* Independence Day. *Somalia:* Union Day. *Suriname:* Freedom Day. *Zambia:* Unity Day. *Multinational:* Bank Holiday (see App. A10).

**4 Fri.** *Philippines:* United States Friendship Day. *United States:* Independence Day. *Yugoslavia:* Freedom Fighters' Day.

**5 Sat.** *Algeria:* Independence Day. *Cape Verde:* Independence Day. *Rwanda:* Unity Day. *Venezuela:* Independence Day.

**6 Sun.** *Comoros:* Independence Day. *Malawi:* Republic Day.

**7 Mon.** *Cayman Islands:* Constitution Day. *Lesotho:* Family Day. *Solomon Islands:* Independence Day. *Tanzania:* Farmers' Day. *Yugoslavia:* Serbian Day. *Zambia:* Heroes' Day.

**10 Thu.** *Bahamas:* Independence Day. *Burma:* Full Moon Day.

**11 Fri.** *Mongolia:* Revolution Day. *Sri Lanka:* Full Moon Poya.

**12 Sat.** *Kiribati:* Independence Day. *Northern Ireland:* Battle of the Boyne Day. *São Tomé:* National Day. *Thailand:* Asalaha Bucha Day.

**13 Sun.** *Thailand:* Khao Phansa Day.

**14 Mon.** *France:* National Day. *Iraq:* Revolution Day.

**15 Tue.** *Brunei:* Sultan's Birthday.

**17 Thu.** *Iraq:* Revolution Day. *Puerto Rico:* Rivera Day. *Slovakia:* Independence Day*. *South Korea:* Constitution Day.

**18 Fri.** *Uruguay:* Constitution Day.

**19 Sat.** *Burma:* Martyrs' Day. *Laos:* Independence Day. *Nicaragua:* Sandinista Day.

**20 Sun.** *Colombia:* Independence Day.

**21 Mon.** *Belgium:* National Day. *Botswana:* President's Day. *Guam:* Liberation Day.

**22 Tue.** *Poland:* Liberation Day. *Zodiac Cusp:* Cancer ends, Leo begins.

**23 Wed.** *Egypt:* Revolution Day. *New Guinea:* Remembrance Day.

**24 Thu.** *Venezuela:* Bolivar Day.

**25 Fri.** *Costa Rica:* Guanacaste Day. *Cuba:* Revolution Day (1st day of 3). *Puerto Rico:* Constitution Day. *Spain:* Santiago Day. *Tunisia:* Republic Day.

**26 Sat.** *Cuba:* Revolution Day (2nd day of 3). *Liberia:* Independence Day. *Maldives:* Independence Day.

**27 Sun.** *Cuba:* Revolution Day (3rd day of 3). *Puerto Rico:* Barbosa Day.

**28 Mon.** *Peru:* Independence Day (1st day of 2). *Virgin Islands (U.S.):* Hurricane Supplication Day. *Far East Islamic:* Hari Raya Puasa (see App. B27). *Islamic:* Eid al Fitr (1st day of 4) (see App. B26).

**29 Tue.** *Peru:* Independence Day (2nd day of 2). *Islamic:* Eid al Fitr (2nd day of 4) (see App. B26).

**30 Wed.** *Vanuatu:* Independence Day. *Islamic:* Eid al Fitr (3rd day of 4) (see App. B26).

**31 Thu.** *Islamic:* Eid al Fitr (4th day of 4) (see App. B26).

# August 2014

**1 Fri.** *Benin:* Independence Day. *Switzerland:* Confederation Day.

**2 Sat.** *Costa Rica:* Virgin of the Angels Day. *Guyana:* Freedom Day. *Trinidad:* Discovery Day.

**3 Sun.** *El Salvador:* Summer Day (1st day of 4). *Guinea-Bissau:* Martyrs' Day. *Niger:* Independence Day. *Tunisia:* President's Birthday.

**4 Mon.** *Bahamas:* Emancipation Day. *Barbados:* Emancipation Day. *Burkina Faso:* Independence Day (1st day of 2). *Canada:* Civic Holiday. *El Salvador:* Summer Day (2nd day of 4). *Ireland:* Public Holiday. *Jamaica:* Independence Day. *Scotland:* Public Holiday.

**5 Tue.** *Burkina Faso:* Independence Day (2nd day of 2). *El Salvador:* Summer Day (3rd day of 4). *Israel:* Tisha Ab. *Jewish:* Tisha Ab.

**6 Wed.** *Bolivia:* Independence Day. *El Salvador:* Summer Day (4th day of 4). *United Arab Emirates:* Accession Day. *Zambia:* Farmers' Day.

**7 Thu.** *Colombia:* Boyaca Day. *Ivory Coast:* Republic Day.

**9 Sat.** *Burma:* Full Moon Day. *Georgia:* Independence Day*. *Singapore:* National Day.

**10 Sun.** *Ecuador:* Independence Day. *Sri Lanka:* Full Moon Poya.

**11 Mon.** *Chad:* Independence Day. *Jordan:* Accession Day. *Zimbabwe:* Heroes' Day (1st day of 2).

**12 Tue.** *Thailand:* Queen's Birthday. *Zimbabwe:* Heroes' Day (2nd day of 2).

**13 Wed.** *Central African Republic:*

Independence Day. *Congo:* Independence Day (1st day of 2). *Tunisia:* Women's Day.

**14 Thu.** *Congo:* Independence Day (2nd day of 2). *Pakistan:* Independence Day.

**15 Fri.** *Congo:* Independence Day (3rd day of 3). *India:* Independence Day. *Liechtenstein:* National Day. *South Korea:* Republic Day. *Christian:* Assumption (see App. A11).

**16 Sat.** *Dominican Republic:* Republic Day.

**17 Sun.** *Argentina:* San Martin's Day. *Gabon:* Independence Day. *Indonesia:* Independence Day.

**20 Wed.** *Hungary:* Constitution Day. *Senegal:* Independence Day.

**21 Thu.** *Estonia:* Independence Day*. *Latvia:* Independence Day*. *Lithuania:* Independence Day*.

**23 Sat.** *Hong Kong:* Liberation Day (1st day of 2). *Romania:* National Day (1st day of 2). *Zodiac Cusp:* Leo ends, Virgo begins.

**24 Sun.** *Kazakhstan:* National Day*. *Liberia:* Flag Day. *Romania:* National Day (2nd day of 2). *Russia:* Independence Day*. *Ukraine:* National Day*.

**25 Mon.** *Belarus:* Independence Day*. *England:* Summer Break. *Hong Kong:* Liberation Day (2nd day of 2). *Northern Ireland:* Summer Break. *Paraguay:* Constitution Day. *Uruguay:* Independence Day. *Wales:* Summer Break.

**27 Wed.** *Moldova:* Independence Day*.

**29 Fri.** *Uzbekistan:* Independence Day*.

**30 Sat.** *Afghanistan:* Children's Day. *Azerbaijan:* Independence Day*. *Peru:* Rose of Lima Day. *Turkey:* Victory Day.

**31 Sun.** *Afghanistan:* Pashtunistan Day. *Kyrgyzstan:* Independence Day*. *Malaysia:* National Day. *Trinidad:* Independence Day.

# September 2014

**1 Mon.** *Canada:* Labour Day. *Libya:* National Day. *Luxembourg:* Fair Day. *Mexico:* President's Message Day. *Syria:* United Arab Republics Day. *United States:* Labor Day.

**2 Tue.** *Vietnam:* Independence Day.

**3 Wed.** *Qatar:* National Day. *San Marino:* Saint Marinus' Day. *Tunisia:* Independence Movement Day.

**6 Sat.** *Pakistan:* Defense Day. *Swaziland:* Independence Day.

**7 Sun.** *Brazil:* Independence Day. *Burma:* Full Moon Day.

**8 Mon.** *Andorra:* National Day. *Malta:* Our Lady of Victory Day. *Sri Lanka:* Full Moon Poya.

**9 Tue.** *Bulgaria:* National Day (1st day of 2). *North Korea:* Independence Day. *Tajikistan:* Independence Day*.

**10 Wed.** *Belize:* National Day. *Bulgaria:* National Day (2nd day of 2).

**11 Thu.** *Chile:* Revolution Day. *Egypt:* New Year's Day (Coptic: 1732). *Ethiopia:* New Year's Day (Ethiopian: 2008). *Pakistan:* Anniversary of Quaid-e-Azam's Death.

**12 Fri.** *Ethiopia:* National Day.

**14 Sun.** *Guatemala:* San Jacinto Day. *Nicaragua:* San Jacinto Day.

**15 Mon.** *Costa Rica:* Independence Day. *El Salvador:* Independence Day. *Guatemala:* Independence Day. *Honduras:* Independence Day. *Japan:* Veneration Day. *Nicaragua:* Independence Day.

**16 Tue.** *Mexico:* Independence Day. *New Guinea:* Independence Day.

**17 Wed.** *Angola:* Heroes' Day. *Marshall Islands:* Independence Day.

**18 Thu.** *Burundi:* Victory of Uprona Day. *Chile:* Independence Day.

**19 Fri.** *Chile:* Armed Forces Day. *Saint Kitts:* Independence Day.

**21 Sun.** *Belize:* Independence Day. *Malta:* Independence Day.

**22 Mon.** *Mali:* Independence Day.

**23 Tue.** *Armenia:* Independence Day*. *Japan:* Autumnal Equinox. *Saudi Arabia:* National Day. *Zodiac Cusp:* Virgo ends, Libra begins.

**24 Wed.** *Dominican Republic:* Mercedes Day. *Guinea-Bissau:* Republic Day.

**25 Thu.** *Israel:* New Year's Day. *Mozambique:* Liberation Day. *Rwanda:* Assembly Day. *Jewish:* Rosh Hashanah (Jewish: 5775).

**26 Fri.** *Ethiopia:* True Cross Day.

**28 Sun.** *Taiwan:* Teachers' Day. *Europe:* Daylight Savings Time ends (retard clocks 1 hour).

**29 Mon.** *Brunei:* Constitution Day. *Paraguay:* Boqueron Battle Day.

**30 Tue.** *Botswana:* Independence Day.

# October 2014

**1 Wed.** *Cameroon:* Unification Day. *China:* National Day (1st day of 2). *Nigeria:* Independence Day. *South Korea:* Armed Forces Day (1st day of 2). *Tuvalu:* Independence Day.

**2 Thu.** *China:* National Day (2nd day of 2). *Guinea:* Independence Day. *India:* Ghandi Day. *South Korea:* Armed Forces Day (2nd day of 2).

**3 Fri.** *Honduras:* Morazan Day. *South Korea:* Foundation Day (1st day of 2). *Asian:* Ancestors' Day (see App. B6).

**4 Sat.** *Israel:* Yom Kippur. *Lesotho:* Independence Day. *South Korea:* Foundation Day (2nd day of 2). *Islamic:* Eid al Adha (1st day of 4) (see App. B28). *Jewish:* Yom Kippur.

**5 Sun.** *Lesotho:* Sports Day. *Macao:* Portuguese Republic Day. *Portugal:* Republic Day. *Far East Islamic:* Hari Raya Haji (see App. B29). *Islamic:* Eid al Adha (2nd day of 4) (see App. B28).

**6 Mon.** *Barbados:* Bank Holiday. *Burma:* Full Moon Day. *Egypt:* Armed Forces Day. *Islamic:* Eid al Adha (3rd day of 4) (see App. B28).

**7 Tue.** *China:* Mid-autumn Day. *Sri Lanka:* Full Moon Poya. *Taiwan:* Mid-autumn Day. *Islamic:* Eid al Adha (4th day of 4) (see App. B28).

**8 Wed.** *Hong Kong:* Mid-autumn Day. *Macao:* Mid-autumn Day.

**9 Thu.** *Israel:* Sukkot. *Peru:* National Dignity Day. *South Korea:* Alphabet Day. *Uganda:* Independence Day. *Jewish:* Sukkot.

**10 Fri.** *Japan:* Health Day. *South Africa:* Kruger Day. *Taiwan:* National Day.

**11 Sat.** *Cuba:* Independence War. *Panama:* Revolution Day.

**12 Sun.** *Equatorial Guinea:* Independence Day. *Spain:* National Day. *Multinational:* Columbus Day (see App. A12).

**13 Mon.** *Canada:* Thanksgiving Day. *Fiji:* Cession Day. *United States:* Bank Holiday. *Virgin Islands (U.S.):* Puerto Rican Friendship Day.

**14 Tue.** *Zaïre:* Founders' Day.

**15 Wed.** *Bosnia and Herzegovina:* Independence Day*. *Tunisia:* Evacuation Day.

**17 Fri.** *Haiti:* Dessalines Day. *Malawi:* Mother's Day.

**20 Mon.** *Guatemala:* Revolution Day. *Jamaica:* Heroes' Day. *Kenya:* Kenyatta Day.

**21 Tue.** *Honduras:* Army Day. *Somalia:* Revolution Day (1st day of 2).

**22 Wed.** *Somalia:* Revolution Day (2nd day of 2). *Vatican:* John Paul II Day. *Hindu:* Deepavali (see App. B21).

**23 Thu.** *Hungary:* Revolution Day. *Thailand:* Chulalongkorn Day. *Zodiac Cusp:* Libra ends, Scorpio begins.

**24 Fri.** *Egypt:* Suez Victory Day.

*Haiti:* United Nations Day. *Zambia:* Independence Day. *Islamic:* New Year's Day (Hegira: 1436) (see App. B22).

**25 Sat.** *Taiwan:* Restoration Day. *Far East Islamic:* New Year's Day (Hegira: 1436).

**26 Sun.** *Austria:* National Day. *Benin:* Revolution Day. *Rwanda:* Government Day. *Canada and United States:* Daylight Savings Time ends (retard clocks 1 hour).

**27 Mon.** *Ireland:* Public Holiday. *New Zealand:* Labour Day. *Saint Vincent:* Independence Day. *Turkmenistan:* Independence Day*. *Zaïre:* Naming Day.

**28 Tue.** *Greece:* Ohi! Day.

**29 Wed.** *Tanzania:* Naming Day. *Turkey:* Republic Day.

**31 Fri.** *Taiwan:* Chiang Kai-shek's Birthday.

# November 2014

**1 Sat.** *Algeria:* Revolution Day. *Antigua:* Independence Day. *Christian:* All Saints' Day (see App. A13). *Islamic:* Ashura (see App. B23).

**2 Sun.** *Brazil:* Memorial Day. *Finland:* All Saints' Eve. *Sweden:* All Saints' Eve. *Christian:* All Souls' Day (see App. A14).

**3 Mon.** *Dominica:* Independence Day. *Ecuador:* Cuenca Independence Day. *Japan:* Culture Day. *Panama:* Independence Day. *Virgin Islands (U.S.):* Liberty Day.

**4 Tue.** *Andorra:* Saint Charles' Day. *Panama:* Flag Day. *Vatican:* John Paul II's Nameday.

**5 Wed.** *Burma:* Full Moon Day. *El Salvador:* Cry of Independence Day.

**6 Thu.** *Liberia:* Thanksgiving Day. *Sri Lanka:* Full Moon Poya.

**7 Fri.** *Bangladesh:* Revolution Day.

**8 Sat.** *Nepal:* Queen's Birthday.

**9 Sun.** *Pakistan:* Iqbal Day.

**10 Mon.** *Panama:* Cry of Independence Day.

**11 Tue.** *Angola:* Independence Day. *Bhutan:* King's Birthday. *Maldives:* Republic Day. *Poland:* Independence Day. *Multinational:* Armistice Day (see App. A15).

**12 Wed.** *Taiwan:* Dr. Sun Yat-sen's Birthday.

**14 Fri.** *Jordan:* King's Birthday.

**15 Sat.** *Brazil:* Republic Day.

**17 Mon.** *Fiji:* Prince Charles' Birthday. *Zaïre:* Armed Forces Day.

**18 Tue.** *Haiti:* Vertieres' Day. *Morocco:* Independence Day. *Oman:* National Day.

**19 Wed.** *Belize:* Garifuna Day. *Germany:* Repentance Day. *Mali:* Army Coup Day. *Monaco:* Prince Ranier's Day. *Puerto Rico:* Discovery Day.

**20 Thu.** *Mexico:* Revolution Day.

**22 Sat.** *Lebanon:* Independence Day. *Zodiac Cusp:* Scorpio ends, Sagittarius begins.

**23 Sun.** *Japan:* Labor Thanksgiving Day.

**24 Mon.** *Zaïre:* New Regime Day.

**25 Tue.** *Suriname:* Independence Day.

**27 Thu.** *United States:* Thanksgiving Day.

**28 Fri.** *Albania:* Independence Day. *Argentina:* Bank Holiday. *Burundi:* Republic Day. *Chad:* Republic Day. *Mauritania:* Independence Day. *Panama:* Independence Day.

**29 Sat.** *Albania:* Liberation Day. *Liberia:* Tubman's Birthday. *Yugoslavia:* Republic Day.

**30 Sun.** *Barbados:* Independence Day. *Benin:* National Day. *Philippines:* Heroes' Day.

# December 2014

**1 Mon.** *Central African Republic:* National Day. *Portugal:* Youth Day. *Ukraine:* Independence Day*.

**2 Tue.** *Laos:* Republic Day. *United Arab Emirates:* National Day.

**5 Fri.** *Burma:* Full Moon Day. *Haiti:* Discovery Day. *Sri Lanka:* Full Moon Poya. *Thailand:* King's Birthday.

**6 Sat.** *Finland:* Independence Day.

**7 Sun.** *Ivory Coast:* Independence Day.

**8 Mon.** *Christian:* Immaculate Conception (see App. A16).

**9 Tue.** *Tanzania:* Independence Day.

**10 Wed.** *Angola:* MPLA Foundation Day. *Equatorial Guinea:* Human Rights Day. *Namibia:* Settlers' Day. *Thailand:* Constitution Day.

**11 Thu.** *Burkina Faso:* National Day.

**12 Fri.** *Kenya:* Independence Day. *Mexico:* Guadalupe Festival.

**13 Sat.** *Malta:* Republic Day.

**16 Tue.** *Bahrain:* National Day. *Bangladesh:* Victory Day. *Nepal:* Constitution Day. *South Africa:* Covenant Day.

**17 Wed.** *Bhutan:* National Day. *Jewish:* Chanukah.

**18 Thu.** *Niger:* Republic Day.

**21 Sun.** *Kazakhstan:* Independence Day*. *Zodiac Cusp:* Sagittarius ends, Capricorn begins.

**23 Tue.** *Japan:* Emperor's Birthday.

**24 Wed.** *Multinational:* Christmas Eve (see App. A17).

**25 Thu.** *Angola:* Family Day. *Congo:* Children's Day. *Pakistan:* Quaid's Birthday. *Taiwan:* Constitution Day. *Multinational:* Christmas Day (see App. A18).

**26 Fri.** *South Africa:* Good Will Day. *Multinational:* Boxing Day (see App. A19).

**30 Tue.** *Madagascar:* Republic Day. *Philippines:* Rizal Day (1st day of 2).

**31 Wed.** *Congo:* Republic Day. *Philippines:* Rizal Day (2nd day of 2). *Multinational:* Bank Holiday and New Year's Eve (see App. A20 & A21).

# January 2015

**1 Thu.** *Cameroon:* Independence Day. *Cuba:* Liberation Day. *Haiti:* Independence Day. *Palau:* Independence Day. *Sudan:* Independence Day. *Taiwan:* Foundation Day (1st day of 2). *Western Samoa:* Independence Day. *Far East Islamic:* Mohammed's Birthday. *Islamic:* Mohammed's Birthday (see App. B24). *Multinational:* Bank Holiday and New Year's Day (see App. A1 & A2).

**2 Fri.** *Japan:* Bank Holiday. *New Zealand:* New Year's Day (2nd day of 2). *Scotland:* New Year's Day (2nd day of 2). *South Korea:* New Year's Day (2nd day of 2). *Switzerland:* Berchtold's Day. *Taiwan:* Foundation Day (2nd day of 2).

**3 Sat.** *Burkina Faso:* Revolution Day. *Burma:* Full Moon Day.

**4 Sun.** *Burma:* Independence Day. *Sri Lanka:* Full Moon Poya. *Zaïre:* Martyrs' Day.

**6 Tue.** *Iraq:* Army Day. *Uruguay:* Children's Day. *Christian:* Epiphany (see App. A3).

**7 Wed.** *Egypt:* Coptic Christmas. *Ethiopia:* Coptic Christmas.

**11 Sun.** *Albania:* Republic Day. *Nepal:* Unification Day. *Puerto Rico:* Hostos Day.

**12 Mon.** *Tanzania:* Revolution Day.

**13 Tue.** *Togo:* Liberation Day.

**15 Thu.** *Japan:* Adult's Day. *Jordan:* Arbor Day.

**19 Mon.** *Ethiopia:* Epiphany. *United*

*States:* Martin Luther King's Birthday.

**20 Tue.** *Mali:* Award Day. *Zodiac Cusp:* Capricorn ends, Aquarius begins.

**21 Wed.** *Dominican Republic:* Altagracia Day.

**22 Thu.** *Saint Vincent:* Discovery Day.

**26 Mon.** *Australia:* Australia Day. *Dominican Republic:* Duarte Day. *India:* Republic Day.

**27 Tue.** *Monaco:* Saint Devota's Day. *Vietnam:* Vietnam Day.

**28 Wed.** *Rwanda:* Democracy Day.

**31 Sat.** *Nauru:* Independence Day.

# February 2015

**2 Mon.** *Burma:* Full Moon Day. *Liechtenstein:* Candlemas. *United States:* Lincoln's Birthday.

**3 Tue.** *Sri Lanka:* Full Moon Poya.

**4 Wed.** *Sri Lanka:* Independence Day.

**5 Thu.** *Mexico:* Constitution Day.

**6 Fri.** *New Zealand:* Waitangi Day.

**7 Sat.** *Grenada:* Independence Day.

**8 Sun.** *Iraq:* Revolution Day.

**9 Mon.** *Lebanon:* Saint Marion's Day.

**10 Tue.** *Malta:* Saint Paul's Day.

**11 Wed.** *Cameroon:* Youth Day. *Japan:* Foundation Day. *Liberia:* Armed Forces Day.

**12 Thu.** *Burma:* Union Day.

**14 Sat.** *International:* Valentine's Day.

**16 Mon.** *United States:* Washington's Birthday. *Christian:* Shrove Monday (see App. B7).

**17 Tue.** *Christian:* Shrove Tuesday (see App. B8).

**18 Wed.** *Gambia:* Independence Day. *Christian:* Ash Wednesday (see App. B9). *Asian:* Chinese New Year Eve (see App. B1).

**19 Thu.** *Nepal:* National Day. *Vietnam:* Tet (1st day of 3). *Asian:* Chinese New Year (Year of the Sheep) (see App. B2). *Zodiac Cusp:* Aquarius ends, Pisces begins.

**20 Fri.** *Vietnam:* Tet (2nd day of 3). *Asian:* 2nd Day of Chinese New Year (see App. B3).

**21 Sat.** *Bangladesh:* Saheed Day. *Vietnam:* Tet (3rd day of 3). *Asian:* 3rd Day of Chinese New Year (see App. B4).

**22 Sun.** *Saint Lucia:* Independence Day.

**23 Mon.** *Brunei:* National Day. *Greece:* Shrove Monday. *Guyana:* Republic Day. *Orthodox:* Shrove Monday.

**25 Wed.** *Kuwait:* National Day.

**27 Fri.** *Dominican Republic:* Independence Day.

# March 2015

**1 Sun.** *South Korea:* Independence Day.

**2 Mon.** *Ethiopia:* Victory of Aduwa Day. *Guam:* Discovery Day. *Morocco:* Independence Day.

**3 Tue.** *Bulgaria:* Liberation Day. *Malawi:* Martyrs' Day. *Morocco:* National Day.

**4 Wed.** *Burma:* Full Moon Day.

**5 Thu.** *Sri Lanka:* Full Moon Poya. *Thailand:* Makha Bucha Day. *Jewish:* Purim.

**6 Fri.** *Ghana:* Independence Day.

**8 Sun.** *Syria:* Revolution Day. *Multinational:* Women's Day (see App. A4).

9 **Mon.** *Gibraltar:* Commonwealth Day.

10 **Tue.** *South Korea:* Labor Day.

11 **Wed.** *Lithuania:* National Day*.

12 **Thu.** *Lesotho:* Moshoeshoe's Day. *Mauritius:* Independence Day.

13 **Fri.** *Grenada:* National Day.

14 **Sat.** *Zambia:* Youth Day.

17 **Tue.** *Ireland:* Saint Patrick's Day. *Northern Ireland:* Saint Patrick's Day.

19 **Thu.** *Christian:* Saint Joseph's Day (see App. A5).

20 **Fri.** *Tunisia:* Independence Day. *Zodiac Cusp:* Pisces ends, Aries begins.

21 **Sat.** *Afghanistan:* New Year's Day (Shamsi: 1394). *Iran:* New Year's Day (Hegira: 1394). *Iraq:* Independence Day. *Japan:* Vernal Equinox. *Mexico:* Juarez Day.

22 **Sun.** *Puerto Rico:* Abolition Day.

23 **Mon.** *Pakistan:* Pakistan Day.

24 **Tue.** *Zambia:* Africa Day.

25 **Wed.** *Cyprus:* Greek Independence Day. *Greece:* Independence Day. *Liechtenstein:* Annunciation.

26 **Thu.** *Bangladesh:* Independence Day.

27 **Fri.** *Angola:* Evacuation Day. *Burma:* Resistance Day.

29 **Sun.** *Central African Republic:* Boganda Day. *Madagascar:* Memorial. *Taiwan:* Youth Day. *Christian:* Palm Sunday. *Europe:* Daylight Savings Time starts (advance clocks 1 hour).

30 **Mon.** *Virgin Islands (U.S.):* Transfer Day.

31 **Tue.** *Malta:* National Day.

# April 2015

1 **Wed.** *Iran:* Republic Day. *San Marino:* National Day.

2 **Thu.** *Christian:* Maundy Thursday (see App. B11).

3 **Fri.** *Burma:* Full Moon Day. *Sierra Leone:* Bank Holiday. *Sri Lanka:* Full Moon Poya. *Christian:* Good Friday (see App. B12).

4 **Sat.** *Hungary:* Liberation Day. *Israel:* Passover. *Senegal:* National Day. *Christian:* Holy Saturday (see App. B13). *Jewish:* Passover.

5 **Sun.** *South Korea:* Arbor Day. *Asian:* Tomb Sweeping Day (see App. A6). *Canada and United States:* Daylight Savings Time starts (advance clocks 1 hour). *Christian:* Easter Sunday (see App. B14).

6 **Mon.** *South Africa:* Founders' Day. *Thailand:* Chakri Day. *Christian:* Easter Monday (see App. B15).

9 **Thu.** *Philippines:* Valour Day. *Tunisia:* Martyrs' Day.

10 **Fri.** *Orthodox:* Good Friday (see App. B20).

11 **Sat.** *Costa Rica:* Heroes' Day. *Uganda:* Liberation Day.

12 **Sun.** *Jordan:* Easter Sunday. *Orthodox:* Easter Sunday.

13 **Mon.** *Chad:* National Day. *Thailand:* Songkrawn (1st day of 2). *Orthodox:* Easter Monday (see App. B20).

14 **Tue.** *Honduras:* Pan American Day. *Thailand:* Songkrawn (2nd day of 2).

15 **Wed.** *Niger:* National Day.

16 **Thu.** *Burma:* New Year's Day (Burmese: 1377). *Cyprus:* Independence Day.

17 **Fri.** *Cambodia:* Independence Day. *Syria:* Independence Day.

18 **Sat.** *Zimbabwe:* Republic Day.

19 **Sun.** *Sierra Leone:* Republic Day. *Uruguay:* Patriots' Day. *Venezuela:* Independence Day.

20 **Mon.** *Zodiac Cusp:* Aries ends, Taurus begins.

21 **Tue.** *Brazil:* Tiradentes Day.

23 **Thu.** *Israel:* Independence Day. *Turkey:* Children's Day.

25 **Sat.** *Australia:* ANZAC Day. *Egypt:* Sinai Day. *Iceland:* Children's Day. *Italy:* Liberation Day.

*New Zealand:* ANZAC Day. *Portugal:* Liberation Day. *Swaziland:* Flag Day.

**26 Sun.** *Tanzania:* Union Day.

**27 Mon.** *Afghanistan:* Independence Day. *Sierra Leone:* Independence Day. *Togo:* Independence Day.

**29 Wed.** *Japan:* Green Day.

**30 Thu.** *Finland:* Vappu Day. *Netherlands:* Queen's Birthday.

# May 2015

**1 Fri.** *Denmark:* All Prayers' Day. *Multinational:* Labor Day (see App. A7).

**2 Sat.** *Burma:* Full Moon Day. *Lesotho:* King's Birthday.

**3 Sun.** *Japan:* Constitution Day. *Sri Lanka:* Full Moon Poya.

**4 Mon.** *Japan:* People's Day. *United Kingdom:* Labour Day. *Zambia:* Labour Day.

**5 Tue.** *Japan:* Children's Day. *Mexico:* Cinco de Mayo. *Netherlands:* Liberation Day. *South Korea:* Children's Day. *Thailand:* Coronation Day.

**6 Wed.** *Lebanon:* Martyrs' Day. *Philippines:* Corregidor Day.

**8 Fri.** *France:* Liberation Day.

**9 Sat.** *Czech Republic:* Liberation Day*. *Slovakia:* Liberation Day*.

**10 Sun.** *Micronesia:* Independence Day. *International:* Mother's Day.

**14 Thu.** *Liberia:* Unification Day. *Malawi:* Kamuzu Day. *Paraguay:* Flag Day. *Christian:* Ascension (see App. B16). *Islamic:* Isra a Majraj (see App. B30).

**15 Fri.** *Paraguay:* Independence Day.

**17 Sun.** *Cayman Islands:* Discovery Day. *Norway:* Constitution Day.

**18 Mon.** *Canada:* Victoria Day. *Haiti:* Flag Day. *Uruguay:* Las Piedras Day.

**19 Tue.** *Finland:* Flag Day. *Turkey:* Youth Day.

**20 Wed.** *Cameroon:* Constitution Day. *Zaïre:* Popular Movement Day.

**21 Thu.** *Chile:* Navy Day. *Zodiac Cusp:* Taurus ends, Gemini begins.

**22 Fri.** *Haiti:* Sovereign Day. *Sri Lanka:* Heroes' Day.

**23 Sat.** *Jamaica:* Labour Day.

**24 Sun.** *Bulgaria:* Culture Day. *Ecuador:* Independence Battle Day. *Israel:* Pentecost. *Christian:* Whitsunday. *Jewish:* Pentecost.

**25 Mon.** *Argentina:* National Day. *Eritrea:* Independence Day*. *Jordan:* Independence Day. *South Korea:* Vesak Day. *Sudan:* Revolution Day. *United Kingdom:* Spring Break. *United States:* Memorial Day. *Christian:* Whitmonday (see App. B18). *Multinational:* Africa Day (see App. A8).

**26 Tue.** *Guyana:* Independence Day.

**27 Wed.** *Nigeria:* Children's Day.

**31 Sun.** *Brunei:* Regiment Day. *South Africa:* Republic Day. *Orthodox:* Pentecost Sunday.

# June 2015

**1 Mon.** *Burma:* Full Moon Day. *Greece:* Pentecost Monday. *Ireland:* Public Holiday. *Kenya:* Madaraka Day. *Malaysia:* Vesak Day. *New Zealand:* Queen's Birthday. *Singapore:* Vesak Day. *Tunisia:* National Day. *Western Samoa:* Independence Day.

**2 Tue.** *Italy:* Republic Day. *Sri Lanka:* Full Moon Poya. *Thailand:* Visakha Bucha Day. *Tunisia:* Youth Day.

3 **Wed.** *Malaysia:* King's Birthday.
4 **Thu.** *Bahamas:* Labour Day. *Tonga:* Independence Day. *Christian:* Corpus Christi (see App. B19).
5 **Fri.** *Denmark:* Constitution Day. *Equatorial Guinea:* President's Birthday. *Seychelles:* Liberation Day.
6 **Sat.** *South Korea:* Memorial Day. *Sweden:* Constitution Day.
7 **Sun.** *Chad:* Revolution Day.
8 **Mon.** *Australia:* Queen's Birthday. *Fiji:* Queen's Birthday. *New Guinea:* Queen's Birthday. *United Kingdom:* Queen's Birthday.
9 **Tue.** *Argentina:* Independence Day.
10 **Wed.** *Macao:* Portugal Day. *Portugal:* Portugal Day.
11 **Thu.** *Libya:* Evacuation Day.
12 **Fri.** *Philippines:* Independence Day.
13 **Sat.** *Hong Kong:* Queen's Birthday (1st day of 2).
15 **Mon.** *Hong Kong:* Queen's Birthday (2nd day of 2).
16 **Tue.** *Islamic:* 1st Day of Ramadan (see App. B25).
17 **Wed.** *Germany:* Unity Day. *Iceland:* Independence Day.
18 **Thu.** *Egypt:* Independence Day.
19 **Fri.** *Algeria:* Righting Day. *Kuwait:* Independence Day. *Uruguay:* Artigas Day.
20 **Sat.** *Argentina:* Flag Day.
21 **Sun.** *Finland:* Midsummer Day (1st day of 2). *Sweden:* Midsummer Day (1st day of 2). *Zodiac Cusp:* Gemini ends, Cancer begins.
22 **Mon.** *Finland:* Midsummer Day (2nd day of 2). *Sweden:* Midsummer Day (2nd day of 2). *Asian:* Dragon Boat Festival (see App. B5).
23 **Tue.** *Luxembourg:* National Day.
24 **Wed.** *Andorra:* Saint John's Day. *Venezuela:* Carabobo Day. *Zaïre:* Constitution Day.
25 **Thu.** *Croatia:* Independence Day*. *Mozambique:* Independence Day. *Slovenia:* Independence Day*.
26 **Fri.** *Chile:* Bank Holiday. *Ecuador:* Bank Holiday. *El Salvador:* Bank Holiday. *Finland:* Bank Holiday. *Madagascar:* Independence Day. *Somalia:* Independence Day.
27 **Sat.** *Djibouti:* Independence Day. *Finland:* Johannus Day.
29 **Mon.** *Seychelles:* Independence Day. *Christian:* Saint Paul's Day (see App. A9).
30 **Tue.** *Burma:* Full Moon Day. *Guatemala:* Army Day. *Sri Lanka:* Bank Holiday. *Zaïre:* Independence Day.

# July 2015

1 **Wed.** *Burundi:* Independence Day. *Canada:* Canada Day. *Ghana:* Republic Day. *Hong Kong:* Half Year Day. *Rwanda:* Independence Day. *Somalia:* Union Day. *Sri Lanka:* Full Moon Poya. *Suriname:* Freedom Day. *Multinational:* Bank Holiday (see App. A10).
4 **Sat.** *Philippines:* United States Friendship Day. *United States:* Independence Day. *Yugoslavia:* Freedom Fighters' Day.
5 **Sun.** *Algeria:* Independence Day. *Cape Verde:* Independence Day. *Rwanda:* Unity Day. *Venezuela:* Independence Day.
6 **Mon.** *Cayman Islands:* Constitution Day. *Comoros:* Independence Day. *Lesotho:* Family Day. *Malawi:* Republic Day. *Zambia:* Heroes' Day.
7 **Tue.** *Solomon Islands:* Independence Day. *Tanzania:* Farmers' Day. *Yugoslavia:* Serbian Day. *Zambia:* Unity Day.
10 **Fri.** *Bahamas:* Independence Day.
11 **Sat.** *Mongolia:* Revolution Day.
12 **Sun.** *Kiribati:* Independence Day. *Northern Ireland:* Battle of the Boyne Day. *São Tomé:* National Day.
14 **Tue.** *France:* National Day. *Iraq:* Revolution Day.

**15 Wed.** *Brunei:* Sultan's Birthday.

**16 Thu.** *Far East Islamic:* Hari Raya Puasa (see App. B27). *Islamic:* Eid al Fitr (1st day of 4) (see App. B26).

**17 Fri.** *Iraq:* Revolution Day. *Puerto Rico:* Rivera Day. *Slovakia:* Independence Day*. *South Korea:* Constitution Day. *Islamic:* Eid al Fitr (2nd day of 4) (see App. B26).

**18 Sat.** *Uruguay:* Constitution Day. *Islamic:* Eid al Fitr (3rd day of 4) (see App. B26).

**19 Sun.** *Burma:* Martyrs' Day. *Laos:* Independence Day. *Nicaragua:* Sandinista Day. *Islamic:* Eid al Fitr (4th day of 4) (see App. B26).

**20 Mon.** *Botswana:* President's Day. *Colombia:* Independence Day.

**21 Tue.** *Belgium:* National Day. *Guam:* Liberation Day.

**22 Wed.** *Poland:* Liberation Day.

**23 Thu.** *Egypt:* Revolution Day. *New Guinea:* Remembrance Day. *Zodiac Cusp:* Cancer ends, Leo begins.

**24 Fri.** *Venezuela:* Bolivar Day.

**25 Sat.** *Costa Rica:* Guanacaste Day. *Cuba:* Revolution Day (1st day of 3). *Puerto Rico:* Constitution Day. *Spain:* Santiago Day. *Tunisia:* Republic Day.

**26 Sun.** *Cuba:* Revolution Day (2nd day of 3). *Israel:* Tisha Ab. *Liberia:* Independence Day. *Maldives:* Independence Day. *Jewish:* Tisha Ab.

**27 Mon.** *Cuba:* Revolution Day (3rd day of 3). *Puerto Rico:* Barbosa Day. *Virgin Islands (U.S.):* Hurricane Supplication Day.

**28 Tue.** *Peru:* Independence Day (1st day of 2).

**29 Wed.** *Burma:* Full Moon Day. *Peru:* Independence Day (2nd day of 2).

**30 Thu.** *Sri Lanka:* Full Moon Poya. *Vanuatu:* Independence Day.

**31 Fri.** *Thailand:* Asalaha Bucha Day.

# August 2015

**1 Sat.** *Benin:* Independence Day. *Switzerland:* Confederation Day. *Thailand:* Khao Phansa Day.

**2 Sun.** *Costa Rica:* Virgin of the Angels Day. *Guyana:* Freedom Day. *Trinidad:* Discovery Day.

**3 Mon.** *Bahamas:* Emancipation Day. *Barbados:* Emancipation Day. *Canada:* Civic Holiday. *El Salvador:* Summer Day (1st day of 4). *Guinea-Bissau:* Martyrs' Day. *Ireland:* Public Holiday. *Jamaica:* Independence Day. *Niger:* Independence Day. *Scotland:* Public Holiday. *Tunisia:* President's Birthday.

**4 Tue.** *Burkina Faso:* Independence Day (1st day of 2). *El Salvador:* Summer Day (2nd day of 4).

**5 Wed.** *Burkina Faso:* Independence Day (2nd day of 2). *El Salvador:* Summer Day (3rd day of 4). *Zambia:* Farmers' Day.

**6 Thu.** *Bolivia:* Independence Day. *El Salvador:* Summer Day (4th day of 4). *United Arab Emirates:* Accession Day.

**7 Fri.** *Colombia:* Boyaca Day. *Ivory Coast:* Republic Day.

**9 Sun.** *Georgia:* Independence Day*. *Singapore:* National Day.

**10 Mon.** *Ecuador:* Independence Day.

**11 Tue.** *Chad:* Independence Day. *Jordan:* Accession Day. *Zimbabwe:* Heroes' Day (1st day of 2).

**12 Wed.** *Thailand:* Queen's Birthday. *Zimbabwe:* Heroes' Day (2nd day of 2).

**13 Thu.** *Central African Republic:* Independence Day. *Congo:* Independence Day (1st day of 2). *Tunisia:* Women's Day.

**14 Fri.** *Congo:* Independence Day (2nd day of 2). *Pakistan:* Independence Day.

**15 Sat.** *Congo:* Independence Day

(3rd day of 3). *India:* Independence Day. *Liechtenstein:* National Day. *South Korea:* Republic Day. *Christian:* Assumption (see App. A11).

**16 Sun.** *Dominican Republic:* Republic Day.

**17 Mon.** *Argentina:* San Martin's Day. *Gabon:* Independence Day. *Indonesia:* Independence Day.

**20 Thu.** *Hungary:* Constitution Day. *Senegal:* Independence Day.

**21 Fri.** *Estonia:* Independence Day*. *Latvia:* Independence Day*. *Lithuania:* Independence Day*.

**23 Sun.** *Romania:* National Day (1st day of 2). *Zodiac Cusp:* Leo ends, Virgo begins.

**24 Mon.** *Kazakhstan:* National Day*. *Liberia:* Flag Day. *Romania:* National Day (2nd day of 2). *Russia:* Independence Day*. *Ukraine:* National Day*.

**25 Tue.** *Belarus:* Independence Day*. *Paraguay:* Constitution Day. *Uruguay:* Independence Day.

**27 Thu.** *Moldova:* Independence Day*.

**28 Fri.** *Burma:* Full Moon Day.

**29 Sat.** *Hong Kong:* Liberation Day (1st day of 2). *Sri Lanka:* Full Moon Poya. *Uzbekistan:* Independence Day*.

**30 Sun.** *Afghanistan:* Children's Day. *Azerbaijan:* Independence Day*. *Peru:* Rose of Lima Day. *Turkey:* Victory Day.

**31 Mon.** *Afghanistan:* Pashtunistan Day. *Kyrgyzstan:* Independence Day*. *England:* Summer Break. *Hong Kong:* Liberation Day (2nd day of 2). *Luxembourg:* Fair Day. *Malaysia:* National Day. *Northern Ireland:* Summer Break. *Trinidad:* Independence Day. *Wales:* Summer Break.

# September 2015

**1 Tue.** *Libya:* National Day. *Mexico:* President's Message Day. *Syria:* United Arab Republics Day.

**2 Wed.** *Vietnam:* Independence Day.

**3 Thu.** *Qatar:* National Day. *San Marino:* Saint Marinus' Day. *Tunisia:* Independence Movement Day.

**6 Sun.** *Pakistan:* Defense Day. *Swaziland:* Independence Day.

**7 Mon.** *Brazil:* Independence Day. *Canada:* Labour Day. *United States:* Labor Day.

**8 Tue.** *Andorra:* National Day. *Malta:* Our Lady of Victory Day.

**9 Wed.** *Bulgaria:* National Day (1st day of 2). *North Korea:* Independence Day. *Tajikistan:* Independence Day*.

**10 Thu.** *Belize:* National Day. *Bulgaria:* National Day (2nd day of 2).

**11 Fri.** *Chile:* Revolution Day. *Pakistan:* Anniversary of Quaid-e-Azam's Death.

**12 Sat.** *Egypt:* New Year's Day (Coptic: 1733). *Ethiopia:* National Day and New Year's Day (Ethiopian: 2009).

**14 Mon.** *Guatemala:* San Jacinto Day. *Israel:* New Year's Day. *Nicaragua:* San Jacinto Day. *Jewish:* Rosh Hashanah (Jewish: 5776).

**15 Tue.** *Costa Rica:* Independence Day. *El Salvador:* Independence Day. *Guatemala:* Independence Day. *Honduras:* Independence Day. *Japan:* Veneration Day. *Nicaragua:* Independence Day.

**16 Wed.** *Mexico:* Independence Day. *New Guinea:* Independence Day.

**17 Thu.** *Angola:* Heroes' Day. *Marshall Islands:* Independence Day.

**18 Fri.** *Burundi:* Victory of Uprona Day. *Chili:* Independence Day.

**19 Sat.** *Chile:* Armed Forces Day. *Saint Kitts:* Independence Day.

**21 Mon.** *Belize:* Independence Day. *Malta:* Independence Day.

**22 Tue.** *Mali:* Independence Day. *Islamic:* Eid al Adha (1st day of 4) (see App. B28).

**23 Wed.** *Armenia:* Independence Day*. *Israel:* Yom Kippur. *Japan:* Autumnal Equinox. *Saudi Arabia:* National Day. *Far East Islamic:* Hari Raya Haji (see App. B29). *Islamic:* Eid al Adha (2nd day of 4) (see App. B28). *Jewish:* Yom Kippur. *Zodiac Cusp:* Virgo ends, Libra begins.

**24 Thu.** *Dominican Republic:* Mercedes Day. *Guinea-Bissau:* Republic Day. *Islamic:* Eid al Adha (3rd day of 4) (see App. B28).

**25 Fri.** *Mozambique:* Liberation Day. *Rwanda:* Assembly Day. *Islamic:* Eid al Adha (4th day of 4) (see App. B28).

**26 Sat.** *Burma:* Full Moon Day.

**27 Sun.** *China:* Mid-autumn Day. *Ethiopia:* True Cross Day. *Sri Lanka:* Full Moon Poya. *Taiwan:* Mid-autumn Day. *Europe:* Daylight Savings Time ends (retard clocks 1 hour).

**28 Mon.** *Hong Kong:* Mid-autumn Day. *Israel:* Sukkot. *Macao:* Mid-autumn Day. *Taiwan:* Teachers' Day. *Jewish:* Sukkot.

**29 Tue.** *Brunei:* Constitution Day. *Paraguay:* Boqueron Battle Day.

**30 Wed.** *Botswana:* Independence Day.

# October 2015

**1 Thu.** *Cameroon:* Unification Day. *China:* National Day (1st day of 2). *Nigeria:* Independence Day. *South Korea:* Armed Forces Day (1st day of 2). *Tuvalu:* Independence Day.

**2 Fri.** *China:* National Day (2nd day of 2). *Guinea:* Independence Day. *India:* Ghandi Day. *South Korea:* Armed Forces Day (2nd day of 2).

**3 Sat.** *Honduras:* Morazan Day. *South Korea:* Foundation Day (1st day of 2).

**4 Sun.** *Lesotho:* Independence Day. *South Korea:* Foundation Day (2nd day of 2).

**5 Mon.** *Barbados:* Bank Holiday. *Lesotho:* Sports Day. *Macao:* Portuguese Republic Day. *Portugal:* Republic Day.

**6 Tue.** *Egypt:* Armed Forces Day.

**9 Fri.** *Peru:* National Dignity Day. *South Korea:* Alphabet Day. *Uganda:* Independence Day.

**10 Sat.** *Japan:* Health Day. *South Africa:* Kruger Day. *Taiwan:* National Day.

**11 Sun.** *Cuba:* Independence War. *Panama:* Revolution Day.

**12 Mon.** *Canada:* Thanksgiving Day. *Equatorial Guinea:* Independence Day. *Fiji:* Cession Day. *Spain:* National Day. *United States:* Bank Holiday. *Virgin Islands (U.S.):* Puerto Rican Friendship Day. *Multinational:* Columbus Day (see App. A12).

**13 Tue.** *Islamic:* New Year's Day (Hegira: 1437) (see App. B22).

**14 Wed.** *Zaïre:* Founders' Day. *Far East Islamic:* New Year's Day (Hegira: 1437).

**15 Thu.** *Bosnia and Herzegovina:* Independence Day*. *Tunisia:* Evacuation Day.

**17 Sat.** *Haiti:* Dessalines Day. *Malawi:* Mother's Day.

**19 Mon.** *Jamaica:* Heroes' Day.

**20 Tue.** *Guatemala:* Revolution Day. *Kenya:* Kenyatta Day.

**21 Wed.** *Honduras:* Army Day. *Somalia:* Revolution Day (1st day of 2).

**22 Thu.** *Somalia:* Revolution Day (2nd day of 2). *Vatican:* John Paul II Day. *Asian:* Ancestors' Day (see App. B6). *Islamic:* Ashura (see App. B23).

**23 Fri.** *Hungary:* Revolution Day. *Thailand:* Chulalongkorn Day. *Zodiac Cusp:* Libra ends, Scorpio begins.

**24 Sat.** *Egypt:* Suez Victory Day. *Haiti:* United Nations Day. *Zambia:* Independence Day.

**25 Sun.** *Taiwan:* Restoration Day. *Canada and United States:* Daylight

Savings Time ends (retard clocks 1 hour).

**26 Mon.** *Austria:* National Day. *Benin:* Revolution Day. *Burma:* Full Moon Day. *Ireland:* Public Holiday. *New Zealand:* Labour Day. *Rwanda:* Government Day. *Sri Lanka:* Full Moon Poya.

**27 Tue.** *Saint Vincent:* Independence Day. *Turkmenistan:* Independence Day*. *Zaïre:* Naming Day.

**28 Wed.** *Greece:* Ohi! Day.

**29 Thu.** *Tanzania:* Naming Day. *Turkey:* Republic Day.

**31 Sat.** *Taiwan:* Chiang Kai-shek's Birthday.

# November 2015

**1 Sun.** *Algeria:* Revolution Day. *Antigua:* Independence Day. *Christian:* All Saints' Day (see App. A13).

**2 Mon.** *Brazil:* Memorial Day. *Finland:* All Saints' Eve. *Sweden:* All Saints' Eve. *Virgin Islands (U.S.):* Liberty Day. *Christian:* All Souls' Day (see App. A14).

**3 Tue.** *Dominica:* Independence Day. *Ecuador:* Cuenca Independence Day. *Japan:* Culture Day. *Panama:* Independence Day.

**4 Wed.** *Andorra:* Saint Charles' Day. *Panama:* Flag Day. *Vatican:* John Paul II's Nameday.

**5 Thu.** *El Salvador:* Cry of Independence Day. *Liberia:* Thanksgiving Day.

**7 Sat.** *Bangladesh:* Revolution Day.

**8 Sun.** *Nepal:* Queen's Birthday.

**9 Mon.** *Pakistan:* Iqbal Day.

**10 Tue.** *Panama:* Cry of Independence Day. *Hindu:* Deepavali (see App. B21).

**11 Wed.** *Angola:* Independence Day. *Bhutan:* King's Birthday. *Maldives:* Republic Day. *Poland:* Independence Day. *Multinational:* Armistice Day (see App. A15).

**12 Thu.** *Taiwan:* Dr. Sun Yat-sen's Birthday.

**14 Sat.** *Jordan:* King's Birthday.

**15 Sun.** *Brazil:* Republic Day.

**16 Mon.** *Fiji:* Prince Charles' Birthday.

**17 Tue.** *Zaïre:* Armed Forces Day.

**18 Wed.** *Germany:* Repentance Day. *Haiti:* Vertieres' Day. *Morocco:* Independence Day. *Oman:* National Day.

**19 Thu.** *Belize:* Garifuna Day. *Mali:* Army Coup Day. *Monaco:* Prince Ranier's Day. *Puerto Rico:* Discovery Day.

**20 Fri.** *Mexico:* Revolution Day.

**22 Sun.** *Lebanon:* Independence Day. *Zodiac Cusp:* Scorpio ends, Sagittarius begins.

**23 Mon.** *Japan:* Labor Thanksgiving Day.

**24 Tue.** *Burma:* Full Moon Day. *Zaïre:* New Regime Day.

**25 Wed.** *Sri Lanka:* Full Moon Poya. *Suriname:* Independence Day.

**26 Thu.** *United States:* Thanksgiving Day.

**27 Fri.** *Argentina:* Bank Holiday.

**28 Sat.** *Albania:* Independence Day. *Burundi:* Republic Day. *Chad:* Republic Day. *Mauritania:* Independence Day. *Panama:* Independence Day.

**29 Sun.** *Albania:* Liberation Day. *Liberia:* Tubman's Birthday. *Yugoslavia:* Republic Day.

**30 Mon.** *Barbados:* Independence Day. *Benin:* National Day. *Philippines:* Heroes' Day.

# December 2015

**1 Tue.** *Central African Republic:* National Day. *Portugal:* Youth Day. *Ukraine:* Independence Day*.

**2 Wed.** *Laos:* Republic Day. *United*

*Arab Emirates:* National Day.

**5 Sat.** *Haiti:* Discovery Day. *Thailand:* King's Birthday.

**6 Sun.** *Finland:* Independence Day. *Jewish:* Chanukah.

**7 Mon.** *Ivory Coast:* Independence Day.

**8 Tue.** *Christian:* Immaculate Conception (see App. A16).

**9 Wed.** *Tanzania:* Independence Day.

**10 Thu.** *Angola:* MPLA Foundation Day. *Equatorial Guinea:* Human Rights Day. *Namibia:* Settlers' Day. *Thailand:* Constitution Day.

**11 Fri.** *Burkina Faso:* National Day.

**12 Sat.** *Kenya:* Independence Day. *Mexico:* Guadalupe Festival.

**13 Sun.** *Malta:* Republic Day.

**16 Wed.** *Bahrain:* National Day. *Bangladesh:* Victory Day. *Nepal:* Constitution Day. *South Africa:* Covenant Day.

**17 Thu.** *Bhutan:* National Day.

**18 Fri.** *Niger:* Republic Day.

**21 Mon.** *Kazakhstan:* Independence Day*.

**22 Tue.** *Islamic:* Mohammed's Birthday (see App. B24). *Zodiac Cusp:* Sagittarius ends, Capricorn begins.

**23 Wed.** *Burma:* Full Moon Day. *Japan:* Emperor's Birthday. *Far East Islamic:* Mohammed's Birthday.

**24 Thu.** *Sri Lanka:* Full Moon Poya. *Multinational:* Christmas Eve (see App. A17).

**25 Fri.** *Angola:* Family Day. *Congo:* Children's Day. *Pakistan:* Quaid's Birthday. *Taiwan:* Constitution Day. *Multinational:* Christmas Day (see App. A18).

**26 Sat.** *South Africa:* Good Will Day. *Multinational:* Boxing Day (see App. A19).

**28 Mon.** *Hong Kong:* Boxing Day.

**30 Wed.** *Madagascar:* Republic Day. *Philippines:* Rizal Day (1st day of 2).

**31 Thu.** *Congo:* Republic Day. *Philippines:* Rizal Day (2nd day of 2). *Multinational:* Bank Holiday and New Year's Eve (see App. A20 & A21).

# Appendix A: Fixed Multinational Holidays

## A1. New Year's Day
*(1st of January)*

Gregorian New Year, the start of the Gregorian year, is the most widely celebrated of the year's holidays—by 172 countries.

Albania
Algeria
Andorra
Angola
Antigua
Argentina
Armenia*
Aruba
Australia
Austria
Azerbaijan*
Bahamas
Bahrain
Barbados
Belgium
Belize
Belarus*
Benin
Bolivia
Bosnia and Herzegovina*
Botswana
Brunei
Bulgaria
Burkina Faso
Burundi
Cambodia
Canada
Cape Verde
Cayman Islands
Central African Republic
Chad
Chile
China
Colombia
Comoros
Congo
Costa Rica
Croatia*
Cyprus
Czech Republic*
Denmark
Djibouti
Dominica
Dominican Republic
Ecuador
El Salvador
Equatorial Guinea
Eritrea*
Estonia*
Fiji
Finland
France

*A1 continued*

Gabon
Gambia
Georgia*
Germany
Ghana
Gibraltar
Greece
Grenada
Guatemala
Guinea
Guinea-Bissau
Guyana
Honduras
Hong Kong†
Hungary
Iceland
India
Indonesia
Ireland
Israel
Italy
Ivory Coast
Jamaica
Japan
Jordan
Kazakhstan*
Kenya
Kiribati
Kuwait
Kyrgyzstan*
Laos
Latvia*
Lebanon
Lesotho
Liberia
Libya
Liechtenstein
Lithuania*
Luxembourg
Macao
Madagascar
Malawi
Malaysia
Maldives
Mali
Malta
Marshall Islands
Mauritania
Mauritius
Mexico
Micronesia
Moldova*
Monaco
Mongolia
Morocco
Mozambique
Nauru
Netherlands
New Guinea
New Zealand
Nicaragua
Niger
Nigeria
North Korea
Norway
Panama
Paraguay
Philippines
Peru
Poland
Portugal
Romania
Russia*
Rwanda
Saint Kitts
Saint Lucia
San Marino
Saint Vincent
São Tomé and Principe
Senegal
Seychelles
Sierra Leone
Singapore
Slovakia*
Slovenia*
Solomon Islands
South Africa
South Korea
Spain
Suriname
Swaziland
Sweden
Switzerland
Syria
Tajikistan*
Tanzania
Thailand§
Togo

Tonga
Trinidad and Tobago
Tunisia
Turkey
Turkmenistan*
Tuvalu
Uganda
United Kingdom
United Arab Emirates
United States
Ukraine*
Uruguay
Uzbekistan*
Vanuatu
Vatican
Venezuela
Vietnam
Yemeni Republic
Yugoslavia
Zaïre
Zambia
Zimbabwe

**Projected holiday.*
*†New Year's Day in Hong Kong is celebrated the first weekday of the new year.*
*§New Year's Day in Thailand has been adopted as the 1st of January for all secular purposes. But the year celebrated is the Pasah one. The Pasah year can be obtained from the Gregorian year by adding 543.*

# A2. Bank Holiday
## *(1st of January)*

Four countries post bank holidays on the first day of the year. The author recommends treating them as full holidays though. It is probably a matter of time (and a short one) before these countries join the foregoing list. They are:

Brazil
Iraq
Pakistan
Somalia

# A3. Epiphany
## *(6th of January)*

Also called Three King's Day, Epiphany marks the arrival of the Maji in Bethlehem according to the Christian faith, and the baptism of Christ according to the Eastern Orthodox faith. A holiday in:

Andorra
Argentina
Austria
Colombia
Cyprus
Equatorial Guinea
Finland
Germany
Greece
Italy
Liechtenstein
Malta
Puerto Rico
Spain
Sweden
Venezuela
Virgin Islands (U.S.)

# A4. Women's Day
*(8th of March)*

Afghanistan
Burkina Faso
Cape Verde
China
Guinea-Bissau
Mauritania
Nepal
Taiwan
Yemeni Republic

# A5. Saint Joseph's Day
*(19th of March)*

Joseph, the husband of Virgin Mary, is honored with a holiday in:

Andorra
Colombia
Costa Rica
Italy
Liechtenstein
Malta
San Marino
Spain
Switzerland
Vatican
Venezuela

# A6. Tomb Sweeping Day
*(5th of April)*

A day set aside to sweep, and otherwise maintain, the grave sites of ancestors. Honored in the four Confucian Asian countries:

China
Hong Kong
Macao
Taiwan

# A7. Labor Day
*(1st of May)*

Also known as May Day, it is set aside to honor the worker. It is the second most widely celebrated of the World's holidays. One hundred sixty-five countries celebrate it:

Afghanistan
Albania
Algeria
Andorra
Angola
Antigua
Argentina
Armenia*
Aruba
Austria
Azerbaijan*
Bahrain
Bangladesh
Barbados
Belarus*
Belgium
Belize
Benin
Bolivia
Bosnia and Herzegovina*
Brazil
Brunei
Bulgaria
Burkina Faso
Burma
Burundi
Cambodia
Cameroon
Cape Verde
Cayman Islands
Central African Republic
Chad
Chile
China
Colombia
Comoros
Congo
Costa Rica
Croatia*
Cuba
Cyprus
Czech Republic*
Djibouti
Dominica
Dominican Republic
Ecuador
Egypt
El Salvador
Equatorial Guinea
Eritrea*
Estonia*
Ethiopia
Fiji
Finland
France
Gabon
Gambia
Georgia*
Germany
Gibraltar
Greece
Grenada
Guatemala
Guinea
Guinea-Bissau
Guyana
Haiti
Honduras
Hungary
Iceland
Iran
Iraq
Italy
Ivory Coast
Jordan
Kazakhstan*
Kenya
Kiribati
Kuwait
Kyrgyzstan*
Laos
Latvia*
Lebanon
Liechtenstein
Lithuania*
Luxembourg
Macao
Malaysia
Mali
Malta
Moldova*
Marshall Islands
Mauritania
Mauritius
Mexico
Micronesia
Monaco
Mongolia
Morocco
Mozambique
Namibia
Nauru

*A7 continued*

Nepal
Nicaragua
Niger
Nigeria
North Korea
Norway
Oman
Pakistan
Palau
Panama
Paraguay
Peru
Philippines
Poland
Portugal
Qatar
Romania
Russia*
Rwanda
Saint Kitts
Saint Lucia
Saint Vincent
San Marino
São Tomé and Principe
Senegal
Seychelles
Singapore
Slovakia*
Slovenia*
Solomon Islands
Somalia
South Africa
Spain Western
Sri Lanka
Suriname
Swaziland
Sweden
Switzerland
Syria
Taiwan
Tajikistan*
Tanzania
Thailand
Togo
Tonga
Trinidad and Tobago
Tunisia
Turkmenistan*
Tuvalu
Uganda
Ukraine*
Uruguay
Uzbekistan*
Vanuatu
Vatican
Venezuela
Vietnam
Western Samoa
Yemeni Republic
Yugoslavia
Zaïre
Zambia
Zimbabwe

**Projected holiday.*

# A8. Africa Day
## *(25th of May)*

Central African Republic
Chad
Equatorial Guinea
Guinea
Liberia
Madagascar
Mali
Mauritania
Namibia
Zambia
Zimbabwe

# A9. Saint Paul's Day
## *(29th of June)*

Also known as Saints Peter's and Paul's Day, it remembers the martyrdom of two of the apostles of Christ. A holiday in:

Andorra
Chile
Colombia
Costa Rica
Ecuador
El Salvador
Guatemala
Italy
Malta
Peru
San Marino
Spain
Switzerland
Vatican
Venezuela

# A10. Bank Holiday
## *(1st of July)*

Egypt
Guatemala
Pakistan
Taiwan
Thailand

# A11. Assumption
## *(15th of August)*

Observed in commemoration of the taking up of the Virgin Mary into heaven according to the Christian faith. A holiday in:

Andorra
Austria
Belgium
Benin
Burkina Faso
Burundi
Cameroon
Chile
Costa Rica
Croatia*
France
Gabon
Gambia
Germany
Greece
Guatemala
Guinea
Haiti
Italy
Ivory Coast
Lebanon
Lithuania*
Luxembourg
Madagascar
Malta
Monaco

*All continued*

Nauru
Paraguay
Poland
Portugal
Rwanda
San Marino
Senegal
Slovenia*
Spain
Togo
Vatican
Venezuela

**Projected holiday.*

# A12. Columbus Day
## *(12th of October)*

Also known as Discoverer's or Discovery Day it marks landing of Christopher Columbus in the Bahamas in 1492. A holiday in:

Argentina
Bahamas
Belize
Bolivia
Brazil
Chile
Colombia
Costa Rica
Ecuador
El Salvador
Guatemala
Honduras
Mexico
Nicaragua
Paraguay
Puerto Rico
United States*
Uruguay
Venezuela

**Columbus Day in the United States is the second Monday in October, and is a bank and federal holiday only.*

# A13. All Saints' Day
## *(1st of November)*

A day set aside by the Christian faith to honor all the Saints canonized by the Christian Church. A holiday in:

Andorra
Argentina
Austria
Belgium
Benin
Bolivia
Burkina Faso
Burundi
Cameroon
Central African Republic
Chad
Chile
Colombia
Congo

Croatia*
Equatorial Guinea
Finland
France
Gabon
Germany
Guatemala
Guinea
Guyana
Haiti
Italy
Ivory Coast
Lebanon
Liberia
Liechtenstein
Lithuania*
Luxembourg
Madagascar
Malta
Mauritius
Mexico
Monaco
Namibia
Nicaragua
Paraguay
Peru
Philippines
Poland
Rwanda
San Marino
Senegal
Seychelles
Slovenia*
Spain
Sweden
Switzerland
Togo
Vatican
Venezuela
Yugoslavia
Zaïre

**Projected holiday.*

# A14. All Souls' Day
## *(2nd of November)*

The Christian equivalent of the Confucian Ancestor Day, All Souls' day honors the souls of the dead. A holiday in:

Belgium
Bolivia
Ecuador
El Salvador
France
Haiti
Luxembourg
Macao
Mexico
San Marino
Uruguay
Vatican

# A15. Armistice Day
## *(11th of November)*

Also known as Veteran's Day, it commemorates the signing of the armistice that ended World War I. A holiday in:

*A15 continued*

Belgium
Bermuda
Canada
El Salvador
France
Macao
Mexico
San Marino
United States
Vatican

## A16. Immaculate Conception
### *(8th of December)*

One of the precepts of Roman Catholicism, the 8th of December commemorates the conception of Christ by the Virgin Mary. Celebrated in:

Andorra
Argentina
Austria
Chile
Colombia
Costa Rica
Croatia*
Equatorial Guinea
Guam
Italy
Lebanon
Liechtenstein
Lithuania*
Macao
Malta
Monaco
Nicaragua
Panama
Paraguay
Peru
Puerto Rico
Seychelles
Slovenia*
Spain
Sweden
Vatican
Venezuela

**Projected holiday.*

## A17. Christmas Eve
### *(24th of December)*

Andorra
Austria
Brazil
Costa Rica
Croatia*
Czech Republic*
Denmark
El Salvador
Finland
France
Germany
Guatemala
Iceland
Italy
Ivory Coast
Liechtenstein
Lithuania*
Luxembourg
Macao
Madagascar

Monaco
Nicaragua
Norway
Panama
Portugal
San Marino
Slovakia*
Slovenia*
Sweden
Switzerland
Uruguay
Vatican
Venezuela

**Projected holiday.*

# A18. Christmas Day
## *(25th of December)*

Christmas commemorates the birth of Christ and is honored in one hundred forty-seven countries:

Andorra
Antigua
Argentina
Armenia*
Aruba
Australia
Austria
Azerbaijan*
Bahamas
Bangladesh
Barbados
Belarus*
Belgium
Belize
Benin
Bolivia
Bosnia and Herzegovina*
Botswana
Brazil
Brunei
Burkina Faso
Burma
Burundi
Cameroon
Canada
Cape Verde
Cayman Islands
Central African Republic
Chad
Chile
Colombia
Costa Rica
Croatia*
Cyprus
Czech Republic*
Denmark
Dominica
Dominican Republic
Ecuador
El Salvador
Equatorial Guinea
Eritrea*
Estonia*
Fiji
Finland
France
Gabon
Gambia
Georgia*
Germany
Ghana
Gibraltar
Greece
Grenada
Guatemala
Guyana
Haiti
Honduras
Hong Kong
Iceland

*A18 continued*

India
Indonesia
Ireland
Italy
Ivory Coast
Jamaica
Jordan
Kazakhstan*
Kenya
Kiribati
Kyrgyzstan*
Latvia*
Lebanon
Lesotho
Liberia
Liechtenstein
Lithuania*
Luxembourg
Macao
Madagascar
Malawi
Malaysia
Mali
Malta
Marshall Islands
Mauritius
Mexico
Micronesia
Moldova*
Monaco
Morocco
Nauru
Netherlands
New Guinea
New Zealand
Nicaragua
Niger
Nigeria
Norway
Palau
Panama
Paraguay
Peru
Philippines
Poland
Portugal
Russia*
Rwanda
Saint Kitts
Saint Lucia
Saint Vincent
San Marino
São Tomé and Principe
Senegal
Sierra Leone
Singapore
Slovakia*
Slovenia*
Solomon Islands
South Africa
South Korea
Spain
Sri Lanka
Sudan
Suriname
Swaziland
Sweden
Switzerland
Syria
Tanzania
Togo
Tonga
Trinidad and Tobago
Turkmenistan*
Tuvalu
Uganda
Ukraine*
United Kingdom
United States
Uruguay
Vanuatu
Vatican
Venezuela
Western Samoa
Zaïre
Zambia
Zimbabwe

**Projected holiday.*

# A19. Boxing Day
## *(26th of December)*

Variously celebrated as a day in honor of Saint Stephen or service workers, the day after Christmas in a holiday in:

Andorra
Australia
Austria
Bahamas
Barbados
Belgium
Belize
Botswana
Canada
Cyprus
Czech Republic*
Denmark
Ecuador
Fiji
Finland
Gabon
Gambia
Germany
Ghana
Gibraltar
Greece
Grenada
Guatemala
Guyana
Hong Kong†
Iceland
Ireland
Italy
Jamaica
Kenya
Lesotho
Liechtenstein
Luxembourg
Macao
Malawi
Namibia
Netherlands
New Guinea
New Zealand
Nigeria
North Korea
Norway
Poland
San Marino
Sierra Leone
Slovakia*
Suriname
Swaziland
Sweden
Switzerland
Uganda
United Kingdom
Vatican
Zambia
Zimbabwe

**Projected holiday*
*†Boxing Day in Hong Kong is the first weekday after Christmas.*

# A20. Bank Holiday
## *(31st of December)*

Argentina
Chile
Colombia
Ecuador
El Salvador
Guatemala
Honduras
Mexico
Paraguay
Sri Lanka

# A21. New Year's Eve
*(31st of December)*

Albania
Benin
Brazil
Czech Republic*
Denmark
Finland
France
Germany
Iceland
Italy
Ivory Coast
Liechtenstein
Madagascar
Monaco
Nicaragua
Norway
Peru
San Marino
Slovakia*
Sweden
Thailand
Turkey
Vatican
Venezuela

**Projected holiday.*

# Appendix B: Algorithmic Holidays

## Asian

### B1. Chinese New Year Eve

*(1 day before Chinese New Year)*

Hong Kong
Macao
South Korea
Taiwan

### B2. Chinese New Year

*(see calendars for January and February or Table C1 in Appendix C)*

Chinese New Year is arguably the noisiest holiday listed in this book, but it's also a time for family get-togethers, paying off debts, honoring elders and children, visiting neighbors, getting your picture taken, and a myriad other more quiet customs. A holiday in:

Brunei
China
Hong Kong
Laos
Macao
Malaysia
Mauritius
Singapore
South Korea
Taiwan

## B3. Second Day of Chinese New Year

*(1 day after Chinese New Year)*

China
Hong Kong
Macao
Malaysia
Singapore
South Korea
Taiwan

## B4. Third Day of Chinese New Year

*(2 days after Chinese New Year)*

China
Singapore
Taiwan

## B5. Dragon Boat Festival

*(6th day of the 4th moon after Chinese New Year)*

*(see calendars for May and June)*

Tuen Ng in romanized Mandarin Chinese, it commemorates the search for the body of a 3rd century Chinese poet/statesman in Tungting Lake. A festival in name only, it's a holiday in:

China
Hong Kong
Macao
Taiwan

## B6. Ancestors' Day

*(9th day of the 8th moon after Chinese New Year)*

*(see calendars for September and October)*

Chung Yeung in Mandarin, a holiday in:

China
Hong Kong
Macao
Taiwan

# Christian

## B7. Shrove Monday

*(48 days before Easter)*

*(see calendars for February and March)*

The second day of the three-day, pre–Lenten, Shrove-tide; Shrove Monday is observed as a holiday in:

Andorra
Argentina
Bolivia
Brazil
Colombia
Ecuador
Panama
Portugal
Uruguay
Vatican
Venezuela

## B8. Shrove Tuesday

*(47 days before Easter)*

*(see calendars for February and March)*

Andorra
Argentina
Bolivia
Brazil
Colombia
Ecuador
Haiti
Liechtenstein
Panama
Portugal
Uruguay
Venezuela

## B9. Ash Wednesday

*(46 days before Easter)*

*(see calendars for February and March or Table C2 in Appendix C)*

The first day of Lent according to the Christian Faith. In:

Brazil
Colombia
Jamaica
Panama
Venezuela

## B10. Palm Sunday
*(7 days before Easter)*
*(see calendars for March and April)*

Palm Sunday commemorates Christ's entry into Jerusalem. Although not a holiday, Palm Sunday is honored in Christian countries, and those having a large Christian population.

## B11. Maundy Thursday
*(3 days before Easter)*
*(see calendars for March and April)*

Observed in commemoration of the day of the institution of the Eucharist (the Last Supper). A holiday in:

Andorra
Argentina
Bolivia
Brazil
Colombia
Costa Rica
Denmark
Ecuador
El Salvador
Finland
Guatemala
Haiti
Honduras
Iceland
Mexico
Nicaragua
Nigeria
Norway
Panama
Paraguay
Peru
Philippines
Portugal
Spain
Sweden
Trinidad and Tobago
Uruguay
Vatican
Venezuela

## B12. Good Friday
*(2 days before Easter)*
*(see calendars for March and April or Table C2 in Appendix C)*

Good Friday is observed as the anniversary of the crucifixion of Christ. A holiday in:

Andorra
Argentina
Armenia*
Aruba
Australia
Bahamas
Barbados
Belarus*
Belize
Bolivia
Botswana
Brazil
Brunei
Cameroon
Canada
Central African Republic
Chile
Colombia
Costa Rica
Croatia*
Denmark
Dominican Republic
Ecuador
El Salvador
Equatorial Guinea
Estonia*
Fiji
Finland
France
Gambia
Germany
Ghana
Gibraltar
Greece
Grenada
Guam
Guatemala
Guyana
Haiti
Honduras
Hong Kong
Iceland
India
Ireland
Jamaica
Kenya
Latvia*
Lebanon
Lesotho
Liberia
Liechtenstein
Lithuania*
Macao
Madagascar
Malawi
Malta
Mexico
Moldova*
Monaco
Netherlands
New Guinea
New Zealand
Nicaragua
Niger
Nigeria
Norway
Panama
Paraguay
Peru
Philippines
Portugal
Puerto Rico
Sierra Leone
Singapore
Slovenia*
South Africa
Spain
Sri Lanka
Suriname
Swaziland
Sweden
Switzerland
Syria
Tanzania
Uganda
United Kingdom
Uruguay
Vatican
Venezuela
Zambia
Zimbabwe

**Projected holiday.*

# B13. Holy Saturday
*(1 day before Easter)*

Armenia*
Australia
Bahamas
Belarus*
Botswana
Brazil
Brunei
Chile
Colombia
Costa Rica
Croatia*
Czech Republic*
Estonia*
Fiji
Guatemala
Guinea
Hong Kong
Iceland
Latvia*
Lithuania*
Macao
Malawi
Malta
Mexico
Moldova*
Nigeria
Panama
Seychelles
Slovakia*
Slovenia*
Spain
Swaziland
Uganda
Uruguay
Vatican
Zambia
Zimbabwe

**Projected holiday.*

# B14. Easter Sunday
*(see calendars for March and April or Table C2 in Appendix C)*

Easter marks the Resurrection of Christ, and is the keystone of the Christian Faith. Although not a holiday, as such, Easter is celebrated in all Christian countries, and those with a large Christian population. Since Easter is a Sunday, the day of rest in most countries—banks, businesses, and schools are closed anyway. Several countries post their national holiday as EASTER MONDAY, and those are tabulated in the next section. Three countries do not fit that description. Their day of rest is on Friday, so for them Easter is a true holiday. They are:

Indonesia
Jordan
Turkey

# B15. Easter Monday

*(1 day after Easter)*

*(see calendars for March and April)*

Andorra
Armenia*
Australia
Austria
Bahamas
Barbados
Belarus*
Belgium
Belize
Benin
Botswana
Burkina Faso
Burundi
Cameroon
Canada
Central African Republic
Chad
Congo
Croatia*
Czech Republic*
Denmark
England
Equatorial Guinea
Estonia*
Fiji
Finland
France
Gabon
Germany
Ghana
Gibraltar
Greece
Grenada
Guyana
Hong Kong
Iceland
India
Ireland
Italy
Ivory Coast
Jamaica
Kenya
Latvia*
Lebanon
Lesotho
Liechtenstein
Lithuania*
Luxembourg
Macao
Madagascar
Malawi
Mali
Moldova*
Monaco
Namibia
Netherlands
New Guinea
New Zealand
Niger
Nigeria
Northern Ireland
Norway
Poland
Rwanda
Senegal
Sierra Leone
Slovakia*
Slovenia*
South Africa
Spain
Sri Lanka
Suriname
Swaziland
Sweden
Switzerland
Tanzania
Togo
Trinidad and Tobago
Uganda
Uruguay
Vatican
Wales
Zaïre
Zambia
Zimbabwe

**Projected holiday.*

# B16. Ascension Thursday

*(39 days after Easter)*

*(see calendars for May and June or Table C2 in Appendix C)*

Ascension is named in commemoration of Christ's ascension into heaven and is observed as a holiday in:

Austria
Andorra
Belgium
Benin
Botswana
Burkina Faso
Burundi
Central African Republic
Cameroon
Chad
Colombia
Congo
Denmark
Equatorial Guinea
France
Finland
Gabon
Germany
Haiti
Iceland
Indonesia
Ivory Coast
Italy
Lebanon
Lesotho
Liechtenstein
Luxembourg
Madagascar
Malta
Monaco
Morocco
Namibia
Netherlands
Norway
Rwanda
Senegal
South Africa
Spain
Swaziland
Sweden
Switzerland
Syria
Togo
Vatican
Venezuela
Zaïre

# B17. Whitsunday

*(49 days after Easter)*

*(see calendars for May and June or Table C2 in Appendix C)*

Also called Pentecost, Whitsunday is commemorated as the beginning of the Christian Church. Although not a holiday, as such, Whitsunday is honored in Christian countries, and those having a large Christian population. Since Whitsunday falls on the day of rest in most countries—banks, businesses, and schools are closed anyway. Several countries post their national holiday as Whitmonday. Those are tabulated in the next section.

# B18. Whitmonday

## *(50 Days after Easter)*

*(see calendars for May and June)*

Andorra
Austria
Bahamas
Barbados
Belgium
Benin
Botswana
Burkina Faso
Cameroon
Canada
Central African Republic
Chad
Congo
Denmark
Finland
France
Gabon
Germany
Grenada
Iceland
Indonesia
Ireland
Ivory Coast
Liechtenstein
Luxembourg
Madagascar
Malta
Monaco
Morocco
Namibia
Netherlands
New Zealand
Norway
Rwanda
Senegal
Sierra Leone
Sweden
Switzerland
Trinidad and Tobago
Zambia

# B19. Corpus Christi

## *(60 days after Easter)*

*(see calendars for May and June or Table C2 in Appendix C)*

The last holiday of the Christian Easter cycle, Corpus Christi, Latin for "the body of Christ," is a holiday in:

Andorra
Austria
Bolivia
Brazil
Chile
Colombia
Costa Rica
Dominican Republic
El Salvador
Equatorial Guinea
Germany
Grenada
Haiti
Italy
Liechtenstein
Monaco
Paraguay
Poland
Portugal
Seychelles

*B19 continued*

Spain
Switzerland
Trinidad and Tobago
Vatican
Venezuela

# Orthodox

## B20. Good Friday

*(2 days before Orthodox Easter)*

## Easter Monday

*(1 day after Orthodox Easter)*

*(see calendars for March and April or Table C3 in Appendix C)*

Only a handful of Mediterranean countries presently celebrate the Orthodox Church's religious holidays. Those celebrating both Good Friday and Easter Monday are:

Greece
Jordan
Lebanon

# Hindu

## B21. Deepavali

*(see calendars for October and November or Table C4 in Appendix C)*

Deepavali, called the Hindu Festival of Lights, and likened to Chanukah and Christmas, is honored in:

India*
Malaysia
Mauritius*
Singapore
Sri Lanka

**Dates of Deepavali in India and Mauritius may be one day later than that shown on the calendars in the eastern parts of those countries.*

# Islamic

## B22. New Year

*(see calendars or Table C5 in Appendix C)*

Afghanistan
Algeria
Azerbaijan*
Bahrain
Bangladesh
Brunei
Comoros
Djibouti
Egypt
Eritrea*
Gambia
Guinea
India
Indonesia
Iran
Iraq
Jordan
Kuwait
Lebanon
Libya
Malaysia
Maldives
Mali
Mauritania
Morocco
Niger
Oman
Pakistan
Qatar
Saudi Arabia
Senegal
Somalia
Sudan
Syria
Tajikistan*
Tunisia
Turkey
United Arab Emirates
Uzbekistan*
Yemeni Republic

*Projected holiday.*

## B23. Ashura

*(see calendars or Table C5 in Appendix C)*

Ashura is observed in commemoration of the end of the flood in the time of Noah mentioned in the Old Testament in:

Afghanistan
Algeria
Bahrain
Iran
Iraq
Lebanon
Libya
Morocco
Pakistan
Syria
Yemeni Republic

# B24. Mohammed's Birthday

*(see calendars or Table C5 in Appendix C)*

The birthday of the Prophet Mohammed is celebrated in:

Afghanistan
Algeria
Azerbaijan*
Bahrain
Bangladesh
Brunei
Burkina Faso
Chad
Comoros
Cyprus
Djibouti
Egypt
Eritrea*
Ethiopia
Fiji
Gambia
Guinea
Guyana
Indonesia
Iran
Iraq
Jordan
Kuwait
Lebanon
Libya
Malaysia
Maldives
Mali
Mauritania
Mauritius
Morocco
Niger
Nigeria
Oman
Pakistan
Saudi Arabia
Senegal
Sierra Leone
Somalia
Sri Lanka
Sudan
Syria
Tajikistan*
Tanzania
Tunisia
Turkey
United Arab Emirates
Uzbekistan*
Yemeni Republic

**Projected holiday.*

# B25. 1st Day of Ramadan

*(see calendars)*

The beginning of the Holy Month of Ramadan, during which the adherents of Islam fast during daylight hours is a holiday in:

Afghanistan
Azerbaijan*
Benin
Eritrea*
Maldives
Pakistan
Saudi Arabia
Tajikistan*
Uzbekistan*

**Projected holiday.*

# B26. Eid al Fitr

*(see calendars or Table C5 in Appendix C)*

Known as Hari Raya Puasa in the Far East (*see* next Table), the end of fasting during the Islamic month of Ramadan is celebrated as a holiday in:

Afghanistan
Algeria
Azerbaijan*
Bahrain
Bangladesh
Benin
Burkina Faso
Burma
Cameroon
Chad
Comoros
Cyprus
Djibouti
Egypt
Eritrea*
Ethiopia
Gabon
Gambia
Guinca
India
Iran
Iraq
Ivory Coast
Jordan
Kenya
Kuwait
Lebanon
Libya
Maldives
Mali
Mauritania
Mauritius
Morocco
Niger
Nigeria
Oman
Pakistan
Qatar
Saudi Arabia
Senegal
Sierra Leone
Somalia
Sri Lanka
Sudan
Syria
Tajikistan*
Tanzania
Trinidad
Tunisia
Turkey
Uganda
United Arab Emirates
Uzbekistan*
Yemeni Republic

**Projected holiday.*

# B27. Hari Raya Puasa

*(see calendars)*

Brunei
Indonesia
Malaysia
Singapore

# B28. Eid al Adha

*(see calendars or Table C5 in Appendix C)*

Known as Hari Raya Haji in the Far East (*see* next Table), it is observed in commemoration of Abraham sending his son Ishmael into the desert, one of the precepts of Islam. A holiday in:

Afghanistan
Algeria
Azerbaijan*
Bahrain
Bangladesh
Benin
Burkina Faso
Cameroon
Chad
Comoros
Cyprus
Djibouti
Egypt
Eritrea*
Gambia
Guinea
Guyana
India
Iran
Iraq
Jordan
Kenya
Kuwait
Lebanon
Libya
Maldives
Mali
Mauritania
Mauritius
Morocco
Niger
Nigeria
Oman
Pakistan
Qatar
Saudi Arabia
Senegal
Sierra Leone
Somalia
Sri Lanka
Sudan
Syria
Tanzania
Tajikistan*
Tunisia
Turkey
United Arab Emirates
Uzbekistan*
Yemeni Republic

**Projected holiday.*

# B29. Hari Raya Haji

*(see calendars)*

Brunei
Indonesia
Malaysia
Singapore

# B30. Isra a Majraj

*(see calendars or Table C5 in Appendix C)*

Observed in commemoration of the night journey of Mohammed to heaven, one of the precepts of Islam. Isra a Majraj is a holiday in:

- Brunei
- Djibouti
- Indonesia
- Jordan
- Kuwait
- Libya
- Oman
- United Arab Emirates
- Yemeni Republic

# Appendix C: Table of Dates for Selected Algorithmic Holidays (1900 to 2100)

## C1. Chinese New Year

| *Year* | *Date* | *Animal* | *Year* | *Date* | *Animal* |
|---|---|---|---|---|---|
| 1900 | 31 Jan. | rat | 1926 | 13 Feb. | tiger |
| 1901 | 19 Feb. | ox | 1927 | 2 Feb. | hare |
| 1902 | 8 Feb. | tiger | 1928 | 23 Jan. | dragon |
| 1903 | 29 Jan. | hare | 1929 | 10 Feb. | snake |
| 1904 | 16 Feb. | dragon | 1930 | 30 Jan. | horse |
| 1905 | 4 Feb. | snake | 1931 | 17 Feb. | sheep |
| 1906 | 25 Jan. | horse | 1932 | 6 Feb. | monkey |
| 1907 | 13 Feb. | sheep | 1933 | 26 Jan. | rooster |
| 1908 | 2 Feb. | monkey | 1934 | 14 Feb. | dog |
| 1909 | 22 Jan. | rooster | 1935 | 4 Feb. | pig |
| 1910 | 10 Feb. | dog | 1936 | 24 Jan. | rat |
| 1911 | 30 Jan. | pig | 1937 | 11 Feb. | ox |
| 1912 | 18 Feb. | rat | 1938 | 31 Jan. | tiger |
| 1913 | 6 Feb. | ox | 1939 | 19 Feb. | hare |
| 1914 | 26 Jan. | tiger | 1940 | 8 Feb. | dragon |
| 1915 | 14 Feb. | hare | 1941 | 27 Jan. | snake |
| 1916 | 4 Feb. | dragon | 1942 | 15 Feb. | horse |
| 1917 | 23 Jan. | snake | 1943 | 5 Feb. | sheep |
| 1918 | 11 Feb. | horse | 1944 | 25 Jan. | monkey |
| 1919 | 1 Feb. | sheep | 1945 | 13 Feb. | rooster |
| 1920 | 20 Feb. | monkey | 1946 | 2 Feb. | dog |
| 1921 | 8 Feb. | rooster | 1947 | 22 Jan. | pig |
| 1922 | 28 Jan. | dog | 1948 | 10 Feb. | rat |
| 1923 | 16 Feb. | pig | 1949 | 29 Jan. | ox |
| 1924 | 5 Feb. | rat | 1950 | 17 Feb. | tiger |
| 1925 | 24 Jan. | ox | 1951 | 6 Feb. | hare |

| *Year* | *Date* | *Animal* | *Year* | *Date* | *Animal* |
|---|---|---|---|---|---|
| 1952 | 27 Jan. | dragon | 2001 | 24 Jan. | snake |
| 1953 | 14 Feb. | snake | 2002 | 12 Feb. | horse |
| 1954 | 3 Feb. | horse | 2003 | 1 Feb. | sheep |
| 1955 | 24 Jan. | sheep | 2004 | 20 Feb. | monkey |
| 1956 | 12 Feb. | monkey | 2005 | 9 Feb. | rooster |
| 1957 | 31 Jan. | rooster | 2006 | 29 Jan. | dog |
| 1958 | 18 Feb. | dog | 2007 | 18 Feb. | pig |
| 1959 | 8 Feb. | pig | 2008 | 7 Feb. | rat |
| 1960 | 28 Jan. | rat | 2009 | 26 Jan. | ox |
| 1961 | 15 Feb. | ox | 2010 | 14 Feb. | tiger |
| 1962 | 5 Feb. | tiger | 2011 | 3 Feb. | hare |
| 1963 | 25 Jan. | hare | 2012 | 23 Jan. | dragon |
| 1964 | 13 Feb. | dragon | 2013 | 10 Feb. | snake |
| 1965 | 2 Feb. | snake | 2014 | 31 Jan. | horse |
| 1966 | 21 Jan. | horse | 2015 | 19 Feb. | sheep |
| 1967 | 9 Feb. | sheep | 2016 | 8 Feb. | monkey |
| 1968 | 30 Jan. | monkey | 2017 | 28 Jan. | rooster |
| 1969 | 17 Feb. | rooster | 2018 | 16 Feb. | dog |
| 1970 | 6 Feb. | dog | 2019 | 5 Feb. | pig |
| 1971 | 27 Jan. | pig | 2020 | 25 Jan. | rat |
| 1972 | 15 Feb. | rat | 2021 | 12 Feb. | ox |
| 1973 | 3 Feb. | ox | 2022 | 1 Feb. | tiger |
| 1974 | 23 Jan. | tiger | 2023 | 20 Feb. | hare |
| 1975 | 11 Feb. | hare | 2024 | 10 Feb. | dragon |
| 1976 | 31 Jan. | dragon | 2025 | 29 Jan. | snake |
| 1977 | 18 Feb. | snake | 2026 | 17 Feb. | horse |
| 1978 | 7 Feb. | horse | 2027 | 6 Feb. | sheep |
| 1979 | 28 Jan. | sheep | 2028 | 26 Jan. | monkey |
| 1980 | 16 Feb. | monkey | 2029 | 13 Feb. | rooster |
| 1981 | 5 Feb. | rooster | 2030 | 3 Feb. | dog |
| 1982 | 25 Jan. | dog | 2031 | 23 Jan. | pig |
| 1983 | 13 Feb. | pig | 2032 | 11 Feb. | rat |
| 1984 | 2 Feb. | rat | 2033 | 31 Jan. | ox |
| 1985 | 20 Feb. | ox | 2034 | 19 Feb. | tiger |
| 1986 | 9 Feb. | tiger | 2035 | 8 Feb. | hare |
| 1987 | 29 Jan. | hare | 2036 | 28 Jan. | dragon |
| 1988 | 17 Feb. | dragon | 2037 | 15 Feb. | snake |
| 1989 | 6 Feb. | snake | 2038 | 4 Feb. | horse |
| 1990 | 27 Jan. | horse | 2039 | 24 Jan. | sheep |
| 1991 | 15 Feb. | sheep | 2040 | 12 Feb. | monkey |
| 1992 | 4 Feb. | monkey | 2041 | 1 Feb. | rooster |
| 1993 | 23 Jan. | rooster | 2042 | 20 Feb. | dog |
| 1994 | 10 Feb. | dog | 2043 | 10 Feb. | pig |
| 1995 | 31 Jan. | pig | 2044 | 30 Jan. | rat |
| 1996 | 19 Feb. | rat | 2045 | 17 Feb. | ox |
| 1997 | 7 Feb. | ox | 2046 | 6 Feb. | tiger |
| 1998 | 28 Jan. | tiger | 2047 | 26 Jan. | hare |
| 1999 | 16 Feb. | hare | 2048 | 14 Feb. | dragon |
| 2000 | 5 Feb. | dragon | 2049 | 2 Feb. | snake |

*Cl continued*

| *Year* | *Date* | *Animal* | *Year* | *Date* | *Animal* |
|---|---|---|---|---|---|
| 2050 | 23 Jan. | horse | 2076 | 5 Feb. | monkey |
| 2051 | 11 Feb. | sheep | 2077 | 24 Jan. | rooster |
| 2052 | 1 Feb. | monkey | 2078 | 12 Feb. | dog |
| 2053 | 19 Feb. | rooster | 2079 | 2 Feb. | pig |
| 2054 | 8 Feb. | dog | 2080 | 21 Feb. | rat |
| 2055 | 28 Jan. | pig | 2081 | 9 Feb. | ox |
| 2056 | 15 Feb. | rat | 2082 | 29 Jan. | tiger |
| 2057 | 4 Feb. | ox | 2083 | 17 Feb. | hare |
| 2058 | 24 Jan. | tiger | 2084 | 6 Feb. | dragon |
| 2059 | 12 Feb. | hare | 2085 | 26 Jan. | snake |
| 2060 | 2 Feb. | dragon | 2086 | 14 Feb. | horse |
| 2061 | 20 Feb. | snake | 2087 | 3 Feb. | sheep |
| 2062 | 9 Feb. | horse | 2088 | 24 Jan. | monkey |
| 2063 | 29 Jan. | sheep | 2089 | 10 Feb. | rooster |
| 2064 | 17 Feb. | monkey | 2090 | 30 Jan. | dog |
| 2065 | 5 Feb. | rooster | 2091 | 18 Feb. | pig |
| 2066 | 26 Jan. | dog | 2092 | 7 Feb. | rat |
| 2067 | 14 Feb. | pig | 2093 | 27 Jan. | ox |
| 2068 | 3 Feb. | rat | 2094 | 15 Feb. | tiger |
| 2069 | 23 Jan. | ox | 2095 | 5 Feb. | hare |
| 2070 | 11 Feb. | tiger | 2096 | 25 Jan. | dragon |
| 2071 | 31 Jan. | hare | 2097 | 12 Feb. | snake |
| 2072 | 19 Feb. | dragon | 2098 | 1 Feb. | horse |
| 2073 | 7 Feb. | snake | 2099 | 20 Feb. | sheep |
| 2074 | 27 Jan. | horse | 2100 | 9 Feb. | monkey |
| 2075 | 15 Feb. | sheep | | | |

# C2. Christian

| *Year* | *Ash Wednesday* | *Good Friday* | *Easter Sunday* | *Ascension Thursday* | *Whit-sunday* | *Corpus Christi* |
|---|---|---|---|---|---|---|
| 1900 | 28 Feb. | 13 Apr. | 15 Apr. | 24 May | 3 June | 14 June |
| 1901 | 20 Feb. | 5 Apr. | 7 Apr. | 16 May | 26 May | 6 June |
| 1902 | 12 Feb. | 28 Mar. | 30 Mar. | 8 May | 18 May | 29 May |
| 1903 | 25 Feb. | 10 Apr. | 12 Apr. | 21 May | 31 May | 11 June |
| 1904 | 17 Feb. | 1 Apr. | 3 Apr. | 12 May | 22 May | 2 June |
| 1905 | 8 Mar. | 21 Apr. | 23 Apr. | 1 June | 11 June | 22 June |
| 1906 | 28 Feb. | 13 Apr. | 15 Apr. | 24 May | 3 June | 14 June |
| 1907 | 13 Feb. | 29 Mar. | 31 Mar. | 9 May | 19 May | 30 May |
| 1908 | 4 Mar. | 17 Apr. | 19 Apr. | 28 May | 7 June | 18 June |
| 1909 | 24 Feb. | 9 Apr. | 11 Apr. | 20 May | 30 May | 10 June |
| 1910 | 9 Feb. | 25 Mar. | 27 Mar. | 5 May | 15 May | 26 May |
| 1911 | 1 Mar. | 14 Apr. | 16 Apr. | 25 May | 4 June | 15 June |
| 1912 | 21 Feb. | 5 Apr. | 7 Apr. | 16 May | 26 May | 6 June |

| Year | Ash Wednesday | Good Friday | Easter Sunday | Ascension Thursday | Whit-sunday | Corpus Christi |
|---|---|---|---|---|---|---|
| 1913 | 5 Feb. | 21 Mar. | 23 Mar. | 1 May | 11 May | 22 May |
| 1914 | 25 Feb. | 10 Apr. | 12 Apr. | 21 May | 31 May | 11 June |
| 1915 | 17 Feb. | 2 Apr. | 4 Apr. | 13 May | 23 May | 3 June |
| 1916 | 8 Mar. | 21 Apr. | 23 Apr. | 1 June | 11 June | 22 June |
| 1917 | 21 Feb. | 6 Apr. | 8 Apr. | 17 May | 27 May | 7 June |
| 1918 | 13 Feb. | 29 Mar. | 31 Mar. | 9 May | 19 May | 30 May |
| 1919 | 5 Mar. | 18 Apr. | 20 Apr. | 29 May | 8 June | 19 June |
| 1920 | 18 Feb. | 2 Apr. | 4 Apr. | 13 May | 23 May | 3 June |
| 1921 | 9 Feb. | 25 Mar. | 27 Mar. | 5 May | 15 May | 26 May |
| 1922 | 1 Mar. | 14 Apr. | 16 Apr. | 25 May | 4 June | 15 June |
| 1923 | 14 Feb. | 30 Mar. | 1 Apr. | 10 May | 20 May | 31 May |
| 1924 | 5 Mar. | 18 Apr. | 20 Apr. | 29 May | 8 June | 19 June |
| 1925 | 25 Feb. | 10 Apr. | 12 Apr. | 21 May | 31 May | 11 June |
| 1926 | 17 Feb. | 2 Apr. | 4 Apr. | 13 May | 23 May | 3 June |
| 1927 | 2 Mar. | 15 Apr. | 17 Apr. | 26 May | 5 June | 16 June |
| 1928 | 22 Feb. | 6 Apr. | 8 Apr. | 17 May | 27 May | 7 June |
| 1929 | 13 Feb. | 29 Mar. | 31 Mar. | 9 May | 19 May | 30 May |
| 1930 | 5 Mar. | 18 Apr. | 20 Apr. | 29 May | 8 June | 19 June |
| 1931 | 18 Feb. | 3 Apr. | 5 Apr. | 14 May | 24 May | 4 June |
| 1932 | 10 Feb. | 25 Mar. | 27 Mar. | 5 May | 15 May | 26 May |
| 1933 | 1 Mar. | 14 Apr. | 16 Apr. | 25 May | 4 June | 15 June |
| 1934 | 14 Feb. | 30 Mar. | 1 Apr. | 10 May | 20 May | 31 May |
| 1935 | 6 Mar. | 19 Apr. | 21 Apr. | 30 May | 9 June | 20 June |
| 1936 | 26 Feb. | 10 Apr. | 12 Apr. | 21 May | 31 May | 11 June |
| 1937 | 10 Feb. | 26 Mar. | 28 Mar. | 6 May | 16 May | 27 May |
| 1938 | 2 Mar. | 15 Apr. | 17 Apr. | 26 May | 5 June | 16 June |
| 1939 | 2 Feb. | 7 Apr. | 9 Apr. | 18 May | 28 May | 8 June |
| 1940 | 7 Feb. | 22 Mar. | 24 Mar. | 2 May | 12 May | 23 May |
| 1941 | 26 Feb. | 11 Apr. | 13 Apr. | 22 May | 1 June | 12 June |
| 1942 | 18 Feb. | 3 Apr. | 5 Apr. | 14 May | 24 May | 4 June |
| 1943 | 10 Mar. | 23 Apr. | 25 Apr. | 3 June | 13 June | 24 June |
| 1944 | 23 Feb. | 7 Apr. | 9 Apr. | 18 May | 28 May | 8 June |
| 1945 | 14 Feb. | 30 Mar. | 1 Apr. | 10 May | 20 May | 31 May |
| 1946 | 6 Mar. | 19 Apr. | 21 Apr. | 30 May | 9 June | 20 June |
| 1947 | 19 Feb. | 4 Apr. | 6 Apr. | 15 May | 25 May | 5 June |
| 1948 | 11 Feb. | 26 Mar. | 28 Mar. | 6 May | 16 May | 27 May |
| 1949 | 2 Mar. | 15 Apr. | 17 Apr. | 26 May | 5 June | 16 June |
| 1950 | 22 Feb. | 7 Apr. | 9 Apr. | 18 May | 28 May | 8 June |
| 1951 | 7 Feb. | 23 Mar. | 25 Mar. | 3 May | 13 May | 24 May |
| 1952 | 27 Feb. | 11 Apr. | 13 Apr. | 22 May | 1 June | 12 June |
| 1953 | 18 Feb. | 3 Apr. | 5 Apr. | 14 May | 24 May | 4 June |
| 1954 | 3 Mar. | 16 Apr. | 18 Apr. | 27 May | 6 June | 17 June |
| 1955 | 23 Feb. | 8 Apr. | 10 Apr. | 19 May | 29 May | 9 June |
| 1956 | 15 Feb. | 30 Mar. | 1 Apr. | 10 May | 20 May | 31 May |
| 1957 | 6 Mar. | 19 Apr. | 21 Apr. | 30 May | 9 June | 20 June |
| 1958 | 19 Feb. | 4 Apr. | 6 Apr. | 15 May | 25 May | 5 June |
| 1959 | 11 Feb. | 27 Mar. | 29 Mar. | 7 May | 17 May | 28 May |
| 1960 | 2 Mar. | 15 Apr. | 17 Apr. | 26 May | 5 June | 16 June |

*C2 continued*

| *Year* | *Ash Wednesday* | *Good Friday* | *Easter Sunday* | *Ascension Thursday* | *Whit-sunday* | *Corpus Christi* |
|---|---|---|---|---|---|---|
| 1961 | 15 Feb. | 31 Mar. | 2 Apr. | 11 May | 21 May | 1 June |
| 1962 | 7 Mar. | 20 Apr. | 22 Apr. | 31 May | 10 June | 21 June |
| 1963 | 27 Feb. | 12 Apr. | 14 Apr. | 23 May | 2 June | 13 June |
| 1964 | 12 Feb. | 27 Mar. | 29 Mar. | 7 May | 17 May | 28 May |
| 1965 | 3 Mar. | 16 Apr. | 18 Apr. | 27 May | 6 June | 17 June |
| 1966 | 23 Feb. | 8 Apr. | 10 Apr. | 19 May | 29 May | 9 June |
| 1967 | 8 Feb. | 24 Mar. | 26 Mar. | 4 May | 14 May | 25 May |
| 1968 | 28 Feb. | 12 Apr. | 14 Apr. | 23 May | 2 June | 13 June |
| 1969 | 19 Feb. | 4 Apr. | 6 Apr. | 15 May | 25 May | 5 June |
| 1970 | 11 Feb. | 27 Mar. | 29 Mar. | 7 May | 17 May | 28 May |
| 1971 | 24 Feb. | 9 Apr. | 11 Apr. | 20 May | 30 May | 10 June |
| 1972 | 16 Feb. | 31 Mar. | 2 Apr. | 11 May | 21 May | 1 June |
| 1973 | 7 Mar. | 20 Apr. | 22 Apr. | 31 May | 10 June | 21 June |
| 1974 | 27 Feb. | 12 Apr. | 14 Apr. | 23 May | 2 June | 13 June |
| 1975 | 12 Feb. | 28 Mar. | 30 Mar. | 8 May | 18 May | 29 May |
| 1976 | 3 Mar. | 16 Apr. | 18 Apr. | 27 May | 6 June | 17 June |
| 1977 | 23 Feb. | 8 Apr. | 10 Apr. | 19 May | 29 May | 9 June |
| 1978 | 8 Feb. | 24 Mar. | 26 Mar. | 4 May | 14 May | 25 May |
| 1979 | 28 Feb. | 13 Apr. | 15 Apr. | 24 May | 3 June | 14 June |
| 1980 | 20 Feb. | 4 Apr. | 6 Apr. | 15 May | 25 May | 5 June |
| 1981 | 4 Mar. | 17 Apr. | 19 Apr. | 28 May | 7 June | 18 June |
| 1982 | 24 Feb. | 9 Apr. | 11 Apr. | 20 May | 30 May | 10 June |
| 1983 | 16 Feb. | 1 Apr. | 3 Apr. | 12 May | 22 May | 2 June |
| 1984 | 7 Mar. | 20 Apr. | 22 Apr. | 31 May | 10 June | 21 June |
| 1985 | 20 Feb. | 5 Apr. | 7 Apr. | 16 May | 26 May | 6 June |
| 1986 | 12 Feb. | 28 Mar. | 30 Mar. | 8 May | 18 May | 29 May |
| 1987 | 4 Mar. | 17 Apr. | 19 Apr. | 28 May | 7 June | 18 June |
| 1988 | 17 Feb. | 1 Apr. | 3 Apr. | 12 May | 22 May | 2 June |
| 1989 | 8 Feb. | 24 Mar. | 26 Mar. | 4 May | 14 May | 25 May |
| 1990 | 28 Feb. | 13 Apr. | 15 Apr. | 24 May | 3 June | 14 June |
| 1991 | 13 Feb. | 29 Mar. | 31 Mar. | 9 May | 19 May | 30 May |
| 1992 | 4 Mar. | 17 Apr. | 19 Apr. | 28 May | 7 June | 18 June |
| 1993 | 24 Feb. | 9 Apr. | 11 Apr. | 20 May | 30 May | 10 June |
| 1994 | 16 Feb. | 1 Apr. | 3 Apr. | 12 May | 22 May | 2 June |
| 1995 | 1 Mar. | 14 Apr. | 16 Apr. | 25 May | 4 June | 15 June |
| 1996 | 21 Feb. | 5 Apr. | 7 Apr. | 16 May | 26 May | 6 June |
| 1997 | 12 Feb. | 28 Mar. | 30 Mar. | 8 May | 18 May | 29 May |
| 1998 | 25 Feb. | 10 Apr. | 12 Apr. | 21 May | 31 May | 11 June |
| 1999 | 17 Feb. | 2 Apr. | 4 Apr. | 13 May | 23 May | 3 June |
| 2000 | 8 Mar. | 21 Apr. | 23 Apr. | 1 June | 11 June | 22 June |
| 2001 | 28 Feb. | 13 Apr. | 15 Apr. | 24 May | 3 June | 14 June |
| 2002 | 13 Feb. | 29 Mar. | 31 Mar. | 9 May | 19 May | 30 May |
| 2003 | 5 Mar. | 18 Apr. | 20 Apr. | 29 May | 8 June | 19 June |
| 2004 | 25 Feb. | 9 Apr. | 11 Apr. | 20 May | 30 May | 10 June |
| 2005 | 9 Feb. | 25 Mar. | 27 Mar. | 5 May | 15 May | 26 May |
| 2006 | 1 Mar. | 14 Apr. | 16 Apr. | 25 May | 4 June | 15 June |

| Year | *Ash Wednesday* | *Good Friday* | *Easter Sunday* | *Ascension Thursday* | *Whit-sunday* | *Corpus Christi* |
|---|---|---|---|---|---|---|
| 2007 | 21 Feb. | 6 Apr. | 8 Apr. | 17 May | 27 May | 7 June |
| 2008 | 6 Feb. | 21 Mar. | 23 Mar. | 1 May | 11 May | 22 May |
| 2009 | 25 Feb. | 10 Apr. | 12 Apr. | 21 May | 31 May | 11 June |
| 2010 | 17 Feb. | 2 Apr. | 4 Apr. | 13 May | 23 May | 3 June |
| 2011 | 9 Mar. | 22 Apr. | 24 Apr. | 2 June | 12 June | 23 June |
| 2012 | 22 Feb. | 6 Apr. | 8 Apr. | 17 May | 27 May | 7 June |
| 2013 | 13 Feb. | 29 Mar. | 31 Mar. | 9 May | 19 May | 30 May |
| 2014 | 5 Mar. | 18 Apr. | 20 Apr. | 29 May | 8 June | 19 June |
| 2015 | 18 Feb. | 3 Apr. | 5 Apr. | 14 May | 24 May | 4 June |
| 2016 | 10 Feb. | 25 Mar. | 27 Mar. | 5 May | 15 May | 26 May |
| 2017 | 1 Mar. | 14 Apr. | 16 Apr. | 25 May | 4 June | 15 June |
| 2018 | 14 Feb. | 30 Mar. | 1 Apr. | 10 May | 20 May | 31 May |
| 2019 | 6 Mar. | 19 Apr. | 21 Apr. | 30 May | 9 June | 20 June |
| 2020 | 26 Feb. | 10 Apr. | 12 Apr. | 21 May | 31 May | 11 June |
| 2021 | 17 Feb. | 2 Apr. | 4 Apr. | 13 May | 23 May | 3 June |
| 2022 | 2 Mar. | 15 Apr. | 17 Apr. | 26 May | 5 June | 16 June |
| 2023 | 22 Feb. | 7 Apr. | 9 Apr. | 18 May | 28 May | 8 June |
| 2024 | 14 Feb. | 29 Mar. | 31 Mar. | 9 May | 19 May | 30 May |
| 2025 | 5 Mar. | 18 Apr. | 20 Apr. | 29 May | 8 June | 19 June |
| 2026 | 18 Feb. | 3 Apr. | 5 Apr. | 14 May | 24 May | 4 June |
| 2027 | 10 Feb. | 26 Mar. | 28 Mar. | 6 May | 16 May | 27 May |
| 2028 | 1 Mar. | 14 Apr. | 16 Apr. | 25 May | 4 June | 15 June |
| 2029 | 14 Feb. | 30 Mar. | 1 Apr. | 10 May | 20 May | 31 May |
| 2030 | 6 Mar. | 19 Apr. | 21 Apr. | 30 May | 9 June | 20 June |
| 2031 | 26 Feb. | 11 Apr. | 13 Apr. | 22 May | 1 June | 12 June |
| 2032 | 11 Feb. | 26 Mar. | 28 Mar. | 6 May | 16 May | 27 May |
| 2033 | 2 Mar. | 15 Apr. | 17 Apr. | 26 May | 5 June | 16 June |
| 2034 | 22 Feb. | 7 Apr. | 9 Apr. | 18 May | 28 May | 8 June |
| 2035 | 7 Feb. | 23 Mar. | 25 Mar. | 3 May | 13 May | 24 May |
| 2036 | 27 Feb. | 11 Apr. | 13 Apr. | 22 May | 1 June | 12 June |
| 2037 | 18 Feb. | 3 Apr. | 5 Apr. | 14 May | 24 May | 4 June |
| 2038 | 10 Mar. | 23 Apr. | 25 Apr. | 3 June | 13 June | 24 June |
| 2039 | 23 Feb. | 8 Apr. | 10 Apr. | 19 May | 29 May | 9 June |
| 2040 | 15 Feb. | 30 Mar. | 1 Apr. | 10 May | 20 May | 31 May |
| 2041 | 6 Mar. | 19 Apr. | 21 Apr. | 30 May | 9 June | 20 June |
| 2042 | 19 Feb. | 4 Apr. | 6 Apr. | 15 May | 25 May | 5 June |
| 2043 | 11 Feb. | 27 Mar. | 29 Mar. | 7 May | 17 May | 28 May |
| 2044 | 2 Mar. | 15 Apr. | 17 Apr. | 26 May | 5 June | 16 June |
| 2045 | 22 Feb. | 7 Apr. | 9 Apr. | 18 May | 28 May | 8 June |
| 2046 | 7 Feb. | 23 Mar. | 25 Mar. | 3 May | 13 May | 24 May |
| 2047 | 27 Feb. | 12 Apr. | 14 Apr. | 23 May | 2 June | 13 June |
| 2048 | 19 Feb. | 3 Apr. | 5 Apr. | 14 May | 24 May | 4 June |
| 2049 | 3 Mar. | 16 Apr. | 18 Apr. | 27 May | 6 June | 17 June |
| 2050 | 23 Feb. | 8 Apr. | 10 Apr. | 19 May | 29 May | 9 June |
| 2051 | 15 Feb. | 31 Mar. | 2 Apr. | 11 May | 21 May | 1 June |
| 2052 | 6 Mar. | 19 Apr. | 21 Apr. | 30 May | 9 June | 20 June |
| 2053 | 19 Feb. | 4 Apr. | 6 Apr. | 15 May | 25 May | 5 June |
| 2054 | 11 Feb. | 27 Mar. | 29 Mar. | 7 May | 17 May | 28 May |

*C2 continued*

| *Year* | *Ash Wednesday* | *Good Friday* | *Easter Sunday* | *Ascension Thursday* | *Whit-sunday* | *Corpus Christi* |
|---|---|---|---|---|---|---|
| 2055 | 3 Mar. | 16 Apr. | 18 Apr. | 27 May | 6 June | 17 June |
| 2056 | 16 Feb. | 31 Mar. | 2 Apr. | 11 May | 21 May | 1 June |
| 2057 | 7 Mar. | 20 Apr. | 22 Apr. | 31 May | 10 June | 21 June |
| 2058 | 27 Feb. | 12 Apr. | 14 Apr. | 23 May | 2 June | 13 June |
| 2059 | 12 Feb. | 28 Mar. | 30 Mar. | 8 May | 18 May | 29 May |
| 2060 | 3 Mar. | 16 Apr. | 18 Apr. | 27 May | 6 June | 17 June |
| 2061 | 23 Feb. | 8 Apr. | 10 Apr. | 19 May | 29 May | 9 June |
| 2062 | 8 Feb. | 24 Mar. | 26 Mar. | 4 May | 14 May | 25 May |
| 2063 | 28 Feb. | 13 Apr. | 15 Apr. | 24 May | 3 June | 14 June |
| 2064 | 20 Feb. | 4 Apr. | 6 Apr. | 15 May | 25 May | 5 June |
| 2065 | 11 Feb. | 27 Mar. | 29 Mar. | 7 May | 17 May | 28 May |
| 2066 | 24 Feb. | 9 Apr. | 11 Apr. | 20 May | 30 May | 10 June |
| 2067 | 16 Feb. | 1 Apr. | 3 Apr. | 12 May | 22 May | 2 June |
| 2068 | 7 Mar. | 20 Apr. | 22 Apr. | 31 May | 10 June | 21 June |
| 2069 | 27 Feb. | 12 Apr. | 14 Apr. | 23 May | 2 June | 13 June |
| 2070 | 12 Feb. | 28 Mar. | 30 Mar. | 8 May | 18 May | 29 May |
| 2071 | 4 Mar. | 17 Apr. | 19 Apr. | 28 May | 7 June | 18 June |
| 2072 | 24 Feb. | 8 Apr. | 10 Apr. | 19 May | 29 May | 9 June |
| 2073 | 8 Feb. | 24 Mar. | 26 Mar. | 4 May | 14 May | 25 May |
| 2074 | 28 Feb. | 13 Apr. | 15 Apr. | 24 May | 3 June | 14 June |
| 2075 | 20 Feb. | 5 Apr. | 7 Apr. | 16 May | 26 May | 6 June |
| 2076 | 4 Mar. | 17 Apr. | 19 Apr. | 28 May | 7 June | 18 June |
| 2077 | 24 Feb. | 9 Apr. | 11 Apr. | 20 May | 30 May | 10 June |
| 2078 | 16 Feb. | 1 Apr. | 3 Apr. | 12 May | 22 May | 2 June |
| 2079 | 8 Mar. | 21 Apr. | 23 Apr. | 1 June | 11 June | 22 June |
| 2080 | 21 Feb. | 5 Apr. | 7 Apr. | 16 May | 26 May | 6 June |
| 2081 | 12 Feb. | 28 Mar. | 30 Mar. | 8 May | 18 May | 29 May |
| 2082 | 4 Mar. | 17 Apr. | 19 Apr. | 28 May | 7 June | 18 June |
| 2083 | 17 Feb. | 2 Apr. | 4 Apr. | 13 May | 23 May | 3 June |
| 2084 | 9 Feb. | 24 Mar. | 26 Mar. | 4 May | 14 May | 25 May |
| 2085 | 28 Feb. | 13 Apr. | 15 Apr. | 24 May | 3 June | 14 June |
| 2086 | 13 Feb. | 29 Mar. | 31 Mar. | 9 May | 19 May | 30 May |
| 2087 | 5 Mar. | 18 Apr. | 20 Apr. | 29 May | 8 June | 19 June |
| 2088 | 25 Feb. | 9 Apr. | 11 Apr. | 20 May | 30 May | 10 June |
| 2089 | 16 Feb. | 1 Apr. | 3 Apr. | 12 May | 22 May | 2 June |
| 2090 | 1 Mar. | 14 Apr. | 16 Apr. | 25 May | 4 June | 15 June |
| 2091 | 21 Feb. | 6 Apr. | 8 Apr. | 17 May | 27 May | 7 June |
| 2092 | 13 Feb. | 28 Mar. | 30 Mar. | 8 May | 18 May | 29 May |
| 2093 | 25 Feb. | 10 Apr. | 12 Apr. | 21 May | 31 May | 11 June |
| 2094 | 17 Feb. | 2 Apr. | 4 Apr. | 13 May | 23 May | 3 June |
| 2095 | 9 Mar. | 22 Apr. | 24 Apr. | 2 June | 12 June | 23 June |
| 2096 | 29 Feb. | 13 Apr. | 15 Apr. | 24 May | 3 June | 14 June |
| 2097 | 13 Feb. | 29 Mar. | 31 Mar. | 9 May | 19 May | 30 May |
| 2098 | 5 Mar. | 18 Apr. | 20 Apr. | 29 May | 8 June | 19 June |
| 2099 | 25 Feb. | 10 Apr. | 12 Apr. | 21 May | 31 May | 11 June |
| 2100 | 10 Feb. | 26 Mar. | 28 Mar. | 6 May | 16 May | 27 May |

# C3. Orthodox

| Year | *Shrove Monday* | *Good Friday* | *Easter Sunday* | *Pentecost Sunday* |
|---|---|---|---|---|
| 1900 | 5 Mar. | 20 Apr. | 22 Apr. | 10 June |
| 1901 | 25 Feb. | 12 Apr. | 14 Apr. | 2 June |
| 1902 | 17 Mar. | 2 May | 4 May | 22 June |
| 1903 | 2 Mar. | 17 Apr. | 19 Apr. | 7 June |
| 1904 | 22 Feb. | 8 Apr. | 10 Apr. | 29 May |
| 1905 | 13 Mar. | 28 Apr. | 30 Apr. | 18 June |
| 1906 | 26 Feb. | 13 Apr. | 15 Apr. | 3 June |
| 1907 | 18 Feb. | 5 Apr. | 7 Apr. | 26 May |
| 1908 | 9 Mar. | 24 Apr. | 26 Apr. | 14 June |
| 1909 | 22 Feb. | 9 Apr. | 11 Apr. | 30 May |
| 1910 | 14 Mar. | 29 Apr. | 1 May | 19 June |
| 1911 | 6 Mar. | 21 Apr. | 23 Apr. | 11 June |
| 1912 | 19 Feb. | 5 Apr. | 7 Apr. | 26 May |
| 1913 | 10 Mar. | 25 Apr. | 27 Apr. | 15 June |
| 1914 | 2 Mar. | 17 Apr. | 19 Apr. | 7 June |
| 1915 | 22 Feb. | 9 Apr. | 11 Apr. | 30 May |
| 1916 | 13 Mar. | 28 Apr. | 30 Apr. | 18 June |
| 1917 | 26 Feb. | 13 Apr. | 15 Apr. | 3 June |
| 1918 | 18 Mar. | 3 May | 5 May | 23 June |
| 1919 | 10 Mar. | 25 Apr. | 27 Apr. | 15 June |
| 1920 | 23 Feb. | 9 Apr. | 11 Apr. | 30 May |
| 1921 | 14 Mar. | 29 Apr. | 1 May | 19 June |
| 1922 | 6 Mar. | 21 Apr. | 23 Apr. | 11 June |

Prior to 1923 there was no general agreement among the various members of the Orthodox Church on the date of Easter. Dates given above are those of the Greek Orthodox Church.

| Year | *Shrove Monday* | *Good Friday* | *Easter Sunday* | *Pentecost Sunday* |
|---|---|---|---|---|
| 1923 | 19 Feb. | 6 Apr. | 8 Apr. | 27 May |
| 1924 | 10 Mar. | 25 Apr. | 27 Apr. | 15 June |
| 1925 | 2 Mar. | 17 Apr. | 19 Apr. | 7 June |
| 1926 | 22 Mar. | 7 May | 9 May | 27 June |
| 1927 | 7 Mar. | 22 Apr. | 24 Apr. | 12 June |
| 1928 | 27 Feb. | 13 Apr. | 15 Apr. | 3 June |
| 1929 | 18 Mar. | 3 May | 5 May | 23 June |
| 1930 | 3 Mar. | 18 Apr. | 20 Apr. | 8 June |
| 1931 | 23 Feb. | 10 Apr. | 12 Apr. | 31 May |
| 1932 | 14 Mar. | 29 Apr. | 1 May | 19 June |
| 1933 | 27 Feb. | 14 Apr. | 16 Apr. | 4 June |
| 1934 | 19 Feb. | 6 Apr. | 8 Apr. | 27 May |
| 1935 | 11 Mar. | 26 Apr. | 28 Apr. | 16 June |
| 1936 | 24 Feb. | 10 Apr. | 12 Apr. | 31 May |
| 1937 | 15 Mar. | 30 Apr. | 2 May | 20 June |
| 1938 | 7 Mar. | 22 Apr. | 24 Apr. | 12 June |
| 1939 | 27 Feb. | 14 Apr. | 16 Apr. | 4 June |
| 1940 | 11 Mar. | 26 Apr. | 28 Apr. | 16 June |

*C3 continued*

| *Year* | *Shrove Monday* | *Good Friday* | *Easter Sunday* | *Pentecost Sunday* |
|---|---|---|---|---|
| 1941 | 3 Mar. | 18 Apr. | 20 Apr. | 8 June |
| 1942 | 23 Feb. | 10 Apr. | 12 Apr. | 31 May |
| 1943 | 15 Mar. | 30 Apr. | 2 May | 20 June |
| 1944 | 28 Feb. | 14 Apr. | 16 Apr. | 4 June |
| 1945 | 19 Mar. | 4 May | 6 May | 24 June |
| 1946 | 11 Mar. | 26 Apr. | 28 Apr. | 16 June |
| 1947 | 24 Feb. | 11 Apr. | 13 Apr. | 1 June |
| 1948 | 15 Mar. | 30 Apr. | 2 May | 20 June |
| 1949 | 7 Mar. | 22 Apr. | 24 Apr. | 12 June |
| 1950 | 20 Feb. | 7 Apr. | 9 Apr. | 28 May |
| 1951 | 12 Mar. | 27 Apr. | 29 Apr. | 17 June |
| 1952 | 3 Mar. | 18 Apr. | 20 Apr. | 8 June |
| 1953 | 16 Feb. | 3 Apr. | 5 Apr. | 24 May |
| 1954 | 8 Mar. | 23 Apr. | 25 Apr. | 13 June |
| 1955 | 28 Feb. | 15 Apr. | 17 Apr. | 5 June |
| 1956 | 19 Mar. | 4 May | 6 May | 24 June |
| 1957 | 4 Mar. | 19 Apr. | 21 Apr. | 9 June |
| 1958 | 24 Feb. | 11 Apr. | 13 Apr. | 1 June |
| 1959 | 16 Mar. | 1 May | 3 May | 21 June |
| 1960 | 29 Feb. | 15 Apr. | 17 Apr. | 5 June |
| 1961 | 20 Feb. | 7 Apr. | 9 Apr. | 28 May |
| 1962 | 12 Mar. | 27 Apr. | 29 Apr. | 17 June |
| 1963 | 25 Feb. | 12 Apr. | 14 Apr. | 2 June |
| 1964 | 16 Mar. | 1 May | 3 May | 21 June |
| 1965 | 8 Mar. | 23 Apr. | 25 Apr. | 13 June |
| 1966 | 28 Feb. | 15 Apr. | 17 Apr. | 5 June |
| 1967 | 13 Mar. | 28 Apr. | 30 Apr. | 18 June |
| 1968 | 4 Mar. | 19 Apr. | 21 Apr. | 9 June |
| 1969 | 24 Feb. | 11 Apr. | 13 Apr. | 1 June |
| 1970 | 16 Mar. | 1 May | 3 May | 21 June |
| 1971 | 1 Mar. | 16 Apr. | 18 Apr. | 6 June |
| 1972 | 21 Feb. | 7 Apr. | 9 Apr. | 28 May |
| 1973 | 12 Mar. | 27 Apr. | 29 Apr. | 17 June |
| 1974 | 25 Feb. | 12 Apr. | 14 Apr. | 2 June |
| 1975 | 17 Mar. | 2 May | 4 May | 22 June |
| 1976 | 8 Mar. | 23 Apr. | 25 Apr. | 13 June |
| 1977 | 21 Feb. | 8 Apr. | 10 Apr. | 29 May |
| 1978 | 13 Mar. | 28 Apr. | 30 Apr. | 18 June |
| 1979 | 5 Mar. | 20 Apr. | 22 Apr. | 10 June |
| 1980 | 18 Feb. | 4 Apr. | 6 Apr. | 25 May |
| 1981 | 9 Mar. | 24 Apr. | 26 Apr. | 14 June |
| 1982 | 1 Mar. | 16 Apr. | 18 Apr. | 6 June |
| 1983 | 21 Mar. | 6 May | 8 May | 26 June |
| 1984 | 5 Mar. | 20 Apr. | 22 Apr. | 10 June |
| 1985 | 25 Feb. | 12 Apr. | 14 Apr. | 2 June |
| 1986 | 17 Mar. | 2 May | 4 May | 22 June |

| Year | Shrove Monday | Good Friday | Easter Sunday | Pentecost Sunday |
|---|---|---|---|---|
| 1987 | 2 Mar. | 17 Apr. | 19 Apr. | 7 June |
| 1988 | 22 Feb. | 8 Apr. | 10 Apr. | 29 May |
| 1989 | 13 Mar. | 28 Apr. | 30 Apr. | 18 June |
| 1990 | 26 Feb. | 13 Apr. | 15 Apr. | 3 June |
| 1991 | 18 Feb. | 5 Apr. | 7 Apr. | 26 May |
| 1992 | 9 Mar. | 24 Apr. | 26 Apr. | 14 June |
| 1993 | 1 Mar. | 16 Apr. | 18 Apr. | 6 June |
| 1994 | 14 Mar. | 29 Apr. | 1 May | 19 June |
| 1995 | 6 Mar. | 21 Apr. | 23 Apr. | 11 June |
| 1996 | 26 Feb. | 12 Apr. | 14 Apr. | 2 June |
| 1997 | 17 Mar. | 2 May | 4 May | 22 June |
| 1998 | 2 Mar. | 17 Apr. | 19 Apr. | 7 June |
| 1999 | 22 Feb. | 9 Apr. | 11 Apr. | 30 May |
| 2000 | 13 Mar. | 28 Apr. | 30 Apr. | 18 June |
| 2001 | 26 Feb. | 13 Apr. | 15 Apr. | 3 June |
| 2002 | 18 Mar. | 3 May | 5 May | 23 June |
| 2003 | 10 Mar. | 25 Apr. | 27 Apr. | 15 June |
| 2004 | 23 Feb. | 9 Apr. | 11 Apr. | 30 May |
| 2005 | 14 Mar. | 29 Apr. | 1 May | 19 June |
| 2006 | 6 Mar. | 21 Apr. | 23 Apr. | 11 June |
| 2007 | 19 Feb. | 6 Apr. | 8 Apr. | 27 May |
| 2008 | 10 Mar. | 25 Apr. | 27 Apr. | 15 June |
| 2009 | 2 Mar. | 17 Apr. | 19 Apr. | 7 June |
| 2010 | 15 Feb. | 2 Apr. | 4 Apr. | 23 May |
| 2011 | 7 Mar. | 22 Apr. | 24 Apr. | 12 June |
| 2012 | 27 Feb. | 13 Apr. | 15 Apr. | 3 June |
| 2013 | 18 Mar. | 3 May | 5 May | 23 June |
| 2014 | 10 Mar. | 25 Apr. | 27 Apr. | 15 June |
| 2015 | 23 Feb. | 10 Apr. | 12 Apr. | 31 May |
| 2016 | 14 Mar. | 29 Apr. | 1 May | 19 June |
| 2017 | 6 Mar. | 21 Apr. | 23 Apr. | 11 June |
| 2018 | 19 Feb. | 6 Apr. | 8 Apr. | 27 May |
| 2019 | 11 Mar. | 26 Apr. | 28 Apr. | 16 June |
| 2020 | 2 Mar. | 17 Apr. | 19 Apr. | 7 June |
| 2021 | 15 Mar. | 30 Apr. | 2 May | 20 June |
| 2022 | 7 Mar. | 22 Apr. | 24 Apr. | 12 June |
| 2023 | 27 Feb. | 14 Apr. | 16 Apr. | 4 June |
| 2024 | 18 Mar. | 3 May | 5 May | 23 June |
| 2025 | 3 Mar. | 18 Apr. | 20 Apr. | 8 June |
| 2026 | 23 Feb. | 10 Apr. | 12 Apr. | 31 May |
| 2027 | 15 Mar. | 30 Apr. | 2 May | 20 June |
| 2028 | 28 Feb. | 14 Apr. | 16 Apr. | 4 June |
| 2029 | 19 Feb. | 6 Apr. | 8 Apr. | 27 May |
| 2030 | 11 Mar. | 26 Apr. | 28 Apr. | 16 June |
| 2031 | 24 Feb. | 11 Apr. | 13 Apr. | 1 June |
| 2032 | 15 Mar. | 30 Apr. | 2 May | 20 June |
| 2033 | 7 Mar. | 22 Apr. | 24 Apr. | 12 June |
| 2034 | 20 Feb. | 7 Apr. | 9 Apr. | 28 May |

*C3 continued*

| *Year* | *Shrove Monday* | *Good Friday* | *Easter Sunday* | *Pentecost Sunday* |
|---|---|---|---|---|
| 2035 | 12 Mar. | 27 Apr. | 29 Apr. | 17 June |
| 2036 | 3 Mar. | 18 Apr. | 20 Apr. | 8 June |
| 2037 | 23 Feb. | 10 Apr. | 12 Apr. | 31 May |
| 2038 | 8 Mar. | 23 Apr. | 25 Apr. | 13 June |
| 2039 | 28 Feb. | 15 Apr. | 17 Apr. | 5 June |
| 2040 | 19 Mar. | 4 May | 6 May | 24 June |
| 2041 | 11 Mar. | 26 Apr. | 28 Apr. | 16 June |
| 2042 | 24 Feb. | 11 Apr. | 13 Apr. | 1 June |
| 2043 | 16 Mar. | 1 May | 3 May | 21 June |
| 2044 | 7 Mar. | 22 Apr. | 24 Apr. | 12 June |
| 2045 | 20 Feb. | 7 Apr. | 9 Apr. | 28 May |
| 2046 | 12 Mar. | 27 Apr. | 29 Apr. | 17 June |
| 2047 | 4 Mar. | 19 Apr. | 21 Apr. | 9 June |
| 2048 | 17 Feb. | 3 Apr. | 5 Apr. | 24 May |
| 2049 | 8 Mar. | 23 Apr. | 25 Apr. | 13 June |
| 2050 | 28 Feb. | 15 Apr. | 17 Apr. | 5 June |
| 2051 | 20 Mar. | 5 May | 7 May | 25 June |
| 2052 | 4 Mar. | 19 Apr. | 21 Apr. | 9 June |
| 2053 | 24 Feb. | 11 Apr. | 13 Apr. | 1 June |
| 2054 | 16 Mar. | 1 May | 3 May | 21 June |
| 2055 | 1 Mar. | 16 Apr. | 18 Apr. | 6 June |
| 2056 | 21 Feb. | 7 Apr. | 9 Apr. | 28 May |
| 2057 | 12 Mar. | 27 Apr. | 29 Apr. | 17 June |
| 2058 | 25 Feb. | 12 Apr. | 14 Apr. | 2 June |
| 2059 | 17 Mar. | 2 May | 4 May | 22 June |
| 2060 | 8 Mar. | 23 Apr. | 25 Apr. | 13 June |
| 2061 | 21 Feb. | 8 Apr. | 10 Apr. | 29 May |
| 2062 | 13 Mar. | 28 Apr. | 30 Apr. | 18 June |
| 2063 | 5 Mar. | 20 Apr. | 22 Apr. | 10 June |
| 2064 | 25 Feb. | 11 Apr. | 13 Apr. | 1 June |
| 2065 | 9 Mar. | 24 Apr. | 26 Apr. | 14 June |
| 2066 | 1 Mar. | 16 Apr. | 18 Apr. | 6 June |
| 2067 | 21 Feb. | 8 Apr. | 10 Apr. | 29 May |
| 2068 | 12 Mar. | 27 Apr. | 29 Apr. | 17 June |
| 2069 | 25 Feb. | 12 Apr. | 14 Apr. | 2 June |
| 2070 | 17 Mar. | 2 May | 4 May | 22 June |
| 2071 | 9 Mar. | 24 Apr. | 26 Apr. | 14 June |
| 2072 | 22 Feb. | 8 Apr. | 10 Apr. | 29 May |
| 2073 | 13 Mar. | 28 Apr. | 30 Apr. | 18 June |
| 2074 | 5 Mar. | 20 Apr. | 22 Apr. | 10 June |
| 2075 | 18 Feb. | 5 Apr. | 7 Apr. | 26 May |
| 2076 | 9 Mar. | 24 Apr. | 26 Apr. | 14 June |
| 2077 | 1 Mar. | 16 Apr. | 18 Apr. | 6 June |
| 2078 | 21 Mar. | 6 May | 8 May | 26 June |
| 2079 | 6 Mar. | 21 Apr. | 23 Apr. | 11 June |
| 2080 | 26 Feb. | 12 Apr. | 14 Apr. | 2 June |

| Year | Shrove Monday | Good Friday | Easter Sunday | Pentecost Sunday |
|---|---|---|---|---|
| 2081 | 17 Mar. | 2 May | 4 May | 22 June |
| 2082 | 2 Mar. | 17 Apr. | 19 Apr. | 7 June |
| 2083 | 22 Feb. | 9 Apr. | 11 Apr. | 30 May |
| 2084 | 13 Mar. | 28 Apr. | 30 Apr. | 18 June |
| 2085 | 5 Mar. | 20 Apr. | 22 Apr. | 10 June |
| 2086 | 18 Feb. | 5 Apr. | 7 Apr. | 26 May |
| 2087 | 10 Mar. | 25 Apr. | 27 Apr. | 15 June |
| 2088 | 23 Feb. | 9 Apr. | 11 Apr. | 30 May |
| 2089 | 14 Mar. | 29 Apr. | 1 May | 19 June |
| 2090 | 6 Mar. | 21 Apr. | 23 Apr. | 11 June |
| 2091 | 26 Feb. | 13 Apr. | 15 Apr. | 3 June |
| 2092 | 10 Mar. | 25 Apr. | 27 Apr. | 15 June |
| 2093 | 2 Mar. | 17 Apr. | 19 Apr. | 7 June |
| 2094 | 22 Feb. | 9 Apr. | 11 Apr. | 30 May |
| 2095 | 14 Mar. | 29 Apr. | 1 May | 19 June |
| 2096 | 27 Feb. | 13 Apr. | 15 Apr. | 3 June |
| 2097 | 18 Mar. | 3 May | 5 May | 23 June |
| 2098 | 10 Mar. | 25 Apr. | 27 Apr. | 15 June |
| 2099 | 23 Feb. | 10 Apr. | 12 Apr. | 31 May |
| 2100 | 15 Mar. | 30 Apr. | 2 May | 20 June |

## C4. Hindu (Deepavali)

(Dates of Deepavali in India and Mauritius may be one day later than that shown below in some eastern parts of those countries.)

| Year | Date | Year | Date | Year | Date |
|---|---|---|---|---|---|
| 1900 | 21 Oct. | 1916 | 25 Oct. | 1932 | 28 Oct. |
| 1901 | 10 Nov. | 1917 | 15 Oct. | 1933 | 18 Oct. |
| 1902 | 30 Oct. | 1918 | 2 Nov. | 1934 | 6 Nov. |
| 1903 | 19 Oct. | 1919 | 22 Oct. | 1935 | 26 Oct. |
| 1904 | 6 Nov. | 1920 | 9 Nov. | 1936 | 14 Oct. |
| 1905 | 27 Oct. | 1921 | 29 Oct. | 1937 | 2 Nov. |
| 1906 | 16 Oct. | 1922 | 19 Oct. | 1938 | 22 Oct. |
| 1907 | 4 Nov. | 1923 | 7 Nov. | 1939 | 10 Nov. |
| 1908 | 24 Oct. | 1924 | 27 Oct. | 1940 | 29 Oct. |
| 1909 | 13 Oct. | 1925 | 16 Oct. | 1941 | 19 Oct. |
| 1910 | 1 Nov. | 1926 | 4 Nov. | 1942 | 7 Nov. |
| 1911 | 21 Oct. | 1927 | 24 Oct. | 1943 | 28 Oct. |
| 1912 | 8 Nov. | 1928 | 12 Oct. | 1944 | 16 Oct. |
| 1913 | 28 Oct. | 1929 | 31 Oct. | 1945 | 3 Nov. |
| 1914 | 18 Oct. | 1930 | 20 Oct. | 1946 | 23 Oct. |
| 1915 | 6 Nov. | 1931 | 8 Nov. | 1947 | 13 Oct. |

*C4 continued*

| *Year* | *Date* | *Year* | *Date* | *Year* | *Date* |
|---|---|---|---|---|---|
| 1948 | 31 Oct. | 1995 | 23 Oct. | 2042 | 11 Nov. |
| 1949 | 20 Oct. | 1996 | 10 Nov. | 2043 | 31 Oct. |
| 1950 | 8 Nov. | 1997 | 30 Oct. | 2044 | 19 Oct. |
| 1951 | 29 Oct. | 1998 | 19 Oct. | 2045 | 7 Nov. |
| 1952 | 17 Oct. | 1999 | 7 Nov. | 2046 | 28 Oct. |
| 1953 | 5 Nov. | 2000 | 26 Oct. | 2047 | 18 Oct. |
| 1954 | 25 Oct. | 2001 | 15 Oct. | 2048 | 5 Nov. |
| 1955 | 14 Oct. | 2002 | 3 Nov. | 2049 | 25 Oct. |
| 1956 | 1 Nov. | 2003 | 24 Oct. | 2050 | 14 Oct. |
| 1957 | 22 Oct. | 2004 | 11 Nov. | 2051 | 2 Nov. |
| 1958 | 10 Nov. | 2005 | 1 Nov. | 2052 | 21 Oct. |
| 1959 | 30 Oct. | 2006 | 21 Oct. | 2053 | 9 Nov. |
| 1960 | 19 Oct. | 2007 | 8 Nov. | 2054 | 29 Oct. |
| 1961 | 7 Nov. | 2008 | 27 Oct. | 2055 | 19 Oct. |
| 1962 | 27 Oct. | 2009 | 17 Oct. | 2056 | 6 Nov. |
| 1963 | 16 Oct. | 2010 | 5 Nov. | 2057 | 27 Oct. |
| 1964 | 3 Nov. | 2011 | 25 Oct. | 2058 | 16 Oct. |
| 1965 | 23 Oct. | 2012 | 14 Oct. | 2059 | 4 Nov. |
| 1966 | 13 Oct. | 2013 | 2 Nov. | 2060 | 23 Oct. |
| 1967 | 1 Nov. | 2014 | 22 Oct. | 2061 | 11 Nov. |
| 1968 | 20 Oct. | 2015 | 10 Nov. | 2062 | 31 Oct. |
| 1969 | 8 Nov. | 2016 | 29 Oct. | 2063 | 20 Oct. |
| 1970 | 29 Oct. | 2017 | 18 Oct. | 2064 | 7 Nov. |
| 1971 | 18 Oct. | 2018 | 6 Nov. | 2065 | 28 Oct. |
| 1972 | 5 Nov. | 2019 | 27 Oct. | 2066 | 18 Oct. |
| 1973 | 25 Oct. | 2020 | 15 Oct. | 2067 | 6 Nov. |
| 1974 | 14 Oct. | 2021 | 3 Nov. | 2068 | 25 Oct. |
| 1975 | 2 Nov. | 2022 | 24 Oct. | 2069 | 14 Oct. |
| 1976 | 22 Oct. | 2023 | 12 Nov. | 2070 | 1 Nov. |
| 1977 | 10 Nov. | 2024 | 31 Oct. | 2071 | 22 Oct. |
| 1978 | 30 Oct. | 2025 | 20 Oct. | 2072 | 9 Nov. |
| 1979 | 20 Oct. | 2026 | 8 Nov. | 2073 | 29 Oct. |
| 1980 | 6 Nov. | 2027 | 28 Oct. | 2074 | 19 Oct. |
| 1981 | 26 Oct. | 2028 | 17 Oct. | 2075 | 7 Nov. |
| 1982 | 16 Oct. | 2029 | 5 Nov. | 2076 | 26 Oct. |
| 1983 | 3 Nov. | 2030 | 25 Oct. | 2077 | 15 Oct. |
| 1984 | 23 Oct. | 2031 | 15 Oct. | 2078 | 3 Nov. |
| 1985 | 11 Nov. | 2032 | 2 Nov. | 2079 | 23 Oct. |
| 1986 | 1 Nov. | 2033 | 22 Oct. | 2080 | 10 Nov. |
| 1987 | 21 Oct. | 2034 | 10 Nov. | 2081 | 31 Oct. |
| 1988 | 8 Nov. | 2035 | 30 Oct. | 2082 | 20 Oct. |
| 1989 | 28 Oct. | 2036 | 18 Oct. | 2083 | 8 Nov. |
| 1990 | 17 Oct. | 2037 | 6 Nov. | 2084 | 28 Oct. |
| 1991 | 5 Nov. | 2038 | 27 Oct. | 2085 | 17 Oct. |
| 1992 | 24 Oct. | 2039 | 16 Oct. | 2086 | 5 Nov. |
| 1993 | 14 Oct. | 2040 | 3 Nov. | 2087 | 25 Oct. |
| 1994 | 2 Nov. | 2041 | 24 Oct. | 2088 | 13 Oct. |

| Year | Date | Year | Date | Year | Date |
|---|---|---|---|---|---|
| 2089 | 1 Nov. | 2093 | 19 Oct. | 2097 | 3 Nov. |
| 2090 | 22 Oct. | 2094 | 7 Nov. | 2098 | 23 Oct. |
| 2091 | 10 Nov. | 2095 | 27 Oct. | 2099 | 11 Nov. |
| 2092 | 29 Oct. | 2096 | 15 Oct. | 2100 | 2 Nov. |

# C5. Islamic

*(all dates subject to local religious review)*

| *Year* | *Hegira Year* | *New Year* | *Mohammed's Birthday* | *Isra a Majraj* | *1st day of Eid al Fitr* | *1st day of Eid al Adha* |
|---|---|---|---|---|---|---|
| 1950 | 1369 | | | 14 May | 16 July | 22 Sep. |
| | 1370 | 11 Oct. | 20 Dec. | | | |
| 1951 | 1370 | | | 3 May | 5 July | 11 Sep. |
| | 1371 | 1 Oct. | 10 Dec. | | | |
| 1952 | 1371 | | | 20 Apr. | 22 June | 29 Aug. |
| | 1372 | 19 Sep. | 28 Nov. | | | |
| 1953 | 1372 | | | 10 Apr. | 12 June | 19 Aug. |
| | 1373 | 8 Sep. | 17 Nov. | | | |
| 1954 | 1373 | | | 31 Mar. | 2 June | 9 Aug. |
| | 1374 | 28 Aug. | 6 Nov. | | | |
| 1955 | 1374 | | | 20 Mar. | 21 May | 28 July |
| | 1375 | 17 Aug. | 26 Oct. | | | |
| 1956 | 1375 | | | 9 Mar. | 11 May | 18 July |
| | 1376 | 6 Aug. | 15 Oct. | | | |
| 1957 | 1376 | | | 25 Feb. | 30 Apr. | 6 July |
| | 1377 | 27 July | 4 Oct. | | | |
| 1958 | 1377 | | | 15 Feb. | 20 Apr. | 27 June |
| | 1378 | 16 July | 24 Sep. | | | |
| 1959 | 1378 | | | 4 Feb. | 9 Apr. | 16 June |
| | 1379 | 6 July | 14 Sep. | | | |
| 1960 | 1379 | | | 24 Jan. | 27 Mar. | 3 June |
| | 1380 | 24 June | 2 Sep. | | | |
| 1961 | 1380 | | | 13 Jan. | 17 Mar. | 24 May |
| | 1381 | 13 June | 22 Aug. | | | |
| 1962 | 1381 | | | 3 Jan. | 7 Mar. | 14 May |
| | 1382 | 2 June | 11 Aug. | 24 Dec. | | |
| 1963 | 1382 | | | | 24 Feb. | 2 May |
| | 1383 | 23 May | 31 July | 13 Dec. | | |
| 1964 | 1383 | | | | 14 Feb. | 22 Apr. |
| | 1384 | 11 May | 20 July | 1 Dec. | | |
| 1965 | 1384 | | | | 2 Feb. | 12 Apr. |
| | 1385 | 1 May | 10 July | 20 Nov. | | |
| 1966 | 1385 | | | | 21 Jan. | 31 Mar. |
| | 1386 | 20 Apr. | 29 June | 9 Nov. | | |

## *C5 continued*

| *Year* | *Hegira Year* | *New Year* | *Mohammed's Birthday* | *Isra a Majraj* | *1st day of Eid al Fitr* | *1st day of Eid al Adha* |
|---|---|---|---|---|---|---|
| 1967 | 1386 | | | | 11 Jan. | 21 Mar. |
| | 1387 | 10 Apr. | 19 June | 30 Oct. | | |
| 1968 | 1387 | | | | | 8 Mar. |
| | 1388 | 29 Mar. | 7 June | 18 Oct. | 20 Dec. | |
| 1969 | 1388 | | | | | 26 Feb. |
| | 1389 | 18 Mar. | 27 May | 8 Oct. | 10 Dec. | |
| 1970 | 1389 | | | | | 16 Feb. |
| | 1390 | 7 Mar. | 16 May | 27 Sep. | 29 Nov. | |
| 1971 | 1390 | | | | | 5 Feb. |
| | 1391 | 25 Feb. | 6 May | 16 Sep. | 19 Nov. | |
| 1972 | 1391 | | | | | 26 Jan. |
| | 1392 | 15 Feb. | 24 Apr. | 4 Sep. | 7 Nov. | |
| 1973 | 1392 | | | | | 14 Jan. |
| | 1393 | 3 Feb. | 14 Apr. | 25 Aug. | 27 Oct. | |
| 1974 | 1393 | | | | | 2 Jan. |
| | 1394 | 23 Jan. | 3 Apr. | 14 Aug. | 16 Oct. | 23 Dec. |
| 1975 | 1395 | 12 Jan. | 24 Mar. | 4 Aug. | 6 Oct. | 13 Dec. |
| 1976 | 1396 | 1 Jan. | 12 Mar. | 24 July | 24 Sep. | 1 Dec. |
| | 1397 | 21 Dec. | | | | |
| 1977 | 1397 | | 1 Mar. | 13 July | 14 Sep. | 21 Nov. |
| | 1398 | 10 Dec. | | | | |
| 1978 | 1398 | | 17 Feb. | 1 July | 2 Sep. | 9 Nov. |
| | 1399 | 30 Nov. | | | | |
| 1979 | 1399 | | 8 Feb. | 21 June | 23 Aug. | 31 Oct. |
| | 1400 | 19 Nov. | | | | |
| 1980 | 1400 | | 28 Jan. | 9 June | 11 Aug. | 19 Oct. |
| | 1401 | 7 Nov. | | | | |
| 1981 | 1401 | | 16 Jan. | 29 May | 31 July | 7 Oct. |
| | 1402 | 27 Oct. | | | | |
| 1982 | 1402 | | 6 Jan. | 20 May | 21 July | 27 Sep. |
| | 1403 | 17 Oct. | 26 Dec. | | | |
| 1983 | 1403 | | | 9 May | 11 July | 17 Sep. |
| | 1404 | 6 Oct. | 15 Dec. | | | |
| 1984 | 1404 | | | 27 Apr. | 29 June | 4 Sep. |
| | 1405 | 25 Sep. | 4 Dec. | | | |
| 1985 | 1405 | | | 17 Apr. | 19 June | 26 Aug. |
| | 1406 | 14 Sep. | 23 Nov. | | | |
| 1986 | 1406 | | | 5 Apr. | 7 June | 14 Aug. |
| | 1407 | 4 Sep. | 13 Nov. | | | |
| 1987 | 1407 | | | 26 Mar. | 28 May | 4 Aug. |
| | 1408 | 24 Aug. | 2 Nov. | | | |
| 1988 | 1408 | | | 15 Mar. | 17 May | 23 July |
| | 1409 | 12 Aug. | 21 Oct. | | | |
| 1989 | 1409 | | | 3 Mar. | 5 May | 12 July |
| | 1410 | 1 Aug. | 10 Oct. | | | |

| Year | *Hegira Year* | *New Year* | *Mohammed's Birthday* | *Isra a Majraj* | *1st day of Eid al Fitr* | *1st day of Eid al Adha* |
|---|---|---|---|---|---|---|
| 1990 | 1410 | | | 22 Feb. | 26 Apr. | 2 July |
| | 1411 | 22 July | 30 Sep. | | | |
| 1991 | 1411 | | | 11 Feb. | 15 Apr. | 22 June |
| | 1412 | 11 July | 19 Sep. | | | |
| 1992 | 1412 | | | 30 Jan. | 3 Apr. | 10 June |
| | 1413 | 30 June | 8 Sep. | | | |
| 1993 | 1413 | | | 19 Jan. | 24 Mar. | 31 May |
| | 1414 | 20 June | 28 Aug. | | | |
| 1994 | 1414 | | | 9 Jan. | 13 Mar. | 20 May |
| | 1415 | 9 June | 18 Aug. | 29 Dec. | | |
| 1995 | 1415 | | | | 1 Mar. | 8 May |
| | 1416 | 29 May | 7 Aug. | 19 Dec. | | |
| 1996 | 1416 | | | | 20 Feb. | 28 Apr. |
| | 1417 | 17 May | 26 July | 7 Dec. | | |
| 1997 | 1417 | | | | 7 Feb. | 16 Apr. |
| | 1418 | 6 May | 15 July | 27 Nov. | | |
| 1998 | 1418 | | | | 29 Jan. | 7 Apr. |
| | 1419 | 26 Apr. | 5 July | 16 Nov. | | |
| 1999 | 1419 | | | | 18 Jan. | 27 Mar. |
| | 1420 | 16 Apr. | 24 June | 5 Nov. | | |
| 2000 | 1420 | | | | 6 Jan. | 15 Mar. |
| | 1421 | 4 Apr. | 13 June | 24 Oct. | 26 Dec. | |
| 2001 | 1421 | | | | | 5 Mar. |
| | 1422 | 25 Mar. | 3 June | 13 Oct. | 15 Dec. | |
| 2002 | 1422 | | | | | 22 Feb. |
| | 1423 | 14 Mar. | 23 May | 3 Oct. | 5 Dec. | |
| 2003 | 1423 | | | | | 10 Feb. |
| | 1424 | 3 Mar. | 12 May | 23 Sep. | 25 Nov. | |
| 2004 | 1424 | | | | | 31 Jan. |
| | 1425 | 20 Feb. | 30 Apr. | 11 Sep. | 13 Nov. | |
| 2005 | 1425 | | | | | 20 Jan. |
| | 1426 | 9 Feb. | 19 Apr. | 31 Aug. | 3 Nov. | |
| 2006 | 1426 | | | | | 9 Jan. |
| | 1427 | 29 Jan. | 9 Apr. | 20 Aug. | 23 Oct. | 30 Dec. |
| 2007 | 1428 | 19 Jan. | 30 Mar. | 10 Aug. | 12 Oct. | 19 Dec. |
| 2008 | 1429 | 8 Jan. | 18 Mar. | 29 July | 30 Sep. | 7 Dec. |
| | 1430 | 27 Dec. | | | | |
| 2009 | 1430 | | 8 Mar. | 19 July | 19 Sep. | 26 Nov. |
| | 1431 | 16 Dec. | | | | |
| 2010 | 1431 | | 24 Feb. | 7 July | 8 Sep. | 15 Nov. |
| | 1432 | 5 Dec. | | | | |
| 2011 | 1432 | | 14 Feb. | 28 June | 30 Aug. | 5 Nov. |
| | 1433 | 25 Nov. | | | | |
| 2012 | 1433 | | 3 Feb. | 16 June | 18 Aug. | 25 Oct. |
| | 1434 | 14 Nov. | | | | |
| 2013 | 1434 | | 21 Jan. | 4 June | 6 Aug. | 14 Oct. |
| | 1435 | 3 Nov. | | | | |

*C5 continued*

| *Year* | *Hegira Year* | *New Year* | *Mohammed's Birthday* | *Isra a Majraj* | *1st day of Eid al Fitr* | *1st day of Eid al Adha* |
|---|---|---|---|---|---|---|
| 2014 | 1435 | | 12 Jan. | 25 May | 28 July | 4 Oct. |
| | 1436 | 23 Oct. | | | | |
| 2015 | 1436 | | 1 Jan. | 14 May | 16 July | 22 Sep. |
| | 1437 | 13 Oct. | 22 Dec. | | | |
| 2016 | 1437 | | | 3 May | 5 July | 11 Sep. |
| | 1438 | 1 Oct. | 10 Dec. | | | |
| 2017 | 1438 | | | 23 Apr. | 25 June | 31 Aug. |
| | 1439 | 20 Sep. | 29 Nov. | | | |
| 2018 | 1439 | | | 12 Apr. | 13 June | 20 Aug. |
| | 1440 | 9 Sep. | 18 Nov. | | | |
| 2019 | 1440 | | | 2 Apr. | 4 June | 11 Aug. |
| | 1441 | 30 Aug. | 8 Nov. | | | |
| 2020 | 1441 | | | 21 Mar. | 23 May | 30 July |
| | 1442 | 19 Aug. | 27 Oct. | | | |
| 2021 | 1442 | | | 9 Mar. | 11 May | 19 July |
| | 1443 | 8 Aug. | 17 Oct. | | | |
| 2022 | 1443 | | | 27 Feb. | 1 May | 9 July |
| | 1444 | 28 July | 6 Oct. | | | |
| 2023 | 1444 | | | 17 Feb. | 21 Apr. | 28 June |
| | 1445 | 17 July | 26 Sep. | | | |
| 2024 | 1445 | | | 6 Feb. | 8 Apr. | 15 June |
| | 1446 | 6 July | 14 Sep. | | | |
| 2025 | 1446 | | | 26 Jan. | 30 Mar. | 6 June |
| | 1447 | 25 June | 3 Sep. | | | |
| 2026 | 1447 | | | 14 Jan. | 19 Mar. | 25 May |
| | 1448 | 15 June | 23 Aug. | | | |
| 2027 | 1448 | | | 4 Jan. | 9 Mar. | 16 May |
| | 1449 | 4 June | 13 Aug. | 24 Dec. | | |
| 2028 | 1449 | | | | 26 Feb. | 4 May |
| | 1450 | 24 May | 2 Aug. | 13 Dec. | | |
| 2029 | 1450 | | | | 13 Feb. | 22 Apr. |
| | 1451 | 13 May | 22 July | 2 Dec. | | |
| 2030 | 1451 | | | | 3 Feb. | 13 Apr. |
| | 1452 | 2 May | 11 July | 22 Nov. | | |
| 2031 | 1452 | | | | 24 Jan. | 2 Apr. |
| | 1453 | 21 Apr. | 1 July | 11 Nov. | | |
| 2032 | 1453 | | | | 12 Jan. | 20 Mar. |
| | 1454 | 10 Apr. | 19 June | 31 Oct. | | |
| 2033 | 1454 | | | | 2 Jan. | 11 Mar. |
| | 1455 | 30 Mar. | 8 June | 20 Oct. | 22 Dec. | |
| 2034 | 1455 | | | | | 1 Mar. |
| | 1456 | 20 Mar. | 29 May | 9 Oct. | 11 Dec. | |
| 2035 | 1456 | | | | | 17 Feb. |
| | 1457 | 10 Mar. | 18 May | 28 Sep. | 30 Nov. | |
| 2036 | 1457 | | | | | 7 Feb. |
| | 1458 | 27 Feb. | 7 May | 17 Sep. | 19 Nov. | |

| Year | Hegira Year | New Year | Mohammed's Birthday | Isra a Majraj | 1st day of Eid al Fitr | 1st day of Eid al Adha |
|---|---|---|---|---|---|---|
| 2037 | 1458 | | | | | 25 Jan. |
| | 1459 | 15 Feb. | 26 Apr. | 6 Sep. | 8 Nov. | |
| 2038 | 1459 | | | | | 15 Jan. |
| | 1460 | 4 Feb. | 15 Apr. | 27 Aug. | 29 Oct. | |
| 2039 | 1460 | | | | | 5 Jan. |
| | 1461 | 24 Jan. | 4 Apr. | 16 Aug. | 18 Oct. | 25 Dec. |
| 2040 | 1462 | 14 Jan. | 24 Mar. | 5 Aug. | 7 Oct. | 14 Dec. |
| 2041 | 1463 | 2 Jan. | 13 Mar. | 25 July | 26 Sep. | 3 Dec. |
| | 1464 | 23 Dec. | | | | |
| 2042 | 1464 | | 2 Mar. | 13 July | 14 Sep. | 21 Nov. |
| | 1465 | 12 Dec. | | | | |
| 2043 | 1465 | | 20 Feb. | 3 July | 4 Sep. | 11 Nov. |
| | 1466 | 1 Dec. | | | | |
| 2044 | 1466 | | 9 Feb. | 21 June | 23 Aug. | 30 Oct. |
| | 1467 | 19 Nov. | | | | |
| 2045 | 1467 | | 29 Jan. | 12 June | 13 Aug. | 20 Oct. |
| | 1468 | 8 Nov. | | | | |
| 2046 | 1468 | | 18 Jan. | 1 June | 3 Aug. | 10 Oct. |
| | 1469 | 29 Oct. | | | | |
| 2047 | 1469 | | 6 Jan. | 20 May | 23 July | 28 Sep. |
| | 1470 | 19 Oct. | 28 Dec. | | | |
| 2048 | 1470 | | | 9 May | 12 July | 18 Sep. |
| | 1471 | 7 Oct. | 16 Dec. | | | |
| 2049 | 1471 | | | 29 Apr. | 1 July | 7 Sep. |
| | 1472 | 27 Sep. | 6 Dec. | | | |
| 2050 | 1472 | | | 17 Apr. | 19 June | 26 Aug. |
| | 1473 | 16 Sep. | 25 Nov. | | | |

# C6. Jewish

| Year | Passover | Pentecost | Tisha Ab | Rosh Hashanah | Yom Kippur | Chanukah |
|---|---|---|---|---|---|---|
| 1900 | 14 Apr. | 3 June | 5 Aug. | 24 Sep. | 3 Oct. | 16 Dec. |
| 1901 | 4 Apr. | 24 May | 25 July | 14 Sep. | 23 Sep. | 7 Dec. |
| 1902 | 22 Apr. | 11 June | 12 Aug. | 2 Oct. | 11 Oct. | 24 Dec. |
| 1903 | 12 Apr. | 1 June | 2 Aug. | 22 Sep. | 1 Oct. | 14 Dec. |
| 1904 | 31 Mar. | 20 May | 21 July | 10 Sep. | 19 Sep. | 3 Dec. |
| 1905 | 20 Apr. | 9 June | 10 Aug. | 30 Sep. | 9 Oct. | 23 Dec. |
| 1906 | 10 Apr. | 30 May | 31 July | 20 Sep. | 29 Sep. | 12 Dec. |
| 1907 | 30 Mar. | 19 May | 21 July | 9 Sep. | 18 Sep. | 1 Dec. |
| 1908 | 16 Apr. | 5 June | 6 Aug. | 26 Sep. | 5 Oct. | 19 Dec. |
| 1909 | 6 Apr. | 26 May | 27 July | 16 Sep. | 25 Sep. | 8 Dec. |
| 1910 | 24 Apr. | 13 June | 14 Aug. | 4 Oct. | 13 Oct. | 26 Dec. |

*C6 continued*

| *Year* | *Passover* | *Pentecost* | *Tisha Ab* | *Rosh Hashanah* | *Yom Kippur* | *Chanukah* |
|---|---|---|---|---|---|---|
| 1911 | 13 Apr. | 2 June | 3 Aug. | 23 Sep. | 2 Oct. | 16 Dec. |
| 1912 | 2 Apr. | 22 May | 23 July | 12 Sep. | 21 Sep. | 4 Dec. |
| 1913 | 22 Apr. | 11 June | 12 Aug. | 2 Oct. | 11 Oct. | 24 Dec. |
| 1914 | 11 Apr. | 31 May | 2 Aug. | 21 Sep. | 30 Sep. | 13 Dec. |
| 1915 | 30 Mar. | 19 May | 20 July | 9 Sep. | 18 Sep. | 1 Dec. |
| 1916 | 18 Apr. | 7 June | 8 Aug. | 28 Sep. | 7 Oct. | 20 Dec. |
| 1917 | 7 Apr. | 27 May | 29 July | 17 Sep. | 26 Sep. | 9 Dec. |
| 1918 | 28 Mar. | 17 May | 18 July | 7 Sep. | 16 Sep. | 30 Nov. |
| 1919 | 15 Apr. | 4 June | 5 Aug. | 25 Sep. | 4 Oct. | 17 Dec. |
| 1920 | 3 Apr. | 23 May | 25 July | 13 Sep. | 22 Sep. | 5 Dec. |
| 1921 | 23 Apr. | 12 June | 14 Aug. | 3 Oct. | 12 Oct. | 25 Dec. |
| 1922 | 13 Apr. | 2 June | 3 Aug. | 23 Sep. | 2 Oct. | 16 Dec. |
| 1923 | 1 Apr. | 21 May | 22 July | 11 Sep. | 20 Sep. | 3 Dec. |
| 1924 | 19 Apr. | 8 June | 10 Aug. | 29 Sep. | 8 Oct. | 21 Dec. |
| 1925 | 9 Apr. | 29 May | 30 July | 19 Sep. | 28 Sep. | 12 Dec. |
| 1926 | 30 Mar. | 19 May | 20 July | 9 Sep. | 18 Sep. | 1 Dec. |
| 1927 | 17 Apr. | 6 June | 7 Aug. | 27 Sep. | 6 Oct. | 19 Dec. |
| 1928 | 5 Apr. | 25 May | 26 July | 15 Sep. | 24 Sep. | 8 Dec. |
| 1929 | 25 Apr. | 14 June | 15 Aug. | 5 Oct. | 14 Oct. | 28 Dec. |
| 1930 | 13 Apr. | 2 June | 3 Aug. | 23 Sep. | 2 Oct. | 15 Dec. |
| 1931 | 2 Apr. | 22 May | 23 July | 12 Sep. | 21 Sep. | 5 Dec. |
| 1932 | 21 Apr. | 10 June | 11 Aug. | 1 Oct. | 10 Oct. | 24 Dec. |
| 1933 | 11 Apr. | 31 May | 1 Aug. | 21 Sep. | 30 Sep. | 13 Dec. |
| 1934 | 31 Mar. | 20 May | 22 July | 10 Sep. | 19 Sep. | 2 Dec. |
| 1935 | 18 Apr. | 7 June | 8 Aug. | 28 Sep. | 7 Oct. | 21 Dec. |
| 1936 | 7 Apr. | 27 May | 28 July | 17 Sep. | 26 Sep. | 9 Dec. |
| 1937 | 27 Mar. | 16 May | 18 July | 6 Sep. | 15 Sep. | 28 Nov. |
| 1938 | 16 Apr. | 5 June | 7 Aug. | 26 Sep. | 5 Oct. | 18 Dec. |
| 1939 | 4 Apr. | 24 May | 25 July | 14 Sep. | 23 Sep. | 6 Dec. |
| 1940 | 23 Apr. | 12 June | 13 Aug. | 3 Oct. | 12 Oct. | 25 Dec. |
| 1941 | 12 Apr. | 1 June | 3 Aug. | 22 Sep. | 1 Oct. | 14 Dec. |
| 1942 | 2 Apr. | 22 May | 23 July | 12 Sep. | 21 Sep. | 5 Dec. |
| 1943 | 20 Apr. | 9 June | 10 Aug. | 30 Sep. | 9 Oct. | 22 Dec. |
| 1944 | 8 Apr. | 28 May | 30 July | 18 Sep. | 27 Sep. | 10 Dec. |
| 1945 | 29 Mar. | 18 May | 19 July | 8 Sep. | 17 Sep. | 1 Dec. |
| 1946 | 16 Apr. | 5 June | 6 Aug. | 26 Sep. | 5 Oct. | 18 Dec. |
| 1947 | 5 Apr. | 25 May | 27 July | 15 Sep. | 24 Sep. | 7 Dec. |
| 1948 | 24 Apr. | 13 June | 15 Aug. | 4 Oct. | 13 Oct. | 26 Dec. |
| 1949 | 14 Apr. | 3 June | 4 Aug. | 24 Sep. | 3 Oct. | 17 Dec. |
| 1950 | 2 Apr. | 22 May | 23 July | 12 Sep. | 21 Sep. | 4 Dec. |
| 1951 | 21 Apr. | 10 June | 12 Aug. | 1 Oct. | 10 Oct. | 23 Dec. |
| 1952 | 10 Apr. | 30 May | 31 July | 20 Sep. | 29 Sep. | 13 Dec. |
| 1953 | 31 Mar. | 20 May | 21 July | 10 Sep. | 19 Sep. | 2 Dec. |
| 1954 | 18 Apr. | 7 June | 8 Aug. | 28 Sep. | 7 Oct. | 20 Dec. |
| 1955 | 7 Apr. | 27 May | 28 July | 17 Sep. | 26 Sep. | 10 Dec. |
| 1956 | 27 Mar. | 16 May | 17 July | 6 Sep. | 15 Sep. | 28 Nov. |

| Year | Passover | Pentecost | Tisha Ab | Rosh Hashanah | Yom Kippur | Chanukah |
|---|---|---|---|---|---|---|
| 1957 | 16 Apr. | 5 June | 6 Aug. | 26 Sep. | 5 Oct. | 18 Dec. |
| 1958 | 5 Apr. | 25 May | 27 July | 15 Sep. | 24 Sep. | 7 Dec. |
| 1959 | 23 Apr. | 12 June | 13 Aug. | 3 Oct. | 12 Oct. | 26 Dec. |
| 1960 | 12 Apr. | 1 June | 2 Aug. | 22 Sep. | 1 Oct. | 14 Dec. |
| 1961 | 1 Apr. | 21 May | 23 July | 11 Sep. | 20 Sep. | 3 Dec. |
| 1962 | 19 Apr. | 8 June | 9 Aug. | 29 Sep. | 8 Oct. | 22 Dec. |
| 1963 | 9 Apr. | 29 May | 30 July | 19 Sep. | 28 Sep. | 11 Dec. |
| 1964 | 28 Mar. | 17 May | 19 July | 7 Sep. | 16 Sep. | 29 Nov. |
| 1965 | 17 Apr. | 6 June | 8 Aug. | 27 Sep. | 6 Oct. | 19 Dec. |
| 1966 | 5 Apr. | 25 May | 26 July | 15 Sep. | 24 Sep. | 7 Dec. |
| 1967 | 25 Apr. | 14 June | 15 Aug. | 5 Oct. | 14 Oct. | 27 Dec. |
| 1968 | 13 Apr. | 2 June | 4 Aug. | 23 Sep. | 2 Oct. | 15 Dec. |
| 1969 | 3 Apr. | 23 May | 24 July | 13 Sep. | 22 Sep. | 6 Dec. |
| 1970 | 21 Apr. | 10 June | 11 Aug. | 1 Oct. | 10 Oct. | 23 Dec. |
| 1971 | 10 Apr. | 30 May | 1 Aug. | 20 Sep. | 29 Sep. | 12 Dec. |
| 1972 | 30 Mar. | 19 May | 20 July | 9 Sep. | 18 Sep. | 2 Dec. |
| 1973 | 17 Apr. | 6 June | 7 Aug. | 27 Sep. | 6 Oct. | 19 Dec. |
| 1974 | 7 Apr. | 27 May | 28 July | 17 Sep. | 26 Sep. | 9 Dec. |
| 1975 | 27 Mar. | 16 May | 17 July | 6 Sep. | 15 Sep. | 29 Nov. |
| 1976 | 15 Apr. | 4 June | 5 Aug. | 25 Sep. | 4 Oct. | 18 Dec. |
| 1977 | 3 Apr. | 23 May | 24 July | 13 Sep. | 22 Sep. | 5 Dec. |
| 1978 | 22 Apr. | 11 June | 13 Aug. | 2 Oct. | 11 Oct. | 24 Dec. |
| 1979 | 12 Apr. | 1 June | 2 Aug. | 22 Sep. | 1 Oct. | 15 Dec. |
| 1980 | 1 Apr. | 21 May | 22 July | 11 Sep. | 20 Sep. | 3 Dec. |
| 1981 | 19 Apr. | 8 June | 9 Aug. | 29 Sep. | 8 Oct. | 21 Dec. |
| 1982 | 8 Apr. | 28 May | 29 July | 18 Sep. | 27 Sep. | 11 Dec. |
| 1983 | 29 Mar. | 18 May | 19 July | 8 Sep. | 17 Sep. | 30 Nov. |
| 1984 | 17 Apr. | 6 June | 7 Aug. | 27 Sep. | 6 Oct. | 19 Dec. |
| 1985 | 6 Apr. | 26 May | 28 July | 16 Sep. | 25 Sep. | 8 Dec. |
| 1986 | 24 Apr. | 13 June | 14 Aug. | 4 Oct. | 13 Oct. | 27 Dec. |
| 1987 | 14 Apr. | 3 June | 4 Aug. | 24 Sep. | 3 Oct. | 16 Dec. |
| 1988 | 2 Apr. | 22 May | 24 July | 12 Sep. | 21 Sep. | 4 Dec. |
| 1989 | 20 Apr. | 9 June | 10 Aug. | 30 Sep. | 9 Oct. | 23 Dec. |
| 1990 | 10 Apr. | 30 May | 31 July | 20 Sep. | 29 Sep. | 12 Dec. |
| 1991 | 30 Mar. | 19 May | 21 July | 9 Sep. | 18 Sep. | 1 Dec. |
| 1992 | 18 Apr. | 7 June | 9 Aug. | 28 Sep. | 7 Oct. | 20 Dec. |
| 1993 | 6 Apr. | 26 May | 27 July | 16 Sep. | 25 Sep. | 8 Dec. |
| 1994 | 27 Mar. | 16 May | 17 July | 6 Sep. | 15 Sep. | 28 Nov. |
| 1995 | 15 Apr. | 4 June | 6 Aug. | 25 Sep. | 4 Oct. | 17 Dec. |
| 1996 | 4 Apr. | 24 May | 25 July | 14 Sep. | 23 Sep. | 7 Dec. |
| 1997 | 22 Apr. | 11 June | 12 Aug. | 2 Oct. | 11 Oct. | 24 Dec. |
| 1998 | 11 Apr. | 31 May | 2 Aug. | 21 Sep. | 30 Sep. | 13 Dec. |
| 1999 | 1 Apr. | 21 May | 22 July | 11 Sep. | 20 Sep. | 4 Dec. |
| 2000 | 20 Apr. | 9 June | 10 Aug. | 30 Sep. | 9 Oct. | 23 Dec. |
| 2001 | 8 Apr. | 28 May | 29 July | 18 Sep. | 27 Sep. | 10 Dec. |
| 2002 | 28 Mar. | 17 May | 18 July | 7 Sep. | 16 Sep. | 30 Nov. |
| 2003 | 17 Apr. | 6 June | 7 Aug. | 27 Sep. | 6 Oct. | 20 Dec. |
| 2004 | 6 Apr. | 26 May | 27 July | 16 Sep. | 25 Sep. | 8 Dec. |

*C6 continued*

| *Year* | *Passover* | *Pentecost* | *Tisha Ab* | *Rosh Hashanah* | *Yom Kippur* | *Chanukah* |
|---|---|---|---|---|---|---|
| 2005 | 24 Apr. | 13 June | 14 Aug. | 4 Oct. | 13 Oct. | 26 Dec. |
| 2006 | 13 Apr. | 2 June | 3 Aug. | 23 Sep. | 2 Oct. | 16 Dec. |
| 2007 | 3 Apr. | 23 May | 24 July | 13 Sep. | 22 Sep. | 5 Dec. |
| 2008 | 20 Apr. | 9 June | 10 Aug. | 30 Sep. | 9 Oct. | 22 Dec. |
| 2009 | 9 Apr. | 29 May | 30 July | 19 Sep. | 28 Sep. | 12 Dec. |
| 2010 | 30 Mar. | 19 May | 20 July | 9 Sep. | 18 Sep. | 1 Dec. |
| 2011 | 19 Apr. | 8 June | 9 Aug. | 29 Sep. | 8 Oct. | 21 Dec. |
| 2012 | 7 Apr. | 27 May | 29 July | 17 Sep. | 26 Sep. | 9 Dec. |
| 2013 | 26 Mar. | 15 May | 16 July | 5 Sep. | 14 Sep. | 27 Nov. |
| 2014 | 15 Apr. | 4 June | 5 Aug. | 25 Sep. | 4 Oct. | 17 Dec. |
| 2015 | 4 Apr. | 24 May | 26 July | 14 Sep. | 23 Sep. | 6 Dec. |
| 2016 | 23 Apr. | 12 June | 14 Aug. | 3 Oct. | 12 Oct. | 25 Dec. |
| 2017 | 11 Apr. | 31 May | 1 Aug. | 21 Sep. | 30 Sep. | 13 Dec. |
| 2018 | 31 Mar. | 20 May | 22 July | 10 Sep. | 19 Sep. | 2 Dec. |
| 2019 | 20 Apr. | 9 June | 11 Aug. | 30 Sep. | 9 Oct. | 22 Dec. |
| 2020 | 9 Apr. | 29 May | 30 July | 19 Sep. | 28 Sep. | 12 Dec. |
| 2021 | 28 Mar. | 17 May | 18 July | 7 Sep. | 16 Sep. | 29 Nov. |
| 2022 | 16 Apr. | 5 June | 7 Aug. | 26 Sep. | 5 Oct. | 18 Dec. |
| 2023 | 6 Apr. | 26 May | 27 July | 16 Sep. | 25 Sep. | 9 Dec. |
| 2024 | 23 Apr. | 12 June | 13 Aug. | 3 Oct. | 12 Oct. | 25 Dec. |
| 2025 | 13 Apr. | 2 June | 3 Aug. | 23 Sep. | 2 Oct. | 15 Dec. |
| 2026 | 2 Apr. | 22 May | 23 July | 12 Sep. | 21 Sep. | 5 Dec. |
| 2027 | 22 Apr. | 11 June | 12 Aug. | 2 Oct. | 11 Oct. | 25 Dec. |
| 2028 | 11 Apr. | 31 May | 1 Aug. | 21 Sep. | 30 Sep. | 13 Dec. |
| 2029 | 31 Mar. | 20 May | 22 July | 10 Sep. | 19 Sep. | 2 Dec. |
| 2030 | 18 Apr. | 7 June | 8 Aug. | 28 Sep. | 7 Oct. | 21 Dec. |
| 2031 | 8 Apr. | 28 May | 29 July | 18 Sep. | 27 Sep. | 10 Dec. |
| 2032 | 27 Mar. | 16 May | 18 July | 6 Sep. | 15 Sep. | 28 Nov. |
| 2033 | 14 Apr. | 3 June | 4 Aug. | 24 Sep. | 3 Oct. | 17 Dec. |
| 2034 | 4 Apr. | 24 May | 25 July | 14 Sep. | 23 Sep. | 6 Dec. |
| 2035 | 24 Apr. | 13 June | 14 Aug. | 4 Oct. | 13 Oct. | 26 Dec. |
| 2036 | 12 Apr. | 1 June | 3 Aug. | 22 Sep. | 1 Oct. | 14 Dec. |
| 2037 | 31 Mar. | 20 May | 21 July | 10 Sep. | 19 Sep. | 2 Dec. |
| 2038 | 20 Apr. | 9 June | 10 Aug. | 30 Sep. | 9 Oct. | 22 Dec. |
| 2039 | 9 Apr. | 29 May | 31 July | 19 Sep. | 28 Sep. | 11 Dec. |
| 2040 | 29 Mar. | 18 May | 19 July | 8 Sep. | 17 Sep. | 1 Dec. |
| 2041 | 16 Apr. | 5 June | 6 Aug. | 26 Sep. | 5 Oct. | 18 Dec. |
| 2042 | 5 Apr. | 25 May | 27 July | 15 Sep. | 24 Sep. | 7 Dec. |
| 2043 | 25 Apr. | 14 June | 16 Aug. | 5 Oct. | 14 Oct. | 27 Dec. |
| 2044 | 12 Apr. | 1 June | 2 Aug. | 22 Sep. | 1 Oct. | 14 Dec. |
| 2045 | 2 Apr. | 22 May | 23 July | 12 Sep. | 21 Sep. | 4 Dec. |
| 2046 | 21 Apr. | 10 June | 12 Aug. | 1 Oct. | 10 Oct. | 23 Dec. |
| 2047 | 11 Apr. | 31 May | 1 Aug. | 21 Sep. | 30 Sep. | 14 Dec. |
| 2048 | 29 Mar. | 18 May | 19 July | 8 Sep. | 17 Sep. | 30 Nov. |
| 2049 | 17 Apr. | 6 June | 8 Aug. | 27 Sep. | 6 Oct. | 19 Dec. |
| 2050 | 7 Apr. | 27 May | 28 July | 17 Sep. | 26 Sep. | 10 Dec. |

| Year | Passover | Pentecost | Tisha Ab | Rosh Hashanah | Yom Kippur | Chanukah |
|---|---|---|---|---|---|---|
| 2051 | 28 Mar. | 17 May | 18 July | 7 Sep. | 16 Sep. | 29 Nov. |
| 2052 | 14 Apr. | 3 June | 4 Aug. | 24 Sep. | 3 Oct. | 16 Dec. |
| 2053 | 3 Apr. | 23 May | 24 July | 13 Sep. | 22 Sep. | 6 Dec. |
| 2054 | 23 Apr. | 12 June | 13 Aug. | 3 Oct. | 12 Oct. | 26 Dec. |
| 2055 | 13 Apr. | 2 June | 3 Aug. | 23 Sep. | 2 Oct. | 15 Dec. |
| 2056 | 1 Apr. | 21 May | 23 July | 11 Sep. | 20 Sep. | 3 Dec. |
| 2057 | 19 Apr. | 8 June | 9 Aug. | 29 Sep. | 8 Oct. | 22 Dec. |
| 2058 | 9 Apr. | 29 May | 30 July | 19 Sep. | 28 Sep. | 11 Dec. |
| 2059 | 29 Mar. | 18 May | 20 July | 8 Sep. | 17 Sep. | 30 Nov. |
| 2060 | 15 Apr. | 4 June | 5 Aug. | 25 Sep. | 4 Oct. | 18 Dec. |
| 2061 | 5 Apr. | 25 May | 26 July | 15 Sep. | 24 Sep. | 7 Dec. |
| 2062 | 25 Apr. | 14 June | 15 Aug. | 5 Oct. | 14 Oct. | 27 Dec. |
| 2063 | 14 Apr. | 3 June | 5 Aug. | 24 Sep. | 3 Oct. | 16 Dec. |
| 2064 | 1 Apr. | 21 May | 22 July | 11 Sep. | 20 Sep. | 3 Dec. |
| 2065 | 21 Apr. | 10 June | 11 Aug. | 1 Oct. | 10 Oct. | 23 Dec. |
| 2066 | 10 Apr. | 30 May | 1 Aug. | 20 Sep. | 29 Sep. | 12 Dec. |
| 2067 | 31 Mar. | 20 May | 21 July | 10 Sep. | 19 Sep. | 3 Dec. |
| 2068 | 17 Apr. | 6 June | 7 Aug. | 27 Sep. | 6 Oct. | 19 Dec. |
| 2069 | 6 Apr. | 26 May | 28 July | 16 Sep. | 25 Sep. | 8 Dec. |
| 2070 | 27 Mar. | 16 May | 17 July | 6 Sep. | 15 Sep. | 29 Nov. |
| 2071 | 14 Apr. | 3 June | 4 Aug. | 24 Sep. | 3 Oct. | 16 Dec. |
| 2072 | 3 Apr. | 23 May | 24 July | 13 Sep. | 22 Sep. | 5 Dec. |
| 2073 | 22 Apr. | 11 June | 13 Aug. | 2 Oct. | 11 Oct. | 24 Dec. |
| 2074 | 12 Apr. | 1 June | 2 Aug. | 22 Sep. | 1 Oct. | 15 Dec. |
| 2075 | 31 Mar. | 20 May | 21 July | 10 Sep. | 19 Sep. | 2 Dec. |
| 2076 | 18 Apr. | 7 June | 9 Aug. | 28 Sep. | 7 Oct. | 20 Dec. |
| 2077 | 8 Apr. | 28 May | 29 July | 18 Sep. | 27 Sep. | 11 Dec. |
| 2078 | 29 Mar. | 18 May | 19 July | 8 Sep. | 17 Sep. | 30 Nov. |
| 2079 | 16 Apr. | 5 June | 6 Aug. | 26 Sep. | 5 Oct. | 18 Dec. |
| 2080 | 4 Apr. | 24 May | 25 July | 14 Sep. | 23 Sep. | 7 Dec. |
| 2081 | 24 Apr. | 13 June | 14 Aug. | 4 Oct. | 13 Oct. | 27 Dec. |
| 2082 | 14 Apr. | 3 June | 4 Aug. | 24 Sep. | 3 Oct. | 16 Dec. |
| 2083 | 3 Apr. | 23 May | 25 July | 13 Sep. | 22 Sep. | 5 Dec. |
| 2084 | 20 Apr. | 9 June | 10 Aug. | 30 Sep. | 9 Oct. | 23 Dec. |
| 2085 | 10 Apr. | 30 May | 31 July | 20 Sep. | 29 Sep. | 12 Dec. |
| 2086 | 30 Mar. | 19 May | 21 July | 9 Sep. | 18 Sep. | 1 Dec. |
| 2087 | 17 Apr. | 6 June | 7 Aug. | 27 Sep. | 6 Oct. | 20 Dec. |
| 2088 | 6 Apr. | 26 May | 27 July | 16 Sep. | 25 Sep. | 8 Dec. |
| 2089 | 26 Mar. | 15 May | 17 July | 5 Sep. | 14 Sep. | 27 Nov. |
| 2090 | 15 Apr. | 4 June | 6 Aug. | 25 Sep. | 4 Oct. | 17 Dec. |
| 2091 | 3 Apr. | 23 May | 24 July | 13 Sep. | 22 Sep. | 5 Dec. |
| 2092 | 22 Apr. | 11 June | 12 Aug. | 2 Oct. | 11 Oct. | 24 Dec. |
| 2093 | 11 Apr. | 31 May | 2 Aug. | 21 Sep. | 30 Sep. | 13 Dec. |
| 2094 | 1 Apr. | 21 May | 22 July | 11 Sep. | 20 Sep. | 4 Dec. |
| 2095 | 19 Apr. | 8 June | 9 Aug. | 29 Sep. | 8 Oct. | 21 Dec. |
| 2096 | 7 Apr. | 27 May | 29 July | 17 Sep. | 26 Sep. | 9 Dec. |
| 2097 | 28 Mar. | 17 May | 18 July | 7 Sep. | 16 Sep. | 30 Nov. |
| 2098 | 17 Apr. | 6 June | 7 Aug. | 27 Sep. | 6 Oct. | 20 Dec. |

*C6 continued*

| *Year* | *Passover* | *Pentecost* | *Tisha Ab* | *Rosh Hashanah* | *Yom Kippur* | *Chanukah* |
|---|---|---|---|---|---|---|
| 2099 | 5 Apr. | 25 May | 26 July | 15 Sep. | 24 Sep. | 7 Dec. |
| 2100 | 24 Apr. | 13 June | 15 Aug. | 4 Oct. | 13 Oct. | 26 Dec. |

# C7. Theravada (Thai) Buddhist

| *Year* | *Makha Bucha* | *Visakha Bucha* | *Asalaha Bucha* | *Khao Phansa* |
|---|---|---|---|---|
| 1900 | 14 Feb. | 13 May | 11 July | 12 July |
| 1901 | 4 Mar. | 1 June | 30 July | 31 July |
| 1902 | 22 Feb. | 21 May | 19 July | 20 July |
| 1903 | 11 Feb. | 10 May | 9 July | 10 July |
| 1904 | 1 Mar. | 29 May | 27 July | 28 July |
| 1905 | 19 Feb. | 18 May | 16 July | 17 July |
| 1906 | 8 Feb. | 7 May | 6 July | 7 July |
| 1907 | 27 Feb. | 27 May | 25 July | 26 July |
| 1908 | 17 Feb. | 15 May | 13 July | 14 July |
| 1909 | 6 Mar. | 3 June | 1 Aug. | 2 Aug. |
| 1910 | 24 Feb. | 23 May | 21 July | 22 July |
| 1911 | 13 Feb. | 12 May | 10 July | 11 July |
| 1912 | 2 Mar. | 30 May | 28 July | 29 July |
| 1913 | 20 Feb. | 19 May | 17 July | 18 July |
| 1914 | 9 Feb. | 8 May | 7 July | 8 July |
| 1915 | 28 Feb. | 28 May | 26 July | 27 July |
| 1916 | 18 Feb. | 16 May | 5 July | 6 July |
| 1917 | 7 Feb. | 6 May | 4 July | 5 July |
| 1918 | 25 Feb. | 25 May | 23 July | 24 July |
| 1919 | 15 Feb. | 14 May | 12 July | 13 July |
| 1920 | 4 Mar. | 1 June | 30 July | 31 July |
| 1921 | 22 Feb. | 21 May | 19 July | 20 July |
| 1922 | 11 Feb. | 10 May | 9 July | 10 July |
| 1923 | 2 Mar. | 30 May | 28 July | 29 July |
| 1924 | 20 Feb. | 18 May | 16 July | 17 July |
| 1925 | 8 Feb. | 7 May | 6 July | 7 July |
| 1926 | 27 Feb. | 27 May | 25 July | 26 July |
| 1927 | 17 Feb. | 16 May | 14 July | 15 July |
| 1928 | 6 Mar. | 3 June | 1 Aug. | 2 Aug. |
| 1929 | 24 Feb. | 23 May | 21 July | 22 July |
| 1930 | 13 Feb. | 12 May | 10 July | 11 July |
| 1931 | 3 Mar. | 31 May | 29 July | 30 July |
| 1932 | 21 Feb. | 19 May | 17 July | 18 July |
| 1933 | 9 Feb. | 8 May | 7 July | 8 July |

| Year | *Makha Bucha* | *Visakha Bucha* | *Asalaha Bucha* | *Khao Phansa* |
|---|---|---|---|---|
| 1934 | 28 Feb. | 28 May | 26 July | 27 July |
| 1935 | 18 Feb. | 17 May | 15 July | 16 July |
| 1936 | 7 Feb. | 5 May | 4 July | 5 July |
| 1937 | 25 Feb. | 25 May | 23 July | 24 July |
| 1938 | 15 Feb. | 14 May | 12 July | 13 July |
| 1939 | 5 Mar. | 2 June | 31 July | 1 Aug. |
| 1940 | 23 Feb. | 21 May | 19 July | 20 July |
| 1941 | 11 Feb. | 10 May | 8 July | 9 July |
| 1942 | 1 Mar. | 29 May | 27 July | 28 July |
| 1943 | 19 Feb. | 18 May | 17 July | 18 July |
| 1944 | 9 Feb. | 7 May | 5 July | 6 July |
| 1945 | 26 Feb. | 26 May | 24 July | 25 July |
| 1946 | 16 Feb. | 15 May | 13 July | 14 July |
| 1947 | 6 Mar. | 3 June | 1 Aug. | 2 Aug. |
| 1948 | 24 Feb. | 22 May | 20 July | 21 July |
| 1949 | 12 Feb. | 11 May | 10 July | 11 July |
| 1950 | 3 Mar. | 31 May | 29 July | 30 July |
| 1951 | 21 Feb. | 20 May | 18 July | 19 July |
| 1952 | 10 Feb. | 8 May | 7 July | 8 July |
| 1953 | 28 Feb. | 28 May | 26 July | 27 July |
| 1954 | 18 Feb. | 17 May | 15 July | 16 July |
| 1955 | 7 Feb. | 6 May | 4 July | 5 July |
| 1956 | 25 Feb. | 24 May | 22 July | 23 July |
| 1957 | 14 Feb. | 13 May | 11 July | 12 July |
| 1958 | 4 Mar. | 1 June | 30 July | 31 July |
| 1959 | 22 Feb. | 21 May | 20 July | 21 July |
| 1960 | 12 Feb. | 10 May | 8 July | 9 July |
| 1961 | 1 Mar. | 29 May | 27 July | 28 July |
| 1962 | 19 Feb. | 18 May | 17 July | 18 July |
| 1963 | 9 Feb. | 8 May | 6 July | 7 July |
| 1964 | 27 Feb. | 26 May | 24 July | 25 July |
| 1965 | 16 Feb. | 15 May | 13 July | 14 July |
| 1966 | 6 Mar. | 3 June | 1 Aug. | 2 Aug. |
| 1967 | 24 Feb. | 23 May | 21 July | 22 July |
| 1968 | 13 Feb. | 11 May | 10 July | 11 July |
| 1969 | 3 Mar. | 31 May | 29 July | 30 July |
| 1970 | 21 Feb. | 20 May | 18 July | 19 July |
| 1971 | 10 Feb. | 9 May | 7 July | 8 July |
| 1972 | 28 Feb. | 27 May | 25 July | 26 July |
| 1973 | 17 Feb. | 16 May | 15 July | 16 July |
| 1974 | 7 Feb. | 6 May | 4 July | 5 July |
| 1975 | 25 Feb. | 25 May | 23 July | 24 July |
| 1976 | 15 Feb. | 13 May | 11 July | 12 July |
| 1977 | 4 Mar. | 1 June | 30 July | 31 July |
| 1978 | 22 Feb. | 21 May | 20 July | 21 July |
| 1979 | 12 Feb. | 11 May | 9 July | 10 July |
| 1980 | 1 Mar. | 29 May | 27 July | 28 July |
| 1981 | 19 Feb. | 18 May | 16 July | 17 July |

*C7 continued*

| *Year* | *Makha Bucha* | *Visakha Bucha* | *Asalaha Bucha* | *Khao Phansa* |
|---|---|---|---|---|
| 1982 | 8 Feb. | 7 May | 5 July | 6 July |
| 1983 | 26 Feb. | 26 May | 24 July | 25 July |
| 1984 | 16 Feb. | 14 May | 12 July | 13 July |
| 1985 | 5 Mar. | 2 June | 31 July | 1 Aug. |
| 1986 | 23 Feb. | 22 May | 20 July | 21 July |
| 1987 | 12 Feb. | 11 May | 10 July | 11 July |
| 1988 | 2 Mar. | 30 May | 28 July | 29 July |
| 1989 | 20 Feb. | 19 May | 17 July | 18 July |
| 1990 | 9 Feb. | 8 May | 7 July | 8 July |
| 1991 | 28 Feb. | 28 May | 26 July | 27 July |
| 1992 | 18 Feb. | 16 May | 14 July | 15 July |
| 1993 | 7 Mar. | 4 June | 2 Aug. | 3 Aug. |
| 1994 | 25 Feb. | 24 May | 22 July | 23 July |
| 1995 | 14 Feb. | 13 May | 12 July | 13 July |
| 1996 | 4 Mar. | 1 June | 30 July | 31 July |
| 1997 | 22 Feb. | 21 May | 19 July | 20 July |
| 1998 | 11 Feb. | 10 May | 8 July | 9 July |
| 1999 | 1 Mar. | 29 May | 27 July | 28 July |
| 2000 | 19 Feb. | 17 May | 16 July | 17 July |
| 2001 | 8 Feb. | 7 May | 5 July | 6 July |
| 2002 | 26 Feb. | 26 May | 24 July | 25 July |
| 2003 | 16 Feb. | 15 May | 13 July | 14 July |
| 2004 | 5 Mar. | 2 June | 31 July | 1 Aug. |
| 2005 | 23 Feb. | 22 May | 21 July | 22 July |
| 2006 | 13 Feb. | 12 May | 10 July | 11 July |
| 2007 | 3 Mar. | 31 May | 29 July | 30 July |
| 2008 | 21 Feb. | 19 May | 17 July | 18 July |
| 2009 | 9 Feb. | 8 May | 7 July | 8 July |
| 2010 | 28 Feb. | 28 May | 26 July | 27 July |
| 2011 | 18 Feb. | 17 May | 15 July | 16 July |
| 2012 | 7 Mar. | 4 June | 2 Aug. | 3 Aug. |
| 2013 | 25 Feb. | 24 May | 22 July | 23 July |
| 2014 | 14 Feb. | 13 May | 12 July | 13 July |
| 2015 | 5 Mar. | 2 June | 31 July | 1 Aug. |
| 2016 | 23 Feb. | 21 May | 9 July | 10 July |
| 2017 | 11 Feb. | 10 May | 8 July | 9 July |
| 2018 | 1 Mar. | 29 May | 27 July | 28 July |
| 2019 | 19 Feb. | 18 May | 16 July | 17 July |
| 2020 | 8 Feb. | 6 May | 5 July | 6 July |
| 2021 | 26 Feb. | 26 May | 24 July | 25 July |
| 2022 | 16 Feb. | 15 May | 13 July | 14 July |
| 2023 | 6 Mar. | 3 June | 1 Aug. | 2 Aug. |
| 2024 | 24 Feb. | 22 May | 21 July | 22 July |
| 2025 | 13 Feb. | 12 May | 10 July | 11 July |
| 2026 | 3 Mar. | 31 May | 29 July | 30 July |
| 2027 | 21 Feb. | 20 May | 18 July | 19 July |

| Year | Makha Bucha | Visakha Bucha | Asalaha Bucha | Khao Phansa |
|---|---|---|---|---|
| 2028 | 10 Feb. | 8 May | 6 July | 7 July |
| 2029 | 27 Feb. | 27 May | 25 July | 26 July |
| 2030 | 17 Feb. | 16 May | 14 July | 15 July |
| 2031 | 7 Mar. | 4 June | 2 Aug. | 3 Aug. |
| 2032 | 25 Feb. | 23 May | 22 July | 23 July |
| 2033 | 14 Feb. | 13 May | 11 July | 12 July |
| 2034 | 4 Mar. | 1 June | 30 July | 31 July |
| 2035 | 22 Feb. | 21 May | 19 July | 20 July |
| 2036 | 11 Feb. | 9 May | 8 July | 9 July |
| 2037 | 1 Mar. | 29 May | 27 July | 28 July |
| 2038 | 19 Feb. | 18 May | 16 July | 17 July |
| 2039 | 8 Feb. | 7 May | 6 July | 7 July |
| 2040 | 27 Feb. | 26 May | 24 July | 25 July |
| 2041 | 16 Feb. | 15 May | 13 July | 14 July |
| 2042 | 6 Mar. | 3 June | 1 Aug. | 2 Aug. |
| 2043 | 24 Feb. | 23 May | 21 July | 22 July |
| 2044 | 13 Feb. | 11 May | 9 July | 10 July |
| 2045 | 2 Mar. | 30 May | 28 July | 29 July |
| 2046 | 20 Feb. | 19 May | 18 July | 19 July |
| 2047 | 10 Feb. | 9 May | 7 July | 8 July |
| 2048 | 28 Feb. | 27 May | 25 July | 26 July |
| 2049 | 17 Feb. | 16 May | 15 July | 16 July |
| 2050 | 8 Mar. | 5 June | 3 Aug. | 4 Aug. |
| 2051 | 26 Feb. | 25 May | 23 July | 24 July |
| 2052 | 15 Feb. | 13 May | 11 July | 12 July |
| 2053 | 4 Mar. | 1 June | 30 July | 31 July |
| 2054 | 22 Feb. | 21 May | 19 July | 20 July |
| 2055 | 11 Feb. | 10 May | 9 July | 10 July |
| 2056 | 1 Mar. | 29 May | 27 July | 28 July |
| 2057 | 19 Feb. | 18 May | 16 July | 17 July |
| 2058 | 8 Feb. | 7 May | 5 July | 6 July |
| 2059 | 26 Feb. | 26 May | 24 July | 25 July |
| 2060 | 16 Feb. | 14 May | 12 July | 13 July |
| 2061 | 5 Mar. | 2 June | 31 July | 1 Aug. |
| 2062 | 23 Feb. | 22 May | 20 July | 21 July |
| 2063 | 12 Feb. | 11 May | 10 July | 11 July |
| 2064 | 2 Mar. | 30 May | 28 July | 29 July |
| 2065 | 20 Feb. | 19 May | 17 July | 18 July |
| 2066 | 9 Feb. | 8 May | 7 July | 8 July |
| 2067 | 28 Feb. | 28 May | 26 July | 27 July |
| 2068 | 18 Feb. | 16 May | 14 July | 15 July |
| 2069 | 7 Mar. | 4 June | 2 Aug. | 3 Aug. |
| 2070 | 25 Feb. | 24 May | 22 July | 23 July |
| 2071 | 14 Feb. | 13 May | 11 July | 12 July |
| 2072 | 3 Mar. | 31 May | 29 July | 30 July |
| 2073 | 21 Feb. | 20 May | 18 July | 19 July |
| 2074 | 10 Feb. | 9 May | 8 July | 9 July |
| 2075 | 1 Mar. | 29 May | 27 July | 28 July |

*C7 continued*

| *Year* | *Makha Bucha* | *Visakha Bucha* | *Asalaha Bucha* | *Khao Phansa* |
|---|---|---|---|---|
| 2076 | 19 Feb. | 17 May | 16 July | 17 July |
| 2077 | 8 Feb. | 7 May | 5 July | 6 July |
| 2078 | 26 Feb. | 26 May | 24 July | 25 July |
| 2079 | 16 Feb. | 15 May | 13 July | 14 July |
| 2080 | 5 Mar. | 2 June | 31 July | 1 Aug. |
| 2081 | 23 Feb. | 22 May | 20 July | 21 July |
| 2082 | 12 Feb. | 11 May | 10 July | 11 July |
| 2083 | 3 Mar. | 31 May | 29 July | 30 July |
| 2084 | 21 Feb. | 19 May | 17 July | 18 July |
| 2085 | 9 Feb. | 8 May | 7 July | 8 July |
| 2086 | 28 Feb. | 28 May | 26 July | 27 July |
| 2087 | 18 Feb. | 17 May | 15 July | 16 July |
| 2088 | 7 Mar. | 4 June | 2 Aug. | 3 Aug. |
| 2089 | 25 Feb. | 24 May | 22 July | 23 July |
| 2090 | 14 Feb. | 13 May | 11 July | 12 July |
| 2091 | 4 Mar. | 1 June | 30 July | 31 July |
| 2092 | 22 Feb. | 20 May | 19 July | 20 July |
| 2093 | 11 Feb. | 10 May | 8 July | 9 July |
| 2094 | 1 Mar. | 29 May | 27 July | 28 July |
| 2095 | 19 Feb. | 18 May | 16 July | 17 July |
| 2096 | 8 Feb. | 6 May | 4 July | 5 July |
| 2097 | 25 Feb. | 25 May | 23 July | 24 July |
| 2098 | 15 Feb. | 14 May | 13 July | 14 July |
| 2099 | 6 Mar. | 3 June | 1 Aug. | 2 Aug. |
| 2100 | 24 Feb. | 23 May | 22 July | 23 July |

# Appendix D: Tables of Holidays Honored by Each Country

## D1. Afghanistan

### (Fixed Holidays)

| | | |
|---|---|---|
| 8 Mar. | Women's Day | multinational |
| 27 Apr. | Independence Day | country-unique |
| 1 May | Labor Day | multinational |
| 30 Aug. | Children's Day | country-unique |
| 31 Aug. | Pashtunistan Day | country-unique |

### (Algorithmic Holidays)

| | | |
|---|---|---|
| 20 or 21 Mar. | New Year's Day | Afghani |
| | Islamic New Year | Islamic |
| | Ashura | Islamic |
| | Mohammed's Birthday | Islamic |
| | 1st Day of Ramadan | Islamic |
| | Eid al Fitr (4 days) | Islamic |
| | Eid al Adha (4 days) | Islamic |

## D2. Albania

### (Fixed Holidays)

| | | |
|---|---|---|
| 1 Jan. | New Year's Day | multinational |
| 11 Jan. | Republic Day | country-unique |
| 1 May | Labor Day | multinational |
| 28 Nov. | Independence Day | country-unique |
| 29 Nov. | Liberation Day | country-unique |
| 31 Dec. | New Year's Eve | multinational |

# D3. Algeria

## (Fixed Holidays)

| | | |
|---|---|---|
| 1 Jan. | New Year's Day | multinational |
| 1 May | Labor Day | multinational |
| 19 June | Righting Day | country-unique |
| 5 July | Independence Day | country-unique |
| 1 Nov. | Revolution Day | country-unique |

## (Algorithmic Holidays)

| | |
|---|---|
| Islamic New Year | Islamic |
| Ashura | Islamic |
| Mohammed's Birthday | Islamic |
| Eid al Fitr (4 days) | Islamic |
| Eid al Adha (4 days) | Islamic |

# D4. Andorra

## (Fixed Holidays)

| | | |
|---|---|---|
| 1 Jan. | New Year's Day | multinational |
| 6 Jan. | Epiphany | Christian |
| 19 Mar. | Saint Joseph's Day | Christian |
| 1 May | Labor Day | multinational |
| 24 June | Saint John's Day | country-unique |
| 29 June | Saint Paul's Day | Christian |
| 15 Aug. | Assumption | Christian |
| 8 Sep. | National Day | country-unique |
| 1 Nov. | All Saints' Day | Christian |
| 4 Nov. | Saint Charles' Day | country-unique |
| 8 Dec. | Immaculate Conception | Christian |
| 24 Dec. | Christmas Eve | multinational |
| 25 Dec. | Christmas Day | multinational |
| 26 Dec. | Boxing Day | multinational |

## (Algorithmic Holidays)

| | | |
|---|---|---|
| Feb.–Mar. | Shrove Monday | Christian |
| Feb.–Mar. | Shrove Tuesday | Christian |
| Mar.–Apr. | Maundy Thursday | Christian |
| Mar.–Apr. | Good Friday | Christian |
| Mar.–Apr. | Easter Monday | Christian |
| May–June | Ascension Thursday | Christian |
| May–June | Whitmonday | Christian |
| May–June | Corpus Christi | Christian |

# D5. Angola

## *(Fixed Holidays)*

| | | |
|---|---|---|
| 1 Jan. | New Year's Day | multinational |
| 27 Mar. | Evacuation Day | country-unique |
| 1 May | Labor Day | multinational |
| 17 Sep. | Heroes' Day | country-unique |
| 11 Nov. | Independence Day | country-unique |
| 10 Dec. | MPLA Foundation Day | country-unique |
| 25 Dec. | Family Day | country-unique |

# D6. Antigua

## *(Fixed Holidays)*

| | | |
|---|---|---|
| 1 Jan. | New Year's Day | multinational |
| 1 May | Labor Day | multinational |
| 1 Nov. | Independence Day | country-unique |
| 25 Dec. | Christmas Day | multinational |

# D7. Argentina

## *(Fixed Holidays)*

| | | |
|---|---|---|
| 1 Jan. | New Year's Day | multinational |
| 6 Jan. | Epiphany | Christian |
| 1 May | Labor Day | multinational |
| 25 May | National Day | country-unique |
| 9 June | Independence Day | country-unique |
| 20 June | Flag Day | country-unique |
| 17 Aug. | San Martin Day | country-unique |
| 12 Oct. | Columbus Day | multinational |
| 1 Nov. | All Saints' Day | Christian |
| 8 Dec. | Immaculate Conception | Christian |
| 25 Dec. | Christmas Day | multinational |
| 31 Dec. | Bank Holiday | multinational |

## *(Algorithmic Holidays)*

| | | |
|---|---|---|
| Feb.–Mar. | Shrove Monday | Christian |
| Feb.–Mar. | Shrove Tuesday | Christian |
| Mar.–Apr. | Maundy Thursday | Christian |
| Mar.–Apr. | Good Friday | Christian |
| Last Fri. in Nov. | Bank Holiday | country-unique |

# D8. Armenia

## *(Projected Holidays)*

### *(Fixed Holidays)*

| | | |
|---|---|---|
| 1 Jan. | New Year's Day | multinational |
| 1 May | Labor Day | multinational |
| 23 Sep. | Independence Day | country-unique |
| 25 Dec. | Christmas Day | multinational |

### *(Algorithmic Holidays)*

| | | |
|---|---|---|
| Mar.-Apr. | Good Friday | Christian |
| Mar.-Apr. | Holy Saturday | Christian |
| Mar.-Apr. | Easter Monday | Christian |

# D9. Aruba

### *(Fixed Holidays)*

| | | |
|---|---|---|
| 1 Jan. | New Year's Day | multinational |
| 1 May | Labor Day | multinational |
| 25 Dec. | Christmas Day | multinational |

### *(Algorithmic Holidays)*

| | | |
|---|---|---|
| Mar.-Apr. | Good Friday | Christian |

# D10. Australia

### *(Fixed Holidays)*

| | | |
|---|---|---|
| 1 Jan. | New Year's Day | multinational |
| 25 Apr. | ANZAC Day | shared with New Zealand |
| 25 Dec. | Christmas Day | multinational |
| 26 Dec. | Boxing Day | multinational |

### *(Algorithmic Holidays)*

| | | |
|---|---|---|
| Mon. after 25 Jan. | Australia Day | country-unique |
| Mar.-Apr. | Good Friday | Christian |

| | | |
|---|---|---|
| Mar.-Apr. | Holy Saturday | Christian |
| Mar.-Apr. | Easter Monday | Christian |
| 2nd Mon. in June | Queen's Birthday | shared with Fiji, New Guinea, and United Kingdom |

# D11. Austria

## *(Fixed Holidays)*

| | | |
|---|---|---|
| 1 Jan. | New Year's Day | multinational |
| 6 Jan. | Epiphany | Christian |
| 1 May | Labor Day | multinational |
| 15 Aug. | Assumption | Christian |
| 26 Oct. | National Day | country-unique |
| 1 Nov. | All Saints' Day | Christian |
| 8 Dec. | Immaculate Conception | Christian |
| 24 Dec. | Christmas Eve | multinational |
| 25 Dec. | Christmas Day | multinational |
| 26 Dec. | Boxing Day | multinational |

## *(Algorithmic Holidays)*

| | | |
|---|---|---|
| Mar.-Apr. | Easter Monday | Christian |
| May-June | Ascension Thursday | Christian |
| May-June | Whitmonday | Christian |
| May-June | Corpus Christi | Christian |

# D12. Azerbaijan

## *(Projected Holidays)*

## *(Fixed Holidays)*

| | | |
|---|---|---|
| 1 Jan. | New Year's Day | multinational |
| 1 May | Labor Day | multinational |
| 30 Aug. | Independence Day | country-unique |
| 25 Dec. | Christmas Day | multinational |

## *(Algorithmic Holidays)*

| | |
|---|---|
| Islamic New Year | Islamic |
| Mohammed's Birthday | Islamic |
| 1st Day of Ramadan | Islamic |

*D12 continued*

| | | |
|---|---|---|
| | Eid al Fitr (4 days) | Islamic |
| | Eid al Adha (4 days) | Islamic |

# D13. Bahamas

## *(Fixed Holidays)*

| | | |
|---|---|---|
| 1 Jan. | New Year's Day | multinational |
| 4 June | Labour Day | country-unique |
| 10 July | Independence Day | country-unique |
| 12 Oct. | Columbus Day | multinational |
| 25 Dec. | Christmas Day | multinational |
| 26 Dec. | Boxing Day | multinational |

## *(Algorithmic Holidays)*

| | | |
|---|---|---|
| Mar.–Apr. | Good Friday | Christian |
| Mar.–Apr. | Holy Saturday | Christian |
| Mar.–Apr. | Easter Monday | Christian |
| May–June | Whitmonday | Christian |
| 1st Mon. in Aug. | Emancipation Day | shared with Barbados |

# D14. Bahrain

## *(Fixed Holidays)*

| | | |
|---|---|---|
| 1 Jan. | New Year's Day | multinational |
| 1 May | Labor Day | multinational |
| 16 Dec. | National Day | country-unique |

## *(Algorithmic Holidays)*

| | | |
|---|---|---|
| | Islamic New Year | Islamic |
| | Ashura | Islamic |
| | Mohammed's Birthday | Islamic |
| | Eid al Fitr (4 days) | Islamic |
| | Eid al Adha (4 days) | Islamic |

# D15. Bangladesh

## *(Fixed Holidays)*

| | | |
|---|---|---|
| 21 Feb. | Saheed Day | country-unique |
| 26 Mar. | Independence Day | country-unique |
| 1 May | Labor Day | multinational |
| 7 Nov. | Revolution Day | country-unique |
| 16 Dec. | Victory Day | country-unique |
| 25 Dec. | Christmas Day | multinational |

## *(Algorithmic Holidays)*

| | |
|---|---|
| Islamic New Year | Islamic |
| Mohammed's Birthday | Islamic |
| Eid al Fitr (4 days) | Islamic |
| Eid al Adha (4 days) | Islamic |

# D16. Barbados

## *(Fixed Holidays)*

| | | |
|---|---|---|
| 1 Jan. | New Year's Day | multinational |
| 1 May | Labor Day | multinational |
| 30 Nov. | Independence Day | country-unique |
| 25 Dec. | Christmas Day | multinational |
| 26 Dec. | Boxing Day | multinational |

## *(Algorithmic Holidays)*

| | | |
|---|---|---|
| Mar.–Apr. | Good Friday | Christian |
| Mar.–Apr. | Easter Monday | Christian |
| May–June | Whitmonday | Christian |
| 1st Mon. in Aug. | Emancipation Day | shared with Bahamas |
| 1st Mon. in Oct. | Bank Holiday | country-unique |

# D17. Belarus

## *(Projected Holidays)*

## *(Fixed Holidays)*

| | | |
|---|---|---|
| 1 Jan. | New Year's Day | multinational |
| 1 May | Labor Day | multinational |

*D17 continued*

| | | |
|---|---|---|
| 25 Aug. | Independence Day | country-unique |
| 25 Dec. | Christmas Day | multinational |

### *(Algorithmic Holidays)*

| | | |
|---|---|---|
| Mar.-Apr. | Good Friday | Christian |
| Mar.-Apr. | Holy Saturday | Christian |
| Mar.-Apr. | Easter Monday | Christian |

## D18. Belgium

### *(Fixed Holidays)*

| | | |
|---|---|---|
| 1 Jan. | New Year's Day | multinational |
| 1 May | Labor Day | multinational |
| 21 July | National Day | country-unique |
| 15 Aug. | Assumption | Christian |
| 1 Nov. | All Saints' Day | Christian |
| 2 Nov. | All Souls' Day | Christian |
| 11 Nov. | Armistice Day | multinational |
| 25 Dec. | Christmas Day | multinational |
| 26 Dec. | Boxing Day | multinational |

### *(Algorithmic Holidays)*

| | | |
|---|---|---|
| Mar.-Apr. | Easter Monday | Christian |
| May-June | Ascension Thursday | Christian |
| May-June | Whitmonday | Christian |

## D19. Belize

### *(Fixed Holidays)*

| | | |
|---|---|---|
| 1 Jan. | New Year's Day | multinational |
| 1 May | Labor Day | multinational |
| 10 Sep. | National Day | country-unique |
| 21 Sep. | Independence Day | country-unique |
| 12 Oct. | Columbus Day | multinational |
| 19 Nov. | Garifuna Day | country-unique |
| 25 Dec. | Christmas Day | multinational |
| 26 Dec. | Boxing Day | multinational |

### (Algorithmic Holidays)

| | | |
|---|---|---|
| Mar.-Apr. | Good Friday | Christian |
| Mar.-Apr. | Easter Monday | Christian |

## D20. Benin

### (Fixed Holidays)

| | | |
|---|---|---|
| 1 Jan. | New Year's Day | multinational |
| 1 May | Labor Day | multinational |
| 1 Aug. | Independence Day | country-unique |
| 15 Aug. | Assumption | Christian |
| 26 Oct. | Revolution Day | country-unique |
| 1 Nov. | All Saints' Day | Christian |
| 30 Nov. | National Day | country-unique |
| 25 Dec. | Christmas Day | multinational |
| 31 Dec. | New Year's Eve | multinational |

### (Algorithmic Holidays)

| | | |
|---|---|---|
| Mar.-Apr. | Easter Monday | Christian |
| May-June | Ascension Thursday | Christian |
| May-June | Whitmonday | Christian |
| | 1st Day of Ramadan | Islamic |
| | Eid al Fitr (4 days) | Islamic |
| | Eid al Adha (4 days) | Islamic |

## D21. Bermuda

### United Kingdom Holidays and:

### (Fixed Holidays)

| | | |
|---|---|---|
| 11 Nov. | Armistice Day | multinational |

## D22. Bhutan

### (Fixed Holidays)

| | | |
|---|---|---|
| 11 Nov. | King's Birthday | country-unique |
| 17 Dec. | National Day | country-unique |

# D23. Bolivia

## (Fixed Holidays)

| | | |
|---|---|---|
| 1 Jan. | New Year's Day | multinational |
| 1 May | Labor Day | multinational |
| 6 Aug. | Independence Day | country-unique |
| 12 Oct. | Columbus Day | multinational |
| 1 Nov. | All Saints' Day | Christian |
| 2 Nov. | All Souls' Day | Christian |
| 25 Dec. | Christmas Day | multinational |

## (Algorithmic Holidays)

| | | |
|---|---|---|
| Feb.–Mar. | Shrove Monday | Christian |
| Feb.–Mar. | Shrove Tuesday | Christian |
| Mar.–Apr. | Maundy Thursday | Christian |
| Mar.–Apr. | Good Friday | Christian |
| May–June | Corpus Christi | Christian |

# D24. Bosnia and Herzegovina

## *(Projected Holidays)*

## (Fixed Holidays)

| | | |
|---|---|---|
| 1 Jan. | New Year's Day | multinational |
| 1 May | Labor Day | multinational |
| 15 Oct. | Independence Day | country-unique |
| 1 Nov. | All Saints' Day | Christian |

# D25. Botswana

## (Fixed Holidays)

| | | |
|---|---|---|
| 1 Jan. | New Year's Day | multinational |
| 30 Sep. | Independence Day | country-unique |
| 25 Dec. | Christmas Day | multinational |
| 26 Dec. | Boxing Day | multinational |

## (Algorithmic Holidays)

| | | |
|---|---|---|
| Mar.–Apr. | Good Friday | Christian |
| Mar.–Apr. | Holy Saturday | Christian |

| | | |
|---|---|---|
| Mar.–Apr. | Easter Monday | Christian |
| May–June | Ascension Thursday | Christian |
| May–June | Whitmonday | Christian |
| 3rd Mon. in July | President's Birthday | country-unique |

## D26. Brazil

### *(Fixed Holidays)*

| | | |
|---|---|---|
| 1 Jan. | Bank Holiday | multinational |
| 21 Apr. | Tiradentes Day | country-unique |
| 1 May | Labor Day | multinational |
| 7 Sep. | Independence Day | country-unique |
| 12 Oct. | Columbus Day | multinational |
| 2 Nov. | Memorial Day | country-unique |
| 15 Nov. | Republic Day | country-unique |
| 24 Dec. | Christmas Eve | multinational |
| 25 Dec. | Christmas Day | multinational |
| 31 Dec. | New Year's Eve | multinational |

### *(Algorithmic Holidays)*

| | | |
|---|---|---|
| Feb.–Mar. | Shrove Monday | Christian |
| Feb.–Mar. | Shrove Tuesday | Christian |
| Feb.–Mar. | Ash Wednesday | Christian |
| Mar.–Apr. | Maundy Thursday | Christian |
| Mar.–Apr. | Good Friday | Christian |
| Mar.–Apr. | Holy Saturday | Christian |
| May–June | Corpus Christi | Christian |

## D27. Brunei

### *(Fixed Holidays)*

| | | |
|---|---|---|
| 1 Jan. | New Year's Day | multinational |
| 23 Feb. | National Day | country-unique |
| 1 May | Labor Day | multinational |
| 31 May | Regiment Day | country-unique |
| 15 July | Sultan's Birthday | country-unique |
| 29 Sep. | Constitution Day | country-unique |
| 25 Dec. | Christmas Day | multinational |

*D27 continued*

### *(Algorithmic Holidays)*

| | | |
|---|---|---|
| Jan.-Feb. | Chinese New Year | Asian |
| Mar.-Apr. | Holy Saturday | Christian |
| | Islamic New Year | Islamic |
| | Mohammed's Birthday | Islamic |
| | Hari Raya Puasa | Far East Islamic |
| | Hari Raya Haji | Far East Islamic |
| | Isra a Majraj | Islamic |

## D28. Bulgaria

### *(Fixed Holidays)*

| | | |
|---|---|---|
| 1 Jan. | New Year's Day | multinational |
| 3 Mar. | Liberation Day | country-unique |
| 1 May | Labor Day | multinational |
| 24 May | Culture Day | country-unique |
| 9 and 10 Sep. | National Days | country-unique |

## D29. Burkina Faso

### *(Fixed Holidays)*

| | | |
|---|---|---|
| 1 Jan. | New Year's Day | multinational |
| 3 Jan. | Revolution Day | country-unique |
| 8 Mar. | Women's Day | multinational |
| 1 May | Labor Day | multinational |
| 4 and 5 Aug. | Independence Days | country-unique |
| 15 Aug. | Assumption | Christian |
| 1 Nov. | All Saints' Day | Christian |
| 11 Dec. | National Day | country-unique |
| 25 Dec. | Christmas Day | multinational |

### *(Algorithmic Holidays)*

| | | |
|---|---|---|
| Mar.-Apr. | Easter Monday | Christian |
| May-June | Ascension Thursday | Christian |
| May-June | Whitmonday | Christian |
| | Mohammed's Birthday | Islamic |
| | Eid al Fitr (4 days) | Islamic |
| | Eid al Adha (4 days) | Islamic |

# D30. Burma

## (Fixed Holidays)

| | | |
|---|---|---|
| 4 Jan. | Independence Day | country-unique |
| 12 Feb. | Union Day | country-unique |
| 27 Mar. | Resistance Day | country-unique |
| 1 May | Labor Day | multinational |
| 19 July | Martyrs' Day | country-unique |
| 25 Dec. | Christmas Day | multinational |

## (Algorithmic Holidays)

| | |
|---|---|
| Full Moon Days | country-unique |
| Eid al Fitr (4 days) | Islamic |

# D31. Burundi

## (Fixed Holidays)

| | | |
|---|---|---|
| 1 Jan. | New Year's Day | multinational |
| 1 May | Labor Day | multinational |
| 1 July | Independence Day | country-unique |
| 15 Aug. | Assumption | Christian |
| 18 Sep. | Victory of Uprona Day | country-unique |
| 1 Nov. | All Saints' Day | Christian |
| 28 Nov. | Republic Day | country-unique |
| 25 Dec. | Christmas Day | multinational |

## (Algorithmic Holidays)

| | | |
|---|---|---|
| Mar.–Apr. | Easter Monday | Christian |
| May–June | Ascension Thursday | Christian |

# D32. Cambodia

## (Fixed Holidays)

| | | |
|---|---|---|
| 1 Jan. | New Year's Day | multinational |
| 17 Apr. | Independence Day | country-unique |
| 1 May | Labor Day | multinational |

# D33. Cameroon

## (Fixed Holidays)

| | | |
|---|---|---|
| 1 Jan. | Independence Day | country-unique |
| 11 Feb. | Youth Day | country-unique |
| 1 May | Labor Day | multinational |
| 20 May | Constitution Day | country-unique |
| 15 Aug. | Assumption | Christian |
| 1 Oct. | Unification Day | country-unique |
| 1 Nov. | All Saints' Day | Christian |
| 25 Dec. | Christmas Day | multinational |

## (Algorithmic Holidays)

| | | |
|---|---|---|
| Mar.–Apr. | Good Friday | Christian |
| Mar.–Apr. | Easter Monday | Christian |
| May–June | Ascension Thursday | Christian |
| May–June | Whitmonday | Christian |
| | Eid al Fitr (4 days) | Islamic |
| | Eid al Adha (4 days) | Islamic |

# D34. Canada

## (Fixed Holidays)

| | | |
|---|---|---|
| 1 Jan. | New Year's Day | multinational |
| 1 July | Canada Day | country-unique |
| 11 Nov. | Armistice Day | multinational |
| 25 Dec. | Christmas Day | multinational |
| 26 Dec. | Boxing Day | multinational |

## (Algorithmic Holidays)

| | | |
|---|---|---|
| Mon. before 25 May | Victoria Day | country-unique |
| Mar.–Apr. | Good Friday | Christian |
| Mar.–Apr. | Easter Monday | Christian |
| May–June | Whitmonday | Christian |
| 1st Mon. in Aug. | Civic Holiday | country-unique |
| 1st Mon. in Sep. | Labour Day | country-unique |
| 2nd Mon. in Oct. | Thanksgiving Day | country-unique |

# D35. Cape Verde

## (Fixed Holidays)

| | | |
|---|---|---|
| 1 Jan. | New Year's Day | multinational |

| | | |
|---|---|---|
| 8 Mar. | Women's Day | multinational |
| 1 May | Labor Day | multinational |
| 5 July | Independence Day | country-unique |
| 25 Dec. | Christmas Day | multinational |

# D36. Cayman Islands

## *(Fixed Holidays)*

| | | |
|---|---|---|
| 1 Jan. | New Year's Day | multinational |
| 1 May | Labor Day | multinational |
| 17 May | Discovery Day | country-unique |
| 25 Dec. | Christmas Day | multinational |

## *(Algorithmic Holidays)*

| | | |
|---|---|---|
| 1st Mon. in July | Constitution Day | country-unique |

# D37. Central African Republic

## *(Fixed Holidays)*

| | | |
|---|---|---|
| 1 Jan. | New Year's Day | multinational |
| 29 Mar. | Boganda Day | country-unique |
| 1 May | Labor Day | multinational |
| 25 May | Africa Day | multinational |
| 13 Aug. | Independence Day | country-unique |
| 1 Nov. | All Saints' Day | Christian |
| 1 Dec. | National Day | country-unique |
| 25 Dec. | Christmas Day | multinational |

## *(Algorithmic Holidays)*

| | | |
|---|---|---|
| Mar.–Apr. | Good Friday | Christian |
| Mar.–Apr. | Easter Monday | Christian |
| May–June | Ascension Thursday | Christian |
| May–June | Whitmonday | Christian |

# D38. Chad

## *(Fixed Holidays)*

| | | |
|---|---|---|
| 1 Jan. | New Year's Day | multinational |

*D38 continued*

| | | |
|---|---|---|
| 13 Apr. | National Day | country-unique |
| 1 May | Labor Day | multinational |
| 25 May | Africa Day | multinational |
| 7 June | Revolution Day | country-unique |
| 11 Aug. | Independence Day | country-unique |
| 1 Nov. | All Saints' Day | Christian |
| 28 Nov. | Republic Day | country-unique |
| 25 Dec. | Christmas Day | multinational |

### *(Algorithmic Holidays)*

| | | |
|---|---|---|
| Mar.–Apr. | Easter Monday | Christian |
| May–June | Ascension Thursday | Christian |
| May–June | Whitmonday | Christian |
| | Mohammed's Birthday | Islamic |
| | Eid al Fitr (4 days) | Islamic |
| | Eid al Adha (4 days) | Islamic |

## D39. Chile

### *(Fixed Holidays)*

| | | |
|---|---|---|
| 1 Jan. | New Year's Day | multinational |
| 1 May | Labor Day | multinational |
| 21 May | Navy Day | country-unique |
| 29 June | Saint Paul's Day | Christian |
| 15 Aug. | Assumption | Christian |
| 11 Sep. | Revolution Day | country-unique |
| 18 Sep. | Independence Day | country-unique |
| 19 Sep. | Armed Forces Day | country-unique |
| 12 Oct. | Columbus Day | multinational |
| 1 Nov. | All Saints' Day | Christian |
| 8 Dec. | Immaculate Conception | Christian |
| 25 Dec. | Christmas Day | multinational |
| 31 Dec. | Bank Holiday | multinational |

### *(Algorithmic Holidays)*

| | | |
|---|---|---|
| Mar.–Apr. | Good Friday | Christian |
| Mar.–Apr. | Holy Saturday | Christian |
| May–June | Corpus Christi | Christian |
| last Fri. in June | Bank Holiday | shared with Ecuador, El Salvador, and Finland |

# D40. China

## (Fixed Holidays)

| | | |
|---|---|---|
| 1 Jan. | New Year's Day | multinational |
| 8 Mar. | Women's Day | multinational |
| 5 Apr. | Tomb Sweeping Day | Asian |
| 1 May | Labor Day | multinational |
| 1 and 2 Oct. | National Days | country-unique |

## (Algorithmic Holidays)

| | | |
|---|---|---|
| Jan.-Feb. | Chinese New Year (3 days) | Asian |
| May-June | Dragon Boat Festival | Asian |
| Sep.-Oct. | Ancestors' Day | Asian |
| Oct. | Mid-autumn Day | Asian |

# D41. Colombia

## (Fixed Holidays)

| | | |
|---|---|---|
| 1 Jan. | New Year's Day | multinational |
| 6 Jan. | Epiphany | Christian |
| 19 Mar. | Saint Joseph's Day | Christian |
| 1 May | Labor Day | multinational |
| 29 June | Saint Paul's Day | Christian |
| 20 July | Independence Day | country-unique |
| 7 Aug. | Boyaca Day | country-unique |
| 12 Oct. | Columbus Day | multinational |
| 1 Nov. | All Saints' Day | Christian |
| 8 Dec. | Immaculate Conception | Christian |
| 25 Dec. | Christmas Day | multinational |
| 31 Dec. | Bank Holiday | multinational |

## (Algorithmic Holidays)

| | | |
|---|---|---|
| Feb.-Mar. | Shrove Monday | Christian |
| Feb.-Mar. | Shrove Tuesday | Christian |
| Feb.-Mar. | Ash Wednesday | Christian |
| Mar.-Apr. | Maundy Thursday | Christian |
| Mar.-Apr. | Good Friday | Christian |
| Mar.-Apr. | Holy Saturday | Christian |
| May-June | Ascension Thursday | Christian |
| May-June | Corpus Christi | Christian |

# D42. Comoros

## (Fixed Holidays)

| | | |
|---|---|---|
| 1 Jan. | New Year's Day | multinational |
| 1 May | Labor Day | multinational |
| 6 July | Independence Day | country-unique |

## (Algorithmic Holidays)

| | |
|---|---|
| Islamic New Year | Islamic |
| Mohammed's Birthday | Islamic |
| Eid al Fitr (4 days) | Islamic |
| Eid al Adha (4 days) | Islamic |

# D43. Congo

## (Fixed Holidays)

| | | |
|---|---|---|
| 1 Jan. | New Year's Day | multinational |
| 1 May | Labor Day | multinational |
| 13 through 15 Aug. | Independence Days | country-unique |
| 1 Nov. | All Saints' Day | Christian |
| 25 Dec. | Children's Day | country-unique |
| 31 Dec. | Republic Day | country-unique |

## (Algorithmic Holidays)

| | | |
|---|---|---|
| Mar.–Apr. | Easter Monday | Christian |
| May–June | Ascension Thursday | Christian |
| May–June | Whitmonday | Christian |

# D44. Costa Rica

## (Fixed Holidays)

| | | |
|---|---|---|
| 1 Jan. | New Year's Day | multinational |
| 19 Mar. | Saint Joseph's Day | Christian |
| 11 Apr. | Heroes' Day | country-unique |
| 1 May | Labor Day | multinational |
| 29 June | Saint Paul's Day | Christian |
| 25 July | Guanacaste Day | country-unique |

| | | |
|---|---|---|
| 2 Aug. | Virgin of the Angels Day | country-unique |
| 15 Aug. | Assumption | Christian |
| 15 Sep. | Independence Day | country-unique |
| 12 Oct. | Columbus Day | multinational |
| 8 Dec. | Immaculate Conception | Christian |
| 24 Dec. | Christmas Eve | multinational |
| 25 Dec. | Christmas Day | multinational |

### *(Algorithmic Holidays)*

| | | |
|---|---|---|
| Mar.-Apr. | Maundy Thursday | Christian |
| Mar.-Apr. | Good Friday | Christian |
| Mar.-Apr. | Holy Saturday | Christian |
| May-June | Corpus Christi | Christian |

## D45. Croatia

### *(Projected Holidays)*

### *(Fixed Holidays)*

| | | |
|---|---|---|
| 1 Jan. | New Year's Day | multinational |
| 1 May | Labor Day | multinational |
| 25 June | Independence Day | country-unique |
| 15 Aug. | Assumption | Christian |
| 1 Nov. | All Saints' Day | Christian |
| 8 Dec. | Immaculate Conception | Christian |
| 24 Dec. | Christmas Eve | multinational |
| 25 Dec. | Christmas Day | multinational |

### *(Algorithmic Holidays)*

| | | |
|---|---|---|
| Mar.-Apr. | Good Friday | Christian |
| Mar.-Apr. | Easter Monday | Christian |
| May-June | Ascension Thursday | Christian |

## D46. Cuba

### *(Fixed Holidays)*

| | | |
|---|---|---|
| 1 Jan. | Liberation Day | country-unique |
| 1 May | Labor Day | multinational |
| 25 through 27 July | Revolution Days | country-unique |
| 11 Oct. | Independence War Day | country-unique |

# D47. Cyprus

## (Fixed Holidays)

| | | |
|---|---|---|
| 1 Jan. | New Year's Day | multinational |
| 6 Jan. | Epiphany | Christian |
| 25 Mar. | Greek Independence Day | shared with Greece |
| 16 Apr. | Independence Day | country-unique |
| 1 May | Labor Day | multinational |
| 25 Dec. | Christmas Day | multinational |
| 26 Dec. | Boxing Day | multinational |

## (Algorithmic Holidays)

| | | |
|---|---|---|
| Apr.-May | Good Friday | Orthodox |
| Apr.-May | Easter Monday | Orthodox |
| | Mohammed's Birthday | Islamic |
| | Eid al Fitr (4 days) | Islamic |
| | Eid al Adha (4 days) | Islamic |

# D48. Czech Republic

## (Projected Holidays)

## (Fixed Holidays)

| | | |
|---|---|---|
| 1 Jan. | New Year's Day | multinational |
| 1 May | Labor Day | multinational |
| 9 May | Liberation Day | country-unique |
| 24 Dec. | Christmas Eve | multinational |
| 25 Dec. | Christmas Day | multinational |
| 26 Dec. | Boxing Day | multinational |
| 31 Dec. | New Year's Eve | multinational |

## (Algorithmic Holidays)

| | | |
|---|---|---|
| Mar.-Apr. | Holy Saturday | Christian |
| Mar.-Apr. | Easter Monday | Christian |

# D49. Denmark

## (Fixed Holidays)

| | | |
|---|---|---|
| 1 Jan. | New Year's Day | multinational |

| | | |
|---|---|---|
| 5 June | Constitution Day | country-unique |
| 24 Dec. | Christmas Eve | multinational |
| 25 Dec. | Christmas Day | multinational |
| 26 Dec. | Boxing Day | multinational |
| 31 Dec. | New Year's Eve | multinational |

### *(Algorithmic Holidays)*

| | | |
|---|---|---|
| Mar.-Apr. | Maundy Thursday | Christian |
| Mar.-Apr. | Good Friday | Christian |
| Mar.-Apr. | Easter Monday | Christian |
| Apr.-May | All Prayers' Day | Christian |
| May-June | Ascension Thursday | Christian |
| May-June | Whitmonday | Christian |

## D50. Djibouti

### *(Fixed Holidays)*

| | | |
|---|---|---|
| 1 Jan. | New Year's Day | multinational |
| 1 May | Labor Day | multinational |
| 27 June | Independence Day | country-unique |

### *(Algorithmic Holidays)*

| | |
|---|---|
| Islamic New Year | Islamic |
| Mohammed's Birthday | Islamic |
| Eid al Fitr (4 days) | Islamic |
| Eid al Adha (4 days) | Islamic |
| Isra a Majraj | Islamic |

## D51. Dominica

### *(Fixed Holidays)*

| | | |
|---|---|---|
| 1 Jan. | New Year's Day | multinational |
| 1 May | Labor Day | multinational |
| 3 Nov. | Independence Day | country-unique |
| 25 Dec. | Christmas Day | multinational |

# D52. Dominican Republic

## (Fixed Holidays)

| | | |
|---|---|---|
| 1 Jan. | New Year's Day | multinational |
| 21 Jan. | Altagracia Day | country-unique |
| 26 Jan. | Duarte Day | country-unique |
| 27 Feb. | Independence Day | country-unique |
| 1 May | Labor Day | multinational |
| 16 Aug. | Republic Day | country-unique |
| 24 Sep. | Mercedes Day | country-unique |
| 25 Dec. | Christmas Day | multinational |

## (Algorithmic Holidays)

| | | |
|---|---|---|
| Mar.–Apr. | Good Friday | Christian |
| May–June | Corpus Christi | Christian |

# D53. Ecuador

## (Fixed Holidays)

| | | |
|---|---|---|
| 1 Jan. | New Year's Day | multinational |
| 1 May | Labor Day | multinational |
| 24 May | Independence Battle Day | country-unique |
| 29 June | Saint Paul's Day | Christian |
| 10 Aug. | Independence Day | country-unique |
| 12 Oct. | Columbus Day | multinational |
| 2 Nov. | All Souls' Day | Christian |
| 3 Nov. | Cuenca Independence Day | country-unique |
| 25 Dec. | Christmas Day | multinational |
| 26 Dec. | Boxing Day | multinational |
| 31 Dec. | Bank Holiday | multinational |

## (Algorithmic Holidays)

| | | |
|---|---|---|
| Feb.–Mar. | Shrove Monday | Christian |
| Feb.–Mar. | Shrove Tuesday | Christian |
| Mar.–Apr. | Maundy Thursday | Christian |
| Mar.–Apr. | Good Friday | Christian |
| last Fri. in June | Bank Holiday | shared with Chile, El Salvador, and Finland |

# D54. Egypt

## (Fixed Holidays)

| | | |
|---|---|---|
| 7 Jan. | Coptic Christmas Day | shared with Ethiopia |
| 25 Apr. | Sainai Day | country-unique |
| 1 May | Labor Day | multinational |
| 18 June | Independence Day | country-unique |
| 1 July | Bank Holiday | multinational |
| 23 July | Revolution Day | country-unique |
| 6 Oct. | Armed Forces Day | country-unique |
| 24 Oct. | Suez Victory Day | country-unique |

## (Algorithmic Holidays)

| | | |
|---|---|---|
| 11 or 12 Sep. | New Year's Day | Coptic |
| | Islamic New Year | Islamic |
| | Mohammed's Birthday | Islamic |
| | Eid al Fitr (4 days) | Islamic |
| | Eid al Adha (4 days) | Islamic |

# D55. El Salvador

## (Fixed Holidays)

| | | |
|---|---|---|
| 1 Jan. | New Year's Day | multinational |
| 1 May | Labor Day | multinational |
| 29 June | Saint Paul's Day | Christian |
| 3 through 6 Aug. | Summer Holidays | country-unique |
| 15 Sep. | Independence Day | country-unique |
| 12 Oct. | Columbus Day | multinational |
| 2 Nov. | All Souls' Day | Christian |
| 5 Nov. | First Cry of Independence Day | country-unique |
| 11 Nov. | Armistice Day | multinational |
| 24 Dec. | Christmas Eve | multinational |
| 25 Dec. | Christmas Day | multinational |
| 31 Dec. | Bank Holiday | multinational |

## (Algorithmic Holidays)

| | | |
|---|---|---|
| Mar.–Apr. | Maundy Thursday | Christian |
| Mar.–Apr. | Good Friday | Christian |
| May–June | Corpus Christi | Christian |
| last Fri. in June | Bank Holiday | shared with Chile, Ecuador, and Finland |

# D56. England

## *United Kingdom Holidays and:*

### *(Algorithmic Holidays)*

| | | |
|---|---|---|
| Mar.–Apr. | Easter Monday | Christian |
| last Mon. in Aug. | Summer Break | shared with Northern Ireland and Wales |

# D57. Equatorial Guinea

### *(Fixed Holidays)*

| | | |
|---|---|---|
| 1 Jan. | New Year's Day | multinational |
| 6 Jan. | Epiphany | Christian |
| 1 May | Labor Day | multinational |
| 25 May | Africa Day | multinational |
| 5 June | President's Birthday | country-unique |
| 12 Oct. | Independence Day | country-unique |
| 1 Nov. | All Saints' Day | Christian |
| 10 Dec. | Human Rights Day | country-unique |
| 8 Dec. | Immaculate Conception | Christian |
| 25 Dec. | Christmas Day | multinational |

### *(Algorithmic Holidays)*

| | | |
|---|---|---|
| Mar.–Apr. | Good Friday | Christian |
| Mar.–Apr. | Easter Monday | Christian |
| May–June | Ascension Thursday | Christian |
| May–June | Corpus Christi | Christian |

# D58. Eritrea

## ***(Projected Holidays)***

### *(Fixed Holidays)*

| | | |
|---|---|---|
| 1 Jan. | New Year's Day | multinational |
| 1 May | Labor Day | multinational |
| 25 May | Independence Day | country-unique |
| 25 Dec. | Christmas Day | multinational |

### (Algorithmic Holidays)

| | |
|---|---|
| Islamic New Year | Islamic |
| Mohammed's Birthday | Islamic |
| 1st Day of Ramadan | Islamic |
| Eid al Fitr (4 days) | Islamic |
| Eid al Adha (4 days) | Islamic |

## D59. Estonia

### (Projected Holidays)

### (Fixed Holidays)

| | | |
|---|---|---|
| 1 Jan. | New Year's Day | multinational |
| 1 May | Labor Day | multinational |
| 21 Aug. | Independence Day | country-unique |
| 25 Dec. | Christmas Day | multinational |

### (Algorithmic Holidays)

| | | |
|---|---|---|
| Mar.-Apr. | Good Friday | Christian |
| Mar.-Apr. | Holy Saturday | Christian |
| Mar.-Apr. | Easter Monday | Christian |

## D60. Ethiopia

### (Fixed Holidays)

| | | |
|---|---|---|
| 7 Jan. | Coptic Christmas Day | shared with Egypt |
| 19 Jan. | Epiphany | country-unique |
| 2 Mar. | Victory of Aduwa Day | country-unique |
| 1 May | Labor Day | multinational |
| 12 Sep. | National Day | country-unique |

### (Algorithmic Holidays)

| | | |
|---|---|---|
| 26 or 27 Sep. | True Cross Day | Coptic |
| 11 or 12 Sep. | New Year's Day | Coptic |
| | Mohammed's Birthday | Islamic |
| | Eid al Fitr (4 days) | Islamic |

# D61. Fiji

## (Fixed Holidays)

| | | |
|---|---|---|
| 1 Jan. | New Year's Day | multinational |
| 1 May | Labor Day | multinational |
| 25 Dec. | Christmas Day | multinational |
| 26 Dec. | Boxing Day | multinational |

## (Algorithmic Holidays)

| | | |
|---|---|---|
| Mar.-Apr. | Good Friday | Christian |
| Mar.-Apr. | Holy Saturday | Christian |
| Mar.-Apr. | Easter Monday | Christian |
| 2nd Mon. in June | Queen's Birthday | shared with Australia, New Guinea, and United Kingdom |
| 2nd Mon. in Oct. | Cession Day | country-unique |
| 3rd Mon. in Nov. | Prince Charles' Birthday | country-unique |
| | Mohammed's Birthday | Islamic |

# D62. Finland

## (Fixed Holidays)

| | | |
|---|---|---|
| 1 Jan. | New Year's Day | multinational |
| 6 Jan. | Epiphany | Christian |
| 30 Apr. | Vappu Day | country-unique |
| 1 May | Labor Day | multinational |
| 19 May | Flag Day | country-unique |
| 1 Nov. | All Saints' Day | Christian |
| 2 Nov. | All Saints' Eve (celebrated the day after All Saints' Day) | shared with Sweden |
| 6 Dec. | Independence Day | country-unique |
| 24 Dec. | Christmas Eve | multinational |
| 25 Dec. | Christmas Day | multinational |
| 26 Dec. | Boxing Day | multinational |
| 31 Dec. | New Year's Eve | multinational |

## (Algorithmic Holidays)

| | | |
|---|---|---|
| Mar.-Apr. | Maundy Thursday | Christian |
| Mar.-Apr. | Good Friday | Christian |

| | | |
|---|---|---|
| Mar.–Apr. | Easter Monday | Christian |
| May–June | Ascension Thursday | Christian |
| May–June | Whitmonday | Christian |
| 20 or 21 June | Midsummer Day 1 | shared with Sweden |
| 21 or 22 June | Midsummer Day 2 | shared with Sweden |
| Sat. nearest 24 June | Johannus Day | country-unique |
| last Fri. in June | Bank Holiday | shared with Chile, Ecuador, and El Salvador |

# D63. France

## *(Fixed Holidays)*

| | | |
|---|---|---|
| 1 Jan. | New Year's Day | multinational |
| 1 May | Labor Day | multinational |
| 8 May | Liberation Day | country-unique |
| 14 July | National Day (also known as Bastille Day) | country-unique |
| 15 Aug. | Assumption | Christian |
| 1 Nov. | All Saints' Day | Christian |
| 2 Nov. | All Souls' Day | Christian |
| 11 Nov. | Armistice Day | multinational |
| 24 Dec. | Christmas Eve | multinational |
| 25 Dec. | Christmas Day | multinational |
| 31 Dec. | New Year's Eve | multinational |

## *(Algorithmic Holidays)*

| | | |
|---|---|---|
| Mar.–Apr. | Good Friday | Christian |
| Mar.–Apr. | Easter Monday | Christian |
| May–June | Ascension Thursday | Christian |
| May–June | Whitmonday | Christian |

# D64. Gabon

## *(Fixed Holidays)*

| | | |
|---|---|---|
| 1 Jan. | New Year's Day | multinational |
| 1 May | Labor Day | multinational |
| 15 Aug. | Assumption | Christian |

*D64 continued*

| | | |
|---|---|---|
| 17 Aug. | Independence Day | country-unique |
| 1 Nov. | All Saints' Day | Christian |
| 25 Dec. | Christmas Day | multinational |
| 26 Dec. | Boxing Day | multinational |

### *(Algorithmic Holidays)*

| | | |
|---|---|---|
| Mar.-Apr. | Good Friday | Christian |
| Mar.-Apr. | Easter Monday | Christian |
| May-June | Ascension Thursday | Christian |
| May-June | Whitmonday | Christian |
| | Eid al Fitr (4 days) | Islamic |

## D65. Gambia

### *(Fixed Holidays)*

| | | |
|---|---|---|
| 1 Jan. | New Year's Day | multinational |
| 18 Feb. | Independence Day | country-unique |
| 1 May | Labor Day | multinational |
| 15 Aug. | Assumption | Christian |
| 25 Dec. | Christmas Day | multinational |
| 26 Dec. | Boxing Day | multinational |

### *(Algorithmic Holidays)*

| | |
|---|---|
| Islamic New Year | Islamic |
| Mohammed's Birthday | Islamic |
| Eid al Fitr (4 days) | Islamic |
| Eid al Adha (4 days) | Islamic |

## D66. Georgia

### ***(Projected Holidays)***

### *(Fixed Holidays)*

| | | |
|---|---|---|
| 1 Jan. | New Year's Day | multinational |
| 1 May | Labor Day | multinational |
| 9 Aug. | Independence Day | country-unique |
| 25 Dec. | Christmas Day | multinational |

# D67. Germany

## (Fixed Holidays)

| | | |
|---|---|---|
| 1 Jan. | New Year's Day | multinational |
| 6 Jan. | Epiphany | Christian |
| 1 May | Labor Day | multinational |
| 17 June | Unity Day | country-unique |
| 15 Aug. | Assumption | Christian |
| 1 Nov. | All Saints' Day | Christian |
| 24 Dec. | Christmas Eve | multinational |
| 25 Dec. | Christmas Day | multinational |
| 26 Dec. | Boxing Day | multinational |
| 31 Dec. | New Year's Eve | multinational |

## (Algorithmic Holidays)

| | | |
|---|---|---|
| Mar.–Apr. | Good Friday | Christian |
| Mar.–Apr. | Easter Monday | Christian |
| May–June | Ascension Thursday | Christian |
| May–June | Whitmonday | Christian |
| May–June | Corpus Christi | Christian |
| 3rd Wed. in Nov. | Repentance Day | country-unique |

# D68. Ghana

## (Fixed Holidays)

| | | |
|---|---|---|
| 1 Jan. | New Year's Day | multinational |
| 6 Mar. | Independence Day | country-unique |
| 1 July | First Republic Day | country-unique |
| 25 Dec. | Christmas Day | multinational |
| 26 Dec. | Boxing Day | multinational |

## (Algorithmic Holidays)

| | | |
|---|---|---|
| Mar.–Apr. | Good Friday | Christian |
| Mar.–Apr. | Easter Monday | Christian |

# D69. Gibraltar

## (Fixed Holidays)

| | | |
|---|---|---|
| 1 Jan. | New Year's Day | multinational |

*D69 continued*

| | | |
|---|---|---|
| 1 May | Labor Day | multinational |
| 25 Dec. | Christmas Day | multinational |
| 26 Dec. | Boxing Day | multinational |

### *(Algorithmic Holidays)*

| | | |
|---|---|---|
| 2nd Mon. in Mar. | Commonwealth Day | country-unique |
| Mar.–Apr. | Good Friday | Christian |
| Mar.–Apr. | Easter Monday | Christian |

## D70. Greece

### *(Fixed Holidays)*

| | | |
|---|---|---|
| 1 Jan. | New Year's Day | multinational |
| 6 Jan. | Epiphany | Christian |
| 25 Mar. | Independence Day | shared with Cyprus |
| 1 May | Labor Day | multinational |
| 15 Aug. | Assumption | Christian |
| 28 Oct. | Ohi! Day | country-unique |
| 25 Dec. | Christmas Day | multinational |
| 26 Dec. | Boxing Day | multinational |

### *(Algorithmic Holidays)*

| | | |
|---|---|---|
| Feb.–Mar. | Shrove Monday | Orthodox |
| Mar.–Apr. | Good Friday | Christian |
| Mar.–Apr. | Easter Monday | Christian |
| Apr.–May | Good Friday | Orthodox |
| Apr.–May | Easter Monday | Orthodox |
| May–June | Pentecost Monday | Orthodox |

## D71. Grenada

### *(Fixed Holidays)*

| | | |
|---|---|---|
| 1 Jan. | New Year's Day | multinational |
| 7 Feb. | Independence Day | country-unique |
| 13 Mar. | National Day | country-unique |
| 1 May | Labor Day | multinational |

| | | |
|---|---|---|
| 25 Dec. | Christmas Day | multinational |
| 26 Dec. | Boxing Day | multinational |

### *(Algorithmic Holidays)*

| | | |
|---|---|---|
| Mar.–Apr. | Good Friday | Christian |
| Mar.–Apr. | Easter Monday | Christian |
| May–June | Whitmonday | Christian |
| May–June | Corpus Christi | Christian |

## D72. Guam

### *United States Holidays and:*

### *(Fixed Holidays)*

| | | |
|---|---|---|
| 21 July | Liberation Day | country-unique |
| 8 Dec. | Immaculate Conception | Christian |

### *(Algorithmic Holidays)*

| | | |
|---|---|---|
| 1st Mon. in Mar. | Discovery Day (also known as Magellan Day) | country-unique |
| Mar.–Apr. | Good Friday | Christian |

## D73. Guatemala

### *(Fixed Holidays)*

| | | |
|---|---|---|
| 1 Jan. | New Year's Day | multinational |
| 1 May | Labor Day | multinational |
| 29 June | Saint Paul's Day | Christian |
| 30 June | Army Day | country-unique |
| 1 July | Bank Holiday | multinational |
| 15 Aug. | Assumption | Christian |
| 14 Sep. | Jacinto Day | shared with Nicaragua |
| 15 Sep. | Independence Day | country-unique |
| 12 Oct. | Columbus Day | multinational |
| 20 Oct. | Revolution Day | country-unique |
| 1 Nov. | All Saints' Day | Christian |
| 24 Dec. | Christmas Eve | multinational |

*D73 continued*

| | | |
|---|---|---|
| 25 Dec. | Christmas Day | multinational |
| 26 Dec. | Boxing Day | multinational |
| 31 Dec. | Bank Holiday | multinational |

### (Algorithmic Holidays)

| | | |
|---|---|---|
| Mar.–Apr. | Maundy Thursday | Christian |
| Mar.–Apr. | Good Friday | Christian |
| Mar.–Apr. | Holy Saturday | Christian |

## D74. Guinea

### (Fixed Holidays)

| | | |
|---|---|---|
| 1 Jan. | New Year's Day | multinational |
| 1 May | Labor Day | multinational |
| 25 May | Africa Day | multinational |
| 15 Aug. | Assumption | Christian |
| 2 Oct. | Independence Day | country-unique |
| 1 Nov. | All Saints' Day | Christian |

### (Algorithmic Holidays)

| | | |
|---|---|---|
| Mar.–Apr. | Holy Saturday | Christian |
| | Islamic New Year | Islamic |
| | Mohammed's Birthday | Islamic |
| | Eid al Fitr (4 days) | Islamic |
| | Eid al Adha (4 days) | Islamic |

## D75. Guinea-Bissau

### (Fixed Holidays)

| | | |
|---|---|---|
| 1 Jan. | New Year's Day | multinational |
| 8 Mar. | Women's Day | multinational |
| 1 May | Labor Day | multinational |
| 3 Aug. | Martyrs' Day | country-unique |
| 24 Sep. | Republic Day | country-unique |

# D76. Guyana

## (Fixed Holidays)

| | | |
|---|---|---|
| 1 Jan. | New Year's Day | multinational |
| 23 Feb. | Republic Day | country-unique |
| 1 May | Labor Day | multinational |
| 26 May | Independence Day | country-unique |
| 2 Aug. | Freedom Day | country-unique |
| 1 Nov. | All Saints' Day | Christian |
| 25 Dec. | Christmas Day | multinational |
| 26 Dec. | Boxing Day | multinational |

## (Algorithmic Holidays)

| | | |
|---|---|---|
| Mar.-Apr. | Good Friday | Christian |
| Mar.-Apr. | Easter Monday | Christian |
| | Mohammed's Birthday | Islamic |
| | Eid al Adha (4 days) | Islamic |

# D77. Haiti

## (Fixed Holidays)

| | | |
|---|---|---|
| 1 Jan. | Independence Day | country-unique |
| 1 May | Labor Day | multinational |
| 18 May | Flag Day | country-unique |
| 22 May | Day of Sovereignty | country-unique |
| 15 Aug. | Assumption | Christian |
| 17 Oct. | Dessalines Day | country-unique |
| 24 Oct. | United Nations Day | country-unique |
| 1 Nov. | All Saints' Day | Christian |
| 2 Nov. | All Souls' Day | Christian |
| 18 Nov. | Vertieres' Day | country-unique |
| 5 Dec. | Discovery Day | country-unique |
| 25 Dec. | Christmas Day | multinational |

## (Algorithmic Holidays)

| | | |
|---|---|---|
| Feb.-Mar. | Shrove Tuesday | Christian |
| Mar.-Apr. | Maundy Thursday | Christian |
| Mar.-Apr. | Good Friday | Christian |
| May-June | Ascension Thursday | Christian |
| May-June | Corpus Christi | Christian |

# D78. Honduras

## (Fixed Holidays)

| | | |
|---|---|---|
| 1 Jan. | New Year's Day | multinational |
| 14 Apr. | Pan American Day | country-unique |
| 1 May | Labor Day | multinational |
| 15 Sep. | Independence Day | country-unique |
| 3 Oct. | Morazan Day | country-unique |
| 12 Oct. | Columbus Day | multinational |
| 21 Oct. | Army Day | country-unique |
| 25 Dec. | Christmas Day | multinational |
| 31 Dec. | Bank Holiday | multinational |

## (Algorithmic Holidays)

| | | |
|---|---|---|
| Mar.–Apr. | Maundy Thursday | Christian |
| Mar.–Apr. | Good Friday | Christian |

# D79. Hong Kong

## (Fixed Holidays)

| | | |
|---|---|---|
| 5 Apr. | Tomb Sweeping Day | Asian |
| 1 July | Half Year Day | country-unique |
| 25 Dec. | Christmas Day | multinational |

## (Algorithmic Holidays)

| | | |
|---|---|---|
| 1st weekday in Jan. | New Year's Day | country-unique |
| Jan.–Feb. | Chinese New Year Eve | Asian |
| Jan.–Feb. | Chinese New Year (2 days) | Asian |
| Mar.–Apr. | Good Friday | Christian |
| Mar.–Apr. | Holy Saturday | Christian |
| Mar.–Apr. | Easter Monday | Christian |
| May–June | Dragon Boat Festival | Asian |
| 2nd Sat. in June | Queen's Birthday Sat. | country-unique |
| Mon. after 2nd Sat. in June | Queen's Birthday Mon. | country-unique |
| Sat. before last Mon. in Aug. | Liberation Day 1 | country-unique |
| last Mon. in Aug. | Liberation Day 2 | country-unique |
| Sep.–Oct. | Ancestors' Day | Asian |
| Oct. | Mid-autumn Day | Asian |
| 1st weekday after Christmas | Boxing Day | country-unique |

# D80. Hungary

## (Fixed Holidays)

| | | |
|---|---|---|
| 1 Jan. | New Year's Day | multinational |
| 4 Apr. | Liberation Day | country-unique |
| 1 May | Labor Day | multinational |
| 20 Aug. | Constitution Day | country-unique |
| 23 Oct. | Revolution Day | country-unique |

# D81. Iceland

## (Fixed Holidays)

| | | |
|---|---|---|
| 1 Jan. | New Year's Day | multinational |
| 25 Apr. | Children's Day | country-unique |
| 1 May | Labor Day | multinational |
| 17 June | Independence Day | country-unique |
| 24 Dec. | Christmas Eve | multinational |
| 25 Dec. | Christmas Day | multinational |
| 26 Dec. | Boxing Day | multinational |
| 31 Dec. | New Year's Eve | multinational |

## (Algorithmic Holidays)

| | | |
|---|---|---|
| Mar.–Apr. | Maundy Thursday | Christian |
| Mar.–Apr. | Good Friday | Christian |
| Mar.–Apr. | Holy Saturday | Christian |
| Mar.–Apr. | Easter Monday | Christian |
| May–June | Ascension Thursday | Christian |
| May–June | Whitmonday | Christian |

# D82. India

## (Fixed Holidays)

| | | |
|---|---|---|
| 1 Jan. | New Year's Day | multinational |
| 26 Jan. | Republic Day | country-unique |
| 15 Aug. | Independence Day | country-unique |
| 2 Oct. | Ghandi Day | country-unique |
| 25 Dec. | Christmas Day | multinational |

## (Algorithmic Holidays)

| | | |
|---|---|---|
| Mar.–Apr. | Good Friday | Christian |

*D82 continued*

| | | |
|---|---|---|
| Mar.–Apr. | Easter Monday | Christian |
| Oct.–Nov. | Deepavali | Hindu |
| | Islamic New Year | Islamic |
| | Eid al Fitr (4 days) | Islamic |
| | Eid al Adha (4 days) | Islamic |

## D83. Indonesia

### *(Fixed Holidays)*

| | | |
|---|---|---|
| 1 Jan. | New Year's Day | multinational |
| 17 Aug. | Independence Day | country-unique |
| 25 Dec. | Christmas Day | multinational |

### *(Algorithmic Holidays)*

| | | |
|---|---|---|
| Mar.–Apr. | Easter Sunday | Christian |
| May–June | Ascension Thursday | Christian |
| May–June | Whitmonday | Christian |
| | Islamic New Year | Islamic |
| | Mohammed's Birthday | Islamic |
| | Hari Raya Puasa | Far East Islamic |
| | Hari Raya Haji | Far East Islamic |
| | Isra a Majraj | Islamic |

## D84. Iran

### *(Fixed Holidays)*

| | | |
|---|---|---|
| 1 Apr. | Republic Day | country-unique |
| 1 May | Labor Day | multinational |

### *(Algorithmic Holidays)*

| | | |
|---|---|---|
| 20 or 21 Mar. | New Year's Day | Iranian |
| | Islamic New Year | Islamic |
| | Ashura | Islamic |
| | Mohammed's Birthday | Islamic |
| | Eid al Fitr (4 days) | Islamic |
| | Eid al Adha (4 days) | Islamic |

# D85. Iraq

## (Fixed Holidays)

| | | |
|---|---|---|
| 1 Jan. | Bank Holiday | multinational |
| 6 Jan. | Army Day | country-unique |
| 8 Feb. | Revolution Day | country-unique |
| 1 May | Labor Day | multinational |
| 14 July | Revolution Day | country-unique |
| 17 July | Revolution Day | country-unique |

## (Algorithmic Holidays)

| | | |
|---|---|---|
| 20 or 21 Mar. | New Year's Day | Iranian |
| | Islamic New Year | Islamic |
| | Ashura | Islamic |
| | Mohammed's Birthday | Islamic |
| | Eid al Fitr (4 days) | Islamic |
| | Eid al Adha (4 days) | Islamic |

# D86. Ireland

## (Fixed Holidays)

| | | |
|---|---|---|
| 1 Jan. | New Year's Day | multinational |
| 17 Mar. | Saint Patrick's Day | shared with Northern Ireland |
| 25 Dec. | Christmas Day | multinational |
| 26 Dec. | Boxing Day | multinational |

## (Algorithmic Holidays)

| | | |
|---|---|---|
| Mar.–Apr. | Good Friday | Christian |
| Mar.–Apr. | Easter Monday | Christian |
| May–June | Whitmonday | Christian |
| 1st Mon. in June | Public Holiday | country-unique |
| 1st Mon. in Aug. | Public Holiday | shared with Scotland |
| last Mon. in Oct. | Public Holiday | country-unique |

# D87. Israel

## (Fixed Holidays)

| | | |
|---|---|---|
| 1 Jan. | New Year's Day | multinational |

*D87 continued*

## *(Algorithmic Holidays)*

| | | |
|---|---|---|
| Sep.–Oct. | New Year's Day (also known as Rosh Hashanah) | Jewish |
| Sep.–Oct. | Yom Kippur | Jewish |
| Sep.–Oct. | Sukkot | Jewish |
| Mar.–Apr. | Passover | Jewish |
| Apr.–May | Independence Day | |
| May–June | Pentecost (also known as Shavuot) | Jewish |
| July–Aug. | Tisha Ab | Jewish |

# D88. Italy

## *(Fixed Holidays)*

| | | |
|---|---|---|
| 1 Jan. | New Year's Day | multinational |
| 6 Jan. | Epiphany | Christian |
| 19 Mar. | Saint Joseph's Day | Christian |
| 25 Apr. | Liberation Day | country-unique |
| 1 May | Labor Day | multinational |
| 2 June | Republic Day | country-unique |
| 29 June | Saint Paul's Day | Christian |
| 15 Aug. | Assumption | Christian |
| 1 Nov. | All Saints' Day | Christian |
| 8 Dec. | Immaculate Conception | Christian |
| 24 Dec. | Christmas Eve | multinational |
| 25 Dec. | Christmas Day | multinational |
| 26 Dec. | Boxing Day | multinational |
| 31 Dec. | New Year's Eve | multinational |

## *(Algorithmic Holidays)*

| | | |
|---|---|---|
| Mar.–Apr. | Easter Monday | Christian |
| May–June | Ascension Thursday | Christian |
| May–June | Corpus Christi | Christian |

# D89. Ivory Coast

## *(Fixed Holidays)*

| | | |
|---|---|---|
| 1 Jan. | New Year's Day | multinational |

| | | |
|---|---|---|
| 1 May | Labor Day | multinational |
| 7 Aug. | Republic Day | country-unique |
| 15 Aug. | Assumption | Christian |
| 1 Nov. | All Saints' Day | Christian |
| 7 Dec. | Independence Day | country-unique |
| 24 Dec. | Christmas Eve | multinational |
| 25 Dec. | Christmas Day | multinational |
| 31 Dec. | New Year's Eve | multinational |

### *(Algorithmic Holidays)*

| | | |
|---|---|---|
| Mar.–Apr. | Easter Monday | Christian |
| May–June | Ascension Thursday | Christian |
| May–June | Whitmonday | Christian |
| | Eid al Fitr (4 days) | Islamic |

## D90. Jamaica

### *(Fixed Holidays)*

| | | |
|---|---|---|
| 1 Jan. | New Year's Day | multinational |
| 23 May | Labor Day | country-unique |
| 25 Dec. | Christmas Day | multinational |
| 26 Dec. | Boxing Day | multinational |

### *(Algorithmic Holidays)*

| | | |
|---|---|---|
| Feb.–Mar. | Ash Wednesday | Christian |
| Mar.–Apr. | Good Friday | Christian |
| Mar.–Apr. | Easter Monday | Christian |
| 1st Mon. in Aug. | Independence Day | country-unique |
| 3rd Mon. in Oct. | Heroes' Day | country-unique |

## D91. Japan

### *(Fixed Holidays)*

| | | |
|---|---|---|
| 1 Jan. | New Year's Day | multinational |
| 2 Jan. | Bank Holiday | country-unique |
| 15 Jan. | Adult's Day | country-unique |
| 11 Feb. | Foundation Day | country-unique |
| 29 Apr. | Green Day | country-unique |
| 3 May | Constitution Day | country-unique |

*D91 continued*

| | | |
|---|---|---|
| 4 May | People's Day | country-unique |
| 5 May | Children's Day | country-unique |
| 15 Sep. | Veneration Day | country-unique |
| 10 Oct. | Health Day | country-unique |
| 3 Nov. | Culture Day | country-unique |
| 23 Nov. | Labour Thanksgiving Day | country-unique |
| 23 Dec. | Emperor's Birthday | country-unique |

### *(Algorithmic Holidays)*

| | | |
|---|---|---|
| 20 or 21 Mar. | Vernal Equinox | country-unique |
| 22 or 23 Sep. | Autumnal Equinox | country-unique |

## D92. Jordan

### *(Fixed Holidays)*

| | | |
|---|---|---|
| 1 Jan. | New Year's Day | multinational |
| 15 Jan. | Arbor Day | country-unique |
| 1 May | Labor Day | multinational |
| 25 May | Independence Day | country-unique |
| 11 Aug. | Accession Day | country-unique |
| 14 Nov. | King's Birthday | country-unique |
| 25 Dec. | Christmas Day | multinational |

### *(Algorithmic Holidays)*

| | | |
|---|---|---|
| Mar.-Apr. | Easter Sunday | Christian |
| Apr.-May | Easter Sunday | Orthodox |
| | Islamic New Year | Islamic |
| | Mohammed's Birthday | Islamic |
| | Eid al Fitr (4 days) | Islamic |
| | Eid al Adha (4 days) | Islamic |
| | Isra a Majraj | Islamic |

## D93. Kazakhstan

### *(Projected Holidays)*

### *(Fixed Holidays)*

| | | |
|---|---|---|
| 1 Jan. | New Year's Day | multinational |

| | | |
|---|---|---|
| 1 May | Labor Day | multinational |
| 24 Aug. | National Day | country-unique |
| 21 Dec. | Independence Day | country-unique |
| 25 Dec. | Christmas Day | multinational |

# D94. Kenya

## *(Fixed Holidays)*

| | | |
|---|---|---|
| 1 Jan. | New Year's Day | multinational |
| 1 May | Labor Day | multinational |
| 1 June | Madaraka Day | country-unique |
| 20 Oct. | Kenyatta Day | country-unique |
| 12 Dec. | Independence Day | country-unique |
| 25 Dec. | Christmas Day | multinational |
| 26 Dec. | Boxing Day | multinational |

## *(Algorithmic Holidays)*

| | | |
|---|---|---|
| Mar.-Apr. | Good Friday | Christian |
| Mar.-Apr. | Easter Monday | Christian |
| | Eid al Fitr (4 days) | Islamic |
| | Eid al Adha (4 days) | Islamic |

# D95. Kiribati

## *(Fixed Holidays)*

| | | |
|---|---|---|
| 1 Jan. | New Year's Day | multinational |
| 1 May | Labor Day | multinational |
| 12 July | Independence Day | country-unique |
| 25 Dec. | Christmas Day | multinational |

# Korea *see* North Korea and South Korea

# D96. Kuwait

## *(Fixed Holidays)*

| | | |
|---|---|---|
| 1 Jan. | New Year's Day | multinational |

*D96 continued*

| | | |
|---|---|---|
| 25 Feb. | National Day | country-unique |
| 1 May | Labor Day | multinational |
| 19 June | Independence Day | country-unique |

### *(Algorithmic Holidays)*

| | |
|---|---|
| Islamic New Year | Islamic |
| Mohammed's Birthday | Islamic |
| Eid al Fitr (4 days) | Islamic |
| Eid al Adha (4 days) | Islamic |
| Isra a Majraj | Islamic |

## D97. Kyrgyzstan

### *(Projected Holidays)*

### *(Fixed Holidays)*

| | | |
|---|---|---|
| 1 Jan. | New Year's Day | multinational |
| 1 May | Labor Day | multinational |
| 31 Aug. | Independence Day | country-unique |
| 25 Dec. | Christmas Day | multinational |

## D98. Laos

### *(Fixed Holidays)*

| | | |
|---|---|---|
| 1 Jan. | New Year's Day | multinational |
| 1 May | Labor Day | multinational |
| 19 July | Independence Day | country-unique |
| 2 Dec. | Republic Day | country-unique |

### *(Algorithmic Holidays)*

| | | |
|---|---|---|
| Jan.–Feb. | Chinese New Year | Asian |

# D99. Latvia

## (Projected Holidays)

### (Fixed Holidays)

| | | |
|---|---|---|
| 1 Jan. | New Year's Day | multinational |
| 1 May | Labor Day | multinational |
| 21 Aug. | Independence Day | country-unique |
| 25 Dec. | Christmas Day | multinational |

### (Algorithmic Holidays)

| | | |
|---|---|---|
| Mar.–Apr. | Good Friday | Christian |
| Mar.–Apr. | Holy Saturday | Christian |
| Mar.–Apr. | Easter Monday | Christian |

# D100. Lebanon

### (Fixed Holidays)

| | | |
|---|---|---|
| 1 Jan. | New Year's Day | multinational |
| 9 Feb. | Saint Marion's Day | country-unique |
| 1 May | Labor Day | multinational |
| 6 May | Martyrs' Day | country-unique |
| 15 Aug. | Assumption | Christian |
| 1 Nov. | All Saints' Day | Christian |
| 22 Nov. | Independence Day | country-unique |
| 8 Dec. | Immaculate Conception | Christian |
| 25 Dec. | Christmas Day | multinational |

### (Algorithmic Holidays)

| | | |
|---|---|---|
| Mar.–Apr. | Good Friday | Christian |
| Mar.–Apr. | Easter Monday | Christian |
| Apr.–May | Good Friday | Orthodox |
| Apr.–May | Easter Monday | Orthodox |
| May–June | Ascension Thursday | Christian |
| | Islamic New Year | Islamic |
| | Ashura | Islamic |
| | Mohammed's Birthday | Islamic |
| | Eid al Fitr (4 days) | Islamic |
| | Eid al Adha (4 days) | Islamic |

# D101. Lesotho

## (Fixed Holidays)

| | | |
|---|---|---|
| 1 Jan. | New Year's Day | multinational |
| 12 Mar. | Moshoeshoe's Birthday | country-unique |
| 2 May | King's Birthday | country-unique |
| 4 Oct. | Independence Day | country-unique |
| 5 Oct. | Sports Day | country-unique |
| 25 Dec. | Christmas Day | multinational |
| 26 Dec. | Boxing Day | multinational |

## (Algorithmic Holidays)

| | | |
|---|---|---|
| Mar.-Apr. | Good Friday | Christian |
| Mar.-Apr. | Easter Monday | Christian |
| May-June | Ascension Thursday | Christian |
| 1st Mon. in July | Family Day | country-unique |

# D102. Liberia

## (Fixed Holidays)

| | | |
|---|---|---|
| 1 Jan. | New Year's Day | multinational |
| 11 Feb. | Armed Forces Day | country-unique |
| 14 May | Unification Day | country-unique |
| 25 May | Africa Day | multinational |
| 26 July | Independence Day | country-unique |
| 24 Aug. | Flag Day | country-unique |
| 1 Nov. | All Saints' Day | Christian |
| 29 Nov. | Tubman's Birthday | country-unique |
| 25 Dec. | Christmas Day | multinational |

## (Algorithmic Holidays)

| | | |
|---|---|---|
| Mar.-Apr. | Good Friday | Christian |
| 1st Thu. in Nov. | Thanksgiving Day | country-unique |

# D103. Libya

## (Fixed Holidays)

| | | |
|---|---|---|
| 1 Jan. | New Year's Day | multinational |
| 11 June | Evacuation Day | country-unique |
| 1 Sep. | National Day | country-unique |

### (Algorithmic Holidays)

| | |
|---|---|
| Islamic New Year | Islamic |
| Ashura | Islamic |
| Mohammed's Birthday | Islamic |
| Eid al Fitr (4 days) | Islamic |
| Eid al Adha (4 days) | Islamic |
| Isra a Majraj | Islamic |

## D104. Liechtenstein

### (Fixed Holidays)

| | | |
|---|---|---|
| 1 Jan. | New Year's Day | multinational |
| 6 Jan. | Epiphany | Christian |
| 2 Feb. | Candlemas | country-unique |
| 19 Mar. | Saint Joseph's Day | Christian |
| 25 Mar. | Annunciation | country-unique |
| 1 May | Labor Day | multinational |
| 15 Aug. | National Day | country-unique |
| 1 Nov. | All Saints' Day | Christian |
| 8 Dec. | Immaculate Conception | Christian |
| 24 Dec. | Christmas Eve | multinational |
| 25 Dec. | Christmas Day | multinational |
| 26 Dec. | Boxing Day | multinational |
| 31 Dec. | New Year's Eve | multinational |

### (Algorithmic Holidays)

| | | |
|---|---|---|
| Feb.-Mar. | Shrove Tuesday | Christian |
| Mar.-Apr. | Good Friday | Christian |
| Mar.-Apr. | Easter Monday | Christian |
| May-June | Ascension Thursday | Christian |
| May-June | Whitmonday | Christian |
| May-June | Corpus Christi | Christian |

## D105. Lithuania

### (Projected Holidays)

### (Fixed Holidays)

| | | |
|---|---|---|
| 1 Jan. | New Year's Day | multinational |
| 11 Mar. | National Day | country-unique |

*D105 continued*

| | | |
|---|---|---|
| 1 May | Labor Day | multinational |
| 15 Aug. | Assumption | Christian |
| 21 Aug. | Independence Day | country-unique |
| 1 Nov. | All Saints' Day | Christian |
| 8 Dec. | Immaculate Conception | Christian |
| 24 Dec. | Christmas Eve | multinational |
| 25 Dec. | Christmas Day | multinational |

### *(Algorithmic Holidays)*

| | | |
|---|---|---|
| Mar.-Apr. | Good Friday | Christian |
| Mar.-Apr. | Easter Monday | Christian |
| May-June | Ascension Thursday | Christian |

## D106. Luxembourg

### *(Fixed Holidays)*

| | | |
|---|---|---|
| 1 Jan. | New Year's Day | multinational |
| 1 May | Labor Day | multinational |
| 23 June | National Day | country-unique |
| 15 Aug. | Assumption | Christian |
| 1 Nov. | All Saints' Day | Christian |
| 24 Dec. | Christmas Eve | multinational |
| 25 Dec. | Christmas Day | multinational |
| 26 Dec. | Boxing Day | multinational |

### *(Algorithmic Holidays)*

| | | |
|---|---|---|
| Mar.-Apr. | Easter Monday | Christian |
| May-June | Ascension Thursday | Christian |
| May-June | Whitmonday | Christian |
| Mon. after 27 Aug. | Fair Day | country-unique |

## D107. Macao

### *(Fixed Holidays)*

| | | |
|---|---|---|
| 1 Jan. | New Year's Day | multinational |
| 5 Apr. | Tomb Sweeping Day | Asian |

| | | |
|---|---|---|
| 1 May | Labor Day | multinational |
| 10 June | Portugal Day | shared with Portugal |
| 5 Oct. | Portuguese Republic Day | shared with Portugal |
| 1 Nov. | All Saints' Day | Christian |
| 11 Nov. | Armistice Day | multinational |
| 8 Dec. | Immaculate Conception | Christian |
| 24 Dec. | Christmas Eve | multinational |
| 25 Dec. | Christmas Day | multinational |
| 26 Dec. | Boxing Day | multinational |

### *(Algorithmic Holidays)*

| | | |
|---|---|---|
| Jan.–Feb. | Chinese New Year Eve | Asian |
| Jan.–Feb. | Chinese New Year (2 days) | Asian |
| Mar.–Apr. | Good Friday | Christian |
| Mar.–Apr. | Holy Saturday | Christian |
| Mar.–Apr. | Easter Monday | Christian |
| May–June | Dragon Boat Festival | Asian |
| Sep.–Oct. | Ancestors' Day | Asian |
| Oct. | Mid-autumn Day | Asian |

## D108. Madagascar

### *(Fixed Holidays)*

| | | |
|---|---|---|
| 1 Jan. | New Year's Day | multinational |
| 29 Mar. | Memorial Day | country-unique |
| 25 May | Africa Day | multinational |
| 26 June | Independence Day | country-unique |
| 15 Aug. | Assumption | Christian |
| 1 Nov. | All Saints' Day | Christian |
| 24 Dec. | Christmas Eve | multinational |
| 25 Dec. | Christmas Day | multinational |
| 30 Dec. | Republic Day | country-unique |
| 31 Dec. | New Year's Eve | multinational |

### *(Algorithmic Holidays)*

| | | |
|---|---|---|
| Mar.–Apr. | Good Friday | Christian |
| Mar.–Apr. | Easter Monday | Christian |
| May–June | Ascension Thursday | Christian |
| May–June | Whitmonday | Christian |

# D109. Malawi

## (Fixed Holidays)

| | | |
|---|---|---|
| 1 Jan. | New Year's Day | multinational |
| 3 Mar. | Martyrs' Day | country-unique |
| 14 May | Kamuzu Day | country-unique |
| 6 July | Republic Day | country-unique |
| 17 Oct. | Mother's Day | country-unique |
| 25 Dec. | Christmas Day | multinational |
| 26 Dec. | Boxing Day | multinational |

## (Algorithmic Holidays)

| | | |
|---|---|---|
| Mar.–Apr. | Good Friday | Christian |
| Mar.–Apr. | Holy Saturday | Christian |
| Mar.–Apr. | Easter Monday | Christian |

# D110. Malaysia

## (Fixed Holidays)

| | | |
|---|---|---|
| 1 Jan. | New Year's Day | multinational |
| 1 May | Labor Day | multinational |
| 31 Aug. | National Day | country-unique |
| 25 Dec. | Christmas Day | multinational |

## (Algorithmic Holidays)

| | | |
|---|---|---|
| Jan.–Feb. | Chinese New Year (2 days) | Asian |
| 1st Wed. in June | King's Birthday | country-unique |
| May–June | Vesak Day | shared with Singapore |
| Oct.–Nov. | Deepavali | Hindu |
| | Islamic New Year | Islamic |
| | Mohammed's Birthday | Islamic |
| | Hari Raya Puasa | Far East Islamic |
| | Hari Raya Haji | Far East Islamic |

# D111. Maldives

## (Fixed Holidays)

| | | |
|---|---|---|
| 1 Jan. | New Year's Day | multinational |

| | | |
|---|---|---|
| 26 July | Independence Day | country-unique |
| 11 Nov. | Republic Day | country-unique |

### *(Algorithmic Holidays)*

| | |
|---|---|
| Islamic New Year | Islamic |
| Mohammed's Birthday | Islamic |
| 1st Day of Ramadan | Islamic |
| Eid al Fitr (4 days) | Islamic |
| Eid al Adha (4 days) | Islamic |

## D112. Mali

### *(Fixed Holidays)*

| | | |
|---|---|---|
| 1 Jan. | New Year's Day | multinational |
| 20 Jan. | Award Day | country-unique |
| 1 May | Labor Day | multinational |
| 25 May | Africa Day | multinational |
| 22 Sep. | Independence Day | country-unique |
| 19 Nov. | Army Coup Day | country-unique |
| 25 Dec. | Christmas Day | multinational |

### *(Algorithmic Holidays)*

| | | |
|---|---|---|
| Mar.–Apr. | Easter Monday | Christian |
| | Islamic New Year | Islamic |
| | Mohammed's Birthday | Islamic |
| | Eid al Fitr (4 days) | Islamic |
| | Eid al Adha (4 days) | Islamic |

## D113. Malta

### *(Fixed Holidays)*

| | | |
|---|---|---|
| 1 Jan. | New Year's Day | multinational |
| 6 Jan. | Epiphany | Christian |
| 10 Feb. | Saint Paul's Day | country-unique |
| 19 Mar. | Saint Joseph's Day | Christian |
| 31 Mar. | National Day | country-unique |
| 1 May | Labor Day | multinational |
| 29 June | Saint Paul's Day | Christian |
| 15 Aug. | Assumption | Christian |

*D113 continued*

| | | |
|---|---|---|
| 8 Sep. | Our Lady of Victory Day | country-unique |
| 21 Sep. | Independence Day | country-unique |
| 1 Nov. | All Saints' Day | Christian |
| 8 Dec. | Immaculate Conception | Christian |
| 13 Dec. | Republic Day | country-unique |
| 25 Dec. | Christmas Day | multinational |

### *(Algorithmic Holidays)*

| | | |
|---|---|---|
| Mar.–Apr. | Good Friday | Christian |
| Mar.–Apr. | Holy Saturday | Christian |
| May–June | Ascension Thursday | Christian |
| May–June | Whitmonday | Christian |

## D114. Marshall Islands

### *(Fixed Holidays)*

| | | |
|---|---|---|
| 1 Jan. | New Year's Day | multinational |
| 1 May | Labor Day | multinational |
| 17 Sep. | Independence Day | country-unique |
| 25 Dec. | Christmas Day | multinational |

## D115. Mauritania

### *(Fixed Holidays)*

| | | |
|---|---|---|
| 1 Jan. | New Year's Day | multinational |
| 8 Mar. | Women's Day | multinational |
| 1 May | Labor Day | multinational |
| 25 May | Africa Day | multinational |
| 28 Nov. | Independence Day | country-unique |

### *(Algorithmic Holidays)*

| | |
|---|---|
| Islamic New Year | Islamic |
| Mohammed's Birthday | Islamic |
| Eid al Fitr (4 days) | Islamic |
| Eid al Adha (4 days) | Islamic |

# D116. Mauritius

## (Fixed Holidays)

| | | |
|---|---|---|
| 1 Jan. | New Year's Day | multinational |
| 12 Mar. | Independence Day | country-unique |
| 1 May | Labor Day | multinational |
| 1 Nov. | All Saints' Day | Christian |
| 25 Dec. | Christmas Day | multinational |

## (Algorithmic Holidays)

| | | |
|---|---|---|
| Jan.–Feb. | Chinese New Year | Asian |
| Oct.–Nov. | Deepavali | Hindu |
| | Mohammed's Birthday | Islamic |
| | Eid al Fitr (4 days) | Islamic |
| | Eid al Adha (4 days) | Islamic |

# D117. Mexico

## (Fixed Holidays)

| | | |
|---|---|---|
| 1 Jan. | New Year's Day | multinational |
| 5 Feb. | Constitution Day | country-unique |
| 21 Mar. | Juarez Day | country-unique |
| 1 May | Labor Day | multinational |
| 5 May | Cinco de Mayo | country-unique |
| 1 Sep. | Presidential Message Day | country-unique |
| 16 Sep. | Independence Day | country-unique |
| 12 Oct. | Columbus Day | multinational |
| 20 Nov. | Revolution Day | country-unique |
| 1 Nov. | All Saints' Day | Christian |
| 11 Nov. | Armistice Day | multinational |
| 12 Dec. | Our Lady of Guadalupe Day | country-unique |
| 25 Dec. | Christmas Day | multinational |
| 31 Dec. | Bank Holiday | multinational |

## (Algorithmic Holidays)

| | | |
|---|---|---|
| Mar.–Apr. | Maundy Thursday | Christian |
| Mar.–Apr. | Good Friday | Christian |
| Mar.–Apr. | Holy Saturday | Christian |

# D118. Micronesia

## *(Fixed Holidays)*

| | | |
|---|---|---|
| 1 Jan. | New Year's Day | multinational |
| 1 May | Labor Day | multinational |
| 10 May | Independence Day | country-unique |
| 25 Dec. | Christmas Day | multinational |

# D119. Moldova

## *(Projected Holidays)*

## *(Fixed Holidays)*

| | | |
|---|---|---|
| 1 Jan. | New Year's Day | multinational |
| 1 May | Labor Day | multinational |
| 27 Aug. | Independence Day | country-unique |
| 25 Dec. | Christmas Day | multinational |

## *(Algorithmic Holidays)*

| | | |
|---|---|---|
| Mar.–Apr. | Good Friday | Christian |
| Mar.–Apr. | Holy Saturday | Christian |
| Mar.–Apr. | Easter Monday | Christian |

# D120. Monaco

## *(Fixed Holidays)*

| | | |
|---|---|---|
| 1 Jan. | New Year's Day | multinational |
| 27 Jan. | Saint Devota's Day | country-unique |
| 1 May | Labor Day | multinational |
| 15 Aug. | Assumption | Christian |
| 1 Nov. | All Saints' Day | Christian |
| 19 Nov. | Prince Ranier's Day | country-unique |
| 8 Dec. | Immaculate Conception | Christian |
| 24 Dec. | Christmas Eve | multinational |
| 25 Dec. | Christmas Day | multinational |
| 31 Dec. | New Year's Eve | multinational |

## *(Algorithmic Holidays)*

| | | |
|---|---|---|
| Mar.–Apr. | Good Friday | Christian |
| Mar.–Apr. | Easter Monday | Christian |

| | | |
|---|---|---|
| May–June | Ascension Thursday | Christian |
| May–June | Whitmonday | Christian |
| May–June | Corpus Christi | Christian |

# D121. Mongolia

## *(Fixed Holidays)*

| | | |
|---|---|---|
| 1 Jan. | New Year's Day | multinational |
| 1 May | Labor Day | multinational |
| 11 July | Revolution Day | country-unique |

# D122. Morocco

## *(Fixed Holidays)*

| | | |
|---|---|---|
| 1 Jan. | New Year's Day | multinational |
| 2 Mar. | Independence Day (Independence from France) | country-unique |
| 3 Mar. | National Day | country-unique |
| 1 May | Labor Day | multinational |
| 18 Nov. | Independence Day (Independence from Spain) | country-unique |
| 25 Dec. | Christmas Day | multinational |

## *(Algorithmic Holidays)*

| | | |
|---|---|---|
| May–June | Ascension Thursday | Christian |
| May–June | Whitmonday | Christian |
| | Islamic New Year | Islamic |
| | Ashura | Islamic |
| | Mohammed's Birthday | Islamic |
| | Eid al Fitr (4 days) | Islamic |
| | Eid al Adha (4 days) | Islamic |

# D123. Mozambique

## *(Fixed Holidays)*

| | | |
|---|---|---|
| 1 Jan. | New Year's Day | multinational |
| 1 May | Labor Day | multinational |

*D123 continued*

| | | |
|---|---|---|
| 25 June | Independence Day | country-unique |
| 25 Sep. | Liberation Day | country-unique |

# Myanmar *see* Burma

# D124. Namibia

## *(Fixed Holidays)*

| | | |
|---|---|---|
| 1 May | Labor Day | multinational |
| 25 May | Africa Day | multinational |
| 1 Nov. | All Saints' Day | Christian |
| 10 Dec. | Settlers' Day | country-unique |
| 26 Dec. | Boxing Day | multinational |

## *(Algorithmic Holidays)*

| | | |
|---|---|---|
| Mar.–Apr. | Easter Monday | Christian |
| May–June | Ascension Thursday | Christian |
| May–June | Whitmonday | Christian |

# D125. Nauru

## *(Fixed Holidays)*

| | | |
|---|---|---|
| 1 Jan. | New Year's Day | multinational |
| 31 Jan. | Independence Day | country-unique |
| 1 May | Labor Day | multinational |
| 15 Aug. | Assumption | Christian |
| 25 Dec. | Christmas Day | multinational |

# D126. Nepal

## *(Fixed Holidays)*

| | | |
|---|---|---|
| 11 Jan. | Unification Day | country-unique |
| 19 Feb. | National Day | country-unique |
| 8 Mar. | Women's Day | multinational |
| 1 May | Labor Day | multinational |

| | | |
|---|---|---|
| 8 Nov. | Queen's Birthday | country-unique |
| 16 Dec. | Constitution Day | country-unique |

## D127. Netherlands

### *(Fixed Holidays)*

| | | |
|---|---|---|
| 1 Jan. | New Year's Day | multinational |
| 30 Apr. | Queen's Birthday | country-unique |
| 5 May | Liberation Day | country-unique |
| 25 Dec. | Christmas Day | multinational |
| 26 Dec. | Boxing Day | multinational |

### *(Algorithmic Holidays)*

| | | |
|---|---|---|
| Mar.–Apr. | Good Friday | Christian |
| Mar.–Apr. | Easter Monday | Christian |
| May–June | Ascension Thursday | Christian |
| May–June | Whitmonday | Christian |

## D128. New Guinea

### *(Fixed Holidays)*

| | | |
|---|---|---|
| 1 Jan. | New Year's Day | multinational |
| 23 July | Remembrance Day | country-unique |
| 16 Sep. | Independence Day | country-unique |
| 25 Dec. | Christmas Day | multinational |
| 26 Dec. | Boxing Day | multinational |

### *(Algorithmic Holidays)*

| | | |
|---|---|---|
| Mar.–Apr. | Good Friday | Christian |
| Mar.–Apr. | Easter Monday | Christian |
| 2nd Mon. in June | Queen's Birthday | shared with Australia, Fiji, and United Kingdom |

## D129. New Zealand

### *(Fixed Holidays)*

| | | |
|---|---|---|
| 1 Jan. | New Year's Day | multinational |
| 2 Jan. | New Year's Day | country-unique |
| 6 Feb. | Waitangi Day | country-unique |

*D129 continued*

| | | |
|---|---|---|
| 25 Apr. | ANZAC Day | shared with Australia |
| 25 Dec. | Christmas Day | multinational |
| 26 Dec. | Boxing Day | multinational |

### *(Algorithmic Holidays)*

| | | |
|---|---|---|
| Mar.–Apr. | Good Friday | Christian |
| Mar.–Apr. | Easter Monday | Christian |
| May–June | Whitmonday | Christian |
| 1st Mon. in June | Queen's Birthday | country-unique |
| last Mon. in Oct. | Labour Day | country-unique |

## D130. Nicaragua

### *(Fixed Holidays)*

| | | |
|---|---|---|
| 1 Jan. | New Year's Day | multinational |
| 1 May | Labor Day | multinational |
| 19 July | Sandinista Day | country-unique |
| 14 Sep. | Jacinto Day | shared with Guatemala |
| 15 Sep. | Independence Day | country-unique |
| 12 Oct. | Columbus Day | multinational |
| 1 Nov. | All Saints' Day | Christian |
| 8 Dec. | Immaculate Conception | Christian |
| 24 Dec. | Christmas Eve | multinational |
| 25 Dec. | Christmas Day | multinational |
| 31 Dec. | New Year's Eve | multinational |

### *(Algorithmic Holidays)*

| | | |
|---|---|---|
| Mar.–Apr. | Maundy Thursday | Christian |
| Mar.–Apr. | Good Friday | Christian |

## D131. Niger

### *(Fixed Holidays)*

| | | |
|---|---|---|
| 1 Jan. | New Year's Day | multinational |
| 15 Apr. | National Day | country-unique |
| 1 May | Labor Day | multinational |
| 3 Aug. | Independence Day | country-unique |

| | | |
|---|---|---|
| 18 Dec. | Republic Day | country-unique |
| 25 Dec. | Christmas Day | multinational |

### *(Algorithmic Holidays)*

| | | |
|---|---|---|
| Mar.–Apr. | Good Friday | Christian |
| Mar.–Apr. | Easter Monday | Christian |
| | Islamic New Year | Islamic |
| | Mohammed's Birthday | Islamic |
| | Eid al Fitr (4 days) | Islamic |
| | Eid al Adha (4 days) | Islamic |

## D132. Nigeria

### *(Fixed Holidays)*

| | | |
|---|---|---|
| 1 Jan. | New Year's Day | multinational |
| 1 May | Labor Day | multinational |
| 27 May | Children's Day | country-unique |
| 1 Oct. | Independence Day | country-unique |
| 26 Dec. | Boxing Day | multinational |

### *(Algorithmic Holidays)*

| | | |
|---|---|---|
| Mar.–Apr. | Maundy Thursday | Christian |
| Mar.–Apr. | Good Friday | Christian |
| Mar.–Apr. | Holy Saturday | Christian |
| Mar.–Apr. | Easter Monday | Christian |
| | Mohammed's Birthday | Islamic |
| | Eid al Fitr (4 days) | Islamic |
| | Eid al Adha (4 days) | Islamic |

## D133. North Korea

### *(Fixed Holidays)*

| | | |
|---|---|---|
| 1 Jan. | New Year's Day | multinational |
| 1 May | Labor Day | multinational |
| 9 Sep. | Independence Day | country-unique |
| 26 Dec. | Boxing Day | multinational |

# D134. Northern Ireland

## *United Kingdom Holidays and:*

### *(Fixed Holidays)*

| | | |
|---|---|---|
| 17 Mar. | Saint Patrick's Day | shared with Ireland |
| 12 July | Battle of the Boyne Day | country-unique |

### *(Algorithmic Holidays)*

| | | |
|---|---|---|
| Mar.–Apr. | Easter Monday | Christian |
| last Mon. in Aug. | Summer Break | shared with England and Wales |

# D135. Norway

### *(Fixed Holidays)*

| | | |
|---|---|---|
| 1 Jan. | New Year's Day | multinational |
| 1 May | Labor Day | multinational |
| 17 May | Constitution Day | country-unique |
| 24 Dec. | Christmas Eve | multinational |
| 25 Dec. | Christmas Day | multinational |
| 26 Dec. | Boxing Day | multinational |
| 31 Dec. | New Year's Eve | multinational |

### *(Algorithmic Holidays)*

| | | |
|---|---|---|
| Mar.–Apr. | Maundy Thursday | Christian |
| Mar.–Apr. | Good Friday | Christian |
| Mar.–Apr. | Easter Monday | Christian |
| May–June | Ascension Thursday | Christian |
| May–June | Whitmonday | Christian |

# D136. Oman

### *(Fixed Holidays)*

| | | |
|---|---|---|
| 1 May | Labor Day | multinational |
| 18 Nov. | National Day | country-unique |

### (Algorithmic Holidays)

| | |
|---|---|
| Islamic New Year | Islamic |
| Mohammed's Birthday | Islamic |
| Eid al Fitr (4 days) | Islamic |
| Eid al Adha (4 days) | Islamic |
| Isra a Majraj | Islamic |

## D137. Pakistan

### (Fixed Holidays)

| | | |
|---|---|---|
| 1 Jan. | Bank Holiday | multinational |
| 23 Mar. | Pakistan Day | country-unique |
| 1 May | Labor Day | multinational |
| 1 July | Bank Holiday | multinational |
| 14 Aug. | Independence Day | country-unique |
| 6 Sep. | Defense Day | country-unique |
| 11 Sep. | Quaid e Azam's Death | country-unique |
| 9 Nov. | Iqbal Day | country-unique |
| 25 Dec. | Quaid e Azam's Birthday | country-unique |

### (Algorithmic Holidays)

| | |
|---|---|
| Islamic New Year | Islamic |
| Ashura | Islamic |
| Mohammed's Birthday | Islamic |
| 1st Day of Ramadan | Islamic |
| Eid al Fitr (4 days) | Islamic |
| Eid al Adha (4 days) | Islamic |

## D138. Palau

### (Fixed Holidays)

| | | |
|---|---|---|
| 1 Jan. | Independence Day | country-unique |
| 1 May | Labor Day | multinational |
| 25 Dec. | Christmas Day | multinational |

## D139. Panama

### (Fixed Holidays)

| | | |
|---|---|---|
| 1 Jan. | New Year's Day | multinational |

*D139 continued*

| | | |
|---|---|---|
| 1 May | Labor Day | multinational |
| 11 Oct. | Revolution Day | country-unique |
| 3 Nov. | Independence Day (Independence from Colombia) | country-unique |
| 4 Nov. | Flag Day | country-unique |
| 10 Nov. | First Cry of Independence Day | country-unique |
| 28 Nov. | Independence Day (Independence from Spain) | country-unique |
| 8 Dec. | Immaculate Conception | Christian |
| 24 Dec. | Christmas Eve | multinational |
| 25 Dec. | Christmas Day | multinational |

### *(Algorithmic Holidays)*

| | | |
|---|---|---|
| Feb.-Mar. | Shrove Monday | Christian |
| Feb.-Mar. | Shrove Tuesday | Christian |
| Feb.-Mar. | Ash Wednesday | Christian |
| Mar.-Apr. | Maundy Thursday | Christian |
| Mar.-Apr. | Good Friday | Christian |
| Mar.-Apr. | Holy Saturday | Christian |

## Papua–New Guinea *see* New Guinea

## D140. Paraguay

### *(Fixed Holidays)*

| | | |
|---|---|---|
| 1 Jan. | New Year's Day | multinational |
| 1 May | Labor Day | multinational |
| 14 May | Flag Day | country-unique |
| 15 May | Independence Day | country-unique |
| 15 Aug. | Assumption | Christian |
| 25 Aug. | Constitution Day | country-unique |
| 29 Sep. | Boqueron Battle Day | country-unique |
| 12 Oct. | Columbus Day | multinational |
| 1 Nov. | All Saints' Day | Christian |
| 8 Dec. | Immaculate Conception | Christian |
| 25 Dec. | Christmas Day | multinational |
| 31 Dec. | Bank Holiday | multinational |

### (Algorithmic Holidays)

| | | |
|---|---|---|
| Mar.–Apr. | Maundy Thursday | Christian |
| Mar.–Apr. | Good Friday | Christian |
| May–June | Corpus Christi | Christian |

## D141. Peru

### (Fixed Holidays)

| | | |
|---|---|---|
| 1 Jan. | New Year's Day | multinational |
| 1 May | Labor Day | multinational |
| 29 June | Saint Paul's Day | Christian |
| 28 and 29 July | Independence Days | country-unique |
| 30 Aug. | Rose of Lima Day | country-unique |
| 9 Oct. | National Dignity Day | country-unique |
| 1 Nov. | All Saints' Day | Christian |
| 8 Dec. | Immaculate Conception | Christian |
| 25 Dec. | Christmas Day | multinational |
| 31 Dec. | New Year's Eve | multinational |

### (Algorithmic Holidays)

| | | |
|---|---|---|
| Mar.–Apr. | Maundy Thursday | Christian |
| Mar.–Apr. | Good Friday | Christian |

## D142. Philippines

### (Fixed Holidays)

| | | |
|---|---|---|
| 1 Jan. | New Year's Day | multinational |
| 9 Apr. | Valour Day | country-unique |
| 1 May | Labor Day | multinational |
| 6 May | Battle of Corregidor Day | country-unique |
| 12 June | Independence Day | country-unique |
| 4 July | United States Friendship Day | country-unique |
| 1 Nov. | All Saints' Day | Christian |
| 30 Nov. | Heroes' Day | country-unique |
| 25 Dec. | Christmas Day | multinational |
| 30 and 31 Dec. | Rizal Days | country-unique |

*D142 continued*

### *(Algorithmic Holidays)*

| | | |
|---|---|---|
| Mar.-Apr. | Maundy Thursday | Christian |
| Mar.-Apr. | Good Friday | Christian |

## D143. Poland

### *(Fixed Holidays)*

| | | |
|---|---|---|
| 1 Jan. | New Year's Day | multinational |
| 1 May | Labor Day | multinational |
| 22 July | Liberation Day | country-unique |
| 15 Aug. | Assumption | Christian |
| 1 Nov. | All Saints' Day | Christian |
| 11 Nov. | Independence Day | country-unique |
| 25 Dec. | Christmas Day | multinational |
| 26 Dec. | Boxing Day | multinational |

### *(Algorithmic Holidays)*

| | | |
|---|---|---|
| Mar.-Apr. | Easter Monday | Christian |
| May-June | Corpus Christi | Christian |

## D144. Portugal

### *(Fixed Holidays)*

| | | |
|---|---|---|
| 1 Jan. | New Year's Day | multinational |
| 25 Apr. | Liberation Day | country-unique |
| 1 May | Labor Day | multinational |
| 10 June | Portugal Day | shared with Macao |
| 15 Aug. | Assumption | Christian |
| 5 Oct. | Republic Day | shared with Macao |
| 1 Dec. | Youth Day | country-unique |
| 24 Dec. | Christmas Eve | multinational |
| 25 Dec. | Christmas Day | multinational |

### *(Algorithmic Holidays)*

| | | |
|---|---|---|
| Feb.-Mar. | Shrove Monday | Christian |
| Feb.-Mar. | Shrove Tuesday | Christian |

| | | |
|---|---|---|
| Mar.–Apr. | Maundy Thursday | Christian |
| Mar.–Apr. | Good Friday | Christian |
| May–June | Corpus Christi | Christian |

# D145. Puerto Rico

## *United States Holidays and:*

### *(Fixed Holidays)*

| | | |
|---|---|---|
| 11 Jan. | Hostos Day | country-unique |
| 6 Jan. | Epiphany | Christian |
| 22 Mar. | Abolition Day | country-unique |
| 17 July | Rivera Day | country-unique |
| 25 July | Constitution Day | country-unique |
| 27 July | Barbosa Day | country-unique |
| 12 Oct. | Columbus Day | multinational |
| 19 Nov. | Discovery Day | country-unique |
| 8 Dec. | Immaculate Conception | Christian |

### *(Algorithmic Holidays)*

| | | |
|---|---|---|
| Mar.–Apr. | Good Friday | Christian |

# D146. Qatar

### *(Fixed Holidays)*

| | | |
|---|---|---|
| 1 May | Labor Day | multinational |
| 3 Sep. | National Day | country-unique |

### *(Algorithmic Holidays)*

| | |
|---|---|
| Islamic New Year | Islamic |
| Eid al Fitr (4 days) | Islamic |
| Eid al Adha (4 days) | Islamic |

# D147. Romania

### *(Fixed Holidays)*

| | | |
|---|---|---|
| 1 Jan. | New Year's Day | multinational |

*D147 continued*

| | | |
|---|---|---|
| 1 May | Labor Day | multinational |
| 23 and 24 Aug. | National Days | country-unique |

# D148. Russia

## *(Projected Holidays)*

### *(Fixed Holidays)*

| | | |
|---|---|---|
| 1 Jan. | New Year's Day | multinational |
| 1 May | Labor Day | multinational |
| 24 Aug. | Independence Day | country-unique |
| 25 Dec. | Christmas Day | multinational |

# D149. Rwanda

### *(Fixed Holidays)*

| | | |
|---|---|---|
| 1 Jan. | New Year's Day | multinational |
| 28 Jan. | Democracy Day | country-unique |
| 1 May | Labor Day | multinational |
| 1 July | Independence Day | country-unique |
| 5 July | Unity Day | country-unique |
| 15 Aug. | Assumption | Christian |
| 25 Sep. | Assembly Day | country-unique |
| 26 Oct. | Government Day | country-unique |
| 1 Nov. | All Saints' Day | Christian |
| 25 Dec. | Christmas Day | multinational |

### *(Algorithmic Holidays)*

| | | |
|---|---|---|
| Mar.-Apr. | Easter Monday | Christian |
| May-June | Ascension Thursday | Christian |
| May-June | Whitmonday | Christian |

# D150. Saint Kitts

### *(Fixed Holidays)*

| | | |
|---|---|---|
| 1 Jan. | New Year's Day | multinational |
| 1 May | Labor Day | multinational |

| | | |
|---|---|---|
| 19 Sep. | Independence Day | country-unique |
| 25 Dec. | Christmas Day | multinational |

# D151. Saint Lucia

## *(Fixed Holidays)*

| | | |
|---|---|---|
| 1 Jan. | New Year's Day | multinational |
| 22 Feb. | Independence Day | country-unique |
| 1 May | Labor Day | multinational |
| 25 Dec. | Christmas Day | multinational |

# D152. Saint Vincent

## *(Fixed Holidays)*

| | | |
|---|---|---|
| 1 Jan. | New Year's Day | multinational |
| 22 Jan. | Discovery Day | country-unique |
| 1 May | Labor Day | multinational |
| 27 Oct. | Independence Day | country-unique |
| 25 Dec. | Christmas Day | multinational |

# D153. San Marino

## *(Fixed Holidays)*

| | | |
|---|---|---|
| 1 Jan. | New Year's Day | multinational |
| 19 Mar. | Saint Joseph's Day | Christian |
| 1 Apr. | National Day | country-unique |
| 1 May | Labor Day | multinational |
| 29 June | Saint Paul's Day | Christian |
| 15 Aug. | Assumption | Christian |
| 3 Sep. | Saint Marinus' Day | country-unique |
| 1 Nov. | All Saints' Day | Christian |
| 1 Nov. | All Saints' Day | Christian |
| 11 Nov. | Armistice Day | multinational |
| 24 Dec. | Christmas Eve | multinational |
| 25 Dec. | Christmas Day | multinational |
| 26 Dec. | Boxing Day | multinational |
| 31 Dec. | New Year's Eve | multinational |

# D154. São Tomé and Principe

## *(Fixed Holidays)*

| | | |
|---|---|---|
| 1 Jan. | New Year's Day | multinational |
| 1 May | Labor Day | multinational |
| 12 July | National Day | country-unique |
| 25 Dec. | Christmas Day | multinational |

# D155. Saudi Arabia

## *(Fixed Holidays)*

| | | |
|---|---|---|
| 23 Sep. | National Day | country-unique |

## *(Algorithmic Holidays)*

| | |
|---|---|
| Islamic New Year | Islamic |
| Mohammed's Birthday | Islamic |
| 1st Day of Ramadan | Islamic |
| Eid al Fitr (4 days) | Islamic |
| Eid al Adha (4 days) | Islamic |

# D156. Scotland

## *United Kingdom Holidays and:*

## *(Algorithmic Holidays)*

| | | |
|---|---|---|
| 2nd weekday of New Year | New Year's Day 2 | country-unique |
| 1st Mon. in Aug. | Public Holiday | shared with Ireland |

# D157. Senegal

## *(Fixed Holidays)*

| | | |
|---|---|---|
| 1 Jan. | New Year's Day | multinational |
| 4 Apr. | National Day | country-unique |
| 1 May | Labor Day | multinational |

| | | |
|---|---|---|
| 15 Aug. | Assumption | Christian |
| 20 Aug. | Independence Day | country-unique |
| 1 Nov. | All Saints' Day | Christian |
| 25 Dec. | Christmas Day | multinational |

### *(Algorithmic Holidays)*

| | | |
|---|---|---|
| Mar.-Apr. | Easter Monday | Christian |
| May-June | Ascension Thursday | Christian |
| May-June | Whitmonday | Christian |
| | Islamic New Year | Islamic |
| | Mohammed's Birthday | Islamic |
| | Eid al Fitr (4 days) | Islamic |
| | Eid al Adha (4 days) | Islamic |

## D158. Seychelles

### *(Fixed Holidays)*

| | | |
|---|---|---|
| 1 Jan. | New Year's Day | multinational |
| 1 May | Labor Day | multinational |
| 5 June | Liberation Day | country-unique |
| 29 June | Independence Day | country-unique |
| 1 Nov. | All Saints' Day | Christian |
| 8 Dec. | Immaculate Conception | Christian |

### *(Algorithmic Holidays)*

| | | |
|---|---|---|
| Mar.-Apr. | Holy Saturday | Christian |
| May-June | Corpus Christi | Christian |

## D159. Sierra Leone

### *(Fixed Holidays)*

| | | |
|---|---|---|
| 1 Jan. | New Year's Day | multinational |
| 19 Apr. | Republic Day | country-unique |
| 27 Apr. | Independence Day | country-unique |
| 25 Dec. | Christmas Day | multinational |
| 26 Dec. | Boxing Day | multinational |

### *(Algorithmic Holidays)*

| | | |
|---|---|---|
| Mar.-Apr. | Good Friday | Christian |

*D159 continued*

| | | |
|---|---|---|
| Mar.–Apr. | Easter Monday | Christian |
| 1st Fri. in Apr. | Bank Holiday | country-unique |
| May–June | Whitmonday | Christian |
| | Mohammed's Birthday | Islamic |
| | Eid al Fitr (4 days) | Islamic |
| | Eid al Adha (4 days) | Islamic |

# D160. Singapore

## *(Fixed Holidays)*

| | | |
|---|---|---|
| 1 Jan. | New Year's Day | multinational |
| 1 May | Labor Day | multinational |
| 9 Aug. | National Day | country-unique |
| 25 Dec. | Christmas Day | multinational |

## *(Algorithmic Holidays)*

| | | |
|---|---|---|
| Jan.–Feb. | Chinese New Year (3 days) | Asian |
| Mar.–Apr. | Good Friday | Christian |
| May–June | Vesak Day | shared with Malaysia |
| Oct.–Nov. | Deepavali | Hindu |
| | Hari Raya Puasa | Far East Islamic |
| | Hari Raya Haji | Far East Islamic |

# D161. Slovakia

## *(Projected Holidays)*

## *(Fixed Holidays)*

| | | |
|---|---|---|
| 1 Jan. | New Year's Day | multinational |
| 1 May | Labor Day | multinational |
| 9 May | Liberation Day | country-unique |
| 17 July | Independence Day | country-unique |
| 24 Dec. | Christmas Eve | multinational |
| 25 Dec. | Christmas Day | multinational |
| 26 Dec. | Boxing Day | multinational |
| 31 Dec. | New Year's Eve | multinational |

### (Algorithmic Holidays)

| | | |
|---|---|---|
| Mar.-Apr. | Holy Saturday | Christian |
| Mar.-Apr. | Easter Monday | Christian |

## D162. Slovenia

### (Projected Holidays)

### (Fixed Holidays)

| | | |
|---|---|---|
| 1 Jan. | New Year's Day | multinational |
| 1 May | Labor Day | multinational |
| 25 June | Independence Day | country-unique |
| 15 Aug. | Assumption | Christian |
| 1 Nov. | All Saints' Day | Christian |
| 8 Dec. | Immaculate Conception | Christian |
| 24 Dec. | Christmas Eve | multinational |
| 25 Dec. | Christmas Day | multinational |

### (Algorithmic Holidays)

| | | |
|---|---|---|
| Mar.-Apr. | Good Friday | Christian |
| Mar.-Apr. | Easter Monday | Christian |
| May-June | Ascension Thursday | Christian |

## D163. Solomon Islands

### (Fixed Holidays)

| | | |
|---|---|---|
| 1 Jan. | New Year's Day | multinational |
| 1 May | Labor Day | multinational |
| 7 July | Independence Day | country-unique |
| 25 Dec. | Christmas Day | multinational |

## D164. Somalia

### (Fixed Holidays)

| | | |
|---|---|---|
| 1 Jan. | Bank Holiday | multinational |
| 1 May | Labor Day | multinational |
| 26 June | Independence Day | country-unique |

*D164 continued*

| | | |
|---|---|---|
| 1 July | Union Day | country-unique |
| 21 and 22 Oct. | Revolution Days | country-unique |

### *(Algorithmic Holidays)*

| | |
|---|---|
| Islamic New Year | Islamic |
| Mohammed's Birthday | Islamic |
| Eid al Fitr (4 days) | Islamic |
| Eid al Adha (4 days) | Islamic |

## D165. South Africa

### *(Fixed Holidays)*

| | | |
|---|---|---|
| 1 Jan. | New Year's Day | multinational |
| 6 Apr. | Founders' Day | country-unique |
| 1 May | Labor Day | multinational |
| 31 May | Republic Day | country-unique |
| 10 Oct. | Kruger Day | country-unique |
| 16 Dec. | Day of the Covenant | country-unique |
| 25 Dec. | Christmas Day | multinational |
| 26 Dec. | Good Will Day | country-unique |

### *(Algorithmic Holidays)*

| | | |
|---|---|---|
| Mar.–Apr. | Good Friday | Christian |
| Mar.–Apr. | Easter Monday | Christian |
| May–June | Ascension Thursday | Christian |

## D166. South Korea

### *(Fixed Holidays)*

| | | |
|---|---|---|
| 1 Jan. | New Year's Day | multinational |
| 2 Jan. | New Year's Day | country-unique |
| 1 Mar. | Independence Day | country-unique |
| 10 Mar. | Labor Day | country-unique |
| 5 Apr. | Arbor Day | country-unique |
| 5 May | Children's Day | country-unique |
| 6 June | Memorial Day | country-unique |
| 17 July | Constitution Day | country-unique |

| | | |
|---|---|---|
| 15 Aug. | Republic Day | country-unique |
| 1 and 2 Oct. | Armed Forces Days | country-unique |
| 3 and 4 Oct. | Foundation Days | country-unique |
| 9 Oct. | Alphabet Day | country-unique |
| 25 Dec. | Christmas Day | multinational |

### *(Algorithmic Holidays)*

| | | |
|---|---|---|
| Jan.–Feb. | Chinese New Year Eve | Asian |
| Jan.–Feb. | Chinese New Year (2 days) | Asian |
| Apr.–May | Vesak Day | country-unique |

## D167. Spain

### *(Fixed Holidays)*

| | | |
|---|---|---|
| 1 Jan. | New Year's Day | multinational |
| 6 Jan. | Epiphany | Christian |
| 19 Mar. | Saint Joseph's Day | Christian |
| 1 May | Labor Day | multinational |
| 29 June | Saint Paul's Day | Christian |
| 25 July | Santiago Day | country-unique |
| 15 Aug. | Assumption | Christian |
| 12 Oct. | National Day | country-unique |
| 1 Nov. | All Saints' Day | Christian |
| 8 Dec. | Immaculate Conception | Christian |
| 25 Dec. | Christmas Day | multinational |

### *(Algorithmic Holidays)*

| | | |
|---|---|---|
| Mar.–Apr. | Maundy Thursday | Christian |
| Mar.–Apr. | Good Friday | Christian |
| Mar.–Apr. | Holy Saturday | Christian |
| Mar.–Apr. | Easter Monday | Christian |
| May–June | Ascension Thursday | Christian |
| May–June | Corpus Christi | Christian |

## D168. Sri Lanka

### *(Fixed Holidays)*

| | | |
|---|---|---|
| 4 Feb. | Independence Day | country-unique |
| 22 May | Heroes' Day | country-unique |

*D168 continued*

| | | |
|---|---|---|
| 1 May | Labor Day | multinational |
| 30 June | Bank Holiday | country-unique |
| 25 Dec. | Christmas Day | multinational |
| 31 Dec. | Bank Holiday | multinational |

### *(Algorithmic Holidays)*

| | | |
|---|---|---|
| Mar.-Apr. | Good Friday | Christian |
| Mar.-Apr. | Easter Monday | Christian |
| Oct.-Nov. | Deepavali | Hindu |
| | Mohammed's Birthday | Islamic |
| | Eid al Fitr (4 days) | Islamic |
| | Eid al Adha (4 days) | Islamic |
| | Full Moon Poya Days | country-unique |

## D169. Sudan

### *(Fixed Holidays)*

| | | |
|---|---|---|
| 1 Jan. | Independence Day | country-unique |
| 25 May | Revolution Day | country-unique |
| 25 Dec. | Christmas Day | multinational |

### *(Algorithmic Holidays)*

| | |
|---|---|
| Islamic New Year | Islamic |
| Mohammed's Birthday | Islamic |
| Eid al Fitr (4 days) | Islamic |
| Eid al Adha (4 days) | Islamic |

## D170. Suriname

### *(Fixed Holidays)*

| | | |
|---|---|---|
| 1 Jan. | New Year's Day | multinational |
| 1 May | Labor Day | multinational |
| 1 July | Freedom Day | country-unique |
| 25 Nov. | Independence Day | country-unique |
| 25 Dec. | Christmas Day | multinational |
| 26 Dec. | Boxing Day | multinational |

### (Algorithmic Holidays)

| | | |
|---|---|---|
| Mar.–Apr. | Good Friday | Christian |
| Mar.–Apr. | Easter Monday | Christian |

## D171. Swaziland

### (Fixed Holidays)

| | | |
|---|---|---|
| 1 Jan. | New Year's Day | multinational |
| 25 Apr. | Flag Day | country-unique |
| 1 May | Labor Day | multinational |
| 6 Sep. | Independence Day | country-unique |
| 25 Dec. | Christmas Day | multinational |
| 26 Dec. | Boxing Day | multinational |

### (Algorithmic Holidays)

| | | |
|---|---|---|
| Mar.–Apr. | Good Friday | Christian |
| Mar.–Apr. | Holy Saturday | Christian |
| Mar.–Apr. | Easter Monday | Christian |
| May–June | Ascension Thursday | Christian |

## D172. Sweden

### (Fixed Holidays)

| | | |
|---|---|---|
| 1 Jan. | New Year's Day | multinational |
| 6 Jan. | Epiphany | Christian |
| 1 May | Labor Day | multinational |
| 6 June | Constitution Day | country-unique |
| 1 Nov. | All Saints' Day | Christian |
| 2 Nov. | All Saints' Eve (celebrated the day after All Saints' Day) | shared with Finland |
| 8 Dec. | Immaculate Conception | Christian |
| 24 Dec. | Christmas Eve | multinational |
| 25 Dec. | Christmas Day | multinational |
| 26 Dec. | Boxing Day | multinational |
| 31 Dec. | New Year's Eve | multinational |

### (Algorithmic Holidays)

| | | |
|---|---|---|
| Mar.–Apr. | Maundy Thursday | Christian |
| Mar.–Apr. | Good Friday | Christian |

*D172 continued*

| | | |
|---|---|---|
| Mar.–Apr. | Easter Monday | Christian |
| May–June | Ascension Thursday | Christian |
| May–June | Whitmonday | Christian |
| 20 or 21 June | Midsummer Day 1 | shared with Finland |
| 21 or 22 June | Midsummer Day 2 | shared with Finland |

# D173. Switzerland

## *(Fixed Holidays)*

| | | |
|---|---|---|
| 1 Jan. | New Year's Day | multinational |
| 2 Jan. | Berchtold's Day | country-unique |
| 19 Mar. | Saint Joseph's Day | Christian |
| 1 May | Labor Day | multinational |
| 29 June | Saint Paul's Day | Christian |
| 1 Aug. | Confederation Day | country-unique |
| 1 Nov. | All Saints' Day | Christian |
| 24 Dec. | Christmas Eve | multinational |
| 25 Dec. | Christmas Day | multinational |
| 26 Dec. | Boxing Day | multinational |

## *(Algorithmic Holidays)*

| | | |
|---|---|---|
| Mar.–Apr. | Good Friday | Christian |
| Mar.–Apr. | Easter Monday | Christian |
| May–June | Ascension Thursday | Christian |
| May–June | Whitmonday | Christian |
| May–June | Corpus Christi | Christian |

# D174. Syria

## *(Fixed Holidays)*

| | | |
|---|---|---|
| 1 Jan. | New Year's Day | multinational |
| 8 Mar. | Revolution Day | country-unique |
| 17 Apr. | Independence Day | country-unique |
| 1 May | Labor Day | multinational |
| 1 Sep. | United Arab Republics Day | country-unique |
| 25 Dec. | Christmas Day | multinational |

### (Algorithmic Holidays)

| | | |
|---|---|---|
| Mar.–Apr. | Good Friday | Christian |
| May–June | Ascension Thursday | Christian |
| | Islamic New Year | Islamic |
| | Ashura | Islamic |
| | Mohammed's Birthday | Islamic |
| | Eid al Fitr (4 days) | Islamic |
| | Eid al Adha (4 days) | Islamic |

## D175. Taiwan

### (Fixed Holidays)

| | | |
|---|---|---|
| 1 and 2 Jan. | Foundation Days | country-unique |
| 8 Mar. | Women's Day | multinational |
| 29 Mar. | Youth Day | country-unique |
| 5 Apr. | Tomb Sweeping Day | Asian |
| 1 May | Labor Day | multinational |
| 1 July | Bank Holiday | multinational |
| 28 Sep. | Teachers' Day | country-unique |
| 10 Oct. | National Day | country-unique |
| 25 Oct. | Restoration Day | country-unique |
| 31 Oct. | Chaing Kai-shek's Birthday | country-unique |
| 12 Nov. | Dr. Sun Yat-sen's Birthday | country-unique |
| 25 Dec. | Constitution Day | country-unique |

### (Algorithmic Holidays)

| | | |
|---|---|---|
| Jan.–Feb. | Chinese New Year Eve | Asian |
| Jan.–Feb. | Chinese New Year (3 days) | Asian |
| May–June | Dragon Boat Festival | Asian |
| Sep.–Oct. | Ancestors' Day | Asian |
| Oct. | Mid-autumn Day | Asian |

## D176. Tajikistan

### *(Projected Holidays)*

### (Fixed Holidays)

| | | |
|---|---|---|
| 1 Jan. | New Year's Day | multinational |
| 1 May | Labor Day | multinational |
| 9 Sep. | Independence Day | country-unique |

*D176 continued*

### *(Algorithmic Holidays)*

| | |
|---|---|
| Islamic New Year | Islamic |
| Mohammed's Birthday | Islamic |
| 1st Day of Ramadan | Islamic |
| Eid al Fitr (4 days) | Islamic |
| Eid al Adha (4 days) | Islamic |

## D177. Tanzania

### *(Fixed Holidays)*

| | | |
|---|---|---|
| 1 Jan. | New Year's Day | multinational |
| 12 Jan. | Revolution Day | country-unique |
| 26 Apr. | Union Day | country-unique |
| 1 May | Labor Day | multinational |
| 7 July | Farmers' Day | country-unique |
| 29 Oct. | Naming Day | country-unique |
| 9 Dec. | Independence Day | country-unique |
| 25 Dec. | Christmas Day | multinational |

### *(Algorithmic Holidays)*

| | | |
|---|---|---|
| Mar.–Apr. | Good Friday | Christian |
| Mar.–Apr. | Easter Monday | Christian |
| | Mohammed's Birthday | Islamic |
| | Eid al Fitr (4 days) | Islamic |
| | Eid al Adha (4 days) | Islamic |

## D178. Thailand

### *(Fixed Holidays)*

| | | |
|---|---|---|
| 1 Jan. | New Year's Day | multinational |
| 6 Apr. | Chakri Day | country-unique |
| 13 and 14 Apr. | Songkrawn | country-unique |
| 1 May | Labor Day | multinational |
| 5 May | Coronation Day | country-unique |
| 1 July | Bank Holiday | multinational |
| 12 Aug. | Queen's Birthday | country-unique |
| 23 Oct. | Chulalongkorn's Day | country-unique |

| | | |
|---|---|---|
| 5 Dec. | King's Birthday | country-unique |
| 10 Dec. | Constitution Day | country-unique |
| 31 Dec. | New Year's Eve | multinational |

### *(Algorithmic Holidays)*

| | | |
|---|---|---|
| Feb.-Mar. | Makha Bucha Day | country-unique |
| May-June | Visakha Bucha Day | country-unique |
| July-Aug. | Asalaha Bucha Day | country-unique |
| July-Aug. | Khao Phansa Day | country-unique |

## D179. Togo

### *(Fixed Holidays)*

| | | |
|---|---|---|
| 1 Jan. | New Year's Day | multinational |
| 13 Jan. | Liberation Day | country-unique |
| 27 Apr. | Independence Day | country-unique |
| 1 May | Labor Day | multinational |
| 15 Aug. | Assumption | Christian |
| 1 Nov. | All Saints' Day | Christian |
| 25 Dec. | Christmas Day | multinational |

### *(Algorithmic Holidays)*

| | | |
|---|---|---|
| Mar.-Apr. | Easter Monday | Christian |
| May-June | Ascension Thursday | Christian |

## D180. Tonga

### *(Fixed Holidays)*

| | | |
|---|---|---|
| 1 Jan. | New Year's Day | multinational |
| 1 May | Labor Day | multinational |
| 4 June | Independence Day | country-unique |
| 25 Dec. | Christmas Day | multinational |

## D181. Trinidad and Tobago

### *(Fixed Holidays)*

| | | |
|---|---|---|
| 1 Jan. | New Year's Day | multinational |
| 1 May | Labor Day | multinational |

*D181 continued*

| | | |
|---|---|---|
| 2 Aug. | Discovery Day | country-unique |
| 31 Aug. | Independence Day | country-unique |
| 25 Dec. | Christmas Day | multinational |

### *(Algorithmic Holidays)*

| | | |
|---|---|---|
| Mar.–Apr. | Maundy Thursday | Christian |
| Mar.–Apr. | Easter Monday | Christian |
| May–June | Whitmonday | Christian |
| May–June | Corpus Christi | Christian |
| | Eid al Fitr (4 days) | Islamic |

## D182. Tunisia

### *(Fixed Holidays)*

| | | |
|---|---|---|
| 1 Jan. | New Year's Day | multinational |
| 20 Mar. | Independence Day | country-unique |
| 9 Apr. | Martyrs' Day | country-unique |
| 1 May | Labor Day | multinational |
| 1 June | National Day | country-unique |
| 2 June | Youth Day | country-unique |
| 25 July | Republic Day | country-unique |
| 3 Aug. | President's Birthday | country-unique |
| 13 Aug. | Women's Day | country-unique |
| 3 Sep. | Independence Movement Day | country-unique |
| 15 Oct. | Evacuation Day | country-unique |

### *(Algorithmic Holidays)*

| | |
|---|---|
| Islamic New Year | Islamic |
| Mohammed's Birthday | Islamic |
| Eid al Fitr (4 days) | Islamic |
| Eid al Adha (4 days) | Islamic |

## D183. Turkey

### *(Fixed Holidays)*

| | | |
|---|---|---|
| 1 Jan. | New Year's Day | multinational |
| 23 Apr. | Children's Day | country-unique |

| | | |
|---|---|---|
| 19 May | Youth Day | country-unique |
| 30 Aug. | Victory Day | country-unique |
| 29 Oct. | Republic Day | country-unique |
| 31 Dec. | New Year's Eve | multinational |

### *(Algorithmic Holidays)*

| | | |
|---|---|---|
| Mar.–Apr. | Easter Sunday | Christian |
| | Islamic New Year | Islamic |
| | Mohammed's Birthday | Islamic |
| | Eid al Fitr (4 days) | Islamic |
| | Eid al Adha (4 days) | Islamic |

## D184. Turkmenistan

### *(Projected Holidays)*

### *(Fixed Holidays)*

| | | |
|---|---|---|
| 1 Jan. | New Year's Day | multinational |
| 1 May | Labor Day | multinational |
| 27 Oct. | Independence Day | country-unique |
| 25 Dec. | Christmas Day | multinational |

## D185. Tuvalu

### *(Fixed Holidays)*

| | | |
|---|---|---|
| 1 Jan. | New Year's Day | multinational |
| 1 May | Labor Day | multinational |
| 1 Oct. | Independence Day | country-unique |
| 25 Dec. | Christmas Day | multinational |

## D186. Uganda

### *(Fixed Holidays)*

| | | |
|---|---|---|
| 1 Jan. | New Year's Day | multinational |
| 11 Apr. | Liberation Day | country-unique |
| 1 May | Labor Day | multinational |
| 9 Oct. | Independence Day | country-unique |

*D186 continued*

| | | |
|---|---|---|
| 25 Dec. | Christmas Day | multinational |
| 26 Dec. | Boxing Day | multinational |

### *(Algorithmic Holidays)*

| | | |
|---|---|---|
| Mar.-Apr. | Holy Saturday | Christian |
| Mar.-Apr. | Good Friday | Christian |
| Mar.-Apr. | Easter Monday | Christian |
| | Eid al Fitr (4 days) | Islamic |

## D187. Ukraine

### *(Projected Holidays)*

### *(Fixed Holidays)*

| | | |
|---|---|---|
| 1 Jan. | New Year's Day | multinational |
| 1 May | Labor Day | multinational |
| 24 Aug. | National Day | country-unique |
| 1 Dec. | Independence Day | country-unique |
| 25 Dec. | Christmas Day | multinational |

## D188. United Arab Emirates

### *(Fixed Holidays)*

| | | |
|---|---|---|
| 1 Jan. | New Year's Day | multinational |
| 6 Aug. | Accession Day | country-unique |
| 2 Dec. | National Day | country-unique |

### *(Algorithmic Holidays)*

| | |
|---|---|
| Islamic New Year | Islamic |
| Mohammed's Birthday | Islamic |
| Eid al Fitr (4 days) | Islamic |
| Eid al Adha (4 days) | Islamic |
| Isra a Majraj | Islamic |

# D189. United Kingdom

## (Fixed Holidays)

| | | |
|---|---|---|
| 1 Jan. | New Year's Day | multinational |
| 25 Dec. | Christmas Day | multinational |
| 26 Dec. | Boxing Day | multinational |

## (Algorithmic Holidays)

| | | |
|---|---|---|
| Mar.-Apr. | Good Friday | Christian |
| 1st Mon. in May | Labour Day | country-unique |
| last Mon. in May | Spring Break | country-unique |
| 2nd Mon. in June | Queen's Birthday | shared with Australia, Fiji, and New Guinea |

# D190. United States

## (Fixed Holidays)

| | | |
|---|---|---|
| 1 Jan. | New Year's Day | multinational |
| 4 July | Independence Day | country-unique |
| 11 Nov. | Armistice Day (also known as Veteran's Day) | multinational |
| 25 Dec. | Christmas Day | multinational |

## (Algorithmic Holidays)

| | | |
|---|---|---|
| 3rd Mon. in Jan. | Martin Luther King's Birthday | country-unique |
| 1st Mon. in Feb. | Lincoln's Birthday | country-unique |
| 3rd Mon. in Feb. | Washington's Birthday | country-unique |
| last Mon. in May | Memorial Day | country-unique |
| 1st Mon. in Sep. | Labor Day | country-unique |
| 2nd Mon. in Oct. | Bank and Federal Holiday (also known as Columbus Day) | country-unique |
| 4th Thu. in Nov. | Thanksgiving Day | country-unique |

# D191. Uruguay

## (Fixed Holidays)

| | | |
|---|---|---|
| 1 Jan. | New Year's Day | multinational |

*D191 continued*

| | | |
|---|---|---|
| 6 Jan. | Children's Day | country-unique |
| 19 Apr. | Patriots' Day | country-unique |
| 1 May | Labor Day | multinational |
| 18 May | Las Piedras Day | country-unique |
| 19 June | Artigas Day | country-unique |
| 18 July | Constitution Day | country-unique |
| 25 Aug. | Independence Day | country-unique |
| 12 Oct. | Columbus Day | multinational |
| 1 Nov. | All Saints' Day | Christian |
| 24 Dec. | Christmas Eve | multinational |
| 25 Dec. | Christmas Day | multinational |

### *(Algorithmic Holidays)*

| | | |
|---|---|---|
| Feb.-Mar. | Shrove Monday | Christian |
| Feb.-Mar. | Shrove Tuesday | Christian |
| Mar.-Apr. | Maundy Thursday | Christian |
| Mar.-Apr. | Good Friday | Christian |
| Mar.-Apr. | Holy Saturday | Christian |
| Mar.-Apr. | Easter Monday | Christian |

## D192. Uzbekistan

### ***(Projected Holidays)***

### *(Fixed Holidays)*

| | | |
|---|---|---|
| 1 Jan. | New Year's Day | multinational |
| 1 May | Labor Day | multinational |
| 29 Aug. | Independence Day | country-unique |

### *(Algorithmic Holidays)*

| | |
|---|---|
| Islamic New Year | Islamic |
| Mohammed's Birthday | Islamic |
| 1st Day of Ramadan | Islamic |
| Eid al Fitr (4 days) | Islamic |
| Eid al Adha (4 days) | Islamic |

## D193. Vanuatu

### *(Fixed Holidays)*

| | | |
|---|---|---|
| 1 Jan. | New Year's Day | multinational |

| | | |
|---|---|---|
| 1 May | Labor Day | multinational |
| 30 July | Independence Day | country-unique |
| 25 Dec. | Christmas Day | multinational |

# D194. Vatican

## (Fixed Holidays)

| | | |
|---|---|---|
| 1 Jan. | New Year's Day | multinational |
| 19 Mar. | Saint Joseph's Day | Christian |
| 1 May | Labor Day | multinational |
| 29 June | Saint Paul's Day | Christian |
| 15 Aug. | Assumption | Christian |
| 22 Oct. | John Paul II Day | country-unique |
| 1 Nov. | All Saints' Day | Christian |
| 1 Nov. | All Saints' Day | Christian |
| 4 Nov. | John Paul II Nameday | country-unique |
| 11 Nov. | Armistice Day | multinational |
| 8 Dec. | Immaculate Conception | Christian |
| 24 Dec. | Christmas Eve | multinational |
| 25 Dec. | Christmas Day | multinational |
| 26 Dec. | Boxing Day | multinational |
| 31 Dec. | New Year's Eve | multinational |

## (Algorithmic Holidays)

| | | |
|---|---|---|
| Feb.-Mar. | Shrove Monday | Christian |
| Mar.-Apr. | Maundy Thursday | Christian |
| Mar.-Apr. | Good Friday | Christian |
| Mar.-Apr. | Holy Saturday | Christian |
| Mar.-Apr. | Easter Monday | Christian |
| May-June | Ascension Thursday | Christian |
| May-June | Corpus Christi | Christian |

# D195. Venezuela

## (Fixed Holidays)

| | | |
|---|---|---|
| 1 Jan. | New Year's Day | multinational |
| 6 Jan. | Epiphany | Christian |
| 19 Mar. | Saint Joseph's Day | Christian |
| 19 Apr. | Independence Day | country-unique |
| | (also known as the Declaration of Independence Day) | |
| 1 May | Labor Day | multinational |

*D195 continued*

| | | |
|---|---|---|
| 24 June | Carabobo Day | country-unique |
| 29 June | Saint Paul's Day | Christian |
| 5 July | Independence Day | country-unique |
| 24 July | Bolivar Day | country-unique |
| 15 Aug. | Assumption | Christian |
| 12 Oct. | Columbus Day | multinational |
| 1 Nov. | All Saints' Day | Christian |
| 8 Dec. | Immaculate Conception | Christian |
| 24 Dec. | Christmas Eve | multinational |
| 25 Dec. | Christmas Day | multinational |
| 31 Dec. | New Year's Eve | multinational |

### *(Algorithmic Holidays)*

| | | |
|---|---|---|
| Feb.-Mar. | Shrove Monday | Christian |
| Feb.-Mar. | Shrove Tuesday | Christian |
| Feb.-Mar. | Ash Wednesday | Christian |
| Mar.-Apr. | Maundy Thursday | Christian |
| Mar.-Apr. | Good Friday | Christian |
| May-June | Ascension Thursday | Christian |
| May-June | Corpus Christi | Christian |

## D196. Vietnam

### *(Fixed Holidays)*

| | | |
|---|---|---|
| 1 Jan. | New Year's Day | multinational |
| 27 Jan. | Vietnam Day | country-unique |
| 1 May | Labor Day | multinational |
| 2 Sep. | Independence Day | country-unique |

### *(Algorithmic Holidays)*

| | | |
|---|---|---|
| Jan.-Feb. | Tet (3 days) | country-unique |

## D197. Virgin Islands (U.S.)

### *United States Holidays and:*

### *(Fixed Holidays)*

| | | |
|---|---|---|
| 6 Jan. | Epiphany (also known as Three Kings Day) | Christian |

### *(Algorithmic Holidays)*

| | | |
|---|---|---|
| last Mon. in Mar. | Transfer Day | country-unique |
| 4th Mon. in July | Hurricane Supplication Day | country-unique |
| 2nd Mon. in Oct. | Puerto Rico Friendship Day | country-unique |
| 1st Mon. in Nov. | Liberty Day | country-unique |

## D198. Wales

### *United Kingdom Holidays and:*

### *(Fixed Holidays)*

| | | |
|---|---|---|
| Mar.–Apr. | Easter Monday | Christian |
| last Mon. in Aug. | Summer Break | shared with England and Northern Ireland |

## D199. Western Samoa

### *(Fixed Holidays)*

| | | |
|---|---|---|
| 1 Jan. | Independence Day | country-unique |
| (If the weather is inclement on the January date, the holiday is celebrated in June.) | | |
| 1 May | Labor Day | multinational |
| 1 June | Independence Day | country-unique |
| 25 Dec. | Christmas Day | multinational |

## D200. Yemeni Republic

### *(Fixed Holidays)*

| | | |
|---|---|---|
| 1 Jan. | New Year's Day | multinational |
| 8 Mar. | Women's Day | multinational |
| 1 May | Labor Day | multinational |

*D200 continued*

### *(Algorithmic Holidays)*

| Holiday | Type |
|---|---|
| Islamic New Year | Islamic |
| Mohammed's Birthday | Islamic |
| Eid al Fitr (4 days) | Islamic |
| Eid al Adha (4 days) | Islamic |
| Isra a Majraj | Islamic |
| Ashura | Islamic |

## D201. Yugoslavia

### *(Fixed Holidays)*

| Date | Holiday | Type |
|---|---|---|
| 1 Jan. | New Year's Day | multinational |
| 1 May | Labor Day | multinational |
| 4 July | Freedom Fighters' Day | country-unique |
| 7 July | Serbian Day | country-unique |
| 1 Nov. | All Saints' Day | Christian |
| 29 Nov. | Republic Day | country-unique |

## D202. Zaïre

### *(Fixed Holidays)*

| Date | Holiday | Type |
|---|---|---|
| 1 Jan. | New Year's Day | multinational |
| 4 Jan. | Martyrs' Day | country-unique |
| 1 May | Labor Day | multinational |
| 20 May | MPR Day | country-unique |
| 24 June | Constitution Day | country-unique |
| 30 June | Independence Day | country-unique |
| 14 Oct. | Founders' Day | country-unique |
| 27 Oct. | Naming Day | country-unique |
| 1 Nov. | All Saints' Day | Christian |
| 17 Nov. | Armed Forces Day | country-unique |
| 24 Nov. | New Regime Day | country-unique |
| 25 Dec. | Christmas Day | multinational |

### *(Algorithmic Holidays)*

| Date | Holiday | Type |
|---|---|---|
| Mar.–Apr. | Easter Monday | Christian |
| May–June | Ascension Thursday | Christian |

# D203. Zambia

## *(Fixed Holidays)*

| | | |
|---|---|---|
| 1 Jan. | New Year's Day | multinational |
| 1 May | Labor Day | multinational |
| 25 May | Africa Day | multinational |
| 24 Oct. | Independence Day | country-unique |
| 25 Dec. | Christmas Day | multinational |
| 26 Dec. | Boxing Day | multinational |

## *(Algorithmic Holidays)*

| | | |
|---|---|---|
| 2nd Sat. in Mar. | Youth Day | country-unique |
| 4th Tue. in Mar. | Africa Day | country-unique |
| Mar.-Apr. | Good Friday | Christian |
| Mar.-Apr. | Holy Saturday | Christian |
| Mar.-Apr. | Easter Monday | Christian |
| 1st Mon. in May | Labour Day | country-unique |
| May-June | Whitmonday | Christian |
| 1st Mon. in July | Heroes' Day | country-unique |
| 1st Tue. in July | Unity Day | country-uniquc |
| 1st Wed. in Aug. | Farmers' Day | country-unique |

# D204. Zimbabwe

## *(Fixed Holidays)*

| | | |
|---|---|---|
| 1 Jan. | New Year's Day | multinational |
| 18 Apr. | Republic Day | country-unique |
| 1 May | Labor Day | multinational |
| 25 May | Africa Day | multinational |
| 11 and 12 Aug. | Heroes' Days | country-unique |
| 25 Dec. | Christmas Day | multinational |
| 26 Dec. | Boxing Day | multinational |

## *(Algorithmic Holidays)*

| | | |
|---|---|---|
| Mar.-Apr. | Good Friday | Christian |
| Mar.-Apr. | Holy Saturday | Christian |
| Mar.-Apr. | Easter Monday | Christian |

# Index and Holiday Register

*Bold references are to the Appendices. References to dates are conclusive; i.e., the index "Abolition Day" indentifies the entry* **22 Mar.** *under Puerto Rico, making further look-up unnecessary. An asterisk beside a date indicates a projected date.*


Abolition Day *Puerto Rico* 22 Mar.
Accession Day *Jordan* 11 Aug., *United Arab Emirates* 6 Aug.
Adha, Eid al, countries honoring: **B28**; dates of: **C5**
Adult's Day *Japan* 15 Jan.
Aduwa, Victory of, Day *Ethiopia* 2 Mar.
Afghani New Year's Day *see* New Year's Day, Afghani
*Afghanistan* holidays honored: **D1**
Africa Day (multinational), countries honoring: **A8**, 25 May
Africa Day *Zambia* Fourth Tuesday in Mar.
*Albania* holidays honored: **D2**
*Algeria* holidays honored: **D3**
All Prayers' Day *Denmark* dates of, 26 days after Easter: **C2**
All Saints' Day, countries honoring: **A13**; 1 Nov.
All Saints' Eve *Finland* and *Sweden* 2 Nov.
All Souls' Day, countries honoring: **A14**; 2 Nov.
Alphabet Day *South Korea* 9 Oct.
Altagracia Day *Dominican Republic* 21 Jan.
Ancestors' Day, countries honoring: **B6** *see* Calendars September–October
*Andorra* holidays honored: **D4**
*Angola* holidays honored: **D5**
Annunciation *Liechtenstein* 25 Mar.
*Antigua* holidays honored: **D6**
ANZAC Day *Australia* and *New Zealand* 25 Apr.
Aquarius begins 19 or 20 Jan.
Arbor Day *Jordan* 15 Jan., *South Korea* 5 Apr.
*Argentina* holidays honored: **D7**
Aries begins 20 or 21 Mar.
Armed Forces Day *Chile* 19 Sep., *Egypt* 6 Oct., *Liberia* 11 Feb., *South Korea* 1 and 2 Oct., *Zaïre* 17 Nov.
*Armenia* holidays honored: **D8**
Armistice Day, countries honoring: **A15**; 11 Nov.
Army Coup Day *Mali* 19 Nov.
Army Day *Guatemala* 30 June, *Honduras* 21 Oct., *Iraq* 6 Jan.
Artigas Day *Uruguay* 19 June
*Aruba* holidays honored: **D9**
Asalaha Bucha Day *Thailand* dates of: **C7**
Ascension Thursday, countries honoring: **B16**; dates of: **C2**
Ash Wednesday, countries honoring: **B9**; dates of: **C2**
Ashura, countries honoring: **B23**; dates of: **C5**
Assembly Day *Rwanda* 25 Sep.
Assumption, countries honoring: **A11**; 15 Aug.
*Australia* holidays honored: **D10**

Australia Day *Australia* Monday after 25 Jan.
*Austria* holidays honored: **D11**
Autumnal Equinox *Japan* 22 or 23 Sep.
Award Day *Mali* 20 Jan.
Azam, Quaid-e-, Anniversary of Death of *Pakistan* 11 Sep.
Azam, Quaid-e-, Birthday of *Pakistan* 25 Dec.
*Azerbaijan* holidays honored: **D12**

*Bahamas* holidays honored: **D13**
*Bahrain* holidays honored: **D14**
*Bangladesh* holidays honored: **D15**
Bank Holiday (multinational), countries honoring: **A2**, 1 Jan.; **A10**, 1 July; **A20**, 31 Dec.
Bank Holiday *Argentina* Last Friday in Nov., *Barbados* First Monday in Oct., *Chile* Last Friday in June, *Ecuador* Last Friday in June, *El Salvador* Last Friday in June, *Finland* Last Friday in June, *Japan* 2 Jan., *Sierra Leone* First Friday in Apr., *Sri Lanka* 30 June.
Bank Holiday *Ireland* and *Scotland* ***see*** Public Holiday
Bank Holiday *United Kingdom* ***see*** Spring Break
Bank Holiday *United States* ***see*** Columbus Day
*Barbados* holidays honored: **D16**
Barbosa Day *Puerto Rico* 27 July
Battle of Boqueron Day *Paraguay* 29 Sep.
Battle of Corregidor Day *Philippines* 6 May
Battle of the Boyne Day *Northern Ireland* 12 July
*Belarus* holidays honored: **D17**
*Belgium* holidays honored: **D18**
*Belize* holidays honored: **D19**
*Benin* holidays honored: **D20**
Berchtold's Day *Switzerland* 2 Jan.
*Bermuda* holidays honored: **D21**
*Bhutan* holidays honored: **D22**
Boganda Day *Central African Republic* 29 Mar.
Bolivar Day *Venezuela* 24 July
*Bolivia* holidays honored: **D23**
Boqueron Battle Day *Paraguay* 29 Sep.
*Bosnia and Herzegovina* holidays honored: **D24**
*Botswana* holidays honored: **D25**
Boxing Day (multinational), countries honoring: **A19**, 26 Dec.
Boxing Day *Hong Kong* First weekday after Christmas
Boyaca Day *Colombia* 7 Aug.
Boyne, Battle of the, Day *Northern Ireland* 12 July
*Brazil* holidays honored: **D26**
*Brunei* holidays honored: **D27**
Buddhist ***see*** Theravada Buddhist
*Bulgaria* holidays honored: **D28**
*Burkina Faso* holidays honored: **D29**
*Burma* holidays honored: **D30**
*Burundi* holidays honored: **D31**

*Cambodia* holidays honored: **D32**
*Cameroon* holidays honored: **D33**
*Canada* holidays honored: **D34**
Canada Day *Canada* 1 July
Cancer begins 20 or 21 June
Candlemas *Liechtenstein* 2 Feb.
*Cape Verde* holidays honored: **D35**
Capricorn begins 21 or 22 Dec.
Carabobo Day *Venezuela* 24 June
*Cayman Islands* holidays honored: **D36**
*Central African Republic* holidays honored: **D37**
Cession Day *Fiji* Second Monday in Oct.
*Chad* holidays honored: **D38**
Chaing Kai-shek's Birthday *Taiwan* 31 Oct.
Chakri Day *Thailand* 6 Apr.
Chanukah dates of: **C6**
Charles', Prince, Birthday *Fiji* Third Monday in Nov.
Charles', Saint, Day *Andorra* 4 Nov.
Children's Day *Afghanistan* 30 Aug., *Congo* 25 Dec., *Iceland* 25 Apr., *Japan* 5 May, *Nigeria* 27 May, *South Korea* 5 May, *Turkey* 23 Apr., *Uruguay* 6 Jan.

*Chile* holidays honored: **D39**
*China* holidays honored: **D40**
*China, Republic of* ***see*** *Taiwan*
Chinese New Year, countries honoring: **B2**; dates of: **C1**
Chinese New Year, Second day, of countries honoring: **B3**; dates of: **C1**
Chinese New Year, Third day of, countries honoring: **B4**; dates of: **C1**
Chinese New Year Eve, countries honoring: **B1**; dates of: **C1**
Christian Algorithmic Holidays list of dates: **C2**
Christmas Day, countries honoring: **A18**; 25 Dec.
Christmas Eve, countries honoring: **A17**; 24 Dec.
Chulalongkorn's Day *Thailand* 23 Oct.
Cinco de Mayo *Mexico* 5 May
Civic Holiday *Canada* First Monday in Aug.
*Colombia* holidays honored: **D41**
Columbus Day (multinational), countries honoring: **A12**; 12 Oct.
Columbus Day *United States* Second Monday on Oct.
Commonwealth Day *Gibraltar* Second Monday in Mar.
*Comoros* holidays honored: **D42**
Confederation Day *Switzerland* 1 Aug.
*Congo* holidays honored: **D43**
Constitution Day *Brunei* 29 Sep., *Cameroon* 20 May, *Cayman Islands* First Monday in July, *Denmark* 5 June, *Hungary* 20 Aug., *Japan* 3 May, *Mexico* 5 Feb., *Nepal* 16 Dec., *Norway* 17 May, *Paraguay* 25 Aug., *Puerto Rico* 25 July, *South Korea* 17 July, *Sweden* 6 June, *Taiwan* 25 Dec., *Thailand* 10 Dec., *Uruguay* 18 July, *Zaïre* 24 June
Coptic Christmas Day *Egypt* and *Ethiopia* 7 Jan.
Coptic New Year's Day, ***see*** New Year's Day, Coptic
Coronation Day *Thailand* 5 May
Corpus Christi, countries honoring: **B19**; dates of: **C2**
Corregidor, Battle of, Day *Philippines* 6 May
*Costa Rica* holidays honored: **D44**
Covenant, Day of the *South Africa* 16 Dec.
*Croatia* holidays honored: **D45**
*Cuba* holidays honored: **D46**
Cuenca Independence Day *Ecuador* 3 Nov.
Culture Day *Bulgaria* 24 May, *Japan* 3 Nov.
*Cyprus* holidays honored: **D47**
*Czech Republic* holidays honored: **D48**
*Czechoslovakia* ***see*** *Czech Republic* and *Slovakia*

Day of Sovereignty *Haiti* 22 May
Daylight Savings Time ends *Canada* and *United States* Last Sunday in Oct., *Europe* Last Sunday in Sep.
Daylight Savings Time starts *Canada* and *United States* First Sunday in April, *Europe* Last Sunday in March
Declaration of Independence Day *Venezuela* 19 Apr.
Deepavali, countries honoring: **B21**, dates of: **C4**
Defense Day *Pakistan* 6 Sep.
Democracy Day *Rwanda* 28 Jan.
*Denmark* holidays honored: **D49**
Dessalines Day *Haiti* 17 Oct.
Devota's, Saint, Day *Monaco* 27 Jan.
Dignity, National, Day *Peru* 9 Oct.
Discovery Day *Cayman Islands* 17 May, *Guam* First Monday in Mar., *Haiti* 5 Dec., *Puerto Rico* 19 Nov., *Saint Vincent* 22 Jan., *Trinidad and Tobago* 2 Aug.
*Djibouti* holidays honored: **D50**
*Dominica* holidays honored: **D51**
*Dominican Republic* holidays honored: **D52**
Dragon Boat Festival, countries honoring: **B5** ***see*** Calendars May–June
Duarte Day *Dominican Republic* 26 Jan.

Easter Monday (Christian), countries honoring: **B15** *see* Calendars March–April
Easter Monday (Orthodox), countries honoring: **B20** *see* Calendars April–May
Easter Sunday (Christian), countries honoring: **B14**; dates of **C2**
Easter Sunday (Orthodox) *Jordan* dates of: **C3**
*Ecuador* holidays honored: **D53**
*Egypt* holidays honored: **D54**
Eid *see* Adha, Eid al and Fitr, Eid al
*El Salvador* holidays honored: **D55**
Emancipation Day *Bahamas* and *Barbados* First Monday in Aug.
Emperor's Birthday *Japan* 23 Dec.
*England* holidays honored: **D56**
Epiphany (Christian), countries honoring: **A3**, 6 Jan.
Epiphany (Orthodox) *Ethiopia* 19 Jan.
*Equatorial Guinea* holidays honored: **D57**
Equinox, Autumnal *Japan* 22 or 23 Sep.
Equinox, Vernal *Japan* 20 or 21 Mar.
*Eritrea* holidays honored: **D58**
*Estonia* holidays honored: **D59**
*Ethiopia* holidays honored: **D60**
Evacuation Day *Angola* 27 Mar., *Libya* 11 June, *Tunisia* 15 Oct.

Fair Day *Luxembourg* Monday after 27 Aug.
Family Day *Angola* 25 Dec., *Lesotho* First Monday in July
Farmers' Day *Tanzania* 7 July, *Zambia* First Wednesday in Aug.
*Fiji* holidays honored: **D61**
*Finland* holidays honored: **D62**
First Cry of Independence Day *El Salvador* 5 Nov., *Panama* 10 Nov.
First Republic Day *Ghana* 1 July
Fitr, Eid al countries honoring: **B26**; dates of: **C5**
Flag Day *Argentina* 20 June, *Finland* 19 May, *Haiti* 18 May, *Liberia* 24 Aug., *Panama* 4 Nov., *Paraguay* 14 May, *Swaziland* 25 Apr.
Foundation Day *Japan* 11 Feb., *South Korea* 3 and 4 Oct., *Taiwan* 1 and 2 Jan.
Founders' Day *South Africa* 6 Apr., *Zaïre* 14 Oct.
*France* holidays honored: **D63**
Freedom Day *Guyana* 2 Aug., *Suriname* 1 July
Freedom Fighters' Day *Yugoslavia* 4 July
Friday as day of rest, list of countries honoring: page 3
Full Moon Days *Burma* *see* calendars
Full Moon Poya Days *Sri Lanka* *see* calendars

*Gabon* holidays honored: **D64**
*Gambia* holidays honored: **D65**
Garifuna Day *Belize* 19 Nov.
Gemini begins 20 or 21 May
*Georgia* holidays honored: **D66**
*Germany* holidays honored: **D67**
*Ghana* holidays honored: **D68**
Ghandi Day *India* 2 Oct.
*Gibraltar* holidays honored: **D69**
Good Friday (Christian), countries honoring: **B12**; dates of: **C2**
Good Friday (Orthodox), countries honoring: **B20**; dates of: **C3**
Good Will Day *South Africa* 26 Dec.
Government Day *Rwanda* 26 Oct.
*Greece* holidays honored: **D70**
Greek Independence Day *Cyprus* 25 Mar.
Green Day *Japan* 29 Apr.
Gregorian New Year's Day, *see* New Year's Day, Gregorian
*Grenada* holidays honored: **D71**
Guadalupe, Our Lady of, Day *Mexico* 12 Dec.
*Guam* holidays honored: **D72**
Guanacaste Day *Costa Rica* 25 July
*Guatemala* holidays honored: **D73**
*Guinea* holidays honored: **D74**
*Guinea-Bissau* holidays honored: **D75**
*Guyana* holidays honored: **D76**

*Haiti* holidays honored: **D77**
Half Year Day *Hong Kong* 1 July
Hanukkah ***see*** Chanukah
Hari Raya Haji, countries honoring: **B29**; for dates, ***see*** Eid al Adha in **C5**
Hari Raya Puasa, countries honoring: **B27**; for dates, ***see*** Eid al Fitr in **C5**
Health Day *Japan* 10 Oct.
Heroes' Day *Angola* 17 Sep., *Costa Rica* 11 Apr., *Jamaica* Third Monday in Oct., *Philippines* 30 Nov., *Sri Lanka* 22 May, *Zambia* First Monday in July, *Zimbabwe* 11 and 12 Aug.
Holy Saturday, countries honoring: **B13** ***see*** Calendars March–April
*Honduras* holidays honored: **D78**
*Hong Kong* holidays honored: **D79**
Hostos Day *Puerto Rico* 11 Jan.
Human Rights Day *Equatorial Guinea* 10 Dec.
*Hungary* holidays honored: **D80**
Hurricane Supplication Day *Virgin Islands (U. S.)* Fourth Monday in July

*Iceland* holidays honored: **D81**
Immaculate Conception, countries honoring: **A16**, 8 Dec.
Independence Battle Day *Ecuador* 24 May
Independence Day *Afghanistan* 27 Apr., *Albania* 28 Nov., *Algeria* 5 July, *Angola* 11 Nov., *Antigua* 1 Nov., *Argentina* 9 June, *Armenia* 23 Sep.*, *Azerbaijan* 30 Aug.*, *Bahamas* 10 July, *Bangladesh* 26 Mar., *Barbados* 30 Nov., *Belarus* 25 Aug.*, *Belize* 21 Sep., *Benin* 1 Aug., *Bolivia* 6 Aug., *Bosnia and Herzegovina* 15 Oct.*, *Botswana* 30 Sep., *Brazil* 7 Sep., *Burkina Faso* 4 and 5 Aug., *Burma* 4 Jan., *Burundi* 1 July, *Cambodia* 17 Apr., *Cameroon* 1 Jan., *Cape Verde* 5 July, *Central African Republic* 13 Aug., *Chad* 11 Aug., *Chile* 18 Sep., *Colombia* 20 July, *Comoros* 6 July, *Congo* 13 through 15 Aug., *Costa Rica* 15 Sep., *Croatia* 25 June*, *Cyprus* 16 Apr., *Djibouti* 27 June, *Dominica* 3 Nov., *Dominican Republic* 27 Feb., *Ecuador* 10 Aug., *Egypt* 18 June, *El Salvador* 15 Sep., *Equatorial Guinea* 12 Oct., *Eritrea* 25 May*, *Estonia* 21 Aug.*, *Finland* 6 Dec., *Gabon* 17 Aug., *Gambia* 18 Feb., *Georgia* 9 Aug.*, *Ghana* 6 Mar., *Greece* 25 Mar., *Grenada* 7 Feb., *Guatemala* 15 Sep., *Guinea* 2 Oct., *Guyana* 26 May, *Haiti* 1 Jan., *Honduras* 15 Sep., *Iceland* 17 June, *India* 15 Aug., *Indonesia* 17 Aug., *Israel* ***see*** Calendars April–May, *Ivory Coast* 7 Dec., *Jamaica* First Monday in Aug., *Jordan* 25 May, *Kazakhstan* 21 Dec.*, *Kenya* 12 Dec., *Kiribati* 12 July, *Kyrgyzstan* 31 Aug.*, *Kuwait* 19 June, *Laos* 19 July, *Latvia* 21 Aug.*, *Lebanon* 22 Nov., *Lesotho* 4 Oct., *Liberia* 26 July, *Lithuania* 21 Aug.*, *Madagascar* 26 June, *Maldives* 26 July, *Mali* 22 Sep., *Malta* 21 Sep., *Marshall Islands* 17 Sep., *Mauritania* 28 Nov., *Mauritius* 12 Mar., *Mexico* 16 Sep., *Micronesia* 10 May, *Moldova* 27 Aug.*, *Morocco* 2 Mar. and 18 Nov., *Mozambique* 25 June, *Nauru* 31 Jan., *New Guinea* 16 Sep., *Nicaragua* 15 Sep., *Niger* 3 Aug., *Nigeria* 1 Oct., *North Korea* 9 Sep., *Pakistan* 14 Aug., *Palau* 1 Jan., *Panama* 3 Nov. and 28 Nov., *Paraguay* 15 May, *Peru* 28 and 29 July, *Philippines* 12 June, *Poland* 11 Nov., *Russia* 24 Aug.*, *Rwanda* 1 July, *Saint Kitts* 19 Sep., *Saint Lucia* 22 Feb., *Saint Vincent* 27 Oct., *Senegal* 20 Aug., *Seychelles* 29 June, *Sierra Leone* 27 Apr., *Slovakia* 17 July*, *Slovenia* 25 June*, *Solomon Islands* 7 July, *Somalia* 26 June, *South Korea* 1 Mar., *Sri Lanka* 4 Feb., *Sudan* 1 Jan., *Suriname* 25 Nov., *Swaziland* 6 Sep., *Syria* 17 Apr., *Tajikistan* 9 Sep.*, *Tanzania* 9 Dec., *Togo* 13 Jan., *Tonga* 4 June,

*Trinidad and Tobago* 31 Aug., *Tunisia* 20 Mar., *Turkmenistan* 27 Oct.*, *Tuvalu* 1 Oct., *Uganda* 9 Oct., *Ukraine* 1 Dec.*, *United States* 4 July, *Uruguay* 25 Aug., *Uzbekistan* 29 Aug.*, *Vanuatu* 30 July, *Venezuela* 19 Apr. and 5 July, *Vietnam* 2 Sep., *Western Samoa* 1 Jan. or 1 June, *Zaïre* 30 June, *Zambia* 24 Oct.
Independence, Declaration of, Day *Venezuela* 19 Apr.
Independence Movement Day *Tunisia* 3 Sep.
Independence War Day *Cuba* 11 Oct.
*India* holidays honored: **D82**
*Indonesia* holidays honored: **D83**
Iqbal Day *Pakistan* 9 Nov.
*Iran* holidays honored: **D84**
Iranian New Year's Day, *see* New Year's Day, Iranian
*Iraq* holidays honored: **D85**
*Ireland* holidays honored: **D86**
Islamic Algorithmic Holidays list of dates: **C5**
Islamic New Year's Day, *see* New Year's Day, Islamic
Isra a Majraj, countries honoring: **B30**; dates of: **C5**
*Israel* holidays honored: **D87**
*Italy* holidays honored: **D88**
*Ivory Coast* holidays honored: **D89**

Jacinto Day *Guatemala* and *Nicaragua* 14 Sep.
*Jamaica* holidays honored: **D90**
*Japan* holidays honored: **D91**
Jewish Algorithmic Holidays list of dates: **C6**
Jewish New Year's Day, *see* New Year's Day, Jewish
Johannus Day *Finland* Saturday nearest 24 June
John Paul II Day *Vatican* 22 Oct.
John Paul II Nameday *Vatican* 4 Nov.
John's, Saint, Day *Andorra* 24 June
*Jordan* holidays honored: **D92**
Joseph's, Saint, Day, countries honoring: **A5**, 19 Mar.
Juarez Day *Mexico* 21 Mar.

Kamuzu Day *Malawi* 14 May
*Kazakhstan* holidays honored: **D93**
*Kenya* holidays honored: **D94**
Kenyatta Day *Kenya* 20 Oct.
Khao Phansa Day *Thailand* dates of: **C7**
King's, Martin Luther, Birthday *United States* Third Monday in Jan.
King's Birthday *Bhutan* 11 Nov., *Jordan* 14 Nov., *Lesotho* 2 May, *Malaysia* First Wednesday in June, *Thailand* 5 Dec.
*Kiribati* holidays honored: **D95**
*Korea* *see* *North Korea* and *South Korea*
Kruger Day *South Africa* 10 Oct.
*Kuwait* holidays honored: **D96**
*Kyrgyzstan* holidays honored: **D97**

Labor Day (multinational), countries honoring: **A7**, 1 May.
Labor Day *Bahamas* 4 June, *Canada* First Monday in Sep., *Jamaica* 23 May, *New Zealand* Last Monday in Oct., *South Korea* 10 Mar., *United Kingdom* First Monday in May, *United States* First Monday in Sep., *Zambia* First Monday in May
Labour Thanksgiving Day *Japan* 23 Nov.
*Laos* holidays honored: **D98**
Las Piedras Day *Uruguay* 18 May
*Latvia* holidays honored: **D99**
*Lebanon* holidays honored: **D100**
Leo begins 22 or 23 July
*Lesotho* holidays honored: **D101**
Liberation Day *Albania* 29 Nov., *Bulgaria* 3 Mar., *Cuba* 1 Jan., *Czech Republic* 9 May*, *France* 8 May, *Guam* 21 July, *Hong Kong* Saturday before last Monday in

Aug. and Last Monday in Aug., *Hungary* 4 Apr., *Italy* 25 Apr., *Mozambique* 25 Sep., *Netherlands* 5 May, *Poland* 22 July, *Portugal* 25 Apr., *Seychelles* 5 June, *Slovakia* 9 May*, *Togo* 13 Jan., *Uganda* 11 Apr.
*Liberia* holidays honored: **D102**
Liberty Day *Virgin Islands (U. S.)* First Monday in Nov.
Libra begins 22 or 23 Sep.
*Libya* holidays honored: **D103**
*Liechtenstein* holidays honored: **D104**
Lima, Rose of, Day *Peru* 30 Aug.
Lincoln's Birthday *United States* First Monday in Feb.
*Lithuania* holidays honored: **D105**
*Luxembourg* holidays honored: **D106**

*Macao* holidays honored: **D107**
*Madagascar* holidays honored: **D108**
Madaraka Day *Kenya* 1 June
Magellan Day ***see*** Discovery Day *Guam*
Makha Bucha Day *Thailand* dates of: **C7**
*Malawi* holidays honored: **D109**
*Malaysia* holidays honored: **D110**
*Maldives* holidays honored: **D111**
*Mali* holidays honored: **D112**
*Malta* holidays honored: **D113**
Marinus, Saint, Day *San Marino* 3 Sep.
Marion's, Saint, Day *Lebanon* 9 Feb.
*Marshall Islands* holidays honored: **D114**
Martin, San, Day *Argentina* 17 Aug.
Martyrs' Day *Burma* 19 July, *Guinea-Bissau* 3 Aug., *Lebanon* 6 May, *Malawi* 3 Mar., *Tunisia* 9 Apr., *Zaïre* 4 Jan.
Maundy Thursday, countries honoring: **B11** ***see*** Calendars March–April
*Mauritania* holidays honored: **D115**
*Mauritius* holidays honored: **D116**
Memorial Day *Brazil* 2 Nov., *Madagascar* 29 Mar., *South Korea* 6 June, *United States* Last Monday in May
Mercedes Day *Dominican Republic* 24 Sep.
*Mexico* holidays honored: **D117**
*Micronesia* holidays honored: **D118**
Mid-autumn Day *China, Hong Kong, Macao,* and *Taiwan* ***see*** Calendars September–October
Midsummer Day (First of 2) *Finland* and *Sweden* 20 or 21 June, (Second of 2) *Finland* and *Sweden* 21 or 22 June
Mohammed's Birthday, countries honoring: **B24**; dates of: **C5**
*Moldova* holidays honored: **D119**
*Monaco* holidays honored: **D120**
*Mongolia* holidays honored: **D121**
Morazan Day *Honduras* 3 Oct.
*Morocco* holidays honored: **D122**
Moshoeshoe's Birthday *Lesotho* 12 Mar.
Mother's Day (international) Second Sunday in May
Mother's Day *Malawi* 17 Oct.
*Mozambique* holidays honored: **D123**
MPLA Foundation Day *Angola* 10 Dec.
MPR Day *Zaïre* 20 May
*Myanmar* ***see*** *Burma*

*Namibia* holidays honored: **D124**
Naming Day *Tanzania* 29 Oct., *Zaïre* 27 Oct.
National Day *Andorra* 8 Sep., *Argentina* 25 May, *Austria* 26 Oct., *Bahrain* 16 Dec., *Belgium* 21 July, *Belize* 10 Sep., *Benin* 30 Nov., *Bhutan* 17 Dec., *Brunei* 23 Feb., *Bulgaria* 9 and 10 Sep., *Burkina Faso* 11 Dec., *Central African Republic* 1 Dec., *Chad* 13 Apr., *China* 1 and 2 Oct., *Ethiopia* 12 Sep., *France* 14 July, *Grenada* 13 Mar., *Kazakhstan* 24 Aug.*, *Kuwait* 25 Feb., *Libya* 1 Sep., *Liechtenstein* 15 Aug., *Lithuania* 11 Mar.*, *Luxembourg* 23 June, *Malaysia* 31 Aug., *Malta* 31 Mar., *Morocco* 3 Mar., *Nepal*

19 Feb., *Niger* 15 Apr., *Oman* 18 Nov., *Qatar* 3 Sep., *Romania* 23 and 24 Aug., *San Marino* 1 Apr., *São Tomé and Principe* 12 July, *Saudi Arabia* 23 Sep., *Senegal* 4 Apr., *Singapore* 9 Aug., *Spain* 12 Oct., *Taiwan* 10 Oct., *Tunisia* 1 June, *Ukraine* 24 Aug.*, *United Arab Emirates* 2 Dec.
National Dignity Day *Peru* 9 Oct.
*Nauru* holidays honored: **D125**
Navy Day *Chile* 21 May
*Nepal* holidays honored: **D126**
*Netherlands* holidays honored: **D127**
*New Guinea* holidays honored: **D128**
New Regime Day *Zaïre* 24 Nov.
*New Zealand* holidays honored: **D129**
New Year's Day, Afghani *Afghanistan* 20 or 21 Mar.
New Year's Day, Coptic *Egypt* and *Ethiopia* 11 or 12 Sep.
New Year's Day, Gregorian, countries honoring: **A1**, 1 Jan., *Hong Kong* First Weekday in Jan.
New Year's Day, Iranian *Iran* and *Iraq* 20 or 21 Mar.
New Year's Day, Islamic, countries honoring: **B22**; dates of: **C5**
New Year's Day, Jewish *Israel* dates of: ***see*** Rosh Hashanah in **C6**
New Year's Day Two *New Zealand* 2 Jan., *Scotland* Second Weekday of New Year, *South Korea* 2 Jan.
New Year's Eve, countries honoring: **A21**, 31 Dec.
*Nicaragua* holidays honored: **D130**
*Niger* holidays honored: **D131**
*Nigeria* holidays honored: **D132**
*North Korea* holidays honored: **D133**
*Northern Ireland* holidays honored: **D134**
*Norway* holidays honored: **D135**

Ohi! Day *Greece* 28 Oct.
*Oman* holidays honored: **D136**
Orthodox Algorithmic Holidays, list of dates: **C3**
Our Lady of Victory Day *Malta* 8 Sep.

*Pakistan* holidays honored: **D137**
Pakistan Day *Pakistan* 23 Mar.
*Palau* holidays honored: **D138**
Palm Sunday ***see*** Calendars March–April
Pan American Day *Honduras* 14 Apr.
*Panama* holidays honored: **D139**
*Papua New Guinea* ***see*** *New Guinea*
*Paraguay* holidays honored: **D140**
Pashtunistan Day *Afghanistan* 31 Aug.
Passover *Israel* dates of: **C6**
Patrick's, Saint, Day *Ireland* and *Northern Ireland* 17 Mar.
Patriots' Day *Uruguay* 19 Apr.
Paul's, Saint, Day (multinational), countries honoring: **A9**, 29 June
Paul's, Saint, Day *Malta* 10 Feb.
Pentecost (Christian) ***see*** Whitsunday
Pentecost (Jewish) *Israel* dates of: **C6**
Pentecost (Orthodox) dates of: **C3**
Pentecost Monday (Orthodox) *Greece* ***see*** Calendars May–June
People's Day *Japan* 4 May
*Peru* holidays honored: **D141**
*Philippines* holidays honored: **D142**
Pisces begins 18 or 19 Feb.
*Poland* holidays honored: **D143**
*Portugal* holidays honored: **D144**
Portugal Day *Macao* and *Portugal* 10 June
Portuguese Republic Day *Macao* 5 Oct.
Presidential Message Day *Mexico* 1 Sep.
President's Birthday *Botswana* Third Monday in July, *Equatorial Guinea* 5 June, *Tunisia* 3 Aug.
Public Holiday (known locally as Bank Holidays) *Ireland* First Monday in June, First Monday in Aug., and Last Monday in Oct., *Scotland* First Monday in Aug.
*Puerto Rico* holidays honored: **D145**
Puerto Rico Friendship Day *Virgin Islands (U.S.)* Second Monday in Oct.
Purim ***see*** Calendars February–March

*Qatar* holidays honored: **D146**
Quaid-e-Azam, Anniversary of Death of *Pakistan* 11 Sep.

Quaid-e-Azam, Birthday of *Pakistan* 25 Dec.
Queen's Birthday *Australia* Second Monday in June, *Fiji* Second Monday in June, *Hong Kong* Second Saturday in June and Monday after Second Saturday in June, *Nepal* 8 Nov., *Netherlands* 30 Apr., *New Guinea* Second Monday in June, *New Zealand* First Monday in June, *Thailand* 12 Aug., *United Kingdom* Second Monday in June

Ramadan, 1st day of, countries honoring: **B25**; dates of: **C5**
Ranier's, Prince, Day *Monaco* 19 Nov.
Regiment Day *Brunei* 31 May
Remembrance Day *New Guinea* 23 July
Repentance Day *Germany* Third Wednesday in Nov.
Republic Day *Albania* 11 Jan., *Brazil* 15 Nov., *Burundi* 28 Nov., *Chad* 28 Nov., *Congo* 31 Dec., *Dominican Republic* 16 Aug., *Guinea-Bissau* 24 Sep., *Guyana* 23 Feb., *India* 26 Jan., *Iran* 1 Apr., *Italy* 1 June, *Ivory Coast* 7 Aug., *Laos* 2 Dec., *Madagascar* 30 Dec., *Malawi* 6 July, *Maldives* 11 Nov., *Malta* 13 Dec., *Niger* 18 Dec., *Portugal* 5 Oct., *Sierra Leone* 19 Apr., *South Africa* 31 May, *South Korea* 15 Aug., *Tunisia* 25 July, *Turkey* 29 Oct., *Yugoslavia* 29 Nov., *Zimbabwe* 18 Apr.
*Republic of China* ***see*** *Taiwan*
Resistance Day *Burma* 27 Mar.
Restoration Day *Taiwan* 25 Oct.
Revolution Day *Algeria* 1 Nov., *Bangladesh* 7 Nov., *Benin* 26 Oct., *Burkina Faso* 3 Jan., *Chad* 7 June, *Chile* 11 Sep., *Cuba* 25 through 27 July, *Egypt* 23 July, *Guatemala* 20 Oct., *Hungary* 23 Oct., *Iraq* 8 Feb., 14 July and 17 July, *Mexico* 20 Nov., *Mongolia* 11 July, *Panama* 11 Oct., *Somalia* 21 and 22 Oct., *Sudan* 25 May, *Syria* 8 Mar., *Tanzania* 12 Jan.
Righting Day *Algeria* 19 June
Rivera Day *Puerto Rico* 17 July
Rizal Days *Philippines* 30 and 31 Dec.
*Romania* holidays honored: **D147**
Rose of Lima Day *Peru* 30 Aug.
Rosh Hashanah ***see*** New Year's Day, Jewish
*Russia* holidays honored: **D148**
*Rwanda* holidays honored: **D149**

Sagittarius begins 21 or 22 Nov.
Saheed Day *Bangladesh* 21 Feb.
Saint Charles' Day *Andorra* 4 Nov.
Saint Devota's Day *Monaco* 27 Jan.
Saint John's Day *Andorra* 24 June
*Saint Kitts* holidays honored: **D150**
*Saint Lucia* holidays honored: **D151**
Saint Marinus' Day *San Marino* 3 Sep.
Saint Marion's Day *Lebanon* 9 Feb.
Saint Patrick's Day *Ireland* and *Northern Ireland* 17 Mar.
Saint Paul's Day (multinational), countries honoring: **A9**, 29 June
Saint Paul's Day *Malta* 10 Feb.
*Saint Vincent* holidays honored: **D152**
*San Marino* holidays honored: **D153**
San Martin Day *Argentina* 17 Aug.
Sandinista Day *Nicaragua* 19 July
Santiago Day *Spain* 25 July
*São Tomé and Principe* holidays honored: **D154**
*Saudi Arabia* holidays honored: **D155**
Scorpio begins 22 or 23 Oct.
*Scotland* holidays honored: **D156**
*Senegal* holidays honored: **D157**
Serbian Day *Yugoslavia* 7 July
Settlers' Day *Namibia* 10 Dec.
*Seychelles* holidays honored: **D158**
Shavuot ***see*** Pentecost, Jewish
Shrove Monday (Christian), countries honoring: **B7** ***see*** Calendars February–March
Shrove Monday (Orthodox) *Greece* dates of: **C3**
Shrove Tuesday (Christian), countries honoring: **B8** ***see*** Calendars February–March

*Sierra Leone* holidays honored: **D159**
Sinai Day *Egypt* 25 Apr.
*Singapore* holidays honored: **D160**
*Slovakia* holidays honored: **D161**
*Slovenia* holidays honored: **D162**
*Solomon Islands* holidays honored: **D163**
*Somalia* holidays honored: **D164**
Songkrawn *Thailand* 13 and 14 Apr.
*South Africa* holidays honored: **D165**
*South Korea* holidays honored: **D166**
Sovereignty, Day of *Haiti* 22 May
*Spain* holidays honored: **D167**
Sports Day *Lesotho* 5 Oct.
Spring Break (known locally as Bank Holiday) *United Kingdom* Last Monday in May
*Sri Lanka* holidays honored: **D168**
*Sudan* holidays honored: **D169**
Suez Victory Day *Egypt* 24 Oct.
Sukkot *Israel* ***see*** Calendars September–October
Sultan's Birthday *Brunei* 15 July
Summer Break *Northern Ireland, Wales,* and *England* last Monday in Aug.
Summer Holidays *El Salvador* 3 through 6 Aug.
Sun Yat-sen's, Dr., Birthday *Taiwan* 12 Nov.
*Suriname* holidays honored: **D170**
*Swaziland* holidays honored: **D171**
*Sweden* holidays honored: **D172**
*Switzerland* holidays honored: **D173**
*Syria* holidays honored: **D174**

*Taiwan* holidays honored: **D175**
*Tajikistan* holidays honored: **D176**
*Tanzania* holidays honored: **D177**
Taurus begins 19 or 20 Apr.
Teachers' Day *Taiwan* 28 Sep.
Tet *Vietnam* Dates of: ***see*** Chinese New Year in **C1**
Thai Buddhist ***see*** Theravada Buddhist
*Thailand* holidays honored: **D178**
Thanksgiving Day *Canada* Second Monday in Oct., *Liberia* First Thursday in Nov., *United States* Fourth Thursday in Nov.
Theravada Buddhist Algorithmic Holidays list of dates: **C7**
Three Kings' Day ***see*** Epiphany *Virgin Islands (U. S.)*
Tiradentes Day *Brazil* 21 Apr.
Tisha Ab *Israel* dates of: **C6**
*Togo* holidays honored: **D179**
Tomb Sweeping Day, countries honoring: **A6**; 5 Apr.
*Tonga* holidays honored: **D180**
Transfer Day *Virgin Islands (U.S.)* Last Monday in Mar.
*Trinidad and Tobago* holidays honored: **D181**
True Cross Day (Coptic) *Ethiopia* 26 or 27 Sep.
Tubman's Birthday *Liberia* 29 Nov.
*Tunisia* holidays honored: **D182**
*Turkey* holidays honored: **D183**
*Turkmenistan* holidays honored: **D184**
*Tuvalu* holidays honored: **D185**

*Uganda* holidays honored: **D186**
*Ukraine* holidays honored: **D187**
Unification Day *Cameroon* 1 Oct., *Liberia* 14 May, *Nepal* 11 Jan.
Union Day *Burma* 12 Feb., *Somalia* 1 July, *Tanzania* 26 Apr.
*United Arab Emirates* holidays honored: **D188**
United Arab Republics Day *Syria* 1 Sep.
*United Kingdom* holidays honored: **D189**
United Nations Day *Haiti* 24 Oct.
*United States* holidays honored: **D190**
United States Friendship Day *Philippines* 4 July
*United States Virgin Islands* ***see*** *Virgin Islands (U.S.)*
Unity Day *Germany* 17 June, *Rwanda* 5 July, *Zambia* First Tuesday in July
*Upper Volta* ***see*** *Burkina Faso*
Uprona, Victory of, Day *Burundi* 18 Sep.

*Uruguay* holidays honored: **D191**
*Uzbekistan* holidays honored: **D192**

Valentine's Day *International* 14 Feb.
Valour Day *Philippines* 9 Apr.
*Vanuatu* holidays honored: **D193**
Vappu Day *Finland* 30 Apr.
*Vatican* holidays honored: **D194**
Veneration Day *Japan* 15 Sep.
*Venezuela* holidays honored: **D195**
Vernal Equinox *Japan* 20 or 21 Mar.
Vertieres' Day *Haiti* 18 Nov.
Vesak Day *Malaysia* and *Singapore* *see* Calendars May–June, *Korea* *see* Calendars April–May
Victoria Day *Canada* Monday before 25 May.
Victory, Our Lady of, Day *Malta* 8 Sep.
Victory Day *Bangladesh* 16 Dec., *Turkey* 30 Aug.
Victory of Aduwa Day *Ethiopia* 2 Mar.
Victory of Uprona Day *Burundi* 18 Sep.
*Vietnam* holidays honored: **D196**
Vietnam Day *Vietnam* 27 Jan.
*Virgin Islands (U. S.)* holidays honored: **D197**
Virgin of the Angles Day *Costa Rica* 2 Aug.
Virgo begins 22 or 23 Aug.
Visakha Bucha Day *Thailand* dates of: **C7**

Waitangi Day *New Zealand* 6 Feb.
*Wales* holidays honored: **D198**
Washington's Birthday *United States* Third Monday in Feb.
*Western Samoa* holidays honored: **D199**
Whitmonday, countries honoring: **B18** *see* Calendars May–June
Whitsunday dates of: **C2**
Women's Day (multinational), countries honoring: **A4**; 8 Mar.
Women's Day *Tunisia* 13 Aug.

*Yemeni Republic* holidays honored: **D200**
Yom Kippur *Israel* dates of: **C6**
Youth Day *Cameroon* 11 Feb., *Portugal* 1 Dec., *Taiwan* 29 Mar., *Tunisia* 2 June, *Turkey* 19 May, *Zambia* Second Saturday in Mar.
*Yugoslavia* holidays honored: **D201**

*Zaïre* holidays honored: **D202**
*Zambia* holidays honored: **D203**
*Zimbabwe* holidays honored: **D204**